ALASKA-YUKON
HANDBOOK

ALASKA-YUKON
HANDBOOK

DEKE CASTLEMAN AND DON PITCHER

MOON
PUBLICATIONS INC.

ALASKA-YUKON HANDBOOK

Published by
Moon Publications Inc.
722 Wall Street
Chico, California 95928 U.S.A.
tel. (916) 345-5473

Printed by
Colorcraft Ltd., Hong Kong

Please send all comments,
corrections, additions,
amendments, and critiques to:

DEKE CASTLEMAN
c/o MOON PUBLICATIONS
722 WALL STREET
CHICO, CA 95928 U.S.A.

PRINTING HISTORY
   First Edition—1983
   Second Edition—April 1988
   Third Edition—Feb. 1990
   Reprinted—April 1991
   Fourth Edition—March 1992

Library of Congress Cataloging in Publication Data
   Castleman, Deke, 1952-
   Alaska-Yukon Handbook / Deke Castleman and Don Pitcher. — 4th ed.
      p.   cm.
   Includes bibliographical references and index
   ISBN 0-918373-78-6 : $13.95
   1. Alaska—Guidebooks.   2. Yukon Territory—Guidebooks.
   3. British Columbia—Guidebooks.   I. Pitcher, Don 1953-
II. Title.
F902.3.C37   1992   91-44314
917.9804'5—dc20   CIP

Printed in Hong Kong

Cover Photo: Don Pitcher; all color page photos by Don Pitcher

ACKNOWLDEGEMENTS

Deke Castleman: This is the sound of two hands clapping for the many researchers and readers who've contributed to this fourth edition of *Alaska-Yukon Handbook*. First and foremost on the appreciation scale are Aussies Andrew Hempstead and Nadina Purdon who, like me, have now used Alaska as their training ground for travel writing; Dan Bagatell, budget traveler extraordinaire and writer par excellence; and Egil Dilkestad, for feedback above and beyond (and tiny handwriting). Kudos also go to Renee Smith for persistent intentions; Edith Tjepkema who holds the check-out record (at the Cadillac, Michigan, public library); and Inez Larson for offering the highest compliment of all. Honorable mention should be extended to: Ashley Sloan, Ned McCarthy, Kimball Payne, Ray Leary, Natalia Grocovetsky, and Paul Berger.

Although he had nothing to do with the book, Bruce Van Dyke of KTHX, Reno, provided non-stop morning entertainment. Of the publishing corporation, Anne-Marie Nicoara provided the editing and Mark Voss the design.

Don Pitcher: Many people assisted me in the updating of the Southeast chapter. A few of those who were especially helpful include Linda Mickle of the Alaska Marine Highway, Mike O'Daniel of Skagway Air, Linda Hayes of Glacier Bay Air, Steve Hites of Yukon and White Pass Route, and Kathy of Glacier Bay Tours and Cruises. Many thanks to all of them. Kudos also to the following people who generously assisted me: Joan Gregory, Colleen Blake, Don Hilmer, Alroy DeAngelis, and Ken Crevier.

IS THIS BOOK OUTTA DATE?

Writing a guidebook is a lot like taking a snapshot: freezing the image of a place on a giant frame. At the same time, however, it's also like stopping progress: locking the ever-changing details into print. You can't stop progress, and you can't slow down time. These guidebooks are corrected for every reprint, and completely redone every two years. Although we make herculean efforts to check our facts, the task is an enormous one and sometimes gets away from us. You can help us keep up.

If something we mention no longer exists, if certain suggestions are misleading, if you've uncovered anything new, please write in. Women travelers sometimes run up against situations which warrant special attention and if you share them with us, we'll share them with everyone else. Letters from Alaskans and western Canadians are especially appreciated. Although we try to make our maps as accurate as possible, we are always grateful when readers point out any omissions or inaccuracies. If you feel we've overlooked an entire map, please let us know and we'll try to include it in the next edition.

When writing, always be as specific and accurate as possible. Notes made on the spot are better than later recollections. Write your comments into your copy of *Alaska-Yukon Handbook* as you go along, then send us a summary when you get home. This book speaks for you, the independent traveler, so please help keep us up to date. Address your letters to:

Deke Castleman
c/o Moon Publications
722 Wall Street
Chico, CA 95928

TABLE OF CONTENTS

LIST OF MAPS

LIST OF CHARTS

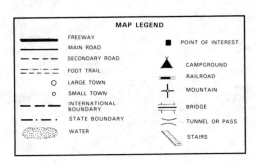

MAP LEGEND

FREEWAY

MAIN ROAD

SECONDARY ROAD

FOOT TRAIL

O   LARGE TOWN

o   SMALL TOWN

INTERNATIONAL
BOUNDARY

STATE BOUNDARY

WATER

■   POINT OF INTEREST

▲   CAMPGROUND

RAILROAD

MOUNTAIN

BRIDGE

TUNNEL OR PASS

STAIRS

To Melissa J. Rubin
1966-1987
Spirit Soar

(GORDY OHLIGER)

INTRODUCTION

THE LAND

The major physical features of western North America continue unbroken into that giant head of land that is Alaska. The Great Plains of the midwestern U.S. extend to become the Mackenzie Lowlands and the North Slope, while the Rockies form an inland spine from deep in Mexico to the Brooks Range. West of the Rocky Mountains a high plateau runs from British Columbia north through the interiors of Yukon and Alaska, then west to the delta of the Yukon River, where it dips into the Bering Sea.

To the west of this plateau, two parallel chains and an intervening depression can be traced all the way from Mexico to Alaska. The Sierra Nevada of California become in turn the Cascades of Oregon and Washington, the Coast Mountains of British Columbia, the St. Elias and Wrangell mountains, the Alaska Range, and finally the Aleutian Range, which then sinks into the Pacific just short of Asia. Closer to the ocean, Cali-

fornia's Coast Range becomes the Olympic Mountains of Washington. Farther north a string of islands from Vancouver to the Queen Charlottes and the Alexander Archipelago runs into the St. Elias Mountains, where the two chains unite into a jagged ice-capped knot. In Alaska they divide again, where the Chugach and Kenai mountains swing southwest toward Kodiak Island. Between these parallel chains is a 3,000-mile-long depression starting with California's Central Valley, then Puget Sound, the Inside Passage, the Susitna Basin in Southcentral Alaska, Cook Inlet, and Southwest Alaska's Shelikof Strait. Only four low-level breaks occur in the Coastal mountains: the valleys of the Columbia, Fraser, Skeena, and Stikine rivers. Most of the places described in this book are within or near this mighty barrier, which contains the highest peaks, largest glaciers, and most of the active volcanos in North America.

Superlatives

Alaska boasts more superlative statistics than any other state in the country (itself a superlative). But all are dwarfed by a single reality: the sheer immensity of the land. Alaska is so huge, so wild, so underpopulated, that it's almost incomprehensible: it falls right off the edge of your imagination. Consider: Alaska's total land area, 591,000 square miles (375,000,000 acres), is double the size of the next largest state, Texas. A little more than four Alaskas could be jammed into the continental U.S., while almost 300 Delawares could be jigsaw-puzzled into the 49th state. Mount McKinley, at 20,306 feet, is the highest point in North America; the Aleutian Trench, plunging to 25,000 feet below sea level, is one of the Pacific's deepest ocean troughs. Juneau, with over 3,000 square miles within its boundaries, has the largest area of any North American city, and the North Slope Borough, at 88,000 square miles (slightly larger than Idaho), is the largest municipally governed entity in the world. Alaska's 45,000-mile coastline is longer than the rest of the country's combined. Though only three percent of the state is covered in glaciers and icefields (debunking the "frozen wasteland" myth—the most common misconception about Alaska), it still has over 100 times more glacial area than the rest of North America. With only 550,000 people (second to last in state residents, behind Wyoming), if Manhattan had a relative population density, 17 people would live there. And if all the Manhattanites were transplanted to Alaska, they'd each have 125 acres. Immense.

Five States In One

This book divides Alaska into five regions: Southeast, Interior, Southcentral, Southwest, and the Arctic Coast. (It also covers Seattle,

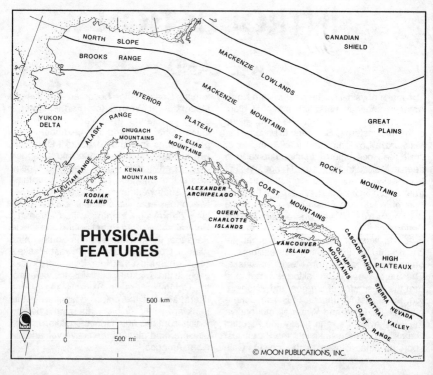

PHYSICAL FEATURES

© MOON PUBLICATIONS, INC.

parts of British Columbia, and the Yukon Territory.) **Southeast** is Alaska's "Panhandle," a coastal region dissected by the Inside Passage. This intricate network of narrow waterways, with rugged, forested mountains rising up from the water's edge, extends along the western edge of Canada from south of Ketchikan up to Skagway. The climate is cool, with very high precipitation. Transportation is limited to ferries and planes. **Interior** is the low rolling country between the northern face of the Alaska Range and the southern slope of the Brooks Range. Population centers huddle on the banks of the mighty Yukon, Tanana, and Kuskokwim rivers. The region has short warm summers, long cold winters, and little precipitation. Transportation is limited to a few roads, bush airlines, and riverboats.

Southcentral stretches along the Gulf of Alaska from the northwest corner of Southeast to the southern edge of the Kenai Peninsula, and up to the peaks of the Alaska Range. The coastal portion is a continuation of Southeast, while the Alaska Range forms the gigantic backbone of the region, with agricultural valleys like the Matanuska and Kenai in between. The climate is mostly coastal maritime, like Southeast's. Transportation is by road, railroad, plane, and ferry.

Southwest includes Kodiak, the Alaska Peninsula, Aleutian Islands, and Bristol Bay area. It's rugged and treeless, with a population mostly of Native Aleut and Inuit. The climate is particularly disagreeable: foggy summers, wind-chilled winters, very stormy, little sun. This area is also one of the world's most active volcano and earthquake zones. Four out of 10 of the world's earthquakes occur here, and 40 active volcanos mark the line where the Pacific tectonic plate bumps up against the North American plate. Transportation is mostly by plane, some by boat.

The **Arctic Coast** regions occupy a huge expanse of sparsely populated bush, up the Bering coast all the way around to Barrow and Prudhoe Bay. The very modest population centers are Nome, Kotzebue, and Barrow, with numerous Native villages scattered throughout. The climate is an extreme version of the Interior's: long cold winters, brief cool summers, and a tiny amount of precipitation. Access is almost entirely by plane.

GEOLOGY

Plate Tectonics

Briefly, the huge Pacific plate (the ocean floor) is drifting slowly northeast. It collides with the North American plate, on which the continent rests, along an arc that stretches from the western Aleutians in the Gulf of Alaska to the Inside Passage—defining one section of the famous Pacific "Ring of Fire." This meeting of plates jams the ocean floor under the continental land mass, and gives rise to violent geologic forces: upthrust of mountains, extensive and large earthquakes, volcanic rumblings and eruptions, and movement along fault lines.

Somewhere in the mists of early geologic time, a particularly persistent and powerful collision between the two plates caused the Brooks Range to rise; erosion has whittled its highest peaks to half the height, at 8,000 feet, they once were. Later, a similar episode thrust the Alaska Range into shape. The Pacific plate even today continues to nose under the continental plate, in the vicinity of Yakutat (near where Southeast meets Southcentral). The force of it pushes Mt. St. Elias, highest peak in Canada, slowly upward.

Earthquakes

One of the world's most seismically active regions, Alaska has withstood some of the most violent earthquakes and largest tidal waves ever recorded. In the last 90 years, 80 Alaskan earthquakes have registered over 7 on the Richter scale (the famous 1906 San Francisco earthquake is estimated at 7.8-8.3). The most destructive occurred at 5:35 p.m. on Good Friday, March 27, 1964. Now listed in history books at an incredible 9.2 on the Richter scale (newer and more sensitive equipment has upgraded it from a "mere" 8.6 recorded at the time), it remains the strongest earthquake ever recorded in North America. The ensuing tsunamis wiped out nearly every coastal village in Southcentral Alaska, wrought havoc all along the Northern Pacific coast, and even created a crest in the canals of Venice in Southern California.

In November 1987, two earthquakes, one 7.5 and the other 7.0, were recorded in the Yakataga Seismic Gap, an active fault zone on the edge of Prince William Sound, in an area where seismologists expect a major quake, over 8.0, to occur any time now.

Volcanos

Like its earthquakes, Alaska's major volcanos occur along the Aleutian chain. In fact, 57 active volcanos stretch along this arc: most have been active in the last 300 years. The largest recorded eruption occurred when Novarupta blew its top in 1912 (see p. 397), the most cataclysmic natural disaster since Krakatoa cracked 30 years earlier. Recently, Mt. Augustine, a gorgeous lone volcanic-cone island just north of Katmai in the southwest Cook Inlet, spewed ash for several days in early 1987. Mount Redoubt, across Cook Inlet from the Kenai Peninsula (110 miles southwest of Anchorage) blew between mid-December 1989 and early January 1990, sending ash 45,000 feet up, blanketing interior Alaska, and threatening airplanes.

Tsunamis

An earthquake deep below the ocean floor in the Gulf of Alaska or the open Pacific is especially dangerous to the coasts of Alaska, Hawaii, and western Canada and the U.S. The activity creates enormous tidal waves (tsunamis) which, though only three to five feet high in open ocean, can travel at speeds exceeding 500 miles an hour. Contrary to popular fears, such a tsunami does not slam into the coast with 20 or 30 feet of water, washing away everything in its path like a flash flood. Instead, the water slowly inundates the land to a depth of four or five feet. Then, after a brief and chilling calm, the wave is sucked back out to sea in one vast undertow. The only survival, and not guaranteed at that, is to ride it out on a boat. Most of the destruction caused by the great Good Friday Earthquake was of this nature, attested to by hair-raising pictures that you'll see in places like Valdez, Seward, and Kodiak.

GLACIATION

A glacier forms in areas of high precipitation and elevation where the snow is allowed to pile up to great depths, compacting the bottom layers into solid ice. The great weight above this ice, along with gravity, pushes it slowly downward like a giant frozen river, scooping out huge valleys and shearing off entire mountainsides. When the rate of advance is balanced by melt-off, the face of the glacier remains more or less stationary. If the glacier flows more quickly than the face melts, it advances; if it melts faster than it flows, the glacier recedes. All air bubbles are squeezed out of the glacier by this tremendous pressure, which makes glacial ice extremely dense. It's so compacted that the higher frequencies of light cannot escape or penetrate it, which explains the dark blue tinge. And because of its density, it also melts at fantastically slow rates; a small chunk or two will keep a beer in a cooler chilled for a week.

Signs Of The Glaciers

As you travel up the coast or hike in the national parks of the Interior, it's satisfying to be able to recognize and identify glacial landforms. While rivers typically erode V-shaped valleys, glaciers gouge out a distinctly U-shaped **glacial trough.** Valleys and ridges branching from the main valley are sliced off to create **hanging valleys** and **truncated spurs.** A side valley which once carried a tributary glacier may be left as a **hanging trough;** from these hanging valleys and troughs waterfalls often tumble. Alpine glaciers scoop out the headwalls of their accumulation basins to form **cirques.** Bare, jagged ridges between cirques are known as **aretes.**

As a glacier moves down a valley it bulldozes a load of rock, sand, and gravel—known as **glacial till**—ahead of it, or carries it on top. The glacial till dumped by a glacier is called a **moraine. Lateral moraines** are pushed to the sides of glaciers, while **terminal moraines** are deposited at the point of the face's farthest advance. A **medial mo-**

raine is formed when a pair of glaciers unite. These ribbon-like strips of rubble can be followed back to the point where the lateral moraines converge between the glaciers.

When looking at a glaciated landscape, watch for gouges and scrape marks on the bedrock, which indicate the direction of glacial flow. Watch, too, for **erratics,** huge boulders carried long distances and deposited by the glacier, which often differ from the surrounding rock. Glacial runoff is often suffused with finely powdered till or **glacial flour,** which gives it a distinctive milky-white color; the abundance of this silt in glacial streams creates a twisting, braided course. With a little practice, you'll soon learn to recognize glacial features at a glance.

Permafrost

To picture permafrost, imagine a veneer of mud atop a slab of ice. In the colder places of the Lower 48, we measure how much surface soil freezes in winter. In Alaska, we measure how much surface soil thaws in summer. True permafrost is ground that has stayed frozen for more than two years. To create and maintain permafrost, the annual average temperature must remain below freezing. The topsoil above the permafrost that thaws in the summer is known as the **active layer.** With the proper conditions, permafrost will penetrate downward until it meets heat from the Earth's mantle. In the Arctic, permafrost begins a few feet below the surface and can extend 2,000 to 5,000 feet deep. This is known as **continuous permafrost,** which almost completely underlies the ground above the Arctic Circle. **Discontinuous permafrost** defines the more southerly stretches of the North, where the permafrost is scattered in patches according to ground conditions.

Frozen ground is no problem—until you need to dig in it. Russian engineers were the first to encounter large-scale problems with permafrost during the construction of the Trans-Siberian Railroad. In Alaska, gold mining, especially in deep placer operations, often required up to two years of thawing hundreds of feet of permafrost before dredging could proceed. Today, houses frequently undermine their own permafrost foundations:

Cirques, aretes, and medial moraines are easily identified in this photograph of spectacular Nabesna Glacier in the Wrangell Mountains.

heat from the house thaws the ground, causing it—and the house above it—to sink. Similarly, road-building clears the insulating vegetation layer and focuses heat on the frozen layer, causing severe "frost heaving," the roller-coaster effect common to roads in Interior Alaska. Most recently, pipeline engineers had to contend with similar effects that the 145° oil flowing through the pipe would have on the permafrost—resulting in potentially disastrous financial and ecological consequences. That's why over half of the Trans-Alaska Pipeline is above ground, supported by a specially designed and elaborate system of heat-reducing pipes and radiators.

LAND ISSUES

Who Owns All This Real Estate?

In the beginning were the Natives, who shared their vast world with the other creatures of earth and sea and sky, and had no concept of owning land. Then came the Russians, who, just by virtue of having arrived, granted themselves ownership of all this earth and sea and sky, and all the creatures in it—including the Natives themselves. Later, the Europeans arrived, and with no less arrogance staked out chunks of Alaska for themselves in the absence of the Russian landlords. Then in 1867 the entire property was sold to the Americans who, over the next 100 years, split up the land into Navy petroleum reserves, Bureau of Land Management parcels, national wildlife refuges, power projects, and the like, to be administered by separate federal agencies, including National Park, Forest, and military services. By the time Alaska became a state in 1959, only .003% of the land was privately owned—mostly homesteads and mining operations, and .01% had been set aside for Native reservations, administered by the Bureau of Indian Affairs.

The Statehood Act allowed Alaska to choose 104 million acres to own. But the selection process finally catalyzed the long-simmering feud between the governments and the Native peoples; that, and the issue of

ownership of the rights-of-way for the Alaska Pipeline, gave birth to the largest settlement ever secured by an indigenous people. The Alaska Native Claims Settlement Act (ANCSA) of 1971 created 12 Native corporations, among which were divided 44 million acres of land, along with just under one billion dollars in federal funds and state oil royalties. People claiming at least one quarter Native blood were entitled to sign up as stockholders in village and regional corporations. "ANCSA sought to bring Natives into the mainstream of the state economy and culture," writes Chelsea Congdon in the *Cultural Survival Quarterly* (No. 4, 1990) "as corporate shareholders of much of Alaska's resource capital."

Today, ANCSA is viewed as a mixed blessing at best. The two important issues facing Alaska's Natives revolve around subsistence rights and the ultimate disposal of Native lands. ANCSA prohibited the sale and taxing of the Native lands for 20 years—until 1991. Now having arrived, it's feared that well-financed buyers will make offers on the mineral-rich lands that shareholders won't be able to refuse, and that financially burdened Native corporations will have to sell some of their lands to pay the new taxes. Recent amendments to ANCSA have set up procedures to prevent the "alienation of Native assets by the Native corporations created to manage them." Subsistence issues are becoming increasingly controversial, since the state has been reluctant to protect Native subsistence claims in the face of federal withdrawals of conservation lands and the growing tourist and fishing industries.

Boomers And Doomers

ANCSA designated 80 million acres to be withdrawn from the public domain and set aside as national-interest lands (conservation property) by 1978. In the mid- to late '70s, in the wake of the completion of the pipeline, this was the raging land issue, generally divided between fiercely independent Alaskans who protested the further "locking-up" of their lands by Washington bureaucrats, and conservationists who lobbied to preserve Alaska's wildlife and wilderness. Finally, 106 million acres were preserved by these so-called "d2" lands (from section 17:d-2 of ANCSA), which included the expansion of Mt. McKinley National Park (renamed Denali), the expansion of Glacier Bay and Katmai national monuments, which became national parks, and the creation of Gates of the Arctic, Kobuk Valley, Wrangell-St. Elias, Kenai Fjords, and Lake Clark national parks, plus numerous national monuments and preserves, scenic and wild rivers, and new wildlife refuges.

Arctic National Wildlife Refuge

Another battle has been brewing for over a decade. At issue is whether or not to allow exploration and drilling for black gold on a 2,300-acre corner of the 1.5-million-acre Arctic National Wildlife Refuge (ANWR), known as Study Area 1002. In a political compromise in 1980, the Alaska National Interest Lands Conservation Act (ANILCA), which set aside millions of acres for parks and wilderness, also called for a federal study to determine if oil and gas could be safely recovered within ANWR. Oil companies are looking ahead to the day when the Prudhoe Bay reserves finally run dry (15 years after the start of oil flowing through the pipeline, the reserves are estimated to be well over half depleted), and claim that the pipeline's 15 years of operation have proven oil development and environmental protection to be compatible (on the North Slope). Also, improved technology has greatly refined development techniques, which further safeguard the wilderness.

Conservationists, on the other hand, know that the caribou herds and 200 other species of wildlife the refuge was installed to protect will be endangered; they argue that this refuge is one of the few places on Earth that protect the complete spectrum of Arctic ecosystems.

Often overlooked in the arguments about caribou and petroleum are the Inupiat, known as the Twilight People, of Kaktovik village on Barter Island, which for thousands of years was a crucial link on the trading route between Greenland and Siberia. The only settlement in the Arctic National Wildlife Refuge, 70% of the villagers depend on subsistence hunting for survival. For a while after the *Exxon Valdez*'s oil spill, the environmentalists held the high moral ground, but the war in the Persian Gulf has recently caused the momentum of the fight to change dramatically. The Bush administration tried desperately to convince Congress to quickly open up ANWR to big oil. But in November 1991, the Senate killed Bennett Johnson's (D-La.) energy "blueprint," which would have opened ANWR for drilling, made it easier to drill offshore, and eased regulations for building nuclear-power plants and gas pipelines. So it looks like ANWR is safe for at least another year, and probably for some time thereafter.

CLIMATE

Granted, over the course of a year, in any given location, Alaska's weather can be extreme and quite unexpected. Because of the predictable harshness of the winters, comfortable travel to many popular destinations is difficult from early Oct. to late April. Contrary to popular misconception, however, the weather can also be quite pleasant. Alaska's spring, summer, and fall are not unlike these seasons elsewhere. It's cool, it's warm; it's wet and dry; sometimes it's windy, sometimes it's muggy, sometimes it's foggy. Maybe it's the worst weather in the world outside, but you're snuggling with your girlfriend in your large new tent after the most exciting raft ride of your life. Maybe it's the crispest, clearest day of your trip, but your camera got soaked in the river and your boyfriend ran off with the tourguide. The weather, here as everywhere, has as much to do with the internal climate as the external. Be happy in the sun. Try to stay happy in the rain. Just keep happy. You're in Alaska.

Superlatives And Trends

It hit 100° F in the state once, in Fort Yukon in 1915. Fairbanks regularly breaks 90° F in July. It gets cold in Fort Yukon too, dropping as low as -78° F (Alaska's record low is -82, recorded in aptly named Coldfoot in 1989). *Any* wind at all at that temperature would make you feel even colder, if that's possible. Thompson Pass near Valdez gets quite a bit of snow, holding the records for the most in 24 hours (five feet), a month (25 feet), and a year (81 feet). But Barrow, at the tip of the proverbial "frozen wasteland," got just three inches of snow in 1936-37. An average 13 feet of rain falls in Ketchikan every year—what they call "liquid sunshine." But again, one year Barrow squeaked by with only an inch.

Though Alaska retains the reputation of the Great Frozen North, a distinct warming trend has had a noticeable effect on the state. Temperatures warmed abruptly in the summer of 1977 and have remained unusually warm ever since, throughout all the seasons. For example, meteorologists report that in the Interior, only on rare occasions over the past 15 years has the mercury dropped below minus 40. Also, the temperature of the permafrost has risen several degrees. These indications, among others, of the greenhouse effect, have been partially attributed to the thinning ozone layer above the Arctic, similar to the "hole" that appears over the Antarctic every spring. Chloroflourocarbons (CFCs) are considered the main culprit; Halon, a CFC found in fire extinguishers, is particularly prevalent in the fire-fighting systems of oil and gas developers. The ozone depletion in the northern hemisphere is thought to have much more dire consequences than in the southern, since the north is much more populated.

Some exceptions to the warming trend have occurred recently. In 1989, both record cold and heat were recorded throughout Alaska. And in Anchorage in August 1989 it

THE PINEAL GLAND

Most Alaskan lifeforms pack a year's worth of living into the five months of light, then hibernate through the seven months of dark and cold. This is not only a cliché; it's also a fact, based on physiology—the physiology of the pineal gland, to be specific. This gland (shaped like a *pine* cone) sits on a short stem in the oldest and most mysterious section of the human brain. It's a lonely gland, a unique, asymmetrical neuronub, surrounded by large masses of advanced symmetrical tissue. Until recently, it was among the most obscure structures in the human neurological frontier; in fact, only 10 years ago it wasn't even considered a gland, but was known only as the pineal "body." This is somewhat surprising, since its function in other vertebrates has been understood for a hundred years. In fish, reptiles, and birds, the pineal "eye" sits on a long stalk close to the brain's outer frontal section, right between the two regular eyes, where a third eye would be. However, it's not connected to the eyes or any other sensory pathways. Rather, the pineal gland is a simple, efficient photoreceptor, which senses and interprets the relative duration, intensity, and polarizing angles of light in the environment—the primary organ responsible for regulating internal circadian and seasonal rhythms. It tells fish how to navigate, birds when to migrate, and mammals when to sleep and reproduce.

The latter two are the key to understanding the gland's function in humans. Our gland produces a single (that we know of) hormone: melatonin. Melatonin circulates through the body and triggers two known reactions: drowsiness and reduced sex drive. What inhibits melatonin production? Light! The more sunlight—the higher its intensity and the steeper its angle—the less drowsiness and the stronger sex drive we feel. This helps explain many interesting general phenomena, such as why we sleep less deeply when it's not dark, the physiology of "spring fever," and why sex is better during the day, as well as specific northern occurrences, such as why an amazing 72% of Alaskan babies are conceived between May and Sept. (as opposed to Nov. and Feb. as is commonly believed), and why you can do with a lot less sleep in Alaska in the summer.

In Inuit mythology the sun is embodied by the female aspect, while the moon is male. The face in this sun is based on a print credited to Johnniebo, a Canadian Inuit (1923-72). Note the tilt of the Earth on its axis; this illustrates why Fairbanks stays light for three solid months in summer, dark for three in winter. (BOB RACE)

rained nearly 10 inches, three inches more than the previous record rainfall. Anchorage sustained a torrential four inches in 24 hours—some people actually kayaked to work!

Climatic Zones

It's possible to generalize about Alaskan weather, and distinguish three climatic zones: coastal maritime, Interior, and Arctic. The main factor affecting the coasts—Southeast, Southcentral, and Southwest—is the warm Japanese Current, which causes temperatures to be much milder than the norm at that latitude. This current also brings continuous rain as the humid Pacific air is forced up over the coastal mountains. For example, it rains in Juneau two out of every three days. However, these mountains shield the Interior plateaus from the maritime air streams, so yearly precipitation there is low, up to a mere 15 inches. The Interior experiences great temperature extremes, from biting cold in winter to summer heat waves. The mountains also protect the coastal areas from cold—and hot!—Interior air masses. The Arctic Zone is characterized by cool, cloudy, and windy summers (averaging 50° F) and cold, windy winters, though not as cold as the Interior.

THE LIGHT AND THE DARK

If you plan to be in Alaska from late May to late July, you can leave the flashlight at home. If you camped at the North Pole for a week on either side of summer solstice, the sun would appear to barely move in the sky, frying you to a crisp from the same spot overhead as if stuck in space. The Arctic Circle, at 67° latitude, is usually defined as the line above which the sun doesn't set on June 21, nor rise on December 21 (though it's also sometimes defined as the line above which no trees grow, or the line above which the mean monthly temperature never exceeds 50° F).

Barrow lies at 71° latitude, four degrees and roughly 270 miles north of the Arctic Circle. Here the sun doesn't dip below the horizon for 84 days, from May 10 to Aug. 2. (You'll definitely see, and probably buy, the famous postcard with the time-lapse photograph showing the sun tracing a very mild curve: "going down" in the north-northwest, hovering above the horizon, and "coming up" in the north-northeast.)

Fairbanks, 140 miles south of the Circle, has 22 hours of direct sunlight on summer solstice, with the sky (if it's clear) going from a bright orange-blue to a sunset purple to a sunrise pink and back to bright orange-blue in continuous two-hour cycles. Even Ketchikan, at around 55° N latitude and probably the southernmost point on most Alaskan itineraries, enjoys over 18 hours of daylight, with the starless dusk a paler shade of twilight. Similarly, in December Ketchikan receives six hours of pale daylight and Fairbanks only three, but at Barrow you wouldn't see the sun at all for nine weeks.

Why?

The explanation for the "midnight sun" lies in the tilted angle at which the Earth rotates on its axis. Because of the off-center tilt, the Arctic Circle leans toward the sun in summer; a complete 24-hour rotation of the planet makes little difference in the angle at which the sun's rays strike the north country. However, the rays do have to travel farther, and they strike Alaska at a lower angle, which you'll notice: the sun never gets nearly as high in the sky here as you're probably used to. Because of the low angle, the rays are diffused over a larger area, thus losing some intensity, which accounts for the cooler air temperatures. And since the sun seems to move across the sky at a low angle, it takes longer to "set" and "rise." In addition, the atmosphere refracts (bends) the sunbeams more dramatically closer to the poles, which causes the low light to linger even after the sun is down. This soft, slanting light is often magical, with sharp shadows, muted colors, silky silhouettes—a photographer's dream (see p. 48-49).

Northern Lights

The continual light is a trippy novelty if you're traveling around Alaska for just a few weeks, but when you're there all summer, to paraphrase the commercial, D-A-R-K spells relief. Stars? What a concept! Headlights? Oy vey! From early August on, though, you start losing daylight quickly, to the tune of an hour a week in Fairbanks. Temperatures drop, berries and rose hips ripen, mushrooms sprout, and there's the possibility of experiencing one of life's all-time great thrills: God's light show, the aurora borealis.

The far-flung Inuit had a variety of mythical explanations for the lights. Many believed that they represented the spirits of ancestors or animals, while others relegated the lights to malevolent forces. Prospectors preferred to think of them as vapors from rich ore deposits. The Japanese, however, have attributed the most romance to them: a marriage consummated under the lights will be especially fulfilling. Scientists have lately raised some controversy over particular aspects of the aurora, such as that the lights never dip below 40 miles above the Earth (though many northerners swear they've seen the lights dancing along the ground); whether or not the lights manifest an electric sound is still a matter of some dissension, and even the experts who believe it don't know why. But these days nearly everyone agrees that the sun, again, is responsible for the show.

When the solar surface sparks, the energy propels a wave of ionized particles (known as the solar wind) through space. When these anxious ions encounter the gases in the Earth's atmosphere, a mad-cap night of oxygen-nitrogen couples dancing begins. The sun's particles and the Earth's gases pair off, with the fastest ions grabbing the highest gases. The ensuing friction causes a red or yellow afterglow. The slower ions infiltrate the lower regions, and those encounters glow green and violet. The waving, shimmering, writhing ribbons of color cannot fail to excite your own ions and gases.

SPARKS IN THE DARK

The stars help guide the northern traveler, and the rhythms of the moon count off the months. But of all the celestial lights, the unpredictable aurora borealis may serve the highest function, stirring our spirits and sparking our imagination in the deadening dark of winter. Some say the northern lights can shine right into the soul and lift a piece of it into the heavens, reflecting there the hope and fear and love and wonder that each of us carries within.

—David and Karen Foster,
ALASKA Magazine, Oct. 1989

FAUNA

INTRODUCTION

If ever Alaska embodied the image of the "last frontier," it's in its animal kingdom. For millenia, Native hunters, with their small-scale weapons and limited needs, had little impact on wildlife populations. Inuit and Aleut villages subsisted comfortably on fish, small mammals, and one or two whales a year; the interior Athabascan bands did well on a handful of moose and caribou. This all changed in the mid-1700s with the coming of the rapacious white man. Sea otters, fur seals, and gray whales were quickly hunted to the verge of extinction. By the 1850s, the Alaskan musk ox, largest member of the sheep family, had been annihilated. Caribou were reduced to a tenth of their original numbers, and wolves, in part because they preyed on the same game as man, were ruthlessly exterminated.

Fortunately, conservation measures have nurtured the numbers, and today Alaska boasts one of the largest concentrations of animal populations remaining on Earth. For example, there are more caribou in Alaska than there are people. There's a moose, and a Sitka black-tailed deer, for every three people. If 80,000 sheep strikes you as an impressive number, consider 40,000 grizzly bears. Bald and golden eagles are commonplace, and while the magnificent trumpeter swan was believed near extinction in the Lower 48, it was thriving in Alaska. Marine mammals, from orcas to the recovering otters, are abundant, and Alaskan waters also contain fish and other sea creatures in unimaginable quantities.

Salmon, halibut, crab, pollock, herring, and smelt, among others, are well known for their positive impact on Alaska's economy; nearly six *billion* salmon, for example, have been harvested in Alaska, representing a dollar value higher than all the gold recovered there. But the economic value of Alaska's wildlife has only recently begun to be appreciated by state managers. Tourism, Alaska's third-largest industry, is based almost entirely on scenery and wildlife. From the "Tundra Wildlife Safari" at Denali National Park to the $7,000 for each big-game animal killed in state, Alaska's fauna is one of the country's greatest renewable resources and will remain so, if handled with care.

Note: Visitors to the north should be aware that wildlife may be encountered, up close, almost anywhere outdoors, and even indoors occasionally. Many animals are well prepared to defend their territories against intruders (you), and even the smallest can bite. Never attempt to feed or touch wildlife. It is seldom good for it, you, or those who follow. Any animal that appears unafraid or "tame" can be quite unpredictable, so keep your distance. If you have a pet along, watch it carefully; dogs unfamiliar to locals are often shot first and questioned afterward. Any mosquitos or other insects reading this are urged not to bother visitors. Hiking in bear country requires special precautions; see p. 292-293. One thing you don't have to worry about is snakes; there are none in Alaska.

LAND MAMMALS

Grizzlies

The grizzly is the symbol of the wild country, the measure of its wildness. Grizzlies once roamed all over North America. In 1800, there were over 100,000 of them; today, less than 300 survive in the Lower 48. Ironically, the grizzly is the state animal of California, where it is now extinct. However, an estimated 32,000 to 43,000 of these magnificent creatures inhabit Alaska.

You're most likely to see a grizzly at Denali National Park. Denali doesn't have a fatally serious bear problem like Glacier or Yellowstone parks. The estimated 200 Denali grizzlies are still wild, mostly in their natural state.

grizzly bear   (MIKE WELLINS)

This is especially important for the continued education of the cubs, who are taught how to dig roots, find berries, catch ground squirrels, and take moose calves. However, Denali grizzlies are not afraid of people, are extremely curious, and some *have* tasted canned beans, vegie burgers, and Oreo cookies. While no one has been killed by a grizzly at Denali, maulings have occurred, usually due to the foolishness of novice hikers and photographers, or as a result of improper food storage. Take care, but don't be afraid to go hiking.

The natural grizzly diet is 80% vegetarian. They eat berries, willows, and roots, as well as preying on anything they can take: from ground squirrels to caribou, from foxes to small black bears. And they're challenged by nothing, except men with high-powered weapons. Grizzlies are racehorse fast and have surprising endurance; they need about 50 square miles for home territory, and travel several miles a night. During the day they like to eat, sleep in the sun—often on snow patches—and entertain tourists on the shuttle buses.

Grizzlies are solitary creatures. Full-grown boars and sows are seen together only during mating season, in July. The gestation period is a little over five months, and the sows give birth in December to one to three cubs. The cubs are hairless, weigh one pound, and remain blind for a week. They stay with the mother for over two and a half years, two full summers. They're then chased away sometime before July of the third summer, when the sow is ready to mate again.

Contrary to popular belief, bears do not hibernate. They do sleep deeply in dens during the winter, sometimes for weeks. But they often get hungry, lonely, or restless, and step outside to forage for frozen roots, berries, and meat. Sometimes a bear will stay out all winter; that's the one that the Natives fear the most: the winter bear. Its fur tends to build up a thick layer of ice, rendering it nearly impenetrable, almost bullet-proof. And of course, sows give birth in the deep winter, which they're certainly awake for.

Grizzlies and brown bears were once thought to be different species, but now are considered the same. Their basic difference is size, due to habitat. Grizzlies themselves are the world's largest land omnivore, growing to heights of six to seven feet tall, and weighing in at 800 to 1,000 pounds. However, they're the smaller of the two, because they live in the interior and feed mostly on vegetation. Brown bears are coastal, and with a rich source of fish protein, have achieved near mythical sizes. Kodiak brown bears retain a reputation for being the largest and most concentrated, reaching heights of over 10 feet and weights of 1,500 pounds. But Admiralty Island brown bears give nothing away in either department.

Moose

The moose is the largest member of the deer family, and Alaska has the largest moose. A bull moose in his prime gets to be about seven feet tall and weighs around 1,200 pounds—all from eating willow stems—about 30 pounds a day of them. They also eat aspen and birch, but willow is the staple of choice. The antlers, which are bone, are shed and renewed every year. Full-size antlers can weigh up to 50 pounds—that's mostly in Sept., during the rut, or impregnation time. Bulls of near-equal rank and size butt their heads together to vie for dominance. You want to be real careful of bulls then. Touchy. The cows have one or two calves, rarely three, in May, and that's when you want to be real careful of the cows, too. The calves stay with the cow exactly a year, then she chases away the yearling. Sometimes at the start of the summer season you spot a huge pregnant cow with a frisky yearling on her heels, and you've never seen a more hassled-looking expression on an animal's face. But that's family life.

Moose don't cover too much territory, about 30 miles a year, mostly in the forest, which provides their natural defense against predators. The word *moose* comes from the Massachusetts Algonquian dialect, and means "muncher of little twigs." By the way, the little flap of hair under the moose's chin is known as the moostache.

The winter of 1989-1990 was something of a disaster for moose on the mainland. The deep snow and bitter cold caused 40-45% of the animals along the railbelt, from Wasilla to Talkeetna, and on the Kenai Peninsula, to perish. Hundreds of moose made their last stand along the snowless railroad tracks and were killed by trains that didn't stop for them. Other hundreds starved to death. Many were hit by cars along roadways; fresh roadkill is butchered and distributed to the local people. Hunting quotas were drastically reduced, and moose numbers have recovered slightly since.

If Alaska moose are the world's largest, Kenai Peninsula moose are Alaska's largest. A Kenai moose holds the Alaskan record: at 10-11 years old, his antlers were just under 75 inches wide, he weighed between 1,500 and 1,600 pounds, and he gave his life for Guiness. Appropriately, the Moose Research Center is on Swanson River Road, about 50 miles from Soldotna on the Kenai Peninsula, in an area that sustained a large forest fire in the late 1940s and in 1969, providing excellent young forage for the prevalent moose. The Research Center was opened in 1969, and has four square-mile and two 15-acre pens, which can comfortably contain a dozen or so moose.

Caribou

Caribou are travelin' fools. They're extremely flighty animals—restless, tireless, fast, and graceful. Run and eat, run and eat, is pretty much all they do, and oh yeah, reproduce. Reindeer, in the same species, are smaller, and often domesticated. Caribou are peaceful critters, and they'll outrun and outdistance their predators, mostly wolves, rather than fight. They like to travel in groups, unlike moose, which are loners. And they cover 10 times as much territory. Their herding and migrating imperatives are similar to the plains bison; they gather in large numbers and think nothing of running 50 miles, almost on a lark. An estimated 550,000 to 600,000 caribou are found in Alaska in 12 major herds.

Caribou are extremely well adapted to their winter environment. They have huge nasal passages and respiratory systems in order to breathe the bitter cold winter air. Thick fur covers almost every inch of their bodies; the fur itself is protected by large, hollow, oily guard hairs. This tends to make caribou look much larger than they really are; a good-size bull weighs 400-500 pounds, cows about half that. They've also got huge prancing hooves, immortalized in the Santa Claus myth, which are excellent for running, swimming, disco dancing, and pawing at the snow to uncover the moss and lichens on which they subsist all through the harsh Arctic winter. Caribou also have the richest milk in the animal kingdom: 20% fat. The word *caribou* comes from the Maine Algonquian dialect and means "scraping hooves."

The caribou is the only member of the deer family whose females grow antlers. Babies are on their feet and nursing within an hour of birth, and at one week they can run 20 miles. If they can't, they'll most likely die, since the herd won't wait. But this helps to keep the herd healthy, controls population growth, and provides food for the carnivores.

The Eskimo are among the caribou's natural predators. The Eskimo, at one time, made use of 99% of a caribou carcass. They ate the meat raw, roasted, and stewed. They ate all the organs, even the half-digested greens from the stomach. The little gobs of fat from behind the eyes were considered a delicacy. They used caribou hide almost exclusively for clothes, rugs, blankets, and tents. The leg skins were used to make *mukluks;* the long strands of stringy sinew provided sewing thread.

Dall Sheep

Named for William H. Dall, one of the first men to survey the lower Yukon (1866), Dall sheep are sometimes called Alaska bighorn sheep, because the Rocky Mountain bighorn are a closely related species. Distinguished by their brilliant white color, the rams grow large curved horns, formed from a specialized skin structure made up of a compacted mass of hair and oil. The horns aren't shed; instead the sheep add another ring to them yearly, so the longer the horns, the older the ram, and the more dominant within the herd. The rams can weigh as much as 300 pounds; the ewes have small spiked horns and average 150 pounds. Their habitat is the high alpine tundra, and they subsist on grasses, mosses, lichens, and flowers. Their bird's-eye view provides an excellent defense. They're also magnificent mountain climbers. Roughly 60,000 to 80,000 Dall sheep reside in the Chugach, Kenai, Alaska, and Wrangell mountain ranges in Alaska. During summer, the rams migrate high into the ranges, leaving the prime lower grazing grounds for the ewes and lambs.

It's natural that they migrate, the same way it's natural that they have predators. Like the caribou, their alpine tundra habitat is very fragile, and takes literally hundreds of years to regenerate after overgrazing. Migration and predation thus keep the flock healthy, control population growth, and guarantee the survival of the habitat.

Wolves

Wolves have traditionally been one of the most misunderstood, misrepresented, and maligned mammals, in both fact and fable. We've come a long way from the days when it was believed that wolves were innately evil, with the visage of the devil himself, eating their hapless prey, or little girls in red hoods, alive. But it wasn't until the mid-1940s, when wildlife biologist Adolph Murie began a long-term and systematic study of the wolves in Mt. McKinley National Park that all the misconceptions comprising the accepted lore about wolves began to change.

For three years Murie tramped mainly on the plains below Polychrome Pass, and became extremely intimate with several wolf families. (His book, *The Wolves of Mount McKinley,* published in 1944, is still considered a classic natural history text.) Though

Murie concluded that a delicate balance is established between predator and prey to their mutual advantage, declining Dall sheep populations, political pressure and, indeed, tradition forced the Park Service to kill wolves, who were considered, against Murie's conclusions, to be the cause of the sheep decline. Typically, though, the wolf population was in just as dire straits as the sheep, and for several years no wolves were killed in the feds' traps *due to their scarcity.*

wolf (BOB RACE)

Since then, many researchers and writers have come to incisive conclusions about the wolf. It's been determined that their social systems—within the pack and with the prey—are amazingly complex and sophisticated. The alpha male and female are the central players in the pack, surrounded by four to seven pups, yearlings, and other adults. The dominant female undergoes a long involved courtship from the dominant male (though he might not necessarily always be the biological father of the pups). Territories can be as small as 200 square miles and as large as 800 square miles, depending on a host of influences.

Perhaps the most complex and fascinating aspect of wolf activity is the hunt. Barry Lopez, author of the brilliant *Of Wolves and Men,* argues persuasively that the individual prey is as responsible for its own killing, in effect "giving itself to the wolf in ritual suicide," as the wolf is in killing it. Lopez maintains that the eye contact between the wolf and its prey "is probably a complex exchange of information regarding the appropriateness of a chase and a kill." Lopez calls this the "conversation of death." Further, he points out that domestic stock have had this interspecies language bred out of them. "The domestic horse, a large animal as capable as a moose of cracking a wolf's ribs or splitting its head open with a kick, will almost always panic and run. It will always be killed. The wolf who has initiated a prescribed ritual has received nothing in return; he has met with ignorance in an animal with no countervailing ritual of its own. So he wounds and kills in anger."

With the advent of radio collaring and tracking from airplanes, the movements of individual wolves and packs have continually surprised wildlife biologists. Wolves often travel five to ten miles an hour for hours at a time. In a matter of days, an individual cut loose from a pack can wind up 500 miles away. Thus wolves are able to select and populate suitable habitats quickly.

Alaska's 6,000-7,000 wolves are reportedly thriving, even though roughly 15% of them are harvested yearly. They've expanded their habitat and their numbers are increasing slowly but surely. They have one extremely fortuitous circumstance in the north country: the lack of a livestock industry. Ranchers have always been the wolf's worst enemy.

Ground Squirrels And Marmots

These two members of the rodent family, unlike brown, grizzly, and polar bears, are true hibernators: they sleep straight for six months, in a deep coma. This separation between life and death is one of the thinnest lines in the animal world. A ground squirrel's heart slows to about six beats a minute, and his body temperature lowers to just above freezing, around 38° F. (In fact, a zoophysicist at University of Alaska-Fairbanks has found that the core temperature of the arctic ground squirrel, the northernmost hibernator, can drop as low as 26° F—six degrees below freezing! Of course, the squirrels don't "freeze," but "supercool.")

He takes a breath every couple of minutes. He uses up half his body weight. If you stuck a needle in a hibernating ground squirrel's paw, it would take him about 10 minutes to begin to feel it.

Ground squirrels provide a large part of the grizzly and wolf diet, and scavenger birds' as well, since they're a common kind of roadkill.

Marmots, similar to woodchucks, are often mistaken for wolverines. They live in large rock outcrops for protection, and have a piercing whistle which warns of approaching predators or other possible danger. Look for marmots around Polychrome Pass at Denali Park; ask the driver where exactly.

Elk

Elk, a common sight in the western Lower 48, were also prevalent in Alaska 10,000 years ago, but disappeared during the last ice age. In the mid-1920s, Alaskans decided that elk would be an attractive addition to the Territory's big-game species, and a handful of elk were imported from Washington state. After a few years of island hopping, the cervids (deer family) were finally transplanted to their permanent homes, Afognak Island off the north coast of Kodiak, and from there they apparently swam to Raspberry Island and Kodiak. Though the country was rugged—wet, windy, and choked with alder—the elk thrived in their new homes, and some grew to 1,000 pounds. Within only 20 years (1950), 27 bulls were culled from the herd by resident hunters. Hunting continued up until the late 1960s, after a series of severe winters had decimated the herds. Ten years' worth of protection and mild winters allowed the herds to regenerate; 1,300 elk today reside on Afognak and Raspberry islands, and around 25 on Kodiak. Roughly 200 elk are harvested a year.

Musk-ox

Musk-ox, a sort of shaggy prehistoric bison, were abundant in the north country until they were hunted into total extinction by the mid-1800s. In the 1930s, several dozen musk-ox were transplanted from Greenland to Nunivak Island in the Bering Sea. Like the elk on Afognak, the musk-ox on Nunivak thrived, and the resident Natives used the soft underwool to establish a small cottage knitting industry of sweaters, scarves, and caps. And that's what it would have remained, a small cottage industry, if it hadn't been for Dr. John J. Teal Jr., a student of arctic explorer Vilhjalmur Stefansson. Stefansson recognized the potential of musk-ox wool, and inspired Teal to experiment with domesticating them. After spending 10 years with musk-ox on his farm in Vermont, Teal concluded that they were amiable, hardy, and easy to domesticate. So in 1964, he started the Musk Ox Project at the U of A in Fairbanks.

The project moved to a farm in the Matanuska Valley in 1984, where musk-ox are bred to produce *qiviut* (KEE-vee-ute), the soft underwool, which is renowned in Alaska for its insulation (eight times warmer by weight than sheep wool) and textural (softer than the finest cashmere) properties. The qiviut is combed from the animals in the spring; four to seven pounds per musk-ox is taken in about three hours. The raw wool is sent to a mill in Rhode Island, and then sold to Oomingmak (the Native word for musk-ox, meaning "bearded one"), a coop consisting of 200 members in villages spread throughout western Alaska. Here the qiviut is knitted into garments, which are sold at retail outlets in Anchorage and at the farm. For more information on visiting both, see pages 327 and 344.

Lynx

The lynx is the northern version of the bobcat, Alaska's only native cat. Lynx are extremely shy and secretive animals, which prey primarily on snowshoe hare. These days, the Kenai Peninsula provides a good example of the continuing danger to fur-bearing animals. The lynx were hunted heavily in the late 1970s when their pelts were worth up to $500 apiece. The diminished lynx population allowed the snowshoe hare to proliferate. But just as the lynx were regenerating, the hare population crashed according to its seven-year cycle, leaving the lynx without its primary food source. And now the lynx have been reported to be active in urban areas such as Soldotna and Sterling, where they raid chicken coops and rabbit pens. The Kenai Peninsula, of course, is a "biological island" only marginally connected to the rest of the Alaska habitat, so Kenai lynx are particularly endangererd.

But with the hare cycle down throughout Alaska, lynx everywhere are hungry in the early 1990s. One of the wild cats actually chased a dog through a pet door into a house near Chugach State Park, and a lynx attacked a domestic goat near Fairbanks.

Mountain Goats

These members of the antelope family number between 13,000 and 15,000 in Alaska. They have snow-white coats, shaggy heads, black-spiked horns up to a foot long, and weigh in between 150 and 300 pounds. They mostly inhabit the coastal ranges and eastern Alaska Range, and are frequently seen high up on cliffs so precipitous that they would probably even scare Dall sheep.

Sitka Black-tailed Deer

This deer is neck and neck with moose for the position of second-most prevalent game animal in Alaska behind caribou, with roughly 150,000 to 175,000 individuals. The Sitka deer prefers a forest environment along the coast—in Southeast, around Prince William Sound, and on Kodiak and surrounding islands—and roam high into the coastal ranges for young shrubs and ripe berries in the late summer months. Males weigh 150 pounds, females 100 pounds.

Black Bear

Sharing the coastal forest habitat with the Sitka black-tailed deer is the black bear, which also comes in cinnamon and glacier blue. Black bears are distinguished from grizzlies and brown bears by their size (much smaller), the shape of their face (much narrower), and by the lack of a shoulder hump. Black bears are actually more dangerous to people than grizzlies: there have been more attacks and maulings in Alaska by black bears than browns.

Others

Alaska has a number of various members of the rodent family: shrews, mice, voles, lemmings (along with squirrels, marmots, and porcupines). Long-tailed and least weasels occupy a wide habitat in the taiga and tundra. Martens are another member of the weasel family, similar to but larger and much more aggressive than mink; the pine marten is one of Alaska's most valuable fur-bearers. Wolverines and badgers are in attendance, though you'd be very lucky to see one. Red fox are common in Interior and Southcentral, and you're likely to see one at Denali Park; the white Arctic fox is a gorgeous animal, though you'll only see one in pictures.

MARINE MAMMALS

Sea Otters

The mass and brutal slaughter of almost *all* of these beautiful creatures by Russian, European, and American traders is especially heart-wrenching, simply because the sea otter, of all the sea mammals in northern waters, is so playfully human-like. James Michener, in his epic *Alaska,* described it thus: "It resembled precisely the face of a bewhiskered old man, one who had enjoyed life and aged gracefully. There was the wrinkled brow, the bloodshot eye, the nose, the smiling lips and, strangest of all, the whispy untended mustache. In fact, this face was so like a man's that later hunters would sometimes be startled by the watery vision and refrain momentarily from killing the otter lest an involuntary murder take place."

Marine member of the weasel family, the sea otter had one characteristic that would seal its doom: a long, wide, beautiful pelt, one of the warmest, most luxurious and durable furs in existence. Otter furs were so valuable that they fetched up to $5000 in London or Canton. Once found from the Aleutians to Mexico, otter fur catalyzed the Russian *promyshleniki* to begin overrunning the Aleutians in the mid- to late-18th century, sealing the doom of the Aleuts as well as the otters. In 1803, Aleksandr Baranov shipped 15,000 pelts back to eastern Russia. Up until the 1840s, otter hunting was the primary industry in the Pacific, and when the Americans purchased Alaska in 1867, nearly a million otters had been killed in the northern Pacific.

(Michener claims that dead sea otters sink and that the number of otters taken represents roughly 20% of those killed. But Jim Rearden, outdoors writer for *ALASKA* Magazine refutes this, stating that sea otters always float when they die.)

During the extreme lawless period in the last quarter of the 19th century, the otters were annihilated. In 1906, schooners cruised the north Pacific for months without taking a single pelt. In 1910, a crack crew of 40 Aleut hunters managed to harvest 16 otters. In 1911, otters were added to the International Fur Seal Treaty, giving them complete protection from everybody. Small, isolated populations of otters had managed to survive in the western Aleutians, and their numbers have increased over the past 80 years to roughly 150,000 sea otters today—to the point where they could start to threaten Alaska's shellfish industry. Still, only Native Alaskans have legal rights to hunt the otter.

The *Exxon Valdez* oil spill claimed 5,500 otters; one of the saddest and most enduring images from the disaster was of the uncomprehending face of an otter peering above jet black, greasy water.

Sea Lions

"George Wilhelm Steller, the first white man to set foot in Alaska, described the northern (Steller) sea lion for science in the spring of 1742," writes Marybeth Holleman in the July/August 1991 issue of *Greenpeace* Magazine. Two marine mammals ended up with his name, the North Pacific (Steller) sea cow, a cold-water relative of the manatee, and the Steller sea lion. "Because of its tameness, its total lack of fear of humans, and the reputed tastiness of its flesh, the sea cow was extinct only 26 years later. Now, 250 years after its discovery, the same fate may await his sea lion."

Steller sea lions, named after the naturalist aboard Vitus Bering's abortive second exploration of Alaska, are pinnipeds—marine mammals with flippers, not feet. Males can weigh up to a ton; females peak at 600 pounds. Sea lions eat several kinds of fish, but mostly pollock. These playful animals were abundant in Alaskan waters up until quite recently. In 1960, for example, an estimated 140,000 sea lions frolicked in the northern Pacific, the Gulf of Alaska, and along the Aleutians. But within 25 years, they had fallen to disturbing levels. Commercial hunting was halted in the mid-1970s, but a mere 68,000 remained in 1985. In only another four years, 25,000 sea lions were counted. That same year, they were listed as a threatened species—with only an estimated 66,000 sea lions remaining worldwide.

Speculation on the reasons for this precipitous decline is mostly centered around starvation: the remaining sea lions are small, anemic, malnourished, and have fewer babies. According to Greenpeace, "the culprit is most likely the burgeoning trawl fishery in the Bering Sea and Gulf of Alaska—a fishery that supplies fast-food filets, imitation crab legs, and highly prized roe to Japan."

The number of trawlers—huge factory ships which drag thousand-foot nets for miles over the ocean floor—have increased from 12 in 1986 to 70 in 1991. They now "clearcut" the ocean of nearly five *billion* pounds of bottomfish every year, over 10% of which is waste. Small wonder why the sea lions, along with harbor and fur seals and many indigenous seabird populations are showing signs of decline.

Whales

The largest summer marine visitors to Alaska are the whales. Each spring **gray whales** are seen migrating north from Baja California; in the fall they return south. Also in the spring **humpback whales** move north from Hawaii and are easily distinguished by their hump-like dorsal fin, large flippers, and huge tail which shows as they dive.

These 50-foot-long creatures often breach (jump) or beat the surface of the water with their tails, as if trying to send a message. Smaller (30-foot) **minke whales** are also common.

The **killer whale (orca),** which is not actually a whale but the largest of the dolphins (up to 24 feet long), travels in groups hunting fish and other mammals. Their six-foot-high, triangular dorsal fin and their black-and-white piebald pattern easily identify them. In the mid-1980s, small black cod and halibut fishing operations (longliners) in Prince William Sound had serious problems with orcas eating the fish caught on the end of the lines (up to 1,800 feet long). In 1986, for example, orcas were thought to have eaten a full third of the black cod or sablefish catch. Depth charges were used to try to scare the killer whales, and some were even shot. But by 1987, the problem seems to have lessened, and has since disappeared.

Fur Seal

The Alaska species of fur seal *(Callorhinus ursinus)* is a kind of "seal bear," as its Latin name suggests. The bulls grow up to seven feet long and 400 pounds. Tens of thousands of these caterwauling creatures return to the Pribilof Islands yearly to breed. The dominant bulls arrive after eight months at sea in early June, and the fight for the prime beach real estate often results in bloody bulls, and is always noisy. The cows show up a couple of weeks later—small (80 pounds), submissive, and steeling themselves for a bloody bounce on the beach. A big stud bull might accumulate 60-70 cows in his harem, and it's exactly as debilitatingly profligate a scene as it sounds: the bulls don't eat, living only off their own fat all summer, and look like Skid Row derelicts by mid-August when they take off to the North Pacific to eat, sleep, and regain their strength.

jumping orca
(BOB RACE)

The gestation period is one year, and the cows return to the same rookery to give birth. The pups swim away in late Oct., and return after a couple of years as "bachelors." Between two and seven years old, they play in the sand and surf, till the young males have grown big and bad enough to do the caveman bit with the cows. (For more information on fur seals and the Pribilofs, see p. 402.)

Walrus

What the Pribilofs are to the fur seal, Round Island in northern Bristol Bay is to the Pacific walrus. Except here, it's a boys-only beach club; the females and babies remain in the northern Bering and Chukchi seas, where they feed at the relatively shallow bottom. Sometimes up to 10,000 of these giant 3,000-pound bulls cram themselves onto narrow beaches at the bottom of steep cliffs around the one- by two-mile island. Tony Dawson, wildlife photographer for *ALASKA* Magazine, writes, "Socially, bull walruses are among the most argumentative in the world, always ready to fight at the drop of a flipper. Most bulls carry dozens of battle scars and scabs on their hides, which are as thick as tire casings. Lips are split and eyes injured or destroyed. Many bulls have chipped, broken, or missing tusks. Earlier breeding battles account for many injuries, but some result from petty disturbances of dozing neighbors."

On the beach, walruses are ungainly, akin to Subaru-sized slugs. But in the water, these big fat fatties are slo-mo smooth.

(To get to Round Island, fly Alaska Air to Dillingham, catch an air taxi to Togiak, and then grab a boat out to the island.)

BIRDS

Alaska is a bird-watcher's paradise. Everywhere you tern, there're not just a few birds to look at, but dozens, or scores, or hundreds of, say, puffins in Kachemak Bay, and even thousands of, for example, bald eagles in Haines (in October), and even millions of murres in the Pribilofs. Over 400 species of birds have been identified in Alaska, of which 200 species return to just the Pribilofs every

eagle   (BOB RACE)

summer. Nearly 100 species visit Potter Marsh just a few miles south of Anchorage.

Thus, it's no surprise that birding is big in the north land. Both birds and birdwatchers travel thousands of miles from all over the world to feed and breed or watch same. Some of the former are extremely rare. The bristle-thighed curlew, for one, has a population of a mere 5,000 worldwide, and their only breeding grounds are in Alaska. Eight of the curlews were banded in the Yukon Delta Wildlife Refuge in 1988, one of which was seen subsequently on Caysan Island in the South Pacific, over 2,000 miles away. Trumpeter swans, for another, were thought to be nearly extinct in the U.S., until several thousand were "discovered" in the Copper River Delta. Many Asian species, such as the greenshank and the Siberian ruby-throat, only foray into the Western Hemisphere as far as western Alaska.

Eagles

As many eagles are found in Alaska as in the rest of the U.S. combined. **Bald eagles** are so common along the coasts that they become almost commonplace—transformed, by familiarity, into the magnificent, high-soaring, scavengers and garbage eaters that they are. Still, with their unmistakable white heads, seven-foot wingspans, and dive-bombing salmon-snatching performances, the thrill is not too quickly gone. Every fall, thousands of bald eagles congregate around

Haines for the late salmon spawning runs nearby, and a lone scraggly black spruce hosting two dozen of the hoary-crowned birds is not unusual.

Golden eagles, found throughout the Interior, come without the distinctive "baldness," but are no less magnificent for their size, scavenging, and soaring habits. Plentiful around Denali Park, golden eagles perched on the tundra, standing more than three feet tall, have been mistaken for everything from grizzly cubs to teenage hikers.

The **white-tailed eagle** is an Asian raptor; Attu Island in the western Aleutians is its only North American habitat.

Trumpeter Swans

The world's largest waterfowl, these swans boast wingspans as wide as eagles (seven feet) and can weigh up to 40 pounds! They're pure white, and so have figured prominently over the centuries in legends, drama, music, and metaphor. They fly as fast as 60 mph and as high as 10,000 feet, on their migrations from Alaska to the Pacific Northwest for the winter (though a group of 500 overwinter in Alaska). They live to be 30 years old, and have a horn-like call, which accounts for their given name.

In 1933, trumpeter populations hit an all-time low in the Lower 48—33 individuals—having been hunted for their meat, down, and quills. But several thousand swans were seen by Alaskan bushplane biologists in the early 1950s, and by the early '70s, trumpeters were removed from the Endangered Species list.

Today, of the nearly 12,000 swans in North America, nearly 10,000 spend their summers in Alaska, of which nearly 2,000 are found in the Copper River Delta. (A great place to see them is on the road from Cordova to the Million Dollar Bridge.)

Geese

The **Aleutian Canada goose** has made a remarkable comeback from the edge of extinction over the past 20 years. Smaller than the Canada goose, Aleutian geese were common throughout the islands up until the 20th century, when decades of fox farming nearly wiped out the geese. Only a few hundred were left alive by the late 1960s, on one fox-free island. Feral foxes were removed from a number of other Aleutians and the geese were reintroduced; by 1987, their numbers (5,800) had regenerated to the point where they were removed from the ranks of the endangered and upgraded to threatened.

Emperor geese, however, have gone the opposite direction. In the past 20 years, their numbers have fallen by half, from 150,000 in the late 1960s, to only 70,000 in the late 1980s. Roughly 90% of the world's population of emperor geese nest in western Alaska, the Aleutians, and Siberia.

Snow geese, on the other hand, are plentiful. Huge flocks totaling up to 100,000 birds migrate roughly 5,000 miles each year from central California through Alaska to their nesting grounds on Wrangel Island (in the Soviet Union).

Ptarmigan

The ptarmigan is the state bird, and one of the most popular targets of small-game hunters. Ptarmigan—willow, rock, and white-tailed—are similar to pheasant, quail, and partridge in the Lower 48. They reproduce in large quantities, molt from winter white to summer brown, and have a very poor sense of self preservation. The various Alaskan place names with "Chicken" are usually referring to ptarmigan, which the namers had too hard a time spelling.

Others

By the end of your travels you'll be able to identify at least a dozen different species of **ducks.** A score of different **seabirds** migrate halfway around the world to nest in their favorite nooks somewhere in Alaska. Crazy **ravens,** frantic **puffins,** divebombing **gulls,** scavenging **magpies,** and lame-brained **ptarmigan** will keep you happily entertained for hours. And you can easily get strung out, lose all sense of time, and miss your tour bus, just by trying to identify all the **finches, sparrows, warblers, thrushes,** and **jays** you see flitting everywhere. *Be sure* to bring a bird book, and also strike up conversations anywhere with anybody about the local avifauna—you're sure to hear some interesting words on birds.

FISH

And if you think birds and bird-talk are plentiful, get someone going on fish—you won't be able to shut him or her up or get a word in edgewise for the whole afternoon, guaranteed. The fisheries program in Alaska is extensive, because commercial, sport, and recreational fishing is important to almost every state resident. Commercial fishing is Alaska's second-largest industry; in 1990, 153 million salmon were caught by professional fishermen in Alaskan waters, for a total of 640 million pounds, worth just over half a billion dollars. These figures are for salmon *alone*—which is actually a depressed market in Alaska, due to the dramatic inroads over the past decade of farmed salmon, primarily in Norway, and the subsequent price collapse. The figures don't include herring, halibut, crab, pollock, smelt, cod, and myriad other commercial fish. Eight million salmon were landed by sport fishermen; along with Arctic char, northern pike, sheefish, steelhead, rainbow, grayling, etc., the annual sportfishing industry is worth nearly $100 million to Alaska. Below is a brief survey of the most popular fish in Alaska's three million lakes, 3,000 rivers, and 40,000 miles of coastline.

Salmon

Five kinds of salmon—king (or chinook), red (or sockeye), pink (or humpie), silver (or coho), and chum (or dog)—return to the same bend in the same little creek where they hatched, to spawn and die, ending one of the most remarkable life cycles and feats of migration and single-minded endurance of any living creature. You'll be steeped in salmon lore if only by osmosis by the end of your trip, and you'll get more than your fill of this most delicious and pretty fish.

The **kings** (also known as chinooks, tyees, and springs) are the world's largest salmon, and the world's largest kings spawn in Alaska waters. The average size for a king is 40-50 pounds, but 100-pounders are not uncommon. Kings generally spend five or six years in salt water before returning to fresh to spawn: the more years spent in the ocean, the larger the fish. They run mostly between mid-May and mid-July.

Reds are the best-tasting salmon and the mainstay of the commercial fishing industry. They average 6-10 pounds, and run in June and July; 50 million reds were caught in 1990.

Pinks are the most plentiful, with massive runs of up to 150 million fish between late June and early September. They're smallish, three to four pounds, with a soft flesh and mild taste; they're mostly canned.

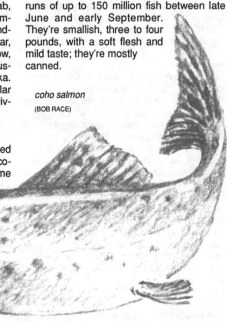

coho salmon
(BOB RACE)

Silvers seem to be the most legendary of the salmon, for their speed, agility, and sixth senses. Their spawning growth rate is no less than fantastic, more than doubling their weight in the last 90 days of their lives. Silvers grow seven to ten pounds and run late, from late July all the way to November.

Chum are the least valued of the five Pacific salmon (*oncorhynchus*), even though they average 10-20 pounds, are extremely feisty, and are the most far-ranging, running way above the Arctic Circle. They're known as dog salmon, as they've traditionally sustained working huskies, but chums remain popular with a hard-core group of sport anglers, who consider them terribly underrated.

A fairly new cottage industry has sprung up locally, in which the skins of pink salmon from Prince William Sound and processed in Cordova are shipped to Korea for tanning into "salmon leather." This luxurious product is more durable (and waterproof) than eelskin, and is used for a variety of products, from watchbands to briefcases. I bought a salmon leather wallet in Kodiak in 1987 for $40, which has only required minor super-glue repairs over the years.

Halibut

Halibut are the favorite monster fish, and can grow so huge and strong that many sportfishermen have an unsurpassed religious experience while catching one. "Chicken halibut" are the common 25-40 pounders, and 100, 200, even 300 pounders are not unusual. (The state record halibut was a 440-pounder, just over eight feet long. And some charter-boat operators swear that out there lurking somewhere is a mythical half-ton halibut.) Even though halibut are huge, and require 80-pound test with 20-ounce lead sinkers, they're not the fiercest fighting fish, and can be caught by just about anyone on a good-day's charter from Kodiak or Homer. It has a very white flesh, with a fine texture (but not too much taste— needs dressing up with a lemony tartar sauce).

Pollock

The mainstay of the bottom-fishing industry, pollock has become big business ever since it began being processed into surimi, or imitation crab and lobster. The "strip mining" of pollock in Alaska waters has recently become an international controversy. Asian trawlers are football-field-long factory fishing boats, which deploy drift nets up to two acres wide and 100 feet deep, and use high-tech fish finders. They trap 20-30 times the sealife that is legal for them to keep, including seabirds and mammals. The male pollock are processed, but the females are stripped of their roe and then the carcasses are dumped overboard (this is now illegal). In 1989, an estimated 111 million pounds of pollock carcasses were dumped. International agreements against drift netting have not been ratified by Japan, Taiwan, and South Korea, evidence of whose trawlers is common around Alaska: fish that are unusually scarred, immature fish on international markets, low runs, and an abnormal amount of fish wastage. Not to mention the recent drastic decline of sea lions and seals.

Smelt

The fattiest fish in northern waters is the Pacific Coast Eulachon, also known as smelt, hooligans, and candlefish (legend claims that the dried fish are so fatty they can be wicked and lit like a candle). These silver and white fish are roughly as long and slender as a pencil, and run in monumental numbers for three weeks in early summer from Northern California to the Pribilofs. A traditional source of oil, the females are dumped into pits or vats by the ton and left to rot for two weeks. Then fresh water is added and the whole mess is boiled, during which the oil rises to the surface. After skimming, straining, filtering, and sterilizing, roughly 20 gallons of oil (reminiscent of cod liver oil) can be processed from a ton of female smelt. The early males, in addition, are good tasting whether cooked, smoked, dried, or salted.

Aquaculture

The commercial growing and harvesting of shellfish—oysters, mussels, clams, scallops, and abalone—and seaweed is slowly gathering momentum in coastal Alaska. Today, nearly 50 "farms" are actively engaged in aquacultural activities, which mostly supply Pacific Northwest markets and restaurants with consistently high-quality shellfish. A veritable swamp of regulatory hurdles, however, has inhibited the ocean farming; the one-plus-billion-dollar commercial fishing industry sees it as unwelcome competition. Still, the potential appears gargantuan.

Byproducts
Fact: one billion pounds of viable fish protein is wasted every year, which adds up to an astounding 80% of that which *isn't* wasted! Some fish byproducts are processed into something usable, such as pet and livestock food and fertilizer. But fish heads, entrails, flesh after filleting, and bones—currently discarded as waste—could be turned into marketable protein, in the form of fish bonemeal, fish oil and solubles, hydrolized protein (surimi), and other products. A large-scale fish byproducts industry would also cut way down on pollution from commercial fisheries. Planning is in its early stages.

FLORA

Vegetation Zones
The vegetation of the North Pacific coast and the Yukon/Alaska Interior can be categorized into four main divisions: rainforest, boreal forest, taiga, and tundra. The lush coastal **rainforests** of British Columbia feature giant conifers: Douglas fir, hemlock, cedar, and spruce. Cedar continues into Southeast Alaska, but spruce and hemlock predominate, and Sitka spruce (Alaska's state tree) rivals California redwoods in height, age, beauty—and commercial value, of course. Sparser forests of hemlock and spruce stretch across Southcentral Alaska, with spruce continuing through northern Kodiak Island but not farther west than the adjacent mainland. Dense thickets of alder and willow grow in the higher, subalpine areas near the coast.

The **boreal forest** of the Interior lowlands consists primarily of scattered open stands of white spruce, paper birch, alpine fir, lodgepole pine, and balsam poplar (cottonwood). **Taiga,** the transition zone between boreal forest and tundra, is characterized by sparse and stunted black spruce, dwarf shrubbery (mostly the ubiquitous willow), and swampy areas known as muskegs.

The lower-elevation **tundra,** also known as the moist tundra, starts at treeline, around 2,500 feet. There you find undergrowth similar to the taiga, without the trees. The higher-elevation alpine tundra consists of grasses, clinging mosses and lichens, and an abundance of tiny psychedelically bright wildflowers, including the unforgettable forget-me-not (state flower), with gaze-catching petals the color of Frank Sinatra's eyes.

Trees
There are actually two treelines in Alaska: one is determined by elevation, the other by latitude. Generally, treeline descends in elevation as the latitude ascends. Although alder and poplar do survive in isolated stands near the Brooks Range, the Arctic region on the North Slope is mostly treeless tundra. Dwarf willow, alder, grasses, and moss give the tundra here the appearance of a shag carpet. This tundra belt continues along the shores of the Bering Sea to the Alaska Peninsula and Aleutian Islands. Southward, the Arctic vegetation is gradually replaced by Pacific coastal varieties.

Sitka spruce continue to be logged and clearcut in Tongass National Forest in Southeast Alaska, a controversial boondoggle involving the National Forest Service, U.S. and Japanese logging companies, and local economies. (For details, see p. 150.) A small cottage industry has developed around white spruce cones. Alaska white spruce cones are harvested locally, then sold to makers of Christmas tree wreaths. Recently, over 5,000 pounds, at $1.15 per pound, were sold.

Mainland birch trees have also attracted the attention of the international lumber market. Birch has traditionally been favored locally for building (and heating) log cabins, for bark baskets and dog sleds, and for syrup. The whiteness of birch wood makes it attractive to use in cabinets, paneling, countertops, and veneers, as well as toothpicks, chopsticks, and tongue depressors; the pulp is especially favored for white paper. Thus far, however, Alaska's birch hasn't met the standards of quality required by the world market.

blackberry
(DIANA LASICH-HARPER)

Cabbage Et Al

In 1941, the managers of the Alaska Railroad offered a $25 prize to the grower of the largest cabbage in the state, and since then cabbage growers have been competing. The usual largest cabbages at the Tanana Valley State Fair (in Fairbanks in mid-August) weigh in at 65-70 pounds, but the state (and world) record-holding cabbage is still 83½ pounds, grown near Wasilla in 1983. Ten-pound celeries, three-pound beets, two-pound turnips, and one-pound carrots are also blue-ribbon earners.

Flowers

Fireweed is a wildflower you'll come to know intimately during your travels in the North. It enjoys sunlight and grows profusely in open areas along roads and rivers. Given proper conditions, tall fireweed can grow to seven feet high; dwarf fireweed is more of a bush. Its long stalk of pink flowers blossoms from bottom to top; sourdoughs claim they can predict the arrival and severity of winter by the speed with which fireweed finishes blooming. In Southcentral and Interior, **prickly rose** is a common sight. The plant grows stems up to four feet high, with sharp stickers. The flowers have five pink petals; the

bright red rose hips ripen in mid-Aug., and contain highly concentrated vitamin C. Pop 'em in, suck off the slightly tart flesh, spit out the pips, and climb a mountain. Three kinds of **primrose,** also a pinkish red, are another common sight on the tundra. Other red wildflowers of the tundra include **purple mountain saxifrage, moss campion,** and large, bright-pink **poppies.**

White flowers include the **narcissus-flowered anemone,** similar to a **buttercup,** which also grows on the tundra. **Mountain avens** are easily recognizable—they look like white roses. A half-dozen different kinds of white **saxifrage** are widespread throughout the state. Be careful of the local **hemlock:** some are harmless, one is deadly poisonous. Similar is the **yarrow,** with its disk of small white flowers and lace-like leaves, which is a medicinal herb. As soon as you identify **Labrador tea,** you'll notice it everywhere in the forest and taiga. **Cotton grass** looks exactly like its name. **Daisies** and **fleabane** complete this group.

Larkspur looks similar to fireweed, only it's a dark purple. It grows on a long stalk and a dwarf bush. **Monkshood** is a beautiful dark-blue flower of the buttercup family; **harebells** and **bluebells** are easily identified around Denali. Three kinds of **violets** grow in the boreal forest. Light-purple **lupine** flowers grow in 20-inch clusters. **Asters,** resembling purple daisies, bloom all over the Interior.

While you're hiking, an excellent book to have along is *Wild Flowers of Alaska* by Christine Heller. The photographs are good, the descriptions are usable (if a little techni-

rose hip
(DIANA LASICH-HARPER)

cal), and the flowers are conveniently arranged by color.

Berries

Berries are the only fruits that grow naturally in Alaska, and luckily the many varieties are abundant, several are edible, a few even taste good, and only one is poisonous. If you're into berry collecting, get to know poisonous **baneberry** immediately. A member of the crowfoot family, it grows mostly in Southeast and central Interior. The white berries look like black-eyed peas; they ripen to a scarlet red. **Juniper berries** grow throughout Alaska, but the **bog** and **Alaska blueberries** and **huckleberries** are much tastier. Blueberries also grow on poorly drained shady alpine slopes, and are generally first to ripen. **Bunchberries** and **elderberries** are good-tasting, but have been known to upset a stomach or two. **Bog cranberries** are best after the first frost, especially when they're a deep purple—delicious-

mountain blueberry
(DIANA LASICH-HARPER)

ly tart. **High-bush cranberries** are common, but are best just before they're completely ripe. **Red raspberries** are a lucky find; a couple of great patches grow around the Denali Park Hotel, but nobody'll tell you where. **Wild strawberries** are even better, if you can get to them before the birds and rodents. The several kinds of **bearberries** (blue and red) are tasteless except to bears, and the **soapberry** will remind you of getting caught saying a dirty word as a kid. Pick up *Alaska Wild Berry Guide and Cookbook* by the editors of *ALASKA* Magazine.

HISTORY

PREHISTORY

The Athabascan Indians of Canada have a legend which tells how, in the misty past, one of their ancestors helped a giant in Siberia to slay a rival. The defeated giant fell into the sea, forming a bridge to North America. The forefathers of the Athabascans then crossed this bridge, bringing the caribou with them. Eventually the giant's body decomposed, but parts of his skeleton were left sticking above the ocean to form the Aleutian Islands.

In less fanciful terms, what probably happened was that low ocean levels during the Pleistocene Epoch (some 30,000-40,000 years ago) offered the nomadic peoples of northeastern Asia a 50-mile-long and 600-mile-wide land "bridge" over the Bering Sea. One of the earliest records of man in the Americas is a caribou bone with a serrated edge found at Old Crow in northern Yukon. Almost certainly used as a tool, carbon dating has placed the bone at 27,000 years old. The interior lowlands of Alaska and the Yukon Valley, which were never glaciated, provided an ice-free migration route. As the climate warmed and the great ice sheets receded toward the Rocky Mountains and Canadian Shield, a corridor opened down the middle of the Great Plains, allowing movement farther south.

The Athabascans

The Athabascans (or Dene) were the first Indian group to cross the Bering land bridge. Their language is spoken today from Interior Alaska to the American Southwest (among Navajos and Apaches). Way back when (anywhere from 40,000 to 12,000 years ago), these Indians of the Interior followed the mastodon, mammoth, and caribou herds which supplied them with most of their necessities. Agriculture was unknown to them, but they did fashion crude implements from the raw copper found in the region. Eventually, certain tribes found their way to the coast. The Athabascan-related Tlingits, for example, migrated down the Nass River near Prince Rupert and then spread north through Southeast Alaska. The rich environment provided them with abundant fish and shellfish, as well as with the great cedar logs from which they fashioned community houses, totem poles, and long dugout canoes.

The Inuit

The Mongoloid Inuit (commonly known as Eskimos) arrived from Asia probably some 10,000 years ago near the end of the last ice age. Today they are found in Siberia and across Alaska and Arctic Canada to Greenland. Their language, which in Alaska is divided into the Inupiak dialect in the north and Yupik dialect in the south, is unrelated to any other in North America except that of the Aleuts. Like the Tlingits, they too lived near the coast, along the migratory routes of the marine mammals they hunted in kayaks and *umiak*. They also relied upon caribou, birds, and fish. Their homes were partly underground and constructed of driftwood, antlers, whale bones, and sod. (The well-known snow-and-ice igloo was exclusive to Canadian Eskimos.) In the summer skin tents were used at fish camps. The Inuit did not utilize dogsleds until the coming of the white man.

The Aleut

Marine mammals and fish provided the Inuit-related Aleuts with food, clothing, and household materials. They were famous for their tightly woven baskets. Prior to the arrival of the Russians in the 1740s, 25,000 Aleut inhabited almost all of the Aleutian Islands; by the year 1800 there were only about 2,000 survivors. The ruthless Russian fur traders murdered and kidnapped the men, enslaved or abandoned the women, and passed on their genes and diseases so successfully that today only 1,000 full-blooded Aleuts remain. The rest intermarried with the conquerors and scattered groups of their descendants are now found in the eastern Aleutians and the Pribilofs to the north.

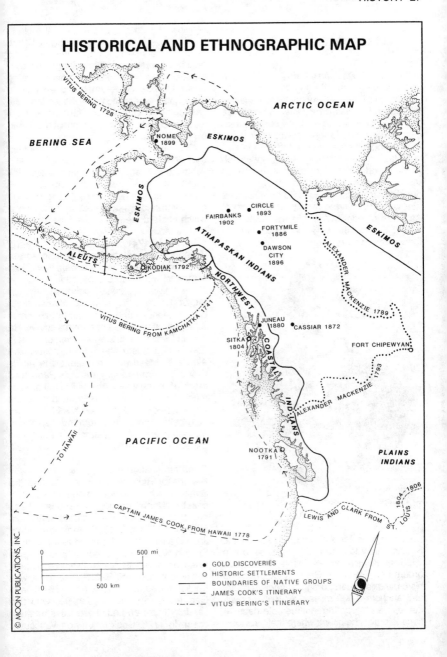

HISTORICAL AND ETHNOGRAPHIC MAP

VITUS BERING 1728

ARCTIC OCEAN

BERING SEA

NOME
1899

ESKIMOS

ESKIMOS

ESKIMOS

ALEUTS

FAIRBANKS
1902

CIRCLE
1893

FORTYMILE
1886

DAWSON
CITY
1896

ATHAPASKAN INDIANS

ALEXANDER MACKENZIE 1789

KODIAK 1792

NORTHWEST

VITUS BERING FROM KAMCHATKA 1741

JUNEAU
1880

CASSIAR 1872

SITKA
1804

COASTAL

FORT CHIPEWYAN

ALEXANDER MACKENZIE 1793

TO HAWAII

INDIANS

PACIFIC OCEAN

NOOTKA
1791

PLAINS
INDIANS

1804–1806

CAPTAIN JAMES COOK FROM HAWAII 1778

LEWIS AND CLARK FROM ST. LOUIS

© MOON PUBLICATIONS, INC.

0   500 mi

0   500 km

●   GOLD DISCOVERIES
○   HISTORIC SETTLEMENTS
—   BOUNDARIES OF NATIVE GROUPS
- - -   JAMES COOK'S ITINERARY
-·-·-   VITUS BERING'S ITINERARY

EUROPEAN EXPLORATION

Vitus Bering

In the early 1700s, long before the New World colonists began manifesting their destiny by pushing the American frontier west to the Pacific coast, Russian *promyshleniki* (explorers and traders) were already busy pushing their own frontier *east* to the Pacific. After these land conquerors had delineated Russia's inhospitable northeastern edges, they were followed by indomitable sea explorers who cast off from the coasts in search of answers to questions that had intrigued Europeans since Marco Polo's *Travels:* mainly, whether or not Asia was joined with America, the mysterious land to the east that was vaguely outlined on then-contemporary maps.

Captain Cook, from Payne's System of Geography *(London, 1791)*

Danish-born Vitus Bering, a sailor in the Russian navy for nearly 20 years, set out in 1725 for Kamchatka Peninsula, Siberia, on orders from Peter the Great. It took him and his crew three years, dragging rigging, cable, and anchors 2,000 miles over trackless wilderness and suffering innumerable deprivations to reach the coast, where their real journey into the uncharted waters of the North Pacific would begin. Bering built his first boat, *Gabriel,* and sailed past St. Lawrence Island (south of present-day Nome) and the Diomedes, but fog prevented him from glimpsing North America. He returned and wintered in Kamchatka, sailed again in the spring, and charted most of the Kamchatka coast, but foul weather and short provisions again precluded exploring farther east.

Over the next 10 years, Bering shuttled between Moscow and his beloved coast, submitting patiently to royal politics and ridicule by the leading scientists and cartographers, while planning and outfitting (though not commanding) a series of expeditions which charted the rest of the Siberian coast and Japan.

Finally, in 1741, at the age of 60, Bering undertook his remarkable voyage to America. Commanding the *St. Peter,* he sailed southeast from Kamchatka, came up south of the Aleutians, passed Kodiak, and sighted Mt. St. Elias on the mainland. By that time, Bering, along with 31 members of his crew, was in the final throes of terminal scurvy. He died in Dec. 1741, and was buried on what is now Bering Island, the westernmost of the Aleutians. Meanwhile, his lieutenant, Alexis Chirikof, commanding the *St. Paul,* had reached all the way to the site of Sitka. After much hardship, survivors from both ships made it back to Siberia—with a load of sea otter pelts. This bounty from the New World prompted a rush of Russian hunters and traders to Alaska.

Conflicting Claims

Reports of Russian advances alarmed the Spanish, who considered the entire west coast of North America theirs. Juan Perez and Bruno Hecata were ordered north from Mexico in 1774 and 1775. Spanish explorer Juan Francisco Quadra sailed as far north as Sitka in 1775 and 1779, but in the end, Spain failed to back up its claim with any permanent settlement north of San Francisco. It was Englishmen James Cook (in 1776-80) and George Vancouver (in 1791-95) who first carefully explored and charted this northern coast. In 1778, Cook landed on Vancouver

Island, then sailed north all the way to what is now called Cook Inlet in Southcentral Alaska, in search of the Northwest Passage from the Atlantic. He continued to the Aleutians and entered the Bering Sea and Arctic Ocean. A decade and a half later, Vancouver, aboard his ship the HMS *Discovery*, charted the coast from California to Southeast Alaska and claimed the region for England. His was the first extensive exploration of Puget Sound and circumnavigation of Vancouver Island; his maps and charts of this confounding coast were so accurate that they were used for another 100 years.

Exploration By Land

Meanwhile, explorers were reaching the Pacific overland from bases in eastern Canada and the United States. In 1789 a Northwest Company trader, Alexander Mackenzie, paddled down the Mackenzie River to the Arctic Ocean. Four years later, in 1793, he became the first person to cross the entire continent by land, reaching the Pacific at Bella Coola, British Columbia. Other employees of the same aggressive Montreal-based company explored farther south. In 1808, Simon Fraser followed the Fraser River, stopping near the present site of the city of Vancouver; in 1810-11 David Thompson traveled from the headwaters of the Saskatchewan River to the mouth of the Columbia, near present-day Portland. In 1803, after the United States purchased 827,000 square miles of territory west of the Mississippi River from France, President Thomas Jefferson ordered a military fact-finding mission into the area. Led by Lewis and Clark, a group of explorers paddled up the Missouri River to its headwaters and crossed to the Columbia, which they followed to the Pacific (1804-06), helping to open vast expanses of western North America. American fur traders followed close behind. (The Alaskan interior, however, was not properly explored until the gold rush at the end of the 19th century.)

The Fur Trade

The excesses of the *promyshleniki*, who had massacred and enslaved the Aleut, prompt-

ed the czar in 1789 to create the Russian America Company, headed by Gregor Shelikof, a fur trader and merchant who in 1784 had established the first permanent settlement in Alaska, at Three Saints Bay on Kodiak Island. Alexander Baranof, a salesman in Siberia, was the first director of the company; he moved the settlement up to present-day Kodiak town, and for the next 20 years, Baranof *was* the law. One of the most powerful men in Alaskan history, he enslaved the remaining Aleuts, warred with the Panhandle Indians, initiated trade with the English, Spanish, and Americans, and sent his trading vessels as far away as Hawaii, Japan, and Mexico. Exhausting the resources of Kodiak and its neighborhood, he moved the company to Sitka, where, according to Merle Colby in his classic 1939 WPA *Guide To Alaska*, ". . . from his wooden 'castle' on the hill surmounting the harbor he made Sitka the most brilliant capital in the new world. Yankee sailors, thrashing around the Horn, beating their way up the California coast, anchored at last in Sitka harbor, and found the city an American Paris, its streets crowded with adventurers from half the world away, its nights gay with balls illuminated by brilliant uniforms and the evening dresses of Russian ladies." Except for the Tlingit Indians, who fought bitterly against Russian imperialism, Baranof's rule, extending from Bristol Bay in western Alaska to Fort Ross, California, was complete. His one last dream—of returning to Russia—was never fulfilled. On the voyage back to the homeland, Baranof died at the age of 72.

THE NINETEENTH CENTURY

Political Units Form

In 1824 and 1825, Russia signed agreements with the U.S. and Britain, fixed the southern limit of Russian America at 54° 40' north latitude, near present-day Ketchikan. But the vast territory south of this line was left up for grabs. The American claim to the Oregon Territory around the Columbia River was based on its discovery by Robert Gray in 1792, and the first overland exploration by Lewis and Clark. Britain based its claim to the region on its effective occupation of the land by the Northwest Company, which in 1821 merged with the Hudson's Bay Company. As American settlers began to inhabit the area, feelings ran high—President Polk was elected in 1846 on the slogan, "Fifty-four Forty or Fight"— referring to the proposed northern boundary between America and British territory in the Pacific Northwest. War between Britain and the U.S. was averted when both agreed to draw the boundary line to the Pacific along the 49th parallel, which remains to this day the Canadian/American border. Vancouver Island went to Britain, and the new Canadian nation purchased all the territorial holdings of the Hudson's Bay Company (Rupert's Land) in 1870. In 1871, British Columbia joined the Canadian Confederation on a promise from the leaders of the infant country of a railroad to extend there from the east.

The Russians Bail Out
1863 was a bad year for the Russian America Company. Back in the motherland, Russia's feudal society was breaking down, threatening the aristocracy's privileged status. In Alaska, competition from English and American whalers and traders was intensifying. Food was scarce and supply ships from California were unreliable and infrequent. Worst, perhaps, were the dwindled numbers of fur seals and sea otters, hunted nearly to extinction over the past century. In addition, bad relations with Britain in the aftermath of the Crimean War (1853-56) prompted Czar Alexander the First to fear for the loss of his far-flung Alaskan possessions to the British by force. Finally, the czar did not renew the Company's charter, and the Russian America Company officially closed up shop.

Meanwhile, American technology was performing miracles. Western Union had laid two cables under the Atlantic Ocean from the U.S. to Europe, but neither had yet worked. So they figured—what the hell, let's go the other way around the world: it was proposed to lay a cable overland through British Columbia, along the Yukon River, across the Bering Strait into Siberia, then east and south into Europe. In 1865, the Western Union

Telegraph Expedition to Alaska, led by William Dall, surveyed the interior of Alaska for the first time, revealing its vast land and resources. This stimulated considerable interest in frontier-minded Washington, D.C. In addition, Czar Alexander's Alaska salesman, Baron Edward de Stoeckl, was spending $200,000 of his own money to make a positive impression on influential politicians and journalists. Secretary of State William H. Seward purchased Alaska on March 30, 1867, for the all-time bargain-basement price of $7,200,000—*two cents* an acre. The American flag was hoisted over Sitka on October 18, 1867. According to Ernest Gruening, first U.S. senator to Alaska, "A year later when the House of Representatives was called upon to pay the bill, skeptical congressmen scornfully labeled Alaska 'Icebergia,' 'Walrussia,' 'Seward's Icebox,' and '[President] Johnson's Polar Bear Garden.' If American forces had not already raised the Stars and Stripes in Sitka, the House might have refused to pick up the tab." (Stoeckl, meanwhile, reimbursed himself the $200,000 he'd invested, and sent the seven million simoleons home to Alexander.) Subsequently, Alaska faded into official oblivion for the next 15 years—universally regarded as a frozen wasteland and a colossal waste of money.

Organic Act Of 1884
This act organized Alaska for the first time, providing a territorial governor and law enforcement (though not a local legislature or representation in Washington). President Chester Arthur appointed federal district court judges, U.S. attorneys, and marshals. From 1884 to 1900, only one U.S. judge, attorney, and marshal managed the whole territory, all residing in the capital, Sitka. The first three appointees to the court in Sitka were removed in disgrace amidst charges of "incompetence, wickedness, unfairness, and drunkenness." A succession of scandals dogged other federal appointees—and that was only in Sitka; the vast Interior had no law at all until 1900, when Congress divided the territory into three legal districts, with courts at Sitka, Nome, and Eagle.

During the Klondike gold rush, tiny cottages and tents crept up the hillsides as Dawson overflowed its narrow plain beside the Yukon River.

William H. Dall wrote of Alaska at that time, "No man could make a legal will, own a homestead or transfer it, or so much as cut wood for his fire without defying a Congressional prohibition; where polygamy and slavery and the lynching of witches prevailed, with no legal authority to stay or punish criminals." Kipling's line, "There's never law of God or man runs north of 53," also refers to the young territory of Alaska. In contrast, Colby in his WPA guide commented that the gold rush stampeders, "although technically without civil authority, created their own form of self-government. The miners organized 'miners' meetings' to enforce order, settle boundary disputes, and administer rough and ready justice. Too often this form of government failed to cope with [serious problems] . . . yet the profound instinct of the American people for self-government and their tradition of democracy made local self-government effective until the creation of the Alaska Legislature in 1912."

The Search For Gold

Alaska's gold rush changed everything. After the California stampede of 1849, the search moved north. In 1858 there was a rush up the Fraser River to the Cariboo goldfields. In 1872, gold was found in B.C.'s Cassiar region. Strikes in Alaska and Yukon followed one another in quick succession: at Juneau (1880), Fortymile (1886), Circle (1893), Dawson City (1896), Nome (1899), Fairbanks (1902), and Iditarod (1908).

A very mobile group of men and women followed these discoveries on riverboats, dogsleds, and foot, creating instant outposts of civilization near the gold strikes. Gold also caused the Canadian and American governments to take a serious look at their northernmost possessions for the first time; the beginnings of the administrative infrastructures of both Yukon and Alaska date from those times. However, in 1896, when Siwash George Carmack and his two Athabascan brothers-in-law discovered gold on Bonanza Creek in Yukon Territory, this vast northern wilderness could barely be called "settled." Only a handful of tiny non-Native villages existed along the Yukon River from Ogilvie and Fortymile in western Yukon to Circle and Fort Yukon in eastern Alaska, and a single unoccupied cabin sat on a beach at the mouth of the Skagway River.

But by the end of 1897, 10,000-20,000 stampeders had skirted the lone cabin on their way to the headwaters of the Yukon and the sure fortunes in gold that awaited them on the Klondike. The two trails from Skagway over the coastal mountains and onto the interior rivers proved to be the most "civilized" and successful routes to Dawson. But the fortune-frenzied hordes proceeded north, uninformed, aiming at Dawson from every direction on the compass. They suffered every conceivable hardship and misery from which death (often by suicide) was sometimes the only relief. And those who finally burst through the barrier and landed at the Klondike and Dawson were already two years too late to partake of the "ready" gold.

But the North had been conquered. And by the time the gold rush had spread to Nome, Fairbanks, Kantishna, Hatcher Pass, and Hope, Alaska could finally be called settled (if not civilized).

THE TWENTIETH CENTURY

In the first decade of the new century, the sprawling wilderness was starting to be tamed. The military set up shop at Valdez and Eagle to maintain law and order, telegraph cables were laid across the Interior, the Northwest Passage had been found, railroads were begun at several locations, vast copper deposits were being mined, and thousands of independent pioneer-types were surviving on their own wits and the country's resources. Footpaths widened into wagon trails. Mail deliveries were regularized. Limited self-government was initiated: the capital moved to Juneau from Sitka in 1905; Alaska's first congressional delegate arrived in Washington in 1906; and a territorial legislature convened in 1912. A year later, the first men stood atop the south peak of Mt. McKinley, and the surrounding area was set aside

as a national park in 1917. At that time, Alaska's white and Native populations had reached equivalency, at around 35,000 each. Judge James Wickersham introduced the first statehood bill to the U.S. Congress in 1916, but Alaska drifted along in federal obscurity until the Japanese bombed Pearl Harbor.

War

It's been said that war is good for one thing: the rapid expansion of communications and mobility technology. Alaska proves the rule. In the early 1940s, military bases were established at Anchorage, Whittier, Fairbanks, Nome, Sitka, Delta, Kodiak, Dutch Harbor, and at the tip of the Aleutians, which brought an immediate influx of military and support personnel and services. In addition, in 1942 alone, the 1,440-mile Alaska Highway from Dawson Creek, B.C., to Delta, Alaska, the 50 miles of the Klondike Highway from Whitehorse to Carcross, the 151-mile Haines Highway, and the 328-mile Glenn Highway from Tok to Anchorage, among others, were punched through the trackless wilderness, finally connecting Alaska by road to the rest of the world. At the war's peak, 150,000 troops were stationed in the territory; all told the U.S. government spent almost a billion dollars there during the war. (For a full description of the actual fighting, see "War in the Aleutians," p. 399.) After the war, as after the gold rush, Alaska's population increased dramatically, with servicemen remaining or returning. The number of residents nearly doubled between 1940 and 1950.

Statehood

The 1950s brought a boom in construction, logging, fishing, and bureaucracy to Alaska. It also saw the discovery of a large oil reserve off the western Kenai Peninsula in the Cook Inlet. The population continued to grow, yet Alaskans still felt like a second-class colony of the U.S., and repeatedly asked for statehood status throughout the decade. Finally, on July 7, 1958, Congress voted to admit Alaska into the Union as the 49th state. President Dwight D. Eisenhower signed the official proclamation on Jan. 3,

BARROW

DEADHORSE • KAKTOVIK

NORTH SLOPE BOROUGH

KOTZEBUE *NORTHWEST ARCTIC BOROUGH*
KOBUK

NOME

FAIRBANKS NORTH STAR BOROUGH

FAIRBANKS • NORTH POLE

SCAMMON BAY

DENALI PARK

ALASKA BOROUGHS

0   200 mi

0   200 km

UNITED STATES / CANADA

MATANUSKA SUSITNA BOROUGH

PALMER

MUNICIPALITY OF ANCHORAGE

OSCARVILLE

ANCHORAGE • CORDOVA

KENAI PENINSULA BOROUGH

SEWARD

PRINCE WILLIAM SOUND

HAINES BOROUGH

SKAGWAY

CITY & BOROUGH OF JUNEAU

JUNEAU

BRISTOL BAY BOROUGH

KING SALMON

KODIAK ISLAND BOROUGH

KODIAK

GULF OF ALASKA

CITY & BOROUGH OF SITKA

KETCHIKAN GATEWAY BOROUGH

KETCHIKAN

DIXON ENTRANCE

© MOON PUBLICATIONS, INC.

1959—43 years after Wickersham had first introduced the idea.

A little over five years later, the Good Friday Earthquake struck Southcentral; at 9.2 on the Richter scale, it remains the largest earthquake ever recorded in the Western Hemisphere. After the tremors and tsunamis had ceased, Anchorage, Whittier, Valdez, Cordova, Seward, and Kodiak lay in shambles, 131 people had died, and damage was estimated at half a billion dollars. But Alaskans quickly recovered and rebuilt with the plucky determination and optimism that still characterize the young state.

The Modern Era

Alaska entered the big time, experiencing its most recent boom, in 1968, when Atlantic Richfield discovered a 10-billion-barrel oil reserve at Prudhoe Bay. In 1969, Alaska auctioned off leases to almost half a million

acres of oil-rich country on the North Slope for $900 million, 10 times more money than all its previous leases combined. A consortium of oil-company leaseholders immediately began planning the Trans-Alaska Pipeline to carry the crude from Prudhoe Bay to Valdez. But conservationists, worried about its environmental impact, and Native groups, concerned about land-use compensation, filed suit, delaying construction for four years.

The upshot of those legal actions was passage in 1971 of the Alaska Native Claims Settlement Act (ANCSA) and the Alaska National Interest Lands Conservation Act (ANILCA) in 1980. The former remains the most extensive compensation to any Native people in the history of the United States. It gave Alaska's aboriginal groups 40 million acres of traditional-use lands, plus a billion dollars to be divided among all American citizens with at least 25% Athabascan, Inuit, or Aleut blood. A dozen Native corporations were established to manage the money and land, in which each recipient of the settlement holds shares. The latter, ANILCA, set aside slightly more than 100 million additional acres of federal property as "public-interest lands," managed by the National Park and National Forest services, Fish and Wildlife, etc.

The pipeline was built from 1974-77. Again, after years of uncertainty due to legal wrangling, Alaska boomed, both in revenues and population. Since then, the state's economic fortunes have risen and fallen with the volatile price of oil. Still, with the Permanent Fund (see "Economy"), rebounding fisheries program, and projects like the Red Dog Mine (see "Kotzebue"), Alaska's financial future seems well assured.

The Oil Spill

On March 23, 1989, at 11 p.m., Captain Joseph Hazelwood turned the 987-foot *Exxon Valdez* supertanker, just a few hours after leaving the pipeline terminal loaded with over 20 million barrels of Prudhoe Bay crude, out of the normal shipping lanes of Prince William Sound to avoid icebergs from Columbia Glacier. Through a tragic series of mistakes, misunderstandings, and ignoring standard procedure, at 12:01 a.m. on March 24, the *Valdez* ran up hard aground on Bligh Reef, opening a tractor trailer-size hole in the ship, which began to leak oil at a rapid rate. It took three hours for the Coast Guard to be notified, and 12 hours for the spill-response team to arrive at the scene. It was a full 72 hours after the oil began to spill before a containment boom was installed to surround the tanker. But as the rest of the oil was offloaded onto the *Exxon Baton Rouge,* the fate of over 1,000 miles of Southcentral coastline had already been sealed. The oil began its inexorable spread.

In the following weeks, the technology available to clean up an environmental disaster of such magnitude proved grossly inadequate. To begin with, Alyeska Pipeline Company's emergency procedures and equipment had completely atrophied over the years. The use of chemical dispersants, a major part of the plan, was not only ineffective, but controversial as well: later in the summer workers who'd handled them began to show symptoms of toxic poisoning. Of the few skimmers that could be deployed (a dozen after a week), those that worked were able to clean up 500 gallons of oil an hour—in the face of millions. And then there were no support facilities for unloading the skimmed crude.

Local fishermen mobilized to try and contain the oil with booms, keeping it away from some of the most bountiful fisheries on Earth at the peak of their seasons. As the oil washed up on the wildlife-rich shorelines of Prince William Sound, crews were sent to attack the thickening, hardening sludge with shovels, buckets, and plastic bags. As early as the first week in June, 24,000 birds and 1,000 sea otters, killed by the oil, had been counted— some so covered with crude that they were impossible to identify. At the height of the summer clean-up, 10,000 workers were engaged in a somewhat futile effort to return the beaches of Prince William Sound, the Kenai and Alaska peninsulas, Kodiak Island, and all the way down to the Shumagin Islands in the Aleutians to their previously pristine state. Garbage clean-up crews were cleaning up after the oil clean-up crews. It's estimated that Exxon spent one and a quarter billion dollars on the effort.

GOVERNMENT

Like Delaware, Wyoming, and North Dakota, Alaska has only one representative to the U.S. Congress, along with two senators. There are 20 state senators and 40 state representatives. They meet in the Capitol in Juneau Jan. through April. Local government is the usual mishmash of Home Rule municipalities (Sitka, Juneau, Anchorage), a total of nine first-, second-, and third-class boroughs, 12 Home Rule cities, 20 first-class cities, 113 second-class cities, and numerous unincorporated villages.

Walter J. Hickel

You've heard of "Wally World," right? *Greenpeace* Magazine (July/Aug. 1991) sums up

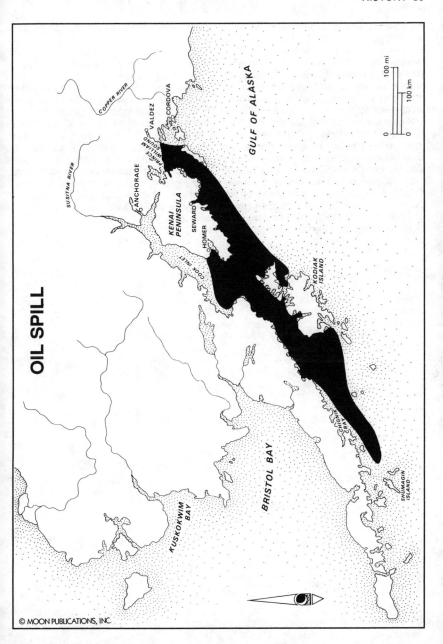

OIL SPILL

© MOON PUBLICATIONS, INC.

the governor of Alaska succinctly: "He was once the people's Hickel, fired by Nixon (from his post as Secretary of the Dept. of Interior) for opposing the Vietnam War. . . . He is now Citizen Hickel, elite champion of the oil and timber industries, and arch-conservative ideologue in the tradition of Ronald Reagan and James Watt."

Hickel denies that his connection to Big Oil is a conflict of interest. Yet, Hickel owns 12% in the pipeline company that would build the gas pipeline from Prudhoe Bay to Valdez. His Commissioner of the Department of Natural Resources is a former ARCO chairman; his Commissioner of the Department of Environmental Conservation has supported clearcutting, strip mining, and oil deregulation; and his Director of the Department of Wildlife Conservation is a notorious wolf killer.

Hickel was elected in 1990 on his promise to open ANWR for drilling by the oil companies. Though many Alaskans are fiercely conservation conscious, most believe that opening the refuge would bring renewed prosperity to the state. After all, profits from the Permanent Fund give every Alaskan a check for nearly $1,000 every single year. However, the wreck of the *Exxon Valdez* will probably remain in the public's consciousness for a long time to come, thwarting the plans of Hickel and his cronies for short-term gain at the expense of the long-term integrity of Alaska's non-renewable resources.

ECONOMY

Cost Of Living

No doubt about it—this place is expensive. In fact, Alaska ranks number one among the states in cost of living. Numerous factors conspire to keep prices high. Most consumer goods must be imported from the Lower 48, and the transportation costs are tacked on all along the line. In addition, the transportation and shipping rates within Alaska are similarly high, which further inflate the cost of goods and services. In more remote regions especially, lack of competition coupled with steady demand ensures top-dollar prices. And let's not forget how long and cold and dark Alaskan winters are; the cost of heat and utilities is an especial hardship. Alaska ranks first in per capita energy consumption for the U.S. Because the cost of living is so high, wages tend to keep pace, which in turn adds to the high cost of goods and services. It's a self-perpetuating cycle.

In comparative terms, Alaskans on the average earn more per hour, per week, and per year ($21,173 in 1989, compared to $17,567 national average) than the rest of the country. Except for Anchorage and Fairbanks, whose large populations and direct transportation allow for slightly more competitive prices, generally the closer you are in the state to Seattle, the lower prices you'll encounter—consumer goods in Ketchikan, for example, can be up to 100% less expensive than in Kotzebue. These financial realities apply to residents much more than to short-term visitors: if you're well prepared, and you provision yourself adequately in the major commercial centers, any time spent in the bush shouldn't be too painful to the pocketbook. For more tips on budget travel in Alaska, see "Other Practicalities."

Employment

Some myths die hard. Thanks to the two huge booms of the past 100 years, many Outsiders still harbor the impression that all you have to do is get to Alaska and you'll automatically make your fortune in the gold mines and oilfields. It was as false in 1898 as it is now. Furthermore, the many (but rarely publicized) busts in the Alaskan economy do not seem to disturb the national misconception. Unemployment figures are usually several percentage points above the national average, even during the peak summer season; in winter they can be double the average. In addition, the highly localized industrial base makes Alaskans especially susceptible to hard times: when logging is in trouble, all Southeast suffers; when the fishing season is disappointing, the whole coastline tightens its belt; when oil prices drop, the entire state gets depressed.

However, the employment picture is not as bleak as many residents and state officials would like the rest of the country to believe. You can still come to Alaska and make a fortune, or just make a living and a life—after all, most Alaskans come from somewhere else (only 33.3% of Alaskans were born in the state—the second-lowest ratio in the country). But the opportunities, it should be stressed, are limited. For example, one out of every three people collecting a paycheck in Alaska works for federal, state, or local government. And the industry that accounts for almost 90% of state revenues (oil and gas) accounts for less than four percent of employment. For a closer look at breaking into the Alaskan job market, see p. 73.

Permanent Fund

In 1976, with oil wealth about to come gushing out of the south end of the pipeline, voters approved a constitutional amendment calling for a percentage of all oil and mineral revenues to be placed in a Permanent Fund. Money from this account can only be used for investment, not for state operating expenses, which explains why during the bust of 1986-87, for example, when hundreds of state workers were laid off and state funds were severely cut back, over seven *billion* surplus dollars sat untouched in the Fund.

The resident dividend program you might hear about distributes half of the interest and capital gains income from Permanent Fund assets to all Alaska residents (including children) in a yearly check. In 1982, the first year of the dividend, each Alaskan received $1,000; in 1985, the dividend came to $425; in 1987, the individual's share of the whopping $1.05 billion in earnings for the 1986 fiscal year was $723. Residents received checks for $906 in 1989.

Fishing

Alaska accounts for nearly 25% of the entire country's commercial fish production—over a billion pounds, worth more than $1.5 billion. Just over a third of the value was in salmon, 23% in shellfish, and the rest in halibut, herring, and bottomfish. Six Alaskan ports are among the country's 50 top producers, with Kodiak again holding down the number-one position, after dropping off to number three for several years. Alaska produces 99% of

ALASKA

© MOON PUBLICATIONS, INC.

the U.S. canned salmon stock (200 million pounds). Fishing is Alaska's largest industry in terms of jobs (80,000), and contributes about 22% of the state's revenues—more than tourism, mining, agriculture, and forestry combined.

Agriculture

The percentage of Alaska's land used for farming is as miniscule as the percentage of Alaska's total economy that is accounted for by agriculture. Of the state's 365,000,000 acres (with 20,000,000 suitable for farming), less than 50,000 acres are occupied by crops; of the nearly $15 billion of gross state product, only $25 million came from agricultural sales. The Matanuska Valley (Palmer/Wasilla) and the Tanana Valley (Fairbanks/Delta) occupy almost 90% of Alaska's usable farmland. Milk, potatoes, hay, and barley are the state's top four crops.

Gold And Minerals

From 1880 to 1980, 30 million ounces of gold were taken from Alaska. Keep in mind, however, that up until 1967, it was never worth more than $35 per troy ounce, while in 1991 it was worth around $400. From 1900-80, 1.38 billion pounds of copper, and from 1920-80, 29.2 million tons of coal, were mined from Alaskan ground. From 1880-1980, *excluding gas and oil*, $20 billion in minerals were recovered in the state.

Alaska is also the only state that produces platinum, more valuable than gold; half a million ounces have been placer mined from southwestern Alaska. Deposits of lead, zinc, jade, molybdenum, chromite, nickel, and uranium have also been located, though the cost of mining in remote Alaska has generally limited these ventures. In fact, Alaska has $300 billion in identified mineral reserves, but ranks 41st among all states in mineral production. The Red Dog Mine, 90 miles north of Kotzebue, is the first major mining project to be undertaken since the early 1900s. An estimated 85 million tons of lead and zinc ore is now being extracted.

Currently, a fierce battle rages between gold miners and environmentalists. An injunction in May 1987 closed nearly all placer mines of over five acres on BLM land until environmental impact statements (mostly concerning the quality of runoff water) could be prepared. A similar injunction closed 90% of mines in Alaska's national parks.

Oil

Everything that moves in Alaska is lubricated with oil, primarily North Slope crude. Without oil, the Alaskan economy would stiffen, shatter, and disappear into thin air. Oil and gas revenues account for roughly 85% of Alaska's entire gross state product. Alaska is so addicted to oil revenue that when the price of a barrel of oil drops $1, the Alaskan budget must be adjusted by $450 million. Yet, this industry only accounts for four percent of the total workforce.

Even pumping over 600 million barrels of oil a year, Alaska was still second in production to Texas; Alaska accounts for roughly 20% of the country's oil. Since commercial drilling in Alaska began in 1902, almost four billion barrels of oil have been produced. In 1976, only 67 million barrels flowed from Alaska; in 1977, during which the pipeline was in operation for nearly half the year, 171 million barrels were pumped out of Alaskan ground. In 1978, however, with the pipeline in full swing, almost 450 million barrels were produced. The Prudhoe Bay oilfield, largest in North America and 18th in the world, has an estimated 10 billion barrels of oil recoverable with today's technology. A little over 70% of that had been pumped through the pipeline by June 1990. Adding up to $23.4 billion, exactly $50,000 for every person in the state, you can see why Alaska is the richest state in the Union.

Tourism

Tourism is Alaska's third-largest industry, behind petroleum production and commercial fishing. In 1986, the largest year ever in Alaska tourism, 800,000 visitors spent roughly $800 million in the state, supporting 13,000-14,000 employees. It's estimated that one restaurant and bar employee in three owes his or her job to the visitor industry, along with one in five workers in the total retail trade industry.

Approximately 75% of visitors (including business travelers) travel independently; the rest come up on package tours. According to the Alaska Visitors Statistics Program, a two-year study conducted for Alaska Division of Tourism, visitors rated Alaska a number six destination out of a possible seven. According to the report, "friendliness and helpfulness" of the people merited a 6.2, "sightseeing and attractions" got a 6.0, and "restaurants and accommodations" averaged 5.1. Favorite activities included flightseeing, day cruising, rafting, fishing, canoeing, and hiking, whereas shopping, dining, and nightlife were low on the list. In order of most visits by all visitors, the top 10 attractions are: Portage Glacier, Inside Passage, Mendenhall Glacier, Glacier Bay, Ketchikan totems, Denali National Park, the pipeline, Sitka's Russian church, UAF Museum in Fairbanks, and Skagway's Gold Rush Historic District.

LANGUAGE

A type of pidgin called "Chinook" evolved in the Pacific Northwest in the 18th century. The language was named after the large, powerful Chinook tribe of the Columbia River, which did business with white traders and the Nootka tribe, which held a monopoly on the shells from which the shell money of the Pacific was manufactured. This pidgin first developed between the Chinooks and Nootkas, and after Europeans arrived, it adopted words from English and French; it was indispensable to traders in Alaska during the entire 19th century. Of the 500 words in the Chinook vocabulary, a few are still used today. Some of the words below have been borrowed from the Inuit (Eskimo) tongue; the rest derive from the colorful frontier slang of the explorers, traders, trappers, prospectors, fishermen, roughnecks, and travel writers.

akutak—Yupik Eskimo word for Eskimo ice cream: a combination of whipped berries, seal oil, and snow.

Alaskan malemute—A particular breed of working dog used to pull sleds.

Alcan—Nickname for the Alaska Highway.

Arctic Circle—An imaginary line, roughly corresponding to 67° N latitude, above which the sun remains entirely above the horizon on summer solstice and entirely below the horizon on winter solstice.

Aurora—Goddess of dawn.

aurora borealis—The scientific term for the northern lights.

baleen—Also known as whalebone, these stiff, flexible whale's "teeth" are woven into baskets by Inuit men, who display great strength and skill to work with this difficult material.

barabara—Traditional Aleut or Inuit shelter, made of driftwood and a sod roof.

bidarka—An Aleut kayak covered with animal skins.

black diamond—Hematite jewelry.

blanket toss—Originally used for spotting game on the tundra, this Native event, where six to eight people holding a large blanket toss high in the air and catch the "spotter," is part of most festivals, and is demonstrated for tourists in Barrow and Kotzebue.

break-up—The period in late April or early May when the river ice suddenly fractures and begins to flow downstream. A particularly muddy, slushy time of year in early spring. Also an apt synonym for divorce, of which Alaska has the country's highest rate (after Nevada, of course).

bunny boot—See "Vapor Barrier Boots."

bush—Borrowed from Africa and Australia, this term generally designates remote areas, but specifically refers to the Arctic tundra where all the vegetation is dwarf shrubbery.

cabin fever—Alaskan-size claustrophobia due to the extreme cold and dark of winter.

cache—Pronounced "cash." A log hut built on tin-wrapped stilts used to store food and supplies beyond the reach of animals.

Nowadays it's a common business name: Book Cache, Photo Cache, Cache 'n' Carry. . . .

Cat—Caterpillar tractor.

Chain, The—Nickname for the Aleutian Islands.

cheechako—A Chinook term meaning "just arrived," used to describe newcomers and visitors.

chinook—A strong warm wind originating in Prince William Sound which can be particularly destructive in Anchorage.

chum—A kind of salmon, also known as dog salmon, to whom it's mostly fed.

clean-up—Reckoning the amount of gold taken at the end of the season; also a phrase that reached mythical proportions during the summer of 1989.

d2—From the section of that name in the Alaska Native Claims Settlement Act, refers to the national interest lands set aside for national parks and forests, wildlife refuges, preserves, and wild and scenic rivers.

Eskimo—From French Canadian *Esquimau,* from northern Algonquin *askimowew,* which means "eater of raw fish." These Natives themselves don't like the name; they refer to themselves as *Inuit,* "people," plural of *inuk,* "person."

fish wheel—An ingenious mechanism that uses the current of the river or stream for power to scoop fish into a tank.

freeze-up—The time of year, mostly in Northwest and Arctic regions, during which all bodies of water are frozen, and the seaports are icebound.

gussuk—Derogatory Inuit term for white person.

hootch—Shortened version of the Chinook word "hootchenoo," meaning home-distilled spirits.

icefog—Caused by an inversion in which warm air traps cold air near the surface, which keeps getting colder and colder . . . until the water vapor in the air freezes, creating floating ice crystals.

iceworm—Originally a joke by sourdoughs on *cheechakos,* the joke was ultimately on the sourdoughs—iceworms actually exist, and you can see specimens of them in the

museum in Juneau and at the Portage Glacier visitor center.

Iditarod—Famous 1,000-mile sled dog race from Anchorage to Nome in February. A "rod" was a measurement of work accomplished in the gold fields; thus the word is actually a sentence: "I did a rod."

igloo—One of the great myths about Alaskan Eskimos, whose shelters are never made of ice (see *"barabara"* above) except in extreme emergencies.

Inupiak—a northern Inuit dialect.

iron dog—Snowmobile.

iron ranger—Collection boxes at state parks.

husky—The generic term for sled dog. A toy poodle hooked up to a sled is technically a husky—for the brief moment before it's eaten by a large **Siberian husky.** Like the malemute, the Siberian husky is a singular breed famous for strength and intelligence.

kupiak—Inuit word for coffee.

kuspuk—Parka worn by Inuit women, often with a small backpack-like pouch for carrying babies.

liquid sunshine—Ketchikan's euphemism for rain.

Lower 48—A slightly hostile/humorous Alaskan term to refer to the rest of the country (except Hawaii).

moose nuggets—Small, round, brown turds, bravely made into jewelry by enterprising (usually bankrupt) local artisans.

mukluk—Boot make by Inuit women with tough sealskin soles, reindeer-hide uppers, fur and yarn trim, all sewed together with caribou sinew.

muktuk—An Inuit delicacy of the rubbery outer layer of whale skin and fat. Very chewy, it's served raw or pickled.

mush—Popularized by Sgt. Preston of the Yukon (and immortalized in the Crusader Rabbit cartoon episode about the small Canadian village, "If Anyone Can, Yukon"), this command means "Let's go!" to anxious dog teams everywhere. It's a Chinook term adapted from the French word *marchons.*

muskeg—Swampy areas covered by moss and scrub.

noseeums—The tiny biting flies which plague Alaska after mosquito season.

nunatak—Lonely rock peak jutting out above icefields.

Outside—Anywhere other than Alaska.

Panhandle—Nickname for Southeast Alaska.

permafrost—Permanently frozen ground, with a layer of topsoil that thaws during the summer.

petroglyphs—Stone-age carvings on rock faces.

poke—A miner's moosehide bag full of gold dust and nuggets.

potlatch—A Native party to celebrate any old thing. Often the hosts would give away all their possessions to their guests. This exercise in the detachment from all worldly goods was simultaneously an exercise in greed, as the event also conferred upon the guests the obligation to host a bigger potlatch with better gifts.

promyshleniki—Early Russian explorers and traders in Alaska.

qiviut—Wool made from musk ox fur, supposedly seven times lighter, warmer, and more expensive than down.

ruff—Fur edge on a parka hood, often of wolf guard hairs.

skookum—A Chinook word meaning strong or worthy.

skookum house—Jail.

solstice—First day of summer (June 21) and winter (Dec. 21).

sourdough—A mixture of flour, water, sugar, and yeast that is allowed to ferment before being used to make bread or hotcakes. A portion of the "sponge," removed to use as a yeast substitute for the next loaf, is called "starter." Also means an old-timer.

squaw candy—Dried or smoked salmon.

taiga—Russian word meaning "land of little sticks," which describes the transition zone between the boreal forest and treeless tundra.

taku wind—Sudden gusts of up to 100 mph that sweep down on Juneau from the nearby icefields.

tillicum—Good friend or partner.

treeline—The elevation (in Alaska, 2,500 feet) and latitude (generally following the Arctic Circle) above which no trees grow.

tundra—Another Russian word meaning "vast treeless plain," used to describe nearly 30% of Alaska's land area.

ugruk—Sealskin used for making *mukluks*.

ulu—A shell-shaped Inuit knife that tourists purchase in record numbers and which airlines disallow in hand luggage.

umiak—An Inuit kayak similar to a *bidarka*.

utilidor—Insulated wooden tunnel through which water and sewer pipes pass.

vapor-barrier boots—Large insulated rubber boots.

visqueen—Thin clear plastic sheeting.

Yupik—The dialect of the Bering Coast Inuit.

PEOPLE

In 1991, Alaska's population was 550,043. Of this, 15.6%, roughly 86,000 people, were of Native descent. There are four groups of Native Alaskans, corresponding to four geographical locations. Southeast Indians consist of **Tlingits, Tsimshians,** and **Haidas.** Interior Indians (who also occupy parts of Southcentral and the Arctic) are **Athabascans. Aleuts** are found along the Alaska Peninsula and Aleutian Chain. And the **Inuit** (or Eskimos) live mostly along the Bering Sea and Arctic Ocean coasts, but are also found inland in small villages around the vast northern and western tundra.

The non-Native population is relatively homogeneous, with only 24,000 (four percent) black and Hispanic residents, 20,000 Asians and Pacific Islanders, and a small number of Scandinavian and Russian descendants.

The typical "Alaskan" is a 26-year-old white male who has lived in Alaska for three and a quarter years. Alaska has the highest male to female ratio in the U.S.: 110 males to 100 females (compared with 95 males to 100 females Outside). But eligible women better hurry: by the year 2000, when Alaska's population is projected to be 625,000, this lopsided ratio will mostly even itself out.

Superlatives

Alaska is the largest and second-least (behind Wyoming) populous of the 50 states, and has the lowest density of people per square mile (0.7), as compared to Wyoming, which has the second smallest (4.7) or New Jersey (986). Alaska's birthrate of 23.7 per thousand loses out only to Utah's 28.6 per thousand. It's also second to last in number of people born in-state (33.3%); Nevada is last at 23%. Nevada also beats out only Alaska for the highest divorce rates: 17.3 per thousand couples in Nevada, 8.8 in Alaska. But Alaska takes first over Nevada in federally owned land, at 85.8% to 85.2%. Alaskans take first place in federal aid per capita ($963) and last place in the civilian labor force (207,000), as well as in its percentage of farm workers (0.1%).

NATIVES

Southeast Natives

Alaska's only Indian reservation is at Metlakatla, near Ketchikan. This group of nearly 1,000 Tsimshian Indians relocated in 1887 from their traditional homeland, slightly south near Prince Rupert, as a result of disagreements between William Duncan, the tribe's main missionary, and his church superiors (see p. 138 for the complete story). These "Natives" are thus the only ones not included in the Alaska Native Claims Settlement Act. Similarly, about 800 Haida Indians live on southern Prince of Wales Island at the southeastern tip of Alaska, and the northern extent of the Haida homeland (see the "Queen Charlotte Islands").

But the Tlingit (pronounced KLINK-it) Indians are the traditional dwellers of Southeast Alaska, related to the Interior Athabascans. Blessed with an incredible abundance of food, fuel, furs, and tools, the Tlingits evolved a sophisticated and complex society, religion, and artistry. The primary social unit was the community house, which typically sheltered 50-100 people. The huge trunks of cedar and spruce provided the house posts, often carved and painted with the clan's totemic symbols; slaves were put in the post holes to cushion the connection between totem and earth. One had to stoop to pass through the single door; no windows punctuated the long structure. Ten or so of these clan houses made up a village, and a number of neighboring villages made up a tribe. But these distinctions held little importance to the Tlingits, who felt connected genetically only to members of the same clan.

All marriages occurred between clans; marrying within the clan was considered incestuous. Descent was matrilineal: children belonged to the mother's clan, and a man's heirs were his sisters' children. Therefore the pivotal male relationship was between uncle and nephews. At the age of 10, boys went to live with an uncle, who taught them the ways of the world. The uncle arranged the boy's marriage to a girl of another clan, who remained with her mother until the wedding. The dowry price was usually a number of blankets; the Tlingits were famous for their weaving and embroidery. Feasts, known as *potlatch,* honored the dead, but feted the living. The Tlingits knew how to party. Often the potlatch continued for days or even weeks, during which the host fed, clothed, and entertained a neighboring, usually wealthier, clan, then "gave away" the clan's most valuable possessions to them. It was understood that the hosted clan would reciprocate eventually, with an even greater degree of festivity and generosity.

The Tlingits had an intensely animistic belief system, in which everything, from glaciers to fish hooks, had a spirit. Tlingit shamans were virtually omnipotent, alternately controlling and beseeching *yek,* or karma, on behalf of the tribe. They also professed a complete understanding of the afterlife, "on authority of men who died and came back." Tlingit arts were expressed by men who carved totems for house posts, through the potlatch and other important events, and by women who weaved exquisite blankets. Unlike the gentle Aleut, the Tlingits were fierce warriors who

Haida hawk ax
(GORDY OHLIGER)

were never completely conquered by invading Russians, going head to head and hand to hand every inch of the way, until they settled into an uneasy coexistence.

Athabascans

A restless people—nomadic hunters and migrants—who developed less of a local cultural cohesion, Athabascans are related to the Tlingit of Southeast Alaska, and the Navajo and Hopi of the American Southwest. These wanderers subsisted on the Interior mammals, mostly caribou and moose, and freshwater fish. They passed the cruel winters in tiny villages of no larger than six houses, with a *kashim,* or community center, as the focal point. They ice-fished and trapped in the dark, using dogsleds as transportation. Their artistic expression was limited mostly to embellishing their clothing with embroidery. The men remained constantly occupied with survival tasks—finding food, building houses, maintaining gear. When the first white explorers and traders arrived in the early 19th century, the Athabascans immediately began to trade with them, learning the new cultures, and in turn educating the newcomers in local customs and skills, not the least of which was dogsledding.

Aleuts

As the Athabascans were almost entirely land-based people, the Aleuts were almost entirely dependent on the sea. Clinging to the edge of tiny, treeless, windswept Aleutian islands, they lived in small dwellings made of sealskin-covered frames, with fireplaces in the middle and steam baths attached on the sides (where marriages were consummated without ceremony). They made sea otter skins into clothing, and processed walrus and seal intestines into parkas. Their kayaks (called *bidarka)* as well were made of marine mammal skins stretched over a wooden or whale-bone frame. Basketry was their highest artistic achievement, and their dances were distinctly martial, with masks, rattles, and knives.

When the Russian *promyshleniki* invaded the Aleutians in the mid-1700s like furies from hell, around 25,000 Aleuts inhabited almost all the Aleutian Islands and the southern portion of the Alaska Peninsula. Within 50 years, over half had died through violence, starvation, or disease. Most of the rest became slaves, and were dispersed around the New World to hunt the sea otter and fight for the Russians. In fact, Aleuts and Koniags (Kodiak Eskimos) traveled as far south as Catalina Island off the Southern California coast, wiping out the peaceful Gabrielino Indians there, along with the entire otter population in 1810. Many of the women served as concubines to the Russian overlords, further diluting the Aleut lineage. Today, most Aleuts carry only half or quarter Aleut blood; only 1,000 are considered full-blooded.

Inuit

Alaskan Inuit are commonly known as Eskimos. The term "Eskimo" comes from the French Canadian *Esquimau,* which in turn is derived from the Algonquin *askimowew,* which means "eaters of raw fish." The Inuit have always considered the name Eskimo derogatory. *Inuit* simply means "people," the plural of *inuk,* or "person." The name the Inuit gave themselves is appropriate in light of their strong traditional sense of community; their society was mostly leaderless, with every able member responsible for contributing to the struggle for survival. The borderline between personal and communal property was fuzzy at best, and theft did not exist. Everything was shared, including wives. All justice was determined by what was deemed best for the community. Marriages, too, were so determined.

A boy entered adulthood after his first kill, and the event was celebrated by a large feast. A girl was considered grown as soon as she began menstruating, which was accompanied by a two-week ritual. The man-child selected a bride, paid a minimal price, and unceremoniously set up house in a hut similar to the Aleuts'—a bone and brush framework covered with moss and grass. "Igloos" made of snow and ice were only used as temporary shelters on the trail (and mostly by central Canadian Eskimos). Fuel was derived from whale oil and driftwood. They ate meat almost exclusively: fish, whale, walrus, caribou, birds. Also, like their relatives the Aleut, they used skin and hides for clothing and boating. Masks are the most visible form of Inuit art, but they apply an aesthetic touch to almost everything they make.

The Russians had little impact on the remote Inuit, but their introduction to Western ways by the Boston whalers around the 1850s was swift and brutal. They quickly succumbed to whiskey, and many Native men were shanghaied while unconscious to labor on the white man's ships. They learned about prostitution (renting the women) and slavery (selling them). They learned how to use firearms and casually kill each other, usually in a drunken fit. They acquired syphilis, white sugar, canned food, and money.

An encounter between the Inuit of St. Lawrence Island and a single whaling vessel in 1880, described by Colby in his classic *Guide to Alaska* (1939), sums up the scene: "The master sent members of his crew ashore with bottles of grain alcohol, [for which] the Eskimos traded ivory, whalebone, and furs. The officers and crew selected a harem from the young women of the village, and paid them in alcohol. When the whaling vessel left, the entire village of 450 Eskimos was dead-drunk and beggared, for they had even cut up their skin boats to trade for liquor. Around them were plenty of hair seal and walrus, but by the time the village had sobered and collected weapons the game was gone. Only about twenty-five villagers survived."

The whaling years ended just before the gold rush began. But the ruin of the Inuit culture was total. Gradually, with the help of missionaries and legislators, the Inuit in the late 19th century turned to reindeer herding, which began to provide income, food, and skins. Today, an estimated 34,000 Inuit live in Alaska, having doubled their number over the past 50 years. The Inuit people live in an arc stretching from Siberia to Greenland. Alaskan Inuit speak two dialects of the common language, Yupik along the Bering coast, and Inupiat along the Arctic coast.

OUTDOOR RECREATION

Since Alaska is the largest state with one of the smallest populations, it stands to reason that it has the most outdoors in the country. Also, because Alaska is so vast, so rugged and diverse, and so anything-goes, the range, breadth, and depth of outdoor sports are mind-boggling. And Alaska has sufficient public transportation—by ground, water, and air—to get you to whatever outdoor location you've chosen for your recreation. If you're experienced and well prepared, you can catch the minivan from, say, Glennallen to Kennicott in Wrangell-St. Elias National Park and backpack for a month without seeing another soul. Or start in Bettles, and walk west across four national parks in the Brooks Range clear to the Chukchi Sea on the west Arctic Coast. Or put your kayak into Resurrection Bay at Seward and paddle around Kenai Fjords National Park for 10 days. Or put a canoe into the Kobuk River at Ambler and float down to Kotzebue. Hiking, backpacking, climbing, skiing, dogsledding, snowmobiling, snowshoeing, fishing, hunting, kayaking, canoeing, flightseeing, photographing, and filming are among the more common activities. Recently, mountain biking, windsurfing, and river rafting have dramatically increased in popularity. And for the extremists among you, some of the wilder opportunities for recreation include paragliding and paraskiing, winter camping and ice fishing, and scuba diving. The possibilities, as they say, are truly limitless.

If you're not all *that* experienced, and would rather leave the planning, preparing, outfitting, and guiding to someone else, you've got a choice of over 500 adventure-travel package operators, offering everything from helicopter skiing on icefields and scuba diving in the Arctic Ocean to ice-climbing on McKinley and skydiving over Turnagain Arm. The best (though still incomplete) compilation of guides and outfitters appears in "Alaska Vacation Planner," put out every year by the Alaska Division of Tourism. Write: Box E, Juneau, AK 99811, tel. (907) 465-2010. Also check the "Guidepost" section of *ALASKA* Magazine.

THE PROPRIETORS

National Parks And Preserves

In the federal scheme of things, the National Park Service gets all the glory. The national parks are the country's scenic showcases, and visitors come by the millions, usually to look, occasionally to experience. An unmistakable carnival atmosphere pervades the most popular national parks—in Alaska's case, Denali and Glacier Bay. Here the Park Service is primarily concerned with crowd control, and they take a hefty cut from the proceeds of the concessionaires, which provide the rides, hot dog stands, souvenir booths, and beds. Such hordes come through these gates that lines are long, rides are packed, facilities are maxed out, and much of the backcountry is closed or seriously limited by the permit system. Other national parks, including Kenai Fjords and Wrangell-St. Elias, are accessible by road; these parks are somewhat new and undeveloped, and they only have visitor centers and a couple of rides. The other eight parks and preserves (Aniakchak, Katmai, Lake Clark, Gates of the Arctic, Noatak, Kobuk Valley, and Yukon-Charley Rivers) are so inaccessible that those with any facilities at all are prohibitively expensive for the average traveler, and the others are really no more than a name and set of boundaries on the map.

People accustomed to Lower 48 national parks are suprised to find that very few trails run through Alaska's baker's dozen. Most of the 54 million acres of national parkland are unforested and in the moist alpine tundra, where trails are not only unnecessary but largely detrimental to the ecology: as soon as the insulating ground cover is removed, the melting permafrost turns the trail into a muddy, impassable morass. Even in Denali, the only trails are around the park entrance and hotel area. Some parks (such as Denali and Katmai) require backpacking permits; in the rest you're on your own. Several of the more accessible parks have designated camping areas, but in the others you can pitch your tent on any level patch. For an excellent overview of Alaska's top eight national parks, check out Sierra Club's beautiful and well-written *Guide to the National Parks of the Pacific Northwest and Alaska*.

Forest Service
If the Park Service is in the carnival business, the Forest Service is a huge lumber corporation. Some of its budget is earmarked for visitor facilities and services, but those frivolities take a definite backseat to timber management. Its 23 million acres in Alaska are divided between the two largest national forests in the country: Tongass in Southeast and Chugach in Southcentral. This land is primarily forested. Trails are numerous. Campgrounds are set in beautiful wooded sites, often on lakes, and cost $5-6 pp per night. The Forest Service also manages a large number of wilderness cabins, a few of which are accessible by road, though most are in the Tongass, accessible only by floatplane or boat. Some in the Chugach are on trails, especially around the Cordova area. You must reserve them well in advance, and they cost $15 per night. Write: Chugach National Forest, 201 E. Ninth Ave., Anchorage, AK 99501, tel. (907) 271-2599, and Tongass National Forest, Box 2097, Juneau, AK 99803, tel. (907) 586-8751. The Forest Service has a beautiful visitor center at Portage Glacier, 40 miles south of Anchorage, and numerous offices around the state.

State Parks And Recreation Sites
The state manages over 100 park sites, from the million-and-a-half-acre Wood-Tikchik State Park outside of Dillingham to the eight-acre Izaak Walton Campground near Sterling on the Kenai Peninsula, and additional lands are continually being added to the system. The state facilities are uniformly better planned, better maintained, more attractive, larger, and less crowded than most of the federally managed park and forest lands, as well as more accessible. About 90% of the sites and parks have trails; about 80% of them have campgrounds.

A usage-fee bill had been rejected by the state Legislature several times over the years, but with declining revenues from the oil-price drop the state's park budget was cut almost in half, and the fees were instituted in 1988. The $6 per night camping fee at all state campgrounds (except Tok at $8, Eagle River outside of Anchorage and Chena Wayside in Fairbanks, which are $10) finally joins Alaska to the other 49 states that charge for their facilities. A $75 annual pass covers camping at all the parks and recreation areas throughout the state, available at the camping areas.

When you have a choice, always head for a state park or recreation site—they're the best outdoor facilities in Alaska.

Others
The largest amount of wilderness in Alaska, 76 million acres, falls under the auspices of Alaska Fish and Game and the U.S. Fish and Wildlife Service, which manage the state and national wildlife refuges. These departments are in the game management business and permit hunting and fishing on their lands. The feds are also somewhat in the oil business, especially within the Kenai National Wildlife Refuge, and maybe one day in the Arctic Refuge (though let's hope not). Some visitor facilities are found at the larger refuges (Kenai and Kodiak): mainly campgrounds ($5), hiking trails, canoe routes, and visitor centers.

Finally, the Bureau of Land Management (BLM) is responsible for whatever land is left over. As a result of the 1980 National Interest Lands Act, BLM's acreage shrunk almost in half. Very few restrictions are imposed by BLM (earning them the derisive nickname of the "Bureau of Logging and Mining"), and much mining takes place on these lands, though the miners are pretty peeved these days at having to comply with new, somewhat strict, court-ordered regulations (mostly concerning the quality of runoff water). These tensions are especially evident out the Steese Highway around Central and Circle. A few trails (such as in the White and

Pinnell mountains outside of Fairbanks) and campgrounds are managed by BLM—minimalist, free.

ON LAND

Respecting The Land

Make it your objective to leave no trace of your passing. Litter is pollution. Whenever you are tempted to leave garbage behind, think of how you feel when you find other people's plastic bags, tin cans, or aluminum foil in *your* yard. If you packed it in, you can pack it out. Burying garbage is useless as animals soon dig it up. Be a caretaker by picking up trash left by less-conscientious visitors. In this way, in part, you thank the land for the experiences it has given you.

Along shorelines, the intertidal zone is the best for campfires and human excrement. Human wastes in other areas should be disposed of at least 100 feet from any trail or water source. Bury wastes and carefully burn the toilet paper, if possible. Try to build your fire on sand or gravel and keep it small and under control. Extreme care should be taken during dry periods and in the forest. Refrain from doing *anything* that might cause even the smallest of accidental fires.

Local People

As you explore, remember that Northerners are fiercely independent people who value their privacy. They can also be overwhelmingly hospitable if you treat them with respect. All Indian reservations are private property; you should always ask the advice of a local resident before camping on one. Never put up your tent in or near a Native village without first asking permission. When visiting a Native village or any small, isolated community, look people straight in the eye and be the first to say hello. Remember, you are the intruder, so you should be the one to make the effort to put them at ease.

Hiking And Camping

Hiking and camping are by far the preferred outdoor recreation for the majority of Alaskans and visitors. These pastimes are available to practically anybody, from three-month

old infants to 83-year-old grannies. Here, you don't have to be in particularly good shape, you don't need a big bank balance, and you don't have to have the latest high-tech equipment. Elevation changes are undramatic in the backcountry, affording as slow, steady, and non-strenuous a pace as required by the weakest hiker. Also, purchasing *everything* in the What To Take section *new* is roughly equivalent to splurging on a fancy weekend in the big city—and properly cared for, the equipment should remain useful for at least a decade.

For the size of the Alaskan outdoors, there are very few *trails*—those totalitarian swaths through the wilderness that supervise, magnetize, and hypnotize. It's easy just to pick a direction, especially in the vast taiga and tundra, and go. Also, the perpetual daylight during hiking season allows for additional deviation from normal hiking-camping cycles, providing further freedom. And the definite possibility of encountering a variety and abundance of wildlife is an incalculable bonus.

The few trails that do exist are covered in their respective travel chapters. For more information about hiking, contact the Alaska Public Lands Information Centers in Anchorage and Fairbanks (see pp. 328 and 264).

Photography

Hand in hand with hiking and camping goes photography—of the gorgeous scenery, the fauna and flora, and the special light. Professional photographers have a literal field day in Alaska, not least because the ideal light conditions—at dawn and sunset everywhere else—continue throughout the long days of low light and long angles in the boreal region. Casual photographers are satisfied with automatic point-and-shoot single-lens reflexes, though the regular 50-55mm lenses don't do justice to either the panoramas or the wildlife. A good set-up would be a couple of camera bodies, a 24mm wide-angle, 80-200mm zoom, and 400mm zoom (a two-ex converter is also handy). A tripod is a must for all the waiting and watching for wildlife; Kodachrome 64 or Fujichrome 100 or 200 will give professional-quality frames. But also take some faster film for those inevitable gray days. And don't be afraid to blow off as much film as your budget can stand, to get those few special shots. A photography class or two are invaluable for learning technique— exposure, bracketing, composition, and the like.

A couple of caveats are in order. A common cause of wildlife *incidents* is foolish photographers either getting too close or having a false sense of security behind the camera. Your backcountry common sense should remain intact with or without a camera in front of you. Besides, there are times and places to *not* use a camera— mostly in order not to separate you from a given experience.

Mountain Biking

This relatively new sport seems to be less controversial in Alaska than in the Lower 48, even on Forest Service trails, which are all open to two-wheelers. This is due in part to the fact that hikers aren't entirely limited to trails and can avoid mountain bikers if they're offended by them, as well as the fact that something about Alaska seems to inspire a certain respect for the environment and sensitivity to other people in those sharing the great outtadoors. In any event, all trails in the state parks system are still closed to mountain bikers (except a few of the wider ones in Chugach State Park near Anchorage); the state parks people consider mountain bikes *vehicles,* which can easily damage trails, tundra, and people. Still, many local trails, especially around Fairbanks and throughout the Kenai Peninsula, are popular mountain-bike venues. Best is to call the local outdoors stores for recommendations.

Hunting

For all the rules, regulations, and seasons, write for "Alaska Game Regulations," Alaska Dept. of Fish and Game, Box 3-2000, Juneau, AK 99802.

IN AND AROUND WATER

Beachcombing

A treasure trove of flotsam and jetsam awaits the savvy and the lucky along the thousands of miles of coastline in Alaska. Prizes include glass-ball floats (used by Oriental fisher-

(GORDY OHLIGER)

men), life preservers, lantern buoys, whale teeth, ambergris, WWII relics, Russian equipment, and notes in bottles. Beachcombing can be developed into a fine art, consisting of weather and tide patterns, wind and storm conditions, beach accessibility and topography. The experts advise that the best beachcombing is in early May, after the snow cover and before the competition from hikers, anglers, and other beachcombers.

Gold Panning

Panning for gold is not only great fun, but it's also a good way to get involved in the history of the North. Besides, there's the chance you'll find a nugget which will become a lifelong souvenir. You might even strike it rich! The amount of equipment required is minimal: an 18-inch plastic gravity-trap gold pan (buy one at any local surplus or sporting goods store for a couple of dollars), tweezers and an eye dropper to pick out the gold flakes, and a small vial to hold them. Ordinary rubber gloves will protect your hands from icy creek water. An automobile oil dipstick bent at one end is handy for poking into crevices, and a small garden trowel helps dig out the dirt under rocks. Look for a gravel bar where the creek takes a turn, for larger rocks forming eddies during high water, for crevices in the bedrock, or for exposed tree roots growing near the waterline. These are places where gold will lodge. Try your luck on any of the old gold-rush creeks; tourist offices can often suggest likely areas. Stay away from commercial mining operations and ask permission if you're obviously on someone's claim.

The principle behind panning is that gold, twice as heavy as lead, will settle to the bottom of your pan. Fill the pan half full of paydirt you've scooped up from a likely spot and cover with water. Hit the rim of the pan seven or eight times, or shake it back and forth. Break up lumps of dirt or clay with your hands and discard any rocks after rinsing them in the pan. Shake the pan again, moving it in a circular motion. Dip the front edge of the pan in the stream and carefully wash off excess sand and gravel until only a small amount of black sand remains. If you see gold specks too small to remove with tweezers, take the black sand out and let it dry. Later dump it on a clean sheet of paper and gently blow away the sand. The gold will remain. That's the basic procedure, though there are many ways to do it. It does take practice; ask a friendly sourdough for advice. Also, many spiked gold-panning facilities are found along the roads in the North—commercial but good places to refine your technique.

Fishing

Fishing is not only great fun but the way to bag some super meals. All you need are a break-down or retractable rod, a variety of hooks, five flies (salmon fly, black fly, mosquito, gnat, nymph), spinners (rooster tail and shannon), spoons, sinkers, line (four- to eight-pound for freshwater, 12- to 30-pound for saltwater—depending on what you're after), and a reel. All but the rod will fit in a small plastic case. For bait, get a small bottle of salmon eggs for freshwater, shrimp for saltwater. Have a knife to clean the fish and a small plastic trowel to bury the fish wastes (but pack out all other garbage). While fishing, watch for protected areas with deadfalls or rocks where fish like to hide. You'll have the best luck in the early morning or late evening, or on cloudy days when the sun

leaks out to shimmer the top of the water. So as not to attract bears, keep your catch on a stringer well downstream.

Locals, as always, are the best advice-givers about fishing technique, spots, and regulations, and might even share some secrets. Generally, look for trout, Dolly Varden, grayling, and whitefish in inland freshwater lakes, the five varieties of northern salmon in bays and rivers, and deep-sea halibut charters mostly in Homer.

Fishing Regulations

Fishing licenses are required almost everywhere. In British Columbia separate licenses are sold for freshwater and saltwater fishing. Non-residents pay C$23 for saltwater, C$27 for freshwater annual licenses, or C$15 for a three-day license. Three-day Alaskan sportfishing licenses cost $15—usually offered by charter fishing operators. Nonresidents can also purchase a two-week license for $30. All-inclusive annual non-resident rates are C$30 in Yukon, US$36 in Alaska. The Alaskan license is valid in national parks; in Canada you need only a special C$4 national park fishing license (a bargain). Licenses are for sale in most outdoor stores. Ask for brochures outlining local fishing regulations when you buy your license. They often include valuable tips for newcomers. Check open and closed seasons, bag limits, etc. to avoid trouble with the law. Shellfish may be poisonous, so get local advice before taking clams, mussels, etc. For the whole thing, spelled out in minute bureaucratic detail, write for a copy of the regulations booklet to Alaska Dept. of Revenue, Fish and Game Licensing, 1111 W. 8th St., Room 108, Juneau, AK 99801, tel. (907) 465-2376. For information on fishing charters, available from every seaport in the state, check with local chambers of commerce, or look in the Guidepost section of *ALASKA* Magazine.

Rafting

Whitewater rafting trips are offered by numerous adventure travel outfitters around the state. A few of the more reasonable, short, and accessible trips include the float down the Nenana River at Denali, down the Kenai

River at Sterling, and down the Lowe River outside of Valdez. A large number of float trip companies and wilderness outfitters offer overnight, several-day, and up to three-week-long trips down the Charley, Kobuk, Tonsina, Chickaloon, and Nova rivers, among others. Check the list in the Alaska Division of Tourism's "Alaska Vacation Planner" for many of their names and addresses.

Canoeing And Kayaking

These take less, more portable, equipment, and less planning than river rafting, and you can easily canoe Alaska's rivers and kayak its fjords and bays on your own. At least one company in each major town rents canoes and kayaks, and they either give lessons themselves or can put you in touch with someone who does. Many companies also offer guided trips. Well-respected outfits include **Alaska Treks 'n' Voyages,** Box 625, Seward, AK 99664, tel. (907) 224-3960; **Ageya Kayak Tours,** 2517 Foraker Dr., Anchorage, AK 99517, tel. (907) 243-3274; and **Alaska Discovery,** 418 Franklin St., Juneau, AK 99801, tel. (907) 586-1911.

Windsurfing

The scenery, the space, and the winds combine to make windsurfing a thrill that Alaskans quickly want more of. Turnagain Arm near Girdwood and Portage is the most attractive locale, though some hardy sorts swear by the waters off the coast of Kodiak. Turnagain Arm boasts six- to eight-foot waves, 10- to 15-mph tides, steady predictable winds, and only a short drive from the Anchorage bowl. Windsurfers can catch some big air in Turnagain Arm; 20 feet isn't unusual. They can also pick up some serious speed; boarders traveling 50 mph have been clocked by passing cars. Turnagain Arm, to be sure, has its dangers as well, primarily the tides, the mudflats, and the biting cold water. But even devoted warm-water boarders swear by the thrills available in Alaskan waters.

Hot Springs

Alaska is a thermally active region, attested to by its more than 100 hot spring sites, of which roughly a dozen are accessible and developed. Accessible, in Alaska, is quite a relative term: possibly the most accessible hot spring in the state is at Chena, 60 miles east of Fairbanks on a well-paved road. But other "accessible" hot springs near Fairbanks include Manley, over 150 hard dirt-road miles, and Arctic Circle, a similar rough distance. Other popular hot springs are in Southeast: White Sulphur and Tenakee on Chichagof Island near Juneau, and Chief Shakes and Baranof on Baranof Island. Contact the Alaska Department of Natural Resources for its map of thermally active areas in Alaska.

IN THE AIR

Flightseeing

Even if you don't go backpacking, rafting, kayaking, gold panning, etc. while you're in Alaska, treat yourself at least once to a small plane or helicopter ride over some spectacular country. Recommended flights include the one from Denali Park around the northern face of the Alaska Range and Mt. McKinley, and the one from Talkeetna around the southern face. The flight over Glacier Bay from Juneau, Haines, or Skagway will leave you hyperventilating for two days. And you won't believe how grand Columbia Glacier really is on the flight over it from Anchorage or Valdez. Scheduled trips such as these usually run between $90 and $120 per person. Chartering a bush plane and pilot for flightseeing routes of your own design can run upwards of $300 an hour for a three- or four-seater; just get a few fellow travelers together and off you go into the wild blue yonder. For more tips on flightseeing, see "Getting Around" p. 69, and the same heading under "Anchorage."

Paragliding And Paraskiing

Two extreme air sports include paraskiing, which involves wearing skis and a parachute and jumping off very steep cornices, and paragliding, which is a cross between hang gliding and parachuting.

ACCOMMODATIONS AND FOOD

Camping

The only consistent way to sleep cheap in the North is to camp. Unless you're on a prepaid package tour, have friends all over, or own a booming gold mine, don't even briefly entertain the remote possibility of going to Alaska without a tent and sleeping bag. One night in the average Alaskan budget hotel can cost the equivalent of up to a week's food or transportation. Two nights pays for a good tent. Tent camping is free or cheap in most areas, and public showers are available in nearly every town you'll find yourself dirty in. The old A-frame tents are sufficient, but the modern self-supporting dome tents are best: they're lightweight, a cinch to erect, don't need to be staked into the often rocky or frozen ground, and you can sit up in them during those long inclement stretches. For peace of mind and dryness of body in those wild and woolly nights in Southeast and Southcentral, make sure the tent is as waterproof as it can be. (Even so, bring a sponge.) A bivouac bag (self-contained sleeping-bag cover, usually Gore-Tex on the outside) is also handy. A three-quarter-length Therma-Rest inflatable pad ($40, 10 ounces) will put a wonderful cushion of air between you and the ground; on top of it you can sleep on gravel, rocks, dead porcupines. . . .

In those few thoughtless towns which don't provide campgrounds within walking distance of the action, you can always wander into the nearby bush and pass the night with relative impunity. Most of the land is owned by some branch of government; so long as you stay out of sight, don't chop down any trees, and are careful with fire, no one is likely to bother you. But avoid places with "No Trespassing" signs, if possible.

In Canada you may camp anywhere on Crown land without a permit; in Alaska camping is allowed on state land and within the national forests. The national parks of both countries ask that you first obtain a free backcountry use permit. Camping on public property within city limits, however, is usually prohibited. The lengths to which officials will go to enforce this varies, but probably the worst that might happen is that you'll be asked to leave. Avoid problems and ensure your privacy by keeping your tent well hidden. A dark green tent attracts the least attention.

Campgrounds

Generally, two distinct types of campgrounds are available. State, provincial, and federal government-operated campgrounds all offer a basic outdoor experience with a minimum of facilities, usually just pit toilets and water from pumps. Municipal and private campgrounds usually offer hot showers, laundromats, stores, dump stations, plug-ins, etc. The latter cater primarily to RV drivers, but most welcome tenters. The government campgrounds in both the U.S. and Canada are usually cheaper (rarely more than $15 nightly) than the commercial variety (rarely less than $10). The showers ($3) at the commercial sites are almost always open to noncampers, and are sometimes the only place in town to rinse off. Whenever you are quoted a fee at a campground always assume, unless told otherwise, that it is for your whole group rather than per person.

Hostels

At last count Alaska had 11 official, though highly varied, youth hostels: at Anchorage, Girdwood, Seward, Soldotna, Fairbanks, Delta, Tok, Haines, Juneau, Sitka, and Ketchikan. There are also hostels in Vancouver, Victoria, Banff, all along the Icefields Parkway, and in Jasper. All are accessible by road or ferry, though a few in Alaska are beyond the reach of public transportation (Delta's, Tok's, and Seward's are at least seven miles outside of town). Males and females have separate dormitories. A sleeping sheet is sometimes required, and always for rent or sale, though you can also use your sleeping bag. All have communal kitchens, reading rooms, and require a small clean-up chore. Some have washing machines and dryers. Most charge around $10 for members, $13 for non-members. Hostels are great places to meet other travelers, but most close during daytime business hours. All addresses and phone numbers are listed in the appropriate travel chapters.

Joining the YH Association before you leave home is recommended. Write: American Youth Hostels, Inc., 133 I St. N.W., Suite 800, Washington, D.C. 20005, USA, or Canadian Hosteling Assn., 333 River Rd., Vanier City, Ontario K1L 8B9, Canada. Wherever and whenever you can, reserve a place at a youth hostel in advance by sending the first-night's price, or calling with a credit card number.

Hotels

Within these pages you'll find reasonably priced hotels wherever they exist. The hotel rates given are usually for the cheapest category of room, with a pay phone in the lobby, TV in the lounge, and shared bathroom down the hall. In other words, it's just like being at home. The older hotels in the big cities look a lot worse than they actually are, but ask to see the room.

In the major package tourist stops *and* off-the-beaten-track places with limited lodging, what's available is often booked way in advance. Unless you've made reservations, don't count on getting any rooms, especially the good cheap ones, at most Alaskan destinations. Be particularly prepared for this at Denali Park, Valdez, Kodiak, and Skagway, where your choice is between an $80 room (in the unlikely event that one is available) or camping.

Other Lodging

Bed and breakfasts are booming throughout Alaska and Canada. They're a great way to spend time with local residents in showcase homes, save a little money on accommodations (most start at around $40), and get breakfast thrown in for the price of a night. Some are listed in the specific travel sections of this book; see "Anchorage" and "Whitehorse" for area-wide associations.

If you're planning to stay a little longer in a particular place, check the classified ads in the newspapers under "Furnished Rooms" or "Rooms for Rent," and the Yellow Pages under "Rooming Houses." You can often get a substantial (50-75%) discount on private rooms (with shared bath and kitchen) for weekly stays.

For indoor sleeping in the great outdoors, check into Forest Service cabins. At $15 per night per cabin, you get up to six bunks, wood stove, wood, table, and outhouse. Of the nearly 200 cabins in the Tongass and Chugach national forests, however, only a few are accessible by road; the rest require flying or boating in. These cabins are popular, and the Forest Service accepts applications for reservations six months in advance. Reservations for some of the most-used cabins, especially during hunting and fishing season, are determined by lottery. For addresses to write for applications, see p. 124.

FOOD

Home Cooking

The cheapest and healthiest way to eat is to buy groceries and prepare your own meals. A lot can just be eaten cold. Peanut butter, anyone? Raw cookie dough? Freeze-dried food is convenient (but expensive and of varying tastiness) for hikers and campers—add water, heat, and then eat the plastic package instead. Canned food can also be handy, though heavy. Carry your own tea bags, instant oatmeal, pancake mix, fresh and dried fruit, and nuts. Most of the large supermarkets (Carrs, Foodland) have extensive health food and bulk sections, plus soup and salad bars where you pay by the pound (usually about $2.50 per). Also, if you can, stop at the roadside produce stands (in Matanuska Valley, mainly) and fish stalls along the coast. The local food won't be cheap, but it will definitely be fresh and tasty, and still less expensive than eating at a restaurant. All hostels have kitchens, or cook on your campstove.

Restaurants

Don't worry, snappy sustenance is found all over Alaska. You'll feel just as foolish and fat after satisfying a craving for Chicken Mc-Nuggets, a Taco Bell Grande, or a bacon quarter-pounder in Anchorage as in your home town. You won't feel quite so dumb after an Arby's roast beef or Burger King salad bar, though. The good-value restaurants are listed in the "Food" sections of the travel chapters, exhaustively researched with gusto and no little guilt. However, Alaska is not known for its large variety of fine cuisine. Even in Anchorage, Juneau, Fairbanks, and other larger towns, the ethnic options are minimal at best, expensive, and often disappointing. Furthermore, after a week of traveling around Alaska and Yukon, you'll think that all the coffee shops, roadhouses, cafes, and beaneries use the same menu, the same ingredients, the same grill and fryolator, and the same short-order cooks. Basic boring bacon-and-eggs breakfasts are usually $5-6; $4.50 is a bargain. Your burger and fries are similarly pricey, though a grilled cheese sandwich (American on white bread with liquid margarine) will be slightly cheaper. Fried chicken will start at $7, but spaghetti could be as little as $5. It's always a good idea to have some emergency munchies on hand. This might save you from going into hypoglycemic shock between eateries, which can be very long distances, or from facing yet another unfaceable meal of road food when you finally get to one.

Salmon Bakes

Splurge on these once or twice. The salmon is usually fresh, thick, and delicious (though the halibut is chunked, breaded, and deep-fried—not great, but it will satisfy your grease quotient). Ribs are messy, but will address those deep carnivorous instincts, especially in this dog-eat-dog wilderness. Some salmon bakes also have reindeer sausage and crab legs. They all have the requisite macaroni, potato, and infernal three-bean salad, carrot and celery sticks, black olives for every finger, and sourdough rolls. Blueberry cake usually tops off the meal. Different bakes have different takes on second helpings; always ask several different cooks and servers for seconds anyway. Soft drinks are usually included, but beer and wine are extra. Expect to pay $10-15 for lunch, $15-20 for dinner. Discount coupons and nights are often advertised; keep your eyes open and jump on them. The one at Alaskaland in Fairbanks is best; Juneau's is a close second.

OTHER PRACTICALITIES

MONEY

The Whale And The Minnow

Prices are high in Alaska, but that doesn't mean you have to pay them. You can get away without spending a lot of money if you try. Planning is half the battle; budgeting is the other half. If you're driving up, take a friend or rider (or two), and your transportation expenses are immediately slashed. A credit card will give you security and extra time to pay when you get back home. If you buy your Greyhound ticket 30 days in advance, you can go anywhere in the U.S. for a totally painless $68. Buy your airline or ferry tickets in the winter or early spring to stretch out the financing of the trip.

Do not even *think* of going to Alaska without a tent. Two nights in a hotel will pay for the tent. Definitely make reservations for the youth hostels in the big towns (Anchorage, Ketchikan, Juneau), and consider becoming a lifetime member of the YH Association, much more economical in the long run. Bring a backpacking stove and cook as much food as you can, and utilize the salad bars at supermarkets. With the money you save you can splash out on an occasional restaurant meal and salmon bake.

Study this book carefully beforehand to help you choose the good-value destinations, attractions, and splurges. Then add up the big transportation chunks, the smaller accommodation bits, and a generous $15-20 a day for food and miscellaneous. With a little creativity, flexibility, and minimalism, you can have a whale of a time on a minnow's worth of money.

The Hard Facts

Unless otherwise stated, all prices in this handbook are in the local currency: Canadian dollars in Canada, U.S. dollars in the United States. (The exchange rate hovers around C$1.30 to US$1.) Assume that all hotel and restaurant prices listed are per person (pp), per day, or per meal. Campground charges are usually per site. The prices and hours of all attractions and services throughout the book refer to the peak season from June through Aug.; discounts are often offered in May and September, when shorter hours are also in effect. Some prices are lower in the off season, but many businesses close. The prices (1991) in this book will be mostly accurate in 1992, but a little low in 1993. Nevertheless, you should find them useful for comparison: what were once the least or most expensive are still likely to be.

Always ask the price of a room, meal, or service before accepting it. Tipping (usually 15% of the bill), as in the Lower 48, is expected at most sit-down eating places fancier than snack bars or takeaway counters. Tourism employees often receive minimum wage and depend on tips for their real income. All transportation fares and traveling times are one way (OW), unless otherwise noted. Be aware that tickets or exact change are required on all forms of public transport in North America; drivers rarely carry change. Read the instructions before using public telephones in the North. Often you do not pay until your party answers; if you put the coin in before that, it will be lost.

Cash, Traveler's Checks, Exchange

Traveler's checks are the best way to carry money, but buy them from a well-known U.S. company such as Bank of America, Visa, or American Express. European or Japanese traveler's checks are very difficult to cash in North America; even Thomas Cook and Barclay Bank checks are sometimes refused.

If you know you will be visiting Canada, be sure to get a few Canadian-dollar traveler's checks, easily arranged at any large American or European bank. It could save you a lot of trouble if you arrive outside banking hours (10-3 Mon.-Thurs., 10-5 Friday). Some Canadian and U.S. cash will make your first few hours in the neighboring country less of a hassle. Note that there are no exchange

MEASUREMENTS

Distances, Weights, And Measures

Alaska, like all of the U.S., employs the "English method" of measuring weights and distances. Basically, dry weights are in ounces and pounds; liquid measures are in ounces, quarts, and gallons; and distances are measured in inches, feet, yards, and miles. The metric system, based on units of 10, is known but is not in general use. The following conversion charts should be helpful.

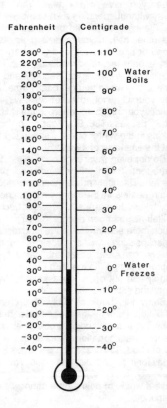

1 inch	=	2.54 centimeters (cm)
1 foot	=	.3048 meters (m)
1 mile	=	1.6093 kilometers (km)
1 km	=	.6214 miles
1 nautical mile	=	1.852 km
1 fathom	=	1.8288 m
1 chain	=	20.1168 m
1 furlong	=	201.168 m
1 acre	=	.4047 hectares (ha)
1 sq km	=	100 ha
1 sq mile	=	2.59 sq km
1 ounce	=	28.35 grams
1 pound	=	.4536 kilograms (kg)
1 short ton	=	.90718 metric ton
1 short ton	=	2000 pounds
1 long ton	=	1.016 metric tons
1 long ton	=	2240 pounds
1 metric ton	=	1000 kg
1 quart	=	.94635 liters
1 U.S. gallon	=	3.7854 liters
1 Imperial gallon	=	4.5459 liters

To compute Centigrade temperatures, subtract 32 from Fahrenheit and divide by 1.8. To go the other way, multiply Centigrade by 1.8 and add 32.

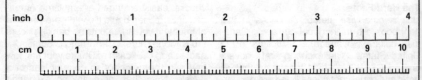

facilities at the borders; Canadians take U.S. dollars at a very poor rate, while Americans often refuse Canadian dollars. Any other currency will most likely be refused. The U.S. dollar hovers around $1.30 Canadian so Americans get a 30% discount (though Canadian prices are generally 20% higher than in the U.S.).

Time And Measurements

In 1983, Alaska went from four time zones to two. From Southeast to the western tip of the mainland is on Alaska Time, one hour earlier than Pacific Time, four hours earlier than Eastern. The western Aleutians are on Hawaii time, two hours behind Pacific Time. British Columbia and Yukon are on Pacific Time. So when you go from Prince Rupert to Ketchikan, or from Dawson to Eagle or Beaver Creek to Tok you gain an hour; from Skagway to Whitehorse you lose an hour.

Just as with currency, all measurements herein are in the local units: metric in Canada, American in the U.S. To compute Celsius temperatures, subtract 32 from Fahrenheit and divide by 1.8. To compute miles from kilometers, multiply by 0.6; to get kilometers from miles multiply by 1.6. Fifty-five mph is 90 km/h. Remember that an imperial gallon is one-fifth larger than a U.S. gallon, so you'll get better mileage!

Mail And Phone

If you would like to receive mail en route, have it addressed to yourself c/o General Delivery via a post office along the way. American post offices hold General Delivery mail 10 days, Canadian post offices 15 days. If you have mail sent to a Canadian post office and think you might not arrive in time, get a "Holding of Mail" card at any Canadian post office and send it to the appropriate address. Postage stamps in the amount of C$1.50 must be affixed to the card for each month you request mail to be held, up to a maximum of three months. This is an excellent service, but don't bother phoning; verbal requests are not honored.

Note that all mail posted in Canada must carry Canadian postage stamps, just as all U.S. mail must have American stamps. Con-

venient General Delivery addresses are: Vancouver, B.C. V6B 3P7; Prince Rupert, B.C. V8J 3P3; Whitehorse, Yukon Y1A 2BO; Seattle, WA 98101; Juneau, AK 99801; Fairbanks, AK 99701; Anchorage, AK 99501. Mail takes several weeks to travel from Alaska to Yukon.

The area code in all of Alaska is 907. British Columbia's is 604. Yukon and Alberta share 403.

BORDER CROSSINGS

Immigration officials are trained to be suspicious, so try to look as much like a legitimate short-term visitor as you can. Never admit (or even imply) that you are going to work, study, do business, or live in a country other than your own. Officials may ask to see your money. If you have less than $250, you stand a chance of being refused entry. Some unscrupulous souls get around this by borrowing $500 or more, using it to buy traveler's checks, and then claiming the checks were lost; they then repay the loan with the replacement checks and use the "dummies" to crash borders with. We don't recommend that you do this as it's illegal and unfair to kindly immigration officers. If you were ever to cash the "lost" checks even by mistake, you would go straight to jail. The best approach is just to be as polite and submissive as you can. Never argue or get angry with an official—it never helps. They have unlimited institutional force on their side and know it. Dissembling is more effective.

Entry Into The U.S.

Everyone other than Canadians requires a passport and visa to enter the United States. Most Western Europeans and Commonwealth country residents can usually obtain from American consulates a six-month travel visa easily. You must have an onward or return ticket. No vaccinations are required, and you can bring an unlimited amount of money (over US$5000 must be registered). Be aware that you can wind up crossing a Canadian/U.S. border four times in each direction (Lower 48 into B.C. or Alberta, back into Southeast Alaska, then into Yukon, then back into mainland Alaska). If you're an overseas visitor, make sure you understand the requirements for *re-entering* the United States. Americans returning from Canada may bring back US$400 worth of duty-free merchandise once every 30 days.

(GORDY OHLIGER)

Entry Into Canada

No visa is required of visitors from Western Europe, most Commonwealth countries, or the United States. Americans can enter Canada by showing a birth certificate or voter registration card; a driver's license may not be sufficient. Everyone else must have a passport. Travelers under 18 must be accompanied by or have written permission from a parent or guardian to enter Canada. Handguns and automatic weapons are not allowed into Canada. Your home country's driver's license is acceptable in Canada.

WHAT TO TAKE

Camping Equipment

Even in summer, weather conditions in the North can change suddenly and you must be well prepared for rain and cold at any time. Water resistance and warmth (in addition to weight) should be your main criteria when purchasing camping equipment and clothing. Categorize and separate all your things in plastic bags or stuff sacks; pack it that way for convenient access and protection from moisture. If you're planning on hiking and traveling by public transportation, your loaded pack should not weigh more than one-quarter your body weight. Walk around the block with it a few times. Next imagine hiking

10 miles uphill into the rain with that load on your back. Now pack again—lighter this time. You'll *still* probably end up sending a few things home.

Practice putting up your tent, cooking on your campstove, etc., *before* you set out. A foam sleeping pad, or better yet, a Therma-Rest inflatable pad, provides comfort, insulation, and protection from moisture—essential qualities in the North. (They also double as inflatable rafts on lakes.) Down sleeping bags are useless when wet, especially problematic in Southeast and Southcentral. But they're much lighter and warmer than synthetic-filled bags, and you can always throw them in a dryer for an hour. Synthetic fiber is warmer when wet, less expensive, but heavier and bulkier.

Clothing

Wearing your clothing in layers allows you to add or remove items, depending on the temperature or your level of exertion. Start out with a T-shirt, thermal, or polypropylene top (and bottom). A wool shirt on top of that is comfortable and warm. A wool sweater and waterproof jacket are lighter and more versatile than a bulky overcoat, and a down vest is worth its weight in gold. Down coats are useless in the rain. Hiking boots are a given. The new lightweight high-tops are efficient, though the old tried-and-true work boots are also adequate. Make sure they're waterproof! A pair of old tennis shoes or scuba divers' rubber booties are handy for crossing streams and muskeg. Wear rubber thongs into public showers, around pools, etc. Bring a wool cap and gloves or mittens. A hooded parka comes in handy, though a poncho is adequate, light, and can double as a ground cloth or awning. Make sure it has a grommeted hole in each corner. Plastic rain pants are light, cheap, and will greatly improve the quality of life. Only the most expensive restaurants in the cities expect dressy attire, so bring a sportcoat, suit, dress, or skirt if you plan to hobnob with the well-heeled or are on a group tour. But a new pair of permanent-press uniform pants goes a long way toward looking casually presentable, rather than the usual scruffy jeans.

WHAT TO TAKE

Camping Equipment
Internal-frame pack
day pack or shoulder bag
nylon tent and rain fly
tent-patching tape
sleeping pad
sleeping bag
YH sleeping sheet
waterproofing compound

Toiletries And Medical Kit
soap in plastic container
toothpaste and toothbrush
unscented stick deodorant
shampoo
white toilet paper
vitamins
nail clippers
insect repellent
ChapStick
a motion-sickness remedy
contraceptives
iodine
water purification pills
Lomotil/diarrhea remedy
Tiger Balm
Vaseline
aspirin or aspirin substitute
Calmitol ointment
an antibiotic
Band-Aids
one large elastoplast or dressing

Documents
passport or birth certificate
youth hostel card
photocopy of important documents
traveler's checks
Canadian and American cash
moneybelt with plastic liner
address book
waterproof notebook, pen or pencil
envelopes
postage stamps
extra ballpoint pen
Alaska-Yukon Handbook

Food Kit
campstove
tin cooking pot
plastic plate
Sierra cup
can and bottle opener
cork screw
pen knife or Swiss Army knife
spoon, fork
canteen or water bottle
waterproof matches
freeze-dried food
tea bags
plastic bags
litter bag
fishing tackle
salt

Accessories
compass
bear bells
pocket flashlight
candle
pocket alarm/calculator
sunglasses
padlock and chain or cable
five yards of rope
towel
powdered laundry soap
sink plug (one than fits all)
sewing kit with mini-scissors
fishing line for sewing heavy gear

Clothing
wool cap, sweater
rain pants, parka
waterproof hiking boots
tennis shoes
rubber thongs
mittens, gloves
poncho with grommets
permanent-press slacks
down vest
socks

Accessories And Documents

A small pocket calculator with a clock/alarm function is always handy. Carrying a bike cable or length of lightweight chain allows you to attach your pack to something solid if you must leave it in public places, and a padlock locks it (and your tent zippers) in place. Rip-offs are infrequent, but they do occur. Take a five-yard length of rope to hang your food up out of reach of brother bruin or to string out for a clothesline.

Make a couple of photocopies of the information page of your passport, identification, YH card, transportation tickets, purchase receipt from traveler's checks, eyeglass and medical prescriptions, etc.—you should be able to get them all on one page. Carry these in different places and leave one at home. A soft pouch-type moneybelt worn under your clothes is very safe and handy, but put the documents inside a plastic bag to protect them from perspiration moisture.

Food Kit

A small campstove is the only way to ensure hot food and drink on the trail. Firewood is often wet or unavailable; other times campfires are prohibited. Look for a stove which is not only lightweight, but burns a variety of fuels. White gas stoves are best. Remember, camping fuel is not allowed on commercial aircraft. Carry your food in lightweight containers. Avoid cans and bottles whenever possible. Dried or freeze-dried foods are light, easy to prepare, and less attractive to animals. Take some high protein/energy foods for hiking. A canteen or plastic water bottle is handy to have along; replenish it whenever you can.

Toiletries And Medical Kit

You'll find a plastic case in which to pack your toiletries or medical kit in the dishware section of any large department or hardware store. Unscented deodorant is best for both bear and bare encounters. Calmitol ointment or aloe gel are good for burns, bites, and rashes. An antibiotic such as sulfatrim apo is useful for serious infections (not VD), but beware of all antibiotics—know when and how to use them. For stomach cramps associated with diarrhea take a pain killer such as imodium. Moleskin is an effective blister preventative. Take an adequate supply of any personal prescription medicines.

HEALTH AND HELP

Hypothermia

The number-one killer of outdoorspeople in the North, accounting for 85% of all wilderness deaths, is hypothermia. Prolonged exposure to wind and cold plus general physical exhaustion can lead to persistent shivering, drowsiness, disorientation, unconsciousness, and eventually death. The most insidious thing about it is that you probably won't even realize that it's happening to you. To prevent hypothermia always carry good raingear, dress in layers (particularly using wool or polypropylene, not cotton), avoid getting wet, and eat nutritious foods. Wet clothes cause you to lose body heat much faster than dry clothes. A full 60% of body heat loss occurs through an uncovered head, so wear a waterproof or wool cap.

If you or someone you're with experiences the early-warning signs, get out of the rain and wind, get to a dry, warm place and remove the wet clothes. Cover the victim with a blanket or sleeping bag and a hat, and don't let him fall asleep. Slowly warm him by placing warm wrapped objects (heated rocks, baked potatoes, etc.) alongside the head, neck, sides, and groin. One of the best ways to rewarm a person is by lying naked next to the victim, using your body heat to warm him (this works best with close friends). Do not try to quickly heat him since this can lead to a heart attack. If at all possible, get the person to a hospital. Be prepared for hypothermia on all overnight hikes; and if making a day hike on a wet day, do not go beyond the point where you can beat a hasty retreat to shelter.

Water

Even clear, cold, free-running streams can be contaminated. The best way to avoid contracting parasites from beavers and muskrats upstream is to boil water for 20 minutes before drinking it. If this is not convenient, treat it with chlorine or (better) iodine (about five drops of either per quart) and let it stand for 30 minutes. Purification pills also do the trick. If you're a real purist, you might take one of the water cleaning devices sold in camping goods stores; First Need works well, and sells for around $35.

Lost In Place

It's easy to become lost in forested areas once you leave the main trail. Do not blunder blindly on, but stop and look around you. Backtrack to a familiar spot, then either continue on the trail carefully, or go completely back to where you began. Don't put your pack down—an excellent way to lose it. Use a compass to find your way to some known point. Panic in the wilderness is a form of culture shock which could spell your end.

Doctors And Mothers

If you're sick or injured and can't afford the prices charged by private doctors and general hospitals, call the local welfare office and ask them to refer you to a low-cost clinic. You may have to wait in line and go during certain limited hours, but there's usually no problem about using their services.

Runaways can send a free message to their parents by calling one of the following toll-free numbers: (800) 231-6946 in the Lower 48; (800) 231-6762 in Alaska/Hawaii. An operator will answer your call and phone your folks anywhere in the U.S. with a message from you. There will be no lectures and nobody will try to find out where you are. Only two questions will be asked, "How are you and do you need anything?" Let your parents know you're alive and okay.

Information

If you have time to write requests, an excellent selection of free maps and brochures is available from the regional tourism authorities: **Tourism B.C.,** 1117 Wharf St., Victoria, B.C. V8W 2Z2, Canada; **Division of Tourism,** Pouch E, Juneau, AK 99881, USA; **Tourism Yukon,** Box 2703, Whitehorse, YT Y1A 2C6, Canada; **TravelArctic,** Government of the North west Territories, Yellowknife, N.W.T. X1A 2L9, Canada.

A free highway **map of Washington** state is available from the Washington State Dept. of Transportation, Transportation Bldg., Olympia, WA 98504, USA. Get a free **map of Canada** from the Canadian Government Office of Tourism, 235 Queen St., O4E, Ottawa, Ont. K1A 0H6, Canada. Write for an index to **maps of Alaska** from the USGS Distribution Branch, Box 25286, Federal Center, Denver, CO 80225, USA.

For information on Alaska's national parks, write: **National Park Service,** 540 W. 5th Ave., Anchorage, AK 99501, USA. Free maps of the Tongass and Chugach national forests may be obtained from the **U.S. Forest Service,** Box 1628, Juneau, AK 99802, USA.

For a **ferry timetable** write: Alaska Marine Highway, Pouch R, Juneau, AK 99811, USA. A list of **Alaskan youth hostels** is available from Anchorage International Hostel, 700 H St., Anchorage, AK 99501, USA.

If you are a member of the American Automobile Assn. (AAA) or Canadian Automobile Assn. (CAA), or have a friend or relative who is, get their *TourBook* and *CampBook* covering western Canada and Alaska, plus detailed maps. Overseas visitors who belong to an affiliated club in their home country can obtain this material free by showing their membership card at an AAA or CAA office in any large city (look in the phone book).

GIARDIA

Although Alaska's lakes and streams may appear clean, you may be risking a debilitating sickness by drinking the water without treatment. The protozoan *Giardia duodenalis* is found throughout the state, spread by both humans and animals (including beaver). Although the disease is curable with drugs, it's always best to carry safe drinking water on any trip or to boil water taken from creeks or lakes. Simply bringing water to a full boil is sufficient to kill Giardia and other harmful organisms. Another option is to use water filters. Note, however, that these may not filter out other organisms such as Campylobacter bacteria that are just 0.2 microns in size. Chlorine and iodine are not always reliable, taste foul, and can be unhealthy.

GETTING THERE

ALASKA PASS

An interesting new concept in Alaskan independent travel was introduced in 1991, known as the Alaska Pass. Nine large carriers (Alaska and B.C. ferries, Alaskon Express, Gray Line, Norline, Island Coach, and Alaska and B.C. railroads) have joined forces and offered substantial (in some cases) discounts for a variety of ground travel options between Bellingham and Fairbanks, including B.C., the Yukon, and mainstream Alaska. Passes range from eight consecutive days ($399, with a $50 surcharge for "starting the clock" in Bellingham) to 21 days of travel out of 45 consecutive days ($839—no surcharge). In 1991, the passes were good for travel starting May 31 and ending Sept. 15. Reservations are the responsibility of the traveler, and no refunds are available (unless the pass is not used at all).

Traveler Dan Bagatell sent in this report about the first year of the Alaska Pass. "Because the passes are so new and not particularly well publicized, a lot of travel agents don't know about them; I only found out along the way and ran into only a handful of people using them. The 12-out-of-21- and 21-out-of-45-day options seem like pretty good deals, especially since they potentially include round-trip ferry down to Vancouver or Bellingham. The continuous-clock options aren't as good a deal because you pay even if you stay somewhere for four days. For the less adventurous traveler staying on a relatively beaten path to major destinations, it's a good deal. For people like me who like playing the budget travel game, you can find cheaper ways to go leg-by-leg, but that takes some effort, and the alternative means might not be as comfortable or fancy (e.g., a beat-up van from Anchorage to Denali for $19 as opposed to the Alaska Railroad for $78). Moreover, the passholder's temptation would be just to use pass-covered transportation, necessitating a fairly strict itinerary, which would eliminate more spontaneous and exciting options along the way, such as the ones that I chose: flying from Juneau to Cordova and going from Fairbanks to Dawson via Eagle."

As Dan points out, because the Alaska Pass doesn't include any air options, and because Alaska is such a gigantic place to travel around completely on the surface, the Alaska Pass could be somewhat limiting. However, with some creativity, very close planning, and comparing of transportation costs, it is certainly possible to come out ahead using this new and interesting brand of travel—falling somewhere between a package tour and complete indpendence.

BY AIR

Five airlines offer nonstop service to Anchorage from as far south as Phoenix, and as far east as Chicago: **Alaska Airlines,** tel. (800) 426-0333, **United,** tel. (800) 241-6522, **Delta,** tel. (800) 221-1212, **Northwest Airlines,** tel. (800) 225-2525, and **Continental,** tel. (800) 525-0280. In Sept. 1991, all were charging $926 for RT regular coach fares Seattle-Anchorage, less than a four-hour flight, and $1212 RT from San Francisco. Don't have an emergency or be in a hurry!

Alaska Airlines has 13 daily flights to Anchorage, as opposed to one a day on United, Continental, and Northwest, and two on Delta. Alaska Air's super-savers (seven-, 14-, and 21-day APEX, non-refundable and non-changeable) were starting at $378 and rising to $538. They also had a red-eye with a 14-day APEX and 100% penalty for $278. Alaska Air was also offering mid-week specials. It's worth your while to start calling early.

Because the one-way coach fare from Seattle and San Francisco was $75 more expensive than the seven-day APEX RT, many people buy roundtrip tickets, with the intention of reselling the unused return portion to someone leaving Alaska by air, at half

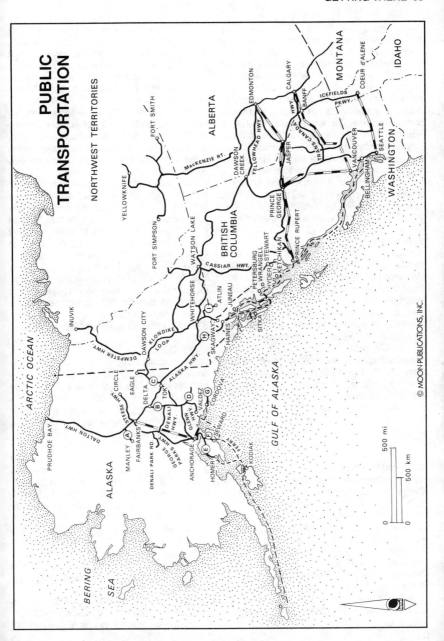

PUBLIC TRANSPORTATION

© MOON PUBLICATIONS, INC.

the roundtrip fare. That's a $75 investment for a possible return of, say, $250—a very good deal for both the seller and the buyer. This is strictly against airline policy, though it's not against the law, which some airline personnel would lead you to believe. Still, airlines are not bound to honor a ticket that is not in your name. It's best to at least be the same gender as the name on the ticket. And you can't change the date or time, without paying a hefty penalty. Check the classifieds in the daily newspapers under "Travel and Transportation" for these bargain tickets.

Alaska Airlines' Mileage Plan is worth knowing about: travel 10,000 miles in Alaska and get a free flight within the state; 15,000 miles gets you one Alaska-mainland ticket.

From Canada

Canadian Airways, tel. (800) 426-7000 in the U.S., flies from most Canadian cities to Whitehorse, Yukon. From Vancouver, the cheapest fare is C$293 RT, with a Saturday minimum and a 30-day maximum stay. (The regular coach fare was $836 RT.) Once in Whitehorse, you can fly **Air North,** tel. (403) 668-2228 to Fairbanks (via Dawson City), C$365 OW (with a 24-hour APEX).

Delta Express, tel. (800) 661-0789 in Canada, (800) 764-1800 in Alaska, flies direct from Whitehorse to Anchorage (and also connects to Yellowknife, Northwest Territories) daily Wed. through Sun., $350 OW, $700 RT, $529 with a seven-day APEX.

BY BUS

Greyhound Lines

This giant company, the largest of its kind in the world, has thousands of buses and stations all over the U.S. and Canada. Bus travel is very flexible—you buy a ticket and you're on your way. And you never need a reservation; if one bus fills up, they just roll out another. Also, they're extremely competitively priced, and always have several special deals going on. For example, in Sept. 1991, their 30-day advance-purchase ticket one-way anywhere was $68, roundtrip $136, $24 cancellation fee, travel Mon. through Thurs. only.

Greyhound also has an unlimited travel Ameripass which is valid throughout the U.S. The Ameripass is sold for periods of 7 days (US$211), 15 days (US$285), and 30 days (US$391), and the ticket is good for one year. Unfortunately, the Ameripass is no longer valid in Canada.

From Vancouver to Whitehorse, the farthest north (and west) that Greyhound goes, is C$192. Or ride to Prince Rupert and grab an Alaska ferry. Check on excursion fares; often some are offered to Banff and eastern destinations.

All Greyhound regular-fare tickets are valid for one year, and unlimited stopovers are allowed. Greyhound buses run around the clock so you can save a lot on hotels. Instead of going straight through, however, stop off once in a while for a night or two in some of the exciting cities along the way. Remember, you're on holiday! There's almost always a YMCA, YWCA, or YH where you can arrange inexpensive accommodations. Greyhound has no nationwide 800 number, except for Spanish-speaking people only—(800) 531-5332. Call your local terminal for information.

Magic Buses

Green Tortoise travel is more than just a bus ride—it's a vacation and a cultural experience in itself. This alternative bus line uses recycled Greyhounds with the seats ripped out and foam-rubber mattresses laid in their place on elevated platforms. Up front there's a lounge area with seats and tables, which converts to another sleeping area at night—just roll out your sleeping bag and forget everything. Food is usually included in the fare for the long-distance trips such as Alaska. Unlike Greyhound, you're allowed to drink beer and wine on board (in moderation), but tobacco smoking is prohibited. One of the best things about these trips is the people—alternative travel attracts good company. The removal of the seats eliminates barriers and leads to new friendships. This is a friendly, unprivate way to travel, though not inexpensive.

Green Tortoise has 10 buses. A shuttle runs between San Francisco and Seattle ($59) four times a week, weekly to Los Angeles ($30).

Alaska Marine Highway's flagship Columbia *sails from Seattle to Skagway once a week in the summer.*

From April to October, there's a weekly trip all the way from San Francisco to New York and Boston ($299 OW plus $81 for food). The journey takes five weeks. They have one trip a summer to Alaska throughout late July and August, for $600 plus $200 for food (breakfast, dinner, and snacks). There are 28 passengers and two drivers, and usually a tour guide. Book in February or March to ensure a space.

Despite the casual approach, Green Tortoise buses are reliable and have a good safety record. For more information write: Green Tortoise Alternative Travel, Box 24459, San Francisco, CA 94124, USA. Telephone numbers are: (415) 821-0803 in California; (206) 324-7433 in Seattle; (212) 431-3348 in New York; (617) 265-8533 in Boston; or toll-free (800) 227-4766 nationwide (outside California).

Others

Alaska Direct connects Anchorage and Minneapolis/St. Paul with a six-day, five-night express bus trip. Call (800) 328-9730 in the Lower 48, (800) 288-1305 in Canada, or (800) 478-7228 in Alaska.

Pacific Coach Lines, tel. (604) 385-4411, offers excellent service the length of Vancouver Island, from Victoria to Port Hardy, with connections in Port Alberni for Long Beach. Once you reach Whitehorse, however, the bus situation goes a little downhill. **Alaskon Express,** Gray Line's public transportation arm, tel. (907) 277-5581, runs into Alaska three times a week. **Norline** runs from Whitehorse up to Dawson. Within Alaska many small companies provide local and short hops around the state; all services are listed in the travel chapters. Note, however, that these companies change with the wind, so always research and reconfirm the information herein.

BY FERRY

Ferries plying the Inside Passage from Bellingham to Skagway cruise up an inland waterway and through fjords far wilder than Norway's, surpassing even a trip down the coast of Chile to Punta Arenas. One difference is that the North American journey is cheaper and more easily arranged than its South American or Scandinavian counterparts. Another difference is the variety of services, routes, and destinations for this 1,000-mile historic cruise. The **Washington State Ferries,** Colman Dock, Seattle, WA 98104, tel. (206) 464-6400 (in Washington call toll-free 800-542-7052) offers regular service throughout Puget Sound and to Vancouver Island. **Black Ball Transport,** 430 Belleville St., Victoria, B.C. V8V 1W9, tel. (604) 386-2202, sails between Victoria and Port Angeles. **B.C. Ferries,** 112 Fort St., Victoria, B.C. V8V 4V2, tel. (604) 669-1211, has commuter service between Vancouver Island and the B.C. mainland, plus long-distance ships through the Canadian Inside Passage from Port Hardy at the northern tip of Vancouver Island to Prince Rupert on the B.C. mainland's north coast, and from Prince Rupert to the Queen Charlotte Islands.

The **Alaska Marine Highway,** Box 25535, Juneau, AK 99802, tel. (800) 642-0066, operates two ferry networks: one from Bellingham throughout Southeast Alaska (see "Southeast Alaska—Introduction" for details), the other through Southcentral Alaska from Cordova to Dutch Harbor. The two systems do not connect, but Alaska Airlines' flight from Juneau to Cordova makes it possible to travel almost the whole distance from Bellingham to Dutch Harbor by regular passenger ferry (ferry Bellingham-Juneau, plane Juneau-Cordova, ferry Cordova-Kodiak-Dutch Harbor). The ferries operate year-round and fares are 25% lower from Oct. to April. Also, a little-known service provided at all the Alaska ferry terminals is a computer printout describing the sights and travel practicalities of all the towns en route. And they're amazingly up to date. Ask when you're there.

BY CAR

Getting to Alaska by car is by far the cheapest, easiest, most dependable, and most flexible means of mobility. Its advantages over public transportation are manifold, so to speak. You can start anywhere, and once there, you can go anywhere there's a road, anytime you feel like it, stopping along the way for however long you decide, carrying anything or anyone you like. The roads in the north country are especially fun, and you have some of them pretty nearly to yourself. On a few roads you rarely see another car. It's very open, unconfined, uninhibiting—a large part of the Spell of the North. All you have to do is keep gas and oil in the car. And a good spare tire.

Highways North

You can drive all the way going to or from or both. Alternatively, put the car on the ferry in the opposite direction. The **Alaska Highway** (nicknamed the Alcan) is now 50 years old. Gone are the days when you had to carry extra fuel and four spare tires, when you had to protect your headlights and windshield with chicken wire, and when facilities were spaced 250 miles apart. Today, almost the entire road is paved and wide enough for two trucks to pass each other without one having to pull over. Gas stations are located almost every 50 miles, and roadhouses and inns are numerous. Still, this road passes through 1,440 miles of somewhat inhospitable wilderness. Frost heaves and potholes are not uncommon. Mechanics are few and far between and parts are even scarcer. Gas prices are no laughing matter. If you're coming from anywhere east of Idaho or Alberta, you can hit mile 0 of the Alaska Highway through Edmonton without having to backtrack east at all. But if you're heading north from the West Coast, or through the Canadian Rockies, you'll probably wind up in Prince George and have to head east a bit to Dawson Creek.

You can also head west out of Prince George on the Yellowhead and take the **Cassiar Highway** north from Meziadin Junction to just west of Watson Lake in Yukon Territory. This 458-mile road is scenically stunning, but 200 miles of it are gravel, and services are a little less frequent than on the Alaska Highway.

Go Prepared

A few common-sense preparations can eliminate all but the most unexpected karmic problems. A gas credit card is invaluable—Chevron, Texaco, and Shell are most useful. You can expect to get hit hard by gas prices, especially along the Alcan and the remoter stretches in Alaska. But along the main Interior and Southcentral thoroughfares, prices are only a few cents higher than Outside. And in the cities, gas may be cheaper than the cheapest in your home town.

A reliable car is a must. If you have the slightest doubt about it, good luck! Get the car closely serviced before setting out; when you ask your mechanic "Will it make it to Alaska?" you won't be kidding. If you get stuck somewhere, there might not be another mechanic for 100 miles. And tow trucks have been known to charge $5 *a mile*. Since you'll be tempted to drive hundreds of miles off-the-beaten track, the best investment you can make in your car is for five steel-belted radial tires. Even with big gashes and holes, they'll still roll under you. Bring a pressure gauge and check the tires frequently. A few spare hoses (and hose tape) and belts take up little room and can come in very handy. Spare gas and oil filters are also useful, due to the amount of dust on the gravel roads in the dry months. Water is an absolute necessity; carry at least a five-gallon jug. Take tools even if you don't know how to use them. Someone usually comes along who doesn't have tools, but knows how. It's a good idea to carry a roll of baling wire and a tube of Superglue, to rehang or rejoin the inevitable part that jars loose, falls off, or drags along the highway.

Be very careful around road construction crews, especially graders. Graders leave a mound of fill in the middle of the road, which they spread along the surface. Occasionally you wind up on the wrong side of the mound, and have to cross over to the right side of the road. Hidden rocks can really tear up the underside of your car. Where there's construction, often a pilot car will lead you through the muddy maze; follow it closely so as not to get stuck. A lot of salt is laid down on the roads, especially in the mountains, so wash the car thoroughly at the first opportunity to minimize the rust, which never sleeps.

Finally, by driving the whole way in one direction, and putting the car on the ferry in the other, you can take different routes up and back.

OTHER WAYS TO ALASKA

By Train

A **Canrailpass** is available in Canada for unlimited travel on VIA Rail trains. During the high summer season, the pass costs C$427, low season C$342. A 30-day pass on the train is C$288 high season, C$235 low season for unlimited travel. Even with the pass, reservations are required; call toll-free in the U.S. (800) 665-0200, in Canada (800) 665-8630. With trains running from both Prince Rupert and Vancouver, a train trip is a creative way to begin or end your journey north. The fare from Vancouver to Prince Rupert is C$171; from Prince Rupert to Jasper is C$107

Driveaways

Driveaway cars are another way of getting around North America. You pick up a car from an agency in one city, pay a deposit, then drive the car to the destination, where your deposit is refunded. If you have a rider or two to share the gas and driving, it's especially cheap and efficient transportation. Non-Canadians and non-Americans are welcome but should have an International Driver's License. Aaacon is one of the largest driveaway agencies in the U.S.; look for others in the Yellow Pages under "Auto Transporters." The classifieds in the daily newspapers of the big cities, especially on the West Coast (under "Travel and Transportation"), often have advertisements for private driveaways and riders to share expenses, sometimes even to Alaska. In Alaska, people looking for drivers or riders to the Lower 48 frequently advertise in the classifieds.

Package Tours

Seven- to 21-day whirlwinds around Alaska-Yukon are available from a growing number of retail and wholesale tour packagers. All will book you onto one of a variety of cruise ships up the Inside Passage, reserve your first-class (for Alaska) hotel rooms, roll you between them on luxury motorcoaches and superdome railcars, and offer options for local and overnight side trips. Many are escorted by tour directors, and some even include all meals in the price. Many people choose this route for convenience, comfort, and security, though they certainly pay for what they get.

Holland America-Westours, 300 Elliot Ave. W., Seattle, WA 98119, tel. (206) 281-3535 or (800) 426-0327, is the granddaddy of the Alaska package program. Chuck West, one of the most colorful characters in the history of Alaska tourism, actually started the entire business in 1948 doing city tours of Fairbanks in his private car, and built Westours into a huge, debt-ridden operation which he had to sell to the shrewd Dutch of Holland America Lines in the early 1970s. In Jan. 1989, Carnival Cruise Lines bought Holland America, including its worldwide cruise ship operation, Alaska Gray Line ground division, and 18-hotel Westmark chain. Changes for the '90s remain to be seen, but if a moderately priced tour is what you want, in many ways their motto—"Westours *is* Alaska"—is accurate.

Chuck West went on to start up another tour company, **TravAlaska,** 808 Fourth and Battery Bldg., Seattle, WA 98121, tel. (206) 441-8687 or (800) 426-0327; you can read all about the fascinating background to the whole Alaska tourism industry in Chuck West's autobiography, *Mr. Alaska, the Chuck West Story,* Weslee Publishing, Seattle.

An excellent package tour, if you can pay the price and get on one of them (book early), is offered by **Tauck Tours,** Box 5027, Westport, CN 06881, tel. (203) 226-6911 or (800) 468-2825, which uses Westours' facilities.

One of the largest domestic package-tourism companies, Tauck's tours are all escorted, and have a system all their own.

The five-star tour is on **Cunard's** *Sagafjord,* Box 999, Farmingdale, NY 11737, tel. (800) 221-4770.

Princess Tours, 2815 Second Ave., Seattle, WA 98121, tel. (800) 421-0522, competes head-on with Westours. I worked at a Westours hotel (now Westmark Fairbanks) for four years, so I'm biased (though I won't say in favor of which!).

Canadians and Germans should contact **Atlas Tours,** Box 4340, Whitehorse, Yukon Y1A 3T5, tel. (403) 668-3161.

Other tour operators include **Exploration Cruise Lines** (see below), **Royal Viking, Sitmar, Admiral,** and **Regency,** among others. For all the info, contact your travel agent, or write for the *Alaska Vacation Planner,* Box E-301, Juneau, AK 99811, tel. (907) 465-2010.

Two tips: It's preferable to take a "southbound" tour, which means you fly into Anchorage, see the mainland first, then finish off with your luxury four-day cruise. That's because the ground portion can be grueling, but then you can just relax on board the ship for the final leg. Also, be aware that the tour companies mostly target the retired market, which can be fun for non-elders who can get into the spirit, but isn't exactly a LoveBoat-type experience for swinging singles. If you're among the latter, and really want to take a cruise (not the ferry), you might try **Exploration Cruise Lines,** 1500 Metropolitan Park Building, Olive and Boren St., Seattle, WA 98101, tel. (206) 624-8551 or (800) 426-0600; they attract a younger crowd. Or take Green Tortoise. If excitement is the buzz, take one of the many outdoor adventure-travel packages advertised in the outdoor and Alaska magazines.

GETTING AROUND

By Plane And Package Tour

In Alaska, often the only way to get from here to there is in the air. To find the best-value fares, always compare the airlines to the big tour companies. You can usually get a better deal from the tour companies, which charge wholesale airfares and then add on the conveniences to compete with the regular coach fare. For example, the best APEX fare between Anchorage and Nome is generally only a few dollars more expensive than the entire Gray Line tour price, which also includes one night's lodging, two city tours, and transfers. The tour groups are mostly made up of friendly, enthusiastic, though sometimes frazzled, elders. It's easy to fall in, for the two-day package, with some of the elderly tourists, and fun when you do. All you need is an approachable attitude—the only way to travel anyway. Also, always check the ads in the daily newspapers, where the tour companies often advertise up to 50% reductions in their local package-tour prices.

Still, when you come right down to it, unless you're really into gold rush history or Eskimo culture, you might rather skip altogether and go flightseeing over Denali and Glacier Bay and cruise Prince William Sound for the same price. (Though you might seriously consider Alaska Airlines' new tours to Russia, starting at $1050!) Even when the airfare alone seems substantially cheaper, by the time you add the Airporter van both ways, and rent a bike or car to see the sights, you might as well take the tour. Besides, the tours themselves can be very good value. All this is contingent, of course, on short time; if you have unlimited days to explore, say, Kodiak, and lots of planning leeway, get the cheapest deal and really stretch your travel dollars.

By Bush Plane

All these factors are, of course, predicated on large domestic carriers flying to your destination. If they don't, you're in for a guaranteed adventure, with the small, local, colorful bush airlines, which almost always deliver exciting, personalized experiences. These airlines have regularly scheduled, mostly competitively priced (though usually expensive) flights to towns and attractions (Eagle or McNeil State Game Preserve, for instance) that either have no public ground transportation or simply can't be reached overland—which accounts for over three-quarters of the state.

The planes usually seat nine, 10, or 16 passengers, and they fly no matter how many passengers are along, for the regular fare (if the weather's cooperating). But if you're heading to a really remote cabin, fjord, river, glacier, or park, that's when you'll encounter the famous Alaskan bush pilots, and the famous Cessna two-, three-, and four-seaters. And their infamous "charter rates," upwards of $300 an hour flying time, which can make Alaska Airlines' fares look like the bargain of the century. But you'll have quite a ride—landing on tiny lakes with pontoons, on snow or ice with skis, on gravel bars with big fat tires, flying through soupy fog by radar or instinct, loaded to the gills with people, equipment, extra fuel, tools, mail, supplies, and anything else under the sun. Make sure you agree on *all* the details beforehand— charges, drop-off and pick-up times and locations, emergency and alternative procedures, tidal considerations, etc. Never be in much of a hurry; time is told differently up here, and many variables come into play, especially weather and maintenance. If you're well prepared for complications, have a flexible schedule, and a loose attitude, one of these bush hops will no doubt be among your most memorable experiences in the north country, worth every penny and minute that you spend.

By Train

Except for the White Pass and Yukon excursion between Skagway and Fraser, and the kids' choo-choo around Alaskaland in Fairbanks, Alaska-Yukon's only train is the Alaska Railroad, running 470 miles between Seward and Fairbanks (with a seven-mile spur between Portage and Whittier). The train—historic and a bit exotic—is also much roomier and slower than the tour buses, but is about the same price (and occasionally even on time). Two daily expresses, one northbound and one southbound, run between Anchorage and Fairbanks (10 hours, $108). Fairbanks to Denali costs $39, Anchorage to Denali $78. Princess Tours and Westours hook their two-deck superdome vistacruiser coaches to the end of the train, for which you pay an additional 35% (meals extra—$9 for brunch, $18 for dinner). There are also plenty of Denali packages, train-plane combinations, and family discounts. A shuttle train transports passengers through the Chugach Mountains between Portage and Whittier several times a day ($8). The train also runs all the way to Seward daily, $35 OW, $60 RT. Write: Alaska Railroad, Passenger Services, Pouch 7-2111, Anchorage, AK 99510, or call (907) 265-2685 in Anchorage, (206) 621-4234 in Seattle.

By Ferry
Alaska Marine Highway serves almost every town in Southeast Alaska, plus most of the coastal towns in Southcentral, Kodiak Island, the Kenai and Alaska peninsulas, all the way out to Dutch Harbor in the eastern Aleutians. The two systems do not interconnect, but the Alaska Airlines flight from Juneau to Cordova is an easy, though very expensive, transition. Five of the nine ferries have staterooms, and eight have a solarium where you can spread out your sleeping bag (or sleep inside in the lounges). Note that the *Bartlett*, which cruises Prince William Sound, doesn't have showers, but the other long-distance ferries do. All except the tiny shuttle between Ketchikan and Metlakatla have food service. It's a very relaxing and friendly way to travel around the state, and prices are extremely reasonable, especially compared to airfare.

Write: Alaska Marine Highway, Box 25535, Juneau, AK 99802, or call (800) 642-0066 for a copy of the schedules and fares, or to make reservations (especially recommended to book staterooms or passage for your car).

Note that the southern terminal of the Alaska ferry system is no longer in Seattle; it's now in Bellingham, WA, 85 miles north; see p. 88.

By Bus
Bus services, highly developed in B.C. and Yukon, become more primitive when you enter Alaska. Nonetheless, you can get to most major destinations by bus or minibus, and most minor destinations (on the road) by van. Except for the big tour companies' buses, plus Alaskon Express (Gray Line), most bus companies are small local affairs, which are covered in the relevant travel sections of this book. Note, however, that some crucial connections (such as Whitehorse to Tok and Anchorage, twice a week) are only infrequently serviced, or not serviced at all by any overland public transportation (such as Dawson City west into Alaska). Also be aware that buses in Alaska and Yukon do not run at night. Everyone arriving from Skagway or Edmonton/Prince George will have to spend a night in Whitehorse. All passengers transiting Yukon to Anchorage must overnight in either Beaver Creek or Tok. Accommodations are at your own expense, so take this into consideration when calculating your costs.

By Car
Your own car is without a doubt the most convenient, reliable, and inexpensive way to get around the small part of Alaska that has roads. It's best to bring the car with you;

trying to buy one at inflated Alaskan prices is not recommended and selling it at the end of your stay is problematic. Rental cars are prohibitively expensive in the outback towns, and can be difficult to come by in the major cities. Gasoline is often cheaper in the larger towns than in the Lower 48, which helps offset the higher prices you pay the closer you get to the end of the roads, and the very high prices beyond the roads. For more info and an in-depth look at bringing your car to Alaska, see "Getting There—By Car" above.

By Bicycle

Inveterate cyclists have a love affair with bike riding that makes the relationship between car and driver look like a one-night stand. If you're indifferent to or can overcome the hardships (hills, trucks, rain and wind, bugs, time, security considerations, sore muscles, etc.), the advantages of bikes are unassailable. They're free to operate, non-polluting, easy to maintain, and are great exercise. They also slow down the world and attract the immediate friendly and curious attention of the locals. Taking along a bicycle is an excellent idea, and most of the ferries will let you bring it at no extra charge. Almost all of the bus companies and railways will carry your bike as accompanied baggage for a nominal amount, although a few ask you to crate it. Most airlines also accept bicycles as luggage, as long as they're boxed before check-in. Before you buy a ticket, compare prices, then ask each about taking a bicycle.

Alaska can be just as hard on bikes as on cars, however, if not harder. Fifteen-speed mountain bikes are recommended to better handle the rough roads. Know how to fix your own bike, and take along a good repair kit as bicycle shops are few and far between. You should have spare tubes and tires, a patch kit, a pump, extra cables, a spare chain, a chain tool, and perhaps even extra wheels. Carry your gear in saddlebag panniers lined with plastic bags. Fenders are nice in wet weather. Warm, waterproof clothing is essential, particularly rain pants, poncho, rain hat, wool shirt, wool socks, and waterproof shoes. Bicycling gloves, shorts, and clear goggles are also necessary. Everything you need may be purchased in Seattle, Vancouver, or Anchorage. Short-distance bicycles are available for rent, usually at no more than $12 per day, in every major town, and are an excellent way to see the local sights, especially in fair weather.

Hitchhiking

One of the best ways to meet the local people and get where you're going at the same time is to stick out your thumb and hitch. Hitchhiking is possible, at least part of the year, throughout the North; mostly what you need is time and patience. If standing by the roadside for hours sounds boring, read a book: *Hitchhiker's Guide to the Galaxy* by Douglas Adams, or Michener's epic *Alaska* are good ones. But be sure to put it down and make eye contact with the drivers. Otherwise, it's easy for them to ignore you. Opinions vary on walking down the road and hitching, but in Alaska it's safer to hitch near civilization, though often easier to get a ride if you're in the middle of nowhere. Most of the North is uninhabited, so if you get stuck you'll have no trouble finding a place to pitch your tent when night falls.

In the hierarchy of hitchhiking, one or two women get rides easiest (but at the most physical risk), then couples, then solo males, then solo males with guitars, then two guys, and last, two guys and a dog. Having small children with you often helps. If you're from somewhere other than Canada or the U.S., a flag on your backpack might assist you in getting a lift. Often the people who stop are former hitchhikers themselves. When you get a ride, offer to contribute for gas, and at stops, try to be the one who pays for cigarettes or soft drinks. Buying the driver lunch will make you both feel good, and is a lot cheaper than a bus ticket. Ask people you meet on ferries and at campgrounds if they can give you a lift. A good number of the motorists leaving the ferry at Haines head for Fairbanks or Anchorage. Tape a notice outside the ship's cafeteria offering to share the gas and driving in exchange for a ride. If you have your own car, save money by looking for riders to share expenses. Notice boards outside tourist offices are great clearinghouses for people offering or looking for rides. In the big towns, check the classifieds in the daily papers.

SUGGESTED ITINERARIES

One Week

If you only have a week, one option is to take the ferry ride from Bellingham to Juneau or Skagway roundtrip (takes six days), or ride the ferry one way, tour Juneau, Glacier Bay, Skagway, or Whitehorse, for example, then fly back from Juneau or Whitehorse. The other option is to fly to and from Anchorage, see the city briefly, then head up to Denali National Park (what most people would do), down to the Kenai Peninsula, or over to Prince William Sound. One week will allow you to do one of the above three leisurely and in depth, two of the three at a steady clip and somewhat superficially, and all three frantically.

Two Weeks

Two weeks is the length of the average package tour to Alaska. In two weeks you can ride the ferry from Bellingham to Skagway, stopping off at, say, Juneau overnight. Spend a night in Skagway, a night in Whitehorse, then go overland to Fairbanks. A few nights in Fairbanks and Denali will get you ready for Anchorage; from there you can choose between the Kenai Peninsula and Prince William Sound as described above. Alternately, you could ride the ferry to Juneau, fly to Cordova and connect up with the Southwest ferry system, and do Prince William Sound and the Kenai Peninsula that way, then wind up in Anchorage. If your planning is tight and your timing is right, you might even be able to jam in Denali. That's starting to get expen-

sive, though. Also, keep in mind that by the end of their package journey, most tourists need a vacation!

Three Weeks

Three weeks is about the minimum required to drive at least one way. It's a long three days from anywhere in the Pacific Northwest up the Alaska or Cassiar highways. But with your own car, you can cover as much ground as you like, as fast as you like. It's light most of the summer, so you don't have to worry about missing the scenery if you drive at night. You can sleep when you're dead. If you really want to crank up the mileage, drive to Whitehorse, then Dawson, then Eagle, then Tok. From Fairbanks, you can get out there, going to hot springs at Manley or Central. Head down to Denali and Anchorage, then take in the whole Kenai Peninsula, and/or put your car on the Bartlett or Tustemena to do the whole Prince William Sound excursion. Riding back on the ferry will save a lot of wear and tear on your wheels and your lower back.

Four Weeks Or More

If you have all this time, and the big bucks, you can get as far out there as you want. Head up the Dempster Highway from Dawson several hundred miles to Inuvik, Northwest Territories, near the Arctic Ocean. Or head up to Coldfoot above the Arctic Circle on the Dalton outside of Fairbanks. Or get to Cordova or Kodiak on the Southwest ferry system. You could also take the *Tustemena* for a week's ride to Dutch Harbor in the Aleutians. Or pay the price and go to McNeil River, Katmai, Nome, Barrow, or the Pribilofs. To travel around Alaska for a month or more, you need to read this whole book very carefully.

EMPLOYMENT

Alaska occupies a special place in the national imagination; a mystique and magnetism surround even the word itself with a singular vibration. Fur, gold, war, statehood, oil, fish, cruise ships—Alaska's life and times are as exotic and electric as the northern lights. For many people, the state assumes a symbolic dimension, vague of correlation yet strong of sensation: somewhere *beyond*. Adventure. The freedom dream. For other people the lure of Alaska is measured directly in dollars: get rich quick in the land of the pipeline and the midnight sun. The wise minority recognizes that the soul of the Alaskan seasonal shuffle, however, is the synthesis of the dream and the dollars.

Boiled down to its essence, at a summer job in Alaska, you'll mostly be working with tourists or fish. The government is another alternative for summer jobs in Alaska, through land-management bureaucracies like the National Park and Forest services.

FISHING AND CANNERIES

For work on fishing boats, there's almost always a waiting list that stretches from the end of the pier through town all the way to cabins in the hills. And everyone on it has at least five years' seniority. Many canneries are unionized, and even if they're not, they may also have waiting lists for entry-level positions. However, it's still eminently possible to find work—a lot of work—at them. Canning is loud, wet, foul, hard, long, hot, cold, and rank . . . which isn't bad if you don't mind that sort of thing. You might, however, lose your appetite for fish. Also, many canneries open and close in a month, depending on the catch; be prepared to relocate occasionally to other canneries to start from scratch. But, in a good season you can make big bucks at canneries, working like 84 hours a week (the infamous "seven twelves") at $6-8 an hour, $9-11 overtime.

You can wind up in some pretty remote places, so find out beforehand whether the company pays for your transportation costs plus housing and food. A lot of fish-processing companies are based in Seattle. Track down the Seattle yellow pages in your local library for applicable listings and call the likely looking—in January, February at the latest, when the fishing companies do their early hiring. Ask as many questions as you can; you'll quickly learn the lay of the Seattle scene. You'll also learn a lot about the seasons: crab, halibut, salmon, cod, pollock, etc. If you're in Seattle in May or early June, you can also call to see who needs latecomers.

After that, the only way to get a cannery job is to go to the canneries themselves, in Cordova, Valdez, Seward, Homer, Dutch, Ketchikan, Juneau, etc. You show up every morning at 5 a.m. until you're hired, and depending on the catch, you work till you drop, or you get laid off the next day. Nothing too secure about it. But if you do lose the one job, you follow the crowd down to the next cannery. If you're in Alaska in the middle of the summer and are serious about working in the commercial fishing industry, a good idea is to call the tourism information people or directory assistance or the library or somebody in each town, get the names of the canneries, and call them. By the end of the day you'll know all you need to know about the work possibilities.

TOURISM JOBS

Tourists don't smell nearly as bad as dead fish, and they tip much more readily. They aren't so cold and slimey, either—most of them, anyway. Every summer, tourists descend on the place by the packed planeload carrying cash, credit cards, and traveler's checks in their pockets. If you position yourself in their path, you can profit from this modern-day gold rush. In addition, the tourist trail for the most part is where adventure

This cannery, photographed in Metlakatla, Alaska, in 1916, was less automated than ones you may work at, but one thing hasn't changed: you might lose your appetite for fish.

awaits: immense and spectacular wilderness areas such as Denali and Glacier Bay national parks; isolated, historic bush communities such as Valdez, Nome, and Juneau; and wild and woolly cityscapes such as Fairbanks and Anchorage.

In order to become a toll collector on the tourist trail, you must first understand that the big money is in the package tourism end of the industry. Your typical Alaskan tourist is a retired senior citizen from the Midwest on a 15- to 17-day package tour which includes 10 or so days busing, railroading, and flying around the state, plus a three- to five-day sail down the Inside Passage on cruise ships. He/she carries two suitcases, sleeps in seven different hotels, rides on nine different buses, eats roughly 30 meals on the mainland, and spends upwards of $500 cash on food, souvenirs, and miscellaneous. The bargain packages pay transportation, lodging, and baggage handling: the expensive tours include meals and gratuity.

Tour Company Jobs

The large package tour companies have numerous entry-level positions: basically warm young bodies to throw at the onslaught of warm old bodies. Jobs are almost entirely centered on transportation and sales and

service. These include bus drivers, expeditors, and tour company sales reps.

Tour-bus driving in Alaska is one of those jobs that *appears* glamorous and exciting, but turns out to be one of the more grueling, burn-out positions on the circuit. Moneywise, however, it's the best entry-level position. First-year drivers for the tour companies generally conduct the "city tour" (Anchorage, Fairbanks, Juneau, Ketchikan), the airport shuttle, and transfers to local attractions. First-year drivers used to do the 375-mile marathon trip between Anchorage and Fairbanks, but this is the exception anymore, now that most package tourists ride the luxury train cars along this run (see below for employment details on the train). Plan to look like a fool all through May and June as you "develop" your rap. It's not unusual to have a busload of tourists (or worse, Alaskans!) behind you, a microphone in front of you, driving along and trying to knowledgeably describe country you've never seen before. And see how far a tour's-worth of sick jokes and Geritol show tunes get you.

Second-year routes are much more lucrative, and much more demanding, than first. On the Fairbanks-Whitehorse-Skagway run, for example, you drive three days (two nights) with the same group, with which—if you're good—you can develop a high-tip rapport. Similar runs include Anchorage-Valdez and the new Fairbanks-Prudhoe Bay overnighter. (The very senior drivers can work up to the three-night Fairbanks-Dawson-Whitehorse run.) Not only do you drive the coach, but you also give the guided narration, spot wildlife, answer the same questions day in and day out, serve lunch, sing, recite Robert Service, cheerlead, and occasionally fish a wallet or bracelet out of the chemical toilet.

Gray Line, Princess Tours, and Alaska Sightseeing run the vast majority of these buses. You must possess a valid bus driver's license before applying, often with stringent clean-record requirements. Plan on $1200-1400 a month to start, with the all-important tips, year-end safety and attendance bonuses, and a small (or no) charge for housing. Bus driving will definitely test your endurance.

Shuttle and tour-bus driver jobs in places like Denali are jealously guarded positions, with five-year employees the norm, 10-year drivers not uncommon, and even 15-year lifers to be found. However, several times in the past decade the shuttle bus concession at the Denali changed hands, at which times all bets were off. The tour-bus system has been under the auspices of Outdoor World/ARA since day one; these positions are highly competitive, and a background in natural science and interpretation is almost mandatory. These days, shuttle drivers too are doing narrations.

Another endurance challenge is the variety of positions on the "domecars"—luxury coaches that are hooked up to the back of the Alaska Railroad to transport the package tourists between Anchorage and Fairbanks. These include car manager, bartender, waitpeople, narrator, and kitchen crew. Schedules are generally as follows: based in Anchorage, you do the 16-hour run to Fairbanks, changing passengers at Denali. You serve three meals, then stay overnight in company apartments in Fairbanks, and do it in reverse the next day. Day off, then another round trip, then three days off. The car manager and waitpeople make good money (though carrying those bowls of soup on

rocking and rolling train cars is *hard* on the legs and nerves), though the hours are long.

Another entry-level possibility in working for the large tour companies is the all-purpose **expeditor** (X.P.) position, a combination greeter, chaperone, cheerleader, trouble-shooter, luggage counter, and gofer. Expediting is possibly the most demanding firing-line job on the tourist trail, with long hours and lots of problems. It's commonly stressful due to the hundreds of tourists needing to be handled at each location at various times of day. But it's a good foot in the door: the pay is fair, you get to see a lot of behind-the-scenes operations, free housing is often included, and some expeditors step right up the ladder into bus driving or management.

Most large hotels in the state have travel desks in their lobbies peopled by **tour company sales reps.** They function as sort of in-house travel agents, selling tours and working closely with other tour companies and the airlines. This is good training for travel agenthood.

A job at **Westours** is the best bet for package tour companies, being Alaska-size and fairly well organized. Holland America/Westours/Gray Line/Westmark Hotels is by far the biggest tour operator in the state. They own numerous cruise ships, countless motorcoaches, and 18 hotels around Alaska. They hire scads of bus drivers, train-car personnel, expeditors, sales and service reps, tour escorts, and some management personnel out of their Seattle office: Personnel, Westours, 300 Elliot Ave. W, Seattle, WA 98119. The hotels do their own hiring on-site.

Other package tour companies based in Seattle with expeditor, bus-driver and/or train-car positions include: Princess Tours, Alaska Travel and Marketing Services (ATMS), Princess Tours/Tour Alaska/Royal Hiway, Alaska Sightseeing, and Exploration Holiday Tours. Most of these companies send out applications starting around Nov., have a filing deadline of Feb. 15, then interview in March and hire in April. That means a two- to three-month wait for word on your first summer; if you survive your dues-paying year, rehire is generally automatic. But for that first year, if you stay loose, and get hired in April, you're going to Alaska in May with a potentially lucrative job in your pocket.

Hotels And Restaurants

Let's face it. Entry-level positions in hotels and restaurants are the dregs. You'll probably be hard-pressed to decide which you'd rather do *less:* housekeeping, laundry, desk clerk, reservations, dishwasher, gift shop, or night kitchen cleaner. For your first year you're pretty much guaranteed a dull, low-paying, drudge of a job. That's the bad news. The good news is, in hotels, there's generally some room to maneuver—in the restaurants and coffee shops, for example. At many places, busing positions are the only shot you'll have at tips your first year. (Not to mention a shot at the restaurant-quality food which, especially as compared to employee food, can be critical to the quality of your experience.) Also, if a waiter or waitress is 86'd, you could be in line for an instant promotion. Similarly, there might be openings for line and prep cooks, sandwich and salad makers, and bakers. It's tough work, but you'll never starve. Bartenders and cocktail waitresses are often replaced every season. Some hotel gift shop positions are open to first-year employees, and offer sales incentives. Even if you do wind up cleaning toilets, at least you'll be *there,* with freedom just outside the door. And if you keep your senses tuned, you're bound to run across some kind of opportunity, like people quitting, or overtime in another department. In addition, if you can just hang in for the 11-14 weeks of your contract, you'll be in a good position to move up the lackey ladder and pick those packaged pockets the following year.

And that's the crux: boastable Alascams take a few seasons to evolve. After you pay your dues the first year, all kinds of doors can open: luggage handler (with an automatic 25-50 cents a head for package tourists), waitperson (with your usual 15% tacked on to grossly overpriced meals), bus driving, even junior management (for career-minded, Horatio Alger types). At that point, you start to experience the essence of scamology Alaska-style—making a year's pay in four to five months, leaving the other seven to eight for school, travel, or just goofing off. In fact, many seasonals really catch the Alaska bug and opt to stay all year.

Most hotels in Alaska, especially the ones open year-round, do their own hiring on-site. It's chancy, but this could be a good way to pick up work if you're mostly interested in traveling and only want to stop to make money if you have to. However, you can get hired in spring in Seattle for, say, Westmark's seasonal hotels (Skagway, Tok, Valdez, etc.).

Where To Do It

The main consideration in determining where you want to work is where you want to live. Would you prefer to be around the coastline, rugged mountains, and glaciers (and rain, rain, rain) of Southeast, Southcentral, and Southwest? Or would you rather bask in the hotter, drier, less spectacular Interior? Another consideration is housing. The large tour companies and outback hotels often provide housing at a nominal (or no) cost to employees. This is the most secure and convenient arrangement, especially your first year. In addition, food plans (three squares a day deducted, with the cost of housing, from your paycheck) are also available. Again, you take your chances finding your own affordable housing after getting a job in a city hotel, most of which don't accommodate their employees.

Best Bets

Denali National Park combines the most favorable conditions for entry-level opportunities in Alaskan tourism. The park itself is the size of Connecticut; you take one 85-mile road in and out, on free shuttle buses. The hiking, wildlife viewing, photography, joy riding, and party possibilities are limitless. The weather is a cross between the wet maritime and dry Interior patterns. Denali is the second-most-popular tourist attraction in the state. The vast majority of package tourists remain only one night, with roughly 500 rooms turning over every 24 hours. Four large hotels (three run by the same company) employ approximately 700 seasonals in positions ranging from dishwashers to waitress/entertainers to oarsmen to tour-bus drivers. There is room to maneuver, even in your first year, and good opportunities for advancement if you decide to make a multi-season commitment (and don't screw up). Numerous smaller lodges, campgrounds, and restaurants offer fall-back and possible moonlighting positions. For applications, write: Personnel, ARA/Outdoor World Ltd., 825 W. 8th Ave., Suite 200, Anchorage, AK 99501, tel. (907) 279-2653; and Personnel, Princess Tours, 2815 2nd Ave. Suite 400, Seattle, WA 98121.

Glacier Bay National Park is equally awesome, but much smaller and more isolated (the only way in is by plane or boat); many flashy tourists nonetheless. Write: Glacier Bay Lodge or Gustavus Inn, Gustavus AK 99826.

FEDERAL GOVERNMENT JOBS

Government workers have always been a mainstay in Alaska's economy. Local, state, and federal employees today comprise a third of the workforce, making the government Alaska's largest employer. These agencies are also important sources of temporary and volunteer employment, accounting for thousands of seasonal jobs each year in Alaska.

Federal Seasonals

Seasonals do much of the grunt work for federal agencies in Alaska: surveying roads, laying out timber sales, fighting fires, building cabins and trails, counting fish, picking up garbage in campgrounds, patrolling backcountry areas, and answering phones. Most of these jobs begin in June and last until mid-September. Much of the work happens outdoors and can be arduous. Clearing a survey line through head-high devil's club is no fun, particularly when you're providing cocktail hour for mosquitos. Even worse is the prospect of returning soaking wet to camp, where you and three others crowd into a small cabin. But for the hard-core outdoor enthusiast, the advantages of getting paid to work in some of the most spectacular country imaginable far outweigh most discomforts and inconveniences.

Applying

Federal government jobs in Alaska have always been attractive to those who enjoy the outdoors. Unfortunately, Alaska's unspoiled beauty is such a drawing card that seasonal jobs are at a premium, and new openings are usually taken by those who have already worked for the federal government in the Lower 48 or as volunteers in Alaska.

The application period for some seasonal positions ends as early as January 15, so be sure to begin your job search very early. Forms vary between the agencies, but it's always a good idea to have a completed SF-171 (Application for Federal Employment) and your resume available for short openings. In most cases your application will be rated by a personnel clerk who scores your qualifications. Often they must go through hundreds of such applications; you're not likely to get VIP treatment. To combat this, make your application as readable as possible (typed is best), and try to address the issues you will be rated on. This means reading the job descriptions carefully and trying to show how you measure up to each qualification.

Once your application has been rated, it is sent to the person who actually does the hiring. The employer looks through those rated most highly and selects the best-qualified person (you, of course). Or so the theory goes. In reality, certain things beyond paper qualifications are at work here. Those with rehire status from the past year are usually given highest priority. Being from Alaska is also a major help (sometimes a requirement), as is being a veteran or of the "correct" race or sex to fulfill hiring quotas. Getting to know the employer can be a great benefit. One way is to directly contact the employer with a letter or phone call. If possible, it's even better to make an appointment and meet with him or her before hiring time. For more information on current federal job openings, contact the individual agencies such as the Park Service or Forest Service (see below for addresses).

VOLUNTEER JOBS

Volunteers are becoming an increasingly important part of the federal seasonal work force all over the nation, and Alaska is no exception. Most of the naturalists on board Alaska's ferry system are volunteers, as are many field workers. The biggest employers of volunteers are the Forest and the Fish and Wildlife services, but the Park Service, Bureau of Land Management, and U.S. Geological Survey also use volunteers. Federal agencies vary greatly in their treatment of volunteers. Some (most egregiously the Park Service) offer only the barest essentials and require that you pay for your own transportation to and from Alaska. The Forest Service has the best volunteer program, which sometimes includes a free ride from your home and back, free food and lodging, and all the adventure you could ask for.

Why You Should Volunteer

Why volunteer for a federal position when you could be putting away money from a cannery job? It all depends on what's most important to you—money, or an interesting and educational job. For many, volunteering is a wonderful opportunity to work in Alaska without having to fight tooth and nail for a job. Non-citizens, too, can volunteer for work in the federal government; paying jobs require U.S. citizenship.

Why You Shouldn't Volunteer

The federal volunteer program has proven immensely popular, but it's not for everyone. For many college students, summers are a time to earn survival money, and they can't afford the time off. Many federal workers are angry that paying jobs are being lost to people willing to work for nothing. At one time, experienced volunteers were able to look forward to a chance for a paying job the following year, but today those prospects are slim. Also, not all volunteer work is enjoyable. At its worst you may be viewed as simply a warm

body willing to slave for three months with no pay. And some employers seem to enjoy testing the mental stability of their volunteers by cooping them up in remote field camps for weeks or months at a stretch. Be sure you find out the specifics before you make a volunteer commitment.

Getting Volunteer Jobs

Short-term volunteer jobs are sometimes available if you're in the right place at the right time. If you have specific skills in such areas as fisheries or wildlife biology, surveying, or carpentry, you may be able to walk into a week-long trip into the wilderness courtesy of Uncle Sam. For longer-term positions you need to apply well in advance (Jan.-March generally). If you have persistence, a few skills, and physical endurance, you're almost assured of a volunteer position—if you start searching early enough and apply to a variety of places. Contacting the agencies directly will give you the best idea of what positions are available and what the work will be like. The **Student Conservation Association**, Box 550C, Charlestown, NH 03603, produces an excellent catalog listing voluntary conservation jobs throughout the U.S., including many in Alaska.

U.S. FOREST SERVICE

Paid Seasonal Positions

The U.S. Forest Service, one of Alaska's largest government employers, has a variety of positions on the Tongass and Chugach national forests. Competition for these jobs is intense. In recent years, fewer than 100 openings have occurred throughout the state, with two-thirds of these going to re-hires. Apply for Forest Service seasonal positions using the standard Federal government application (SF-171). Officially, you can only apply to a single national forest (or area within Tongass National Forest), so try to find out in advance where the jobs are most likely to be open in your area of interest. For information on job openings, when and where to apply, contact the following offices:

Tongass National Forest
  Ketchikan Area Office
  Federal Building
  Ketchikan, AK 99901
  tel. (907) 225-3101

Tongass National Forest
  Chatham Area Office
  Box 1980
  Sitka, AK 99835
  tel. (907) 747-6671

Tongass National Forest
  Stikine Area Office
  Box 309
  Petersburg, AK 99833
  tel. (907) 772-3841

Chugach National Forest
  2221 E. Northern Lights Blvd.
  Anchorage, AK 99508
  tel. (907) 279-5541

Volunteer Positions
Alaska's national forests use hundreds of volunteers each year. There is no central clearinghouse for these applications; you'll need to contact each national forest office for the correct forms and information on the various types of work. You can apply to as many places as you want. Deadlines vary, but the sooner you apply, the better your chances. Many positions are listed in the Student Conservation Association catalog; see above for their address. Write or call the Forest Service volunteer coordinator at any of the above addresses for more specific information and application forms. Since all "hiring" is done at the district level, you may be better off writing to the individual Forest Service district where you would most like to work.

NATIONAL PARK SERVICE

Paid Seasonal Positions
The National Park Service manages 55 million acres of park and preserve land in Alaska. Much of this lies within areas created by the 1980 Alaska National Interests Land Claims Act (ANILCA). Because of the areas' newness and the agency's perennially tight budget, seasonal jobs are few. Alaska's national parks lure many job seekers, so competition for the 300 or so seasonal openings is incredibly intense. Glamour jobs such as studying Dall sheep in the Brooks Range are nearly impossible to get unless you have all the right skills, education, experience, and know the person doing the hiring. Unfortunately, bribery doesn't help.

Most Park Service openings are covered by the standard seasonal application (form 10-139). Be sure to get your application in prior to January 15. Attempts at filling out this application have been known to drive normal people to the brink of insanity. Where else would you be asked to describe everything from your technical rock-climbing ability to your knowledge of colonial pioneer homemaking? A good night's sleep, several cups of coffee, and a willingness to exaggerate should pull you through. Applications are available from:

National Park Service
  Alaska Regional Office
  2525 Gambell St.
  Anchorage, AK 99503
  tel. (907) 261-2691

Volunteers In The Parks (VIPs)
If you don't want to go the insanely competitive paid seasonal route, Alaska's national parks and preserves also offer over 130 volunteer positions each year. Here your chances are better, although still only half of the applicants are accepted. Volunteers are generally "hired" for the entire summer, but the cheapskate agency even makes volunteers pay for their own transportation and food. The NPS does supply lodging (and occasionally a stipend). There is no central application center for VIP work; write to the VIP coordinator in the park where you wish to work. They'll send an application and information on the types of volunteer work available. The addresses are:

Bering Land Bridge National Preserve
  P.O. Box 220
  Nome, AK 99762
  tel. (907) 443-2522

Denali National Park and Preserve
P.O. Box 9
McKinley Park, AK 99755
tel. (907) 683-2294

Gates of the Arctic
National Park and Preserve
P.O. Box 74680
Fairbanks, AK 99707
tel. (907) 452-5363

Glacier Bay National Park and Preserve
Bartlett Cove
Gustavus, AK 99826
tel. (907) 697-3341

Katmai National Park and Preserve
and **Aniakchak National Monument
and Preserve**
P.O. Box 7
King Salmon, AK 99630
tel. (907) 246-3305

Kenai Fjords National Park
P.O. Box 1727
Seward, AK 99664
tel. (907) 224-3874

Klondike Gold Rush
National Historic Park
P.O. Box 517
Skagway, AK 99840
tel. (907) 983-2299

Lake Clark National Park and Preserve
701 C St. Box 61
Anchorage, AK 99513
tel. (907) 271-3751

Northwest Areas Parks:
Kobuk Valley National Park
Cape Krusenstern National Monument
Noatak National Preserve
P.O. Box 287
Kotzebue, AK 99752
tel. (907) 442-3890

Sitka National Historical Park
P.O. Box 73
Sitka, AK 99835
tel. (907) 747-6281

**Wrangell-St. Elias National Park and
Preserve**
P.O. Box 29
Glennallen, AK 99588
tel. (907) 822-5235

Yukon-Charley Rivers National Preserve
P.O. Box 64
Eagle, AK 99738
tel. (907) 547-2233

FISH AND WILDLIFE SERVICE

Paid Seasonal Jobs
The U.S. Fish and Wildlife Service manages
Alaska's 16 national wildlife refuges. These
cover a staggering 77 million acres, many of
them created by the 1980 Alaska National
Interests Land Claims Act (ANILCA). The
Fish and Wildlife Service hires approximately 50 seasonal workers each year as
biological technicians and park technicians,
as well as laborers. The competition is cutthroat, and you'll be battling it out with over
800 qualified applicants! If you're not extremely well qualified (strong wildlife or fisheries biology education plus lots of related
experience), it is probably not worth your
time to apply. Write or call them to get a
complete listing of job requirements and application procedures:

U.S. Fish and Wildlife Service
1011 East Tudor Rd.
Anchorage, AK 99503
tel. (907) 786-3301

Volunteer Jobs
Even the volunteer program for Alaska wildlife refuge work is rather competitive. Each
year the Fish and Wildlife Service selects
approximately 175 volunteers from a pool of
over 300 applicants. The jobs may include
taking census of waterfowl in the Yukon
delta, operating a fish weir, or working with
peregrine falcons. Living conditions vary
greatly, but all food and lodging are supplied
You must supply your own transportation to
and from Alaska, however. Applications
should be submitted before April and most

positions last from June through August. For more information, write or call:

Volunteer Coordinator
U.S. Fish and Wildlife Service
1011 East Tudor Rd.
Anchorage, AK 99503
tel. (907) 786-3399

BUREAU OF LAND MANAGEMENT

The Bureau of Land Management (BLM) manages extensive portions of Alaska, and is responsible for mining activities on all federal land. Unlike the Forest and National Park services, the BLM has a reputation for being more of a holding company than a land management agency. (In the Lower 48, people claim BLM stands for Bureau of Livestock and Mining.) In Alaska, the agency employs only a few seasonals in land management, but is well known for its strong firefighting program based in Fairbanks. Each year the BLM hires approximately 250 firefighters, dispatchers, and smoke jumpers to suppress fires in the northern half of the state. (The Alaska Division of Forestry is responsible for forest fire control in the southern half.) For more on BLM seasonal work, contact:

Personnel Office
Bureau of Land Management
P.O. Box 1150
Fairbanks, AK 99707
tel. (907) 356-2025

OTHER FEDERAL JOBS

National Marine Fisheries Service
The National Marine Fisheries Service hires a number of seasonals each year as biological technicians, fish and wildlife biologists, clerk/typists, and other positions. Contact them at:

U.S. Dept. of Commerce—NOAA
Western Administrative Support Center
7600 Sand Point Way N.E.
Bin C15700
Seattle, WA 98115
tel. (206) 526-6357

Army Corps Of Engineers
The Corps of Engineers is responsible for maintaining navigable waterways, harbors, and rivers. In Alaska, the Corps hires approximately 50 temporary summer employees each year. Most of the jobs are based in Anchorage rather than in the field. Unlike some other agencies, no preference is given to Alaskan residents and most of the hires come from Outside. For more information, contact:

Army Corps of Engineers
Alaska District
Pouch 898
Anchorage, AK 99506
tel. (907) 753-2838

JOBS WITH THE STATE OF ALASKA

Although recent years have seen state funding cutbacks, Alaska continues to be an excellent employer. Wages often run considerably higher than for similar federal jobs, and the perks are noticeably better. Although you must be a resident to apply for nearly all state jobs, the requirement is easily met. A resident is "anyone living in Alaska at the time of application with no intention of permanently leaving." For complete information on state employment, ask for a copy of "How to apply for a job with the State of Alaska" from:

Division of Personnel
Public Services Unit
P.O. Box C
Juneau, AK 99811

Seasonal Jobs
Although most state employees work year-round, some are only employed for a few months each year, primarily the summer. These "permanent seasonals" can be found in a number of state agencies, including Fish and Game, Environmental Conservation, and Natural Resources. The jobs are primarily technical: fish and wildlife technician, park ranger, fish and wildlife enforcement officer, and others. Although the positions are open continuously, it's wise to apply early since

most hiring takes place in spring. Write to the above address to get an application form.

Clerical Work

As in any bureaucracy, the state's clerical staff keeps a semblance of order in the chaos of paper. Each year the State of Alaska hires hundreds of secretaries, clerical aides, document processors, document shredders (just kidding), supply clerks, and others for both permanent and short-term work. The vast majority of these positions is in Juneau, though some are available in Anchorage, Fairbanks, and other cities. Positions are open year-round on both a permanent and temporary basis.

Volunteer Positions

The State of Alaska employs volunteers in a number of positions. Volunteers in the state parks work on trails, as backcountry rangers, at information counters, and as campground hosts. The benefits are quite limited and may not even include lodging. You'll need to apply before April for most jobs. For more info, write or call:

Alaska Division of Parks and Outdoor Recreation
Volunteer Coordinator
P.O. Box 107001
Anchorage, AK 99510
tel. (907) 765-2602

The Alaska Department of Fish and Game also has a few volunteer jobs. For details, contact them at:

Department of Fish and Game
Personnel Office
P.O. Box 3-2000
Juneau, AK 99802
tel. (907) 465-4140

(GORDY OHLIGER)

GATEWAYS

SEATTLE AND VICINITY

Seattle is one of the best places to begin an Alaskan holiday. Highways and bus routes from every corner of the Lower 48, as well as major air routes from Hawaii and the Orient, connect here with two of the largest ferry lines in the world. (Note, however, that the Alaska Marine Highway system's southern terminus moved to Bellingham, 85 miles north, in fall 1989—see below.) The city is also an attraction in its own right, good for several days of adventurous sightseeing. Fascinating day-trips beckon from all sides, and the beauty of Seattle's waterways complements the grandeur of the Olympic Mountains to the west, the Cascades to the east, with Mt. Rainier to the southeast, giving you a taste of the magnificence waiting farther north.

SIGHTS

Downtown
Start your day with breakfast at the **Pike Place Market** at the corner of Pike Place and the waterfront end of Stewart St. downtown.

Lowell's Restaurant, within the market itself is recommended, open Mon.-Sat., 7-5, Sun. 8:30-4 for food, bar till 9 p.m. Mon.-Saturday. Farmers have been bringing their produce here since before WW I; the sensual market, open daily except Sun., is one of Seattle's best free shows: browse among the fruits and vegetables, herbs and spices, fish, baked goods, flowers, and crafts. Take the stairs behind Pike Place (north end) past trendy shops, under the freeway, down to Pier 59 of the waterfront. Although bounded by a noisy overhead freeway and cluttered with kitschy shops, the Seattle waterfront is worth a stroll. A combination ticket ($9) is available for the **Aquarium** and **Omnidome** at Pier 59. Vintage 1927 Aussie streetcars rumble along Alaskan Way. From there, head left (north) and check out **Creative Northwest** at Pier 55—good gift shop of local items. If you haven't been on the ferries yet, go into the Washington State Ferry Terminal on Pier 52 for a look. A roundtrip ferry ride to Bremerton is an excellent, inexpensive scenic cruise.

Keep heading north, past Waterfront Park, schlock shops, fish and chips stands, and harbor tour ticket kiosks, then turn left at Yesler Way, just a little beyond the State Ferry Terminal, to reach **Pioneer Square**—heart of gold-rush Seattle. The totem pole and covered archway are remnants of the city of the 1890s. Henry Yesler established

his sawmill here in 1852 and the logs he slid down Yesler Way led to the naming of the original Skid Road. The great fire of 1889 razed the area, so most of what you now see was built soon after.

For a bird's-eye view of this part of the city, take the elevator to the top of the **Smith Tower** ($1), 2nd Ave. and Yesler Way. Or it

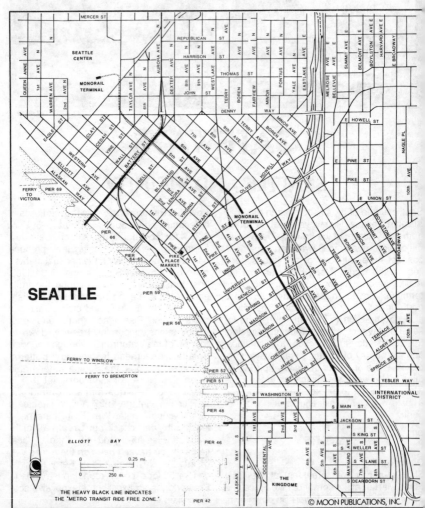

you want to delve a little deeper into the city, take the highly entertaining **Underground Tour** ($5) which begins several times a day at 610 E. 1st Avenue. This is Seattle's answer to the famous Paris sewer tours.

The highlight of the historical district is the **Klondike Gold Rush National Historical Park,** 117 S. Main St., open daily 9-5, free. As soon as you walk in, you're greeted by a huge print of the famous "Golden Stairs" black and white—the most dramatic and enduring image from the gold rush. Wander around to see and hear the story of that mad summer of 1897 when thousands of men dropped what they were doing and answered the call of "Gold!" The park rangers at the Visitor Center are very helpful and will be glad to show you free movies about the gold rush in the adjoining auditorium. A stop here is an absolute must for anyone headed north. To get there, take a right on 1st Ave. from Yesler, walk several blocks, then take a left on Main.

Continue east on Main St. to enter Seattle's **International District.** Head straight for the historic Nippon Kan Theater, 628 S. Washington St. (one block north of Main). A self-guided tour starts here with a 45-minute multi-media show. Other attractions in this one-time Chinatown include the Wing Luke Memorial Museum, 414 8th St., Hing Hay Park, and Uwajimaya Japanese supermarket at King and 6th streets.

Northwest Of Downtown

The Seattle World's Fair took place in 1962 but for the people of Seattle it never ended. The fairgrounds, now the **Seattle Center,** tel. 684-7200, have become a local institution. Get there on a monorail which leaves from 5th Ave. and Pine downtown and costs only 60 cents OW. Entry to the grounds is free. In the **Center House** is a large indoor pavilion with dozens of cheerful fast-food counters selling specialties from around the world; prices are reasonable ($2-5). You can ride up the **Space Needle** ($4.75), or take in the **Pacific Science Center's** museum, IMAX big-screen flick ($6), and Laserium shows ($6). **Seattle Children's Museum** and **Fun Forest** amusement park will keep the kids happy for a while.

When you've had your fill of the Center, walk out to 1st Ave. N and board bus no. 15 or 18, or head up Elliot to 15th Ave. to the south end of Ballard Bridge. The bulk of the Pacific Northwest fishing fleet is based at the Salmon Bay Terminal just west of the bridge. From here grab bus no. 17 or head west on Shilshole Ave. to one of Seattle's most interesting sights, the narrow Hiram M. Chittenden or **Government Locks,** which permit navigation between Puget Sound and Lake Washington. Finished in 1916, they're still very busy. The public is welcome to observe their operation and enjoy the beautiful surrounding gardens daily, free. Its Visitor Center is open 11-5 (closed Tues. and Wed.). At the large fish ladder just on the other side of the locks you can look a salmon in the eye (late summer).

Northeast Of Downtown

Seattle's best museum and one of the finest of its kind anywhere is the **Burke Memorial Museum,** NE 45th St. and 17th Ave. NE in the University District. Open 11-5 Tues. to Fri., 9-4:30 Sat. and Sun., admission free. This well-arranged and colorful collection features Northwest Coastal Indian artifacts. The museum is at the north edge of the large, park-like University of Washington campus, originally the site of the 1909 Alaska-Yukon-Pacific Exposition. Numerous buses, many running north on 3rd Ave., shuttle between downtown and the University District. Or take the exit off I-5 and park in one of the many lots ($4).

Other Sights

West Seattle has scenery, beaches, parks, and bike and strolling paths. **Woodland Park Zoo** and **Green Lake Park** are two of the dozens of city parks awaiting your aching bones—to relax, sunbathe, people-watch. Half a dozen museums, dozens of tours, several breweries and wineries, floating bridges, nearby waterfalls, and of course all the activities on the vast Puget Sound, rugged Olympic Peninsula, mighty Cascades, and the usual city food, shopping, and entertainment will keep you busy till your time and/or money run out—unless you remember in the nick of time that this is only the *beginning* of your journey to Alaska.

INFORMATION

Before you go you can contact, or while you're here you can visit, the **Seattle-Kings County Convention and Visitors Bureau,** 666 Stewart at the corner of 7th and Stewart right next to the Vance Hotel, tel. (206) 461-5840, open Mon. to Friday 8:30-5. Three or four staff members are always behind the desk or manning the phones, and three walls of tempting brochures will provide excellent training weight in your day pack for those wilderness backpacking trips awaiting up north. Be sure to pick up the *Visitors Guide,* and accommodations brochures (including those for the budget YM- and YWCAS and the Seattle International AYH Hostel) plus bed and breakfast lists, all the way up to the $150-a-night Warwick Hotel. Seattle Events Calendar, tour maps, flyers for all the attractions, and schedules for all the public bus transportation and Gray Line tours and airporters are available. There's also a **tourist information** counter in the Washington State Ferry Terminal at Pier 52, open daily 7-7.

Otherwise, a number of guidebooks on the Seattle area and Washington State can fill in all the holes in coverage that are beyond the scope of this book. The best, of course, is Moon Publications' own *Washington Handbook* by Dianne Lyons and Archie Satterfield; see the back pages for ordering information. *Seattle Best Places* and *Northwest Best Places* by Sasquatch Press in Seattle are also adequate. Dozens of other guides, on everything from bed and breakfasts and touring Washington's wine country to hiking, kayaking, and birding in the area, are available at bookstores around town. **Waldenbooks** is at 406 Pine St., and **Dalton's** is at 1533 4th Avenue. A great local bookstore on the walking tour of downtown described above is **Elliot Bay Book Company,** 101 S. Main St., with a huge section on Northwest titles, and books literally overflowing the store on everything under the sun.

A good place for guidebooks, maps, luggage, and travel accessories is **AAA Travel Store,** 330 6th Ave. N.

The **National Parks Information Office,** 1018 1st Ave. at Spring, is open Mon. to Friday 8-5. Go there for maps if you plan to do some hiking in the Olympics or Cascades. For good free maps of British Columbia and Canada, visit the **Canadian Government Tourist Office,** 6th Ave. and Stewart, Plaza 600, 4th floor. For a map of British Columbia go to **Tourism BC,** 720 Olive Way at 8th Ave. (one block from Greyhound). The **Youth Hostel Association** office, 419 Queen Anne Ave. N, Suite 108, near Seattle Center, tel. 281-7306, sells memberships and has local information. They offer some excellent group trips around Washington in the summertime. Office hours are Mon. to Fri. noon-4. **CIEE Student Travel,** 1314 NE 43rd St., Room 210 off University Way, sells cheap air tickets to Europe and Asia. Check out the **Greenpeace** office, 4649 Sunnyside Ave. N in the Good Shepherd Center near Goldies on 45th, for information on local environmental issues.

The **area code** for Seattle and Bellingham is 206.

TRANSPORTATION

Airport

Sea-Tac International Airport is 12 miles south of downtown Seattle, halfway to Tacoma. Metro buses nos. 174 and 194 run from the airport into town every half hour Mon. to Sat., hourly on Sun., $1 OW off-peak, $1.50 peak. Or hop on **Gray Line's** airporter, to six downtown hotels every half hour, $6; the timetable is posted at the stop. A very helpful **tourist information counter** is on the central baggage claim level, north end, open every day 9:30-7:30. They can direct you to other airporters to surrounding suburbs (Everett, Redmond, etc.). The **First National Bank** branch on the ticketing level is open Mon. to Fri. 9-5. **Coin lockers** are available for 75 cents.

By Train And Boat

Amtrak, King St. Station, tel. 464-1930 or (800) USA-RAIL, has daily connections

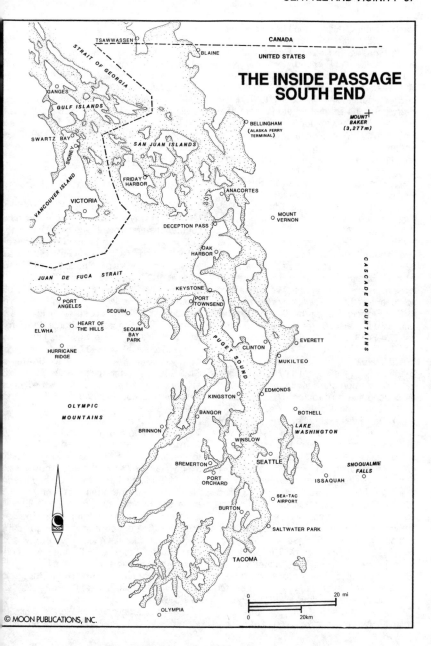

THE INSIDE PASSAGE
SOUTH END

CANADA

UNITED STATES

STRAIT OF GEORGIA

TSAWWASSEN

BLAINE

GANGES

GULF ISLANDS

MOUNT BAKER
(3,277m)

BELLINGHAM
(ALASKA FERRY TERMINAL)

SWARTZ BAY

SIDNEY

SAN JUAN ISLANDS

VANCOUVER ISLAND

FRIDAY HARBOR

ANACORTES

VICTORIA

MOUNT VERNON

DECEPTION PASS

OAK HARBOR

JUAN DE FUCA STRAIT

KEYSTONE

PORT ANGELES

PORT TOWNSEND

SEQUIM

ELWHA

HEART OF THE HILLS

SEQUIM BAY PARK

CASCADE MOUNTAINS

PUGET SOUND

CLINTON

EVERETT

HURRICANE RIDGE

MUKILTEO

OLYMPIC MOUNTAINS

EDMONDS

KINGSTON

BANGOR

BOTHELL

LAKE WASHINGTON

BRINNON

WINSLOW

BREMERTON

SEATTLE

SNOQUALMIE FALLS

PORT ORCHARD

ISSAQUAH

SEA-TAC AIRPORT

BURTON

SALTWATER PARK

TACOMA

MOON

0   20 mi

0   20km

OLYMPIA

© MOON PUBLICATIONS, INC.

south (Chico, Oakland, and Los Angeles) on its *Coast Starlight* and east (Salt Lake City) on its *Pioneer*. The *Mount Rainier* runs between Seattle and Portland.

Two ferry networks originate in Seattle. The **Washington State Ferries** (Pier 52) run to Bremerton every 1½ hours, to Winslow every hour; the Bremerton trip is more scenic. Take your bicycle for 70 cents extra. A ferry leaves West Seattle (Fauntleroy) for Southworth every 40-50 minutes. Also from that dock, a ferry runs over to Vashon Island every half hour.

Again, note that the **Alaska Marine Highway** southern terminus has moved from Pier 48 in Seattle to a new (1989) facility in Bellingham (see below).

By Bus

Greyhound Lines, 8th Ave. and Stewart, tel. 624-3456, offers reliable bus service to cities all over Canada and the U.S., with departures every couple of hours. If you're headed south, one of the cheapest ways from Seattle to San Francisco is on the **Green Tortoise** "magic" bus (see p. 64 for details). In Seattle, call 324-7433.

Local Buses

Seattle has an excellent city bus service. Most buses operate daily from 6 a.m. to 1 a.m. along the main routes. The basic fares are $1 during peak hours (6-9 a.m. and 3-6 p.m.) and 75 cents other hours. Exact change is required. Most of the buses used by visitors leave from the downtown area. If your entire trip is within the "ride free zone" indicated on the city map, you pay no fare till 8 p.m. Whenever you pay a fare, always ask the driver for a free transfer. This will allow you to take any other bus, or return on the same, within two or so hours, or by the time shown on the transfer. The Metro Bus Information Office, 821 2nd St. at Marian, tel. 553-3000, is open 24 hours. This office also sells a special three-day "visitor's pass" ($3)—good value. Buy the pass after noon and they give you an extra half day free. On Sat., Sun., and holidays, All-Day Passes ($1.50) are available from bus drivers for unlimited Metro bus travel—a real bargain.

Others

Check out what opportunities are available for driveaways (see main "Introduction" for an explanation) by looking under the travel section of the classifieds in the daily newspapers. **Aaacon Transport,** 1904 3rd Ave., Suite 630, tel. 682-2277, has driveaway cars to all points in the Lower 48. You pay the gas and leave a $100 refundable deposit. Also try **A-1 Auto Movers** in Renton, tel. 243-0150, and **Auto Driveaway,** 13470 Empire Way S, tel. 235-0880.

BELLINGHAM

The MV *Columbia,* flagship of the Alaska Marine Highway fleet, now runs from the new southern terminus of the Southeast ferry line, Bellingham. Seattle had served in this capacity for 20 years, during which Bellingham had twice bid for, and lost, the honor. But the third time, in 1987, was the charm. The Alaskan economy was reeling from the drop in oil revenues, and Bellingham not only underbid Seattle, but also proposed to build a new terminal. They offered to charge the ferry only $100,000 a year to lease the facility, as opposed to Seattle's $390,000; operating expenses would be $57,000 to Seattle's $120,000. Also, this picturesque town, 85 miles north of Seattle and 55 miles south of Vancouver, slices five hours off the sailing time to Skagway. Seattle's loss is Bellingham's major gain.

The new home of the Alaska ferry is at **Fairhaven Terminal,** on the edge of the historical district of Bellingham. To get there, simply take the Old Fairhaven Parkway, Exit 250, from I-5, go right on 12th St. and left on Harris Ave. down to the waterfront. A much more scenic and satisfying (though longer) route is to cruise to and from I-5 on Chuckanut Drive. Or from downtown Bellingham it's about four miles; just head north on 12th and State streets. Stock up for the ferry ride at the nearby grocery store.

The **Visitor's and Convention Bureau** is located off I-5 exit 253 at 904 Potter St., tel. 671-3990.

Great budget accommodation is available at the new IYHF youth hostel in a beautiful location in the Fairhaven Rose Garden, tel. 671-1750, a long walk uphill from the ferry terminal (or take Bus 1 from the downtown city bus terminal—25 cents). Someone's there to answer the phone all day on weekends, but only after 5 or 5:30 p.m. weekdays. Note that the hostel fills up fast on the Thursday night before the Friday sailing of the *Columbia.*

There's a **Motel 6,** 3701 Bryon St., tel. 671-4494, $26 s, $32 d. In the same price range is **Aloha Motel,** 315 N. Samish Way (off exit 252), tel. 733-4900, and **Lions Inn Motel,** 2419 Elm, tel. 733-2330. Best Western's **Heritage Inn,** 151 E. McLeod, tel. 647-1912, has rooms starting at $45; also contact **Accommodations Northwest,** tel. 671-8689, for local B&Bs.

Greyhound is at the corner of State and Magnolia right downtown, tel. 733-5251; the city bus terminal is across the street. **Whatcom County Transportation Authority,** tel. 676-RIDE, services the local area, including the new ferry terminal. **Bellingham International Airport** is a few miles north of town just off of I-5 (exit 258). PSA flies in and out. Or if you're flying into Seattle, catch the

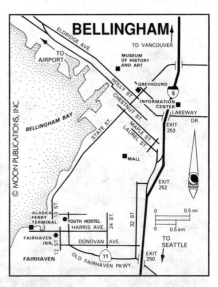

Bellingham/Sea-Tac Airporter, which does five roundtrips daily between the airports, $18.50 one way.

VANCOUVER

Canadians consider Vancouver their most beautiful city, and certainly no other in North America is so spectacularly located. A wall of snowcapped mountains faces Vancouver on the north, and wide bays and inlets encircle it on the other three sides. Abundant park lands and beaches offer outdoor experiences not usually associated with thriving metropolises, but with unforgettable vistas of modern buildings clustered against the forested hillsides.

Vancouver is still a young city. Although Capt. George Vancouver sailed into Burrard Inlet in 1792 and made the area known to the world, permanent white settlers did not arrive until 70 years later. A rough-and-tumble loggers' shantytown established itself on the site about that time, but it was the settlements along the Fraser River which received early official attention and benefited from the 1858 Cariboo gold rush. All this changed in 1887, when Canada's first transcontinental railway reached Vancouver and the city became the country's major Pacific port. Today Vancouver is Canada's third-largest city, its half-million people comprising a third of the province's population. It is an exciting city to visit and, for Canadians, the gateway to the Pacific coast. Also, due to U.S. maritime laws, all Inside Passage cruise ships tie up to Vancouver's piers at Canada Place.

SIGHTS

The West End
For many, the highlight of the city is beautiful **Stanley Park** (bus no. 11 from W. Pender St.), occupying a large peninsula jutting out into Burrard Inlet. A walk along the seawall promenade offers totem poles, beaches, honking geese, and a series of splendid views. Stanley Park also has a zoo (free), an aquarium ($6.50), snack bars, and lots of

lawns and scenic spots where you can sit and watch the world go by. If you like your action a little faster, rent a bicycle from the shop at the foot of Alberni St., or try a tandem for a lark. You can also rent scooters and mopeds from the rental place at 1896 Georgia Street.

Walk back to town along Robson St. for Vancouver's best window-shopping. Locally known as Robsonstrasse, many delicatessens, tea rooms, and small shops have a European flavor. In summer the restaurants move some of their tables into the open air.

Downtown

Landscaping and a balance between open spaces and offices help make **Robson Square** the architectural showplace of the city. Filling three city blocks along Howe, south from Georgia St., features include the restored old courthouse (now the Vancouver Art Gallery), the central plaza with its excellent Food Fair, and the sloping glass roof of the Provincial Courthouse which now houses the Vancouver Art Gallery, on Hornby Street. Walk through Eaton's Department Store on the east side of Robson Square out onto the Granville Mall and down to the waterfront. Take a quick look in the old Canadian Pacific Railway station, now the Sea Bus Terminal (see "North Vancouver" below), and continue east hugging the waterfront into **Gastown**.

Vancouver got its start near the intersection of Water and Carrall streets, there's now a statue of notorious saloon and hotel keeper Gassy Jack Deighton, for whom Gastown was named. Today, Water St. is lined with art galleries, boutiques, and fancy restaurants crowded with chic residents and tourists. All of the original buildings from Gassy Jack's time disappeared in the great fire of 1886 and in the building boom which followed the arrival of the railway, but the restored old warehouses and hotels from the 1890s and early years of this century offer an evocative glimpse into history. Continue along Carrall St. to Pender. At 8 W. Pender is the "narrowest building in the world."

Continue a few blocks along the waterfront to get to **Canada Place,** the wild-looking "sailbuilding" at the edge of Burrard Inlet.

Canada's pavilion at Expo86, it now hosts the convention center, the many-starred Pan Pacific Hotel, an IMAX screen, and the docking facilities for cruise ships.

Chinatown runs along Pender St. for three blocks from Carrall to Gore; second only in size to San Francisco's, its many restaurants, markets, and emporia are worth a leisurely look.

North Vancouver

Take Hwy. 1 across the Second Narrows Bridge (or the Sea Bus from the old CPR station at the foot of Seymour across Burrard Inlet) to North Vancouver. Check out **Lonsdale Quay Market,** a new waterfront development, with parks, pubs, stalls, shops, rooms, and food food food.

Continue by car (or transfer to bus no. 228 or 229) to **Lynn Canyon Park.** The park has forests, trails, and a river where you can swim. The highlight is the Ecology Center, with films and exhibits on all aspects of the local environment, open daily 10-5.

Wend your way west (or take bus no. 228 or 229 back to Lonsdale Ave. where you can transfer to a no. 232 Queens bus) to Nancy Green Way and the **Grouse Mountain Skyride.** The cable car ($8.50) to the ski resort on Grouse Mountain operates in the summer for sightseers and day-trippers. It's a memorable ride if you can spare the money, but look up the hill before buying a ticket: if the trees disappear into the clouds, visibility on top will be zero. Much of the forest has been cleared for ski runs and the area available to hikers is limited.

From the Skyride head back down two km to **Cleveland Dam** (1954) and **Lake Capilano**, Vancouver's water supply. The dam is impressive in itself, but be sure to take the dirt road below the dam to the south and look for the signposted trail to the fish hatchery on the right. The **Capilano Salmon Hatchery** (free) is worth a visit anytime for its informative displays and striking setting, but it's best from July to Oct. when you can watch the returning fish fighting their way up a fish ladder into the holding tanks. There is an excellent 30-minute walk along the river here—consult the trail guide

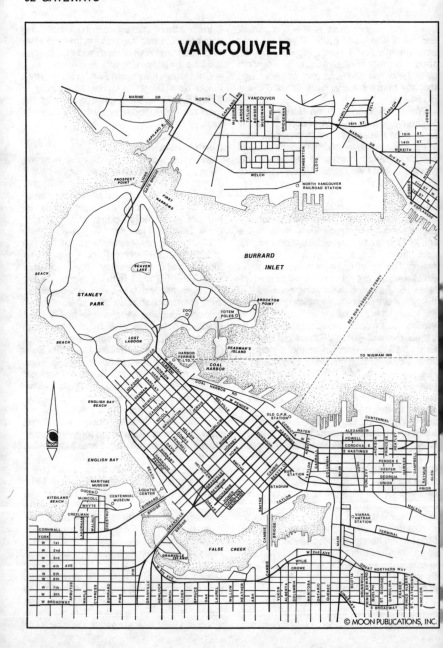

VANCOUVER

© MOON PUBLICATIONS, INC.

sign opposite the hatchery. This lovely area along the Capilano River should not be missed.

The much-touted "Capilano Suspension Bridge" ($5) is farther south. If you're on foot, after the hatchery it's a 15-minute walk up a paved road to the highway. Walk south on Capilano Rd. to Ridgewood Dr., where you can get a no. 246 Highland bus running across the Lions Gate Bridge back to Vancouver. Bus routes in North Vancouver can be a little confusing, so tell the drivers where you are going and ask them to let you know when to get off.

University And Museums

Drive out W. 10th Ave. (or take a no. 10 10th Ave. bus from Granville St.) to the University of British Columbia (UBC). Go via the clock tower and rose garden (in bloom from June to Sept.) to the **Museum of Anthropology,** open 11-9 Tues., 11-5 Wed. through Sun., $5. This museum has a fantastic display of Northwest Coastal Indian sculpture and a large research collection open to visitors. Around the east side of the building and in back is a great view of the Strait of Georgia from the adjacent cliff. Just to the left is a steep stairway down to the beach. Walk south along Wreck Beach, with its nude sunbathing, huge driftwood logs, and high wooded cliffs—so wild you hardly know you're on the edge of a big city. Another stairway leads back up to the UBC campus. When you get to the top of the stairs turn left and walk between the red brick residences to the **Nitobe Japanese Garden** on campus. The UBC campus covers a large, beautifully landscaped area with many buildings worth looking into. Wander at will. If you're weary and hungry, try the Student Union Building with its large cafeteria **(The Subway)** and pub **(The Pit).**

From UBC head back on the coast road along English Bay (or on a no. 14 Hastings bus back along Broadway to MacDonald, where you transfer to a no. 22 Knight bus to go as far as Cypress St.). Go due north on Cypress to the totem pole flanking a group of museums on the south side of English Bay at the entrance to False Creek. The **Centennial** **Museum** has exhibits on Vancouver history and a good cafeteria with a fine view. The $4 admission includes a small **Maritime Museum** nearby. The RCMP ship *St. Roch,* first to traverse the difficult Northwest Passage between the Pacific and Atlantic oceans in both directions (during the 1940s), can be seen at no charge every day in the same building as the Maritime Museum. All these facilities are open daily 10-5. The unusual mushroom dome over the Centennial Museum contains a planetarium. If the sun is shining, walk west along the shore to Kitsilano Beach to join the local sun worshippers. There's also an outdoor saltwater swimming pool here which you may use for a buck.

Along Howe Sound

A good day-trip from Vancouver and one which no rail buff will want to miss is on the *Royal Hudson,* an authentic 1930s' steam locomotive. This is a six-hour RT excursion from North Vancouver station to the logging town of Squamish. From May to Sept., Wed. to Sun., the train pulls out at 10 a.m. for the two-hour journey past Horseshoe Bay and up Howe Sound to Squamish. In Squamish there is ample time for lunch and a visit to the local pioneer museum in the park near the station. Although the trip may be a little touristy, at $9.50 RT it's still a good value and the scenery is hard to beat. Tickets are available from Tourism B.C. at Robson Square; the seller will explain where to catch the city bus to the station.

Up Indian Arm

Harbor Ferries Ltd., on Coal Harbor just beyond the Bayshore Inn, offers a six-hour day trip up and down Indian Arm, 90 km to the Wigwam Inn. The boat leaves daily at 10 a.m. ($14 RT) and reservations are not necessary. The two-hour journey up the fjord gives you a taste of what to expect on the Inside Passage cruise to Skagway—snowcapped mountains, thick forests, eagles, and seals. You also get to see Vancouver Harbor from end to end with a knowledgeable commentary from the captain. There's a two-hour stopover at the Wigwam Inn but the food is expensive, so bring along a picnic lunch. A short trail behind the lodge leads straight up to a waterfall viewpoint. You could extend your trip by hiking for two days along a logging road from Wigwam to Squamish and then catch the *Royal Hudson.* There's a high pass to cross, so do this only from mid-June on. An alternative way of getting to the trailhead is to call Jim Patterson, tel. (604) 929-3911 or 929-1520, and arrange to have his water taxi take you from Deep Cove (bus no. 211 or 212 from Phibbs Exchange) to the top of Indian Arm for about $8 pp.

INFORMATION

By far the best source of information about Vancouver, Victoria, Vancouver Island, and the rest of British Columbia is Moon Publications' *British Columbia Handbook,* by Jane King. This guide is absolutely indispensable for anyone going overland to the Yukon and Alaska: across to Victoria, up Vancouver Island, then back across to Prince Rupert, and onto the Alaska ferries to Haines or Skagway; or train to Prince Rupert and ferry to Alaska; or driving up the Cassiar or Alaska highways. At US$13.95, this is the best investment you could make in your trip through B.C. (see the back of this book for ordering information).

Five **Travel Infocentres** are scattered around Vancouver, the best places to get face-to-face information on Vancouver and the province. The main one is at 562 Burrard St., tel. (604) 683-2000, open Mon.-Sat. 8-5. Be sure to collect a map of the city (free), the *Accommodations* booklet for B.C. (invaluable), and all the brochures, schedules, etc. that you have room for. A Deak International Currency Exchange is located inside. The other Infocentres are located at Delta, Richmond, Coquitlam, and North Vancouver.

Detailed topographical maps for hikers are available from the **Government Agent,** Room 222, Robson Square. For free maps of Alaska and all other U.S. destinations, go to **Travel USA,** Room 84 of the old CPR station at the foot of Seymour St. (Mon.-Fri. 9-5).

Greenpeace, 2623 W. 4th Ave., publishes information sheets on local environmental issues. The **Vancouver Public Library,** Robson and Burrard streets, is open Mon.-Thurs. 9:30-9:30, Fri. and Sat. till 6 p.m. **Duthie Books,** Robson and Hornby, is the best bookstore in the city. The **Pack and Boots** store, 3425 W. Broadway, sells camping equipment, guidebooks, and youth hostel membership cards.

The arrival of the first train on May 23, 1887, heralded Vancouver's becoming the major metropolis of western Canada.

The most knowledgeable travel agency in Vancouver is **Westcan Treks,** 3415 W. Broadway, tel. 734-1066, beside the Pack and Boots store.

The **area code** for all of B.C. is 604.

TRANSPORTATION

By Air

Vancouver International Airport (YVR) is 20 km south of downtown Vancouver. Transit bus no. 100/800 leaves from outside the terminal's upper level (departures) to the right. Pay 75 cents (exact change only) and ask for a transfer. Just after the large bridge change to the no. 25 Victoria bus which runs straight up Granville into town. The no. 100/800 bus leaves the airport every 30 minutes Mon.-Sat., hourly on Sun.; service continues until after midnight. Alternatively, grab the **Express Bus** airporter from Level Two, leaving every half hour for downtown, $7.

The **information counter,** on Level Three, is open daily 8 a.m.-11 p.m.—very helpful with maps and brochures. There is no bank, but a currency exchange booth opens 6 a.m.-10:30 p.m. daily, which gives about two percent less than the banks downtown. Coin lockers are plentiful and cost 50 cents a day. The airport is open 24 hours a day so crash here if you're arriving or leaving in the wee hours. Don't feel guilty about stretching out your sleeping bag because they charge $12.50 airport tax on international flights. On domestic flights the charge is eight percent of the ticket price, or $23, whichever is lower. If you bought your ticket abroad and weren't charged, don't worry—Air Canada collects the money when you check in.

By Boat

B.C. Ferries has frequent service throughout the day from Tsawwassen, 30 km south of Vancouver, to the Gulf Islands and Swartz Bay (for Victoria). The ferry to Nanaimo on Vancouver Island leaves frequently from Horseshoe Bay, a 10-minute drive west of Vancouver, as does the ferry to Langdale (for the Sunshine Coast). To get to the Tsawwassen ferry terminal by public transportation, take bus no. 601 South Delta from Howe St. to Ladner Exchange where you transfer to a no. 640 bus to the ferry. West Vancouver Transit has frequent service, usually every 30 minutes daily, to Horseshoe Bay. Look for the blue bus (65 cents) in front of the Hudson's Bay Co. at Georgia and Seymour streets.

The **Sea Bus** crosses Burrard Inlet to North Vancouver from the old railroad station at the foot of Seymour Street. There is service every 15 minutes weekdays, every 30 minutes evenings and weekends. The fare is $1.35 and city bus transfers are both given and accepted.

By Bus

Greyhound Lines, 150 Dunsmuir St., tel. 662-3222, sells tickets to Prince Rupert ($139), Whitehorse, Yukon ($142), and points throughout Canada. **Pacific Coach Lines,** tel. 662-8074, has service every hour between 5:45 a.m and 5:45 p.m. from the Greyhound terminal to Victoria ($19.70, includes ferry and tax). **Maverick Coach Lines,** tel. 255-1171, has a bus from the same terminal twice a day to Powell River. The 8:30 a.m. bus is the one to take if you want to see anything along the way. (It lays over in Powell River for two hours, then returns to Vancouver by 10 p.m.) The fare, $23.25, includes both ferries.

Local

All Vancouver city buses, the SkyTrain, and Sea Bus charge a flat rate of $1.35 (exact *change* required—no bills) regardless of distance traveled in off-peak hours, and go up to $2.50 for way-out travel during rush hour. All give a transfer valid for stopovers and roundtrips for up to one and a half hours. Ask about Day Passes and Explorer Packs—good value if you're using public transportation to get around.

Other Travel Options

VIA Rail has service to all points east and north of Vancouver. The terminal is at 1150 Station St. near Main and Pryor behind the SkyTrain station, tel. (800) 561-8630 in Canada, (800) 361-3677 in the U.S. One way to Prince Rupert is $171, to Jasper $156, and all the way to the other end of the line at

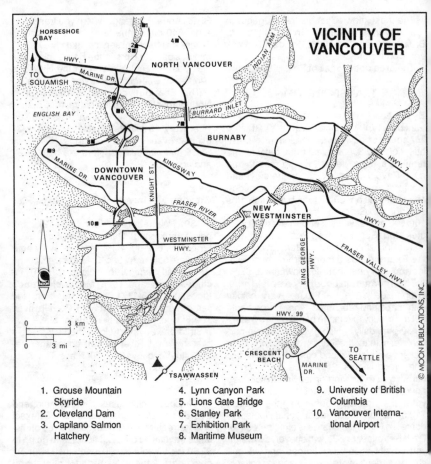

VICINITY OF VANCOUVER

© MOON PUBLICATIONS, INC.

1. Grouse Mountain Skyride
2. Cleveland Dam
3. Capilano Salmon Hatchery
4. Lynn Canyon Park
5. Lions Gate Bridge
6. Stanley Park
7. Exhibition Park
8. Maritime Museum
9. University of British Columbia
10. Vancouver International Airport

Halifax, Nova Scotia, $532. The Canrail Pass, $287, is good for 30 days.

Auto Driveaway, 211 W. 1st St., North Vancouver (three blocks from the Sea Bus terminal), has driveaway cars to Toronto, Montreal, and Los Angeles. You must put up a $250 refundable deposit and pay the gas, but otherwise it's free transportation. Europeans should have an International Driver's License. Call 985-0936 for information. Many other such agencies are listed in the Yellow Pages of the phone book under "Automobile Transporters and Driveaway Companies."

Hitchhiking is prohibited on the Trans-Canada Highway east out of Vancouver. However, if you're determined, take bus no. 330 Ferguson (no Sun. service) from Hastings St. and get off at the first stop after the Port Mann Bridge. Walk back to the highway and smile. To reach the White Rock/Blaine border crossing into the U.S., take bus no. 351 North Bluff from Howe St. to Johnston and King George Highway. From there it's easy to hitch to the border.

VANCOUVER ISLAND

Vancouver is the largest island off the west coast of North America. Lying parallel (northwest-southeast) to mainland B.C., it's 454 km long and an average of 97 km wide. The island was discovered by Capt. Cook in 1776, but it was Capt. George Vancouver who, by entering Discovery Passage near Campbell River and sailing on through Johnstone Strait, proved it was not connected to the mainland. Today, roughly 350,000 people live on the island, mostly around Victoria and along the east coast. Logging is the main industry, with clearcutting prevalent in the north, followed by fishing, tourism, and mining. A spine of snowcapped mountains runs down the center of the island, isolating the wild, rugged west coast. Much of the west coast is inaccessible, making Pacific Rim National Park a haven for backpackers.

Vancouver Island is an entire vacation destination of its own, and if you're tempted to halt your northbound progress here, you'll find enough wilderness, coast and ocean, villages, medium-sized towns, and cosmopolitan capitals to keep you happily occupied for the whole summer; just have *British Columbia Handbook* along for company. Otherwise, grit your teeth, maybe spend a few days checking out the highlights, and make your way to Port Hardy at the northern tip—where the trip to Alaska officially kicks off.

VICTORIA

Without a doubt the most intriguing and unusual place on the entire island is Victoria itself, with its British civility, island-type homey familiarity, and its large and wild backyard. Victoria was established in 1843 as a Hudson's Bay Company fort. Agricultural lands were soon developed nearby, but the little settlement didn't gain momentum until 1858, when a gold rush on the Fraser River brought a flood of American miners through the town. In 1868, Victoria was made capital of the crown colony of British Columbia.

Today, nearly three-quarters of the people on Vancouver Island live in this small city of a quarter million and on the adjacent Saanich Peninsula. The many historic sites, parks and gardens, tourist sideshows, and inexpensive facilities, along with a distinct European air and compact size make Victoria an inspiring gateway to the Inside Passage and beyond.

Downtown Sights

Most walking tours begin at the **Parliament Buildings** (1898), which dominate Victoria's Inner Harbor. Together with the **Empress Hotel** (1908), they lend the city a monumental air. Free tours of Parliament leave regularly every day from the front door and are well worth taking. Across the street is the ultra-modern **Royal B.C. Natural and Human History Museum,** tel. 387-3014, open 9:30-7 in summer, 10-5:30 in winter, $5. Largest in western Canada, and one of the best around, the rich collection of art, artifacts, and photos envelops all of your senses in the entire realm of living history of British Columbia; allow half a day here.

Thunderbird Park, beside the museum, has totem poles and replicas of large Northwest Indian houses. Helmcken House (1852), just behind the totem poles, is one of the oldest houses in the province still at its original location (open daily except Mon., free). Just a block south on Douglas St. is the entrance to **Beacon Hill Park.** This century-old reserve extends all the way to the Juan de Fuca Strait. From the shore is a splendid view of the Olympic Mountains. A 39-meter-high totem pole, numerous ponds, and flower gardens add to the park's allure.

Bastion Square, heart of the 1890s' city at Yates and Wharf, gets its name from a bastion of old Fort Victoria (1843) which once stood here. Today the old courthouse (1889) there is the **Maritime Museum,** and the square with its trees and benches is a perfect picnic or people-watching place. **Centennial Square,** a few blocks north at Pandora and Government streets, is another

VICTORIA

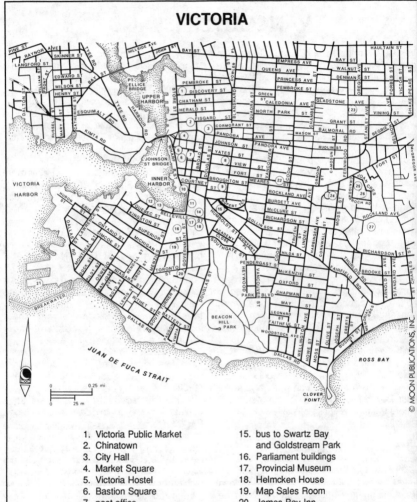

© MOON PUBLICATIONS, INC.

1. Victoria Public Market
2. Chinatown
3. City Hall
4. Market Square
5. Victoria Hostel
6. Bastion Square
7. post office
8. St. Andrew's Cathedral
9. public library
10. tourist office
11. Empress Hotel
12. Seattle Ferry
13. Port Angeles Ferry
14. bus station
15. bus to Swartz Bay
    and Goldstream Park
16. Parliament buildings
17. Provincial Museum
18. Helmcken House
19. Map Sales Room
20. James Bay Inn
21. cruise ship wharf
22. antique shops
23. Prancing Pony Restaurant
24. Victoria Art Gallery
25. Craigmyle Guest House
26. Craigdarroch Castle
27. Government House

historic district. Victoria's colorful **Chinatown** is just north of here at Government and Fisgard streets. Downtown Victoria is full of side-show "attractions," such as Undersea Gardens, Miniature World, Glass Garden, Classic Car Museum, and Royal Wax Museum—all are expensive. If you're still in the mood for tourist attractions, check out Sealand and Fable Cottage Fairy Estate up the east coast.

To The Castle
Walk up Courtney St. to the impressive facade of **Christ Church Anglican Cathedral.** Many old tombstones from Victoria's first cemetery stand in the park beside the church. Continue east on Rockland Ave. for 15 minutes through a peaceful residential area to **Government House,** home of the lieutenant-governor. The beautiful gardens surrounding the estate are open to the public daily (free). Leave the gardens through the second gateway and head north on Joan Crescent to **Craigdarroch Castle** at no. 1050. This towering Victorian mansion, built by coal magnate Robert Dunsmuir in 1890, is now open daily for tours ($3). Ask if you can shoot a little nine-ball in the rumpus room. Walk back to town along Fort St. past many antique shops.

Butchart Gardens
These famous gardens, 20 km north of Victoria on Saanich Inlet, originated almost 90 years ago, when Canadian cement pioneer Butchart and his wife began collecting flora from around the world and planting it at their quarry. Today, the gardens contain roughly 5,000 varieties of flowers, trees, and shrubs, many rare and exotic. They're open from 9-9 in summer, 9-5 in winter. The best time to go is in the early evening, to appreciate the fading light and the nighttime illumination effects. Admission is $8 in summer. Take Highway 17 north and follow the signs.

Information
The **Tourism Victoria Travel Information Centre,** 812 Wharf St. on the Inner Harbor, tel. 382-1131, is open daily 9-7. They have stacks of maps and promo brochures on Vic-

toria and the surrounding area. **Ministry of the Environment,** 810 Blanshard St., provides free brochures on B.C. wildlife. Whether you need a topographical map for hiking or only a big souvenir map of the island, the **Map Sales Room,** 553 Superior St. behind the Parliament Buildings, will have it. **Greenpeace,** the **Sierra Club,** and the **South Pacific Peoples Foundation of Canada** all have offices at 620 View Street.

TRANSPORTATION

By Boat
The Port Angeles ferries dock at adjoining wharfs in Victoria's Inner Harbor. **Black Ball Transport's** Port Angeles ferry leaves three times daily year-round, passenger US$6 OW, car and driver US$24; call (206) 457-4491 in the U.S. and (604) 386-2202 in Victoria for information. Clear U.S. Immigration at Port Angeles.

The Anacortes ferry to Friday Harbor, San Juan Island (US$5), leaves Sidney daily at 12:30 p.m. Twelve ferries run daily between Swartz Bay (Vancouver Island) and Tsawwassen (Lower Mainland), $4 OW, car and driver $19. For ferries to and from Vancouver, see above.

Bus Connections
Bus no. 70 Pat Bay Highway ($1.50) runs from Douglas St. in downtown Victoria right to the Swartz Bay ferry terminal hourly every day. This same bus passes within a block of the Sidney ferry terminal for the Washington State ferry to Anacortes. At Tsawwassen, catch the no. 640 Valley-To-Sea bus (75 cents), also hourly every day, to Ladner Exchange, where you transfer to the bus to downtown Vancouver. If you're going to the Vancouver YH hang onto your transfer and ask the driver where you change to the 4th Ave. bus.

Long-distance Buses And Trains
Pacific Coach Lines (PCL), 710 Douglas St., Victoria, tel. 385-4411, has a bus every two hours to Vancouver, $19.70. Five PCL buses a day run from Victoria to Campbell

River ($31); and one a day goes all the way to Port Hardy ($70), leaving Victoria at 8:10 a.m., arriving at Port Hardy at the island's northern end at 6:30 p.m. Stopovers are allowed. There are coin lockers (75 cents) at the PCL depot behind the Empress Hotel, if you need a place to leave your luggage for the day. If you prefer trains, a diesel rail car goes from Esquimalt to Courtenay daily at 8:15 a.m., $23 OW. No bicycles are carried. Take bus no. 23, 24, or 25 to the station. Call 383-4324 for reservations.

Local Buses And Hitching
The Victoria local bus system publishes *Rider's Guide* and *By Bus* brochures, which you can have for the asking at the Infocentre. Or call 382-6161 for specific questions. Usual fares are 85 cents; they also sell day passes and offer tourist discounts.

To hitch north to Nanaimo, take bus no. 50 Goldstream to Brock and Jacklin, very close

to the Trans-Canada Highway. To hitch to Port Renfrew for the West Coast Trail, take a no. 61 Sooke bus from Western Exchange to Sooke ($1.50), which is on Highway 14 on the way to the trailhead. The Sooke bus only runs every couple of hours, so call 382-6161 for the schedule before leaving. Timetables for all bus routes are available free at the tourist information offices.

The Route North
You can drive/bus to Port Angeles and then connect to the ferry to Victoria from there. Or take the B.C. ferry from Tsawwassen southwest of Vancouver to Swartz Bay northeast of Victoria. Whichever you choose, once on Vancouver Island you'll drive, bus, or hitch up the highway to Port Hardy on the far north tip, where the B.C. ferry *Queen of the North* runs to Prince Rupert every other day from May to September. From there, you can catch Greyhound up the Yellowhead to the Alaska

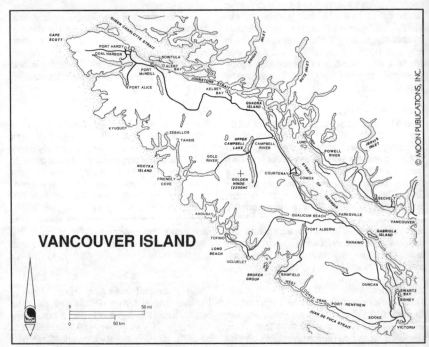

VANCOUVER ISLAND

© MOON PUBLICATIONS, INC.

Highway as far as Whitehorse, or connect to the Alaska State Ferries through Southeast Alaska as far as Haines or Skagway, both of which have road connections to mainland Alaska.

TOWARD THE MIDNIGHT SUN

Gulf Islands

These 100-plus islands off the east coast of Vancouver Island were once part of the main island but became separated by glaciation. The scenery is magnificent, with long channels and inlets flowing between hillsides covered in pine. But it's the peace and easy-going pace which most attract droves of city people. B.C. Ferries has service to the Gulf Islands several times a day from Swartz Bay and Tsawwassen. The Swartz Bay ferry calls at Montague Harbor on Galiano (good camping near the terminal), and at Pender, Mayne, and Saturna islands. The Tsawwassen ferry stops at Sturdies Bay on Galiano, Long Harbor on Saltspring (largest and most populous island), and at Pender and Mayne. Instead of sailing directly from Swartz Bay to Tsawwassen, stop off at a Gulf island at no extra cost. If you're not going to Vancouver, the morning run from Swartz Bay around the islands is an excellent and inexpensive scenic cruise. There's no bus service on the Gulf Islands themselves, but hitchhiking on them is easy—everybody stops.

Nanaimo

Founded in 1852 as a coal-mining settlement, downtown Nanaimo and its Small Boat Harbor are attractive, with excellent views. Don't judge the city by the jumble of parking lots, shopping centers, and strip suburbia you find on the outskirts. Old Nanaimo is worth a stopover. Along the waterfront past the **museum** is the **Bastion,** a wooden fort built in 1853 by the Hudson's Bay Company to protect the coal-mining families against Indian attack.

Excellent hiking and camping are found on **Newcastle Island,** just offshore from downtown Nanaimo. A self-guide folder for the nine-km nature trail on Newcastle is available free from the Nanaimo tourist office. June to

Captain George Vancouver was first to circumnavigate Vancouver Island. His negotiations with the Spaniard Quadra, at Nootka Sound in 1792, laid the groundwork for British domination of this coast. From 1792-94, he explored and charted the entire Inside Passage from Puget Sound to Glacier Bay.

Aug. an hourly passenger ferry goes from Nanaimo to the island ($2.50 RT). The entire island is a provincial park, with no cars to contend with. The Gabriola ferry ($1 RT) leaves approximately every hour from the landing adjoining the bus station in downtown Nanaimo. Campsites ($6) without shower are available at Taylor Bay Lodge, on Gabriola, tel. 247-9211, an easy three-km walk from the ferry.

The ferry to Horseshoe Bay (Vancouver) leaves hourly during summer from Departure Bay, about three km north of downtown Nanaimo; catch bus no. 2 to Stewart Ave. and Brechlin Rd., closest stop to the terminal. **Pacific Coach Lines** has three buses daily to Port Alberni ($9), six daily to Campbell River ($17), and nine daily to Victoria ($13).

Across The Island

The road from Parksville to Port Alberni traverses superb forested countryside along the north slope of Mt. Arrowsmith (1,806 meters), which dominates this part of Vancou-

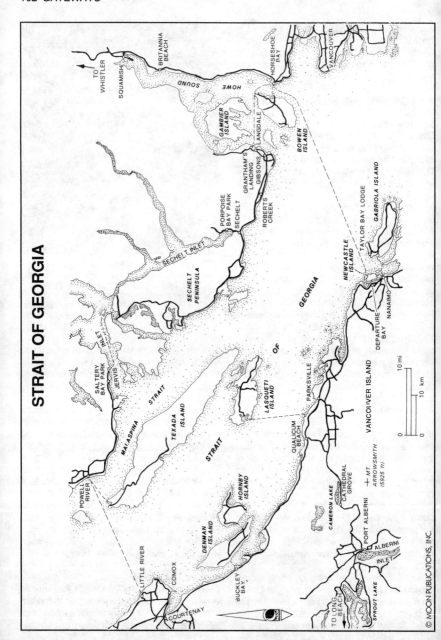

STRAIT OF GEORGIA

© MOON PUBLICATIONS, INC.

ver Island. Just beyond lovely Cameron Lake is MacMillan Provincial Park (Cathedral Grove), with 850-year-old Douglas firs. The cross-island highway cuts right through the middle of this ancient forest. There isn't much to see in Port Alberni itself; generally it's only a place you come to to catch the boat down to Alberni Inlet. The MV *Lady Rose,* a passenger-carrying cargo boat built in Scotland in 1937, leaves from the wharf at the bottom of Argyle St. for four-hour runs down Alberni Inlet; check departure days (usually only three times a week), times, and fares at any tourist information office in B.C. On the Ucluelet trip the ship sails among the beautiful Broken Group Islands, now part of Pacific Rim National Park. A bus also runs from Port Alberni to Tofino.

Ucluelet (yoo-CLOO-let) and **Tofino** are two small picturesque villages on the island's west coast, with limited but adequate facilities. **Long Beach,** the best on Canada's coast, stretches 11 km between them, with several campgrounds accommodating RVers and tenters. The **West Coast Trail** from Bamfield to Port Renfrew was built in 1907-12 as a lifesaving trail for shipwrecked seamen from ships which often foundered on this windswept coast. Today, it's a favorite of intrepid backpackers, and forms part of Pacific Rim National Park. Be prepared, however, as this is no Sunday outing. Six days is the minimum required to do the trail and most hikers take eight. Rain and fog are possible anytime and no supplies are sold anywhere along the route. Beach hiking and camping are the most popular activities and there is plenty of driftwood for campfires. Be aware of tidal conditions to avoid being cut off below cliffs by rising waters. The Sierra Club puts out an excellent trail guide. Copies can be purchased at the Pack and Boots store in Vancouver. Pick up a copy of the tide tables for Tofina, B.C., while you're at it.

Central Vancouver Island
Courtenay is a communications and supply center halfway up the east coast. The Powell River ferry lands at Little River, 11 km northeast of Courtenay. Comox Taxi Ltd. runs a jitney service back to the Courtenay bus sta-

tion. The bus to Campbell River (45 km) is only $3. There's also a train to Courtenay from Victoria.

Campbell River is a boomtown at the top of the Strait of Georgia, the northernmost large settlement of Vancouver Island's populated east coast; the excellent 236-km highway from Campbell River to Port Hardy runs largely through undeveloped and uninhabited logging country. The downtown area faces Discovery Passage, through which Capt. George Vancouver sailed in 1792, proving that Vancouver was an island. An hourly ferry runs across Discovery Passage to Quadra Island, leaving from the east side of Tyee Plaza.

The paved road to **Gold River** follows the south shore of Upper Campbell Lake near Strathcona Provincial Park, affording some splendid views of the mountains, forests, and rivers of central Vancouver Island. Numerous trails crisscross the park and backcountry camping is permitted anywhere over 800 meters off the main roads. Gold River is a modern bedroom community for the employees of the big pulp mill on Muchalat Inlet, 16 km southwest. There's no public transportation between Campbell River and Gold River. The freighter MV *Uchuck III* runs scenic cruises around Friendly Cove, and carries passengers from Gold River to Tahsis.

On Broughton Strait
Just two km off the Island Highway, **Port McNeill** is primarily a gateway to several offshore islands. From the landing in the center of town, a ferry crosses Broughton Strait to Sointula and Alert Bay throughout the day. **Sointula,** on Malcolm Island, is a friendly little community descended from Finnish settlers who came looking for utopia in the early years of this century. Many still speak Finnish and the blond heads and Nordic landscape make it easy to imagine you're in Scandinavia. **Alert Bay,** on five-km-long Cormorant Island near the mouth of the Nimpkish River, was established in 1870 when a salmon saltery was set up. In 1878 the Kwakiutl Indian mission was moved here from Fort Rupert near Port Hardy. Today the population of 1,800 is half Indian, half white. The

picturesque town with its large frame houses and fishing boats winds along the water's edge; the Indian village is to the left of the ferry landing, the white man's town to the right. Alert Bay is probably the most intriguing coastal town in northern B.C., but you won't read much about it in the offical tourist brochures because the locals want to keep it to themselves.

Port Hardy

Port Hardy, near the north end of Vancouver Island 485 km from Victoria, is a medium-size tourist town where you catch the B.C. ferry to Prince Rupert on the northern coast of mainland Canada. Since the ferry departs at 7:30 a.m. you'll need to spend the night, and since the arriving ferry from Rupert pulls up around 10:30 p.m., accommodations can get rather

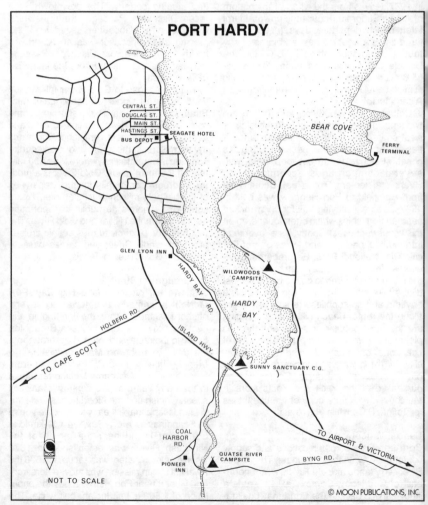

PORT HARDY

CENTRAL ST.
DOUGLAS ST.
MAIN ST.
HASTINGS ST.
BUS DEPOT   SEAGATE HOTEL

BEAR COVE

FERRY TERMINAL

GLEN LYON INN

HARDY BAY RD.

WILDWOODS CAMPSITE

HARDY BAY

HOLBERG RD.

ISLAND HWY

SUNNY SANCTUARY C.G.

TO CAPE SCOTT

TO AIRPORT & VICTORIA

COAL HARBOR RD.

PIONEER INN

QUATSE RIVER CAMPSITE

BYNG RD.

NOT TO SCALE

© MOON PUBLICATIONS, INC.

tight on turnaround night. The best campground is halfway (four km) between the ferry terminal at Bear Cove and downtown: **Quatse River Campsite,** on Coal Harbor Rd. (go left at the totem pole fork, then turn left into the campground), tel. 949-8233, has 55 large sites under towering spruce trees, $7, showers in the trailer at the entrance. Just across the street is the **Pioneer Inn,** tel. 949-7271, which has rooms for $34 s, $36 d, and an excellent cafeteria-style coffee shop where the "trucker's breakfast" will keep you stuffed until dinner time. **Wildwoods Campsite** is only three km down Bear Cove Rd. from the ferry terminal, but it isn't particularly comfortable for tenting. And **Sunny Sanctuary Campground,** just before Coal Harbor Rd., is an RV parking lot that looks like a wagon train in a defensive circle. **Seagate Hotel,** right on the wharf, tel. 949-6348, has rooms for $25 s, $33 d; **Airport Inn** on Byng Rd. south of Port Hardy, tel. 949-9434, charges $30 s and d. The coffee shop at **Glen Lyon Inn,** on Hardy Bay Rd. along the waterfront, tel. 949-7115, $40 s, $45 d, has an excellent view of the Small Boat Harbor.

You can see the new Bear Cove ferry terminal from the waterfront at Port Hardy, but it's eight km around by road. A minibus ($3) conveniently leaves the bus station on Market St. 90 minutes prior to all ferry sailings; if you call 949-6300 they'll pick you up from any of the area campgrounds or hotels at no extra cost. This minibus and the big Pacific Coach Lines buses to Campbell River ($39) and Victoria ($70) also meet arrivals of the ferry from Prince Rupert.

Queen Of The North

Flagship of the huge B.C. Ferry fleet, this comfortable vessel can accommodate 750 passengers and 160 cars. It departs Port Hardy once every two days (in June, July, and Sept. on odd-numbered days, in Aug. on even-numbered days) at 7:30 a.m., $80 OW, $165 car OW, and arrives in Prince Rupert at

The Kwakuitl Indians of coastal B.C. painted these huge, one-and-a-half-meter-long raven dance masks black, red, and white. Shredded cedar bark fell to the shoulders; a long cape covered the body. The spectacle of a line of squatting dancers, masks swinging from side to side, hinged beaks opening and clapping shut to the beat of their batons, must have been overwhelming.

10:30 p.m. Lately, they've been allowing drivers to check in between 9:30 and 11 p.m. the night before the sailing. You are assigned a place in line and can camp in the parking lot in your vehicle; they wake you when they start loading.

It's a lovely trip 274 nautical miles up the almost uninhabited middle Inside Passage, especially if the weather's clear. The route enters open Pacific just beyond the north end of Vancouver Island and can be particularly rough during the two-hour sail through Queen Charlotte Sound. Open Pacific is also encountered for an hour at Milbanke Sound. Have breakfast in the cafeteria, then splurge on the lunch buffet around 2 p.m.—it's a better deal than the dinner buffet. The individual john compartments on the "'tween decks" are large and private enough that activities therein are only limited by your imagination. Pick up from the gift shop the excellent *B.C. Ferries Guide to the Inside Passage,* 50 cents. And study the "wall of history" about the discovery and exploration of the Inside Passage.

(GORDY OHLIGER)

PRINCE RUPERT AND THE NORTH COAST

Rainy Rupert! Prince Rupert is a fair-sized city on Kaien Island near the mouth of the large Skeena River, at the north end of the Canadian Inside Passage. Hooked up to the rest of the world by road, rail, ferry, and airline, most travelers pass through Rupert on their way to or from Vancouver Island, the Queen Charlottes, the B.C. interior, and Alaska. Being such a major crossroads and gateway, the city has abundant and reasonable facilities for travelers and plenty of action. You couldn't ask for a better place to cool your heels while waiting for a connection. Prince Rupert is called the "City of Rainbows," though as one local put it, "It doesn't *stop* raining long enough for any rainbows to shine."

History

This area had been an important trade center for thousands of years before the Hudson's Bay Co. built Fort Simpson, 30 km north of present- day Prince Rupert, in 1834. The local Tsimshian Indians had evolved into prosperous middlemen in the trade of precious metals, furs, slaves, etc. between the powerful tribes to the north and south. An uneasy truce prevailed between the Indians and the settlers, as Fort Simpson, the most important post between Vancouver and Sitka, began to attract the inevitable missionaries, prospectors, loggers, fishermen, and homesteaders. William Duncan of Metlakatla fame (see below) served here until 1862. A gold strike up the Skeena River (Skeena means "River of Trouble," as many Indians died after eating poisonous shellfish found near its mouth) in the 1870s led to the opening of the first sawmill on the north coast in 1875, eight km north of Fort Simpson, which continued to mill cedar, spruce, and hemlock till 1969.

The Grand Trunk Railroad, Canada's second transcontinental line, was originally intended to terminate at Fort Simpson, until at the last moment it was decided that a better harbor was situated at Kaien Island. The western end of the line was begun in 1906, and a national contest was sponsored to name the new city; $250 was awarded for "Prince Rupert," named for the first governor of Hudson's Bay Company. The tent town, strictly overseen by the railroad company, was finally put up for sale in 1909, and the boom was on. The first lots, sold for $500 in 1910, fetched $17,000 a year later. The first train pulled into Rupert in April 1914, but by then WW I had halted the boom, and poor management bankrupted the Grand Trunk by 1919, which was reorganized into the

Canadian National Railway in 1923. Fishing and logging became the economic bases, and today Rupert's role as a transportation hub still accounts for numerous canneries, a monstrous pulp mill, and trans-shipment terminals for much of Canada's grain and coal.

SIGHTS

First visit the **Museum of Northern B.C.** (donation), 100 1st Ave. E, tel. 624-3207, open Mon.-Sat. 9-9, Sun. 9-5 in summer, and Mon.-Sat. 10-5 the rest of the year. The area's history is graphically displayed in a number of excellent exhibits, especially those on the Tsimshian Indians and Fort Simpson. Don't miss the great videos of constructing the

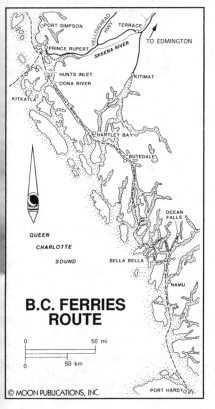

B.C. FERRIES ROUTE

0   50 mi

0   50 km

© MOON PUBLICATIONS, INC.

Grand Trunk and of early halibut and salmon fishing. An art gallery is in the back room, and a good selection of local-interest books is sold in the gift shop. The **Visitors Information Office,** tel. 624-5637, in the lobby is very helpful; read the bulletin board and brochures closely, then ask, ask, ask.

Behind the museum is a **carving shed,** where totems are sometimes in progress. Walk around the courthouse beside the museum to enjoy the attractive gardens and scenic views. The "sunken gardens" were an ammunition dump during WW II. Across 1st Ave. from the museum and overlooking the harbor is the **Northern Mariners Memorial Park,** a tribute to those who have lost their lives at sea.

To dig really deep into Rupert's past, head for the **Regional Archives,** 123 3rd St., tel. 624-3326, open 10-4. Then go over two blocks to 5th St. and head up to **Roosevelt Park.** Prince Rupert was an important Allied transportation base during WW II and at one time 7,000 U.S. soldiers slept in the barracks on this hill. Stop off at the map to orient yourself and read some history, then continue up to **Totem Park,** across from the hospital, a little higher with a less obstructed view of town and the harbor.

Get High

But for the high point of Prince Rupert, head down McBride St. (or grab the no. 53 bus to the Civic Centre), and go two km on the access road to **Mt. Hays Gondola,** $6. The gondola runs daily 10-10 (midnight on weekends). In seven minutes flat, the whole city and harbor, and the islands and mountains in the distance open up before you—a taste of what's to come up the Inside Passage. Or try the hard three-hour hike up the second-steepest gondola ground in North America. The coffee shop at the chalet has some worthwhile books and exhibits on wildflowers (but bring lunch). Follow the T-bar left to the B.C. Tel service road to their communications apparatus on the peak (732 meters).

Hiking

Get your map of the Linear Trails from the infocentre. These trails link the Prince Rupert township to the ferry terminal via Park Avenue Campground, and the Gondola to Roosevelt Park. A linear trail also starts at Seal Cove. To get there, take the no. 51 Seal Cove bus to the seaplane base at the end of the line. The road southeast from the bus stop leads past a series of abandoned WW II ammunition bunkers to the Dept. of Fisheries wharf. Walk back to the corner where the bus turns and continue along the abandoned railway line. This follows the shoreline below a high wooded bluff back past the Small Boat Harbor to Cow Bay and cannery row.

About two km south of the Alaska/B.C. ferry terminals is an overgrown concrete bunker and gun emplacement built during the war to protect Prince Rupert against a Japanese naval strike. A hike this way also offers excellent views of Chatham Sound and the surrounding waterways. Follow the railway tracks past two "No Trespassing" signs and keep going until you see the bunker above you to the left. More bunkers are several km farther down the line near Ridley Island, but they can be hard to find. If you're determined, continue south until you reach three small bunkers beside the tracks. Just beyond these is a bridge over the railway. Scramble up onto the bridge and look back to the northwest. Many wartime fortifications are swallowed by the bush here. Hitch a ride back to town on the road from Ridley Island and you'll have gone right around Kaien Island. Or, if you're willing to risk arrest or a fatal accident, walk boldly along the railway tracks past the pulp mill to Prince Edward. But don't stop on the railway bridge to admire the rushing waters at the narrows, as a sudden train could spell your end. Continue down the road seven km to the cannery museum, or catch a bus back to town.

PRACTICALITIES

Accommodations

Prince Rupert has an amazing amount of reasonable accommodations—but being such a crossroads town, it can be eventful trying to find a good cheap room if you don't have reservations. You should know when you'll be here, since you'll either be arriving or departing on a scheduled ferry. Do yourself a favor and call ahead to reserve your bed.

Cheapest is **Pioneer Rooms,** 167 3rd Ave. E, around the corner from the Museum of Northern B.C., tel. 624-2334, $15 s, $20 d, shared bath on each of their three floors ($3 for a shower alone). Even though it's a $4-5 cab ride from the ferry terminal, this place fills up fast after the ferries arrive.

If that happens, try: **Ocean View Hotel,** 950 1st Ave. W, tel. 624-6259, $28 s, $30 d without bath, $39 d with; The **Aleeda Motel,** 900 3rd Ave. W, tel. 627-1367, is recommended, $38 s, $44 d, all with bath and some with kitchenettes, which you can sometimes get for no extra charge. The **Slumber Lodge,** tel. 627-1711, across the road from the Aleeda, is $49 s, $53 d; the **Rupert Motor Inn,** 720 1st Ave. W., tel. 624-9107, has views over the harbor for $50 s, $56 d. If you want to splurge, try a 10th-floor room atop the **Highliner,** tel. 624-9060, for $75 d.

The **Park Avenue Municipal Campground** is a one-km, 10-minute walk toward town from the ferry terminals, tel. 624-5861. It's open to register from 9 a.m. to midnight, $12 for full hookups, $9 for tent sites, which includes showers. Showers alone are $2. Good for city camping—treeless, grassy, some tents, mostly RVs. The alternative is **Prudhomme Lake Provincial Park** ($8), 20 km out of town on Hwy. 16.

Food, Dude

Breakfast around town is good and cheap— $4 for bacon and eggs. **Smitty's Pancake House** is in Pride O' the North Mall. The **Slumber Inn** restaurant is good and opens at 5 a.m. The coffee shop at **Moby Dick Motor Inn,** on 2nd Ave., also serves big but budget boring bacon-and-eggs breakfasts, open 24 hours. Or try **Raffles Inn** on 3rd Ave. with specials starting at $3.

The **Stardust** has good Chinese—cheap and plentiful. **Zorba's** is recommended for good authentic Greek, but get your Greek pizza at **Rodhos.** At **La Gondola,** flash your headlights from the carpark to place your order for takeaway food. **Smiles Seafood** is recommended highly by Rupertites. Shop at

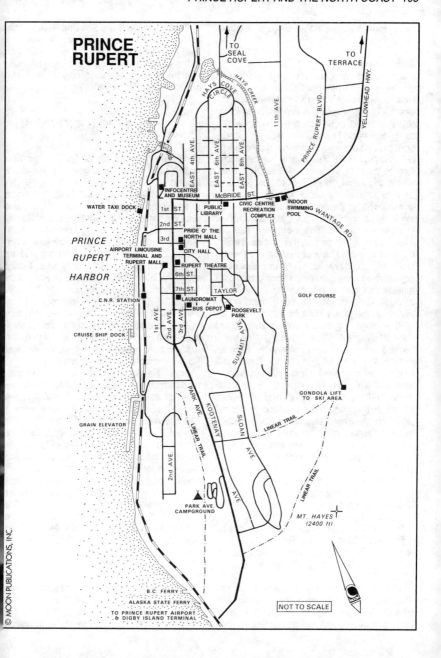

the Rupert Mall, or Safeway near the museum, open daily.

Entertainment

Drink, dance, and try not to get your face punched in. **Popeye's Pub** in the Rupert Hotel is where the 21-year-olds hang out, the kind of place where the hard-rocking band plays its heart out, ends every song with a bang, and nobody claps (not even the dancers), though one drunk guy invariably shouts out, "Rock 'n' roll!" **Surf Club,** corner of 2nd Ave. W and 5th St., is for the over-30 crowd, where the band plays Top 40, or '50s and '60s rock, ends a song with a bang, but doesn't wait for the crowd not to clap, launching instead right into a sick joke or another two-minute classic. **The Belmont,** 725 3rd Ave. W, has the size and the bodies, though depending on the local crowd it can either be crammed or cavernous. At the **Empress** across the street, you're on your own. For a quieter experience, head out to **Solly's Pub** at Seal Cove, or look for out-of-town entertainers at the **Moby Dick Inn.**

Play bingo nightly at **Totem Bingo,** 3rd Ave. W and 1st Street. Hang out with the 15-year-olds at **Fourth Avenue Amusements,** 2nd Ave. W and 4th St., for pinball, foosball, or eight-ball. Or play some serious nine-ball with the 17-year-olds at **International Billiards,** 2nd Ave. W and 6th Street. In fact, Rupert has more pool tables per capita than anywhere else in the North, including a beautiful giant snooker table at the Belmont. **Rupert Cinemas,** 2nd Ave. W and 5th St., tel. 624-6770, shows three separate films, $7.50.

Services And Information

You're never wanting for the time or temp. here: both are displayed from the top of the landmark Highliner Inn. They might not be right, which is *more* fun. For info on the infocentre see "Sights" above. Another infocentre is found at Park Avenue Campground.

The **library** is on McBride between 6th and 7th. Rupert has a good bookstore, too: **Star of the West,** 518 3rd Ave. W, tel. 624-9053, open 9-5. Also check out the gallery in back.

Public showers are $2 at the Park Avenue Campground or $3 at Pioneer Rooms. The **Earl Mah Aquatic Centre,** McBride St. next to the Civic Centre, has a pool, hot tub, saunas, and fitness machines, only $3 for the lot; call 627-7946 for hours.

TRANSPORTATION

By Air

Canadian Airlines, tel. 624-9181, has three flights daily from Vancouver via Terrace to Rupert (and back to Vancouver), $250 OW; the APEX fare starts at $225 RT. The airport is on Digby Island across the harbor; Canadian Air has a check-in at the Rupert Square Mall, 2nd Ave. W between 3rd and 6th streets, two hours before departure. From there, a bus transfers you via ferry to the airport. The bus is technically free, though the ferry charges $9 pp, which you pay to the bus driver. Go figure. **Air B.C.,** 112 6th St. tel. 624-4554, flies the same route. **Water Taxi,** tel. 624-3337, has a workers' ferry several times a day from the second dock south from the foot of McBride St. ($2), if you want to try to save a few bucks—it's a five-km walk from the drop-off to the airport.

Local air transportation is provided by a few seaplane companies at Seal Cove (see "Hiking" above). **Trans-Provincial Airlines** tel. 627-1341, is the largest, with service to Ketchikan ($110) and Port Simpson ($29). They fly to Sandspit and Queen Charlotte City ($94 OW), and Masset ($76) on the Queen Charlotte Islands; their Masset service operates three times daily, permitting you to combine sea (ferry to Skidegate), land (hitch to Masset), and air (seaplane back to Rupert) travel on a visit to these islands. You can also charter their various planes for scenic flights, from $310 an hour. **North Coast Air Services,** tel. 627-1357, flies all the same routes.

By Sea

Both the B.C. and Alaska ferry terminals are two km from downtown. City buses show up once every two to three hours, if that, but an **Allwest** shuttle bus ($2) meets all arrivals. A cab to downtown costs $5, to Pioneer Rooms at the far end of town, $6. If it's late and you're camping, just walk the one km to the campground. Or walk the km to the corner of Pillsbury and Kootenay, where bus no. 52 passes every half hour 7:30-5:30, except Sunday.

B.C. Ferries' (tel. 624-9627) *Queen of the North* makes a roundtrip between Port Hardy on Vancouver Island and Prince Rupert every two days. Southbound, the ferry leaves Prince Rupert on even-numbered days in June, July, and Sept., odd-numbered days in Aug., at 7:30 a.m. and arrives Port Hardy 10:30 p.m.; northbound just reverse the ports and days. The ferry makes a stop in Bella Bella, a surprisingly large town, once a week. The fare is $80 OW, car $165.

Queen of Prince Rupert sails to Skidegate Landing on the Queen Charlottes four to six days a week, depending on the month. The 6½-hour ride leaves Rupert at 11 a.m (9 p.m. on Mon., 2 p.m. on Wed.), $16 OW, $77 car and driver. From Skidegate, the ferry leaves at 11 a.m. on Mon. and Tues., 11 p.m. on Thurs., Fri. (and Sat. in Aug.).

For local ferry trips, see "Vicinity of Prince Rupert." For Alaska Marine Highway information, see p. 66 and p. 120.

By Rail
The **VIA Rail** depot is at the foot of 2nd St.; a wooden ramp descends right down to the water, tel. 627-7304. The train leaves at Tues., Wed., and Fri. 11:30 a.m., $62 to Prince George, $100 to Jasper. Connect with the train to Vancouver at Prince George on Wed. and Fri.; you must overnight in Prince George. You travel along the historic Skeena River route; get a window seat on the right for best views. The train arrives in Rupert at 3:45 p.m. Mon., Thurs., and Sunday. For further information and reservations, call (800) 561-3630 anywhere in B.C. The depot is open all day and has a few coin lockers.

By Bus
The **Greyhound** bus depot is at 822 3rd Ave., tel. 624-5090. The depot is open weekdays 8-5 and on weekends for the buses and has a few coin lockers. Two buses a day go in and out of Prince Rupert. All buses these days are non-smoking. Two buses arrive daily, at 9:25 a.m. and 6:45 p.m. Two depart too, at 11:15 a.m. and 8:30 p.m. It's 12 hours to Prince George ($64) where you connect to Vancouver ($67) or Whitehorse ($168).

Getting Around
Prince Rupert has an adequate local transit system, which can get you practically anywhere in and around town within an hour. Fare is 75 cents, exact change, or $2 to ride all day. Buses run commuter hours during the week, later on Fri. nights, limited on Sat., not at all on Sunday. Schedules/route maps are available on any bus, or call 624-3343 for info. **Budget** rents cars, starting at $40 a day plus 25 cents per km, tel. 627-7400, with an office in Rupert Mall. **Tilden's** rates are the same, tel. 624-5318.

For transportation to and from the ferry docks, see "By Sea" above.

Tours
To reach **Gray Line,** call 624-6124. A number of charter and tour boats operate out of Rupert, all organized into **Prince Rupert Charter Operators.** Fishing charters run $40-60 an hour pp, $150 pp per day; check the Yellow Pages. A two-hour harbor tour is $50 pp (minimum four people), and a crab-fishing picnic is $60 pp (minimum four). For more info, call 627-7777.

VICINITY OF PRINCE RUPERT

Around Chatham Sound
Digby Island is the one to the left as the ferry arrives. Site of an old Norwegian settlement, many of the old houses remain, as does Wahl's Boatyard (now closed) at Dodge Cove, where wooden fishing boats were once built. An old wharf and more dilapidated buildings are at Casey Cove, one bay over. There are some interesting hikes around the cove area. Rupert Water Taxi leaves from its dock (at the foot of McBride St., 7:30 a.m. noon, and 3:30 Mon.-Fri. ($2) for Dodge Cove, and makes for a cheap harbor ride.

Port Simpson, 30 km north of Rupert, was a Coast Tsimshian settlement, before Hudson's Bay Co. built a fort there in 1834. The white population grew steadily till the turn of the century, but quickly subsided as soon as the Grand Trunk Railroad terminus was located at Prince Rupert. The fort was abandoned in 1904, burned down in 1912, and now it's again a settlement of the Coast Tsimshian. A fish-processing plant there is owned by the Indians. A small B.C. ferry, *Sisayda Lady,* runs from Rupert to Port Simpson every Mon. and Fri., leaving the second dock south from the foot of McBride St. (look for the walkway over the tracks and down the stairs to the dock) at 8:30 a.m., returning by 11:30 p.m., $9.50 RT.

Centurion 4 is the other small B.C. ferry that departs Prince Rupert from the small downtown dock for Kincolith, a small Indian settlement up the Portland Inlet. It departs Mon. and Fri. at 8 a.m., arriving back in Rupert around 3:30 p.m., $18 RT. There is no longer a B.C. ferry up the spectacular Portland Canal to Stewart, though you can catch an Alaska ferry in Ketchikan to Hyder.

Metlakatla

This small Indian village, eight km west of Rupert by boat, was founded in 1862 by Anglican missionary William Duncan on an ancient Tsimshian site. A sawmill and trading post were set up, and these people became self-supporting. The church Duncan built in 1874 seated 1,200 people, at the time the largest church west of Chicago and north of San Francisco. In later years Duncan clashed with church authorities who wanted to impose the elaborate Episcopalian ritual on the Indians. When Duncan demurred, the Episcopal bishop had local officials seize the land on which the mission sat in an attempt to force Duncan to obey. Instead, he traveled to Washington, D.C., where he received permission for the Tsimshian to homestead in Alaska. In 1887, Duncan led 823 Indians to Annette Island, Alaska, where they founded a new Metlakatla (see p. 138). The original town burned down in 1901, and today no buildings remain from Duncan's time.

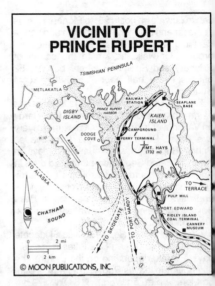

VICINITY OF PRINCE RUPERT

© MOON PUBLICATIONS, INC.

A small ferry operated by the Indian community leaves the Water Taxi dock (second dock south from the foot of McBride St. in Rupert) Mon., Tues., and Wed. at 8:30 a.m., overnights in Metlakatla, then returns at 7:45 the next morning, $3 OW. You need a permit to stay overnight in the village.

Port Edward

A scenic 20-km ride from Rupert brings you to the **North Pacific Cannery Museum,** 1889 Skeena Dr., tel. 628-3538, open daily 9-5, till 9 in July and August. Built in 1889, this is the oldest salmon cannery remaining of more than 200 such plants on the B.C. coast. At its peak, the cannery employed 400 workers of several nationalities. It canned its last fish in 1972; a museum society to sponsor its restoration was formed in 1985, and in July 1987 ownership was transferred to Port Edward village. In the cannery building itself are the displays, including a 10-meter relief map of local salmon-spawning routes, a seven-meter map of the Skeena River hand-drawn on sailcloth, early maritime charts, and salmon fishing artifacts. Also check out the Iron Chink and can-making machinery in the back room. Walk along the boardwalk past

Missionary William Duncan converted the Tsimshians into model Christians, but obliterated all trace of Indian culture in the process.

he former living quarters, which now house an art gallery, coffee shop, and store—note he ledgers with 1937 prices: six cents for a package of Jello, 20-cent bottles of vinegar, 5-cent bottles of ketchup. The large wharf is a fine place to get a tan from sitting in the English rain.

Far West Bus Lines does a roundtrip to Port Edward four times on weekday, twice on weekends, \$1.25 OW, tel. 624-6400. The Cannery Museum is 6½ km down the road from the bus stop at Port Edward, slightly upwind from the giant pulp mill.

THE QUEEN CHARLOTTE ISLANDS

The Queen Charlotte Islands (pop. 6,000) form a chain 300 km long, separated from the Canadian mainland continental shelf by the stormy 50- to 130-km-wide Hecate Channel. Although there are 150 islands in all, the two largest, Graham and Moresby, account for most of the group's land area. Narrow Skidegate (SKID-uh-git) Channel slices these two apart near the middle of the group.

Snowcapped mountains run down the west coast of the archipelago, with a wide area of lowland and rolling hillside on the east toward the middle and northern end of the chain. For the most part, the Queen Charlotte Islands are a remote, wild, and natural land where deer and eagles still outnumber people, where the world's largest black bears are found, and where the temperate rainforest grows like a thick green jungle. If you are looking for a unique experience, this is the place.

History

Juan Perez was the first European to sight the islands, in 1774; however, the Charlottes had been the homeland of the Haida Indians for centuries. The Haida are considered by contemporary anthropologists as having evolved one of the world's most sophisticated hunter-gatherer societies. The natural abundance on the Queen Charlottes makes this easy to understand: the rich fisheries of Hecate Strait, the teeming life in the tidepools, mushrooms and berries, and prolific game animals provided the Haida with a rich pantry. This allowed the Haida to develop an advanced artistic tradition, especially in the carving of argillite, a soft black slate. They also constructed huge longhouses and some of the world's largest canoes—up to 25 meters long and two meters across—that could easily transport 40 people and two tons of baggage, and which they used for trading, raiding, and whaling.

When Capt. George Dixon named the archipelago after his ship, the *Queen Charlotte,* in 1787, an estimated 8,000 Haida inhabited these islands. But missionaries and white officials proscribed the art and customs of the Haidas; by 1915 cultural degeneration and European diseases had reduced their numbers to 588. Today their descendants live in Haida village, near Masset, and in Skidegate; 5,000 whites also inhabit the group, mostly along Skidegate and Masset inlets.

Preparations

Bring as much as you can of what you'll need to the Queen Charlottes—these islands are remote. Especially be prepared for *rain—*

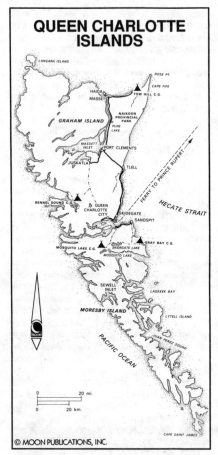

QUEEN CHARLOTTE ISLANDS

LANGARA ISLAND

ROSE PT.

CAPE FIFE

HAIDA
MASSET

TOW HILL C.G.

NAIKOON
PROVINCIAL
PARK

GRAHAM ISLAND

PURE
LAKE

MASSETT
INLET
PORT CLEMENTS

JUSKATLA

TLELL

FERRY TO PRINCE RUPERT

HECATE STRAIT

RENNEL SOUND C.G.

QUEEN
CHARLOTTE
CITY

SKIDEGATE

SANDSPIT

MOSQUITO LAKE C.G.

SKIDEGATE LAKE

GRAY BAY C.G.

MOSQUITO LAKE

SEWELL
INLET

LASKEEK BAY

MORESBY ISLAND

LYTELL ISLAND

PACIFIC OCEAN

JUAN PEREZ SOUND

MOON

0   20 mi.

0   20 km.

CAPE SAINT JAMES

© MOON PUBLICATIONS, INC.

which is always happening somewhere on the islands, usually where *you* are. A good raincoat and waterproof rubber boots are a must. August and Sept. are the best months to take your chances with the weather; bring a sponge, anyway. Also bring food, camping equipment, and basic supplies. For the most part, prices are only slightly higher than on the mainland, but selections are limited.

Skidegate

B.C. Ferries' *Queen of Prince Rupert* docks at Skidegate Landing. The **Queen Charlotte**

Islands Museum ($2), just 500 meters east of the ferry landing, is open weekdays 10-5, weekends 1-5. The museum has a good collection of argillite carvings, century-old totem poles, and fascinating displays of fauna, insects, and birds. Skidegate village, a small Haida community (pop. 350), is 2½ km up the road. The **Band Council Office** on the waterfront is built in the form of a traditional longhouse. A new totem pole stands in front. A lavish feast is served for dinner (5-6 p.m., $20) in Old Skidegate Hall on Thurs. nights in summer.

The ferry MV *Kwuna,* which leaves the landing 12 times daily from 7:30 a.m. to 10:30 p.m. on its 20-minute trip over to Alliford Bay and the road to Sandspit ($2 RT, $8 car and driver), is the only public transportation on the islands. Also check out the numerous tours that leave from the Landing.

Queen Charlotte City

Second-largest town on the islands (pop. 1,000), Q.C. City is five km west of the ferry landing and an easy hitch. Most of the islands' government offices are here, plus half a dozen small lodging houses. But make your first stop at the travel infocentre at friendly **Joy's Island Jewelry,** and be sure to buy the *Guide to the Queen Charlotte Islands* for only $3.95. Make your arrangements here in Q.C. City for over 40 kayaking, fishing, sailing, flightseeing, or sightseeing tours. Call **Kallahin Expeditions,** tel. 559-8455, for any info and to book ahead.

Stay at **Spruce Point Lodge,** on 7th St. tel. 559-8234, for $12.50 (dorm bed) or $50 d (bed and breakfast), or the **Premier Hotel** 3rd Ave., tel. 559-8415, $25 or $56 d, with sweeping views of the harbor. **Gracie's Place,** 3rd Ave., tel. 559-4262, captures the essence of the Queen Charlottes, at $45 d. **Haydn Turner Park** at the west end of the road through Q.C. City has 10 sites ($3), pit toilets, and huge trees. You can also camp at Joy's Island Jewelry for $5 pp. Eat at **Margaret's Cafe** or **Lucy's Place.**

Sandspit

It's 13 km by paved road from the ferry landing on Moresby Island to the island's only settlement, Sandspit, a logging and communications town (pop. 550) with good beaches. South Moresby Island has recently been designated a National Park Reserve—a victory for the Haida and environmentalists, a setback for the logging companies. Sandspit also boasts the only airstrip in the group. Best of several B&Bs is **Moresby Island Guesthouse** on Beach Rd., tel. 637-5305, $40 s, $50 d, or ask about the fold-out beds for $10 a night, including breakfast if you're lucky. The stunning **Sandspit Inn,** tel. 637-5334, will put you up for the night while putting you back $55 d. Or head down to **Gray Bay Campground** on a secluded beach 15 km south of Sandspit. Gray Beach is as far south as you can drive on Moresby Island; the rest of the way south to Cape St. James, accessible only on tours or by sea kayak, could be the wildest land in the North Pacific. The logging road heads west from Gray Bay by Skidegate Lake and down to Moresby Camp on Mosquito Lake, then back up to the ferry landing. This is a long day's drive, and an even longer hitchhike.

An information facility is on Beach Rd., tel. 637-5436. Canadian Airlines flies jets in and out of the airport to Prince Rupert and Vancouver. Budget Rent-A-Car has an office here, tel. 626-5688. Again, a dozen tour operators offer tours of the island and park; contact Kallahin Expeditions in Q.C. to lead you in the right direction.

Naikoon Park

Naikoon ("Long Nose") Provincial Park covers a large flat area in the northeast corner of Graham Island. Park HQ, tel. 557-4390, is in Tlell, 40 km north of Skidegate, where there's a 31-site campground ($8) and picnic area. Tlell is home to a number of back-to-the-land weavers, potters, and artisan types, which provides a welcome contrast to the island's rough-and-ready loggers. The **Bellis Lodge** provides accommodations near Tlell River for YHA members from May to Oct., $12 pp, $17 for non-members, $2 showers. Call 557-4434 for reservations. **Tlell River House,** tel. 557-4211, has a bar, restaurant, and lodging, $52 s, $60 d.

A five-km trail leads up the north side of Tlell River onto the beach and past the wreck of the *Pesuta,* a log barge grounded during a fierce storm in 1928. The East Beach Hike starts here and goes all the way to Tow Hill at the northern tip of the island, a four- to eight-day hike (89 km). The beach is open to 4WDs, which use it very regularly.

To Tow Hill

Continue northwest to **Port Clements** (pop. 550)—check out the museum (open 2-4 p.m., donation), the market, a couple of bars and a restaurant. Stay at the **Golden Spruce Motel,** tel. 557-4325, $36 s, $40 d. Then head up to **Masset** (pop. 1,600), largest settlement on Graham Island. Stop in at the infocentre in the small van. Accommodations are limited; try **Naikoon Park Motel,** tel. 626-5187, $45 d, or **Copper Beach House** by the dock, tel. 626-3225. The town itself has little of interest, but the surrounding countryside more than makes up for it. Do head to **Haida** or Old Masset, two km west of Masset, to visit the museum, crafts shops, and a few totem poles. **Trans-Provincial Airlines,** tel. 626-3944, flies to Prince Rupert twice daily, $65 OW.

Tow Hill is 26 km east of Masset, the last 13 along a gravel road. Three trails begin by the Heillen River bridge at the base of the hill. The **Blow-hole Trail** (one km) leads down to fantastic rock formations by the shore and a view of the spectacular basalt cliff on the north side of Tow Hill (109 meters). From here a second trail climbs to the top of Tow Hill for a view of the sandy beaches which arch in both directions along the north coast of Graham Island for as far as you can see. The longest trail is the **Cape Fife Trail** (10 km) which cuts across to the east side of the island. From there you can hike up to Rose Point at the very northeastern tip of the archipelago, where the Haida believe the world began. Then come back down North Beach to Tow Hill, a total of 31 km, a one- to three-day hike.

An established campground (windy) is beside the road just west of Tow Hill, but backcountry camping is allowed anywhere in Naikoon Park. For more info, contact **Nai-**

koon Park HQ, Box 19, Tlell, B.C. V0T 1Y0, tel. 557-4390.

Transportation

Except for the local ferry between Skidegate and Alliford Bay, there is no public transportation. The locals are good about picking up hitchhikers, but cars can be few. Hitching the main (gravel) roads is a piece of cake, though, compared to getting really out there on the logging roads, especially when you remember how many black bears are around. Most logging roads are open to the public on weekends and after 6 p.m. weekdays. During working hours, on Moresby Island, you must get permission from Fletcher Challenge's office in Sandspit to travel on them, tel. 637-5323. MacMillan-Bloedel controls most of the logging roads on Graham Island and has offices in Q.C. City, tel. 559-4224, and in Juskatla, tel. 557-4212.

Queen Charlotte City and Masset have **bicycle rentals.**

You might consider renting a car from **Budget,** which has offices in Q.C. City, Sandspit, and Masset, tel. 559-4675, starting at $52.95 plus 25 cents a km; pick-up trucks and 4WDs start at $56.95 plus 30 cents. Make your reservations far in advance.

Most people arrive on the excellent B.C. Ferries' service from Prince Rupert at Skidegate landing ($16, $77 car and driver) which runs five to six times a week in summer, three in the off-season. The ferries remain overnight at Skidegate, enough time to see the town. While a quick roundtrip is certainly better than nothing, campers and naturalists will want to spend longer in the islands.

Canadian and **Air B.C.** have daily flights from Vancouver to Sandspit, from $250 RT. All flights are met at the airport by Twin Ser vices, which transports passengers to Q.C. City for $5. **Wag Air,** tel. 663-2875, has daily flights from Vancouver via Bella Bella and Port Hardy to Masset ($360 RT). **Trans-Provincial Airlines,** tel. 626-3944, flies to Prince Rupert twice daily from Q.C. City and Sandspit ($94 OW), or Masset ($76 OW) and has other scheduled flights around the islands. **South Moresby Air Charters,** tel 559-4222, in Q.C. City flies everywhere; popular charters include Hot Spring Island, from $260 RT for three people, and Anthony Is land, from $422 RT.

For information on the Queen Charlottes write to the Chamber of Commerce, Box 357 Queen Charlotte City, B.C. V0T 1S0, tel. 559 4661. And be sure to pick up their excellen *Guide to the Queen Charlotte Islands,* $2.95 which has everything you need to know, in cluding exact distances between towns.

Rennell Sound

A logging road leads northwest from Q.C City, 55 km to Port Clements through the heart of Graham Island. Halfway along in , road, which leads as far west as it is possible to drive in Canada, to Rennell Sound. Th final descent to this rugged piece of coastline is a mere 24% gradient. (Pick up your ' survived the Rennell Sound Hill" sticker from the infocentre.) Here you'll find grea beachcombing (Japanese glass floats ar the prize) and a free campground with p toilets along the shoreline. Back on the mai logging road, continue past Justkatla to th unfinished Haida canoe, and one of th world's only golden spruce trees.

(GORDY OHLIGER)

SOUTHEAST ALASKA

INTRODUCTION

For many people, the name Alaska conjures up images of bitterly cold winters and sunshine-packed summers, of great rivers, enormous snow-capped mountains, and of open tundra reaching to the horizon. If that is your vision of the state, you've missed its Garden of Eden: the Southeast. Almost entirely boxed in by British Columbia, Southeast Alaska's "Panhandle" stretches 500 miles along the North American coast. Everything about this beautifully lush country is water based: the rain that falls on the land, the glaciers that drop from giant icefields, and the ocean that surrounds it all. Gray-blue clouds play a constant game of hide and seek with the verdant islands; deep fjords drive up between snow-covered summits; waterfalls plummet hundreds of feet through the evergreen forests to feed rivers rich in salmon; brown bears prowl the creeks in search of fish; bald eagles perch on treetops beside the rugged, rocky coastline; and

great blue glaciers press down toward the sea.

The Land
Southeast Alaska is comprised of a mountainous mainland and hundreds of islands, varying from rocky reefs that barely jut out of the sea at low tide to some of the largest islands in North America. Collectively, these islands are called the Alexander Archipelago. This ragged shoreline is more than 11,000 miles long and includes over 1,000 named islands, the largest being Prince of Wales, Chichagof, Baranof, Admiralty, Revillagigedo, and Kupreanof—names that reflect the Englishmen, Russians, and Spaniards who explored the area.

The Rainforest
Much of Southeast is covered with dense rainforests of Sitka spruce (the state tree), western hemlock, Alaska yellow-cedar, and

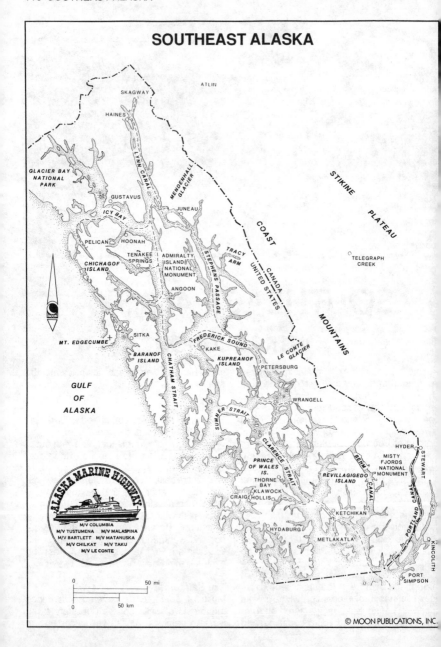

SOUTHEAST ALASKA

western red cedar. Interspersed through the rainforests are open boggy areas known as muskegs, with a scattering of stunted lodgepole pines and cedars. Above the treeline (approx. 2,500 feet) are rocky peaks covered with fragile flowers and other alpine vegetation. Shorelines often have a fringe of grass dotted with flowers during the summer.

The rainforests here are choked with a dense, ankle-grabbing understory of huckleberry, devil's club, and other shrubs. Berry lovers will enjoy a feast in late summer as the salmonberries, red and blue huckleberries, and thimbleberries all ripen. If you're planning a hike, learn to recognize devil's club, a lovely, abundant plant with large maple-shaped leaves and red berries. Barbed spines cover devil's club plants, and when touched they feel like a bee sting. The spines become embedded and are difficult to remove, often leaving a nasty sting for several days. If you're planning a cross-country hike, wear leather gloves to protect your hands. Surprisingly, mosquitoes are not nearly as abundant in Southeast as they are, for example, in Alaska's Interior. They can, however, make your life miserable some of the time, especially during noseeum season.

Climate

The tourist brochures invariably show happy folks cavorting around gleaming glaciers under a brilliantly blue sky. Photographers often wait weeks to capture all three elements. Southeast Alaska is rain country! Expect rain or mist at least half of the time. In much of the region, blue-sky days come only once a week, if that. The cool maritime climate brings rain in the summer, and rain and snow in winter. Most towns in Southeast get 30 inches or more of precipitation, and of the major towns, Ketchikan takes top honors with 162 inches per year. That averages out to half an inch every day of the year. The tiny fishing settlement of Port Alexander on the south end of Baranof Island drowns in 220 inches per year!

Weather patterns vary greatly in Southeast; Skagway gets just 22 inches a year, but only a few miles away, precipitation tops 160 inches annually on the peaks bordering Canada. Fortunately, the driest months are generally June through August. Recent years have seen an alternating pattern of wet and dry summers. If it's any comfort, the summer of 1991 was one of the wettest ever. Don't make any plans based on this theory, however. This isn't the *Farmer's Almanac*.

Residents learn to tolerate Southeast's rain, which they call "liquid sunshine." You won't see many umbrellas, but heavy raingear and red rubber boots are appropriate dress for almost any occasion. (Not surprisingly, the best raingear is sold around Southeast.) If you ask, locals will admit to a grudging appreciation for the rain; it not only creates the lush green countryside and provides ample streamflow for the vital salmon runs, but it also keeps the region relatively safe from overcrowding—with the drier-minded set.

The People

Southeast Alaska has only 65,000 people. Nearly half live in Juneau, with the rest spread over nearly two dozen isolated towns and settlements strung along the Inside Passage. Much of the economy is based upon fishing, logging, governing, and tourism. The towns are dependent upon the sea for their survival, not only for the fish it provides, but as a way to transport huge rafts of logs to the mills. Ninety-five percent of the goods brought to Southeast arrive by barge or ship and most of the visitors arrive aboard cruise ships or state ferries.

Southeast corresponds almost exactly to the ancestral homeland of the Tlingit (pronounced KLINK-it) Indians, and signs of their culture—both authentic and visitor-oriented—are common. Almost every town has at least one totem pole, and some have dozens! Tlingit artwork generally includes carvings, beadwork, sealskin moccasins, and silver jewelry. It doesn't include the *ulus,* Eskimo dolls, and other paraphernalia frequently sold in local tourist shops.

Accommodations

Every summer Southeast Alaska is inundated with travelers and thousands of young people looking for jobs. Accommodations are tight. Once you forsake camping and youth hostels, expect to pay a minimum of $40 s or $50 d for a stark room with shared bath. Discounts or weekly rates are hard to come by, particularly if you arrive after mid-June. An excellent option for couples is to stay at one of the many bed and breakfasts throughout Southeast. Contact the **Alaska Bed and Breakfast Association,** Box 21890, Juneau, AK 99802, tel. (907) 586-2959, for a list of places and prices. Rates start around $40 s or $50 d.

For those on a tighter budget, campgrounds are plentiful throughout Southeast, and most main towns have youth hostels. (Note, however, that most campgrounds and hostels are open only from mid-May to mid-September.) Camping is allowed anywhere in the Tongass National Forest except day-use areas, but is generally prohibited within city limits. If you have more money and are willing to spend it, some incredible places to bed down are available. These include remote lodges and resorts where the scenery is grand and the service impeccable.

ALASKA MARINE HIGHWAY

Visitors come to Southeast by three primary means: cruise ship, jet, and ferry. Cruise ships are easily the most popular method— well over 200,000 folks travel this way each year—but also the most expensive and the least personal. The smaller ships, such as those operated by **Alaska Sightseeing Tours,** tel. (800) 426-7702, offer more personal voyages that emphasize the natural world. But they're still the most expensive.

The second option, by air, is more popular with independent travelers. Both **Alaska Airlines,** tel. (800) 426-0333, and **Delta Airlines,** tel. (800) 221-1212, have daily flights into Juneau. Alaska also flies to five other towns in Southeast: Ketchikan, Wrangell, Petersburg, Sitka, and Gustavus. Float-planes connect these towns to smaller places and provide access to even the most remote corners of the Panhandle, such as Elfin Cove and Port Alexander. These flights are detailed in subsequent chapters.

Only three Southeast towns (Haines, Skagway, and Hyder) are connected by road to the rest of the continent. All the others (including Juneau, the state capital) are accessible only by boat or plane. This lack of roads (hopefully they will never be built) has led to an efficient public ferry system, the best in the Western Hemisphere and the longest in the world. Most ferries sail between Prince Rupert, B.C., and Skagway, stopping along the way in the major towns. There is also once-weekly service from Bellingham, Washington all the way to Skagway. Less popular, but more scenic, is the weekly summertime service from Hyder. In the larger towns, summer service is almost daily, but in the smallest settlements ferries may be up to two weeks apart.

History

One of the first actions of the newly created Alaska State government in 1959 was to establish a state ferry system. Originally i' consisted of just a single boat, the 100-foot-long snub-nosed *Chilkat* (no longer in ser vice), but after passage of a 1960 state bond three new ships were built: the *Matanuska, Malaspina,* and *Taku.* Over the next decade the *Tustumena, Bartlett, Le Conte,* and the flagship *Columbia* (418 feet long with a capacity of 1,000 passengers) were added to the fleet. The newest of the eight ships, the *Aurora,* was christened in 1977. Service has gradually expanded over the years so that today the only substantial Southeast town without ferry service is Gustavus—where residents don't want the influx of RVers i would bring.

The Ferry System

Southeast Alaska is served by the *Columbia, Malaspina, Matanuska, Taku, Le Conte,* and *Aurora.* The *Tustumena* and *Bartlett* operate between Southcentral Alaskan ports. The smaller vessels (*Le Conte* and *Aurora*) primarily serve the more remote villages such as Hoonah, Pelican, or Angoon. All the vessels carry vehicles and have a cafeteria, free shower facilities (except the *Bartlett*), lockers, and a cocktail lounge, but the larger ships also have private or shared dorms and

Erecting your own nylon stateroom on deck outside the solarium is a common practice on the long journey north from Bellingham up the Inside Passage.

more spacious facilities. The *Le Conte* and *Aurora* take you to quieter villages relatively untouched by the glamorizing effects of tourism. You'll be able to talk with more locals and can walk right up to the ship's prow to watch the islands slip by.

Ferries generally stop for one or two hours in the larger towns, but less than an hour in the smaller villages. Lockers are available in most of the larger ferry terminals, except Ketchikan (where bags are left in a central area). The ferry terminals are generally well stocked with local free information brochures. Most open only for ship arrivals, closing with their departure.

Life Onboard

Most young travelers and backpackers think of the ferry as a floating motel—a place to dry off, wash up, relax, sleep, and meet other travelers, while at the same time moving on to new sights and new adventures. Ferry food is reasonable (by Alaskan standards) and varies in quality from mediocre to fairly good. Many folks stock up on groceries before they board to save both money and their appetites. For a bit of entertainment, try flying a kite from the back deck. Be sure it's a cheap one, however, since you can't chase it if it gets away from you. Another popular toy is a hackey sack. And if you bring an instrument along, *you'll* provide the entertainment. Be sure to also bring earplugs if you are a light sleeper since things can get pretty noisy sometimes.

Staterooms aren't necessary since there's plenty of space to stretch out a sleeping bag in the recliner lounge (an inside area with airline-type seats), and in the solarium. The solarium—a covered and heated area high atop the ship's rear deck—has several dozen lawn chairs to sit and sleep on, making it a favorite hangout for backpackers, budget travelers, cannery workers, travel writers, and high school basketball teams. It's also a great place to make new friends of the opposite sex. It's the *in* place to sleep, providing the best views of the passing panorama and plenty of fresh air. The solarium is so popular that at some embarkation points (particularly Bellingham), there's often a mad dash up the stairs to grab a place before all the chairs are taken. When the weather is good you're also likely to see the rapid development of a tent-city on the rear deck.

Reader-adventurer Dan Bagatel writes, "The *Columbia* can be a pretty abysmal experience. During peak season, the boat is an absolute zoo: to win a solarium deck chair you need to be in line by 4 p.m. for the 9 p.m. sailing. People sleep in the aisles, under the stairs, in the Forest Service center; going to the bathroom is like running an obstacle course. The solarium roof leaks badly, and the deck chairs are in lousy shape." (For alternate routes, see Suggested Itineraries.)

Between June 1 and Labor Day (first Monday in Sept.) the *Columbia, Malaspina, Matanuska,* and *Taku* have Forest Service interpreters on board. They provide videos and slide shows, give talks, answer questions, hand out Smokey Bear pins to the kids, and generally spoon-feed Forest Service propaganda. Be sure to pick up a **"Tongass National Forest map"** ($2) from them, and take a look at their "Opportunity Guide" for up-to-date info on each town. This is a good place to ask about various Forest Service cabins in Southeast (see below).

Getting Tickets

Make ferry reservations by calling (800) 642-0066, or by writing to Alaska Marine Highway, Box 25535, Juneau, AK 99802. Since most travel in Southeast centers around the ferry schedules, it's a good idea to request a copy of the schedule before making any solid travel plans. *The Milepost* (available in bookstores or from Alaska Northwest Publishing Co., P.O. Box 3007, Bothell, WA 98041-9912) also lists the current ferry schedules and rates. Before you get ready to board, it's always a good idea to call the local ferry terminal to make sure the ferry is on schedule.

Relatively unknown outside Alaska are the substantial discounts for people over 65 or handicapped. This only applies to travel within Alaska, not between Ketchikan and Prince Rupert or Bellingham. You do not need to be from Alaska to obtain the discounts. Contact the ferry system for further details.

Although there is usually space for walk-on passengers, it's a good idea to make advance reservations for ferries out of Bellingham. Reservations are required for anyone with a vehicle, and are generally available six months in advance. If you can't get on in Bellingham, take a ferry to Victoria on Vancouver Island, a bus (or hitch) to Port Hardy, and a ferry to Prince Rupert. This will cost slightly more, but will be far more exciting. Foot passengers do not require reservations out of Prince Rupert or within Southeast (the only exception to this is during the Southeast Alaska State Fair which jams all Haines-bound ferries in mid-August). The ferry system now charges an extra fee of up to $52 (the amount varies depending upon your destination) to carry bicycles, canoes, kayaks, and inflatable boats aboard. These are listed in the schedule as "alternate means of conveyance."

A careful reading of the ferry passenger schedule may save you a few bucks, particularly if you plan to make several stops in some of the more remote destinations. For example, Bellingham-Hollis ($168), Hollis-Ketchikan ($18), and Ketchikan-Skagway ($90) totals $276, while Bellingham-Ketchikan ($154), Ketchikan-Hollis ($18), and Hollis-Skagway ($90), totals $262, a $14 savings for the same destinations.

Another way to save money is by riding the ferry during the off-season (Oct. 1-May 15) when rates drop 15-20% for passengers. During the summer, drivers of vehicles must pay for both the car and themselves, but in the off-season they only pay for the car, a total savings of almost 40%. Note also that each fall and spring the *Tustumena* makes a special run that connects Southeast Alaska with Yakutat, Seward, and other Southcentral towns (heading north in spring and south in fall). These offer the unusual opportunity to sail along some of Alaska's wildest coastlines (bring seasickness pills) for very reasonable rates: $68 from Juneau to Yakutat, or $128 from Juneau to Seward.

TONGASS NATIONAL FOREST

Three times larger than any other national forest in the country, Southeast Alaska's Tongass National Forest is America's rainforest masterpiece. Within these 16.8 million acres are magnificent coastal forests, dozens of glaciers, snowcapped peaks, an abundance of wildlife, hundreds of verdant islands, and a wild beauty that has long since been lost elsewhere. Originally named Alexander Archipelago Forest Reserve in 1902, the area became Tongass National Forest in 1907 by proclamation of President Theodore Roosevelt. It was later enlarged to include most of the Panhandle. Between the Forest and Park services, nearly 95% of Southeast is federal property.

Recreation

The Tongass is a paradise for those who love the outdoors. It has dozens of scenic hiking trails and over 1,000 miles of logging roads accessible by mountain bike (if you don't mind the clearcuts and can avoid the logging trucks and flying gravel). The islands contain hundreds of crystal-clear lakes, many with Forest Service cabins on them. Fishing enthusiasts will enjoy catching salmon and other fish from these lakes, the ocean, and the thousands of streams that empty into bays. The Inside Passage is composed of a wonderful maze of semi-protected waterways, making it a sea kayaker's dream come true. Particularly popular with kayakers are Misty Fjords National Monument, Glacier Bay National Park, and the waters around Sitka and Juneau, but outstanding sea kayaking opportunities can be found throughout Southeast. If you have a sea kayak, access is easy, since they can be carried on the ferries. Ask the Forest Service recreation staff in the local district offices for info on nearby routes and conditions.

Wilderness Areas

Less than five percent of the Tongass has been logged or otherwise developed, so it isn't necessary to visit an official wilderness area to see truly wild country. However, 21 wilderness areas total well over five million acres in the national forest, offering outstanding recreational opportunities. The largest are Misty Fjords National Monument (2.1 million acres) near Ketchikan, and Admiralty Island National Monument (956,000 acres) near Juneau. Other major wildernesses include Tracy Arm-Ford's Terror (653,000 acres) south of Juneau, Stikine-Le Conte (449,000 acres) near Wrangell, Russell Fjord (349,000 acres) near Yakutat, South Baranof (320,000 acres) south of Sitka, and West Chichagof-Yakobi (265,000 acres) near Pelican. Six new wilderness areas (totalling over 300,000 additional acres) were created when

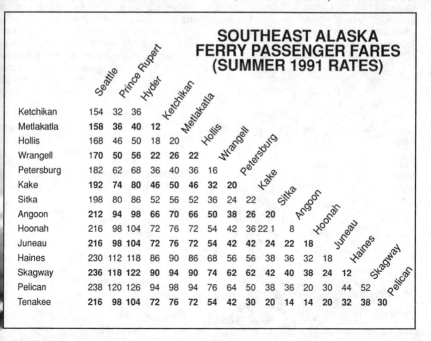

SOUTHEAST ALASKA FERRY PASSENGER FARES (SUMMER 1991 RATES)

From	Seattle	Prince Rupert	Hyder	Ketchikan	Metlakatla	Hollis	Wrangell	Petersburg	Kake	Sitka	Angoon	Hoonah	Juneau	Haines	Skagway	Pelican
Ketchikan	154	32	36													
Metlakatla	158	36	40	12												
Hollis	168	46	50	18	20											
Wrangell	170	50	56	22	26	22										
Petersburg	182	62	68	36	40	36	16									
Kake	192	74	80	46	50	46	32	20								
Sitka	198	80	86	52	56	52	36	24	22							
Angoon	212	94	98	66	70	66	50	38	26	20						
Hoonah	216	98	104	72	76	72	54	42	36	22	1	8				
Juneau	216	98	104	72	76	72	54	42	42	24	22	18				
Haines	230	112	118	86	90	86	68	56	56	38	36	32	18			
Skagway	236	118	122	90	94	90	74	62	62	42	40	38	24	12		
Pelican	238	120	126	94	98	94	76	64	50	38	36	20	30	44	52	
Tenakee	216	98	104	72	76	72	54	42	30	20	14	14	20	32	38	30

Congress passed the Tongass Timber Reform Act of 1990.

Several wilderness areas, such as the remote islands off the west coast of Prince of Wales (Coronation, Maurelle, and Warren islands), are exposed to the open ocean and are inaccessible for much of the year, even by floatplane. Others, such as the Stikine-Le Conte, Admiralty Island, Russell Fjord, and Petersburg Creek-Duncan Salt Chuck wilderness areas are relatively accessible. There are developed trails or canoe/kayak routes within Misty Fjords, Admiralty Island, Stikine-Le Conte, Tebenkof Bay, and Petersburg Creek-Duncan Salt Chuck wilderness areas. See subsequent chapters for specific information.

Forest Service Cabins

Tongass National Forest has close to 200 public recreation cabins located throughout Southeast. Most of these are one-room Pan-Adobe cabins 12 by 14 feet in size with bunk space for four to six people. The rustic cabins generally have a woodstove with cut firewood (some have oil stoves), an outhouse,

and rowboats (at cabins along lakes). You'll need to bring your own bedding, cooking utensils, food, and mousetraps. Many of the cabins can only be reached by floatplane. These flights can be very expensive, averaging approximately $230/hour in a Cessna 185 (two people and gear) or $350/hour in a Beaver (five people and gear), but even those on a tight budget should plan to spend some time at one of these cabins. A few can be reached by hiking from town (in Ketchikan, Petersburg, and Juneau), cutting out the expensive flight. If you're considering a flight-seeing trip anyway, make it a trip to one of these remote cabins where you get to see what the country is really like. This is one splurge you won't regret.

Cabin reservations can be made in person at any ranger district office (Ketchikan/Misty Fjords, Thorne Bay, Craig, Wrangell, Petersburg, Sitka, Hoonah, Juneau/Admiralty Island, or Yakutat), or by writing to one of the area offices listed below. The Forest Service charges $20 per night for the cabins, with all fees going toward the maintenance of these facilities. They are reserved on a first-come, first-served basis up to six months in advance. Some of the most popular cabins are even chosen by lottery. The area offices publish brochures describing nearby recreation facilities and can also supply Tongass National Forest maps ($2) that show the locations of all Forest Service cabins. Write to:

Forest Supervisor-Ketchikan Area
Tongass National Forest
Federal Building
Ketchikan, AK 99901
tel. (907) 225-3101

Forest Supervisor-Stikine Area
Tongass National Forest
P.O. Box 309
Petersburg, AK 99833
tel. (907) 772-3841

Forest Supervisor-Chatham Area
Tongass National Forest
204 Siginaka Way
Sitka, AK 99835
tel. (907) 747-6671

(GORDY OHLIGER)

KETCHIKAN

After the 40-hour ferry ride up from Bellingham, Ketchikan is most first-timers' introduction to Alaska. Along the way they've heard tales from sourdoughs (and those who claim to be), talked to Forest Service naturalists, and watched the logging towns and lush green islands of British Columbia float past. As the ferry pulls into Tongass Narrows an air of expectancy grows among the newcomers, who are about to take their first steps in Alaska. The state's fifth largest town (pop. 7,700), Ketchikan bills itself as "Alaska's First City," and even its zip code (99901) seems to bear this out. Many ferry passengers don't bother to stop here, instead hurrying on toward Juneau and points north. Because downtown is two miles away, they only have time for a superficial bus tour or a walk to the grocery stores for provisions. But with its great scenery, fine local trails, unusual museums, the world's largest collection of totem poles, a bustling downtown, and famous

Misty Fjords nearby, Ketchikan deserves a longer stay.

The Setting

Located 90 miles north of Prince Rupert, Ketchikan clings to a steep slope along Tongass Narrows, on Revillagigedo (ruh-vee-ya-he-HAY-do) Island; locals shorten the name to "Revilla." Fortunately, it doesn't bear the one-time Viceroy of Mexico's full name: Don Juan Vicente de Guemes Pacheco de Pedilla y Horcasitas, Count of Revilla Gigedo! The town is "three miles long and three blocks wide," with a continuous strip along the waterfront from the ferry terminal to beyond Thomas Basin. Because of this, Tongass Avenue—the only through street—is one of the busiest in the entire state. Be ready for traffic jams.

Much of Ketchikan is built on fill, on pilings over the water, or on hillsides with steep winding ramps for streets. Fishing boats jam

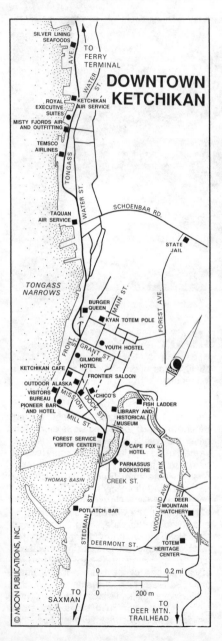

DOWNTOWN KETCHIKAN

SILVER LINING SEAFOODS

TO FERRY TERMINAL

ROYAL EXECUTIVE SUITES

KETCHIKAN AIR SERVICE

MISTY FJORDS AIR AND OUTFITTING

TEMSCO AIRLINES

WATER ST.

TONGASS AVE.

TAQUAN AIR SERVICE

SCHOENBAR RD.

STATE JAIL

TONGASS NARROWS

BURGER QUEEN

MAIN ST.

KYAN TOTEM POLE

FOREST AVE.

FRONT ST.

GRANT ST.

YOUTH HOSTEL

GILMORE HOTEL

KETCHIKAN CAFE

FRONTIER SALOON

OUTDOOR ALASKA

MISSION ST.

VISITORS BUREAU

CHICO'S

PIONEER BAR AND HOTEL

DOCK ST.

FISH LADDER

MILL ST.

LIBRARY AND HISTORICAL MUSEUM

FOREST SERVICE VISITOR CENTER

CAPE FOX HOTEL

PARNASSUS BOOKSTORE

THOMAS BASIN

CREEK ST.

POTLATCH BAR

STEDMAN ST.

PARK AVE.

WOODLAND AVE.

DEER MOUNTAIN HATCHERY

DEERMONT ST.

TOTEM HERITAGE CENTER

0   0.2 mi

0   200 m

TO SAXMAN

TO DEER MTN. TRAILHEAD

© MOON PUBLICATIONS, INC.

the three boat harbors (there are almost as many boats as cars in Ketchikan), and the two canneries and two cold-storage plants run at full throttle during the summer. Float-planes seem to take off constantly from the narrows. At the large pulp mill five miles north, spruce and hemlock are processed and shipped all over the world for the production of rayon and cellophane. The pulp is even used in sandwich spreads and ice cream, so beware when you hear of a new high-fiber food product!

Ketchikan is one of the rainiest places in Alaska, with more than 13 feet a year. Luckily, May to August are the driest months, but expect to get wet. Locals adapt with "Ketchikan sneakers" (red rubber boots) and Helley Hanson raingear; umbrellas are a sure sign of a tourist. Residents pride themselves on almost never cancelling baseball games, and enjoy weekend picnics at Ward Lake in a downpour. Weather predicting is easy in Ketchikan: if you can't see the top of Deer Mountain, it's raining; if you can, it's *going to* rain.

History

The name Ketchikan comes from *Kitcxan,* A Tlingit word meaning "Where the Eagles' Wings Are," a reference to the shape of a sandspit at the creek mouth. The sandspit was dredged in the 1930s to create Thomas Basin Boat Harbor. Rumor has it that several bodies were found then, and suspicious fingers were pointed toward the denizens of nearby Creek Street, the local red-light district. One of Southeast Alaska's youngest major towns, Ketchikan began with the construction of the first of many salmon canneries at the mouth of Ketchikan Creek in 1885. By the 1930s it had become the "Salmon Capital of the World" (13 canneries), and Alaska's largest town. Overfishing caused salmon populations to crash in the 1940s, and the fishing industry was supplanted in the 1950s by a new pulp mill that made the town a major logging center. More recently, fishing has rebounded due to strict fishing controls and increased hatchery production. Tourism has also become increasingly important in the past decade, and cruise ships deliver hordes of people onto downtown Ketchikan each summer day.

SIGHTS

Creek Street

Ketchikan's best-known and most-photographed section has wooden houses on pilings along Ketchikan Creek. A boardwalk connects the buildings, and affords views of salmon and steelhead in the creek. Now a chain of tourist shops, Creek Street once housed the red-light district, during Prohibition the only place to buy booze. Local jokesters call it "the only place where both salmon and men came up from the sea to spawn." By 1946 more than 30 "female boarding houses" operated here. Prostitution on Creek Street was stopped in 1954, and the house of **Dolly Arthur** was eventually turned into a small museum ($2). Inside are antiques, secret liquor caches, and risqué colors. It's open only when cruise ships are in port, and it's fun to tour the museum with the grandmothers. A new **cable car** now connects Creek Street with the luxurious Westmark Cape Fox Lodge, where you'll discover impressive vistas over Ketchikan and Tongass Narrows.

Downtown

The small **Tongass Historical Museum** at 629 Dock St. (the library building), tel. 225-5600, is open Sun. 1-5, Mon.-Sat. 8:30-5 in the summer, and Wed.-Fri. 1-5, and Sat. and Sun. 1-4 in the winter. Admission is $1; free on Sunday. The museum contains local historical items plus permanent exhibits on Native culture and the commercial fishing industry. Outside the museum/library is **Raven Stealing the Sun Totem**, and not far away stands the newly re-carved **Chief Johnson Pole.**

Check out some of Ketchikan's many long aerobic **stairways** up to hillside homes and outstanding vistas. The best ones start from the tunnel at Front and Grant streets, and directly behind the **Chief Kyan Totem Pole** at Main and Pine streets. Legend has it that those who touch this totem will come into money within a day—it's worth a try. If you

have a bike (or better yet a skateboard), you may want to test your mettle on Schoenbar Rd., the route blasted out of a very steep hillside behind town.

Get to picturesque **Thomas Basin Boat Harbor** (on the south end of town) by turning right on Thomas St. just beyond the Salvation Army building. While there, head to the **Potlatch Bar** for a game of pool or a beer with local fishermen. Farther down Stedman St. notice the colorful mural, *Return of the Eagle* (1978) at Ketchikan Community College. It was painted by Ray Troll. For more artwork, head to the gallery at the **Ketchikan Area Arts Council,** 338 Main St., tel. 225-2211. "Wearable art" is on sale here too.

Totem Heritage Center

One of the highlights of the Ketchikan area, the Totem Heritage Center, tel. 225-5900, is a quarter-mile walk up Deermount Street. It's open Sun. 9-5, Mon.-Sat. 8-5 (Tues.-Fri. 1-5 in winter), admission $2 (free on Sunday). The center was established in 1976 to preserve a collection of 33 original totem poles and house posts retrieved from abandoned village sites. Unlike other totems in the area, these works are not brightly painted copies or restorations, but were instead carved more than a century ago to record Tlingit and Haida events and legends. Guides answer your questions and put on a short video about the totem recovery program. During the winter, the center has special classes in carving, basketry, beading, and other Native crafts. Surrounding the building is a short trail with signs identifying local plants. Out front is the Raven-Woman pole, crafted by noted carver Nathan Jackson.

Hatchery

Just across a footbridge from the Totem Heritage Center is Deer Mountain Hatchery on Ketchikan Creek. Signboards explain and illustrate the process of breeding and rearing king and coho salmon. Kings arrive from the Pacific Ocean to spawn at the hatchery late in the summer; look for them in the creek. A fish ladder to help them get past the falls is visible from the Park Ave. bridge. If too many fish return to spawn, the state opens Ketchi-

Saxman Totem Pole

kan Creek to dipnet fishing by locals, creating a rather astounding scene. Thousands of pink (humpback) salmon also spawn in the creek. Another good place to see salmon is Hoadly Creek, a half mile south of the ferry terminal.

Totem Bight
Totem Bight State Historical Park, eight miles northwest of the ferry terminal (free), has 15 Haida and Tlingit totems, plus a realistic replica of a clan house complete with a brightly painted facade and cedar-scented interior. Be sure to pick up the fine brochure describing the poles and their meaning. The totems, carved from 1938 to 1941, are replicas of older poles. They are surrounded by a stand of young hemlock trees and a view across Tongass Narrows. Although hundreds of tour buses come here each summer, no city bus-

es reach Totem Bight, so you'll have to walk or hitch here unless you have wheels.

Saxman
This Native village (ironically named for a white schoolteacher) is a 2½-mile walk or hitch south of Ketchikan. Saxman is crowded with the largest collection of standing totem poles in the world—more than two dozen. Most were brought from their original sites in the 1930s and restored by Native CCC workers; others came from a second restoration project in 1982. The oddest pole is topped with a figure of Abraham Lincoln in commemoration of the settlement of a war begun by the U.S. revenue cutter *Lincoln*. Probably the most photographed is the Rock Oyster Pole, which tells the story of a man who drowned after his hand became caught in an oyster. Two aging and unrestored totems are the Eagle Tree and Halibut poles at the abandoned Chief Kahshakes house nearby.

Saxman (pop. 300) has recently thrown itself into the tourism maelstrom with the completion of a cedar Beaver Clan House (first clan house built in Alaska in 50 years), a pleasant gift shop selling quality Native handicrafts, and a **carving shed** for totems, masks, and other woodworking. The carving shed (free; open Mon.-Fri. 9-4) is a must-see, especially when master carver Nathan Jackson is at work. Tours of Saxman ($20; mainly for the cruise-ship crowd) include performances in the clan house by the Cape Fox Dancers. Get tickets at the gift shop.

TRAILS AND CABINS

Deer Mountain
The best hike from Ketchikan is up to the 3,000-foot summit of Deer Mountain (six miles and a minimum of three hours RT). Begin by following the Ketchikan Lakes Rd. a half mile up toward the city dump from Deermount and Fair streets. The dump is a good place to watch for ravens, crows, eagles, black bears, and garbage trucks. Note that there are no brown bears on Revilla Island. Take the first left—the road to Ketchikan Lakes, source of the town's drinking

water—and then an immediate right. The trail starts from a small parking lot and climbs along an excellent but strenuous path through dense Sitka spruce and western hemlock forests. There's an incredible view in all directions from the top of Deer Mountain, but right into July you'll have to cross snowbanks to reach the summit. (Raingear works great for sledding down again.)

Just before the final climb to the peak, a trail to the left leads around the north slope and on to **Blue Lake** and **John Mountain** (3,238 feet). Entirely above the timberline, this portion can be hazardous for inexperienced hikers. Carry a map and compass since it's easy to become disoriented if the clouds drop down. A Forest Service A-frame **cabin** ($20) is at Deer Mountain below the north slope a half mile beyond the fork; space for eight hikers. No stove, but the cabin is well insulated. Make reservations at the Forest Service office in Ketchikan. You can also find places to camp near the summit of Deer Mountain and at Blue Lake.

Another 1½ mile beyond Blue Lake is a steep drop-off that requires careful climbing. After this, the trail continues to John Mountain and then down to Lower Silvis Lake where it meets a gravel road. Follow this road the final two miles to the Beaver Falls Powerplant and a Fish and Game salmon hatchery (ask to take a look inside). With luck you can hitch the 13 miles back to town from here. Total trail length is 11½ miles. If you do the trek in the opposite direction, you'll need to sign the log book next to the hatchery and then go past a gate labelled "Extreme Danger, Construction Area, High Voltage, Keep Out."

Ward Lake Area
Two good trails are near the Forest Service campground at Ward Lake. The 1½-mile **Ward Lake Nature Trail** is an easy loop with interpretive signs and good steelhead and salmon fishing. **Perseverance Lake Trail** begins on the right side just before Three-C's Campground. Park on the left side of the road. The two-mile climb follows a "Stairway-to-Heaven" boardwalk, passing through several muskegs along the way. Unfortu-

nately, the interesting trail ends in a quagmire at Perseverance Lake, so don't plan on camping there. To get an idea of how the Saxman-based Cape Fox Native Corporation is mismanaging its lands, head another four miles up the road beyond Ward Lake. This unbelievably huge clearcut is so bad that even the Forest Service makes it a point to put up boundary signs saying "Entering Private Land." Unfortunately, this sort of operation is typical of Native corporations in Alaska.

Naha River
The Naha River watershed, 20 miles north of Ketchikan, contains one of the finest trail and cabin systems in Southeast. The river once supported astounding runs of sockeye salmon and is still a popular salmon, steelhead, and trout fishing area for locals. At one time the town of Loring (established 1888) at its mouth had the world's largest fish cannery and was the main point of entry into Alaska. Today, it's a tiny settlement of vacation homes and retirees. **Heckman Lake,** six miles upriver, had the world's largest and most costly salmon hatchery at the turn of the century. The hatchery failed, however, and all that remains are the overgrown ruins. The pleasant 5½-mile **Naha River Trail** begins at Naha Bay, follows the shore of Roosevelt Lagoon, and then climbs gently up to Jordon and Heckman lakes. Both lakes have Forest Service cabins ($20) with rowboats. Approximately half the trail is boardwalk. At the mouth of Roosevelt Lagoon is an interesting salt chuck where the direction of water flow changes with the tides. Covered picnic tables are nearby. More picnic tables are two miles up the trail at a small waterfall, a good place to watch black bears catching salmon late in the summer. Access to the Naha area is either by sea kayak, by floatplane (approximately $230 RT), or by having someone drop you off in a skiff (approx. $120 RT through charters from Knudsen Cove Marina, tel. 225-8500).

Other Cabins
Lake Shelokum, 40 miles north of Ketchikan, has a free shelter near a hot springs. A

two-mile trail stretches from the shelter to Bailey Bay, passing the scenic lake and a very impressive waterfall. Be prepared for lots of mosquitos. Access is expensive, approximately $450 RT for a Cessna 185 with space for two people and gear. Ketchikan Ranger District has many other cabins worth visiting. My favorites include Lake McDonald, Reflection Lake, Helm Creek, and Blind Pass. Contact the district office for details.

PRACTICALITIES

Accommodations

The **Ketchikan Youth Hostel,** downtown in the basement of the Methodist church at Grant and Main, tel. 225-3319, costs $4 for members and $7 for nonmembers. Open 6 p.m. to 8:30 a.m., doors are locked at 11 p.m.; if your ferry gets in after that, call the hostel and they'll open them. The hostel,

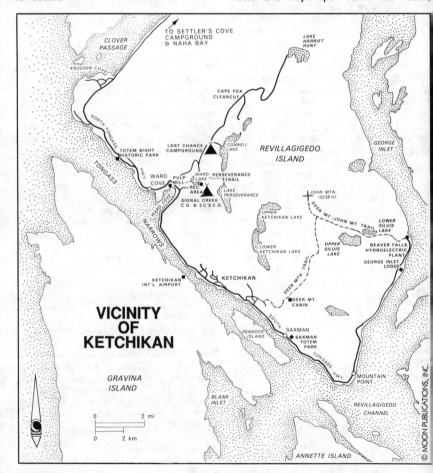

VICINITY OF KETCHIKAN

open from Memorial to Labor days, is nothing fancy—we're talking mattresses on the floor—but is very friendly, with free coffee, kitchen facilities, and showers. It's a good place to meet other travelers. There is a four-night maximum stay.

One step up from the hostel in facilities and a giant leap in price is **Rain Forest Inn,** 2311 Hemlock St. (just up the hill from Sea Mart), tel. 225-9500. The crowded dorms are $21 pp; space for 14 men and two women, a reflection of Alaska's skewed demographics! Private rooms are $45 s or d. During mid-summer, spaces may not be available so you should reserve in advance. The inn has a TV, kitchen facilities, no curfew, and lots of chain-smokers. No alcohol allowed.

Ketchikan Bed and Breakfast, Box 3213, Ketchikan, AK 99901, tel. 225-8550, lists a variety of local homes starting for $50 s and $60 d. This is a great way to get an insider's view of life in Ketchikan. The newest (and most elaborate) digs in Ketchikan can be found at **Westmark Cape Fox Lodge,** accessible by a free cable car from Creek Street.

If you're on a very tight budget and need a place for a week or more, you might try **Union Rooms Hotel,** 319 Mill St., tel. 225-3580. Built in 1906, this isn't the fanciest place around, but only charges $100 s or $190 d for a week's lodging. Take a look at the rooms before putting down any money. The other boarding houses in Ketchikan tend even further toward the unlivable end of the spectrum.

Camping

There are no campsites in town, but in a pinch folks have been known to camp in the small city park a few blocks uphill and directly across from the ferry terminal. Don't leave a tent up during the day if you try this.

The Forest Service operates three excellent campgrounds in the scenic Ward Lake area. All cost $5/night and have running water, outhouses, and picnic tables. Hitching from town is relatively easy. Head five miles north from the ferry terminal and turn right just before the pulp mill at Ward Creek Road. Ward Cove is a good place to see eagles and salmon, so stop for a look before heading up to the lake. The first and most popular camping area is **Signal Creek Campground,** three-quarters of a mile up the road, and along the shore of Ward Lake. A quarter mile farther is the tiny **Three-C's Campground.** During the winter this is the only one open. Another 1½ miles is **Last Chance Campground,** used as an overflow during the peak season. Note that when the wind is blowing the wrong way these campgrounds are occasionally inundated with pungent smoke from the pulp mill.

Settler's Cove State Park, 16 miles north of the ferry, charges $7 for campsites, but is primarily used by RVers. The beach here is a popular picnic spot. While at Settler's Cove, be sure to hike the 100-yard trail that ends at a platform overlooking an impressive falls. The creek is a good place to watch pink salmon spawn.

There are two private RV parking lots in the Ketchikan area: **Clover Pass Resort,** 15 miles north of town, tel. 247-2234, and **Ketchikan RV Park,** next to Sea Mart, tel. 225-6166.

Food

Although not renowned for its food, Ketchikan has a number of places worth a visit. Start the morning with the locals at **Ketchikan Cafe,** 314 Front St., where the grub is reasonable and well prepared. Try French toast for breakfast or a Reuben (on homemade bread) for lunch. **Latitude 56** at 2050 Sea Level Dr. next to the bowling alley has good buffet breakfasts. On Sundays 9-2, the **VFW Hall** at 311 Tongass (one-half mile south of the ferry) serves up filling all-American breakfasts. If you just want to relax and enjoy looking over busy Tongass Narrows, stop by **Coffee Connections,** 521 Water St., for a cup of espresso or a pastry. **Five Star Cafe,** on Creek St., serves fresh sandwiches, soups, and coffees in what was once a bawdy house. **June's Cafe,** also on Creek St., has overpriced and not particularly notable food, but you should go there anyway just for the experience. Trust me. The best local burgers are at **Burger Queen**—a small truck parked next to the tunnel on Front Street.

KETCHIKAN ACCOMMODATIONS

Name	Address	Phone	Rates	Features
Ketchikan Youth Hostel	Grant and Main	225-3319	$4-7 pp	hostel facility
Rain Forest Inn	2311 Hemlock St.	225-9500	$21 pp	crowded dorms
Main St. B&B	Box 7473	225-8484	$50 s, $60 d	full breakfast
Bowey's B&B	2021 1st Ave.	225-3494	$50 s, $60 d	summer only
North Tongass B&B	Ward Cove	225-2467	$50 s $70 d	various homes
Alaskan Home Fishing B&B	12 miles north	225-6919 (800) 876-0925	$55+ s $75+ d	courtesy van spa
Gilmore Hotel	326 Front St.	225-9423	$58+ s or d	courtesy van
The Landing (Best Western)	3434 Tongass	225-5166	$62 s $66 d	AAA approved courtesy van
Pioneer Hotel	118 Front St.	225-2336	$65 s or d	bath down hall
Royal Executive Suites	1471 Tongass	225-1900	$75+ s or d	
Super 8 Motel	2151 Sea Level	225-9088 (800) 843-1991	$76 s $81 d	courtesy van
Ingersoll Hotel	303 Mission St.	225-2124	$76 s $86 d	AAA approved continental b'fast courtesy van small rooms
Island Cottages	350 Bawden St.	225-2800	$84 s or d	includes kitchen
Salmon Falls Resort	17 miles north	225-2752 (800) 247-9059	$109 s $139 d	elaborate resort
Westmark Cape Fox Lodge	800 Venetia Way	225-8001 (800) 544-0970	$102 s $112 d	AAA approved courtesy van, cable car

McDonald's is in the shopping mall, three-quarters of a mile south of the ferry.

Jeremiah's is directly across from the ferry terminal and upstairs from **The Landing Restaurant**—a popular breakfast place. Jeremiah's has a Thursday night all-you-can-eat Mexican buffet that's worth a look. For more authentic Mexican food, head to **Chi-co's,** 435 Dock Street. Chico's also serves pizza, as does **Harbor Lights,** 2131 Tongass. The latter has a great selection of beers at decent prices and a fine view of Bar Harbor. **Cape Fox Westmark,** 800 Venetia Way, tel. 225-8001, serves outstanding seafood and steak dinners with huge portions, but the prices match the quality. To splurge on a weekend dinner, make reservations at **George Inlet Lodge,** 12 miles south of town, tel. 225-6077. For $20 you get a great filling dinner served family-style in an old float house decorated like a logging camp. The setting and view are authentically Alaskan; loons call from the inlet most evenings. After dinner, sit back and enjoy accordion music performed by the owner.

Groceries And Fresh Seafood

The closest store to the ferry (one-quarter mile north) is **Super Valu Foods,** open 24 hours. **Sea Mart,** three-quarters of a mile south of the ferry, has a salad bar for $3/pound and the best selection of groceries in town. Prices are a bit lower at **Market Foods,** a few hundred feet closer to the ferry. **Silver Lining Seafoods,** 1705 Tongass, has the finest local seafood (both fresh and smoked), but be ready for sky-high prices. For a fee, Silver Lining will also smoke, freeze, or can fish that you bring in. They also have the complete collection of local artist Ray Troll's wonderfully wacky posters, cards, and T-shirts.

Entertainment

With a 5 a.m. closing time for many of its bars, lots of free-spending fishermen, and no cover charges, Ketchikan is known as something of a party town. The live music scene changes each year, but something is always happening downtown. Just follow your ears. For starters check the rowdy **Bank Shot Tavern,** 127 Main St., tel. 225-1938, for rock and roll. There are pool tourneys on Monday nights, and the upper deck is a good place to check out the action on the big dance floor below. The **Pioneer Bar,** 122 Front St., tel. 225-3210, often has a country band rolling through the tunes. If Dave Rubin and his rockin' Potlatch Band are playing at the **Potlatch Bar** next to Thomas Basin, tel. 225-4855, beat tracks in that direction. You won't regret it, but you may have a hard time finding space to breathe.

Jeremiah's, across from the ferry, tel. 225-6530, has mellow rock tunes five nights a week. It's a nice place to get romantic. Another quiet and classy place is **Charley's,** 208 Front St., tel. 225-5090. Dance to golden oldies here on weekends. The finest bar views are from the **Cape Fox Westmark,** overlooking town above Creek Street. The **Arctic Bar** near the tunnel, tel. 225-4709, has a pleasant patio hanging over Tongass Narrows, and attracts the biker/fisherman crowd. Surprise your friends back home with one of their risqué baseball caps. For a bit more spice, head to the **Marine Bar,** 740 Water St., the local strip joint.

During the summer, a local theatre group, First City Players, tel. 225-4792, puts on two lighthearted melodramas. **"Frontier Follies"** runs daily, while **"Fish Pirate's Daughter"** plays on Fridays. Both cost $6 pp, and are performed at 338 Main Street. During the fall and winter, the First City Players produce more serious stuff.

Services

Showers are available at **Highliner Laundromat,** 2703 Tongass Ave., ($2) or **The Mat,** 989 Stedman St. ($2.50). A better option is to head up Madison St. to the high school **swimming pool,** tel. 225-2010, where a swim, sauna, and shower cost $2-4.50. **Ketchikan Job Service,** 2030 Sea Level Dr., tel. 225-3181, lists cannery jobs, crew positions on boats, logging work, tourism jobs, and much more. Fishermen tend to hang out at the Potlatch Bar or Arctic Bar, or you might try checking local bulletin boards on the public docks. The **Seamen's Center,** 423 Mission St., tel. 225-6003, is a great place to go if you live on the sea. There's a TV room, showers, washers and dryer, plus a library. Those looking for work on a boat might try talking to folks here. **Mountain Point,** 5½ miles south of Ketchikan, is a good spot to try your luck at salmon fishing from the shore. The **Phone Connection,** 636 Dock St., has inside booths where you can call home at a discount. Locals do much of their shopping at **Plaza Portwest Mall,** centering around Sea Mart and McDonald's, with a couple dozen other shops.

Seacops

This Ketchikan-based nonprofit organization works to publicize the destruction caused by illegal Taiwanese, Korean, and Japanese fleets on the high seas. Totaling nearly 1,000 large boats, these pirates claim to be fishing for squid, with each vessel setting nets that may reach for 60 miles every night. The drift-nets (illegal in the U.S. and Canada) destroy everything in their path, including tens of thousands of marine mammals and perhaps 800,000 seabirds each year. Until recently, the U.S. government has taken almost no action against the Asian "squid" boats, even though there is strong evidence that perhaps 22 million immature salmon and steelhead are being illegally caught and sold each year. As a result, Alaskan and Canadian fisheries have seen dramatic declines in recent years. You can join Seacops to help halt this pillage for $25/year. Write (or visit) them at 700 Water St., Ketchikan, AK 99901.

Information

The **Ketchikan Visitors Bureau** is right on the downtown dock at 141 Front St., tel. 225-6166. It's open daily in summer 8-5 (and later when cruise ships are docked). Their free map of Ketchikan includes a good walking tour of local sites. Pick up a copy of the free *Ketchikan Guide* here, published annually. In the Federal Building, corner of Mill and Stedman streets, is the **Forest Service Visitor Center,** tel. 225-3101, with a few displays on Tongass National Forest. It's open Mon.-Fri. 7:30-4:30. Pick up a Tongass map ($2) and make Forest Service cabin reservations here for the Ketchikan area (including Prince of Wales and Misty Fjords). The **Forest Service offices** for Ketchikan and Misty Fjords ranger districts (open Mon.-Fri. 8-5) are a half mile south of the ferry at 3031 Tongass, tel. 225-2148. Be sure to talk to the staff there if you're planning a hiking or kayaking trip into the surrounding country. An elaborate new Southeast Alaska Public Lands Information Center is under construction downtown, and should open in 1993.

Books

Ketchikan's **public library**, 629 Dock St., tel. 225-3331, is open Mon. and Wed. 10-8, Tues., Thurs., and Fri. 10-6, and Sat. noon-5 (closed Sunday). Inside, find an excellent collection of Alaskana. An afternoon of reading at the tables along the big windows overlooking Ketchikan Creek is a pleasant alternative to soaking in the rain. You can also watch videos on a TV (with headphones). A book-lover's bookstore, **Parnassus Bookstore and Coffeehouse,** is upstairs next to Dolly's House on Creek Street. Sit down to talk with the friendly owner, Lillian Ference, about the latest Ketchikan news, while sipping a cappuccino. Two other good bookstores in town are the **Voyageur Bookstore,** 405 Dock St., and **Waldenbooks** in Plaza Portwest Mall.

Events

Ketchikan's 4th of July boasts the usual parade and fireworks, plus a **Timber Carnival** held at the ball field (corner of Fair St. and Schoenbar Rd.). Events include axe throwing, pole climbing, and a variety of chainsaw contests, ending with a dramatic pole-felling event. In mid-August, check out the **Blueberry Festival,** complete with slug races, pie-eating contests, art and craft exhibitions, and folk music. Ketchikan also has two king salmon derbies and a halibut derby each summer. **Festival of the North** arrives in February, complete with music, art shows, and various workshops.

TRANSPORTATION

Ferry

The ferry terminal (tel. 225-6182, or 225-6181 for recorded info) is two miles northwest of downtown. During the summer, the ferries provide weekly service to Hyder and almost daily runs to Prince Rupert, Hollis, Metla-katla, Wrangell, and points north. Ferry service to Bellingham is twice weekly. There are no coin lockers in the ferry terminal, but you can leave bags at a central storage area inside. The terminal is open Mon-Fri. 9-4:30, and when ships are in port.

Buses And Tours

The **city bus** ($1) runs from the ferry terminal to town every half hour Mon.-Sat. 6:45 a.m.-6:45 p.m. In town, catch it at the library or near the tunnel at Front and Grant streets.

Cab fare from **Alaska Cab Co.,** tel. 225-2133, or **Sourdough Cab,** tel. 225-5544, is about $7 from the ferry to downtown or $42 per hour (up to five people). It's usually quite easy to hitch in Ketchikan. Because Ketchikan's sights are so spread out, renting a car is a good idea if you're able to get several folks together on the deal. **Alaska Car Rental,** 2828 Tongass, tel. 225-5000 or (800) 478-0007 (in Alaska), charges $35/day with 100 free miles. **Avis,** at the airport, tel. 225-4515 or (800) 331-1212, costs $44/day and up, with 100 free miles.

Local tour buses meet most ferries and provide 1½-hour city tours for $18. **Orca Tours** (the folks with the fin-topped buses) are the most aggressive and least expensive of the lot, but get decidedly mixed reports from travelers. **North Wind Expeditions,** tel. 225-4751, offers a 2½-hour tour that includes a short rainforest walk and a visit to Saxman for $29 pp. The **Airporter Bus,** tel. 225-5429, provides 90-minute Fishing Industry Tours ($22 pp) that include a stroll through the Silver Lining Seafood processing plant. Tours of the Ketchikan Pulp Mill are also available locally, but you aren't likely to hear about who dumped toxic chemicals in Ward Cove in front of the plant, or why the trees are dying behind the mill.

By Air

Ketchikan Airport is on Gravina Island, directly across Tongass Narrows from the ferry terminal. The airport ferry, $2 RT, operates every 15 minutes Sun. 6:45 a.m.-9:45 p.m. and Mon.-Sat. 5:45 a.m.-8:45 p.m. The **Airporter Bus,** tel. 225-5429, has shuttle service into town from the airport for an exorbitant $11 each way.

Alaska Airlines, tel. (800) 426-0333, has flights from Ketchikan to Juneau ($122), Petersburg ($97), Sitka ($122), Wrangell ($97), and other cities in Alaska and the Lower 48. **Taquan Air Service,** 1007 Water St., tel. 225-9668 or (800) 478-0668, flies daily to Craig/Klawock ($72), Hollis ($44), Kasaan, ($40), Metlakatla ($22), and Thorne Bay ($45). **Ketchikan Air Service,** 1427 Tongass Ave., tel. 225-6600, has daily scheduled service to Craig/Klawock ($72 from the airport),

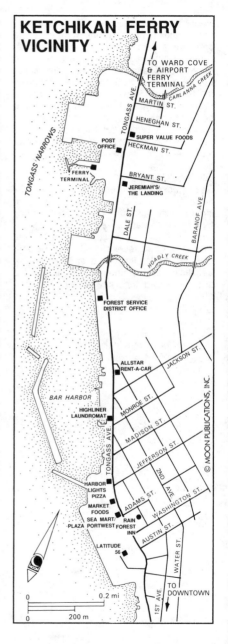

Hollis ($49), Petersburg ($99), Thorne Bay ($44), and Wrangell ($87). Both of these companies also fly to the many logging camps, fishing villages, and resorts on Prince of Wales. These companies, plus **Misty Fjords Air and Outfitting,** 1285 Tongass, tel. 225-5155, all have flightseeing trips to Misty Fjords (see below) and offer air-taxi service to nearby Forest Service cabins. Expect to pay around $250/hour for a Cessna 185 (two people with gear), or $375/hour for a Beaver (up to five people with gear).

On The Water

Geoff Gross of **Southeast Exposure,** 507 Stedman St., tel. 225-8829, offers sea kayaking instruction ($20 for 1½ hours), plus day trips to nearby areas, starting at $50 for a three-hour tour of Tongass Narrows. Rent single fiberglass kayaks for $35/day and doubles for $45/day (less for over three days or for plastic kayaks). Southeast Exposure also does extended trips into Misty Fjord (see below) and to the Barrier Islands along the south end of Prince of Wales. The latter cost $1150 pp for a 10-day expedition (including transportation and supplies).

The best local on-the-water deal is through the **City Parks and Recreation Dept.,** 344 Front St., tel. 228-6650. They rent fully equipped canoes for only $10/day ($4 for additional days) and also offer special sea kayaking classes. During winter, you can rent cross-country skis and snowshoes from them for $10/day. Basketballs and other sports equipment can also be rented at any time. **Knudsen Cove Marina,** tel. 247-8500, 13 miles north of town, and **Salmon Falls Resort,** 15 miles north of town, tel. 225-2752, both rent skiffs for around $70/day. Charter fishing is available from many different outfitters; see the visitor center for their brochures. One of the better operations is **Danika Sailing,** tel. 225-1965, with guided sailing trips aboard a 43-foot yacht for $100 pp/day.

VICINITY OF KETCHIKAN

MISTY FJORDS NATIONAL MONUMENT

The 3,600-square-mile Misty Fjords National Monument is the largest national forest wilderness in the U.S., covering the east side of Revillagigedo Island, the adjacent mainland all the way to the Canadian border, and the long narrow Behm Canal that separates the two. Misty contains a diversity of spectacular scenery—glaciers, rainforests, narrow fjords, and rugged mountains—but is best known for the spectacular cliff faces that rise as high as 3,000 feet from the ocean. Almost unknown until its establishment in 1978, Misty Fjords is today one of the highlights of an Alaskan trip for many visitors. Be forewarned however: it's an expensive highlight.

Seeing It

On any given summer day, flightseeing planes constantly take off from Tongass Narrows for trips over the monument. Although the scenery itself is grand, the almost mystical name, Misty Fjords, attracts many of the sightseers. Hour-and-a-half-long flightseeing trips cost approximately $120 pp from **Taquan Air Service,** tel. 225-9668, **Ketchikan Air Service,** tel. 225-6608, or **Misty Fjords Air and Outfitting,** 225-5155.

An excellent way to see Misty is by boat. Dale Pihlman of **Outdoor Alaska,** 215 Main St., Suite 211, tel. 225-6044, runs top-notch cruises into Misty Fjords from June to early September. Prices begin at $135 pp ($90 for children) with lunch included for a 12-hour cruise, or $175 pp ($130 for children) for a faster trip that includes a flightseeing return back to Ketchikan. They'll give you an impressive 30% discount if you take your chances and book standby the day before.

The best way to see Misty Fjords is from a kayak. You can paddle there from Ketchikan, but only if you're experienced and adequately prepared. For $150, Outdoor Alaska does drop-offs and pick-ups at the head of Rudyerd Bay. Those with folding kayaks may opt for flying one way and taking the boat the other direction. Pick-ups are anywhere along their daily tour route. **Southeast Exposure,** 507 Stedman St., tel. 225-8829, provides four- to ten-day kayak trips into Misty that start for $510 pp. These are coordinated with Outdoor Alaska's drop-off runs, and include a special women-only trip. If you are going on your own, rent kayaks from Southeast Exposure for $35/day for singles or $45/day for doubles (discounts for longer periods). Kayakers should be warned that flightseeing planes and cruise ships may well destroy your wilderness experience in Rudyerd Bay, but other areas get far less use.

Trails, Cabins, And Info

Misty Fjords National Monument has 14 recreation cabins ($20/night). The cabins near magnificent Rudyerd Bay are very popular, and reservations must be made months in advance. There are also nine trails that take you from saltwater to scenic lakes, most with cabins or free three-sided shelters. Two of the best trails lead up to shelters at Punchbowl and Nooya lakes. The one-mile Punchbowl Lake Trail switchbacks up from Rudyerd Bay, passing spectacular Punchbowl Creek Waterfall on the way. Both brown and black bears may be encountered on any of these trails, so be certain to make plenty of noise and to hang all food. The Forest Service maintains a floating bunkhouse/barge for its field crews near Winstanley Island and there is usually someone on board who can answer your questions.

Before heading out on any overnight trips into Misty, talk with staff at the **District Office,** 1817 Tongass, tel. 225-2148, or write to: Misty Fjords National Monument, Box 6137, Ketchikan, AK 99901. They can provide information on trail conditions, campsites, and what to expect. Be sure to request a copy of their excellent map of Misty Fjords ($3).

METLAKATLA

Twelve miles southwest of Ketchikan on the western shore of Annette Island is the planned community of Metlakatla (pop. 1,200). Metlakatla (meaning "Saltwater Channel" in Tsimshian) is Alaska's only Indian reservation, a status that was reaffirmed in 1971 when its residents refused to join other Native groups under the Alaska Native Claims Settlement Act. It is the only predominantly Tsimpshian settlement in Alaska and the only place in the United States where fish traps are still legal. The quiet, conservative town has a strong religious heritage and the air of a pioneer village. Large frame houses occupy big corner lots, while vacant lots yield abundant berry crops. There seems to be a church on every corner—eight in all, but none of them Catholic. Children are also abundant—nearly a third of the population is of grade-school age! Like much of Southeast, Metlakatla boasts a flourishing cannery, cold storage facility, fish hatchery, and sawmill. Most of Annette Island is wooded mountainous terrain reaching up to 3,500 feet, but the town of Metlakatla spreads out across a large, relatively flat portion of the island that contains many muskegs and lakes.

History

In 1887, a Tsimshian Indian group left Canada in search of religious freedom in Alaska. They discovered an abandoned Tlingit settlement on Annette Island offering a sheltered bay, gently sloping beaches, and a beautiful nearby waterfall. Under the direction of Anglican missionary William Duncan, 823 Tsimshian followers began clearing a townsite. The converts took new "Christian" names, dressed up in suits, and abandoned much of their cultural heritage. (For the story of Duncan's activities in Metlakatla, Canada, see "Prince Rupert"). At Metlakatla, Alaska, the settlers established a sawmill to produce lumber for the construction of houses and the first cannery.

The most ambitious building to be erected was a 1,000-seat church, "The Westminster Abbey of Alaska." It burned in 1948, but was replaced by a replica six years later. In 1891,

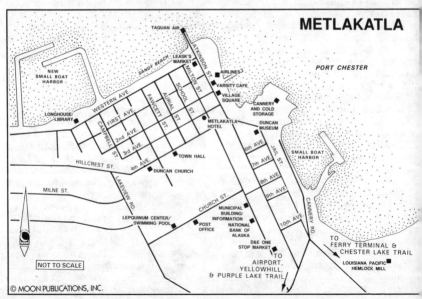

METLAKATLA

the U.S. Congress granted the Tsimshians the entire 86,000-acre island as a reserve, a right they jealously guard to this day. Duncan maintained his paternal hold over most aspects of life here until 1913 when a government school opened. (Duncan's paternalism extended other directions too: rumors persist that the never-married Duncan fathered many Metlakatla children.) He opposed the school, preferring that education remain in the hands of his church. The ensuing conflict led to intervention by the U.S. Dept. of the Interior in 1915 which seized the sawmill, cannery, and other facilities that had been under his personal control. Duncan died three years later, but his memory is still revered by many, and his influence can still be seen in the healthy little Indian settlement of today. For a fascinating account of Father Duncan and the two Metlakatlas, read Peter Murray's *The Devil and Mr. Duncan* (Sono Nis Press, Victoria, B.C.).

During WW II, the U.S. Army constructed a major military base seven miles from Metlakatla on Annette Island. The base included observation towers (to search for Japanese subs), a large airfield, hangers, communications towers, shore batteries, and housing for 10,000 men. At the time the airport was built, t was the most expensive one ever constructed by the government—everything kept sinking out of sight into the marshy muskeg. Until construction of an airport on Gravina Island in 1973, this airfield was used for jet service to Ketchikan, forcing passengers to and on Annette and fly by floatplane to Ketchikan. With the area's notorious weather, delays were common; many times it took onger to get the last dozen miles to Ketchikan than the 600 miles from Seattle to Annette Island.

Sights

Father Duncan's Cottage, tel. 886-6926—where the missionary lived from 1894 until his death in 1918—is open as a museum 10-noon Mon.-Fri. ($1) or by request on weekends at tel. 886-7363. The fascinating assortment of personal items owned by Duncan and the old photographs of Metlakatla make a stop here a must. Mrs. Lavarne Wel-

come, the curator, is always delighted to talk to visitors about the history of Metlakatla. The rather rundown **William Duncan Memorial Church** (built in 1954) stands at the corner of 4th Ave. and Church Street. Duncan's grave is on the left side. Also visit the Small Boat Harbor where a traditional-style **longhouse** (open Mon.-Fri. afternoons) has been erected to stimulate local arts and crafts and to help recover the cultural traditions decimated by Duncan's missionary zeal. Inside is a small library and a model of one of the four floating **fish traps** used on the island. One of these traps is often visible near the ferry terminal. Annette Island Cannery and Cold Storage dominates the waterfront, and the lumber mill is not far away.

Hiking

Unlike almost everywhere else in Alaska, there are no bears on Annette Island, a relief to those who fear encounters with bruins. A short hiking trail runs from the corner of Milton St. and Airport Rd. on the southeast edge of town along **Skaters Lake,** a large pond where native plants and ducks can be observed. **Yellow Hill,** a 540-foot tall fragment of 150-million-year-old sandstone, is unique in Southeast Alaska. The rock is rich in iron and magnesium, giving it a lovely desert-like yellow color set off by gnarled old lodgepole pines. An easy boardwalk trail (20 minutes OW) leads up to its summit where you get panoramic vistas of the western side of Annette, along with the snowcapped peaks of nearby Prince of Wales Island. A noisy wind generator disturbs your peace at the top. Get there by walking or hitching 1½ miles south from town on Airport Rd. to the signed trailhead on the right side. Some people claim to see George Washington's profile in Yellow Hill.

Two trails access alpine lakes in the mountains east of Metlakatla. The **Chester Lake Trail** starts at the end of the road, a quarter mile beyond the ferry terminal. From the trail you get views over the impressive Chester Lake Falls that first attracted Duncan's flock to Annette Island. The trail climbs very steeply up steps and a slippery path along a waterline used for power generation. Plan on 45 minutes to reach beautiful Chester Lake, where there is a small dam. From this point, the country is above timberline and it's possible to climb along several nearby ridges for even better views. Good camping sites are available, but be careful coming up the steep, slippery path with a pack.

Farther afield and not quite as scenic is the **Purple Lake Trail.** Take Airport Rd. four miles south of town and turn left near the quonset huts at the unmarked Purple Mt. Road. Follow it two miles to the powerplant. The unmarked trail heads directly upslope along a steep jeep road. After a 30-minute climb, you reach a saddle and from there you can head up adjacent ridges into the alpine or drop down to Purple Lake (10 minutes). Another place worth a look is the aptly named **Sand Dollar Beach** on the southwest end of the island. Ask locally for directions.

By Bike
The flat country around Metlakatla contains a labyrinth of dirt roads built during WW II, and if you have a mountain bike or car, they're well worth exploring. You'll find abandoned structures of all types: huge communication towers, strangely quiet empty hangers, old gun emplacements, and a major airport with no planes. Sort of like the Twilight Zone. From the south end of the road network are excellent views of Prince of Wales and Duke Islands, as well as out into the open sea beyond Dixon Entrance. This is the southernmost road in Alaska.

Practicalities
Metlakatla Hotel, tel. 886-3456, has rooms for $85 s or d. Locals often rent rooms out. Try Bernita Brendible, tel. 886-7563, who also makes traditional spruceroot baskets. Several other locals produce craftwork: Ray Holt, Jack Hudson, and Jimmy Casperson; ask locally for directions. Meals (mainly burgers and Mexican fare) are available at D&E's One Stop, the Village Source, Junior Varsity, and Ma Ma Jo's. The **Village Source** is the best of the lot, and even has health foods. **D&E's** has a great old jukebox. In general, you're better off heading to **Leask's Market** for food. Check the bulletin board here for

such items as hand-carved fossil ivory or fresh Ooligan grease (if you don't know what it is, you probably won't like it). Note that Metlakatla is officially a dry town, and alcoholic beverages are not allowed on the island.

The mayor's office in the municipal building, tel. 886-4868, may be able to provide some local information. **Camping** is discouraged, and visitors who want to stay on Annette Island more than five days must obtain a special permit from the city. A local sponsor is required, and fishing is not allowed. The **Lepquinum Activity Center** ($2) next to the high school houses an Olympic-size swimming pool, plus a weight room, sauna, and showers. Out front is Raven and the Tide Woman Totem, with a descriptive plaque. Although Metlakatla is only a dozen miles away from Ketchikan, it gets 118 inches of precipitation per year, 44 inches less than Ketchikan. Townfolks celebrate the establishment of Metlakatla each year on **Founder's Day,** August 7. As with most other American towns Metlakatla also has festivities on the **4th of July.**

Transport
Metlakatla's **ferry terminal** is a mile east of town. There are no storage lockers and ferries generally stop for only a half hour or so. During the summer, the *Aurora* connects Metlakatla and Ketchikan four days a week for $12 OW. Local cops often check for smuggled booze on arrival. On Saturdays the ferry schedule allows for an early Ketchikan departure and a return trip that evening offering a good chance to visit this interesting little town. **Taquan Air,** tel. 225-9668 or (800) 478-0668, flys daily between Ketchikan and Metlakatla for $22 OW or $33 RT.

HYDER AND STEWART

The twin towns of Hyder, Alaska, and Stewart, British Columbia, lie at the head of the long, narrow Portland Canal that separates Canada and the United States. The area's remoteness has kept it one of the relatively undiscovered gems of the entire Pacific

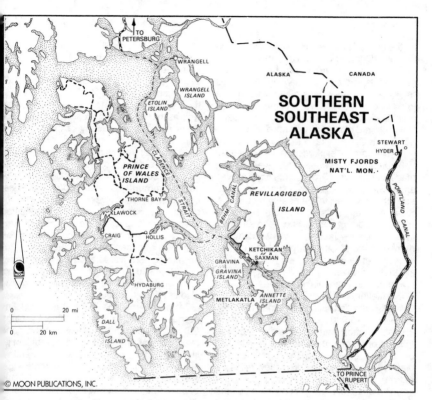

© MOON PUBLICATIONS, INC.

Northwest coast. Most people arrive via the stunning drive down Highway 37A from Meziadin Junction into Stewart, passing beautiful lakes, majestic glaciers, the narrow Bear River Canyon, and finally the mountain-rimmed, water-trimmed towns. The ferry trip through Portland Canal gives close-up vistas of one of the wildest stretches along the British Columbia and Alaska coastlines. Early in the season numerous black bears frolic along the shore, and porpoises are common in the fjord.

The town of Stewart, B.C. (pop. 2,200), lies at the mouth of the Bear River, while tiny Hyder, Alaska (pop. 90), is three km down the road next to the Salmon River. They are as different as two towns could possibly be. Stewart is the "real" town with a hospital,

churches, schools, a museum, a pharmacy, a bank, and the other necessities of life; it bills itself as Canada's northernmost ice-free port. In contrast, Hyder, "the friendliest ghost town in Alaska," makes the most of its flaky reputation. Between the two settlements lies an international boundary that is virtually ignored. There are no border check stations. Residents buy their liquor in Alaska and send their kids to school in British Columbia. Everyone uses Canadian currency and the Canadian phone system (area code 604). The Royal Canadian Mounted Police patrol both Stewart and Hyder. You can, however, mail letters from a post office in either country, saving postage and the hassles of shipping parcels internationally.

History

In 1793, Capt. George Vancouver, searching for the fabled Northwest Passage, turned into Portland Canal. For days his men worked their boats up the narrow fjord, but when they reached its end after so many miles he was "mortified with having devoted so much time to so little purpose." Over a century later the area finally began to develop. In 1896, Capt. David Gilliard of the Army Corps of Engineers (for whom Gilliard Cut in the Panama Canal was later named) explored the region and left behind four stone storehouses, Alaska's first masonry buildings. Prospectors soon arrived and found an incredible wealth of gold, silver, and other minerals in the nearby mountains. Stewart received its name from two of its earliest settlers, Robert and John Stewart. The adjacent Alaskan town was initially named Portland City, but postal authorities, wary of yet another Portland, vetoed it. Instead, the town was named for Frederick B. Hyder, a Canadian mining engineer.

Gold fever and the prospect of a transcontinental Canadian railway terminus attracted more than 10,000 newcomers to the area. The steep, mountainous terrain was difficult to build on; much of Hyder was constructed on pilings driven into the tideflats. The planned railroad only made it a few miles out of town, but in 1919 prospectors struck it rich. The Premier Gold and Silver Mine was, until its 1948 closure, the largest gold mine in North America. After it shut down, the local population dwindled to less than a thousand until development of the Granduc copper mine in the 1960s. To reach the rich Leduc ore vein, workers dug the longest tunnel ever built from one end, 18 km. A devastating avalanche in 1965 buried 40 men in a tunnel entrance, killing 27 of them. The mine operated until 1984 when it was closed down, completely dismantled, and the site restored to a relatively natural condition.

The spectacular Stewart/Hyder area has been used for the filming of several B-movies: Bear Island, The Thing, and Iceman. Recent years have also seen sporadic promises of new gold, silver, or coal mines, but much of the economy now depends upon the shipping of asbestos from Cassiar and nearby logging operations that strip-mine timber from British Columbia hillsides.

Sights And Information

The fine **Stewart Historical Society Museum** ($1) at Columbia and 6th, tel. 636-2568, is housed in the old Fire Hall (1910). It has wildlife specimens on the first floor as well as numerous historical items both upstairs and out front. Many of the items are from the region's rich mining history. The museum also serves as an information center for the area. It is open Mon.-Fri. 1-4 p.m., Sat. and Sun noon-5 or by appointment. Hyder's **Community Center** is home to the post office, library, and Hyder Community Association, tel. 636-9148, which has a limited amount of visitor info. The U.S. Forest Service usually has someone here during the summer who can answer questions. For swimming, showers, and a weight room ($2.50), head to the Stewart High School **pool** on Main Street. The public **library** is also at the high school.

At the international border stands a tiny **stone storehouse** built in 1896 by Capt. Gilliard. The building looks like an old jail, and once served that purpose, but for much of its life it was a shoe repair shop. On the mudflats in front of Hyder are hundreds of old pilings, remnants of what was once a town of 1,000 people. The straight row of pilings in front of Stewart is all that remains of the aborted transcontinental railroad.

Watering Holes

Hyder has three bars (open to 5 a.m.) for fewer than ninety inhabitants. Getting "Hyderized" is an experience that attracts folks from all over the world. Bartenders claim that the tradition began when prospectors would tack up a dollar bill on the wall, in case they were broke next trip into town. Today the walls of both the **Glacier Inn** and the **First and Last Chance Saloon** are papered with over $20,000 in signed bills left by previous initiates, creating the "world's most expensive wallpaper." Becoming Hyderized is cheap ($2) and lasts a lifetime (you even get an official card), but it could also prove expensive if you fail the test.

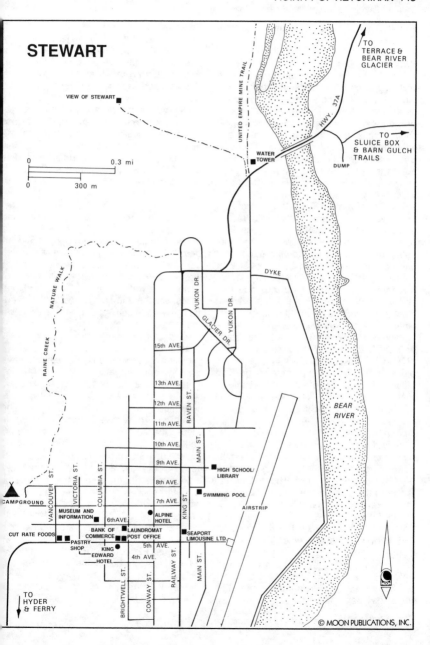

STEWART

VIEW OF STEWART ■

TO TERRACE & BEAR RIVER GLACIER

TO SLUICE BOX & BARN GULCH TRAILS

HWY 37A

DUMP

UNITED EMPIRE MINE TRAIL

WATER TOWER ■

0   0.3 mi

0   300 m

NATURE WALK

RAINE CREEK

DYKE

YUKON DR.

GLACIER DR.

YUKON DR.

15th AVE.

13th AVE.

12th AVE.

11th AVE.

10th AVE.

9th AVE.

8th AVE.

7th AVE.

6th AVE.

5th AVE.

4th AVE.

RAVEN ST.

MAIN ST.

KING ST.

VICTORIA ST.

COLUMBIA ST.

VANCOUVER ST.

BRIGHTWELL ST.

CONWAY ST.

RAILWAY ST.

MAIN ST.

BEAR RIVER

HIGH SCHOOL/ LIBRARY ■

SWIMMING POOL ■

AIRSTRIP

ALPINE HOTEL ●

MUSEUM AND INFORMATION ■

CUT RATE FOODS ■■

PASTRY SHOP ■

BANK OF COMMERCE ■

LAUNDROMAT ■ POST OFFICE

KING EDWARD HOTEL ●

SEAPORT LIMOUSINE LTD. ■

▲ CAMPGROUND

TO HYDER & FERRY

© MOON PUBLICATIONS, INC.

Warning: it involves that frat house favorite, Everclear.

Hiking

The easiest local trail, **Raine Creek Nature Walk,** takes off from the Raine Creek Campground and follows the creek 2½ km to the north end of town. The mountains around Stewart and Hyder are crisscrossed with old mining roads, great both for day hikes and camping. Scenic **Barney Gulch Trail** and **Sluice Box Trail** begin near the dump, just across the Bear River on the north edge of town. The **United Empire Mine Trail** starts from Quarry Rd. north of Stewart.

The **Ore Mountain Trail** starts 13 km east of Stewart at Clements Lake. An attractive campsite (free) is available near the trailhead. This four-km trail gains 1,100 meters as it climbs up along an old mining road to a small alpine lake. Plan on 2½ hours OW for the hike. **Red Top Trail**, 22 km east of Stewart, follows another old mining road that climbs 1,300 meters in just four km. Allow at least two hours to reach the alpine zone where many glaciers are visible, including the Cambria Ice Fields. The **Titan Trail** starts near the bridge over Fish Creek (five km out of Hyder) and climbs eight km up to the alpine. You'll also discover the remains of an old mine up here. For maps and more info on these and other local hikes contact the **Stewart Forest Service Office**, tel. 636-2663.

Accommodations

Stewart Lions Campground in Stewart has tent spaces for $9. It's quietly situated on the edge of town and has a cookhouse, free firewood, and pay showers. The tenting area is across the creek. Some people also camp in the woods near Grizzly Bear Lodge in Hyder, but beware of bears. The best local hotel is the **Grand View Inn** in Hyder, tel. 636-9174. The friendly owner, George Hancock, has plenty of local tales and can direct you to fishing holes. Rooms are also available in Stewart's **King Edward Hotel/Motel**, tel. 636-2244, and **Sealaska Inn**, tel. 636-9003, in Hyder.

Food

Stewart has the excellent **Dutch Pastry Shop** on 5th St. with some of the best breads and flakiest turnovers you'll ever taste. **Fong's Garden** at 5th and Conway serves Chinese food and the **King Eddy** has good burgers. For a meal out, locals often head to Hyder where prices are generally lower. Hyder's **Portland City Dining Emporium** serves big helpings of fresh fish for reasonable prices and the **Grizzly Bear Lodge** serves up traditional American food. For breakfast, head to the **Border Cafe,** just down the street.

Events

Canada's Independence Day (July 1) and the American Independence Day (July 4) provide the opportunity for a four-day party in Stewart and Hyder. **International Days,** as it's called, consists of a wide range of events including beer gardens (with glacial ice), a truckload of Tennessee watermelons, international bed races, salmon and crab bakes, logging contests, "low-tide golf," and even a broom-kicking contest.

Transport

Alaska ferry service to Hyder/Stewart offers an excellent alternative to the usual routes north. Between June and September the *Aurora* sails weekly (US$36 OW) from Ketchikan to the Stewart dock, leaving Ketchikan Thurs. evenings and arriving in Hyder the next morning. It stays approximately four hours before heading back to Ketchikan. Stewart does not have a ferry terminal building and you must purchase tickets on board the ship. Considering a bit of international drug-running on the unguarded Hyder/Stewart border? Be forewarned that U.S. Customs in Ketchikan "greets" all Hyder and Stewart ferry passengers.

Seaport Limousine Ltd., tel. 636-2622, in Stewart provides bus connections to Terrace B.C. Hitching to Terrace is relatively easy. **Temsco Airlines,** the only air connection went out of business in late 1991.

Nearby

About five km out of Hyder is **Fish Creek;** each Aug. its waters are filled with some of the world's largest chum salmon—up to 14 kilograms. A viewing platform here provides an excellent vantage point over an artificial spawning channel where black bears catch salmon. Nearby are remains of an old "cathouse" operated by Dolly, Ketchikan's best-known madam. No Forest Service cabins are near Hyder, but ask at the Hyder Community Center about the beautiful **Chickamin Cabin** on Texas Lake.

The **Premier** and **Big Missouri** gold mines are 48 km beyond Hyder. Before heading out, be sure to ask about the snow level along the road. **Seaport Limousine Ltd.,** tel. 636-2622, has an excellent four-hour bus tour that provides spectacular vistas of Salmon Glacier, lovely alpine meadows, the icebergs of Summit Lake, and a visit to Tide Lake, site of the world's greatest yearly snowfall: 28 meters in 1971!

The gorgeous **Bear River Glacier,** 37 km east of Stewart on Highway 37A, should not be missed. Like its more famous cousin, Juneau's Mendenhall Glacier, it is a "drive-up glacier" with the highway passing close to its base. The small lake in front is often filled with icebergs.

PRINCE OF WALES ISLAND

With more miles of roads than the rest of Southeast Alaska combined, a beautifully wild coastline, deep U-shaped valleys, rugged snow-topped mountains, and a wealth of wildlife, you might expect America's third-largest island (after Kodiak and Hawaii) to be a major tourist attraction. Instead, Prince of Wales (POW) has a reputation as a place to avoid. The island provides over half the timber cut on Forest Service land in Alaska, and is a major source of timber for Native corporations such as Sealaska. As a result, much of the island has been heavily logged, with huge clearcuts gouged out of the hillsides, particularly along the extensive road network.

Actually, POW's notoriety is its saving grace as well: the towns are authentically Alaskan, with no pretext of civility for the tourists. People are friendly, and the many roads offer good opportunities for a variety of recreation not available elsewhere in Southeast. Mountain bikers will enjoy riding on the logging roads when they aren't in use. The island is very popular with hunters from other parts of Southeast and the roads provide easy access to many bays for fishing. Black bears and deer are common sights, and wolves are occasionally seen.

POW has several small towns along with many logging camps, some on float houses and others with more permanent structures.

State land sales and a strong timber market have helped turn POW into an economically booming area in recent years. The island's largest settlement is Craig, on the island's western coast, but Klawock, Thorne Bay, and Hydaburg are also growing. Rainfall amounts on POW range from 60 to 200 inches per year, depending upon local topographic conditions.

CRAIG

Just across a short bridge from the western shore of POW Island lies the town of Craig (pop. 1,400), overflowing Craig Island. Named after Craig Miller—founder of an early fish cannery here—it was originally called the even more prosaic "Fish Egg," after the herring eggs found here and considered a Tlingit delicacy. Fishing and logging are the mainstays of Craig's economy, giving it a likeable rough edge. The town has two fish-processing plants where jobs are sometimes available. Black bears are often seen at the dump, located a mile north of town (look for the "Entering Klawock Heenya Land" sign). The Forest Service's **Craig District Office,** tel. 826-3271, faces the south boat harbor. Folks here can supply maps and recreation info. You can thank Shaan-Seet Inc. for the giant clearcut glaring down on Craig.

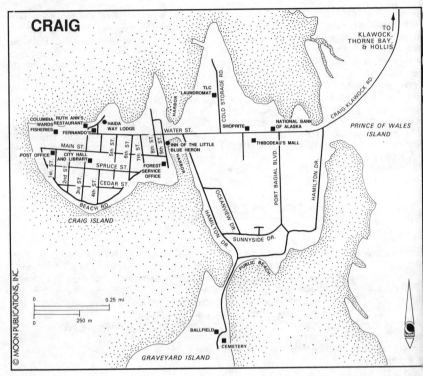

Accommodations

Travelers often camp in the trees near Craig's ballfield. Simple rooms are available at **TLC Laundromat** on Cold Storage Rd., tel. 826-2966, for $35 s or $45 d. Showers here cost $3 if you're camping. Nicer rooms are $65 s or d at **Ruth Ann's Motel,** tel. 826-3377, or stay at **Haida Way Lodge,** tel. 826-3268, for $70 s or $76 d. The homiest place to spend a night is **Inn of the Little Blue Heron,** tel. 826-3606, which faces the south boat harbor. Rates are $55 s or $65 d, including a substantial continental breakfast.

Food

Meal prices are high on POW, and your best bet is to stock up in Ketchikan or in Craig at **Shoprite**—they have a good deli. **Ruth Ann's Restaurant** downtown serves good food with a front-row view of the harbor. Nice place. You won't go wrong ordering fish and chips ($7.25). A block away is the **Haida Way Lodge,** offering slightly cheaper food (but we're still talking $8 for a lunchtime soup and salad bar). For Mexican dishes, head to **Fernando's Mexican Food and Pizza.** The **Hill Bar** sometimes has live music.

OTHER TOWNS

Klawock

Six miles from Craig is the Tlingit village of Klawock (pop. 760), home to the oldest cannery in Alaska (1878), along with a bustling sawmill, state fish hatchery, and POW's only airport (all other settlements have floatplane service). Klawock is best known for its **Totem Park** (21 poles) that dominates the center of town. These brightly painted poles all originals, were moved from the old abandoned village of Tuxekan (20 miles north) in the 1930s and restored. Showers ($3) are available at **Black Bear Laundromat** next to Thorne Bay Road. Also here is a Quik Stop market. **Log Cabin Resort,** tel. (800) 544-2205, rents rustic cabins along the beach for $35 and tent spaces for $10 (showers and kitchen included). Rent one of their canoes ($20/day) or skiffs ($65/day) and explore Big Salt Lake and nearby islands. Other gear, including fishing poles and even crabpots, can also be rented. The **Fireweed Lodge,** tel. 755-2930, has rooms for $75 s or d, and bunkhouse space for $25 pp. The restaurant serves breakfast and dinner. **Klawock Bed & Breakfast,** tel. 755-2287, also has local accommodations.

Thorne Bay

The growing settlement of Thorne Bay (pop. 500) calls itself "the biggest logging camp in the U.S." It's also billed as a "planned city," but the plan seems based upon chaos, mud, abandoned vehicles, and a heavy dose of mobile homes and shacks. Thorne Bay has to be one of the ugliest settlements in Southeast; that alone should be reason enough for a visit! There's a small grocery store called—appropriately enough—the **Clear Cut Market,** plus **Gallagher's Galley Restaurant** and the **Riptide Bar.** McFarland's **Floatel B&B,** tel. 828-3335, has deluxe log cabins for $120 (sleeps four). They rent skiffs for $75/day. Lodging is also available at **Gloria's Bed and Breakfast,** tel. 828-3375. The town hosts the **POW Island Fair and Logging Show** each August. Ten miles north of Thorne Bay on Forest Hwy. 30 is **Sandy Beach Picnic Area,** an attractive beach (rare in Southeast) where you can pitch a tent.

Hydaburg

Forty-two miles south of Craig, Hydaburg (pop. 500) is the largest Haida settlement in Alaska. The Haida Indians are relative newcomers to the state, arriving in this Tlingit land around 1700. Originally from Canada's Queen Charlotte Islands, they were given parts of POW in compensation for the accidental killing of a Haida chief by the Tlingits.

Hydaburg was established in 1911 when three nearby Haida villages combined into one. Hydaburg has the prettiest setting on POW, situated along scenic Sukkwan Strait. Most of the houses, however, are very plain BIA-style boxes. The gravel road to Hydaburg was only completed in 1983, opening the town to the outside world. In town is a nice collection of totems restored by the CCC in the 1930s, along with a new one erected in 1991. For food you're best off heading to **Do Drop Inn Groceries,** but fast food is available at **JJ's** or the **Sweet Shop.** The latter has a pool table. Ask for **Marlene Edenshaw,** tel. 285-3254, or **Fran Sanderson,** tel. 285-3139, if you need a place to stay. They charge around $70 pp for boarders, including three big meals a day.

Logging And Fishing Towns

The tiny logging communities of **Whale Pass** (pop. 90) and **Coffman Cove** (pop. 270) each have a general store, gas pumps, and lodging. On the far northern end of POW are the miniscule fishing/retirement villages of **Port Protection** and **Point Baker.** Both have small general stores and a number of float houses, but are accessible only by boat or floatplane. If you have the bucks (we're talking over $2,000 for three nights!), **Waterfall Resort,** tel. (800) 544-5125, is pretty hard to beat. Located on the south end of POW in a refurbished fish cannery, Waterfall has become extremely popular with the elite crowd. Great fishing, three big meals daily, and positively pampered guests.

TRANSPORTATION

Ferry

The Alaska state ferry *Aurora* connects POW with Ketchikan almost daily during the summer months. Reservations for vehicles are highly recommended. Ferries to Petersburg generally depart on Mondays and are less crowded. The ferry terminal is in **Hollis,** tel. 530-7115, and is open a half hour before arrivals and one hour prior to departures. No services in Hollis (other than phones and a toilet), and it's 25 miles to Klawock, the nearest town. Make reservations in Craig, down-

Klawock totems (GORDY OHLIGER)

stairs in Thibodeau's Mall, tel. 826-3432; open Mon.-Fri. 9-5 only.

The *Aurora* tends to arrive and depart late at night, making hitching somewhat difficult; in general, however, hitching is fairly easy on the island, though you may have to wait awhile for a ride. **Prince of Wales Transporter** in Klawock, tel. 755-2348, has vans that meet most ferry dockings. Rates are: Hollis-Craig $17 OW, Hollis-Thorne Bay $25 pp for two people, and Hollis-Hydaburg $25 pp for two people. Call in advance from Ketchikan to be sure they'll be meeting your ferry.

By Air
Two air taxi operators, **Ketchikan Air Service,** tel. 225-6608, and **Taquan Air Service,** tel. 225-9668 or (800) 478-0668, fly every day between Ketchikan and the major towns on POW, offering rates within a few dollars of each other: Craig ($65), Hollis ($40), Hydaburg ($65), Klawock ($65), and Thorne Bay ($40). In addition, all three also have daily flights to the many logging camps and fishing communities that dot the island. Folks with a folding sea kayak may want to take advantage of these flights as an inexpensive way to reach remote parts of POW. Example roundtrip airfare from Ketchikan to the Karta Bay cabin will set you back $330 for a charter flight, but just $75 if you buy seat fare to nearby Kasaan on these daily flights!

The Road System
For a good road map, pick up the **"Prince of Wales Road Guide"** ($3) at Forest Service offices in Ketchikan, Craig, or Thorne Bay. Be sure to check out the photo on the back cover that shows a logging truck heading up a POW road. It's labeled "A Forest At Work"— as though this were the sole purpose of publicly owned forests! Pretty obvious that "non-working" forests—such as wilderness areas—are lazy and good for nothing. Because of its extensive road network (over 2,000 miles and increasing at 80 miles per year), some visitors take mountain bikes to POW. There are some excellent stretches of paved road (including the entire distance from Hollis to Craig), and enjoyable vistas but be prepared for wet weather, huge logging trucks, and many miles of rutted and rough gravel roads. Ask at the Forest Service offices in Ketchikan or Craig where logging is going on. Avoid these roads, unless you don't mind watching a loaded logging truck bearing down on you! Some travelers to POW rent a car from **Rent-A-Dent** in Klawock, tel. 826-3555.

(previous page) Glaciers crowd the mountain country within Glacier Bay National Park.
(top) Mt. McKinley dominates the landscape of Interior Alaska.
(bottom) The 9,077-foot summit of Devil's Thumb rises behind Petersburg.

ACTIVITIES

Camping

You can camp almost anywhere on POW's National Forest land, but avoid trespassing on Native lands (these are generally quite easy to identify since all the trees have been logged for miles in all directions). The new **Eagles Nest Campground** ($5/night) is just east of the intersection of the Klawock-Thorne Bay road and the Coffman Cove Road. Also here is a pleasant pair of lakes (Balls Lakes—named for, well, you figure it out) with a short path down to tent platforms overlooking the water. This is a good place for canoeing.

Hiking And Cabins

There are only a few trails on POW. One of the best and most accessible is the 1½-mile-long **One Duck Trail** southwest of Hollis. The trailhead is on the east side of the Hydaburg Rd., two miles south of the junction with the Craig-Hollis Road. It heads up sharply to a new Adirondack shelter (free) on the edge of the alpine where the scenery is grand and the hiking is easy. Be sure to wear rubber boots since the trail can be mucky. The **Soda Springs Trail** (marked) begins approximately 14 miles south of the junction along the Hydaburg Road. The 2½-mile trail leads to a fascinating collection of bubbling soda springs covering several acres. There are colorful tufa deposits (calcium carbonate primarily) similar to those in Yellowstone, but on a much smaller scale. **Control Lake**, at the junction of the Thorne Bay and Big Salt Lake roads, has a nice state-owned cabin ($20/night) with a rowboat. Twenty other Forest Service cabins are scattered around POW, most accessible only by floatplane or boat. For world-class steelhead and salmon fishing, reserve one of the four cabins in the Karta River area north of Hollis. The five-mile-long **Karta River Trail** connects Karta Bay to the Salmon Lake Cabin and provides panoramic views of surrounding mountains. This is now part of the newly designated **Karta Wilderness** (40,000 acres).

Canoeing

Most of the major watersheds on POW have been entered by loggers. An area that remains untouched (probably not for long, alas) encompasses Hatchery Creek and the upper Thorne River. This is a popular place for canoeists who paddle and portage the 42-mile-long **Honker Divide Canoe Route**. The route begins near Coffman Cove at the bridge over Hatchery Creek on Forest Road 30, and works up Hatchery Creek to Lake Galea, which has a Forest Service cabin ($20/night). You may need to line the canoe up shallow sections of the creek. The route then continues over Honker Divide on a mile-long portage to the upper Thorne River before heading downstream all the way to Thorne Bay. There is a two-mile portage to avoid dangerous rapids and falls. The route is strenuous and should only be attempted by experienced canoeists. (By the way, the record time for running this route is 13 hours!) A second canoe route (15 miles) is being completed in the Sarkar Lakes area along POW's northwestern shore. For more information on either of these routes, contact the **Thorne Bay Ranger District Office** at Box 1, Thorne Bay, AK 99950, tel. 828-3304.

Sea Kayaking

With hundreds of miles of rugged coastline, and numerous small islands, inlets, and bays, POW offers tremendous opportunities for sea kayakers. One of the wildest areas is the 98,000-acre **South Prince of Wales Wilderness**, but access is difficult and much of the area is exposed to fierce ocean storms. Nearby Dall Island has exploring possibilities, but parts of it are being logged. On beaches exposed to the open sea, one occasionally finds beautiful Japanese glass fishing floats that have washed ashore. **Southeast Exposure**, 507 Stedman St., Ketchikan, tel. 225-8829, offers sea kayaking trips to the myriad of Barrier Islands on the south end of Prince of Wales. These trips cost $1,150 pp for a 10-day expedition (including transportation and supplies). Highly recommended.

In Craig, you can rent sea kayaks from Cheryl Fecko, tel. 826-3425. Sylvia Geraghty in New Tokeen also rents sea kayaks. Tiny New Tokeen (pop. 3!) has a small store for fishermen, and is accessible by boat from Naukati or floatplane. It's a good place to start explorations of fascinating Sea Otter Sound. Three other wilderness areas along POW's outer coast—**Maurelle Islands, Warren Island,** and **Coronation Island**—offer remote and almost unvisited places to see whales, sea otters, and nesting colonies of seabirds. You're likely to see a few fishermen, but nobody else.

A CLEARCUT ISSUE

One commonly hears Prince of Wales Island described as "nuked." The logging policies of both the U.S. Forest Service and the Native corporations are to blame. Logging—practiced in one form or another for over 100 years—is a major economic pillar in Southeast Alaska. In towns such as Ketchikan, Craig, Thorne Bay, and Kake, employment opportunities are scarce and logging, mill work, or stevedoring provide well-paying jobs. The first large-scale logging on Tongass National Forest began during WW II, when Sitka spruce was needed for airplane construction, but until the 1950s, logging's impact was minor. In 1954 the first pulp mill opened in Ketchikan. A Japanese corporation built a second in Sitka five years later, and today more than 4,500 people work in the timber industry in Southeast. To supply these mills, the Forest Service signed unprecedented 50-year contracts giving the two companies nearly 300 million board-feet of timber each year at prices well below timber management costs. This controversial boondoggle was institutionalized in 1980 with passage of the Alaska National Interest Lands Conservation Act (ANILCA), which mandated a 450 million board-foot cut each year on the Tongass, to be funded by a $40 million annual appropriation to the Forest Service for road building and timber management. After years of pressure, the Tongass Timber Reform Act of 1990 put an end to the worst of this. The battle, however, is far from over, and

loggers continue to move into previously untouched watersheds.

Clearcutting is not only an eyesore visible from the ferries and roads, but it also results in the loss of the vital old-growth ecosystem. Within 20 years after logging, the cut-over land is densely covered with trees and bushes. Although these provide wildlife habitat for awhile, as the trees grow taller an impenetrable thicket develops. Thinning crews attempt to open up these stands by cutting out the smaller and weaker trees. Once these forests reach 50 years of age they appear similar to old-growth forest from a distance, but inside they differ greatly. Old-growth forests have an almost continuous understory of huckleberry, devil's club, salmonberry, skunk cabbage, rusty menziesia, and other plants that provide food and cover for many animals. In contrast, second-growth forests lack many of these understory plants, making for great hiking, but very poor wildlife habitat.

One of the most infamous clearcuts on Forest Service land anywhere in the country is the six-square-mile scalping at Staney Creek near the center of Prince of Wales. Due to persistent criticism, the Forest Service has now reduced clearcut sizes to less than 40 acres. Unfortunately, private corporations created by the Alaska Native Claims Settlement Act of 1971 have taken the lead in the cut-and-run game. Unlike the Forest Service—which ostensibly manages its lands for multiple-use and is accountable to the public—private corporations are managing much of their land for only one purpose: cutting the timber as fast as possible to make as much money as possible. The timber is almost gone from most of the village corporation lands, and even timber giant Sealaska's supply—300,000 acres of trees—will only last another decade or so.

The big profiteers out of this are the Japanese and Korean corporations who get Alaskan timber for fire-sale prices. The big losers are the Native people who will have decimated their land for a short-term boom. The resulting eyesores have prompted even the Forest Service to distance itself by placing "Entering Private Land" signs on Sealaska

Corporation borders. It's too late for many areas, but people are finally becoming aware that cutting all the trees on all your land at once does not provide a long-term economic base. Two things are certain for the future: clearcut logging will continue to be one of the major uses of forest land in Southeast, and it will continue to generate controversy.

WRANGELL

With a strong base in logging and fishing, great scenery, a vibrant Native culture, and a small-town friendliness that could be Anyplace, USA, the town of Wrangell (pop. 3,100) seems to epitomize life in Southeast Alaska. Wrangell's streets are filled with folks in pickup trucks, their dogs hanging out the back, and country tunes on the radio. Its inner harbor comes alive with salmon- and shrimp-processing plants, fishing boats, seaplanes, and totem poles. Surrounding the harbor are old buildings on piles, wooded hillsides, and snowcapped mountains. Wrangell is compact enough that visitors can hoof it around to the most interesting sites in an hour or two and still have time to buy beer for the ferry. To see the area right, however, you should spend a couple of days, or longer if you're interested in visiting the mighty Stikine River.

History

Third-oldest community in Alaska, Wrangell is the only one to have been governed by four nations: Tlingit, Russian, British, and American. Tlingit legends tell of an ancient time when glaciers forced them to abandon their coastal life and move to what is now British Columbia. As the ice retreated following the last ice age, the Stikine River was their entryway back to the newly reborn land. When the Tlingits discovered that the river suddenly disappeared under a glacier, they sent old women to explore, expecting never to see them again. One can only imagine their astonishment when the women returned to lead canoes full of people out to the coast.

For many centuries the Tlingits lived in the Stikine River area, paddling canoes upstream to catch salmon and trade with interior tribes. Similarly, the river figured strongly in Wrangell's founding. Russians began trading with Stikine Indians in 1811; by 1834 the British were trying to move in on their lucrative fur trading monopoly. To prevent this, Lt. Dionysius Zarembo and a band of men left New Archangel (present-day Sitka) to establish a Russian fort near the Stikine River mouth. The settlement, later to become Wrangell, was originally named Redoubt St. Dionysius. When the British ship *Dryad* anchored near the river, the Russians boarded the vessel and refused to allow access to the Stikine. The *Dryad* was forced to return south, but an opening had been wedged in Russia's Alaskan empire. Five years later the Hudson's Bay Co. acquired a long-term lease to the coastline from the Russian government. Redoubt St. Dionysius became Fort Stikine, and the Union Jack flew from town flagpoles.

The discovery of gold on Stikine River gravel bars in 1861 brought a boom to Fort Stikine. Hundreds of gold-seekers arrived, but the deposit proved relatively small, and most soon drifted on to other areas. With the transfer of Alaska to American hands in 1867, Fort Stikine was renamed Wrangell, after Baron Ferdinand Petrovich von Wrangel, governor of the Russian-American Company. Its population dwindled until 1872 when gold was again discovered in the Cassiar region of British Columbia. Thousands of miners quickly flooded the area, traveling on steamboats up the Stikine. Wrangell achieved notoriety as a town filled with hard-drinking rabble-rousers, gamblers, and "shady ladies." When the naturalist John Muir visited in 1879 he called it "the most inhospitable place at first sight I had ever seen . . . a lawless draggle of wooden huts and houses, built in crooked lines, wrangling around the boggy shore of the island for a mile or so in the general form of the letter S, without the slightest subordination to the points of the compass or to building laws of any kind."

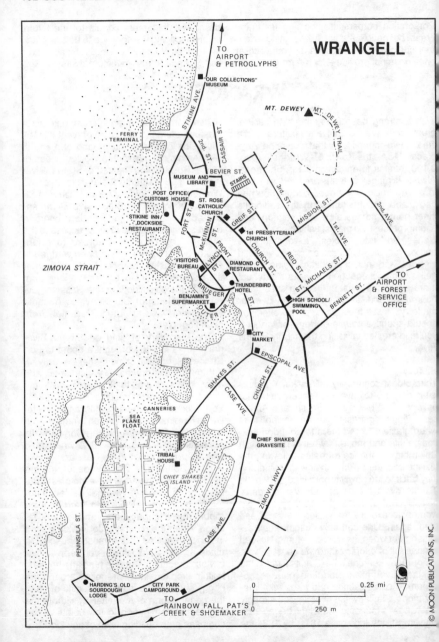

WRANGELL

TO
AIRPORT
& PETROGLYPHS

"OUR COLLECTIONS"
MUSEUM

MT. DEWEY ▲ MT. DE WEY TRAIL

FERRY
TERMINAL

STIKINE AVE.

2nd ST.

CASSAIR ST.

3rd ST.

MISSION ST.

2nd AVE.

BEVIER ST.

MUSEUM AND
LIBRARY

STAIRS

POST OFFICE/
CUSTOMS HOUSE

ST. ROSE
CATHOLIC
CHURCH

GREIF ST.

1st Presbyterian
CHURCH

1st AVE.

REID ST.

FORT ST.

McKINNON ST.

STIKINE INN/
DOCKSIDE
RESTAURANT

CHURCH ST.

ST. MICHAELS ST.

ZIMOVA STRAIT

VISITORS
BUREAU

LYNCH ST.

DIAMOND C
RESTAURANT

FRONT ST.

TO
AIRPORT
& FOREST
SERVICE
OFFICE

BENNETT ST.

BENJAMIN'S
SUPERMARKET

BRUEGER ST.

THUNDERBIRD
HOTEL

OUTER DR.

HIGH SCHOOL/
SWIMMING
POOL

CITY
MARKET

EPISCOPAL AVE.

SHAKES ST.

CASE AVE.

CHURCH ST.

CANNERIES

SEA
PLANE
FLOAT

CHIEF SHAKES
GRAVESITE

TRIBAL
HOUSE

CHIEF SHAKES
ISLAND

ZIMOVIA HWY.

PENINSULA ST.

CASE AVE.

HARDING'S OLD
SOURDOUGH
LODGE

CITY PARK
CAMPGROUND

TO
RAINBOW FALL, PAT'S
CREEK & SHOEMAKER

0   0.25 mi

0   250 m

© MOON PUBLICATIONS, INC.

By the late 1880s, the second gold rush had subsided and lumbering and fishing were getting started as local industries. The Klondike gold rush of the late 1890s brought another short-lived boom to Wrangell as the Stikine was again tapped for access to interior Canada, but Skagway's Chilkoot Trail became the preferred route. With its rowdy days behind, Wrangell settled into the 20th century as a home to logging and fishing operations, still mainstays of the local economy. Rebuilt after destructive fires in 1906 and 1952, much of downtown is now on rockfill and pilings. In the 1980s, Wrangell re-emerged as a mining supply center, spurred by the opening of several new mines in nearby British Columbia. One of Wrangell's strangest sights is an enormous freight-hauling hovercraft (the only one in existence) that makes two runs daily up the Stikine River to the Snip Gold Mine. Each run returns with partially processed ore worth $75,000.

SIGHTS

Chief Shakes Island is the centerpiece of picturesque Wrangell harbor. A footbridge at the bottom of Front St. near Wrangell's cannery and cold storage plants gives access to the island. Here you'll find the **Tribal House of the Bear**, an old-style Native log house built in 1939-40 by the CCC. Inside are various artifacts, including the original house posts carved over 200 years ago. The house ($1) is usually open for ferries or cruise ships in port over an hour, or by appointment (tel. 874-3770). Outside are seven totems, CCC reproductions of older poles from the area. Shakes Island is especially beautiful at night, surrounded by the town and harbor. The Shakes lineage was established over 300 years ago, after the Stikine Tlingits defeated Niska invaders and then forced the vanquished chief, We-Shakes, to give away his name in exchange for peace. **Chief Shakes VI's grave** is around on Case Ave. opposite the Hansen Boat Shop. Two carved killer whales watch silently over the site. Several impressive totem poles stand in front of the town library (2nd St.), carved by

the CCC. Wrangell's newest **totem park** (1987), next to the City Market along Front St., has four poles.

Petroglyphs
Hundreds of petroglyphs (ancient rock carvings) are found on Wrangell Island, but precisely who carved them or when is uncertain. They may date back more than 8,000 years. The best nearby carvings are only a 20-minute walk away. To get there, turn left (north) from the ferry terminal and walk two-thirds of a mile to a small parking area on the left. Follow the signed boardwalk to the beach where you'll easily find a dozen petroglyph rocks along upper parts of the beach, especially those on the right side (facing the water). Most face seaward and are near the high-tide line. One of the best (a killer whale) lies on the edge of a grassy lawn to the right of the path. Other petroglyphs are in the Wrangell Museum and in front of the library. Petroglyph rubbings can be created by placing rice paper (available in local stores) over the carvings and rubbing lightly with ferns found near the beach.

Museum
Given the size of Wrangell, its museum ($1) is a surprise. Housed in the town's first schoolhouse (1906), it is open Wed. and Thurs. 1:30-3, and Fri. 10:30-noon, or whenever a ferry or cruise ship docks for over an hour. Petroglyphs, old photographs, Tlingit artifacts, and local relics are crowded into this provocative museum. The staff is also a good source for information about the town. A slide program of Wrangell is shown on request and the museum shop sells books on local and regional history.

Mount Dewey
A half-mile path winds up **Mt. Dewey** (actually more of a hill) from 3rd Street. It's a steep 15-minute climb up to this viewpoint over Wrangell. You could probably find a place to camp up here in a pinch. On a wild stormy night in 1879, John Muir did just that. He, however, also decided to build a huge bonfire atop the hill, its flames dancing off the clouds. Muir later wrote, "Of all the thousands of

campfires I have elsewhere built none was just like this one, rejoicing in triumphant strength and beauty in the heart of the rain-laden gale." To the Native people below, however, the fire ignited fears of evil spirits, and as Muir's partner noted, the Tlingits "ever afterward eyed Muir askance, as a mysterious being whose ways and motives were beyond all conjecture." During the 1920s, a dance pavilion crowned the top of Mt. Dewey; nothing remains of it today.

Other Sights

Wrangell is home to the oldest Protestant church building in Alaska, the **First Presbyterian Church**, as well as the oldest Roman Catholic parish, **St. Rose of Lima Catholic Church**. Located on Church St. (of course), both were founded in 1879. The large red neon cross atop the Presbyterian church is one of only two in the world used as a navigational aid (the other is in Rio). For something completely different you might want to stop in at **Our Collections,** (free) on your way to the petroglyphs. The place looks like a cross between granny's attic and a bad yard sale, and represents 50 years of collecting by the Bigelow family.

As you step off the ferry you will be greeted by local kids selling **garnets**. These imperfect but attractive stones come from a nearby garnet ledge along the Stikine River, deeded to the Boy Scouts in 1962 by a former mayor. Local children may collect the stones for free, but adults must pay $10 for a permit (available at the museum). At one time the mine was owned by the Alaska Garnet Mining and Manufacturing Co., the world's first corporation composed entirely of women.

TRAILS AND CABINS

Anan Creek Bear Observatory

Anan Creek, 30 miles south of Wrangell on the mainland, has an observation platform that provides a good place to watch black and brown bears catching salmon and steelhead. The best viewing is a half-mile upstream from this, below a second falls, but be sure to make lots of noise when walking up this primitive trail to keep from surprising a bear. No food is allowed along these trails. The best time to visit is mid-July through mid-August. A nearby Forest Service cabin is often booked months in advance, so make reservations early. Many visitors to Anan Creek arrive by floatplane (approximately $300 RT for three people and gear), but the **Stikine Princess**, tel. 874-3455, also offers day trips to Anan Creek on the water ($125 pp/day). Those with a sea kayak may want to paddle along the east side of Wrangell Island to Anan Bay. En route, be sure to visit scenic **Berg Bay**, an area rich in moose, mountain goats, grizzly, deer, geese, and other wildlife. A Forest Service **cabin** ($20) is available here, and a trail leads from the cabin along Berg Creek for several miles into a cirque basin with old mine ruins.

Hiking Trails

Scenic **Rainbow Falls Trail**, a moderately steep three-quarter-mile hike, begins across the road from Shoemaker Bay Campground, five miles south of town. More ambitious bodies can continue 3½ miles up the trail to **Shoemaker Overlook** (1,500 feet). The trail accesses large ridgetop muskeg areas and ends at a new Adirondack-style shelter offering a panoramic vista of Zimovia Strait. The trail and shelter provide an excellent opportunity for an overnight camping trip. The trail is steep and often muddy, but is being rebuilt with a boardwalk. Check with the Forest Service for current conditions.

Logging roads crisscross most of Wrangell Island, providing good opportunities for mountain bike enthusiasts—if you enjoy seeing cut-over land. Check with the Forest Service to see where logging is currently going on, so you can avoid close encounters with behemoth logging trucks. Those with wheels may want to visit several areas on the island. **Long Lake Trail**, 28 miles southeast of Wrangell along Forest Road 6271, is a half-mile boardwalk that ends at an Adirondack shelter complete with a rowboat, fire grill, and outhouse. In the same vicinity is a 300-foot path to **Highbrush Lake,** where you'll find a small boat to practice your Olympic rowing skills. Handicapped individuals may want to try fishing at **Salamander Creek,** 19 miles south of town on Forest Road 6265, where ramps lead right up to a pad along the creek. Good fishing for king salmon here. For info on cabins and other trails around Wrangell, visit the Forest Service district office at 525 Bennett St. (on the way to the airport).

Cabins
The closest Forest Service cabin to Wrangell is at **Virginia Lake**, a $225 RT flight for three people and gear. See below for air taxi companies. Another nearby place is **Kunk Lake,** across Zimovia Strait from the south end of the Wrangell Island road system. Access is by kayak, or skiff if you can get someone to run you across. A 1½ mile trail climbs to a new three-sided shelter at the lake. From here, it's a relatively easy climb into high elevation muskeg and alpine areas that cross Etolin Island.

PRACTICALITIES

Motels and Lodges
The least expensive place to stay in Wrangell is **Clarke Bed and Breakfast**, 732 Case Ave., tel. 874-2125, for $40 s or $50 d. **Thunderbird Hotel,** 223 Front St., tel. 874-3322, charges $50 s or $57 d. **Roadhouse Lodge,** four miles south of town, tel. 874-2335, has rooms for $50 s or $58 d, including transport from town. It also has a restaurant and bar. **Harding's Old Sourdough Lodge**, tel. 874-3613, charges $55 s or d ($63 s including breakfast). This is a friendly, down-home sort of place that includes a sauna and steam bath, plus free pickup from the ferry or airport. **Stikine Inn** on Front St., tel. 874-3388, costs $73 s and $78 d (weekend specials for $48 s or $53 d). Families may prefer to stay at **Harbor House,** 645 Shakes St., tel. 874-2277, where a furnished house costs $110 d, plus $5 pp for children.

Camping
Free tent camping is allowed (no vehicles) at **City Park** just beyond the ball field, two miles south of the ferry on the water side of the main highway. The official limit is 24 hours, but this is not strictly enforced. More free camping (RV parking too) at **Shoemaker Bay,** five miles south of town, but you'll find yourself right alongside the highway. One advantage of this camping site is its proximity to trails to Rainbow Falls and Shoemaker Overlook (see above). The unmaintained **Pat's Creek Campground** (free), 11 miles south of town, isn't worth the trip unless you have an RV. Pat's Creek is, however, a good place to see spawning salmon.

Food
Wrangell restaurants leave much to be desired, but the **Dock Side Restaurant** at Stikine Inn, tel. 874-3737, has decent breakfasts. The **Diamond C**, just up the street, tel. 874-3677, may be a better bet for breakfasts and other meals. Try their homemade soups at lunchtime. The **Pizza and Ice Cream Shop,** on Front St., tel. 874-2353, sells homemade pizza by the pie or slice, or you might try **J&W's** (a couple of doors down) for greasy fast food. Get pastries and espresso coffee (at least that's what they call it) at **Dreyer's Doughnuts,** also on Front St., tel. 874-3010. **Harding's Old Sourdough Lodge,** tel. 874-3455, serves family-style dinners. Ask around the harbor for local fishermen selling fresh shrimp (Wrangell's specialty) or salmon. **Benjamin's Supermarket**, on Outer Dr., tel. 874-2341, has a deli with inexpensive sandwiches. **City Market** on Front St., tel. 874-3336, is Wrangell's other grocery store.

Entertainment
The **Stikine Inn Lounge,** tel. 874-3388, offers live music and dancing six nights a week (no cover). Locals also hang out in the **Marine Lounge,** 274 Shakes St., tel. 874-3005, and the **Brig Bar**, 532 Front St., tel. 874-3442.

Information And Services
The **Wrangell Visitor Center**, tel. 874-3901, is downtown in an A-frame beside the 65-foot-tall Kiksadi totem pole. It's open Mon.-Fri. 10-4, but skip it and get information at the museum instead. The **library** has a good collection of books about Alaska; ask about their cartoon shows complete with fresh pop-

corn (25 cents). For excellent local info, pick up a copy of *The Wrangell Guide* (free) at the ferry terminal. The **Forest Service Ranger district office**, tel. 874-2323, is on Bennett St., three-quarters of a mile from town on the left side of the road. They have info on local hiking trails, the Stikine River, and 23 nearby recreation cabins ($20). Wrangell's excellent **swimming pool** at the high school, tel. 874-2381, costs $2, and is the place to go for showers if you're camping out. For quality Alaskan crafts and jewelry, stop by **Jays Fine Gifts,** across from Stikine Inn. Fishing and sightseeing **charters** are available through a number of local outfits; get brochures from the visitor center. Rates aren't cheap: around $200 for two people on a half-day trip.

Transportation

Wrangell's **ferry terminal** is right in town, and has coin lockers inside. Ferries head both north and south almost daily during the summer months. The terminal opens 1½ hours before ferries arrive, and recorded ferry departure info is available at tel. 874-3711. **Star Cab**, tel. 874-3622, and **Porky's Cab,** tel. 874-3603, both charge $5 to transport a car load of people and gear to the campsites in City Park.

The airport is a mile from town on Bennett Street. **Alaska Airlines**, tel. (800) 426-0333, has daily flights from Wrangell to Juneau ($112), Ketchikan ($97), Petersburg ($62), and Sitka ($105), along with other Alaskan and Lower 48 cities. **Ketchikan Air Service**, tel. 874-2369, or (800) 478-2360, has daily service to Kake ($90), Ketchikan ($87), Klawock ($143), and Petersburg ($55). Both Ketchikan Air Service and **Sunrise Aviation**, tel. 874-2319, provide charter flights to nearby Forest Service cabins. Forty-five-minute Le Conte Glacier and Stikine River flightseeing trips cost around $60 pp. **Allstar Rent-A-Car**, tel. 874-3975, has cars for $40/day with 50 free miles. Rent bikes from **Pedal Power**, tel. 874-3986.

THE STIKINE RIVER

Wrangell is only seven miles from the mouth of the Stikine River, one of the top 10 wild rivers of Canada and the fastest navigable river in North America. The river begins its 330-mile journey to the sea high inside British Columbia's Spatsizi Wilderness Park. The 55 mile-long Grand Canyon of the Stikine, just above Telegraph Creek, B.C., has thousand-foot walls enclosing fierce whitewater. River travel is easier below Telegraph Creek, all the way to Wrangell, between high peaks of the coast range, past glaciers and forested hills. At one spot on the river, 21 different glaciers are visible! These glaciers dump tons of silt into the river, coloring it a milky gray; at the mouth of the Stikine, the sea takes on this color for miles in all directions. So much for the advertisements about glacially pure water!

Running The River

The Stikine River is a popular destination for kayakers, canoeists, and river rafters. (It is even more popular with local jetboaters, so don't expect peace and quiet in the lower reaches.) You can either float down the river from Telegraph Creek, B.C. or work your way upriver to the Canadian border (30 miles) and then float back. (You will need to go through customs at the Wrangell airport if you cross the border.) Heading upriver is not as difficult as it might sound, and the route is well documented. Be extremely cautious, however, when crossing the mouth of the Stikine by canoe, especially during the bigger tides and when the wind is blowing. The Forest Service publishes an excellent **guide and map** ($3) of Stikine canoe/kayak routes, available from the Wrangell Ranger District, Box 51, Wrangell, AK 99929. Canoe or kayak rentals are not available in Wrangell (the insurance companies strike again!), but you can bring your own along on the ferry at a small extra charge. Another possibility is to rent a skiff ($75/day from Harbor House, tel. 874-2277) and motor up the river, carefully avoiding the sandbars and submerged logs.

The lower Stikine is a multi-channeled, silt-laden river nearly a mile wide in places. The route is spectacular, wildlife crowds the banks, campsites are numerous, and 13 Forest Service cabins ($20) are available. One of the finest is the **Mt. Rynda Cabin** along crystal-clear Andrew Creek, a spawning area for king salmon. You may also want to stay in one of the two cabins near **Chief Shakes Hot Springs**. At the springs you'll discover two wooden hot tubs (one enclosed), making a great place to soak those aching muscles. Note, however, that macho Wrangellites run loud jetboats up here, and the facility is often crowded and dirty on summer weekends, especially when the river is high enough to get boats up the side channels (generally in mid-July). It is the local party place. Also beware that the river is run twice each day by a very noisy hovercraft that carries supplies to, and ore from, a gold mine on the Iskut River, and creates a large wake. You can escape the crowds at the main hot springs by finding your own undeveloped springs in surrounding areas.

The upper portion of the Stikine is a vastly different river, with less noise and development than on the U.S. side of the border, and a drier, colder climate. The vegetation reflects this. The settlement of Telegraph Creek is accessible by road from the rest of B.C., or you can charter a small plane from Wrangell. Well-prepared, intrepid river runners with rafts might put in off the Cassiar Highway; canoeists and kayakers intent on running the river would do best to begin at Telegraph Creek.

Tours

Stikine Riversong Lodge in Telegraph Creek, tel. (604) 235-3196, will help you set up raft trips down the Stikine. They also have lodging, supplies, and a pleasant cafe. Several charter boat operators in Wrangell provide day trips or longer voyages by power boats up the Stikine River. Guided day-trips up the river from Wrangell will set you back $125 pp. Contact **TH Charters,** tel. 874-3455, or **Terry Buness,** tel. 874-3061, for specifics. These companies, along with **Frank Gleason** in Telegraph Creek, tel. (604) 778-7316, will also pick up canoes in Wrangell and haul you upriver so you can float back. **Tel-Air,** in Telegraph Creek, tel. (604) 235-3296, will fly you and your canoe to Telegraph Creek for the put in.

PETERSBURG

Southeast Alaska's picture-postcard town, Petersburg (pop. 3,500) sits at the north tip of Mitkof Island along the Wrangell Narrows. Great white walls of snow and ice act as a dramatic backdrop for the town. "Peter's Burg" was named after Peter Buschmann, who built a sawmill in 1897, followed by a cannery three years later. With ample supplies of fish, timber, and glacial ice, the cannery proved an immediate success—32,750 cases of salmon were shipped that first season. Unlike boom-and-bust Wrangell, the planned community of Petersburg has kept pace with its expanding fishing base. Many of the present inhabitants are descended from Norwegian fishermen, who found that the place reminded them of their native land. The language is still occasionally heard on Petersburg's streets, and Norwegian rosemaling (floral painting) can be found on window shutters of the older homes.

Petersburg is a prosperous and squeaky-clean town with green lawns (a rarity in Alaska), tidy homes, and a hard-working heritage that may appear a bit cliquish to outsiders. Although the town has a lumber mill, fishing is still the main activity here, with salmon, halibut, herring, crab, and shrimp all landed. The odor of fish hangs in the air. Petersburg has the most canneries in Southeast Alaska (four) and is home to the world's largest halibut fleet. It is a self-sufficient, inward-looking community, that only tolerates tourism instead of promoting it.

Wrangell Narrows

Between Wrangell and Petersburg the ferry passes through tortuous Wrangell Narrows, a 46-turn nautical obstacle course that resembles a pinball game played by ship. This is one of the highlights of the Inside Passage trip, and is even more exciting at night when the zigzag course is lit up like a Christmas tree. Be up front to see it. The larger cruise ships are too big to negotiate these shallow waters between Kupreanof and Mitkof islands, thus sparing Petersburg from the tourist blitz and glitz other Southeast towns endure.

SIGHTS

In Town

Petersburg's main attraction is its gorgeous harbor and spectacular setting. The sharply pointed peak visible behind Petersburg is **Devil's Thumb,** a 9,077-foot mountain 30 miles away on the U.S.-Canadian border. The **Sons of Norway Hall** (1911), built on pilings over scenic Hammer Slough, bears traditional Norwegian rosemaling designs on the exterior. Inside is the **Husfliden** craft shop which sells locally made Scandinavian handicrafts. **Clausen Memorial Museum,** 2nd and Fram streets, tel. 772-3598, is open Mon.-Fri. 1-5 and Tues. 8:30-10:30 p.m. (donation). Inside, find the world's largest king salmon (a 126-pound monster) and chum salmon (36 pounds), along with the impressive old Cape Decision lighthouse lens and other historical exhibits. Outside is an 11-foot bronze sculpture and fountain by Carson Boysen. The new visitor information center is next door. Check with Patti Norheim at **Tongass Traveller,** tel. 772-4680, for local cannery tours. A good place to watch eagles is **Eagle's Roost Park,** near the Petersburg Fisheries cannery. Upwards of 30 eagles have been seen at one time along here when the tide is low.

Nearby

South of town, the main road is paved for 18 miles and a gravel road continues for another 16 miles to the southeast end of Mitkof Island. From this point you have excellent views of the nearby Stikine River mouth and the white-capped peaks of the Coast Range. Canoeists or kayakers (with transportation) may want to start their trip up the Stikine from here rather than Wrangell (see "Wrangell" for details). A **trumpeter swan observatory** is set up on Blind Slough 16 miles south of Petersburg. Approximately 20 pairs of these majestic birds overwinter here and other waterfowl abound during spring and fall migrations. **Crystal Lake Fish Hatchery,** 18 miles south of Petersburg, produces king, coho, and chum salmon, plus steelhead trout.

Le Conte Glacier

Le Conte Glacier, the southernmost tidewater glacier in North America, dips into Le Conte Bay on the mainland, 25 miles east of Petersburg. Part of the vast Stikine Icefield, the glacial ice was once used by local fishermen to keep their catches cold on the way to market in Seattle. Today, locals use it to cool their drinks. Le Conte Bay is home to 2,000 harbor seals. The entire area is included with the 448,841-acre **Stikine-Le Conte Wilderness.** There are no Forest Service cabins in Le Conte Bay, but an excellent one is on **Mallard Slough,** near its entrance. A 1½-mile trail connects the cabin and Le Conte Bay, where you're likely to find icebergs high and dry at low tide. A fine trip for experienced sea kayakers is to head up the Stikine River from Wrangell and then into Le Conte Bay, 10 miles north, before crossing Frederick Sound and continuing on to Petersburg. Total distance is approximately 50 miles (longer if you explore the Stikine River or Le Conte Bay).

The visitor center has a complete listing of boat charters for fishing or other sightseeing around the area. Outback Expeditions, Box 16343, Seattle, WA 98116, offers guided trips to Le Conte Bay. If you want to do it yourself, rent a skiff from **Tides Inn,** tel. 772-4288, for $125/day. **Ron Compton,** tel. 772-3978, (11 miles out of town) has a canoe for rent. **Alaska Island Air,** tel. 772-4222, **Nordic Air,** tel. 772-3535, and **Pacific Wing,** tel. 772-9258, all charge around $150 for a 45-minute flightseeing trip of the glacier (up to three people).

Nearby Hiking And Cabins

See the Forest Service district office (upstairs from the post office) for detailed maps of local hiking trails and nearby cabins. A pleasant one-mile walk takes off from Nordic Dr. (just beyond Sandy Beach) and continues along a boardwalk to **Frederick Point.** Along the way, you get a taste of muskeg, rainforest, and a creek that's packed with salmon in August. You can return to town along the beach.

Petersburg has one of the few Forest Service cabins in Southeast Alaska that can be reached by hiking from town. The **Ravens Roost** cabin lies 1,600 feet above sea level at the end of a four-mile trail that starts near the red-and-white water tower next to the airport. Camping is permitted on Forest Service land anywhere out of sight of the trail and well away from the cabin. The trail traverses muskeg for the first mile, becomes very steep (and often mucky) for the next mile through the forest, before breaking into open muskeg again along a ridge. Here the trail is in better condition and you are treated to grand views of Devil's Thumb and the surrounding country. Keep your eyes open for wolf tracks. The path ends at a two-level Forest Service cabin with space for up to eight people. Allow three hours for the hike up and be sure to make advance reservations for the cabin through the Forest Service ($20 per night). Come wintertime, Ravens Roost cabin becomes a popular cross-country ski center, with access either by skis or a local helicopter company.

A five-mile ski/snowmobile trail connects the cabin to **Twin Creek Road** (7½ miles south of Petersburg). A second ski route provides a three-mile loop trip from Twin Creek Road. Both of these trails can also be hiked in the summer. Very popular with locals for picnicking, fishing, and berry picking is the beautiful **Three Lakes Recreation Area** along Forest Service Road 6235, located 33 miles southeast of town. You can hitch there, but it's a long hike back to town if your thumb is numb. Each lake has a rowboat and picnic table and you may want to camp nearby at the old three-sided shelter built by the CCC along tiny Shelter Lake. An easy three-mile boardwalk loop trail connects the lakes; a brushed-out primitive trail continues from Sand Lake to nearby Ideal Cove, 1½ miles away. Be sure to wear your rubber boots. The three main lakes (Sand, Hill, and Crane) are named after the cranes that announce each spring.

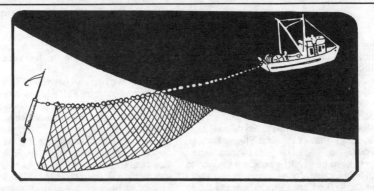

Three types of salmon-fishing boats are commonly seen along the Pacific coast. The gillnetter is easily recognized by the large drum at the stern of the boat. Fish are caught by the gills in the long nylon net played out from the drum and removed by hand as the net is wound back in.

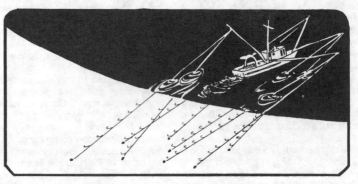

Trollers use tall poles that stick straight up from the boat when not in use. To catch fish they are extended over the sides with up to 8 trailing lines and hooks. The hooked fish are pulled in either hydraulically (power trollers) or by hand (hand trollers).

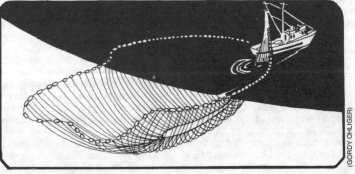

(GORDY OHLIGER)

The purse seiner is the largest of the types. It is recognized by the power block in the rigging to haul the net in, and by a skiff that is usually perched astern. A net with floats along the top edge and weights at the bottom is pulled out around a school of fish by a man in a skiff. When the fish are surrounded, the bottom is closed like a purse and the net is pulled out by the power block.

Kupreanof Island Trails

On nearby Kupreanof Island, the **Petersburg Mountain** and **Petersburg Lake** trails provide good hiking and great views. Both paths begin at the State Boat Dock on Bayou Point directly across Wrangell Narrows. Ask around Petersburg harbor for people willing to provide skiff transportation for a fee. For Petersburg Mountain, walk north (right) up the road 1½ miles to the trail marker. Be prepared for a very steep, muddy, and brushy path, rising 3,000 feet in a distance of only 2½ miles. From the top, however, you'll be rewarded with outstanding views of the entire Petersburg area.

Petersburg Creek Trail provides an easy 6½-mile hike to a Forest Service cabin ($20 a night) on Petersburg Lake, within the 46,777-acre **Petersburg Creek-Duncan Salt Chuck Wilderness.** Check with the Forest Service for current conditions, since it is being rebuilt. A diamond-shaped sign marks the trailhead along the shore. Fish the creek for coho salmon, steelhead, and cutthroats. Another option is to fly in to Petersburg Lake (approximately $100 for three people and gear) and hike back out. From Petersburg Lake it's possible to continue another 10½ miles along a primitive but brushed-out trail to the Forest Service's Salt Chuck West cabin. The trail is nearly level the entire distance and offers spectacular views of Portage Mountain.

On the south end of Kupreanof Island is **Kah Sheets Lake,** where the Forest Service has an A-frame cabin ($20/night) that is now wheelchair accessible. The cabin is a 30-minute flight from Petersburg (approximately $200 RT for three people and gear). A three-mile trail leads from the lake to Kah Sheets Bay where you can fish for coho and sockeye salmon. A second Forest Service cabin sits along the bay.

PRACTICALITIES

Accommodations

With nearly a thousand transient cannery workers clamoring for housing in Petersburg, travelers often have a hard time finding a place to stay. Unfortunately, there is no youth hostel in Petersburg, and no cheap lodging. **Jewell's by the Sea,** 1106 Nordic Dr., tel. 772-3620, has beachfront rooms for $50 s or $60 d, including a full breakfast. **Beachcomber Inn,** three miles south of the ferry, has rooms starting for $50 s or $60 d including courtesy van service. **Narrows Inn,** across from the ferry terminal, tel. 772-4284, has rooms for $55 s or $65 d. **Scandia House,** on Main St., tel. 772-4281, has rooms with bath down the hall for $55 s or $70 d, including a continental breakfast and courtesy van service. The AAA-approved **Tides Inn** at 1st and Dolphin streets, tel. 772-4288, charges $65 s or $75 d, including a continental breakfast. **Mountain Point Bed and Breakfast,** along scenic Wrangell Narrows, tel. 772-9382, costs $65 s or $75 d. For something different, groups may want to try **Green Rocks Lodge,** tel. 772-3245. A flat rate of $200 for up to four people includes a full breakfast, access to a skiff with fishing gear, and transport from Petersburg. This is quite a bargain.

Camping

Finding a place to camp in Petersburg can be a problem during the summer. The only designated camping area close to town is **Tent City,** about two miles out, between the airport and Sandy Cove. This campground (alias "Visqueen Acres") consists of 38 wooden tent platforms built over the wet muskeg and connected by boardwalk to a covered cooking/partying area with cold running water, firewood, and toilets. There are no showers or phones. The facility becomes home to dozens of cannery workers during the summer and is often full by June. Travelers often have a hard time finding space, and those who do should be ready for a very noisy night. Tent City costs $5/tent pad (two people) or $35/week. City Cab has a CB at Tent City that you can use to call for a ride to town ($4 for two people) or to check on times to report for work at the canneries. It may not be legal, but good camping sites can also be found by walking east a half-mile along the beach from Sandy Beach Recreation Area. The sites are in the woods near the beach.

Look around, and you may find ancient petroglyphs on nearby stones.

Those with a vehicle or willing to try hitching should head south 22 miles to the Forest Service's excellent **Ohmer Creek Campground.** It's free and provides a quiet place in a flower-filled meadow along Blind Slough. Water is available. Not far away is the quarter-mile long, wheelchair-accessible **Ohmer Creek Trail,** complete with interpretive signs. RVers often head to **Le Conte RV Park,** 4th St. and Haugen Dr., tel. 772-4680, or **Twin Creek RV Park,** seven miles south of town,

tel. 772-3244, where full hookups cost $15/night.

Food And Entertainment

For a good greasy-spoon meal, visit the **Homestead Café** downtown on Main St. (open 24 hours). Try their fish and chips basket for lunch. **The Coffee Cache,** next door, has pastries (including delicious Norwegian krumkak), along with soups, salads, sandwiches, and fresh shrimp cocktails. **Helse Café** at Sing Lee Alley and Gjoa St., tel. 772-3444, serves inexpensive earthy

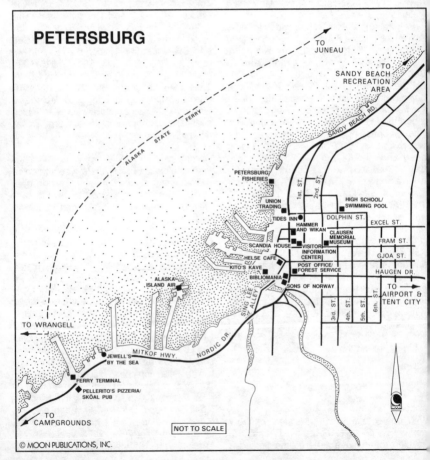

PETERSBURG

TO JUNEAU

TO SANDY BEACH RECREATION AREA

ALASKA STATE FERRY

SANDY BEACH RD.

PETERSBURG FISHERIES

UNION TRADING

TIDES INN

HAMMER AND WIKAN

SCANDIA HOUSE

HELSE CAFE

KITO'S KAVE

ALASKA ISLAND AIR

BIBLIOMANIA

CLAUSEN MEMORIAL MUSEUM

VISITORS INFORMATION CENTER

POST OFFICE/ FOREST SERVICE

SONS OF NORWAY

1st. ST.

2nd. ST.

HIGH SCHOOL/ SWIMMING POOL

DOLPHIN ST.

EXCEL ST.

FRAM ST.

GJOA ST.

HAUGEN DR.

3rd ST.

4th ST.

5th ST.

6th ST.

TO AIRPORT & TENT CITY

SING LEE ALLEY

NORDIC DR.

TO WRANGELL

JEWELL'S BY THE SEA

MITKOF HWY.

FERRY TERMINAL

PELLERITO'S PIZZERIA/ SKÖAL PUB

TO CAMPGROUNDS

NOT TO SCALE

MOON

© MOON PUBLICATIONS, INC.

lunches with homemade soup and bread. Don't miss Friday's fish chowder and thick, hearty bread for $4. Try the downtown street vendors around lunch for a cheap quick meal. Budget watchers should head down to the docks to buy fresh-caught salmon, halibut, or shrimp.

The Beachcomber Inn, tel. 772-3888, four miles south of Petersburg, serves up delicious fish, and has live music most nights. They even provide free van service to and from town. Another excellent choice for fresh seafood and steak is **The Quay,** 1103 Nordic, tel. 772-4600. For some of the best pizzas in Alaska, head to **Pellerito's Pizzaria,** across from the ferry terminal. Order downstairs and head up to the **Skoal Pub and Disco** for a beer. The bartender will call out your name when it's ready. This is a good place to watch sporting events on the TVs, and their disco is open most evenings. Live music, booze, and a clientele of local toughs make for good fights in **Kito's Kave** on Sing Lee Alley. For something more relaxing, **Scandia House,** 110 Nordic Dr., tel. 772-4281, has hot tubs for $9.50 pp/hr ($16/hr for two people).

Prices for food and other items are higher in Petersburg than other Southeast towns. The friendliest place for groceries is **Hammer and Wikan** on Main St., tel. 772-4246, but **Trading Union,** tel. 772-3881, (two blocks farther down) tends to be a little cheaper. Get natural foods at **Helse Foods** on Sing Lee Alley, tel. 772-3444.

Events

Petersburg's **Little Norway Festival,** held each year on the weekend nearest Norwegian Independence Day (May 17), is the town's biggest event. The three-day festivities include boat races, a pseudo-Viking ship, folk dancing, Norwegian costumes, pancake breakfasts, and a big seafood smorgasbord. The American **Independence Day** (July 4) is another time for fun and games, and the annual **salmon derby** (late May) is always popular with locals.

Information And Services

The new **Petersburg Visitor Information Center** is on 1st and Fram streets, tel. 772-

3646, and is open Mon.-Fri., 7:30-5. For up-to-date local info pick up a copy of Petersburg's free **"Viking Visitor Guide"** here or at the ferry terminal. The Forest Service publishes a **map** ($3) of the Petersburg area ("Mitkof Island Road Guide"), available from their office upstairs in the post office building on Main St., tel. 772-3871. It details the whys and wherefores of logging on the island, and even describes a tour of local clearcuts for the truly dedicated timber beast. (The title on the back cover gives you an idea of its biases: "Timber Harvest Prepares the Way.") The map is a must if you're planning to ride a mountain bike around the island.

Sing Lee Alley Bookstore, tel. 772-4440, next to the Sons of Norway Hall, has an excellent collection of Alaskan books and other choice reading material. The town **library,** open Mon.-Thurs. noon-9, Fri. and Sat. 1-5, is upstairs in the municipal building on Main Street. Coin-operated **showers** are available downtown next to the harbormaster's office ($1 gives you eight minutes of hot water). For a better deal, head to the public **swimming pool** ($2) at Petersburg High School, tel. 772-3304.

Transportation

Petersburg is strung out along Wrangell Narrows, with the ferry terminal a mile south of town center. During the summertime, ferries run almost daily both north- and southbound from Petersburg. They usually stop for an hour or two, long enough to walk into town or at least check out the nearby harbor. The ferry terminal, tel. 772-3855, does not have storage lockers, but it's usually OK to leave things inside while it's closed. The terminal opens two hours prior to ship arrivals. **City Cab,** tel. 772-3003, charges $4 pp for transport from the ferry to Tent City. Rent cars from **Rent-A-Dent,** tel. 772-4281, or **Avis,** tel. 772-4716, or (800) 331-1212.

Petersburg Airport is a mile southeast of town on Haugen Drive. **Alaska Airlines,** tel. (800) 426-0333 has daily service to Juneau ($103), Ketchikan ($97), Sitka ($99), Wrangell ($65), and other places in Alaska and the Lower 48. **Alaska Island Air,** tel. 772-3130, flies daily to Kake ($47), while **Ketchikan Air Service,** tel. 772-3443, has daily flights to Kake ($45), Ketchikan ($90), and Wrangell ($55). **Wings of Alaska,** tel. 772-3536, flies to Juneau ($97) and Kake ($47). **Alaska Island Air,** along with **Pacific Wing,** tel. 772-9258, and **Kupreanof Flying Service,** tel. 772-3396, all provide air charter service to Forest Service cabins and nearby sites (around $200/hour for two people and gear).

KAKE

The small Tlingit village of Kake (pop. 670) lies along the northwest shore of Kupreanof Island, halfway between Petersburg and Sitka. Kake's single claim to fame is being home to the world's tallest totem pole, exhibited at the 1970 World's Fair in Osaka, Japan. The 132-foot pole is unique in that it contains figures representing all the Tlingit clans on a single pole. Kake is also the starting point for sea kayak trips into two large wilderness areas on nearby Kuiu Island.

History
During the 1800s the Kake tribe had a reputation as one of the fiercest in Southeast. Richard Meade (1871) recorded the following incident: "In 1855 a party of Kakes, on a visit south to Puget Sound, became involved in some trouble there, which caused a United States vessel to open fire on them, and during the affair one of the Kake chiefs was killed. This took place over 800 miles from the Kake settlements on Kupreanof Island. The very next year the tribe sent a canoe-load of fighting men all the way from Clarence Straits in Russian America to Whidby's Island in Washington Territory, and attacked and beheaded an ex-collector—not of internal revenue, for that might have been pardonable—but of customs, and returned safely with his skull and scalp to their villages. Such people are, therefore, not to be despised, and are quite capable of giving much trouble in the future unless wisely and firmly governed." John Muir later described a visit to a Kake village where human bones were scattered all over the ground, reminders of previ-

ous battles: "Chief Yana Taowk seemed to take pleasure in kicking the Sitka bones that lay in his way, and neither old nor young showed the slightest trace of superstitious fear of the dead at any time." Needless to say, the people of Kake treat outsiders in a more friendly manner today.

Practicalities
New Town Inn, tel. 785-3472, has rooms for rent, and the **Nugget Inn,** tel. 785-6469, serves meals. In town are three grocery stores; **SOS Value-Mart** is the largest. Kake has a laundromat and liquor store, but no bank. For local info contact the City of Kake, Box 500, Kake, AK 99830, tel. 785-3804. Camping facilities are not available and much of the land around Kake is privately owned, but camping is permitted on Forest Service land, two miles south of town. Charters and tours are becoming available as Kake residents begin to enter the tourism business. Kake is one of the drier towns in Southeast, with 50 inches per year of precipitation. The town has a fish hatchery and cold-storage plant but no Forest Service office. Ask at the Forest Service office in Petersburg about the Cathedral Falls, Goose Lake, and Hamilton River trails. **Big John Cabin** ($20/night) on Big John Bay is accessible from the Kake road network.

Transportation
The ferry *Le Conte* visits Kake twice a week, heading both east to Petersburg and west to Sitka. The ferry docks 1½ miles from the center of town. There is only a covered shelter area with no phone or storage lockers. The *Le Conte* usually stops just long enough to load and unload cars (a half-hour or so). There are daily flights between Kake and Petersburg (around $47) by **Alaska Island Air,** tel. 772-3130 (in Petersburg), **Ketchikan Air Service,** tel. 785-3284, and **Wings of Alaska,** tel. 772-3536 or (800) 478-9464. **BellAir,** tel. 747-8636 in Sitka, flies daily between Sitka and Kake for $86.

Kuiu Island
If you have the time, equipment, and skill, nearby Kuiu (pronounced Q-U) Island pro-

vides excellent kayaking and canoeing opportunities. The area is filled with an enjoyable network of islands and waterways. The Forest Service has cleared four portages (ranging from one to four miles in length), making it possible to do a variety of loop trips. Plan on at least a week and be sure to check with the Forest Service on current trail conditions, especially the Alecks Creek Portage. Be cautious along portions of Kuiu Island exposed to ocean swells, particularly near Pt. Ellis. Three Forest Service cabins ($20/night) are along the route. Also of interest are the protected waters of scenic **Rocky Pass,** separating Kupreanof and Kuiu islands. Because of the numerous reefs the pass is treacherous for boats, but can be run in a kayak if you traverse with the tidal flows. Some supplies are available at the Gedney Harbor Fish Buying Scow, but check with Petersburg Fisheries in Petersburg first to see what is available.

Two wilderness areas encompass the south and west sides of Kuiu Island; other parts have been very heavily logged in recent years. Dozens of interesting islands, islets, and coves crowd the west side of Kuiu in the 67,000-acre **Tebenkof Bay Wilderness,** while the south end includes the newly established 60,000-acre **Kuiu Wilderness.** Wilderness rangers patrol these areas from kayaks. The Forest Service publishes a detailed map of Kuiu Island with descriptions of all portages and routes. Get a copy of **"Kuiu Island/ Tebenkof Bay Canoe/Kayak Routes"** ($1) from Petersburg Ranger District, Box 1328, Petersburg, AK 99833, tel. 772-3871. Experienced kayakers will enjoy the paddle between Kake and Petersburg around the south end of Kupreanof Island. There is open water in places, but a good portion of the route is protected, and the state ferry makes it easy to get between Kake and Petersburg.

SITKA

Sitka (population 8,400) is everybody's favorite Southeast Alaska town. Look out on the gem-like setting of Sitka Sound on a typical summer day. Fishing boats head out to sea from the three harbors, passing the hundreds of islands that dot the sound. Tugboats pull huge log rafts toward the nearby pulp mill. Cruise ships steam by, their decks crowded with tourists as they pass the Mt. Fuji-like snowcapped volcano that adorns Sitka's outer waters. Back in town, other visitors glance inside the Russian church that dominates Sitka's center, wander along totem-pole-lined paths in Sitka National Historical Park, and climb up the sharply rising wooded peaks. The people who make this their home are similarly diverse, ranging from laid-back post-hippie boat builders to tough-as-nails loggers ready to spit in the eye of "environ-meddlers from Outside." This surprising diversity and the gorgeous setting make Sitka a detour well worth the effort. Be forewarned, however, to expect rain—the town soaks in 94 inches a year. (By the way, Sitka lays claim to being the "largest city in America"; its boundaries encircle Baranof Island, fully 4,710 square miles!)

Located on the western shore of Baranof Island, "Sitka-by-the-Sea" is one of Southeast Alaska's most remote ferry stops, and the only major Southeast town to front on the Pacific Ocean. Getting to Sitka by ferry requires a long detour through the scenic but treacherous Sergius Narrows that separates Baranof and Chichagof islands— a great place to watch for eagles perched on trees along the shore. During larger tides, fierce currents prevent ferries from going through, and the ships must time their passage to coincide with a high or low slack tide. This has one side benefit: the ferry is forced to stay for three hours in Sitka, long enough for you to get a taste of this fascinating town.

History

First established as a base for collecting sea otter pelts, Sitka has a long and compelling history. In 1799, Alexander Baranof—head of the Russian American Company—founded the settlement under a charter from the czar. Baranof built his original fort, Redoubt St. Michael, near the present Alaska ferry terminal, only to see it destroyed by a Tlingit attack in 1802. (There is evidence that the British, long enemies of the Russians, assisted the Tlingits in the fort's destruction.) Two years later Baranof returned with 120 soldiers and 800 Aleuts in 300 baidarkas, defeating the Tlingits in what was to become the last major resistance by any Northwest Coast Indians. The Russians rebuilt the town, then called New Archangel, on the present site and constructed a stockade enclosing what is now downtown Sitka. New Archangel soon became the capital of Russian America and a vital center for the sea otter and fur seal trade with China. Although the Tlingits were invited back in 1821, the groups coexisted uneasily. Tlingits built their houses just outside the stockade, facing a battery of eight Russian cannons.

Once labeled the "Paris of the North Pacific," New Archangel quickly became the Northwest's most cosmopolitan port. By 1840, it was already home to a library of several thousand volumes, a museum, a meteorological observatory, two schools, a hospital, an ar-

Russian emblem
(LOUISE FOOTE)

mory, two orphanages, and dozens of other buildings. The wealthier citizens lived in elaborate homes filled with crystal and fine lace, but as with czarist Russia itself, the opulence of Sitka did not extend beyond a select few. Slave-like working and living conditions were forced upon the Aleut sea otter hunters.

An emotional ceremony at Sitka in 1867 marked the passage of Alaska from Russian to American hands, and most of the Russians returned to their motherland, including many third-generation Sitkans. Even today, however, one still occasionally hears Russian spoken on Sitka's streets. Although the town served as Alaska's first capital city for three decades, its importance declined rapidly under the Americans, almost becoming a ghost town by the turn of the century. The state government was moved to the then-booming mining town of Juneau in 1900.

During WW II, Sitka became a major link in the defense of Alaska against Japan. Hangars remain from the large amphibious air base just across the bridge on Japonski Island (Ft. Ray), and the barracks that once housed 3,500 soldiers were turned into Mt. Edgecumbe High School, Alaska's only boarding high school for Natives. The boarding school is now fully integrated. The Japanese may have failed in their military quest, but Sitka's Japanese-owned pulp mill (five miles east of town) is today a mainstay of the economy. Unfortunately, the mill has also gained national attention for dumping large quantities of cancer-causing dioxin into nearby Silver Bay, and for being one of the primary forces behind the clearcut logging of Tongass National Forest. In addition to jobs at the pulp mill, many Sitkans work in the fishing and tourism industries, and for the government.

SIGHTS

St. Michael's Cathedral

The most striking symbol of Russian influence in Sitka is St. Michael's Cathedral. Originally built in 1848, the building burned in 1966, but was replaced by an identical replica a decade later. The original Russian artifacts and icons, including the Sitka Madonna

St. Michael's Cathedral

(purportedly a miraculous healer), were saved from the fire and have been returned to their original setting in this, the mother church for all of Alaska's 20,000 Russian Orthodox members. The church ($1 donation), tel. 747- 8120, is open Sun. 7:30-1 and Mon.-Sat. 11-3, with longer hours when cruise ships are in port.

Other Downtown Sights

One of the finest views of Sitka is from the unusual cable-stayed, girder-span bridge that crosses Sitka harbor to Japonski Island. On a clear day, you'll have a hard time deciding which direction to look: the mountains of Baranof Island rise up behind the town, while the perfect volcanic cone of Mt. Edgecumbe (3,000 feet) on Kruzof Island dominates the opposite vista. Beside the old post office on

Lincoln St. a stairway leads up to **Castle Hill**, a tiny state park commemorating the spot where the ceremony transferring Alaska to the U.S. was held on October 18, 1867. The Kiksadi Indian clan inhabited this hill for many generations prior to the Russian arrival. After defeating the Indians, Baranof built his castle-like house here, but the building burned in 1894. The splendid view makes Castle Hill a must.

The most prominent downtown feature is the large yellow **Alaska Pioneers Home** (built in 1934), housing elderly Alaskans with 15 or more years of state residence. The Pioneer Home craft shop is open weekdays 8-5. The famous **Prospector** statue out front was based upon William "Skagway Bill" Fonda, an Alaskan pioneer. Across the road is a totem pole bearing the Russian coat of arms, three old English anchors, and a couple of Indian petroglyphs.

On a hill just west of the Pioneer Home stands a reconstructed Russian **blockhouse** from the stockade that kept the Indians restricted to the area along Katlian Street. It's open Sun. afternoons during the summer. **Kogwantan and Katlian streets,** directly below the blockhouse, are a picturesque mixture of docks, fish canneries, shops, and old houses, one with its exterior entirely covered in Tlingit designs. The main **Russian Orthodox cemetery** (400 graves dating from 1848) caps the wooded hill at the end of Observatory Street. The grave of the Russian Princess Maksoutoff is at the end of Princess St., and a few other old graves are near the blockhouse. Cemetery buffs might also be interested in the small **Sitka National Cemetery,** accessible via Jeff Davis St. beside Sheldon Jackson College. It's the oldest national cemetery west of the Mississippi.

When cruise ships are in town, Centennial Hall auditorium comes alive with half-hour performances of traditional Russian choreography by the **New Archangel Dancers** ($4). The 32 dancers are all women, though some dress in men's costumes. For a very different dance program, the Tlingit **Noow Tlein Native Dancers** give periodic performances through the summer months ($5 including fish chowder and fry bread) at the **Alaska Native Brotherhood** (ANB) hall on Katlian St., tel. 747-5302.

The **Isabel Miller Museum,** tel. 747-6455, in the Centennial Building, is open Mon.-Fri. 8-5, Sat.-Sun. 9-5 in summer, and Mon.-Fri. 10-4 in winter. A donation is requested. The museum houses a small collection of interesting local artifacts from the past 120 years. The scale model of Sitka in 1867 (the year Alaska became a U.S. territory) is especially evocative of the Russian period. A beautiful old chair made entirely of whale bones is also notable. Out front is a 50-foot carved and painted replica of a Tlingit war canoe.

Russian Bishop's House
Now administered by the National Park Service (no charge), the Russian Bishop's House is Sitka's oldest building. Built in 1842, the carefully restored building was home to Ivan Veniaminov, Bishop of Alaska, and later head of the entire Russian Orthodox Church hierarchy in Moscow. It's one of just four Russian buildings still standing in North America. The first floor houses a museum describing the building and its occupants, as well as the exploits of Russia's American colony. The second floor has been fully restored to its 1853 appearance and is filled with original furnishings and artifacts. The Bishop's House is open daily 8:30-5 during the summer or by reservation in the winter.

Sheldon Jackson Museum
Farther along the waterfront is Sheldon Jackson College, with its distinctive brown and white buildings. Established in 1878 as a place to train Alaska's Natives, this is the oldest educational institution in the state. Author James Michener lived here while researching his best-selling novel, *Alaska.*

The outstanding Sheldon Jackson Museum, tel. 747-8981, is open daily 8-5 in the summer, (Tues.-Fri. 12-4 and Sat. 9-4 in the winter). Admission is $2, or free with student ID. Dr. Sheldon Jackson (1834-1909) worked as both a Presbyterian missionary and as the first General Agent for Education in Alaska. His extensive travels throughout the territory between 1888 and 1898 allowed him to acquire thousands of Eskimo, Athabaskan,

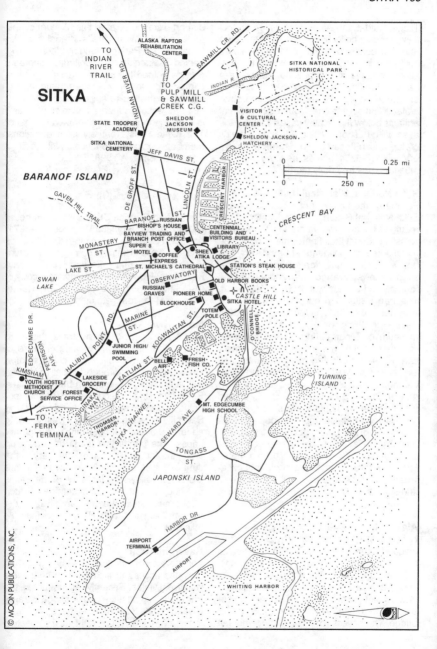

Tlingit, Haida, and Aleut artifacts. To protect this priceless collection, a fireproof museum (the first concrete structure in Alaska) was built here in 1895. Alaska's oldest, the museum contains an exceptional selection of kayaks, hunting tools, dog sleds, baskets, bentwood boxes, Eskimo masks, and other artifacts. Be sure to check out the drawers of artifacts below the display cases. Also here is a small gift shop selling Alaskan jewelry, crafts, and notecards. The **salmon hatchery,** tel. 747-5254, across the street from the museum, has free daily tours.

Sitka National Historical Park

For many, the highlight of a visit to Sitka is Sitka National Historical Park, located at the mouth of Indian River where the Tlingits and Russians fought their final battle in 1804. The Indians kept the invaders at bay for a week, but with their ammunition exhausted and resupply efforts thwarted, they abandoned the fortress and silently withdrew to Peril Strait. The free visitor and cultural center on the site, tel. 747-6281, is open daily 7:30-6 (Mon.-Sat. 8-5 in winter). It includes a small museum of Tlingit culture and a workshop (summers only) where Native craftworkers can be seen producing bead blankets, jewelry, and woodcarving. The 10-minute historical slide show, "Battle of Sitka," is very informative. Out front are totems originally carved for the 1904 St. Louis World's Fair. Behind the visitor center is a one-mile loop trail past 11 more totem poles set in the second-growth spruce forest. There are good views of picturesque Sitka Sound. The old Indian fort site where the battle was held (not excavated) is along the nearby Indian River. You'll find spawning pink salmon in the river late in the summer.

Alaska Raptor Rehabilitation Center

Located at 1101 Sawmill Creek Rd., this unique facility has a dozen or so bald eagles (and a screech owl) at any given time, most recovering from gunshots, car accidents, or steel-trap wounds. Get there by walking out of town along Sawmill Creek Rd. and a couple hundred feet beyond the Indian River bridge. The access road takes off to your left

a short distance beyond this. A more scenic route is to follow the trails through the National Historic Park or along the Indian River behind Sheldon Jackson College. Volunteers provide guided tours of the facilities, or you can pay $10 for the full tour and film (this is mainly for the cruise ship crowd). Call 747-8662 for details. When a cruise ship or ferry is in town, there is always someone on hand. The center exists entirely from donations; memberships cost $15 a year. Write them at Box 2984, Sitka, AK 99835.

HIKING

The **Forest Service Supervisors Office,** at Katlian St. and Siginaka Way, tel. 747-6671, has up-to-date info on the more than 40 miles of local trails, ranging from gentle nature walks to treks that take you high up onto nearby peaks. While there, pick up a copy of the Sitka Trails Recreation Opportunity Guide ($1) for complete details.

Indian River Trail

One of the finest of Sitka's trails, this is an easy valley hike within walking distance of town. The route follows a clear salmon spawning stream through typical rainforest, with a chance to see brown bear and deer. Begin by taking Indian River Rd. (unmarked) beside the Public Safety Academy along Sawmill Creek Road. Follow it past the gate about a half-mile to the city water pumphouse. The gentle trail leads from here up along the Indian River and a tributary to the right as far as a lovely 80-foot waterfall in a V-shaped valley. The last mile of the trail is brushed out, but not well maintained. Watch for berries along the trail and fish in the stream. Allow six hours RT to cover the 5½-mile trail.

Gaven Hill Trail

For the more adventurous, Gaven Hill Trail provides access to alpine areas near Sitka with great vistas. Recently reconstructed, the trail starts just past the house at 508 Baranof St. and climbs three miles to the top of 2,500-foot Gaven Hill. (Bear right at the junction with the Cross Trail just under a mile up.) Gaven Hill Trail then switchbacks to a long ridge that opens onto subalpine meadows before a steep final climb up the last 200 feet of elevation. From here, it's relatively easy to follow rock cairns on through the alpine, connecting to the Harbor Mountain Trail. This makes an outstanding loop hike with impressive vistas of Sitka Sound.

Harbor Mountain Trail

One of the easiest and most scenic ways to get into the alpine is via Harbor Mountain Trail. Built by the Army during World War II, the road originally provided access to a lookout post for invading Japanese ships and submarines (none were ever seen, though a whale was once mistakenly bombed after the spotters thought it an enemy submarine). Get to the trailhead by heading four miles northwest of Sitka along Halibut Point Rd. and turning right onto Harbor Mountain Road. The gravel road climbs five miles up the mountain to an elevation of 2,000 feet, but it is closed until June by snow. On sunny days the view over Sitka Sound is breathtaking. Those without a car or mountain bike should be able to hitch a ride up the road with locals. A trail begins at the parking area on top and switchbacks up a side hill before leveling out in the subalpine meadows. A spur trail heads to an overlook here, but the main trail turns right and continues past the ruins of wartime lookout buildings. Beyond this, rock cairns follow the ridge, and the path eventually connects with the Gaven Hill Trail back to town. It takes approximately six hours to hike from Harbor Mountain parking area to town via the Harbor Mountain and Gaven Hill trails. A small survival hut (no stove) provides a camping place approximately three miles in.

Mount Verstovia Trail

On a clear day get spectacular views out across Sitka Sound to Mt. Edgecumbe from the Mt. Verstovia Trail, a strenuous climb to this high, pointed peak overlooking Sitka. The steep 2½ mile trail begins on the west side of the Kiksadi Club, two miles east of town on Sawmill Creek Road. Although re-

cently brushed-out, the path can be confusing in spots. You'll pass some old Russian charcoal pits (signposted) only a quarter mile from the trailhead. The route switchbacks to a ridge, which you follow to the "shoulder" of Mt. Verstovia. The true summit is farther northeast along the ridge. Allow four hours for the return trip as far as the "shoulder" (2,000 feet), six hours RT to the top (2,550 feet).

NEARBY CABINS

Detailed information and reservations for the 20 nearby Forest Service cabins ($20/night) are available through the Sitka District Office, 204 Siginaka Way, Sitka, AK 99835, tel. 747-6671. Five of these are brand new cabins.

Redoubt Lake Cabin

One of the nicest nearby cabins is at the end of a six-mile trail that starts in Silver Bay (10 miles southeast of Sitka), goes along the shore of Salmon Lake, and then over a 600-foot saddle to the Redoubt Lake cabin. If you have (or can rent) a sea kayak, an easier way to reach the cabin is by paddling past the hundreds of small islands along the shore south of Silver Bay and into Redoubt Bay, where a short portage will take you to Redoubt Lake.

Mount Edgecumbe

Mt. Edgecumbe, a 3,000-foot volcanic cone that looks like Mt. Fuji, can be climbed along a 6½-mile trail that starts on the southeast shore of Kruzof Island. The last mile is above timberline through red volcanic ash. The island is 10 miles west of Sitka and can be reached by kayak (beware of ocean swells) or by arranging for a skiff drop-off (approximately $125 RT) through a local charter boat operator. Stay in the **Fred's Creek Cabin** at the trailhead, or in a free three-sided shelter halfway up the peak. Wonderful views from atop this dormant volcano. (Note: the Fred's Creek Cabin frequently gets trashed out by local partiers, so be sure to check with the Forest Service on its current condition.)

Lake Eva Cabin

The Lake Eva Handicap Access Cabin, 27 miles northeast of Sitka on Baranof Island, is unique in Southeast Alaska. The cabin, dock, outhouse, and fishing platform are entirely wheelchair accessible and have guard rails. It's also a great place for those with young children or physical handicaps. Good fishing for sockeye salmon, cutthroats, and steelhead. On the east side of Lake Eva (opposite the cabin) a trail leads three miles through beautiful old-growth forests to Hanus Bay. Lake Eva is a half-hour float-plane trip from Sitka (approximately $440 RT for two people and gear).

Plotnikof Lake Cabin

One of the most scenic local cabins is on the edge of Plotnikof Lake, a narrow four-mile-long lake bordered by steep mountain sides and many waterfalls. The cabin is an expensive 45-minute floatplane trip from Sitka in the spectacularly rugged South Baranof Wilderness Area. Bring fuel oil for the oil-burning stove here. A one-mile trail connects Plotnikof Lake to the similarly impressive Davidof Lake, which also has a Forest Service cabin.

PRACTICALITIES

Accommodations

See the chart for a complete listing of Sitka accommodations. The **Sitka Youth Hostel** (open June 1 to Aug. 31 only) is in the Methodist church at 303 Kimsham Rd., tel. 747-8356. Follow Halibut Point Rd. out of town toward the ferry and turn right on Peterson St. just beyond McDonald's. Kimsham St. is an immediate left from there. The hostel is on the left side of the road, just beyond Wachusetts Avenue. Lodging is $5 for members, $8 for nonmembers, sleeping bag required. The hostel is open from 6 p.m. to 8 a.m. with an 11 p.m. curfew. There are no cooking facilities. Beyond the hostel, prices rise dramatically. Least expensive is the **Bunkhouse,** but nine different bed and breakfast places offer more homey surroundings. **Sitka Hotel** is relatively inexpensive, but take a look inside

first since it has a reputation as a flop house at times.

Camping

No campgrounds are near downtown Sitka, but the Forest Service provides camping at each end of the road. The excellent **Starrigavan Campground** ($5/night) is seven miles northwest of town and three-quarters of a mile beyond the ferry terminal. Campsites to the left of the road face onto a rocky beach while those to the right border Starrigavan Creek where you can watch spawning coho salmon in late summer. Starrigavan fills up with RVs in July and Aug., but there are six walk-in sites on the ocean side of the campground (water isn't available on this side of the road, however.) Interpretive display signs mark the site of **Old Sitka** (burned by the Tlingits in 1802) between the ferry and campground.

The unmaintained and little-used **Sawmill Creek Campground** (free, but no water) is up Blue Lake Rd. beyond the pulp mill (which gives off a distinctive reminder of its presence), six miles east of town. The campground is a bit remote, making it hard to reach on foot, and the road is too rough for RVs. An excellent three-quarter-mile trail climbs up to **Beaver Lake** from the bridge at this campground. Park RVs ($10/night) at **Sealing Cove** on Japonski Island or **Sportsman's Campground** a block south of the ferry terminal.

Restaurants

For a reasonably priced breakfast, locals head to **Revard's,** downtown at 324 Lincoln St., tel. 747-3449, or to **Judy's Valley Restaurant** at 327 Seward St., tel. 747-8533. **Coffee Express,** 104 Lake St., tel. 747-3343, is a pleasant place to relax over a cup of cappuccino and a sandwich. Another good place to spend time is in the small coffee shop behind Old Harbor Books on Lincoln Street.

Staton's Steak House, at the foot of the bridge to Japonski Island, has outstanding halibut fish and chips. This is the real thing, Alaskan style. Lunch here is the best deal in town. The **Channel Club,** three miles out on

SITKA ACCOMMODATIONS

Name	Address	Phone	Rates	Features
Youth Hostel	303 Kimsham St.	747-8356	$5-8 pp	Open June-Aug. only
The Bunkhouse	3302 Halibut Pt. Rd.	747-8796	$32 s $39 d	
Hannah's B&B	504 Monastery St.	747-8309	$40 s $50 d	
Mt. View B&B	201 Cascade Cr. Rd.	747-8966	$40 s $50 d	Apartments available
Bed Inn	518 Monastery St.	747-3305	$43 s $54 d	B&B
Karra's B&B	230 Kogwantan St.	747-3978	$43 s $54 d	
Sitka Hotel	118 Lincoln St.	747-3288	$45 s $50 d	Very plain
Sitka House B&B	325 Seward St.	747-4937	$45 s $55 d	Summer only
Creek's Edge Guest House	109 Cascade Creek	747-6484	$45 s $55 d	B&B
Biorka B&B	611 Biorka St.	747-3111	$50 s $55 d	
Seaview B&B	203 Harbor Dr.	747-8020	$50 s $55 d	
Helga's B&B	2821 Halibut Pt. Rd.	747-5497	$50 s $60 d	
Potlatch Motel	713 Katlian St.	747-8611	$59 s $67 d	Recently remodeled
Super 8 Motel	404 Sawmill Cr. Rd.	747-8804	$61 s $66 d	
Westmark Shee Atika	330 Seward St.	747-6241	$96 s $102 d	AAA approved, very nice

Halibut Point Rd., tel. 747-9916, broils up great steaks and seafood, or you can do some grazing on the large salad bar. **Bayview Restaurant,** tel. 747-5440, upstairs in Bayview Trading, 407 Lincoln St., serves every possible type of burger (including one with caviar). For Russian fare, try their borscht ($3.25 a bowl) or piroshki ($7). While in the building, get a free cup of "Russian Tea," a sweet concoction of questionable authenticity containing instant tea, spices, and Tang.

For Chinese food, head to **Twin Dragon Restaurant,** tel. 747-5711, next to the Pioneer Bar on Katlian Street. **El Dorado,** at 714 Katlian St., tel. 747-5070, across from the Forest Service office, has decent Mexican food and pizzas at Alaskan prices. More au-

thentic fare at **Los Amigos,** 1305 Sawmill Creek Rd., tel. 747-3113, next to the post office. They also serve margaritas and the best local pizzas. If you're on your way into or out of town by jet, stop by the airport's **Nugget Restaurant,** tel. 966-2480, where the fresh-baked pies are famous. Get burgers and other fast food at **Lane 7 Snack Bar,** tel. 747-6310, next to the bowling alley downtown. Of course, there is always the **McDonald's** a mile out on Halibut Point Rd. for industrial-strength junk food.

Grocers

Sea Mart, two miles from town along Halibut Point Rd., tel. 747-6266, has a salad bar ($3/lb), deli, bakery, and the most complete selection of groceries in Sitka. Closer to town are **Lakeside Grocery,** 705 Halibut Point Rd., tel. 747-3317, and **Market Center Supermarket,** 210 Biorka St., tel. 747-6686. The **Fresh Fish Company,** behind Murray Pacific on Katlian St., sells fresh local salmon, halibut, shrimp, snapper, and smoked salmon and black cod. They can also smoke fish that you bring in.

On The Town

The **Kiksadi Club,** tel. 747-3285, two miles out on Sawmill Creek Rd., has live music six nights a week in a raucous atmosphere. In town, fishermen (and would-be crewmembers) hang out at the rowdy **Pioneer Bar,** tel. 747-3456, on Katlian Street. The **Shee Atika,** 330 Seward St., tel. 747-6241, also offers lounge-lizard music and rock some nights.

Events

Each June, the renowned **Sitka Summer Music Festival** attracts musicians from all over the world. Chamber music concerts ($10) are given Tues., Fri., and Sat. evenings in the Centennial Building, but the most fun is the annual Houseparty Concert ($30 with wine and cheese). Reserve early. Concert tickets may be hard to come by, but you can always visit rehearsals for free. For advance tickets and more info contact Sitka Summer Music Festival, Box 3333, Sitka, AK 99835, tel. 747-6774. Another cultural event is the **Sitka Writers Symposium** in mid-June which attracts nationally known writers.

In late May, visitors can join locals in the **Sitka Salmon Derby** where the top fish is often a 60-plus-pound king salmon. For an enjoyable slice of macho bravado by some of the nation's top loggers (some from as far away as New Zealand), be sure to see the **All-Alaska Logging Championships,** generally held the last weekend in June at the Elementary School grounds on Baranof Street. Contests include tree topping, axe chopping, speed climbing, choker setting, and others. Entrance costs $4. **July 4** is, of course, another time for fun, with a parade, races, tug-of-war, live music, and dancing. As the town where Alaska was officially transferred from Russian to American hands,

Sitka is also the place to be on **Alaska Day.** A celebration is held each October 18 with dances, a crab feed, Russian costumes, a parade, and a reenactment of the brief transfer ceremony.

Information

The modern Centennial Building houses the **Sitka Visitors Bureau,** tel. 747-5940, open daily 9-5. During summer, the Forest Service and National Park Service jointly operate a small information booth on the corner of Lake and Harbor Streets. The **Forest Service's Sitka office** is in a bright red building at Katlian St. and Siginaka Way, tel. 747-6671. For up-to-date local info pick up the summer newspaper supplement, **"All About Sitka"** (free) at the ferry terminal or visitors bureau. For the latest weather info (in great detail), push the button at the box above the ramp to Crescent Harbor (downtown).

Services

Showers are available at Homestead Laundry ($2) on Katlian St. near the Forest Service office, and Duds and Suds ($1.25) across from McDonald's on Halibut Point Road. A better deal is the public **pool** (tel 747-5677) in the junior high school at 601 Halibut Point Rd. where you can swim and shower for $1.25. The pool at Sheldon Jackson College is also open to the public daily for $2. The new main **post office** is on Sawmill Creek Rd., 1½ miles south of town, but a sub-station is in McDonald's Bayview Trading Co., corner of Lincoln and Lake streets. For fishing or cannery work head to the **Job Service Office** in the Municipal Building at 304 Lake St. (tel. 747-3423), or talk with folks on the docks and in local bars.

Booked Up

Old Harbor Books on Lincoln St. has a fine collection of books on Alaska and a small coffee shop in the back. The owner is a local Greenpeace activist, so this is a great place to catch up on environmental issues affecting Southeast Alaska. The public **library,** tel 747-8708, next to the Centennial Building downtown has a free paperback exchange with plenty of titles along with a phone for free local calls. They also have binoculars to watch whales, seals, and porpoises from the library windows that overlook the bay. The curved benches out back make a pleasant lunch spot when it isn't raining. Library hours are Sun. 1-5 p.m., Mon.-Thurs. 10-9, Fri 10-5, and Sat. noon-5.

Ferry Service

State ferries reach Sitka three or four times a week during the summer. The larger ferries usually stop for three hours; the Saturday "turn-around" runs put the *Le Conte* in Sitka for six hours. (It's used by residents of Hoonah and Angoon for a shopping visit to the big city.) The ferry terminal, tel. 747-8737 (live) or 747-3300 (recording), is open weekdays 9-5:30 and two hours prior to ship arrivals.

The terminal is seven miles north of town, but despite the distance you'll have time for a quick tour of town, even if you don't stay. Most folks ride the tour buses that meet the main ferries for $5 RT or $8 with a tour that includes the cathedral and Sitka National Historical Park. Hitching both into and out of town is easy and almost always faster than the buses. Besides, this gives you a chance to talk with locals rather than getting a canned package tour. Taxis cost approximately $12 OW from the ferry to town or $35 for a one-hour tour.

For car rentals, **Baranof Motors**, 216 Gavern St., 747-8228 has compacts at $29 a day with unlimited mileage. **Allstar Rent-A- Car**, tel. 966-2552, and **Avis**, tel. 966-2404, have cars for $40/day with unlimited miles. Book ahead since they are busy in the summer. **Bikes** ($19/day) can be rented from a van parked near Crescent Harbor or at Southeast Diving and Sports, 203 Lincoln St., tel. 747-8279.

By Air

The airport is on Japonski Island, just under a mile from town by road. **Alaska Airlines**, tel. (800) 426-0333, flies to Juneau ($85), Ketchikan ($122), Petersburg ($99), Wran-

gell ($100), and other cities in Alaska and the Lower 48. **BellAir**, 475 Katlian St., tel. 747-8636, has scheduled daily floatplane service to the nearby villages of Angoon ($76), Freshwater Bay ($86), Kake ($86), Pelican ($95), Port Alexander ($86), Port Walter ($86), Rowan Bay ($86), and Tenakee Springs ($76). Both BellAir and **Mountain Aviation** at the airport (cheaper rates), tel. 966-2288, provide charter flights to nearby Forest Service cabins, and flightseeing trips. Expect to pay around $240/hour for two people with gear in a Cessna 185 or $345/hour for a Beaver which seats four or more with gear.

On The Water

The protected waters near Sitka provide excellent kayak access to many Forest Service cabins and trails. Larry Edwards of **Baidarka Boats** rents double fiberglass kayaks for $45/day or $245/week and singles for $35/day or $175/week. Folding double kayaks are also available for $55/day or $355/week. Call 747-8996, or write him at Box 6001, Sitka, AK 99835 to reserve a kayak. This is also the only place in the U.S. to buy Nautiraid folding kayaks, a superior design to the better-known Kleppers. Request Baidarka's catalog detailing the various kayaks and kayaking equipment.

Alaskan Waters Unlimited, 1809A Edgecumbe Dr., tel. 747-5777 has a variety of local trips, including harbor tours ($35 pp), and trips to the tufted puffin colonies on **St. Lazaria Islands National Wildlife Refuge**, ($80 pp). Other wildlife commonly seen along the way are storm petrels, auklets, whales, seals, and sea lions. This area is a favorite of birdwatchers. For other charter boat and fishing opportunities, pick up a listing from the visitors bureau. Boat trips start at $70 for a half-day. Recommended is **Sitka's Secrets**, tel. 747-5089, which is run by two experienced wildlife biologists. A different option is to sail aboard the 30-foot **Miishka**, tel. 747-3608. Bareboat charters are also available.

JUNEAU

Considered by many people the nation's most beautiful state capital, Juneau (pop. 30,000) is a thriving slice of civilization surrounded by rugged Inside Passage scenery. The city perches precariously on a thin strip of land at the mouth of Gold Creek. Behind it rise the precipitous summits of Mt. Juneau and Mt. Roberts; out front Gastineau Channel separates it from Douglas Island and the town of Douglas. The city abounds with cultural and artistic attractions, and the adjacent wild country provides a broad sampling of Southeast Alaska, from glacially capped mountains to protected coves where sea kayakers relax.

Juneau is a government town, where nearly half the people work in state, federal, or city agencies. Tourism provides another mainstay for the local economy, fed by an annual influx of more than a quarter-million visitors, primarily aboard luxury cruise ships. On summer days, up to five different ships tie up simultaneously. Juneau has a small fishing fleet, and seems poised for a possible return to its old glory days of mining. The huge Greens Creek Mine—North America's largest silver mine—employs hundreds of Juneauites who commute by boat to Admiralty Island. Active plans are also afoot to reopen the long-abandoned AJ Gold Mine in Juneau and to develop the Kensington Mine 35 miles north of town near scenic Berners Bay. Local opinion is very fractured, with environmentalists fearing that the mines could damage popular recreation areas and fish habitat and exacerbate already crowded housing problems.

Juneau may be small in population, but its boundaries extend to the Canadian border covering 3,100 square miles—larger than any other American city (except Sitka, with a staggering 4,710 sq. miles). Less than half of Juneau's population actually lives downtown. The rest are spread into Douglas (across the channel), Mendenhall Valley (10 miles northwest), and other surrounding areas. As might be expected, these areas exhibit diverse personalities. Even the weather varies, with an average of 92 inches of rain each year downtown, but only 55 inches in nearby Mendenhall Valley.

Downtown Juneau is dominated by a mix of modern government offices and older wood en structures, many dating from the turn of the century. Across the Douglas Bridge is Douglas Island and the bedroom community of Douglas. The town now consists of a few shops, but at its peak in 1915 when the Treadwell Gold Mine was operating, Douglas housed 15,000 hardrock miners. The road north from downtown Juneau is Southeast's only divided highway. Heading north, you first reach Mendenhall Valley, Juneau's version of suburbia: three shopping malls, a slew of fast fooderies, and hundreds of pseudo-rustic split-level homes and condos. But spilling out of the massive Juneau Icefield is something most suburbs don't have: a drive-up glacier. The road continues north from Mendenhall Valley for another 30 miles, passing Auke Lake, the ferry terminal, and scattered homes along the way, and ending at scenic Echo Cove.

HISTORY

Gold In The Hills

In October 1880, two prospectors—Joe Juneau and Richard Harris—arrived at what would later be called Gold Creek. Along its banks was a small Tlingit fishing camp of the Auke tribe. Chief Kowee showed the prospectors gold flakes in the creek, and the resulting discovery turned out to be one of the largest gold deposits ever found. Harris and Juneau quickly staked a 160-acre townsite. The first boatloads of prospectors arrived the next month, and almost overnight a town sprouted along the shores of Gastineau Channel. Three giant hard-rock gold mines were developed in the area, eventually producing some seven million ounces of gold, worth over $3 *billion* at today's prices! Compare that to the $7.2 million the U.S. paid Russia for Alaska only 13 years before the discovery.

The **Alaska Juneau (AJ) Mine** proved the most successful, operating for more than 50 years. Built in Last Chance Basin behind Juneau, its three tunnels connected the ore source to the crushing and recovery mill site on Gastineau Channel. Inside the mine itself was a maze of tunnels that eventually reached over 100 miles long. Because the ore was low grade—it could take 28 tons of ore to yield one ounce of gold—enormous quantities of rock had to be removed. At its peak, the mill (still visible just south of town) employed 1,000 men to process 12,000 tons of ore a day. Tailings from the mill were used as the fill upon which much of downtown Juneau was constructed. (Franklin St. was originally built on pilings along the shore.) The AJ closed down in 1944 due to wartime labor shortages and never reopened. But considerable low-grade ore remains, and recently Echo Bay Mines Ltd. announced highly controversial plans to reopen the AJ by the mid-1990s. The tailings would be dumped in scenic Sheep Creek Valley south of Juneau.

The **Perseverance Mine** operated between 1885 and 1921, with a two-mile tunnel carrying ore from Gold Creek to the mill four miles south of Juneau. It eventually ran into low-grade ore and was forced to close.

The most famous Juneau-area mine was the **Treadwell,** on Douglas Island. The Treadwell Complex consisted of four mines and five stamping mills to process the ore. It employed some 2,000 men who were paid $100 a month, some of the highest wages anywhere in the world at the time. The men enjoyed such amenities as a swimming pool, Turkish baths, tennis courts, bowling alley, gymnasium, and a 15,000-volume library. The giant Treadwell stamping mills where the ore was pulverized made so much noise that people in downtown Douglas had to shout to be heard. Everything changed on April 21, 1917, when the ground atop the mines suddenly began to collapse, swallowing first the gymnasium and swimming pool, then the fire hall. Sea water rushed in, filling the tunnels as the miners ran for their lives. Amazingly, all apparently escaped alive. (The only missing miner was reportedly later seen in a nearby tavern before he skipped town.) Only one of the four mines was not destroyed in the collapse, and that one closed five years later.

Later Years

Juneau became the capital of Alaska in 1906 as a result of its rapid growth and the simultaneous decline of Sitka. Several attempts have been made to move the capital closer to the state's present power center—Anchorage. The most recent began with the 1976 statewide voter approval of a new site just north of Anchorage. Six years later, however, when expectations for petro-billions had settled into reality, voters thought better of the move and refused to fund it. Juneauites breathed a sigh of relief and went on a building spree that only ended with the sudden drop in state oil revenue from the 1986 oil price plummet. Recent years have seen ever-increasing tourism and a renewed focus on mining developments. Juneau's robust economy did not even feel the 1991 recession that hit other parts of the nation.

SIGHTS

Museums

Anyone new to Juneau should not miss the **Alaska State Museum,** at 395 Whittier St., tel. 465-2901. It's open summers Mon.-Fri. 9-6, Sat. and Sun. 10-6, and winters Tues-Sat. 10-4; admission $2 (students free). Inside, you'll find an impressive collection of Native artifacts, including a collection of wildly creative Yupik Eskimo spirit masks. Upstairs are exhibits relating to the Russian-American period and other aspects of Alaskan history. There is also a gallery of contemporary fine arts. The highlight of the museum is a full-size bald eagle nest and other wildlife in the circular stairwell.

The fine **Juneau-Douglas City Museum** ($1), tel. 586-3572, at 4th and Main streets is open summers Mon.-Fri. 9-5, Sat. and Sun. 11-5, and winters Thurs.-Sat. 12-4:30. Inside is a good collection of maps, artifacts, photos, and videos from Juneau's rich mining history. Check out the three-dimensional model of Perseverance Mine with its intricate system of tunnels. Also take a look through the museum's historic postcards from the 1920s, available for $3 apiece. The museum has free brochures describing walking tours of historic Juneau; 60 remaining downtown buildings were built before 1904!

Downtown Attractions

Enter the modernistic **State Office Building** (locally known as the SOB, a title also applied by Alaskans to the current governor, Wally Hickel) from Willoughby Ave. and take the

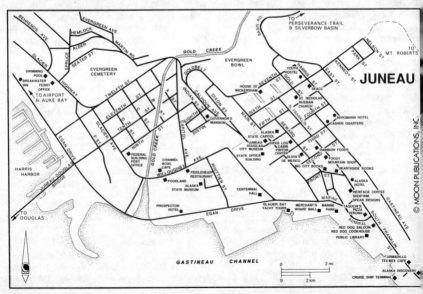

elevator up to the eighth floor. Here you'll discover a 1928 Kimball organ, a lovingly preserved totem pole from the 1880s, the Alaska State Library, and an incredible panoramic view from the observation deck (great for bag lunches). The huge airy lobby is also a fine place to stay dry on a rainy day; Friday at noon you'll enjoy the added bonus of an organ recital.

Just up Calhoun Ave. from the SOB is the large white **Governor's Mansion.** Built in 1912 in the New England colonial style, it overlooks much of Juneau from its hilltop location. The mansion is open for free guided tours if you reserve a couple of weeks in advance by calling 465-3500. Out front is a totem pole carved in 1939-40. Near its base are the figures of a mosquito and a man, representing the Tlingit tale of the cannibalistic giant Guteel, and his capture by hunters in a pit. The hunters built a fire to kill him, but just before he died he warned "Even though you kill me, I'll continue to bite you." His ashes swirled into the air, becoming the mosquitoes that fulfill Guteel's promise. More than 20 other totems are scattered around downtown. Most are recent carvings, but some date to the 19th century. Pick up the "Totem Pole Walking Tour" brochure from the Juneau-Douglas City Museum to find them all.

Back on 4th St. is the marble **Alaska State Capitol,** built in 1930 as the Federal and Territorial Building. Not at all like a traditional capitol, from the outside, it could be easily mistaken for an ostentatious Midwestern bank. Free tours are available every half hour daily between 8:30 and 5. Check out the impressive historical photos by Winter and Pond on the second floor. You may sit in on the legislature when they are in session (Jan. to May).

The historic **House of Wickersham,** 213 7th St., tel. 586-9001, offers a good view of Juneau and the surrounding country. The house ($1) is open Sun.-Fri. 12-5, and Sat. 10-2, with brief tours. This was home to Judge James Wickersham (1857-1939), a man who had a major impact upon Alaskan history. As Alaska's longtime delegate to Congress he introduced the first statehood bill in 1916—43 years before it passed—and

was instrumental in the establishment of a territorial legislature, McKinley National Park, the University of Alaska, and the Alaska Railroad. Be sure to notice the beautiful ivory carvings that Judge Wickersham collected from around the state.

One of Juneau's most photographed sights is **St. Nicholas Russian Orthodox Church** (built in 1894) at 5th and Gold. Open Mon.-Sat. 10-5; admission $1. Inside are icons and artwork, some dating from the 1700s. **Marine Park,** along Shattuck Way, with its lively mix of people and picturesque views, is a good place to relax after your tour of downtown. Directly across the street a bright mural depicts the Haida creation legend. **Evergreen Cemetery,** between 12th and Seatter streets on the north side of town, has the graves of Juneau's founders: Joe Juneau, Richard Harris, and Chief Kowee.

Gastineau Salmon Hatchery

Juneau is home to a brand new $7 million Douglas Island Pink and Chum (DIPAC) salmon hatchery located three miles north of town at 2697 Channel Drive, tel. 463-4810. Here you can learn about salmon spawning and commercial fishing, watch fish moving up Alaska's largest fish ladder, and check out the saltwater aquariums and underwater viewing windows. The facility (open Sun.-Fri. 10-6, Sat. 12-5) includes several shops and a visitor center. Entrance costs $2.25 for adults or $1 for kids.

Mendenhall Glacier

Southeast's best-known drive-up block of ice, Mendenhall Glacier is without a doubt Juneau's most impressive sight. This moving river of ice pushes down from the 1,200-square-mile Juneau Icefield and is 12 miles long and up to 1½ miles wide. Since 1750, the glacier has been receding and is now several miles farther up Mendenhall Valley. It is presently retreating at more than 100 feet each year, although some scientists believe that it may begin advancing within the next decade.

There are free videos plus a large relief map of the area in the **Mendenhall Visitor Center,** tel. 789-0097 (open daily 9-6 in summer, or winter weekends only 9-6). Use the spotting scopes to check the slopes of nearby Bullard Mt. for mountain goats. Forest Service naturalists lead walks on nearby trails and can answer your questions. Walk up at least one of the excellent trails in the area if you want to come away with a deeper appreciation of Mendenhall Glacier (see "Hiking and Cabins" below).

Although it's 11 miles northwest of town, the glacier is easily accessible by city bus. Have the driver let you off when the bus turns left one mile up Mendenhall Loop Road. It's a one-mile walk up the road from here to the glacier. Buses run both directions around Mendenhall Loop Road. On the way back you can catch a bus heading either direction since both eventually drop you off downtown. All local tour buses go to Mendenhall; see "Tours and Treks" below for details.

Floating Mendenhall River
Alaska Travel Adventures, tel. 789-0052, provides 3½-hour raft trips down the Mendenhall River during the summer. The cost is $75 pp for adults or $48 pp for children. Experienced rafters and canoeists also float the river, but be sure to ask the Forest Service for the details. The river is not particularly treacherous, but people die in boating accidents here almost every year.

University
The campus of the University of Alaska Southeast (2,600 students) is a dozen miles northwest of Juneau on beautiful Auke Lake. The view across the lake to Mendenhall Glacier makes it one of the most attractive campuses anywhere. City buses reach the university hourly Mon.-Saturday. Also here is **Chapel By The Lake,** a popular place for weddings with a dramatic backdrop of mountains and the Mendenhall Glacier. Across the highway, **Auke Bay Fisheries Lab** has a small saltwater aquarium and various fisheries displays. It's open Mon.-Fri. 8-4:30.

Eaglecrest
Come wintertime, the Eaglecrest Ski Area, tel. 586-5284, provides excellent skiing op-

portunities on Douglas Island. There are 30 ski trails with a maximum vertical drop of 1,400 feet. Lift tickets cost $20 per day. Cross-country skiers can get a special two-ride pass for $5 that takes them into the beautiful alpine meadows. Eaglecrest is generally open Thanksgiving to early April. Call 586-5330 for a recording of current snow conditions. The lifts no longer operate during the summer.

Alaskan Brewery
For something completely different, take the city bus to Anka St. in Lemon Creek and walk two blocks to Shaune Drive. Follow it a block to the small Alaskan Brewery (formerly called Chinook Brewery) building on the left. Alaska's only brewery, their amber beer has won top prize in several national competitions. Free tours are given every half hour between 11 and 5 (tel. 780-5866), and you're given a glass of beer at the end of the tour. Bottling takes place on Thursdays. Available only in Alaska and the Pacific Northwest, the beer is pricey ($7 a six-pack), but is very popular with both locals and visitors. The brewery also sells T-shirts with their attractive logo.

Shrine Of St. Terese
Twenty-three miles northwest of Juneau is a beautiful Catholic chapel built in 1939, the Shrine of St. Terese, tel. 780-6112. The cobblestone chapel hides within a bucolic little wooded island connected to the mainland by a 400-foot causeway. It's open daily, with Sunday service at 1 p.m. This is a nice, quiet place to soak up the scenery or to try your hand at fishing for salmon from the shore. The trail to Peterson Lake is nearby.

HIKING AND CABINS

The Juneau area has an amazing wealth of hiking trails leading into the surrounding mountains. For a complete listing, pick up a copy of **"Juneau Trails"** ($2) from the Forest Service Information Center in Centennial Hall at 101 Egan Dr., tel. 586-8751. See "Information" below for specifics. Rubber boots (rent

(top) Anchorage's skyline reveals its big-city status.
(bottom) Skagway's downtown contains many historic buildings.

(top) Ketchikan's Creek Street is a favorite Southeast Alaska attraction.
(bottom) Wrangell at night

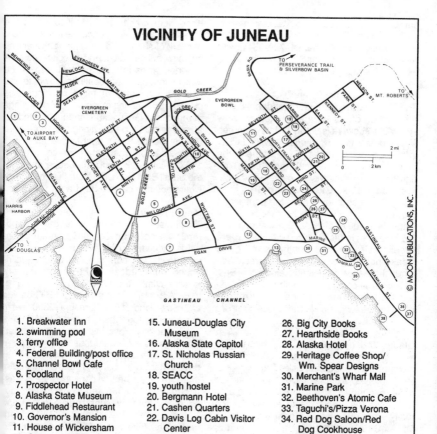

VICINITY OF JUNEAU

1. Breakwater Inn
2. swimming pool
3. ferry office
4. Federal Building/post office
5. Channel Bowl Cafe
6. Foodland
7. Prospector Hotel
8. Alaska State Museum
9. Fiddlehead Restaurant
10. Governor's Mansion
11. House of Wickersham
12. Centennial Hall
13. Glacier Bay Yacht Tours
14. State Office Building
15. Juneau-Douglas City Museum
16. Alaska State Capitol
17. St. Nicholas Russian Church
18. SEACC
19. youth hostel
20. Bergmann Hotel
21. Cashen Quarters
22. Davis Log Cabin Visitor Center
23. Olivia's de Mexico
24. Rainbow Foods
25. Foggy Mountain Shop
26. Big City Books
27. Hearthside Books
28. Alaska Hotel
29. Heritage Coffee Shop/ Wm. Spear Designs
30. Merchant's Wharf Mall
31. Marine Park
32. Beethoven's Atomic Cafe
33. Taguchi's/Pizza Verona
34. Red Dog Saloon/Red Dog Cookhouse
35. public library
36. Armadillo
37. Alaska Discovery

able at Alaska Discovery) are recommended
or all these trails, though you could get by
vith leather boots on some of the paths when
he weather is dry.

Guided Hikes

The **City Parks and Recreation Department** offers guided day hikes in the summer
and wintertime cross-country ski trips into
areas around Juneau every Wed. and Sat.
:30-3. The Wednesday hikes are for adults

only. Pick up a schedule of hikes from their
office at 155 S. Seward St., tel. 586-5226, or
check the Thursday edition of the *Juneau
Empire*. Karla and Betty Lou Hart of **Alaska
Rainforest Tours,** tel. 463-3466, will be
happy to lead you on 6- to 10-mile hikes
around Juneau for $100 pp/day, lunch,
raingear, and boots included. They can also
arrange all sorts of other activities in surrounding settlements, from Angoon to Tenakee Springs. Call them well in advance to

set up a personalized trip to Alaska geared to your interests. Recommended. Another option is **Alaska Up Close,** tel. 789-9544, with half-day nature tours for $49 pp, and guides who are fluent in German.

Mendenhall Glacier Trails

The short **nature trail** near Mendenhall Visitor Center offers a fine chance to view spawning sockeye salmon in late summer. (An elaborate underwater fish-viewing facility is in the planning stages.) Even shorter is the handicapped-accessible **Photo Point Trail** right in front of the visitor center. The relatively easy **East Glacier Loop Trail** (3½ miles RT), also begins near the center and provides good views of the glacier. For a longer hike, follow the East Glacier Loop Trail 1½ miles out to the junction with the **Nugget Creek Trail.** This trail continues along the creek another four miles to a decrepit Adirondack shelter. Vegetation along the East Glacier Trail consists of brush and trees established since the glacier's recent retreat, while trees along the Nugget Creek Trail are much older.

My favorite Mendenhall trail is the **West Glacier Trail** (seven miles RT), which begins from the end of Montana Creek Rd., just beyond the Mendenhall Lake Campground: incredible views of the glacier and icefalls en route. Experienced ice climbers use the path to access the glacier itself. Finally, for the really ambitious there's a primitive route up **Mt. McGinnis** (3,228 feet) from the end of the West Glacier Trail, an additional four miles (six hours) RT. This trail is generally covered with snow until late summer, but offers panoramic vistas of the entire Juneau area—on clear days.

Douglas

Remains of the **Treadwell Mine,** destroyed by the collapse and flood of 1917, are well worth exploring. Pick up the "Treadwell Mine Historic Trail" brochure from the Juneau-Douglas City Museum for a description of the area. The trail starts from the south end of St. Ann's Ave. in Douglas. Get there by catching the hourly Douglas bus ($1) in Juneau and riding it to the end of the line at Sandy Beach.

Keep right on the main trail to reach the Treadwell Glory Hole, once the entrance to a network of shafts under Gastineau Channel, but now full of water and wrecked cars. A waterfall drops into the hole. Return to the fork in the trail and continue down to the shore for remains of more buildings and pieces of old mining machinery. Mine tailings dumped into Gastineau Channel created an attractive sandy beach along the shore here (Sandy Beach Park). Just to the south is a steep-sided pit where the mine collapsed in 1917. Walk back along the beach and past the Small Boat Harbor to Douglas Post Office where you can catch a bus back to Juneau.

Mount Roberts

The most convenient way to get a panoramic view of Juneau and Gastineau Channel is by climbing Mt. Roberts, directly behind town. On summer weekends, you're bound to meet dozens of others on this enjoyable climb, including ironman-type joggers. A 2½-mile trail (five hours RT) begins at the east end of 6th St., rising 2,500 feet in elevation through the rainforest. It ends at a large wooden cross just above the timberline. The hike is strenuous, but you're rewarded with spectacular views on clear days. There may be snow above this point until late July. The trail continues up to Gastineau Peak (3,666 feet), six miles (four hours RT) from town, then on along the ridge to the summit of Mt. Roberts (3,819 feet) nine miles (five hours RT) from town. Experienced hikers with a map and compass may want to continue along the ridge, eventually connecting up with other trails in the area. Weather conditions change rapidly on these ridgetops, so be aware of incoming clouds and never hike into fog.

Up Gold Creek

Some of the finest hiking around Juneau is found in the old gold mining areas up beyond the end of Basin Rd., a pleasant half hour walk from town. You could easily spend several days exploring this scenic area. In Last Chance Basin, 1½ miles up Basin Rd., are the fascinating remains of the **AJ Mine.** A number of paths lead around the compressor building, a locomotive repair shop, and a variety of remains from the heyday of gold mining. For more details of the area, pick up the "Last Chance Basin Walking Tour" brochure from the Juneau-Douglas City Museum.

Perseverance Trail leads past Last Chance Basin to Silverbow Basin, site of the Perseverance Mine, three miles away (three hours RT). The **Mt. Juneau Trail** branches off from Perseverance Trail a half mile up. It's very steep and only suitable for experienced backpackers, but offers unparalleled vistas across Gastineau Channel. Plan on seven hours RT. Directly across from the Mt. Juneau trailhead is a short path down to Ebner Falls. Continue another mile out Perseverance Trail to the **Granite Creek Trail** (1½ miles OW) which follows the creek up past several waterfalls into the alpine. Just before Silverbow Basin yet another side trail leads right to the Glory Hole, which is connected to the AJ Mine by a tunnel. Old mining ruins are at the end of the trail, but signs warn of potential hazards from toxic tailings at the old mines.

Point Bridget State Park

Newly created in 1988, Point Bridget is a delightful park located 38 miles north of Juneau along Lynn Canal. It's a great place to hike if you have the wheels to get there or want to try hitching. Several paths lace this 2,850-acre park, including the **Point Bridget Trail** (seven miles RT) which takes hikers out to a fine vantage point across Lynn Canal to the Chilkat Mountains. Sea lions, harbor seals, and humpback whales are often seen from here. Before heading out, pick up a park map from the Department of Natural Resources, 400 Willoughby Ave., tel. 465-4563.

Hike-in Cabins

The Juneau area has four very popular Forest Service cabins ($20) that can be reached by hiking trails or in the winter on skis. Be sure to make advance reservations, especially for weekends. Some of these fill up eight months in advance. Located on a scenic alpine ridge, the **John Muir Cabin** overlooks Auke Bay and the surrounding islands. Get there by following the Spaulding Trail a half mile, turning left onto the Auke Nu Trail, and continuing another 2½ miles to the cabin. The trail starts from a parking area on the right side of the road 12 miles northwest of town and just beyond the Auke Bay Post Office.

The **Peterson Lake Cabin** lies at the end of a 4½-mile trail. Although it's mostly boardwalk, rubber boots are highly recommended. The trailhead is on the right, 24 miles northwest of town, and just beyond the Shrine of St. Terese. Experienced hikers or cross-country skiers with a map and compass may want to cross the alpine ridges from Petersburg Lake to the John Muir Cabin (three miles away), where they can head back along the Auke Nu and Spaulding trails.

The **Dan Moller Cabin** on Douglas Island lies at the end of a three-mile trail. Get there by taking the Douglas bus to West Juneau. Debus on Cordova St. (across from the Breeze Inn) and hike three blocks up the street. Turn left onto Pioneer Ave; the trail begins from a small parking lot next to 3185 Pioneer Ave. One of the most popular wintertime skiing trails in the area, it leads up to the beautiful alpine country of central Douglas Island.

The newest cabin (completed in 1991) is **Eagle Glacier Cabin,** facing this magnificent glacier. It is accessed via the Amalga (Eagle Glacier) Trail which begins 28 miles north of town. The 7½-mile path (OW) is relatively easy to hike, and ends at the Eagle Glacier. The cabin faces across a lake to the glacier, offering some of the most dramatic vistas anywhere. Wear rubber boots for the often muddy trail.

In addition to these four cabins, there are four other Forest Service cabins on the mainland around Juneau, plus another 15 on nearby Admiralty Island. Access to these cabins is by floatplane or sometimes by sea kayak. For more details on all Forest Service cabins in the area contact the Forest Service Information Center downtown or the district office near Nugget Mall. The closest and most popular (they fill up several months in advance) are two cabins on **Turner Lake,** 20 miles east of Juneau. Great fishing for cutthroat trout and incredible waterfall-draped rock faces on all sides. The flight in takes you past the enormous Taku Glacier, an added bonus. Expect to pay $250 RT (two people and gear) for a floatplane into the cabin. See "Transportation" for a list of local air taxi operators.

ACCOMMODATIONS

A full range of options is available to travelers staying in Juneau. See the chart for a complete listing of Juneau lodging places. Note that an 11% tax is added to these prices. Bags and backpacks can be stored at the Alaskan Hotel, 167 S. Franklin St., tel. 586-1000 ($1.50/bag/day). During the off-season, the Davis Log Cabin Visitor Center will temporarily store bags for free.

Hostel
One of the finest youth hostels in Alaska, **Juneau International Hostel** is in a lovely old home at 614 Harris St., tel. 586-9559, just a few blocks up the hill from downtown. In addition to dorm space for 40 people, the hostel has a comfortable community room, kitchen facilities, washer and drier. It's open year-round, but is closed daily 9-5. The doors are locked at 11 p.m. (10:30 p.m. in winter), putting a damper on your nightlife. Members pay $8 per night and nonmembers $11 (maximum stay three nights). Showers are 50 cents extra. Highly recommended.

Bed And Breakfasts
Couples traveling together may want to spend the extra money to stay in one of more than 20 B&Bs in Juneau. Prices start at $40 s or $50 d and accommodations run the gamut from old miners' cabins to gorgeous log hillside homes with views out over Juneau. For details contact the **Alaska Bed & Breakfast Association,** Box 21890, Juneau, AK 99802, tel. 586-2959. It's a good idea to reserve ahead during the summer. The B&B Association can make reservations for many other Alaskan towns. The downtown visitor center has brochures describing half-a-dozen of the nicest B&Bs around Juneau.

Hotels
Hotel prices in Juneau match those elsewhere in Alaska—they are expensive. The least expensive places are **Inn at the Waterfront** and **Alaskan Hotel.** Built in 1913, the Alaskan is Juneau's oldest lodging place. It was recently renovated, returning it to its traditional Victorian glory. The Alaskan also has a hot tub, jacuzzi, and sauna available ($21 an hour for two people; half price weekdays noon-4).

Camping
Both of the Forest Service's campgrounds in the Juneau area are far from downtown and open only mid-May to mid-September. (You can pitch a tent here for free in the off-season, but will have to haul your own water.) The campgrounds charge $5 per site and have firewood, water, and toilets. **Auke Village Campground** (11 sites) is 16 miles out Glacier Highway on Point Louisa. Get there by turning left from the ferry and walking or hitching two miles on the road. The area is secluded, with a nice beach and views of nearby islands. Its only problem is access to Juneau—the nearest city bus stop is four miles away. **Mendenhall Lake Campground,** a larger area with great views across Mendenhall Lake to the glacier and access to many hiking trails, has seven backpacker units and 54 sites for vehicles. From the ferry terminal, turn right and go two miles to De Hart's Store, then left onto Loop Road. Follow it three miles to Montana Creek Rd., then another three-quarters of a mile to the campground. From Juneau, take the city bus to where Montana Creek Rd. intersects Mendenhall Loop Road. Walk up Montana Creek Rd., bear right at the "Y" after a half mile, then continue another half mile to the campground (well marked). Note that the rifle range is near the Mendenhall Lake Campground, so you may be awakened by gunfire some mornings. Don't worry, the drug wars haven't come to Juneau yet.

Although there are no official campgrounds closer to Juneau, backpackers sometimes head up Basin Rd., with several

JUNEAU ACCOMMODATIONS

Name	Address	Phone	Rates	Features
Juneau Youth Hostel	614 Harris St.	586-9559	$8-11 pp	Inexpensive, 11 p.m. curfew
Inn at the Waterfront	455 S. Franklin St.	586-2050	$34+ s, $56+ d	
Alaska B&B Assoc.	Box 21890	586-2959	$40+ s, $50+ d	20 different homes
Alaskan Hotel	167 S. Franklin St.	586-1000 (800) 327-9347	$40 s $50 d	bath down the hall, kitchenettes, free airport shuttle
Cashen Quarters	315 Gold St.	586-9863	$45 s, $54 d	
Bergmann Hotel	434 3rd St.	586-1690	$45 s $55 d	kitchen facilities, airport shuttle
Driftwood Lodge		586-2280	$49 s, $62 d	
Super 8 Motel	2295 Trout St.	789-4858 (800) 843-1991	$72 s $85 d	close to airport
Breakwater Inn		586-6303	$75 s, $85 d	AAA approved
Prospector Hotel	375 Whittier St.	586-3737	$75 s $95 d	AAA approved, free airport shuttle
Silverbow Inn	120 2nd St.	586-4146	$85 s $95 d	AAA approved, Continental b'fast, historic building
Best Western Country Inn	9300 Glacier Hwy.	789-5005 (800) 528-1234	$95 s $99 d	jacuzzi and pool free airport shuttle
Airport Travelodge	9200 Glacier Hwy.	789-9700	$95 s $105 d	AAAapproved whirlpool, pool
Baranof Hotel	127 N. Franklin St.	586-2660	$105 s $115 d	AAA approved free airport shuttle
Westmark Juneau	51 W. Egan Dr.	586-6900	$132 s $144 d	AAA approved free airport shuttle

tolerable spots in the trees nearby. Farther afield, you'll find places to pitch a tent up the Mt. Roberts or Perseverance trails. Some people also camp at beautiful Echo Cove, 40 miles northwest of Juneau on the Glacier Highway. Getting there without wheels is the primary drawback.

RVs can generally overnight in Juneau shopping mall parking lots for free, and the city of Juneau maintains limited RV facilities at Savikko Park and Norway Point for $5. Full service facilities ($15) are available at **Auke Bay RV Park,** tel. 789-9467, located 1½ miles south from the ferry terminal. Get details from the RV Information Center in Nugget Mall.

FOOD

One of Juneau's strong points is a good variety of restaurants with quality food and moderate (for Alaska) prices. Hang out with the bureaucrats at the cheapest and blandest place in town, the **cafeteria,** Room 241 in the Federal Building at 9th St. and Glacier Ave. (open Mon.-Fri. 7-3:30). The absolute best place to get a breakfast or lunch in Juneau is the **Channel Bowl Cafe,** 608 Willoughby Ave., tel. 586-6139. In spite of its location (in the bowling alley on Willoughby Ave.) and its decor (1950s-style Naugahyde diner stools and Formica counters), the Channel has great all-American cooking. You're likely to meet everyone from fishermen to state legislators inside. Be ready to be insulted by owner/clown Laurie Berg. There is always some irreverent witticism posted on the sign out front. Just up the street at 429 Willoughby Ave. is the **Fiddlehead Restaurant and Bakery,** tel. 586-3150, with a nouvelle cuisine menu of fresh sourdough breads, locally caught seafoods, homemade soups, and vegetarian specialties. Be prepared to drop $25 pp or more for dinner. Definitely recommended if you have the bucks.

Downtown Juneau has several street vendors who sell quick takeaway food at rock-bottom prices. Particularly popular over the lunch hour is **Mickey's Bagel Bistro,** usually on the corner of 1st and Seward streets. The **Cook House,** tel. 463-3658, beside the Red Dog Saloon downtown, serves up gigantic burgers (at a humongous $13 price), steaks, and fish specials. Over in Douglas is **Mike's Place,** 1102 2nd St., tel. 364-3271, owned by the same family since 1914. Fine steaks and seafood, along with a big salad bar.

Mexican Food
Armadillo Tex-Mex Cafe, 431 S. Franklin St., tel. 586-1880, is well known for its delicious south-of-the-border fare, especially tasty nachos with a spicy salsa. Most meals start around $10, but a cup of homemade chili and cornbread is a good deal for $3.50.

Extremely popular with both locals and travelers. **Olivia's de Mexico,** downstairs at 222 Seward St., tel. 586-6870, has more traditional Mexican food, fair prices, and big portions.

Italian And Pizza
TJ's Restaurant, 230 Seward St., tel. 586-9555, offers Italian lunches and dinners. With entrees starting around $8, **Taguchi's Fine Chow,** 25 S. Franklin St., has the best Chinese food in town. Juneau's best-known pizza place is **Bullwinkle's,** tel. 586-2400, directly across from the State Office Building on Willoughby Ave. and also in Mendenhall Valley next to Super Bear Market. Daily lunch pizza specials start around $5 and the popcorn is always free. You'll get better and more authentic pizza at **Pizza Verona,** 256 S. Franklin St., tel. 586-2816. A small cheese pizza costs $10. **Vito 'N Nick's,** 299 N. Franklin, tel. 463-5051, makes tasty deep-dish pizzas, along with sandwiches, Italian dinners, and monstrous homemade cinnamon rolls (famous locally). If quantity is more important than quality, stuff yourself at **Pizza Pizzaz** in the Nugget Mall, tel. 789-3555, with their $6.79 all-you-can-eat lunch special that includes a soup and salad bar.

Salmon
Almost every town in Southeast has a daily salmon bake during the summer, and Juneau has two of the best. Both offer an all-you-can-eat dinner of salmon, salad, bread, beer, and more, plus free transport from town. **Thane Ore House Salmon Bake,** tel. 586-3442, four miles south of town, charges $16 pp, while the **Gold Creek Salmon Bake,** tel. 586-1424, in Last Chance Basin behind town, charges $19 pp (kids $9). Gold Creek is a favorite of locals as well as visitors. Two local places sell freshly smoked salmon: **Taku Smokeries,** 230 S. Franklin, tel. 463-3474, and **Alaska Seafood Co.,** 5434 Shaune Dr. (across from the Alaskan Brewery), tel. 780-5111.

Coffee Shops
Several pleasant coffee shops serve espresso and pastries in Juneau. **Heritage Coffee**

Co. at 174 S. Franklin St., tel. (800) 478-5282, is easily the most popular and crowded, and is open till 11 most nights during the summer. A great place to meet tree-huggers, state government yuppies, hip high schoolers, and Gortex-clad touristas. Walk down the halls here to discover some wonderful historic photos lining the walls. Out in Nugget Mall near the airport is **Vintage Fare Cafe,** which offers good breakfasts and lunches, plus espresso coffees.

Fast Food

If all Juneau's fine food is not to your liking, and you just want a cheap burger, be assured that Juneau also has two **McDonald's** restaurants (downtown and in Mendenhall Valley), along with a **Burger King** on Franklin St. and a **Taco Bell** in Mendenhall Mall.

Grocers

You'll find the cheapest groceries (and the most harried clerks) at **Fred Meyer** (open 24 hours), nine miles northwest of town along Glacier Highway. Nearby, notice the old hip-roofed barn that was once home to the Juneau Dairy. **Family Grocer,** near the airport, has discount prices. In town, head to friendly **Foodland Supermarket,** 615 Willoughby Ave., for the most complete selection of fresh produce and meats. **Rainbow Foods,** Franklin and 2nd streets is an overpriced natural foods market.

ENTERTAINMENT AND RECREATION

The Bar Scene

Juneau has an active nightlife, with plenty of live music almost every night of the week. The famous **Red Dog Saloon,** tel. 463-3777, on S. Franklin St. has sawdust on the floor and honky-tonk or rock music in the air every day and night during the summer. Quite a scene when the cruise ships are in town!

A block up the street is the **Alaskan Bar,** 167 S. Franklin, tel. 586-1000, a much quieter place with blues or folk music most nights. It is very popular with locals, who head here in the summer to escape the

hordes at the Red Dog. The Alaskan has a turn-of-the-century decor and you can hear lawyer shoptalk from any seat in the place during the legislative session. For a dose of instant culture-schlock, traipse a couple of doors down to the old Senate Building (Burger King is here now) and take the elevator four flights up. The **Penthouse,** tel. 586-5656, has windows overlooking the city lights, Top-40 rock videos, a glitzy dance floor, and a decor that looks like it was borrowed from *Saturday Night Fever.* The cover charge is $2. Across the street is the **Rendezvous,** 184 S. Franklin, tel. 586-1270, where you'll find very loud rock 'n roll. **Fiddlehead Restaurant and Bakery,** 429 W. Willoughby Ave., tel. 586-3150, often has live jazz ($5 cover charge) in its upstairs room. This is a fine place for a romantic getaway. The **Sandbar,** 2525 Industrial Blvd., tel. 789-3411 (behind the Nugget Mall near the airport), offers country or rock music nightly. Nearby is the **Landing Strip,** 9121 Glacier Hwy., tel. 789-2820, for higher-octane rock and roll (bring earplugs).

Happy hours are no longer legal in Alaska, so several enterprising Juneau bars have taken to offering free hors d'oeuvres early each evening. This is a good way to save money on food costs while throwing back a few drinks with the locals. Try lounges at the **Breakwater Inn,** 1711 Glacier Ave., tel. 586-6303, and **Prospector Hotel,** 320 Whittier Street, tel. 586-3737.

Musicals

Of the dozen or so musical melodramas in Alaska, Juneau's **"Lady Lou Revue"** ($14 adults; $7 kids) is one worth seeing. The acting is top-notch in this amusing musical spoof of the Klondike Gold Rush era. Held in Merchant's Wharf on Marine Way, showtimes vary depending on cruise ship schedules. Call 586-3686 for details. The actors are members of Perseverance Theater, a respected Douglas-based group that performs more serious productions between September and May. Call 364-2421 for the scoop on their other productions. Every Friday evening from 7 to 8:30, **Marine Park** in downtown Juneau comes alive with free musical performances, ranging from classical to middle eastern folk. Call 586-2787 to see who's playing.

Playing Around

Rent bikes from **OM Cycles,** tel. 586-2277, located right across from the library in downtown Juneau. They cost $4/hour or $25 for all day. Very friendly guys. See the Davis Log Cabin Visitor Center for a complete listing of the more than two dozen **charter boat** operators in Juneau. They provide all sorts of options, from half-day fishing ventures to two-week cruises around Southeast. Day rates start around $175 pp. Rent kayaks from Alaska Discovery (see below). Golfers may want to head to **Mendenhall Golf Course,** tel. 789-7323, a nine-hole course near the airport.

Events

Call 586-JUNO for a recording listing upcoming events and activities in Juneau. **July 4** is Juneau's day to play. There are the usual parades and fireworks (see them from Douglas Island for the most impressive backdrop), along with such events as float races down Gold Creek and a highly competitive sandcastle contest at Sandy Beach Park. If you're around in April, don't miss the week-long **Alaska State Folk Festival** which attracts musicians from Alaska and the Pacific Northwest. Performances are free, and you can also attend workshops and dance to some of the hottest folk and bluegrass bands anywhere. Lots of fun. Each May, culture comes to town with the **Juneau Jazz and Classics,** a 10-day long series of performances and workshops by local musicians and guest artists. Entrance fees are $8-12. Those who like to fish should throw in their line at the annual **Salmon Derby** in early August where a top prize of $10,000 makes it the big summer event for locals. Even Robert Redford once took part.

OTHER PRACTICALITIES

Services

The main **post office** is in the downtown Federal Building and a branch post office is on Seward St. behind Ace Hardware. Both **The Connection,** 287 S. Franklin St. and **The Phone Connection,** 171 Shattuck Way, #108, have discount long-distance calling rates. Use their booths and then pay, rather than having to feed the phone with quarters. Coin-operated showers ($1.50) are available at **Harbor Wash Board,** 1100 Glacier Ave., **Portside Laundromat,** 1711 Glacier Ave., and at the **Auke Bay Harbormaster's Office.** A better deal is the **Augustus Brown Swimming Pool,** at the high school, 1619 Glacier Ave., tel 586-2055. In addition to showers, the facility has an excellent pool ($3), sauna, and weight-lifting equipment.

Arts And Crafts

Wm. Spear Designs at 174 S. Franklin St., tel. 586-2209, (upstairs from Heritage Coffee Shop) has the complete collection of colorful enameled pins by this local artisan with an international reputation. A former lawyer, Spear's work covers the spectrum from UFOs to dinosaurs. Check out the flying eyeball and the painting of bikers eating puffins (!) for a bit of his twisted humor. The **Rie Munoz Gallery,** 233 S. Franklin, tel. 586-2112, features works by several of Alaska's finest artists, including prints by Rie Munoz and JoAnn George. Scads of other galleries and gift shops sell artwork and trinkets to the cruise ship crowd. The quality varies widely, but nearly everything is overpriced, particularly anything by a Native artisan. Unfortunately, the romanticized paintings, carvings, and sculpture depicting these original Alaskans hunting seals in kayaks or carving totem poles meets head-on against a much sadder picture of inebriated Natives leaning against the windows of downtown Juneau bars.

Shopping

Most locals do their shopping in Mendenhall Valley at Nugget Mall, Mendenhall Mall, or the huge Fred Meyer store. The **Salvation Army Thrift Store** beside Channel Bowl on Willoughby Ave. sells warm clothes, paperbacks, and more. More bargains near the airport at **St. Vincent De Paul's,** 8617 Teel, tel., 789-5535. The **Foggy Mountain Shop,** 134 N. Franklin St., sells camping gear, topographic maps, and sports equipment. They also rent ski equipment and rollerblades. The best place for rugged raingear, boots, and outdoor clothes is the **Nugget Store** in Nugget Mall. While there, check out the mall's nine-foot-tall stuffed brown bear. **Taku Tailor**, 217 5th St., does a nice job on repairs of packs and tents. For something completely different, take a peek inside **Alaskins Leather**, 478 S. Franklin, tel. 586-1700, where fish skins are made into leather items of all types, even swimsuits.

The Literary Scene
Juneauites enjoy three different public libraries. The award-winning **main library,** tel. 586-5249, is on the top floor of the parking garage on S. Franklin Street. There's a wonderful view of all the activity in Gastineau Channel from the outside walkway. Visitors may want to stop by the freebie shelves near the entrance for a trashy novel to read. Hours are Mon.-Thurs. 11-9, Fri. and Sat. noon-5. The **valley branch** in Mendenhall Mall, tel. 789-0125, is open Sun. noon-5, Mon.-Thurs. noon-9, Fri. 10-5 and Sat. 11-5. The **Douglas library** at 3rd and E streets, tel. 586-5249, is open Mon.-Wed. 3-9, Thurs. 11-5, Sat. and Sun. 1-5. The **Alaska State Library** is on the eighth floor of the State Office Building. **Big City Books,** 100 N. Franklin St., has a good selection of Alaskan books and topographic maps. A few doors down is **Hearthside Books,** which also has a store in the Nugget Mall near the airport. The **Alaskan Heritage Bookshop,** 174 S. Franklin, has a fine choice of old books, including the world's largest collection of Robert Service's volumes, plus old prints, maps, and photos. A real treat for collectors. For bargain-basement prices on used books, stop by the library's secondhand bookshop in Mendenhall Mall.

SEACC
The Southeast Alaska Conservation Council (SEACC), 419 6th St., tel. 586-6942, has material on environmental issues and activist T-shirts. This is the primary environmental group in Southeast and has a reputation as a highly effective organization both locally and in Washington, D.C. Members receive a quarterly newsletter and periodic notices of important environmental issues. You can join for $25/year. Their mailing address is Box 21692, Juneau, AK 99802.

Information
Juneau's **Visitor Information Center** is in the Davis Log Cabin at 134 3rd St., tel. 586-2201. Modeled after Juneau's first church (rebuilt in 1980), this picture-perfect log cabin is itself a tourist attraction. Hours are Mon.-Fri. 8:30-5, Sat.-Sun. 10-5 during the summer. Three other locations in Juneau are staffed by visitors bureau personnel during the summer months: the kiosk in Marine Park (open daily 9-6), in the Cruise Ship Terminal on S. Franklin St. (open daily 8-6), and at the airport (open for flight arrivals). RVers may want to stop at the Good Sam RV Info Center in Nugget Mall. For up-to-date local information, pick up a copy of the annual **"Juneau Guide"** (free) at the ferry terminal or the visitor center. A "Juneau Walking Tour" map is also available at the visitor center, with German and Japanese translations.

The **U.S. Forest Service Information Center** in Centennial Hall at 101 Egan Dr., tel. 586-8751, is open daily 9-5 during the summer. Inside, find a tremendous amount of information on recreation activities throughout Southeast. The staff has both Forest Service and National Park Service personnel able to answer almost any question about the outdoors. This is the place to make reservations for Forest Service cabins, find out about trips to Glacier Bay or Tracy Arm, pick up free brochures and maps, or buy books on local hiking trails. On rainy days, stop by to watch Native craft demonstrations, along with films on whales, eagles, glaciers, bears, and other topics. Special events are held here throughout the winter months. The **Forest Service District offices** for Juneau Ranger District and Admiralty Island National Monument are at 8465 Old Dairy Rd., tel. 789-3111, 10 miles northwest of town near Nugget Mall. The folks here have a first-hand knowledge of the local terrain and can also make cabin reservations. Call 465-4116 for recorded fishing information courtesy of the Alaska Department of Fish and Game.

TRANSPORTATION

By Air

Juneau airport is nine miles northwest of downtown Juneau and has lockers available where you can store bags for 24 hours. Express city buses ($1) arrive hourly in front of the airport between 7:45 a.m. and 5:45 p.m. On weekends or later hours (till 11:15 p.m.) you can catch the regular city bus at Nugget Mall, a half mile away. If you're in a hurry, **Eagle Express Line,** tel. 586-2660, has shuttle service to town for $6. Juneau airport closes from 10 p.m.-5 a.m., so forget trying to sleep here. Inside the terminal, take a look at the glass cases with various stuffed critters, including a huge polar bear (upstairs). The upstairs cafeteria offers impressive vistas out across Mendenhall Glacier. A good place to see waterfowl and eagles is the **Mendenhall Wetlands** that surround the airport. An overlook provides a view from Egan Highway on the way into Juneau or you can jog along a scenic dirt road behind the airport's floatplane pond.

Both **Alaska Airlines,** tel. (800) 426-0333, and **Delta,** tel. (800) 221-1212, have daily flights into Juneau and on to Anchorage and Fairbanks. Alaska's jets also connect Juneau with Sitka ($85), Gustavus ($43), Wrangell ($115), Petersburg ($103), Ketchikan ($122), and points south all the way to Mexico. Alaska's flights to Anchorage stop at Yakutat and Cordova (pray for good weather, or consider motion-sickness medication if you're easily nauseated). A one-way ticket to Cordova, though painfully expensive at $173, is an excellent way to connect to Southcentral Alaska. You get to see out-of-the-way Cordova, the spectacular Copper River delta country, and you can catch the southwest ferry to Valdez ($28) and on to Whittier via Columbia Glacier ($56), then through to Portage ($8) via Alaska Railroad. Catch a bus in Portage to Anchorage for another $20 (or hitchhike). The total transportation cost for this route ($285) is only $67 more than a one-way plane ticket from Juneau to Anchorage, plus you get to explore stunning Prince

William Sound. This can be cut even more if you miss Valdez and the Columbia Glacier by going directly by ferry from Cordova to Whittier ($34).

There are many options for small plane service to communities around Juneau. **Air North,** tel. 789-2007 or (800) 764-0407, flies between Juneau and Whitehorse, Yukon, on Sun., Wed., and Fri. afternoons. If you can plan ahead, their seven-day advance purchase fare is a steal: $130 RT. **Wings of Alaska,** tel. 789-0790 or (800) 478-9464, has daily service to Angoon ($72), Elfin Cove ($88), Gustavus ($56), Haines ($61), Hoonah ($41), Kake ($85), Pelican ($75), Petersburg ($97), Skagway ($72), and Tenakee Springs ($61). **Glacier Bay Airways,** tel. 789-9009, has daily flights to Excursion Inlet ($55), Gustavus ($60), and Pelican ($75), and **Skagway Air,** tel. 789-2006, flies to Skagway ($80) and Haines ($70) each day. Knock $10 off Skagway Air's prices for cash. **L.A.B. Flying Service,** tel. 789-9160, has daily service to Angoon ($73), Gustavus ($55), Haines ($60), Hoonah ($45), Kake ($95), and Skagway ($71).

Flightseeing Trips

Charter service to nearby Forest Service cabins and flightseeing trips are available from the above-listed companies and from two others: **Alaska Coastal Airlines,** tel. 789-7818, and **Ward Air,** tel. 789-9150. (Both of these also have excellent safety records and have been around for many years.) Expect to pay around $330/hour for a Beaver (seats six people or four with gear) or $240/hour for a Cesna 206 (seats four people or two with gear). Fixed-wing flightseeing trips (45 minutes) over the Juneau Icefield cost $70-100 pp. Glacier Bay tours are available for around $145 pp, but you'll find lower rates and shorter flying distances out of Haines or Skagway. **Temsco Helicopters,** tel. 789-9501, has 50-minute Mendenhall Glacier tours costing $125 pp, while **ERA Helicopters,** tel. 586-2030, offers hour-long tours of the Juneau Icefield for $145 pp. Either company can also provide access to the glaciers for heli-hiking or skiing.

By Ferry

Juneau's ferry terminal, tel. 789-7453, is 14 miles northwest of town at Auke Bay. Ferries arrive and depart daily during the summer, headed both north to Haines ($18) and Skagway ($24) and south to Sitka ($24) and other towns. Arrivals are often very late at night, so be ready to stumble off in a daze. Ferries generally stay one to two hours in Auke Bay. The terminal is open Mon.-Fri. 8:30-4, and at other times two hours before ship arrivals. Several covered picnic tables are behind the terminal where you can crash out if you have an early-morning departure. Inside are storage lockers (50 cents). Call 465-3940 for recorded ferry schedule info.

Taxis And Transit

A local bus company, **MGT**, tel. 789-5460, meets all ferries year-round and charges $5 for the ride into town. They can also deliver you to the ferry from Juneau if you call ahead. MGT offers a hurried two-hour tour of Juneau and the Mendenhall Glacier ($9) for those foolish enough not to lay over in Juneau. Another company, **Eagle Express Line**, tel. 789- 5720, charges $8 for transportation to or from town. You'll need to make reservations the day before to be sure they meet your ferry. The local taxi companies are **Taku Taxi**, tel. 586-2121, **Glacier Cab**, tel. 586-2121, and **Capital Cab**, tel. 586-2772. A cab ride to town will set you back $20 or so. Hitching to or from town is relatively easy during the day. You can also walk the two miles to De Hart's Store where hourly city buses ($1) will pick you up Mon.-Sat. between 7 a.m. and 11:30 p.m.

Transit buses ($1) operate Mon.-Sat. connecting Juneau, Douglas, and Mendenhall Valley. If you're accustomed to surly service on big city buses, you'll be surprised at the friendliness of Juneau's drivers. Buses to and from Mendenhall Valley run every half-hour from 7 a.m. to 11 p.m., with both regular and express service. Service to Douglas is hourly. For details, call 789-6901 or pick up route maps and schedules from the various visitor centers. Schedules are also posted at the bus stop outside the downtown Federal Building. During the summer, free **Nugget Mall shuttle buses** provide connections every half hour (except Saturdays) from downtown to this shopping mall near the airport. It is primarily used by cruise ship passengers, but is available to anyone.

Tours And Treks

Ptarmigan Ptransport and Ptours, tel. 789-5427, **MGT**, tel. 789-5460, and **Eagle Express Lines,** tel. 789-5720, run 2½-hour sightseeing tours of the city and Mendenhall Glacier for $9 pp. The **MV** *Fairweather* cruises north from Juneau to Skagway every other day. A roundtrip cruise plus lunch on the boat and a night's lodging at Skagway's Westmark Inn costs $169 s or $238 d. Also included is a bus tour of Juneau. This is a good bargain for Alaska. Call 586-3773 for details.

Car Rentals

With nearly 100 miles of roads in the Juneau area, renting a car is a smart idea, especially if you can get several people in on the deal. **Rent-A-Wreck,** tel. 789-4111, has the cheapest rates (and the oldest cars): $30 a day with 100 free miles. Also try **Mendenhall Auto Center**, 8725 Mallard St., tel. 789-1386 or (800) 478-1386, where compacts go for $40/day with unlimited mileage. **Evergreen Ford**, 8895 Mallard St., tel. 789-9386, rents Festivas for $30/day or $180/week with unlimited mileage. Hot tip: cars rented in Skagway or Haines have mileage restrictions, so people on a budget sometimes rent a car in Juneau for a week or two, put it on the ferry to Haines, and drive all over Alaska and the Yukon before returning to Juneau. Many of the national chains also have offices at the airport: **Allstar** (800) 722-0741, **Avis** (800) 331-1212, **Budget** (800) 527-0700, **Hertz** 789-9494 or (800) 654-8200, **National** (800) 227-7368, and **Payless** (800) 729-7219. Most of these companies can pick up or drop off visitors downtown or at the airport (by prior arrangement). Rates start around $40/day.

TRACY ARM-FORDS TERROR WILDERNESS

Located 50 miles southeast of Juneau, the 653,000 acre Tracy Arm-Fords Terror Wilderness contains country that rivals both Glacier Bay National Park and Misty Fjords National Monument. The wilderness consists of a broad bay that splits into two long glacially carved arms—Tracy Arm and Endicott Arm. (Fords Terror splits off as a separate bifurcation halfway up Endicott Arm.) Within Tracy Arm, steep-walled granite canyons plummet 2,000 feet to incredibly deep and narrow fjords. We're talking rocks-to-the-waterline here. The fjords wind past waterfalls to massive glaciers, their icebergs dotted with hundreds of hair seals. Humpback whales are a common sight, as are killer whales. Look closely on the mountain slopes and you're bound to see mountain goats, especially near North Sawyer Glacier. John Muir noted that the fjord was "shut in by sublime Yosemite cliffs, nobly scuptured, and adorned with waterfalls and fringes of trees, bushes, and patches of flowers, but amid so crowded a display of novel beauty it was not easy to concentrate the attention long enough on any portion of it without giving more days and years than our lives can afford." Modern-day visitors come away equally impressed. Two glaciers—Sawyer and South Sawyer—cap the end of Tracy Arm. Both of these are retreating up-bay at 85 to 300 feet annually. Contact the Forest Service Information Center in Juneau, tel. 586-8751, for details on Tracy Arm, or talk to people at Alaska Discovery, tel. 586-1911, where you can also rent sea kayaks.

Boat Trips

Visitors to Tracy Arm can choose from three very different boats. The best and most personal trip is aboard the six-passenger *Wilderness Swift.* Trips are specifically geared to showing visitors the magic of this wild area. In addition to day-long Tracy Arm trips ($139 pp), they can drop off kayakers for $75 each way (more if you get dropped off farther upbay). Call 463-3466 for details. Definitely

recommended. On Sundays, the luxurious *Spirit of Glacier Bay,* a 50-passenger boat, runs two-day, one-night trips from Juneau to Tracy Arm for $160 pp and up. For details, contact Alaska Sightseeing Tours, Merchant's Wharf, Juneau, tel. 586-6300, or (800) 426-7702. A final option for trips into Tracy Arm is the 65-foot long **MV Stephanie Anne,** tel. 586-3311. Choose between a day-long cruise (around $140) or a combination cruise-and-fly trip (around $200). Lunch or dinner are served onboard.

On Your Own

There are no trails in the Tracy Arm-Fords Terror Wilderness, but experienced sea kayakers discover spectacular country that rivals Glacier Bay. Unfortunately, kayakers camping in Tracy Arm should be prepared for a constant parade of giant cruise ships, leaving large wakes and plenty of engine noise to contend with. (Sound travels a long ways over the water. Wilderness rangers report being startled to suddenly hear loud speakers announcing, "Margaritas will be served at 1630 in the aft lounge.") You can, however, escape the boats by hiking up the ravines into the high country, or by heading into the less-congested waters of Endicott Arm where the big cruise ships rarely stray.

Camping sites are available along the shore throughout Tracy Arm, although there are fewer places to pull out as you approach the glaciers themselves at the upper end. Many boaters anchor in No Name Cove near the entrance to Tracy Arm. Kayakers will probably prefer to head to the middle part of the fjord and away from the motorboats. Ambitious folks (with a topo map) may want to try the steep half-mile cross-country climb up to scenic Icefall Lake, 1,469 feet above sea level.

Massive Dawes Glacier jams the top of Endicott Arm with thousands of bergs of all sizes and shapes, making it tough to get close to the face of the glacier. There are fewer camping spots along Endicott Arm than in Tracy Arm. Fords Terror is a turbulent but spectacular inlet that angles away from Endicott Arm. Tidal changes create wild water conditions near the entrance, so kayakers and boaters need to take special precautions. Only run the narrows at slack tides, when the water is relatively calm. (The narrows are named for the terror felt by H.R. Ford, who rowed into the inlet one day in 1889 when the water was calm, but nearly died while fighting the currents, whirlpools, and icebergs on the way back out.) There are no tidewater glaciers in Fords Terror, but numerous hanging glaciers and craggy peaks are visible.

Chuck River Wilderness

Twelve miles south of Tracy Arm is Windham Bay, entrance to the newly designated Chuck River Wilderness. This small wild area currently receives very little use, but offers good fishing for all five species of salmon, and a chance to explore the ruins of Southeast's oldest mining community, Windham Bay.

Endicott River Wilderness

Although it encompasses 94,000 acres, this is believed to be the least-visited wilderness area anywhere in America. A few hunters (mainly in search of brown bears and moose) are the primary visitors each year. The wilderness borders on Glacier Bay National Park and includes the Endicott River watershed along the eastern slope of the Chilkat Range. The country is spruce and hemlock forests, mixed with alders. There are no trails, and access from Lynn Canal is very difficult. See the Forest Service's Juneau Ranger District for access routes and other information on this decidedly off-the-beaten-track area.

ADMIRALTY ISLAND AND VICINITY

Just 20 miles west of Juneau lies the northern end of Admiralty Island National Monument, and the massive Kootznahoo Wilderness. At nearly a million acres, the wilderness covers 90% of Admiralty, making it the only large island in Southeast that has not been extensively logged or developed. The Tlingit name for Admiralty—Kootznahoo—means "Bear Fortress." The island is aptly named: it has perhaps 1,500 brown bears, giving it some of the highest bear densities anywhere on Earth. Eagles are extraordinarily abundant along the shoreline, and the cries of loons haunt Admiralty's lakes. This is truly one of the gemstones of Southeast Alaska.

ANGOON

Located along Admiralty's southwestern shore, the Tlingit village of Angoon (pop. 650), is the island's lone town. It sits astride a peninsula guarding the entrance to Kootznahoo Inlet, an incredible wonderland of small islands and saltwater passages. Tourism is not encouraged in Angoon but people are friendly. Locals have cable TVs and microwave ovens, but smokehouses sit in front of many houses and you'll hear older people speaking Tlingit. Angoon weather generally lives up to its reputation as Southeast Alaska's "Banana Belt"; yearly rainfall averages only 38 inches, compared to three times that in Sitka, only 40 miles away. By the way, the word "hootch" originated from the potent whiskey distilled by the "Hoosenoo" Indians of Admiralty in the 19th century. Today, Angoon is a dry town with a reputation as a place where traditional ways are encouraged.

History
The village of Angoon still commemorates an infamous incident that took place more than a century ago. While working for the Northwest Trading Company, a local shaman was killed in a seal hunting accident. The villagers

demanded 200 blankets as compensation and two days off to honor and bury the dead man. To ensure payment, they seized two hostages. Unaware of Tlingit traditions, the company manager fled to Sitka and persuaded a U.S. Navy boat to "punish them severely." On October 26, 1882, the town was shelled, destroying most of the houses. All the villagers' canoes were smashed and sunk, and all their winter supplies burned. Six children died from the smoke and the people nearly starved that winter. In a U.S. Congressional investigation two years later, the shelling was called "the greatest outrage ever committed in the United States upon any Indian tribe." Finally, in 1973, the government paid $90,000 in compensation for the shelling, but the Navy has never formally apologized.

Unlike most other villages in Southeast, the people of Angoon have fought hard to preserve their island from logging and development. Unfortunately, they were unable to stop the timber-mining presently destroying some of Admiralty's most scenic country. **Atikon Forest Products,** a Native-owned corporation, has already logged right down to the water around Peanut and Kathleen lakes (30 miles north of Angoon), and beautiful Lake Florence stands poised to be the final victim. An ardent effort by environmentalists, the U.S. Forest Service, and many others may well be defeated by the greed of this rapacious corporation. On the north end of Admiralty Island the less-controversial **Greens Creek Mine** is one of the largest silver mines in the country, employing some 250 miners who ride special high-speed catamarans to and from Juneau each day. Aside from these developments and a few other old logging scars and homesites, Admiralty Island is pristine wilderness.

Sights
Even if you don't stay overnight in Angoon, get off the ferry and walk across the road and down to the beach. From there you can

(GORDY OHLIGER)

TOTEM POLES

These largest of all wooden sculptures were carved in cedar by the Tlingit, Haida, Tsimshian, Kwatkiutl, and Bella Bella peoples of the Pacific Northwest. Their history is not completely known, but early explorers found poles in villages throughout Southeast. Apparently, totem-pole carving reached its heyday in the late 19th century with the arrival of metal woodworking tools. The animals, birds, fish, and marine mammals on the poles were totems that symbolized clan and, in combination, conveyed a message. Totem poles were very expensive and time-consuming to produce; a clan's status could be determined in part by the size and elaborateness of their poles. In a society without written words to commemorate people or events, the poles served a variety of purposes. Some totem poles told of a family's history, others of local legends, and still others served to ridicule an enemy or debtor. In addition, totems were used to commemorate the dead, with a special niche at the back to hold ashes of a revered ancestor. Totem poles were never associated with religion, yet early missionaries destroyed many and, as recently as 1922, the Canadian government outlawed the art in an attempt to make the Natives more submissive. Realizing that a rich heritage was being lost due to neglect, skilled Native carvers worked with the CCC during the 1930s to restore older totems and create new ones. Today, active carving and restoration programs are taking place in Saxman, Ketchikan, Sitka, and Haines.

look up to a small cemetery with old gravestones and fenced-in graves. Another interesting cemetery is near the end of the peninsula a half-mile behind the Russian Orthodox church in town. A number of rustic old houses line the shore, one with killer whales painted on the front. A hundred feet uphill from the post office are five memorial totems topped by representations of different local clans. Near Angoon Trading you get a great view of the narrow passage leading into Kootznahoo Inlet where tides create dangerous rapids.

Practicalities

Angoon has two places to stay. **Favorite Bay Inn,** tel. (800) 423-3123, on the edge of town near the boat harbor, charges $49 s or $89 d with breakfast included. **Kootznahoo Inlet Lodge,** tel. 789-3501, a few hundred feet closer to town, costs $56 s or $66 d. It also has skiffs available for $75/day and may serve meals. Angoon has no official camping facilities, but people sometimes pitch tents at the rather trashed-out picnic area just to the right of the ferry terminal along the beach. By road it is 2½ miles to town or a pleasant 1½-mile walk north along the rocky beach. **Angoon Trading** (closed Sundays) has a limited and rather expensive selection of groceries and other supplies. Get fishing gear at the **White Raven.** The **Forest Service** operates a small office, tel. 788-3166, in the old city hall with a friendly staff and a variety of brochures.

Transportation

The ferry *Le Conte* visits Angoon four times a week (twice in each direction), staying just long enough to unload and load vehicles. There is no ferry terminal, and the dock is 2½ miles out of town; so you won't get to see Angoon up close unless you disembark. "Taxis" meet most ferries, or you can hitch or walk the dirt road to town. Both **Wings of Alaska,** tel. 788-3164 or (800) 478-9464, and **L.A.B. Flying Service,** tel. 788-3501, have daily floatplane service between Angoon and Juneau for $73. **BellAir,** tel. 788-3641, flies to Sitka every day for $76.

Cross-Admiralty Canoe Route

Admiralty Island is ideally suited for people who enjoy canoeing or sea kayaking. Kootznahoo Inlet reaches back behind Angoon through a labyrinth of islands and narrow passages, before opening into expansive Mitchell Bay. From there you can continue to Salt Lake or Kanalku Bay, or begin the Cross-Admiralty Canoe Route—a chain of scenic lakes connected by portages (one over three miles long). Using this 42-mile route you should reach Seymour Canal in 4-6 days (the record is 12 hours). Along the way are six Forest Service cabins (\$20) and six Adirondack shelters (free), so you won't have to sleep out in the rain all the time.

Kootznahoo Inlet

Twice each day, tidal fluctuations push water through the narrow passages of Kootznahoo Inlet into Mitchell Bay and Salt Lake. At full flood or ebb tide, the water becomes a torrent that creates some of the fastest-flowing stretches of salt water in the world (13 knots). These strong tidal currents create eddies, whirlpools, standing waves, and even falls, depending upon the tides and the stage. To avoid these Class III whitewater conditions, be sure you reach the narrow passages at slack tide. Use a tide chart, adding approximately two hours to the Juneau times for the passage through the inappropriately named Stillwater Narrows. Inside Mitchell Bay and at Salt Lake the tides are delayed even longer, up to three hours beyond Juneau tides. If you aren't sure how to read the tide charts, talk to folks at the monument office in Juneau or at Alaska Discovery when you rent the canoes.

Practicalities

Be sure to make cabin reservations well in advance by contacting **Admiralty Island National Monument** at 8461 Old Dairy Rd., Juneau, AK 99801, tel. 586-8790. Also be certain to request a copy of their "Admiralty Island National Monument Canoe/Kayak Route" map (\$2). It includes detailed info on navigating Kootznahoo Narrows and crossing the island. Trail conditions may vary along the canoe route. The Distin Lake to Thayer Lake trail is in poor condition and the Mole Harbor to Lake Alexander trail can be quite muddy. Other trails on the route are in excellent condition, with long stretches of puncheon or boardwalk. Canoes can be rented in Juneau (and perhaps in Angoon) through **Alaska Discovery,** tel. 463-5500, or you can bring your own along on the ferry.

Thayer Lake Lodge makes an excellent break in the middle of the canoe route (if you take a bit of a detour). The facilities are comfortably rustic and you get three big meals a day plus use of the lodge's boats and fishing gear. Besides, you get to meet some real old-time Alaskans. Highly recommended if you have the cash. For reservations, contact Thayer Lake Lodge, Box 5416, Ketchikan, AK 99901, tel. 225-3343.

If you're really ambitious (and experienced) it's possible to cross Admiralty Island and then continue up Seymour Canal, eventually reaching Juneau. Only a few hardy souls try this, however, because the canoes that work so well on the lakes can be dangerous in the open water of Seymour Canal, and sea kayaks are impractical for the long portages of the canoe route.

Guided Trips

Alaska Discovery, 418 S. Franklin St., Juneau, AK 99801, tel. 586-1911, offers professionally guided canoe trips within Admiralty Island National Monument, supplying everything but personal gear and sleeping bags. Their seven-day Cross-Admiralty canoe trip costs \$1,000 pp, while a five-day canoe trip around Seymour Canal (including Pack Creek) is \$950 pp. These prices include airfare from Juneau. If you have the cash and are not sure you could handle the wilderness on your own, this is a fine way to explore Admiralty.

SEYMOUR CANAL

The Seymour Canal area is popular with sea kayakers, offering beautiful country, relatively protected waters, and the chance to see eagles, brown bears, and other wildlife. Most kayakers head south from Juneau, crossing the often-rough Stevens Passage and entering Oliver Inlet. A boat tramway makes it easy to bring kayaks across to upper Seymour Canal, a mile away. Alaska State Parks maintains the **Oliver Inlet Cabin** ($20) at the northern tip of Seymour Canal. For reservations contact Alaska State Parks, 400 Willoughby Center, Juneau, AK 99801, tel. 465-4563.

In Seymour, you'll find many coves and islands to explore, plus a chance to view bears that are protected from hunting. If you're adventurous, climb up the nearby peaks to get fantastic views of the entire area. A three-sided shelter (free) is available in Windfall Harbor. Bears can be a real problem in Seymour so be sure to select camping spots carefully (preferably on a small island) and hang all food.

Pack Creek

Located along the west side of Seymour Canal, this is one of the better known places to see brown bears in Alaska. Pack Creek fills with spawning humpback and chum salmon during July and August, and this in turn attracts the bears, which in turn attract people. Most visitors arrive on day-trips from Juneau via the local air taxi operators. Others come aboard kayaks and boats, or with commercially guided groups such as Alaska Discovery (see above). Because of its popularity with both bears and people—and the potential for conflicts between the two—Pack Creek has very stringent rules. Get the details along with permits (free) from Admiralty Island National Monument, 8461 Old Dairy Rd., Juneau, AK 99801, tel. 586-8790. Bring raingear and rubber boots, even if you're only coming for the day.

HOONAH

The predominantly Tlingit village of Hoonah (pop. 900) nestles in Port Frederick on Chichagof Island, 20 miles south of Glacier Bay. Port Frederick has served as a home for the Tlingits since the last ice age drove them out of Glacier Bay and across Icy Strait to the north coast of Chichagof Island. There they found a protected bay that they called Huna, meaning "Place Where the North Wind Doesn't Blow." The Northwest Trading Company opened a store here in 1880 and missionaries added a church and school the following year. A cannery opened in 1912, operating until 1953. The attractive old cannery still stands a mile north of town on the entrance to Port Frederick, but the old village and many priceless Tlingit cultural items were destroyed by a fire in 1944. The people rebuilt their village on the ashes.

Today Hoonah is far from being the prettiest town in Alaska. The weathered clapboard houses are unpainted, and junk cars pile up in the yards. It's the sort of town where the eagle calls blend with the sounds of motor boats and mufflerless dump trucks. There are dogs in every house and children playing on every porch. The liquor store has a sign out front: "No cork boots." Life in Hoonah follows a slow pace—residents half-complain that they are unable to go anywhere without meeting someone who wants to talk the hours away. Hoonah's economy is a blend of logging, commercial fishing, and traditional activities such as deer hunting, fishing, and berry picking.

The impressive cliff faces of Elephant Mt. (2,775 feet) guard the southern flank of Hoonah. Unfortunately, two Native corporations, Huna Totem and Sealaska, have logged much of their land near town, selling off a heritage that reaches back for hundreds of years to pay off debts resulting from appeals to their land claims. Hoonah is now surrounded by a spider web of logging roads on both Native and Forest Service land, making this a good place to explore by mountain bike if you're ready for clearcuts and can dodge the many logging trucks.

Practicalities

The **Hoonah Cultural Center,** tel. 945-3600, has a small free museum with local artifacts, open Mon.-Fri. 10-3. There are no campgrounds, but you should be able to find a camping spot above the upper edge of town. For Hoonah info, head to **City Hall,** tel. 945-3664. The **Forest Service Hoonah District Office,** Box 135, Hoonah, AK 99829, tel. 945-3631, at the south end of town has limited local trail and kayaking information. Get a copy of the detailed **"Hoonah Area Road Guide"** map ($2) from them if you plan to spend any time in the Hoonah or Tenakee area.

Mary's Inn Restaurant, a non-profit vocational school and boarding house for local youths, is a good place to get burgers, fresh baked goods, or more substantial meals while helping out a great program. **Huna Totem Lodge,** tel. 945-3636, has rooms for rent and serves meals in its restaurant. Hoonah has two small grocery stores (including the L. Kane Store established in 1893) and a laundromat with coin-operated showers. Showers are also available in the new harbor building, or at the **swimming pool** ($1), next to the high school. One of the oddest places in Hoonah is the "Beauty Combo," a combination tanning booth, barber shop, and U-bake pizza shop! Hoonah also has a bank, a tavern, a variety store, a liquor store, a cold storage facility (mostly local hires), and a logging camp. A few miles southwest of town near Game Point is the only agricultural commune in Southeast, Mt. Bether Bible Center.

Transportation

The tiny ferry terminal, tel. 945-3293, (no lockers) is a half mile from town. The *Le Conte* arrives four days a week and generally stops for approximately 45 minutes, long enough for a quick jog into town and back. Across from the ferry terminal is a tiny but interesting old cemetery. Two air-taxi operators fly every day into Hoonah. Both **Wings of Alaska,** tel. (800) 478-9464, and **L.A.B. Flying Service,** tel. 945-3661, have flights between Juneau and Hoonah for around $45.

Nearby

The Hoonah area has almost nothing in the way of developed trails or other recreation facilities. If you have a car, the quarter-mile **Bear Paw Lake Trail,** 18 miles south of town on Road 8508, leads to a good lake where you can catch trout or coho salmon. Kayakers and canoeists may want to paddle the 40 miles from Hoonah to Tenakee Springs. The route goes to the head of Port Frederick,

where there is a 100-yard portage into Tenakee Inlet. Neka Estuary in Port Frederick is a good place to see bears. A Forest Service cabin ($20) is available at nearby **Salt Lake Bay,** but a considerable amount of logging has beaten you there. Ask at the Hoonah Forest Service office for details on these and other possible kayak trips in the area.

PELICAN

If you're looking for a place to get away from it all, it's hard to get more remote than the tiny, picturesque fishing village of Pelican (pop. 300) inside narrow Lisianski Inlet on the western shore of Chichagof Island. During the summer Pelican's population doubles with the arrival of fishermen and cold storage workers. (Pelican received it name from *The Pelican,* a fishing boat owned by the town's founder; there are no pelicans in Alaska.) Tiny Pelican has achieved notoriety as a party town, particularly when festivities reach their peak each July 4. Featured attractions include a beer-can-throwing contest, a tug-of-war that is inevitably won by the women, and a wet T-shirt contest.

The centerpiece of Pelican's boardwalk thoroughfare is the rowdy **Rosie's Bar and Grill,** where Rosie still holds down the fort. Rosie's, tel. 735-2265 rents rooms, or you can stay at **Harbor Bed & Breakfast,** tel. 735-2257. Pelican Seafoods operates a large cold storage plant and the town also has a general store, laundromat, and restaurant. Rent sea kayaks at the float house. **Lisianski Lodge,** tel. 735-2266, three miles north of Pelican, offers a pricey but idyllic setting for a splurge trip. They also rent skiffs. Showers are available at the laundromat, or try the steambaths at the local liquor store (no joke).

Ferry service to Pelican arrives only twice a month. The *Le Conte* usually stays for two hours and then turns around for the return trip to Juneau. **Glacier Bay Airways,** tel. 789-9009, and **Wings of Alaska,** tel. (800) 478-9464, have daily flights between Juneau and Pelican for $75, and **BellAir,** tel. 747-8636, flies from Sitka for $95.

West Chichagof-Yakobi Wilderness

On the northwestern shore of Chichagof Island is the wildly rugged 264,747-acre West Chichagof-Yakobi Wilderness. The coastline is swept by ocean storms and winds. Sea otters have been reintroduced to portions of this scenic shore and sea lions, marten, brown bears, and deer are common. The coast is deeply indented with many small bays, lagoons, and inlets. It also supports areas of distinctive open spruce forest with grassy glades. Except for White Sulfur Springs, this wilderness gets very little recreational use due to its remoteness and the storms that frequently make it a dangerous place for small boats and kayaks.

One of the most popular Forest Service cabins in Southeast (make reservations well in advance) is at **White Sulfur Springs,** accessible only by boat, sea kayak, or helicopter (at an astronomical $525/hour for the 40-minute OW flight from Sitka). The springs are a 20-mile kayak trip from Pelican. Much of the trip is through the protected waters of Lisianski Inlet and Strait, but the last five miles are exposed to the open ocean and require great care. The cabin ($20) has a wonderful hot springs bathhouse overlooking Bertha Bay just 50 feet away. Note, however, that the springs can be used by anyone for free, so fishermen, kayakers, and others from nearby Pelican will probably disturb your solitude.

Elfin Cove

This tiny fishing settlement (pop. 50) tops the north end of Chichagof Island, and is considered one of Alaska's prettiest towns. The setting is pretty hard to beat, right on the edge of the wild waters of Cross Sound and yet protected within a narrow harbor. The town has two grocery stores, lodging facilities, plus showers and a sauna during the summer months. During the summer, **Wings of Alaska,** tel. 789-0790 or (800) 478-9464, has daily service to Elfin Cove for $88 OW. The waters of Cross Sound and Icy Strait separate Chichagof Island from Glacier Bay National Park. They are some of the best places to see whales in Southeast Alaska,

especially near Pt. Adolphus. Charter boats offer day trips from Glacier Bay to Elfin Cove during the summer months. Also nearby is the 23,000-acre **Pleasant-Lemesurier-Inian Islands Wilderness,** created in 1990.

TENAKEE SPRINGS

The tiny hamlet of Tenakee Springs (pop. 120) has retirees and counter-culture devotees, along with a few local fishermen. Many Juneau folks have second homes here. Tenakee's houses stand on stilts along the shoreline; some have "long-drop" outhouses over the water. The town has only one street, a dirt path barely wide enough for Tenakee's three vehicles (its oil truck, fire truck, and dump truck). Everyone else walks or uses three-wheelers and bicycles. This simplicity is by choice—when rumors arose that the Forest Service would complete a road to Hoonah, locals became alarmed and successfully blocked the idea. Tenakee is best known for its hot **mineral springs** located in a building right beside the dock. The springs feed a small concrete pool with an adjacent changing room. There are separate hours for men (2-6 p.m. and 10 p.m.-9 a.m.) and women (6-10 p.m. and 9 a.m.-2 p.m.), but after midnight the rules tend to relax a bit. If the ferry is in town for more than a half-hour, be sure to take a quick dip in the pool.

Practicalities

You can pitch your tent two miles east of town along Indian River, but be sure to hang your food since brown bears are sometimes a problem. Trails extend out of town for several miles in both directions along the shore. The trail south of town reaches eight miles to an old cannery and a homestead at Coffee Cove. Beside the dock is **Snyder Mercantile Co.,** tel. 736-2205, which has groceries and supplies, and rents cottages. Tenakee Springs has a small library, an impressive new hillside grade school, and two bars. The imposing Victorian-style **Tenakee Inn,** tel. 736-2241 or (800) 327-9347, has dorm facilities ($15) or separate rooms ($40 s, $45 d).

Each room has a private bath and kitchenette. Be sure to reserve rooms well in advance for either place. Tenakee Inn rents kayaks ($35 a day or $25 a day for guests), bikes ($5 a day), and skiffs. Showers are $3. **Rosie's Blue Moon Cafe** serves good meals, or you can try the Tenakee Inn for burgers and pub grub. Tenakee does not have a Forest Service office, but if you are considering a kayak trip in the area, contact the Hoonah District Office, Box 135, Hoonah, AK 99829, tel. 945-3631, for a detailed guide that includes Tenakee, the "Hoonah Area Road Map" ($2).

Transportation

Tenakee is a popular weekend vacation spot for both Juneauites and travelers. The ferry *Le Conte* arrives in Tenakee three times a week with a schedule that makes it possible to stop-over for a Fri. night before returning to Juneau the following evening ($40 RT). There is no ferry terminal and cars cannot be off-loaded. The ferry usually stays in town for only a brief time, sometimes not even long enough to get off the boat for a walk. **Wings of Alaska,** tel. (800) 478-9464, has daily flights between Juneau and Tenakee for $61, while **BellAir,** tel. 747-8636 (in Sitka), flies every day between Sitka and Tenakee for $76.

(DIANA LASICH-HARPER)

GLACIER BAY NATIONAL PARK

America's national parks are this country's version of Mecca, places where hordes of pilgrims are drawn, in search of a fulfillment that seems to come from experiencing these shrines of the natural world. Since Glacier Bay's discovery by John Muir in 1879, the spectacles of stark rocky walls, deep fjords, and giant rivers of ice calving massive icebergs into the sea have never ceased to inspire and humble visitors.

Established as a national park in 1925, Glacier Bay received major additions in the Alaska National Interest Lands Conservation Act (ANILCA) of 1980. The park and preserve now cover more than 3.3 million acres and contain 18 glaciers that reach the ocean, making this the largest concentration of tidewater glaciers on Earth. These glaciers originate in the massive snowcapped Fairweather Range, sliding down the slopes and carving out giant troughs that become fjords when the glaciers retreat. Mount Fairweather, rising 15,320 feet, is Southeast Alaska's tallest peak. On a clear day, it is prominently visible from park headquarters, 72 miles away. The vegetation of Glacier Bay varies from a 200-year-old spruce and hemlock forest at Bartlett Cove to freshly exposed moraine where tenacious plant life is just starting to take hold. (Around Bartlett Cove you'll see extensive areas of Sitka spruce killed by a recent bark beetle infestation.) Wildlife is abundant in the park: humpback whales, harbor porpoises, harbor seals, and bird rookeries can be seen from the excursion boats and kayaks. Black bears are fairly common.

History

Glacier Bay has not always looked as it does today. When Capt. George Vancouver sailed through Icy Strait in 1794, he found a wall of ice more than 4,000 feet thick and 20 miles wide. Less than 100 years later (1879) when Hoonah Indian guides led John Muir into the area, he discovered that the glaciers had retreated nearly 50 miles, creating a new land and a giant bay splitting into two deep

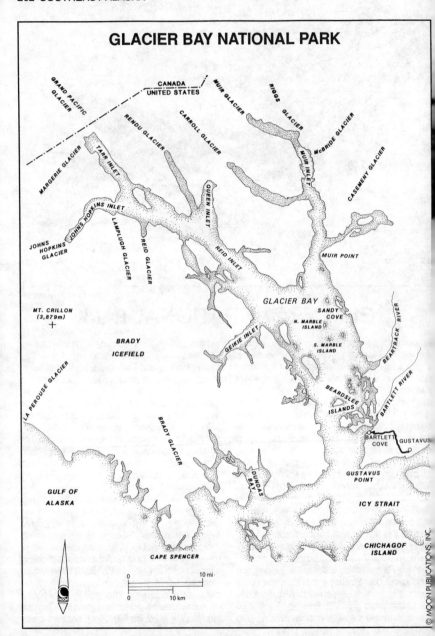

GLACIER BAY NATIONAL PARK

GRAND PACIFIC GLACIER

CANADA
UNITED STATES

MUIR GLACIER

RIGGS GLACIER

RENDU GLACIER

CARROLL GLACIER

McBRIDE GLACIER

MUIR INLET

MARGERIE GLACIER

TARR INLET

CASEMENT GLACIER

JOHNS HOPKINS INLET

QUEEN INLET

JOHNS HOPKINS GLACIER

LAMPLUGH GLACIER

REID GLACIER

REID INLET

MUIR POINT

MT. CRILLON
(3,879m)
+

GLACIER BAY

SANDY COVE

N. MARBLE ISLAND

BEARTRACK RIVER

BRADY ICEFIELD

GEIKIE INLET

S. MARBLE ISLAND

BARTLETT RIVER

LA PEROUSE GLACIER

BEARDSLEE ISLANDS

BARTLETT COVE

GUSTAVUS

BRADY GLACIER

DUNDAS BAY

GUSTAVUS POINT

GULF OF ALASKA

ICY STRAIT

CHICHAGOF ISLAND

CAPE SPENCER

0   10 mi
0   10 km

MOON

fjords on its upper end. The bay was shrouded by low clouds, but anxious to see farther into the country, he climbed a peak on its western shore: "All the landscape was smothered in clouds and I began to fear that as far as wide views were concerned I had climbed in vain. But at length the clouds lifted a little, and beneath their gray fringes I saw the berg-filled expanse of the bay, and the feet of the mountains that stand about it, and the imposing fronts of five huge glaciers, the nearest being immediately beneath me. This was my first general view of Glacier Bay, a solitude of ice and snow and newborn rocks, dim, dreary, mysterious. I held the ground I had so dearly won for an hour or two, sheltering myself from the blast as best I could, while with benumbed fingers I sketched what I could see of the landscape, and wrote a few lines in my notebook. Then, breasting the snow again, crossing the shifting avalanche slopes and torrents, I reached camp about dark, wet and weary and glad." Today's traveler is less likely to take such pains to see this grand place.

The rapid retreat of the glaciers over the last 200 years has caused the land to rebound, much like a sponge that has been squeezed and then re-forms. The process is astoundingly rapid by geological standards; around Bartlett Cove it is rising nearly two inches a year and even faster farther up the bay.

Visiting Glacier Bay

The vast majority of the 140,000 visitors who come to Glacier Bay each year arrive aboard luxury cruise ships; they're given a talk by a Park Service naturalist as the ship heads up the west arm of the bay and never set foot on the land itself. Most other visitors stay in Glacier Bay Lodge, venturing out only to walk the two short trails in Bartlett Cove or cruise up to the glaciers on a speeding tour boat. The tiny percentage who come to actually see and touch their national park rather than view it in a park naturalist's slide show are often prevented from doing so by prohibitive costs. It is somewhat ironic that the park is most accessible not to those who really want to experience the place on the ground and

on the water, but to those who would rather look out on its glaciers from their stateroom windows.

The nearest tidewater glacier is 40 miles from park headquarters at Bartlett Cove. To see these glaciers, expect to spend at least $200 from Juneau for a three-day trip up bay and $40 a day more to include a sea kayak trip. This assumes you'll be camping. Lodging starts at $24 per night in crowded dorm facilities and ascends to a lofty $106 for your own room. A visit to Glacier Bay is a highly recommended experience, but there are few options for the budget traveler, and you should probably make other plans if you're pinched for cash. Note also that things wind down after Labor Day, as facilities close for the winter months and boats stop running up the bay.

Bartlett Cove Hiking Trails

There are several enjoyable walks in the Bartlett Cove area. The mile-long **Forest Trail** loops between the lodge and the campground. **Bartlett River Trail** (three miles RT) leads from near the backcountry office to the river mouth, with opportunities to observe wildlife. For a satisfying beach walk, head south from the campground along the shore. If you're ambitious, it is possible to walk to Pt. Gustavus (six miles) or on to Goode River (13 miles). Follow the river upstream a mile to Gustavus, where you can walk or hitch back on the road. Beach walking is easiest at low tide; the backcountry office has tide charts. Note that none of these trails go anywhere near the tidewater glaciers for which the park is famous.

Campground

An excellent free campground at Bartlett Cove comes complete with bear-proof food storage caches, outhouses, and a three-sided shelter with a wood stove (great for drying your gear after a kayak trip up the bay). The campground is only a half mile from Glacier Bay Lodge and almost always has space. Running water is available next to the nearby backcountry office. All cooking must be done below the high tide line (where the odors are washed away every six hours) to reduce the chance of bear problems. See "Hiking" below for info on camping elsewhere within the park.

GUSTAVUS AREA

There are two basic centers for visitors to Glacier Bay: **Gustavus** (outside the park) and **Bartlett Cove** (10 miles away and inside the park boundaries). The airport, main boat dock, small store, and several lodging houses are in the unincorporated community of Gustavus (pop. 220). The town consists of equal parts park employees, fishermen, and folks dependent upon the tourism trade. It is one of the only places in Southeast Alaska that has enough flat country to raise cows— Opal and Ruby are shared cooperatively by six local families! Bartlett Cove has Park Service Headquarters, a campground, Glacier Bay Lodge (with bar and restaurant), boat dock, and a **backcountry office** (open daily 8 a.m. to 7 p.m. during the summer). The Park Service offers interpretive walks every day plus evening talks and slide shows upstairs in the lodge. Bartlett Cove and Gustavus are connected by a shuttle bus ($7.50 OW).

Lodging
During the summer Glacier Bay is packed with flashy tourists, so don't expect any bargains. The least expensive place (after camping) is **Glacier Bay Lodge,** tel. (800) 622-2042, where $24 gets you dorm space (jammed eight to a room). The lodge is located right in Bartlett Cove (park headquarters), and has an overpriced restaurant, a nice bar, plus a big stone fireplace that makes a cozy place to sit on a rainy evening, even if you're not a guest. Laundry facilities and coin-operated **showers** ($1) are available at Glacier Bay Lodge. Luggage or gear storage for $2/day, or you can store things for free in the shed next to the backcountry office (not locked, however).

Several other lodging options are available in nearby Gustavus; see the chart for a complete listing. Contact the **Gustavus Visitors Association,** Box 167, Gustavus, AK 99826 for a complete listing of local establishments. If this is your honeymoon or time for a major

splurge, you may should look into staying at one of the excellent upscale lodges that serve three big gourmet meals each day: **Gustavus Inn,** tel. 697-2254, or **Glacier Bay Country Inn,** tel. 697-2288. These places get a lot of favorable press, and advance reservations are essential, especially for Gustavus Inn, the oldest and most famous. Its picturesque garden provides fresh vegetables all summer long.

Food And Supplies
In Gustavus, the **Open Gate Café,** tel. 697-2227, is a fine place for a cup of coffee and fresh pastries in the morning. Try the battered halibut sandwich for lunch, or stop by on Wednesday night for a homemade pizza. It's open year-round, but closed on Sundays. Lunches and dinners are also available at **Hitching Post Restaurant** and **Glacier Bay Lodge** in Bartlett Cove. The small grocery store at Gustavus, **Beartrack Mercantile,** tel. 697-2358, sells essentials (including tofu for the vegetarian crowd), but it's better to bring all your own food from Juneau. They don't sell booze, so bring your own, or head to the bar at Glacier Bay Lodge for drinks. For outstanding gourmet seafood dinners, make reservations at **Gustavus Inn,** where a few spots are held for non-guests willing to pay $22.50 apiece.

Fishing
Fishing is a big attraction for many visitors, and most of the lodges offer special package deals for anglers. Halibut and salmon fishing are the main attraction. Charter boat operators include: **Grand Pacific Charters,** tel. 697-2288, **Glacier Bay Puffin Charters,** 697-2260, **Fairweather Lodge & Adventures,** tel. 697-2334, **Alaska Seair Adventures,** tel. 697-2215, and **Glacier Bay Lodge,** tel. (800) 622-2042.

TRANSPORTATION

Getting There
There is no state ferry service to either Glacier Bay or Gustavus, and locals receive most of their supplies by barge every two

GLACIER BAY ACCOMMODATIONS

Note: all addresses are for Gustavus, AK 99826.
Most provide free transport to and from the Gustavus airport,
and bikes to ride on the many dirt roads.

Name	Address	Phone	Rates	Features
Glacier Bay Lodge	76 Egan Dr. Juneau	(800) 622-2042	$24 $106 s, $126 d	dorm space private rooms
Puffin's Bed and Breakfast	Box 3	697-2260	$40/cabin	simple cabins
Salmon River Cabins	Box 13	697-2245	$40/cabin	sleeps four
Goode Riverbed & Breakfast	Box 37	697-2241	$40 s $60 d	elegant log home
Annie Mae Lodge	Box 80	(800) 478-2346	$100 s, $175 d	three meals
W.T. Fugarwe Lodge	Box 280	697-2244	$105 pp	three meals
Gustavus Inn	Box 60	697-2254	$110 pp	cabins, three meals
Glacier Bay Bed & Breakfast	Box 60	697-2255	$70 pp	full breakfast
Glacier Bay Country Inn	Box 5	697-2288	$129 s $184 d	three meals

veeks. See "Getting to the Glacier" below for boat transport to Glacier Bay from Juneau. Most visitors fly by jet from Juneau to Gustavus on **Alaska Airlines,** tel. (800) 426-0333, or a bargain-basement price of $86 RT. Book ahead to be sure of getting on these very popular flights. The trip takes only 15 minutes in the air, so the flight attendants don't even have time to throw bags of peanuts at you. More rewarding are flights by **Glacier Bay Airways,** tel. 789-9009, **Wings of Alaska,** tel. 789-0790, and **L.A.B. Flying Service,** tel. 789-9160 (all Juneau phone numbers). They offer more personal service and the small planes fly lower, providing excellent sightseeing for around $120 RT, or $15 less if you pay cash. Note that it's illegal to transport white gas and other potentially explosive fuels in any commercial aircraft so be

sure your gas stove and fuel bottles are empty before you reach the airport. White gas can be purchased in Bartlett Cove next to the visitor center or in Gustavus at Beartrack Mercantile.

The airport in Gustavus is 10 miles from Park Service Headquarters at Bartlett Cove. A **shuttle bus** meets all Alaska Airlines flights, transporting you to Bartlett Cove for an absurd $7.50 each direction. Add $18 each way if you're carrying a hardshell kayak. Hitching eliminates this extortion, but traffic can be downright scarce in tiny Gustavus. Actually, it is easier to hitch to Gustavus from Bartlett Cove, so you may want to pay the $7.50 to get to Bartlett Cove and then hitch back when you leave. **TLC Taxi,** 697-2239, provides passenger and kayak transport from anywhere in the Gustavus area.

Flightseeing

Glacier Bay Airways, tel. 697-2249, offers flightseeing trips from Gustavus. The price is $110 pp for a 1¼-hour flight. Other companies providing flightseeing trips are **Alaska Seair Adventures,** tel. 697-2215, and **L.A.B. Flying Service,** tel. 789-9160 (in Juneau). Flightseeing trips over Glacier Bay are also available from Juneau, Haines, and Skagway, but prices are generally higher since you will need to fly farther. If you have a folding kayak, these companies can provide drop-offs up the bay if you want to charter a flight. Most people travel to the head of Glacier Bay on boats instead.

Getting To The Glaciers

Most independent travelers touring Glacier Bay travel upbay aboard one of two boats: the *Spirit of Adventure* or the *Spirit of Glacier Bay.* See "Sea Kayaking" (below) for camper drop-off info. Both boats run from late May through early September only, and have Park Service naturalists onboard when the vessels are within park waters. The *Spirit of Adventure,* a 220-passenger high-speed catamaran, sails every day during the summer from Juneau to Glacier Bay and has a Park Service naturalist onboard within the park. Day trips from Bartlett Cove will set you back $142 pp. Make reservations at the lodge or by calling (800) 622-2042. Another option is to pay $249 pp for a day-long trip that includes a flight from Juneau to Gustavus followed by a trip up the bay and another flight back that evening. The same trip spread over two days and including a night at Glacier Bay Lodge will set you back $316 pp. For details, stop by Glacier Bay Tours and Cruises, 76 Egan Dr., Suite 110, tel. 463-5510, or (800) 622-2042. Note that the lunch served on board is nothing special, and that you will need to pay for snacks.

Many people prefer the *Spirit of Glacier Bay,* a slower boat that leaves Juneau on Mondays, Wednesdays, and Fridays from mid-May through early September. One-way fare from Juneau to Gustavus (no one-way returns available) costs $99, but space is limited to six people per trip. Add in another $50 for kayak transportation (or rent one in

Glacier Bay). Much more popular is the three-day, two-night voyage that includes excellent meals (prime rib, seafood, fresh baked bread . . .), stateroom accommodations, and a leisurely cruise up the West Arm of Glacier Bay. The voyage starts for a not-so-leisurely $450 pp. Be sure to reserve months ahead for this very popular trip. The *Spirit of Glacier Bay* has a foredeck that is perfect for watching wildlife or photographing glaciers, and its slow speed (11 knots versus 30 knots for the *Spirit of Adventure*) means the wind doesn't force you inside. Note, however, that the *Spirit of Glacier Bay* does not do kayaker or camper drop-offs, and is not available to folks getting on in Bartlett Cove. For details, contact Alaska Sightseeing Tours, Merchant's Wharf, Juneau, tel 586-6300, or (800) 426-7702.

ON YOUR OWN

There are no trails anywhere in Glacier Bay's backcountry, but Park Service rangers can provide good info on hiking and camping up the bay. Camping is allowed in most areas within the park. Exceptions are the Marble Islands that are closed because of their importance for nesting seabirds, and a few other areas closed because of the potential for bear incidents. A gas stove is a necessity for camping since wood is often not available. Free permits (available at the backcountry office) are recommended before you head out. Park naturalists have special camper orientations each evening, including info on how and where to go, bear safety, and minimum-impact camping procedures. Bears have killed two people within the park in past years, and to lessen the chance of this happening, free bear-proof containers are supplied to all kayakers and hikers before they head out. A small storage shed beside the backcountry office is a good place to store unneeded gear while you are up the bay. Note that firearms are not allowed in Glacier Bay National Park.

Sea Kayaking

An increasingly popular way to visit Glacier Bay is by sea kayak. Some folks bring their

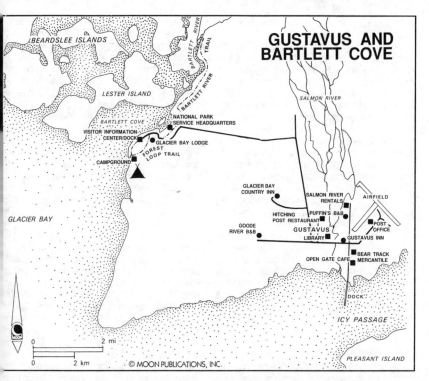

GUSTAVUS AND BARTLETT COVE

BEARDSLEE ISLANDS

LESTER ISLAND

BARTLETT RIVER TRAIL

SALMON RIVER

BARTLETT COVE
VISITOR INFORMATION CENTER/DOCK
NATIONAL PARK SERVICE HEADQUARTERS
GLACIER BAY LODGE
FOREST LOOP TRAIL
CAMPGROUND

GLACIER BAY

GLACIER BAY COUNTRY INN
SALMON RIVER RENTALS
AIRFIELD
HITCHING POST RESTAURANT
PUFFIN'S B&B
POST OFFICE
GOODE RIVER B&B
GUSTAVUS
LIBRARY
GUSTAVUS INN
OPEN GATE CAFE
BEAR TRACK MERCANTILE

DOCK

ICY PASSAGE

PLEASANT ISLAND

0   2 mi
0   2 km
© MOON PUBLICATIONS, INC.

own folding kayaks on the plane, or pay $50 to bring them from Juneau aboard the *Spirit of Glacier Bay,* but most people rent them from **Glacier Bay Sea Kayaks** in Bartlett Cove for $40/day ($35/day for four to six days use). Write them at Box 26, Gustavus, AK 99826, tel. 697-2257, for details. Reservations are needed during mid-summer. Kayak rental includes a two-person boat, paddles, life vests, spray skirts, flotation bags, and a brief lesson.

Heading Up Bay

There are several focal points that kayakers enjoy visiting within Glacier Bay. The **Beardslee Islands,** in relatively protected waters near Bartlett Cove, make for an excellent two- or three-day kayak trip and do not require any additional expenses. Beyond the Beardslees, Glacier Bay becomes much less

protected and you should plan on spending at least a week up bay if you paddle there. (It is 50 miles or more to the glaciers.) Rather than attempting to cross this open water, most kayakers opt for a drop-off at one of three places. These change periodically, so ask at the backcountry office for specifics. The *Spirit of Adventure* (see above) provides daily trips into both arms of Glacier Bay. Roundtrip drop-off and pick-up service costs $166 from Bartlett Cove, or $97 if you get dropped off and paddle back. Muir Inlet (the east arm of Glacier Bay) is preferred by many kayakers because it is a bit more protected and is not used by the cruise ships or most tour boats. The West Arm is more spectacular—especially iceberg-filled Johns Hopkins Inlet—but you'll have to put up with a constant stream of large and small cruise ships. If the boat operators have their way, even more ships can be expected in future years.

Kayaking opportunities at Glacier Bay are described in *Discover Southeast Alaska with Pack and Paddle* by Margaret Piggott. For information on hiking, pick up a copy of *Hiking in Muir Inlet* ($2) at the backcountry office. They also sell topographic maps ($5) of the park and a variety of local guidebooks.

Guided Kayak Trips
Alaska Discovery, 369 S. Franklin St., Juneau, AK 99801, tel. 586-1911, offers several excellent, but pricey guided trips into Glacier Bay National Park and Preserve. Their kayak trips of the bay cost $800 for four days or $1,200 for seven days, airfare from Juneau included. **Spirit Walker Expeditions,** Box 240, Gustavus, AK 99826, tel. 697-2266, also offers excellent sea kayak tours, including overnight trips to nearby Pleasant Island for $250 pp or eight-hour day trips for $85 pp. All sorts of longer trips are available, all the way up to seven-day trips ($1000 pp) to remote islands off Chichagof Island. They do not guide within Glacier Bay National Park.

The Tatshenshini
Along the western edge of Glacier Bay National Park flows the Tatshenshini River, considered one of the world's premier wilderness rafting routes. Bears, moose, mountain goats, and Dall sheep are all visible along the route. The river passes through Class III whitewater and spectacular canyons along its way to the juncture with the Alsek River. Alaska Discovery (see above) has several trips each summer down this spectacular route. A 10-day river-rafting trip isn't cheap—$1500 pp—including a van ride from Haines to the put-in point at Dalton Post in the Yukon. A longer 12-day trip ($1800 pp) includes a helicopter portage (!) around the Class VI rapids of Turnback Canyon before continuing on down the **Alsek River** below its confluence with the Tatshenshini. The latter trip takes you right past the seven-mile wide face of the Alsek Glacier. Both of these trips start in Haines and end in Yakutat, so you'll need to add air fare from Yakutat, unless you're moving there permanently. If so, there are certainly cheaper ways to get to Yakutat.

Many other American and Canadian companies also offer float trips down the "Tat" River. For their addresses and info on running the river on your own, contact **Glacier Bay National Park and Preserve,** Gustavus, AK 99826, tel. 697-3341. If you plan to run the river on your own, contact the Park Service for permit information. Only one launch is allowed per day, with half of these set aside for commercial guides. Alaskon Express can provide bus transportation from Haines to the put-in point at Dalton Post.

(GORDY OHLIGER)

HAINES

The pleasant town of Haines (pop. 1,200) provides a transition point between the lush greenery of Southeast and the more rugged beauty of the Yukon and Alaska's Interior. As the ferry sails north to Haines on the Lynn Canal—at 1,600 feet deep it's the longest and deepest fjord in North America—the Inside Passage gets narrower, and you sense that this unique waterway, and your passage on it, is coming to an end. To the east, waterfalls tumble off the mountainsides, while to the west, glaciers lumber down from the icefields of the Chilkat Range. The long river of ice you see 40 minutes before Haines is Davidson Glacier. Rainbow Glacier, also on the left, hangs from a cliff just beyond. Both originate from the same icefield that forms part of Glacier Bay National Park.

The quiet and conservative town of Haines lies 90 miles north of Juneau, straddling a narrow peninsula between Chilkoot and Chilkat inlets. Its mountain-ringed setting seems to define the word spectacular: from the ferry, you catch a glimpse of the white Victorian buildings of Ft. Seward, while behind the 5,500-foot tall Cathedral Peaks form an incredible backdrop. Haines has a wealth of outdoor experiences, almost as many for those without cash as those with. There are plenty of hiking trails running up surrounding peaks, camping is right next to town, and travelers will discover a pleasant mixture of working stiffs and artisans.

Unlike nearby Skagway where a tidal wave of tourists inundates the town daily, Haines only sees a single large cruise ship each week during the summer. Most Haines visitors arrive by ferry and head on up the highway (or vice versa), but Haines is also becoming a popular weekend getaway for Canadians from Whitehorse. With "only" 60 inches of precipitation a year, Haines weather is decidedly drier than points farther south. And, on top of that, the people of Haines seem to be some of the friendliest in Alaska.

History
Long before the arrival of whites to the Haines area, the Tlingit people of the Chilkoot and Chilkat tribes established villages nearby. Fish were plentiful, as were game animals and berries. The area's "mother village" was Klukwan, 20 miles up the Chilkat

Chilkat blanket
(DIANA LASICH-HARPER)

River, but another large Chilkoot village nestled near Chilkoot Lake, and a summer camp squatted just northwest of present-day Haines. The Chilkats were renowned for their beautiful blankets woven from mountain goat wool and dyed with an inventive mixture of copper nuggets, urine, lichen, and spruce roots. The blankets were (and are) worn during dance ceremonies. Today they are also exceedingly valuable.

In 1879, the naturalist John Muir and the Presbyterian minister Samuel Hall Young reached the end of Lynn Canal. Reverend Young was looking for potential mission sites to convert the Natives to Christianity. Muir was along for the canoe ride, wanting a chance to explore this remote territory. While there, they met with members of the Chilkat tribe at a settlement called Yendestakyeh. Both men gave speeches before the people, but the Chilkats were considerably more interested in Muir's "brotherhood of man" message than Dr. Young's proselytizing. Muir wrote: "Later, when the sending of a missionary and teacher was being considered, the chief said they wanted me, and, as an inducement, promised that if I would come to them they would always do as I directed, follow my councils, give me as many wives as I liked, build a church and school, and pick all the stones out of the paths and make them

smooth for my feet." Two years later the mission was established by two Presbyterian missionaries (Muir had other plans) and the village was renamed Haines, in honor of Mrs. F.E.H. Haines of the Presbyterian Home Missions Board. She never visited her namesake, and some have recently proposed renaming the town Port Chilkoot (won't happen).

During the Klondike Gold Rush, an adventurer and shrewd businessman named Jack Dalton developed a 305-mile toll road between Haines and the Yukon along an old Indian trade route, charging miners $150 each to use his **Dalton Trail.** Armed men never failed to collect. To maintain order among the thousands of miners, the U.S. Army established Fort William H. Seward at Haines. Named for Alaska's "patron saint," it was built between 1900 and 1904 on 100 acres of land deeded to the government by the Haines mission. Renamed Chilkoot Barracks in 1922 (to avoid confusion with the town of Seward), it was the only military base in all of Alaska for the next 20 years.

In 1942-43 the Army built the 150-mile Haines Highway from Haines to Haines Junction as an emergency evacuation route from Alaska in case of invasion by the Japanese. After WW II, the post was declared excess government property and sold to a veterans' group that hoped to form a business cooperative. The venture failed, but many stayed on, making homes in the stately old officers' quarters. The site became a national historic landmark in 1978 and its name was changed back to Ft. Seward.

Today the town of Haines has a diversified economy that includes a sawmill, fishing (no canneries, however), tourism, and government jobs. Haines has also recently become something of a center for the arts, attracting artists and craftsworkers of all types, from creators of stained glass to weavers of Chilkat blankets. Halfway between Haines and Juneau is the site of a large gold mine currently under development. If opened, the Kensington Mine would employ 340 people from Juneau, but would also lead to effluent being dumped into the pristine waters nearby where salmon and halibut are caught.

SIGHTS

The **Sheldon Museum,** tel. 766-2366, on Main St. has a fine collection of Tlingit artifacts (including Chilkat blankets) and items from the gold rush. Downstairs, you can watch the excellent Audubon Society movie, "Last Stronghold of the Eagles," (filmed at the Chilkat Bald Eagle Preserve) continuously most days, or a slide show about local history. The museum ($2) is open daily 1-5 in the summer and Sun., Mon., and Wed. 1-4 in winter. **Lookout Park** (next to the harbor) is a great place to sit on a sunny day to watch the fishing boats, eagles, and scenery. Bring a lunch. Behind it is a small **cemetery** with pioneer graves dating from the 1880s. An old building, all that remains of Yendestakyeh, is just beyond the airport, 3½ miles from town. The **mission bell** (1880) that once called Tlingit peoples to worship now sits out front of the Presbyterian church on 1st Avenue. Ask locally for directions to the set of Walt Disney's **White Fang,** filmed next to Haines in 1990.

Fort Seward

The well-preserved buildings of Ft. Seward make an excellent place to explore. Inside the central parade ground are recent replicas of a Tlingit tribal house, along with a Yukon trapper's cabin complete with pelts and a sod cache. The non-profit **Alaska Indian Arts** (open Mon.-Sat. 9-5), operates from the old hospital building on the southwest side of Ft. Seward. Inside you'll find master woodcarvers, silversmiths, and other craftsworkers with items for sale. The **Wild Iris Shop** here has the most attractive T-shirts in Haines, and has the added bonus of being run by the Haines Borough mayor, Fred Shields. Along the top of the hill is "Officers' Row," the attractive white turn-of-the-century homes that once housed captains, lieutenants, and their families. You'll find **Lowell "Knute" Knutson's** woodworking shop at #5 Officers Row, tel. 766-2288. This is a fun chance to talk to an old time Alaskan logger, craftsman, and character. Ask if he knows any of Robert Service's poems. The Haines visitor bureau has a free detailed historical guide and walking tour of Fort Seward.

HIKING

The Haines area has a number of excellent hikes, ranging from the easy (Battery Point) to the strenuous (Mt. Ripinski). For more details see *Discover Alaska with Pack and Paddle* by Margaret Piggott, or pick up the **"Haines is for Hikers"** pamphlet from the visitor center.

Mount Riley Trails

Three trails lead to the top of 1,760-foot Mt. Riley, from which you get a panoramic view of Lynn Canal, Davidson and Rainbow glaciers, the Chilkat River, Taiya Inlet, and 360 degrees of snowcapped peaks. The shortest and steepest route (two miles, three hours RT) starts three miles southeast of Haines on Mud Bay Road. A small parking area is opposite the marked trailhead. You can also follow FAA Rd. from behind Ft. Seward. This trail is four miles long (approximately four hours RT) and follows the city water supply route for two miles before splitting off to join the more direct trail. A third path (unmarked) starts from the end of the road at Portage Cove and follows the **Battery Point Trail** for two miles. The path to Mt. Riley splits off to the right and climbs steeply to the top. The total length is 5½ miles (five hours RT). You can also continue along the relatively easy Battery Point Trail to a campsite at Kelgaya Point and across pebbly beaches to Battery Point (2½ miles).

Mount Ripinski Trail

The full-day hike up and down Mt. Ripinski (3,900 feet) offers unparalleled views of mountains and inland waterways, but it's strenuous and long (10 miles RT). You may want to camp in the alpine and make this a two-day hike. From Haines, take Young Rd. north till it intersects with a jeep road that follows a buried pipeline around the mountain. The trail begins about a mile along this dirt road and climbs through a spruce/hemlock forest to muskeg and finally alpine at

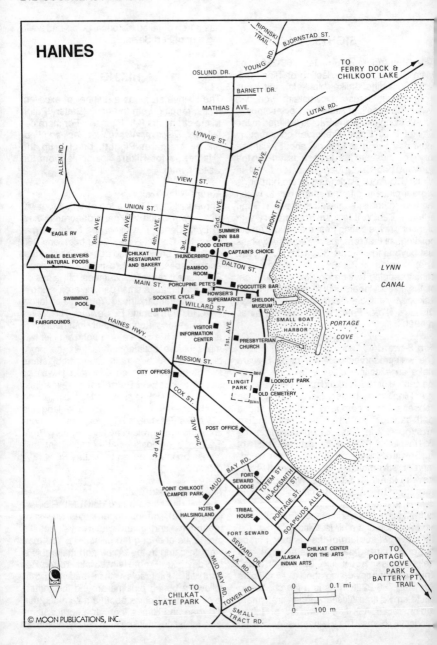

HAINES

RIPINSKI TRAIL
BJORNSTAD ST.
YOUNG RD.
TO FERRY DOCK & CHILKOOT LAKE
OSLUND DR.
BARNETT DR.
MATHIAS AVE.
LUTAK RD.
LYNVUE ST.
1st. AVE.
ALLEN RD.
VIEW ST.
FRONT ST.
UNION ST.
2nd. AVE.
6th. AVE.
5th. AVE.
4th. AVE.
3rd. AVE.
EAGLE RV
SUMMER INN B&B
FOOD CENTER
CAPTAIN'S CHOICE
BIBLE BELIEVERS NATURAL FOODS
CHILKAT RESTAURANT AND BAKERY
THUNDERBIRD
DALTON ST.
BAMBOO ROOM
MAIN ST.
PORCUPINE PETE'S
FOGCUTTER BAR
SWIMMING POOL
SOCKEYE CYCLE
HOWSER'S SUPERMARKET
SHELDON MUSEUM
LIBRARY
WILLARD ST.
LYNN CANAL
FAIRGROUNDS
HAINES HWY.
VISITOR INFORMATION CENTER
1st. AVE.
PRESBYTERIAN CHURCH
SMALL BOAT HARBOR
PORTAGE COVE
MISSION ST.
CITY OFFICES
COX ST.
TLINGIT PARK
LOOKOUT PARK
OLD CEMETERY
3rd. AVE.
2nd. AVE.
POST OFFICE
MUD BAY RD.
FORT SEWARD LODGE
TOTEM ST.
BLACKSMITH
PORTAGE ST.
SOAPSUDS ALLEY
POINT CHILKOOT CAMPER PARK
HOTEL HALSINGLAND
TRIBAL HOUSE
FORT SEWARD
F.A.A. RD.
SEWARD DR.
ALASKA INDIAN ARTS
CHILKAT CENTER FOR THE ARTS
TO PORTAGE COVE PARK & BATTERY PT. TRAIL
MUD BAY RD.
TOWER RD.
TO CHILKAT STATE PARK
SMALL TRACT RD.

0   0.1 mi
0   100 m

© MOON PUBLICATIONS, INC.

2,500 feet. You can continue along the ridge to the north summit (3,160 feet) where there is a register box, or on to the main peak. Return the same way, or via a steep path that takes you down to a saddle and then to the Haines Highway, seven miles northwest of Haines. Mount Ripinski is covered with snow until mid-summer, so be prepared. Don't go in bad weather and do stay on the trail in the alpine areas.

Seduction Point Trail

For a gentle, long, and very scenic beach walk, head to Chilkat State Park campground, seven miles southwest of Haines on Mud Bay Road. Seduction Point is on the end of the peninsula separating Chilkoot and Chilkat inlets, a six-mile hike from the campground. The trail alternates between the forest and the beach, and it's a good idea to check the tides to make sure that you're able to hike the last beach stretch at low tide. This hike also makes a fine overnight camping trip. Call the State Park Office in Haines, tel. 766-2292, for locations of campsites along this trail.

PRACTICALITIES

Accommodations

The "youth hostel" in Haines is 2½ miles southeast of town on Small Tract Road. Called **Bear Creek Camp,** tel. 766-2259, dorm spaces are $10 per night or $12 per night for nonmembers. Ferry pick-ups may be available. Showers cost $2 extra, and limited kitchen facilities are available. The hostel is not particularly clean and definitely on the primitive side, but a few travelers like the rusticity. You may be better off camping if you're on a tight budget. Bear Creek is closed in Jan. and February.

Hotel Halsingland offers the nicest lodging in town. Note, however that the $30 room is very tiny (most other rooms are twice this rate). This beautiful old Victorian hotel was once the commanding officer's quarters at Ft. Seward. Two recommended bed and breakfast places are **Ft. Seward B&B** (a classic Victorian structure), and **Summer Inn B&B** (downtown), built by Tim Vogel, a no-

torious member of Soapy Smith's Skagway gang.

Camping

The best campsite near Haines is at **Portage Cove State Wayside** ($6/night), only three-quarters of a mile from town. Water and outhouses are available, but there is no overnight parking—the site is for hikers and cyclists only. The location is quiet and attractive, and eagles hang around nearby. **Port Chilkoot Camper Park,** tel. (800) 542-6363 (behind Hotel Halsingland) has wooded campsites at $6.50 per tent, showers ($1.50), and a laundromat on the premises. There is always tent space. If you have a vehicle or don't mind hitching, stay at one of the two excellent state-run campgrounds ($6/night), both with drinking water, toilets, and picnic shelters. **Chilkat State Park,** seven miles southeast of Haines, has a fine hiking trail to Seduction Point, and **Chilkoot Lake State Recreation Site,** five miles northwest of the ferry, has good fishing and a lovely view over the turquoise-blue lake. RVers park at the gravel lot named **Oceanside RV Park,** tel. 766-2444, on Main St., or a the fancier but sterile **Haines Hitch-Up RV Park** on Haines Highway, tel. 766-2882, for $12/night. No tents allowed.

Food

Haines has a variety of restaurants with fair prices (by Alaskan standards). For filling breakfasts and lunches, along with friendly service, head to the **Bamboo Room** on 2nd Ave., tel. 766-9101. It's a good place to meet local loggers. Check the board for daily specials. **Lighthouse Restaurant,** at the foot of Main St., tel. 766-2442, is an old favorite that serves famous buttermilk pies. For pizzas, try **Porcupine Pete's** on Main St., tel. 766-9199. **Chilkat Restaurant and Bakery** on 5th Ave., tel. 766-2920, has all-you-can-eat Mexican meals on Friday nights and fresh salmon and halibut other evenings. It's a bit on the pricey side. Their baker rolls out great pastries, and the coffee is free with a wooden nickel (available at the visitor center).

Howser's Supermarket on Main St., tel. 766-2040, has a salad bar and deli, along with most anything else you might need. Cheaper prices and better produce at **Food Center,** 3rd and Dalton, tel. 766-2181. More unusual is **Bible Believers Natural Foods,** 6th and Main, where you'll discover good prices on natural foods, and a stash of used fishing lures for just a buck apiece. Ask around the boat harbor to see who's selling fresh fish or prawns. **Dejon Delights Smokery,** at Fort Seward, tel. 766-2505, has freshly smoked salmon for sale or will smoke fish that you catch. An all-you-can-eat **salmon bake** ($17.50) is held nightly in the tribal house at Fort Seward. Go light on the trimmings to save room for more of the tasty fish. Some of the best local seafood dinners can be found at **Hotel Halsingland,** tel. 766-2000. Pig out at lunchtime on soup, salad, and chili for $6.50. Not far away at **Ft. Seward Lodge,** all-you-can-eat crab dinners ($25) are served nightly.

Entertainment

If you hit the bar at **Ft. Seward Lodge,** be sure to ask for a "Roadkill," the flaming house drink that's guaranteed to set your innards on fire. They also have live music on weekends, along with the **Fogcutter Bar** downtown. The **Chilkat Dancers,** an acclaimed Tlingit dance group, give performances ($7, students $4) Mon., Wed., and Sat. evenings, tel. 766-2160. The costumes (including priceless Chilkat blankets) and dances are all entirely authentic, offering a glimpse of the revitalized Tlingit culture. Lynn Canal Community Players perform the melodramatic **"Lust for Dust,"** on Fri. and Sun. evenings for $5. With characters such as Sgt. Justin Time and Patience Steadfast, you can expect a lighthearted romp through local history. Both groups perform in the **Chilkat Center for the Arts,** one of Alaska's finest performing-arts facilities. It is located in Ft. Seward's old recreation hall, renovated into a theater in 1967.

Southeast Alaska State Fair

Every year some 15,000 visitors from all over Alaska and the Yukon flock to Haines for the five-day long Southeast Alaska State Fair, held the third week in August each year. Events include a horse show, logging contest, farmers' market, parade, pig races, dog show, and hundreds of exhibits of all types. There are daily musical concerts every afternoon featuring nationally known artists at no extra charge.

Services

Showers are available at Port Chilkoot Camper Park for $1.25. Another option is the **swimming pool,** tel. 766-2666, next to the high school, where $2 gets you a shower and swim. The **public library,** on 3rd St., tel 766-2545, is open Mon.-Fri. 10-4:30, Sat. 1-4, and Mon.-Thurs. 7-9 p.m. Get used books for 25 cents. The **post office** is on Haines Highway near Ft. Seward. Get topographic maps from **Jackson's** at 2nd and Main streets.

Information

The **Haines Visitor Information Center,** tel 766-2234, (800) 458-3579 (U.S.), or (800) 478-2268 (Canada), is located on 2nd Avenue. Stop here first to talk to the very friendly and knowledgeable staff. Open daily 8-8 in summer and Mon.-Sat. 8-5 in winter. You can leave notes on the message board for fellow travelers, or get a cup of coffee or tea. Packs can generally be left here while you walk around town. Ask about the free guided walking tours available from the visitor center. For thorough, up-to-date info, pick up a copy of the free **"Haines Sentinel Visitors Guide"** here or at the ferry terminal.

TRANSPORTATION

Ferry Service

The Haines ferry terminal, tel. 766-2111, is 3½ miles north of town on Lutak Highway, has storage lockers. Ferries arrive in Haines almost every day during the summer, heading both north to Skagway and south to Juneau. They generally stop for 1½ hours. **Haines Taxi,** tel. 766-3138 and **The Other Guys Taxi,** tel. 766-3257, both charge $5 to town from the ferry terminal. Rent mountain bikes ($5/hour or $25/day) from **Sockeye Cycle,** tel. 766-2869, in the alley behind Howser's Market. Kayak rentals run $30/day

HAINES ACCOMMODATIONS

Name	Address	Phone	Rates	Features
Bear Creek Camp	3 miles south	766-2259	$12 pp	hostel
Ft. Seward Lodge	Ft. Seward	766-2009	$40+ s, $45+ d	
Hotel Halsingland	Ft. Seward	766-2000 (800) 542-6363	$30+ s, $64+ d $69 s, $74 d	B&B
Eagle's Nest Motel	Haines Hwy.	766-2891	$57 s, $66 d	AAA approved
Mountain View Motel	Mud Bay Rd.	766-2900	$54 s $59 d	
Summer Inn B&B	2nd and Main	766-2970	$55 s, $65 d	historic place
Thunderbird Motel	Dalton St.	766-2131 (800) 327-2556	$56 s $66 d	
Ft. Seward B&B	Ft. Seward	766-2856	$58 s, $68 d	classic Victorian
Captain's Choice Motel	Dalton & 2nd	766-3111 (800) 247-7153	$70+ s, $80+ d	nicest in town AAA approved
Ft. Seward Condos	Ft. Seward	766-2425	$70/unit	3 day min.

The **Haines-Skagway Water Taxi,** tel. 766-3395, is an excellent choice if you need a break from the ferries and don't have a car. The boat connects Haines and Skagway twice each day in summer, and costs $15 OW or $25 RT ($5 extra for bikes). This is a fine way to see wildlife, fjords, glaciers, and waterfalls at a leisurely nine-knot pace. Every Saturday, the *Red Head* offers boat taxi service from Haines to Juneau for $45 RT. The boat returns the same evening. Call 983-2022 for specifics.

By Air
The airport is 3½ miles west of town on the Haines Highway. **Wings of Alaska,** tel. (800) 478-9464, flies daily to Juneau ($61) and Skagway ($35). **Skagway Air,** tel. 789-2006, flies to Skagway ($60) and Juneau ($60) each day ($10 more for plastic). **Haines Airways**, tel. 766-2646, has daily flights to Juneau. **L.A.B. Flying Service,** tel. 766-2222, flies every day between Haines and Juneau ($60) and Skagway ($30). The flight between

Juneau and Haines is pretty spectacular; on clear days you'll be treated to views of glaciers along both sides of Lynn Canal.

Heading North
The paved highway north from Haines is the most direct route to Fairbanks (665 miles) and Anchorage (775 miles). For cyclists it's much easier than the Klondike Highway out of Skagway. The cheapest way to get into Interior Alaska is aboard the vans of **Alaska-Denali Transit.** Call 766-2869 in Haines for ticket information, or 273-3331 in Anchorage for recorded info. They operate vans between Haines and Tok ($65), Anchorage ($115), Denali ($105), Talkeetna ($110), and Homer ($149). Kayaks, (50% extra) and bikes ($10 extra) can also be carried. The vans leave twice a week from the Haines Visitor Center, with an overnight stop at the Tok Youth Hostel (or you can camp). This is a summer-only service.

Alaskon Express, tel. (800) 544-2206, also provides bus service between Haines

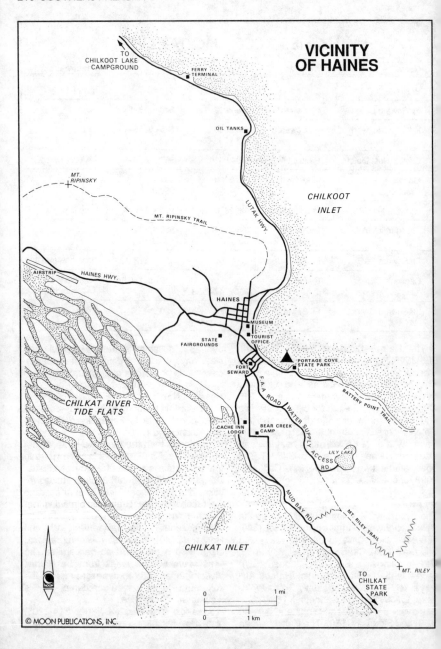

VICINITY OF HAINES

TO CHILKOOT LAKE CAMPGROUND

FERRY TERMINAL

OIL TANKS

MT. RIPINSKY

MT. RIPINSKY TRAIL

LUTAK HWY.

CHILKOOT INLET

AIRSTRIP

HAINES HWY.

HAINES

MUSEUM

STATE FAIRGROUNDS

TOURIST OFFICE

FORT SEWARD

PORTAGE COVE STATE PARK

F.A.A. ROAD

BATTERY POINT TRAIL

CHILKAT RIVER TIDE FLATS

CACHE INN LODGE

BEAR CREEK CAMP

WATER SUPPLY ACCESS RD.

LILY LAKE

MUD BAY RD.

MT. RILEY TRAIL

CHILKAT INLET

MT. RILEY

TO CHILKAT STATE PARK

0   1 mi

0   1 km

© MOON PUBLICATIONS, INC.

and Haines Junction ($54), Whitehorse ($75), Tok ($114), Glennallen ($141), Fairbanks ($156), and Anchorage ($182). You can get off anywhere along the route. In Haines, buses stop at the Wings of Alaska office on Main St. and Hotel Halsingland. Reservations are not required. The buses depart Haines every Tues. and Fri. morning late May to mid-Sept., arriving in Anchorage the next evening after a one-night layover in Beaver Creek, Yukon. Lodging in Beaver Creek is not included in the bus fare (or you can camp). Travelers to Whitehorse catch the same bus in Haines and transfer in Haines Junction, arriving in Whitehorse that afternoon.

It's also possible to hitch north from Haines, but traffic is variable (depending upon ferry arrivals), and the retirees in Winnebagos won't pick you up. You may want to try hitching and catch one of the buses if you get stranded—they can be flagged down en route. Several places in town rent cars; cheapest (around $40/day) are from **Hertz,** (800) 327-2556 and **Eagle's Nest,** tel. 766-2891. The latter company allows Skagway drop-offs. A better deal may be to rent a car in Juneau where there are no mileage restrictions (compacts for $180/week from Evergreen Ford, tel. 789-9386), put it on the ferry, and drive north from there for a week or two before returning to Juneau.

Cruising Into Canada

The Canadian border is 42 miles north of Haines. Both Canadian and U.S. Customs are open 7 a.m. to 11 p.m. (Canada is on Pacific Standard Time). Canadian Customs requires at least $150 cash for 48 hours travel. Customs agents are known to hassle backpackers, so be prepared for lots of questions if you are traveling on the cheap. No handguns are allowed across the Canadian border.

Tours

Chilkat Guides, tel. 766-2491, offers an excellent four-hour float trip down the Chilkat River for $60 ($25 for children). This is a leisurely raft trip (no whitewater) with good views of the Chilkat Mountains, glaciers, and numerous eagles. They also have a two-day, fly-in/raft-out trip that begins with a flight to Leblondeau Glacier, followed by a float trip down the gentle Tsirku River to Klukwan where a van returns you to Haines. This trip is $325 per person. Dan Egolf of **Alaska Nature Tours,** tel. 766-2876, leads educational three-hour trips ($45) to the eagle-viewing area along the Chilkat River and other places. Ask about his longer day-trips and telemark ski tours in the high country. The visitor center has a complete listing of other local guiding companies and charter boat operators.

CHILKAT BALD EAGLE PRESERVE

Each fall on the "Bald Eagle Council Grounds," the Chilkat River north of Haines becomes home to the largest eagle gathering on Earth. Due to upwellings of warm water near the Tsirku River alluvial fan, the lower Chilkat River doesn't freeze over, and a late run of up to 100,000 chum salmon arrive to spawn. The dying salmon attract bears, wolves, gulls, magpies, ravens, and up to 3,500 bald eagles along a four-mile stretch of river just below the Tlingit village of **Klukwan.** The 48,000-acre Chilkat Bald Eagle Preserve protects this unique gathering of eagles. During the peak of the salmon run (Nov.-Jan.), black cottonwoods along the river are filled with hundreds of birds, and many more line the braided riverbanks. The area is very popular with photographers, but be sure to stay off the flats to avoid disturbing these majestic birds. During the summer, local eagle populations are much lower, but, with 80 active nests and up to 400 resident eagles on the river, you're guaranteed of seeing some eagles. A state campground ($6) is at Mosquito Lake, five miles north of Klukwan and three miles off the highway.

SKAGWAY

Occupying a narrow plain by the mouth of the Skagway River at the head of the Lynn Canal, Skagway is a triangle-shaped town that seems to drive a wedge into the sheer slopes that lead to White Pass. Northern terminus of the Inside Passage, Skagway is derived from an Indian word meaning "Home of the North Wind." During the Klondike Gold Rush, the town was the gateway to both the Chilkoot and White Pass trails, a funnel through which thousands of frenzied fortune-seekers passed. Today, the boardwalks, frontier storefronts, restored interiors, museum-quality giftshops, historic films and slide shows, and old-time cars and costumes all in the six-block town center give it the flavor for which it has been famous for nearly a century. Skagway still survives on the thousands of visitors and adventurers who come each summer to continue on the trail that led to gold. This is the most popular cruise port in Alaska, and the 1,500 summer residents (it dwindles to 400 or so in winter) are snowed under by up to 8,000 cruise ship visitors in a single day. Independent travelers often leave Skagway with mixed feelings. The town is fun to visit and has lots to see and do, but seems well on the way to becoming a schmaltzy shadow of its former self, sort of a Disneylandish vision of the gold rush era. If you're looking for authentic Alaska, look elsewhere.

Skagway's weather is decidedly different from the rest of Southeast. It only gets 22 inches of precipitation a year, and alder, willow, and cottonwood carpet the adjacent hillsides. It is very colorful in mid-September when the leaves are turning.

History

An enormous amount of Alaskan history was collapsed into the final decade of the 19th century at Skagway. In August 1896, on the day that George Carmack struck it rich on Bonanza Creek, Skagway consisted of a single cabin, constructed eight years previously by Capt. William Moore, but only occupied sporadically by the transient pioneer. News of the Klondike strike hit Seattle in July 1897; within a month 4,000 people huddled in a haphazard tent city surrounding Moore's lone cabin, and "craft of every description, from ocean-going steamers to little more than floating coffins, were dumping into the makeshift village a crazily mixed mass of humanity." Almost immediately, Frank Reid surveyed and platted the townsite, and the stampeders grabbed 1,000 lots, many within Moore's homestead. There was no law to back up either claims or counterclaims, and reports from the time describe Skagway as "the most outrageously lawless quarter" on the globe.

Into this breach stepped Jefferson Randall Smith, known not as J.R. but as Soapy, Alaska's great bad man. A notorious con artist from Colorado, Soapy Smith oversaw a mind-bogglingly extensive system of fraud, theft, armed robbery, even murder. He had his own spy network, secret police, and army to enforce the strong-arm tactics. Finally, a vigilance committee held a meeting to oppose Soapy. Frank Reid, the surveyor, stood guard. Soapy approached. Guns blazed. Smith, shot in the chest, died instantly, at age 38. Of Soapy, the newspaper reported, "At 9:30 o'clock Friday night the checkered career of 'Soapy' Smith was brought to a sudden end by a 38 calibre bullet from a revolver in the unerring right hand of City surveyor Frank H. Reid. . . ." Reid was shot in the groin and died in agony a week later. His gravestone reads, "He gave his life for the honor of Skagway."

Skagway was the jumping-off point for White Pass, which crossed the Coastal Range to Lake Bennett and the Yukon headwaters. This trail, billed as the "horse route," was the choice of prosperous prospectors who could afford pack animals to carry the requisite "ton of goods." But it was false advertising at best, and death-defying at worst. The mountains were so precipitous, the trail so narrow and rough, and the weather so wild, that the men turned merciless; all 3,000 horses and mules that stepped onto the trail in 1897-98 were doomed to a proverbial fate worse than death. Indeed, men swore that horses leaped off the cliffs on purpose, committing suicide.

The famous Chilkoot Trail, which started in Dyea (die-EE), 15 miles from Skagway, was the "poor-man's route." Stampeders had to backpack their year's worth of supplies 33 miles to Lake Lindeman, which included 40 trips up and down the 45-degree "Golden Stairs" to the 3,550-foot pass. This scene, recorded in black and white, is one of the most dramatic and enduring photographs of the Days of '98. Into this breach stepped Michael J. Heney, the "Irish Prince." An Irish-Canadian contractor with a genius for vision, fund-raising, management, and commanding the loyalty of his workers, Heney punched through the 110-mile narrow-gauge White Pass and Yukon Railway, which connected saltwater Skagway to freshwater White-horse. The route, so treacherous to pack animals, was no less malevolent to railroaders, who worked suspended from the steep slopes by ropes, often in 50 below temperatures, into the force of raging Arctic blizzards, for $3 a day. The job was completed in just under two years, when the final stake was driven in at Carcross, on July 29, 1900, thus ensuring the constant flow of passengers and freight—as well as Skagway's survival. The train shut down when metal prices plummeted in 1982, but reopened again for excursion travel only in 1988. Ore from the Yukon's enormous Cypress Anvil lead mine is now trucked to Skagway for shipment to Japan. The WP&YR is once again Skagway's favorite attraction, and one of the only operating narrow-gauge railroads in North America.

SIGHTS

Skagway town consists of roughly 23 east-west avenues intersected by five north-south streets. Downtown, however, is made up of seven blocks on Broadway, along which are most of the sights. The ferry terminal is at the very bottom of Broadway: a three-minute hike and you're in the heart of beautiful downtown Skagway. Many of the historic buildings are owned and managed by the National Park Service as **Klondike Gold Rush National Historic Park.** Most of the restored structures are leased to private businesses.

On Broadway

The old White Pass and Yukon administration building houses the **National Park Service Visitor Center;** open daily 8-6 (reduced winter hours). Don't miss the excellent "moving slide show" with black-and-white images from the gold rush, shown almost hourly. Narrated by Hal Holbrook, this 30-minute show is an articulate and graphic overview of the mad days of the stampede. Other Park Service activities include talks, films, and twice-a-day 45-minute walking tours of town. Personnel behind the desk have the latest trail, weather, and transportation information, and can probably answer that burning question you've been carrying around all day.

Across Broadway on 2nd is **Soapy Smith's Parlor,** the saloon from where the infamous blackguard supervised his various nefarious offenses. It is not open to the public.

You can't miss **Arctic Brotherhood Hall** between 2nd and 3rd—the only example of turn-of-the-century Alaska driftwood stick architecture. It has to be the most-photographed building in Alaska. The Brotherhood was organized aboard the vessel *City of Seattle,* which waited out the winter of 1899 in Skagway Harbor. The order spread, and local chapters were established in most Alaskan towns. Dues were paid solely in nuggets. The building now houses Skagway's **visitor information center** (open daily 8:30-5:30) where you'll get your fill of local facts. For something more entertaining, pay $2.50 for the combination one man variety show and 25-minute documentary on the WP&YR adventure. Shows are three times a day.

The **Golden North Hotel** bills itself as Alaska's oldest, and is filled with antique gold-rush-era furnishings. Ask about the ghost that roams the halls. Duck into the many gift shops in the next few blocks. Many of the furnishings, display cases, and even some of the stuff for sale are worth a look. **Dedman's Photo Shop,** between 3rd and 4th, has a large selection of black-and-white postcards (50 cents). **Eagle's Hall** at 6th houses "Days of '98" (see "Entertainment" below). **Corrington's Museum of Alaskan History,** on the corner of 5th and Broadway, is a combination giftshop and scrimshaw museum ($1 entrance). The collection includes over 40 exquisitely carved pieces that tell the history of Alaska on walrus ivory. It's well worth a visit. The museum is flanked by a colorful flower garden.

Off Broadway

The original **William Moore cabin,** which was moved under pressure from the early stampeders to its present location, 5th and

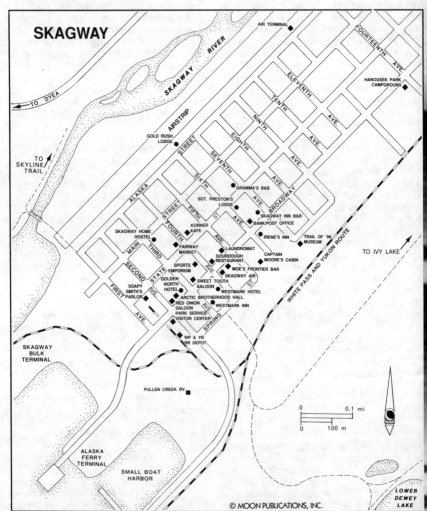

SKAGWAY

© MOON PUBLICATIONS, INC.

Spring, has been refurbished by the Park Service. Its interior walls are papered with newspapers from the 1880s. Continue north two blocks across Pullen Creek to City Hall, an old stone building that is home to the **Trail of '98 Museum** (2nd floor). If you're lucky, your $2 admission ($1 for students) will be collected by Valerie Lawson, a fourth generation Skagwayan—ask her about her great-grandfather! The museum is open daily 8-6. Check out the old gambling equipment, the duckskin blanket, the 1908 map of Skagway and 1916 map of Alaska, the April 9, 1898, edition of *Dyea Trail,* with the account of the catastrophic avalanche, and the July 15 edition of the *Skagway News* with the story of the killing of Soapy ($2). Also here is an amazing salmon-skin parka and an Eskimo mask from Anaktuvuk Pass. Several videos are available if you want to know more about the characters in Skagway's past.

Gold Rush Cemetery
It's right beside the railroad tracks two miles north of town. The largest monument is Frank Reid's, while Soapy Smith only rates a wooden plank. While you're here, be sure to follow the short trail above the cemetery to **Lower Reid Falls.**

White Pass & Yukon Route Railroad
The White Pass & Yukon Route narrow gauge runs twice-daily trains from Skagway to White Pass and back (28 miles each way; three hours RT). Trains run from mid-May till late September only. The tracks follow along the east side of the Skagway River, with stunning vistas that get better and better as the train climbs. Tour guides point out the sights, including portions of the Trail of '98. Be sure to sit on the left side. Excursions leave Skagway at 8:45 a.m. and 1:15 p.m. Get tickets in the restored railroad depot office on 2nd St. for $69. Call (800) 343-7373 in the U.S., or (800) 478-7373 in Canada for details. The gracious old steam locomotive #73 chugs out of town, with video cameras rolling in all directions. (Note, however, that the steam engine is replaced by a more modern diesel engine on the edge of town to save it from wear and tear on the strenuous climb.)

The train will stop to pick up hikers who flag it down.

Through service to Whitehorse ($89 OW) departs Skagway at 1 p.m., arrives in Frasier, British Columbia, at 2:35, where you transfer to buses to Whitehorse, arriving at 6:30. The return schedule is: depart Whitehorse at 8:15 a.m. by bus, transfer to the train in Frasier at 10:25, and arrive in Skagway at 12:10 p.m.

Hiking
A network of well-marked trails on the slopes just east of town offers excellent day-hikes and a place to warm up for the Chilkoot Trail. Cross the small footbridge and railroad tracks beyond the end of 3rd and 4th avenues, then follow the pipeline up the hill. **Lower Dewey Lake** is an easy 20-minute climb. A trail right around the lake branches at the south end off to Sturgill's Landing (three miles) on Taiya Inlet. **Upper Dewey Lake** and the **Devil's Punchbowl** are a steep 2½-mile climb from the north end of the lower lake. Icy Lake is a relatively level two miles from the lower lake, but the trail to Upper Reid Falls is steep and hard to follow. A number of clearings with picnic tables are around the lower lake where camping is possible, as well as at the other lakes and Sturgill's Landing.

At 1st and Alaska streets, cross the airstrip and the suspension bridge over Skagway River. A short hike goes left to Yakutania Point and Smugglers Cove. Go right and head out to Dyea Rd.; you'll see the trailhead in a mile up **A.B. Mountain,** named for the Arctic Brotherhood (the letters "AB" are supposedly visible in snow patches each spring). This five-mile jaunt is steep and strenuous; the summit is 5,100 feet above your starting point (sea level) and a five-hour hike.

Hikers often use the WP&YR train as a way to get into the high country around Skagway. The **Denver Glacier Trail** begins six miles up the tracks (it's illegal to walk on the tracks), and climbs five miles and 2,000 feet to Denver Glacier. You can also get dropped off at **Glacier Station** (14 miles up), where an easy two-mile trail leads to a Forest Service cabin near Laughton Glacier ($20/night). Make cabin reservations at the Park Service visitor center in Skagway. Flag down the train to return.

PRACTICALITIES

Lodging
After years of doing without, Skagway now has a comfortable new home hostel right in town. No smoking or alcohol, and a 10:30 p.m. curfew may put a crimp in your social life, but the folks here are very friendly. There's space for only 10, so its wise to make reservations ahead; write Skagway Home Hostel, Box 231, Skagway, AK 99840, tel. 983-2131. Reservations are required in winter. Register between 5 and 10:30 p.m. They generally accommodate late-arriving ferries. Rates are $10/night for AYH members and $15/night for nonmembers. Beyond the hostel, there are many choices, but none of them cheap. The least expensive rooms are at Irene's Inn, but the local bed and breakfast places are a better deal.

Camping
The Park Service maintains a free campground at **Dyea**, eight miles northeast of Skagway. It is especially popular with hikers along the Chilkoot Trail. Hitching is possible, or those without wheels can contact one of the local taxi companies for a ride ($10 OW). **Hanousek Park** at 14th and Broadway is the tenters' campground in town, with flush toilets and cold running water; $6 if anyone collects. The narrow-gauge tracks border the grounds, making this a good place for photo opportunities. **Pullen Creek RV Park,** next to the ferry terminal, has full hookups for $14. Showers cost $1 here. Quiet, uncrowded campsites are available at **Liarsville,** 2½ miles out on the Klondike Highway, but there is no water.

Food
With so many flash-and-dash tourists running around, it comes as no surprise to find high meal prices in Skagway. **Korner Kafe,** at 4th and State streets is the place to go for burgers and reasonably priced breakfasts. On Broadway, both the **Sweet Tooth Saloon** and the **Prospector** serve good breakfasts.

A very pleasant lunch hangout is **Pack Train Cafe,** on the corner of 4th and Broadway. Close by are "cribs" where you'll find bagels and cream cheese ($2.50) or espresso coffees. The benches here are where all the hip seasonal workers hang out on sunny days. Pizzas and nachos are offered at the **Red Onion. Northern Lights Cafe** serves Greek and Italian dishes, but is on the pricey side. The most popular place in town is the **Sourdough Cafe,** but the food is bland industrial pabulum. **Golden North Hotel** is a fine place for dinners, as is the **Chilkoot Room** in the Westmark Hotel. **Fairway Market** is at 4th and State. Get there on Tuesday for the once-a-week fresh produce deliveries.

Entertainment
The **Red Onion,** 2nd and Broadway, is Skagway's well-known establishment, with an occasional local band on stage practicing in public, and red-light mannequins posing in the second-floor windows. But if you want to get down and dirty and start drinking with the locals at 10 a.m., head across the street and up the block to **Moe's Frontier Bar.** The funnest thing to do at night is to attend the **Days of '98** saloon theater at 6th and Broadway. The great-granddaddy of them all, this production is the oldest running theater in Alaska—over 65 years! Amazing how young the actors have remained. Check the performance schedules posted around town: matinees ($12) are offered most days, and evening performances start at 7:45 p.m., with warm-up gambling with "Soapy money," and the show goes on at 8:30. Splurge on this one.

Services
Sports Emporium on 4th between Broadway and State is the outfitter in town, and sells freeze-dried food for the trail. Books are available at **Skagway News Depot.** Take a **shower** ($1) at Pullen Park, or at the Chevron station on State and 4th streets. **National Bank of Alaska,** 6th and Broadway, changes green dollars into multicolored dollars, but doesn't have an ATM machine. Save some money on your calls home by placing them at the **Alascom** phone center on Broadway. The **library** is at 8th and State, and is open

Mon.-Fri. 1-9, and Sat. 1-5. Get free reading material on the paperback racks inside (and these aren't all bodice-buster novels either). There is no swimming pool in Skagway.

TRANSPORTATION

On The Water
Skagway is the northern terminus of the ferry system, and ferries arrive daily, sometimes twice, during the summer. The ferry terminal, tel. 983-2941, has storage lockers and is right next to town. The **Haines-Skagway Water Taxi,** tel. 766-3395 (in Haines), offers a break from the ferries. The boat connects Haines and Skagway twice each day in summer, and costs $15 OW or $25 RT ($5 extra for bikes). The **Red Head Express,** tel. 983-2231, provides water taxi service ($47 RT) between Skagway and Juneau on Saturdays during the summer. It leaves Skagway at 7 a.m. and gets back that night at 9:30. The MV

Fairweather, tel. 983-2557, offers a daily excursion run between Juneau and Skagway for $125 OW.

Planes, Trains, And Automobiles
See "Yukon and White Pass Route Railroad" above for Skagway's most distinctive means of transport. You can fly daily from Juneau on **Skagway Air,** tel. 983-2218, $80 OW and $120 RT cash (extra if you pay with plastic). Skagway to Haines flights cost $60 OW cash. Two other companies offer connections to Juneau via Haines: **Wings of Alaska,** tel. 789-0790 or (800) 478-9464, and **L.A.B. Flying Service,** tel. 789-9160. Rent cars from **Avis,** tel. 983-2247, at the Westmark Hotel, or from **Sourdough Shuttles,** 6th and Broadway, tel. (800) 4878-2529. Sourdough will also deliver you to Carcross for $30 or Whitehorse for $50. **Alaskon Express** motorcoaches, tel. (800) 544-2206 operate every summer day between Skagway and Whitehorse. The fare is $54 OW.

SKAGWAY ACCOMMODATIONS

Name	Address	Phone	Rates	Features
Skagway Home Hostel	3rd & Main	983-2131	$10-15 pp	youth hostel
Irene's Inn	6th & Broadway	983-2520	$35+ s, $40+ d	
Grammas B&B	7th & State	983-2312	$45 s, $50 d	very nice
Skagway Inn B&B	7th & Broadway	983-2289	$48 s $55 d	full breakfast, historic bordello
Sgt. Preston's Lodge	6th & State	983-2521	$50 s $60 d	
Wind Valley Lodge	22nd & State	983-2236	$50 s $62 d	AAA approved, whirlpool
Golden North Hotel	3rd & Broadway	983-2521	$60 s $70 d	oldest in Alaska
Gold Rush Lodge	6th & Alaska	983-2831	$65 s $70 d	
Westmark Inn	3rd & Broadway	983-2291 (800) 544-0970	$75+ s or d	AAA approved

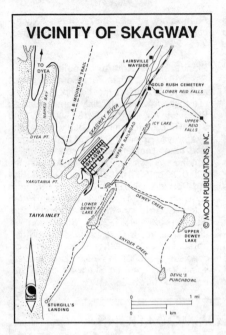

VICINITY OF SKAGWAY

TO DYEA

AIRSVILLE WAYSIDE

A MOUNTAIN TRAIL

NARKO BAY

GOLD RUSH CEMETERY

LOWER REID FALLS

SKAGWAY RIVER

DYEA PT.

ICY LAKE

UPPER REID FALLS

WP&YR RAILROAD

YAKUTANIA PT.

SKAGWAY

LOWER DEWEY LAKE

DEWEY CREEK

TAIYA INLET

SNYDER CREEK

UPPER DEWEY LAKE

DEVIL'S PUNCHBOWL

STURGILL'S LANDING

© MOON PUBLICATIONS, INC.

0   1 mi

0   1 km

Local Tours

A number of local taxi/shuttle companies can run you out to the Chilkoot trailhead for $10. Gray Line, Atlas Tours, and the other biggies all do two-hour city tours for around $15; you'll see these buses stopped in the middle of downtown streets as the driver rattles on. Local tour and taxi companies, including **Pioneer Taxi & Tours,** tel. 983-2623, and **Sourdough Shuttle and Tours,** tel. 983-2523 or (800) 478-2529, will run you around town for $5. Or rent a **bike** from Sourdough and do it yourself. Bikes can also be rented from the van on 2nd St. between Broadway and Spring. More distinctive tours are aboard the 1930s-era White Motor Company cars run by **Skagway Street Car Co.,** tel. 983-2908. The complete trip (including the AB Hall multimedia presentation) costs $34 ($17 for kids) for two hours.

The **Red Head,** tel. 983-2231, offers three-hour boat trips to the Burro Creek hatchery ($59). **Skagway Air,** tel. 983-2218, does 90-minute Glacier Bay flightseeing trips for $110 pp, and 45-minute gold rush tours (to Lake Bennett) for $55 pp.

(GORDY OHLIGER)

YUKON TERRITORY

INTRODUCTION

Yukon Territory covers 483,450 square km (208,000 square miles) of northwestern Canada. This represents just under five percent of Canada's total land area; of the country's 10 provinces and two territories, Yukon ranks number eight in size. Still, Yukon Territory is 25% larger than California. Yet only 29,000 people live here, giving each resident nearly 20 square kilometers. Almost 70% of them live in the capital, Whitehorse; the second-largest town, Watson Lake, has all of 1,700 people. Some 5,000 are native Indians, mostly Athabaskan. The name Yukon comes from *yuckoo*, an Indian word for "clear water." The wild, unpopulated, and open countryside makes a lasting impression on everyone who experiences it. The Yukon also has the mightiest mountain range in Canada, great herds of caribou and tiny wriggling iceworms, and beautiful wildflowers which paint the landscape bright pink in the summertime.

The Land
Yukon Territory sits like a great upside-down wedge, bordered by Alaska, British Columbia, Northwest Territories, and the Arctic Ocean. The massive St. Elias Mountains pass through the territory's southwest corner, with Canada's highest peak, Mt. Logan (5,950 meters), and the world's largest non-polar icecap. The rest of Yukon is a huge expanse of rolling hills, long narrow lakes, and thick forests (except for the tundra above the Arctic Circle), with the mighty Yukon River draining the southwestern section and the Peel and Mackenzie rivers draining the northeastern. The Dempster Highway runs 726 km north from Dawson City to Inuvik, Northwest Territories, on the Arctic Ocean, making Canada the only contiguous country in the world with road access to three oceans.

THE YUKON

© MOON PUBLICATIONS, INC.

History

The most ancient archaeological evidence (50,000 years old) in the Americas was unearthed at Old Crow, establishing Yukon Indians as the earliest residents of North America. But it wasn't until 1842 that civilization arrived, when Robert Campbell of Hudson's Bay Company opened the first fur trading post in this uncharted wilderness. Six years later he opened a second, Fort Selkirk, at the confluence of the Yukon and Pelly rivers, near present-day Pelly Crossing. In 1870 Canada purchased Rupert's Land, of which Yukon was a part, from the Company. The government didn't show much interest in the area until 1887-88 when George Dawson was sent north at the head of the Canadian Yukon Exploration Expedition. By this time, mining had already replaced fur trading as the region's economic lure; the first prospectors, moving continually north ahead of the peaking gold rushes in British Columbia and southeast Alaska, began cresting the Chilkoot Pass and floating down the Yukon River and filtering into the Klondike Valley.

On Aug. 17, 1896, a sourdough named George Carmack and his two Indian brothers-in-law, Skookum Jim and Tagish Charlie, found gold in the Klondike Valley on a tip from fellow prospector Robert Henderson. This sparked North America's last great gold rush, which saw upwards of 40,000 stampeders from all points of the compass descend on Dawson, having burst through the barrier of this immense wilderness to open the last frontier. Since the strike, over $300 million has been recovered from these goldfields. In 1898 Yukon was separated from Canada's Northwest Territories and Dawson City was made the capital.

The Alaska Highway

After 1900, mining went into a slow decline and nobody paid much attention to the territory until early 1942, when an anticipated Japanese invasion prompted President Roosevelt to order construction of a military road northwest through Canada to Alaska. By November, a mere eight months later, the road opened in a ceremony at Soldiers' Summit beside Kluane Lake. Upgrading work continued and by the following year all 2,437 km (1,511 miles) from Dawson Creek, B.C., to Fairbanks had been gravel surfaced and the 130 bridges had been completed. Some 25,000 men labored on the road for 20 months, at a cost to the U.S. of $140 million.

Throughout the year 1992 a giant party the length of the road (and beyond) will celebrate the 50th anniversary of its construction. Opening ceremonies will be held at Dawson Creek on Feb. 16, and nearly a full year of floatplane rallies and competitions, international airshows and airmadas, convoys, reenactments, rendezvous, and festivals will culminate at the Rededication Ceremony at Soldiers Summit on Nov. 20. For more information on Rendezvous '92, contact Yukon Anniversaries Commission, Bag 1992, Whitehorse, Yukon, Y1A 5L9, tel. (403) 668-1992, or Great Alaska Highways Society, Box 74250, Fairbanks, AK 99707, tel. (907) 452-8000.

The Alaska Highway (or "Alcan") had an impact on the Yukon equivalent to that of the Klondike gold rush. Whitehorse replaced Dawson City as the capital in 1953. Road improvements began in earnest in the mid-'70s, and today, the Alaska Highway is almost completely paved, except where ongoing construction is replacing stretches of cracked, buckled, and patched road. But although the highway is the vital link Roosevelt foresaw and a highly scenic route in its own right, to discover the Yukon that Robert

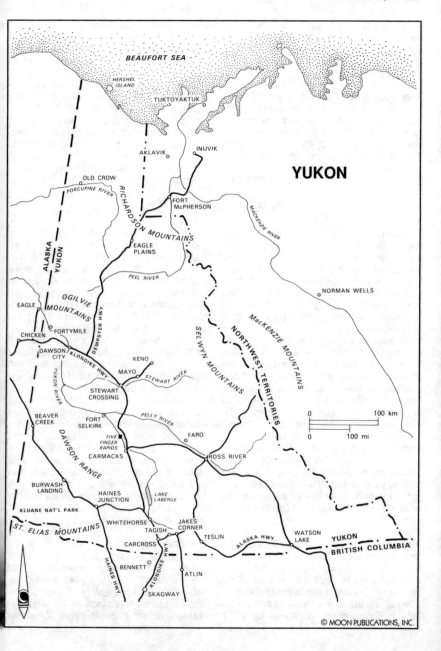

© MOON PUBLICATIONS, INC.

Service expressed so well, you must take to the rivers and trails where the real country is waiting.

General Information

For info concerning crossing the Canadian border, see p. 58. For a complete 112-page booklet on visiting Yukon, including all hunting, fishing, and camping regulations, contact Tourism Yukon, Box 2703, Whitehorse, Canada Y1A 2C6, tel. (403) 667-5340. The area code for the entire Yukon is 403. Yukon Time is the same as Pacific Time, an hour later than Alaska. Beware of arriving in Yukon without enough Canadian currency to tide you over until you can get to a bank. There are no exchange facilities at the borders and businesspeople give discouraging rates. Large banks in America and Europe will sell you Canadian dollars at the current rate. Canadian immigration officials may ask to see your money to guarantee you will not compete for scarce jobs or already strained social benefits. All prices in this chapter, unless specified as US$, are in Canadian dollars. Also, distances are listed in kilometers for Canada and miles for Alaska—sorry if it looks schizophrenic near the borders.

WATSON LAKE

This is the first town in Yukon Territory for all drivers: both the Alaska and Cassiar highways converge here. These days the second-largest town in the territory (the number-two spot flip-flops back and forth with Dawson) with just under 1,700 residents, Watson Lake was originally inhabited by Kaska Indians, whose lives were permanently disrupted by the Cassiar gold rush of the 1870s. The town itself was created in 1940, with the construction of one of a string of airfields across the northern vastness of Canada, and its existence was ensured when the Alcan was routed through to service the airfield. Today, Watson Lake is the hub of a large area of southwestern Yukon, southeastern Northwest Territories, and northern British Columbia. Indeed, Watson Lake is a welcome sight after the several hundred kilometers of gravel on the Cassiar and the all-day ride from Ft. Nelson on the Alaska Highway. The telling statistic reveals that 75% of the 175,000 visitors to Watson Lake (1990) stayed for one night, and the rest stayed for two or more.

Sights

Stop first at the **Alaska Highway Interpretive Centre,** at the corner of the Alaska and Campbell highways, tel. 536-7469, open daily 9-9, May to Sept. 15. Here you'll get your whole lesson in the monumental engineering feat that is the Alcan. Outside is the famous **Sign Forest,** originated by a G.I. working on the highway who, when given the task of repainting the road's directional sign, added the direction and mileage to his hometown of Danville, Illinois. Since then, more than 10,000 other signs have been added to the collection—with town signs, license plates, posters, driftwood, pie tins, gold-panning pans, mufflers, driftwood, even flywheels stating where the contributor is from and who he/she is. You can put up your addition personally, or take it inside the visitor center and have them put it up for you. The Reenactment of the Creation of the Sign Forest is slated for Sept. 11-13, 1992.

One block north of the Sign Forest, across from the Watson Lake Hotel, is the **Heritage House Wildlife and History Museum,** tel. 536- 2400, open daily 9-9, May 1 to Aug. 31, 9-5 Sept. 1 through Oct. 15. Reposited in the oldest house in Watson Lake are a number of stuffed animals, including the world's second-largest stone sheep, plus a gift shop with native and nugget souvenirs. Check with the visitor center for all the local fishing, photo, hiking, and camping hotspots.

Practicalities

Coming into Watson Lake from the road, you'll be tired and hungry, guaranteed; I had the best night's sleep of my life at the Gateway in late April one year. Half a dozen motels, several campgrounds, and a handful of restaurants are there to serve. Cheapest place to stay is the **Upper Liard River Resort,** Mile 642 Alaska Hwy., tel. 536-2271, $40 d in summer, or $6 to camp, and a $12 salmon bake. Both the **Cedar Lodge,** 536-7406, and **Gateway Motor Inn,** tel. 536-7744, charge upwards of $60 d. **Watson Lake Hotel,** tel. 536-7781, goes up to $90. **Downtown RV Park,** tel. 536-2646, has full hookups, laundry, and showers. **Green Valley Trailer Park,** tel. 536-2276, is 15 km west of town at Km 1032. the **Recreation Park** turnoff is at Km 1025, then head in three km to the provincial campground: 50 gravel sites, water, pit toilets, $6.

The Nugget restaurant serves okay Chinese food at reasonable prices, till 10 p.m. daily. The **Watson Lake Hotel** serves three meals from 6 a.m. to 10 p.m., as does the **Gateway** (except it opens at 7). **Pizza Pantry** stays open till 2 a.m. Mon.-Sat., midnight on Sunday. And **Watson Lake Foods** will sell you groceries Mon.-Sat. 8-9 and on Sun. 10-5.

To Whitehorse

It's 454 km from Watson Lake to Whitehorse, passing by the Cassiar Mountains, motel and gas and provincial campground (Km 1144), Great River Divide (Km 1163), lodges at Km 1181 and 1252, and **Teslin** at Km 1294. Teslin has several motels, cafes, and gas stations, along with camping, a salmon bake, a small museum, and one of the highest percentages of Natives supported by traditional lifestyles in the territory.

There's a campground with laundry and showers at Km 1346, a motel, gas station, and coffee shop at Km 1392, a large RV park, motel, and restaurant at Km 1414, several provincial campgrounds at Km 1366, 1432, and 1459; finally you come to Whitehorse at Km 1470.

The sun's rays hit the Earth at the equator in short, straight, and hot beams; they reach the north country in longer, more angled, and less intense beams. This explains the low rays and golden light of Alaska in the summer—a photographers dream.

(TODD CLARK)

(GORDY OHLIGER)

WHITEHORSE

Windy Whitehorse is a friendly oasis in the heart of an unforgiving land. With a little more than 20,000 residents, Whitehorse is the largest city in northern Canada. It squats on the western bank of the Yukon, hemmed in by 60-meter bluffs which create something of a wind tunnel along the river. To the east, the bare rounded hulk of Grey Mountain (1,494 meters) fills the horizon. Whitehorse has its share of gold rush history and nostalgia, but is not dominated by it; as capital of Yukon Territory for the past 35 years, this growing city has a brash, modern frontier energy all its own. It's easy to slip into Whitehorse's strong stream of hustle and bustle, which seems to keep pace with the powerful Yukon itself. Yet the town has a warm, homespun vitality to it, like huddling around the fire on a cold Yukon night.

History
The 25,000 stampeders who braved the Chilkoot or White Pass trails wintered on the banks of Lindeman or Bennett lakes, building boats and waiting for break-up. A veritable

armada set sail in late May 1898, and quickly encountered Miles Canyon and rapids, some of the roughest waters on the entire Yukon. The name White Horse was given to the rapids, which reminded miners of the flowing manes of white horses. An entry in an early edition of the *Klondike Nugget* described the scene. "Many men who ran these dangerous waters had never handled a boat in their lives until they stopped at Lake Bennett to figure out which end of their oar went into the water. . . . The boats filed into that tremendous first section of the canyon, dodged the whirlpool in the middle, rushed down the second section of the canyon, tossed around for a while in the seething water of the rapids, made that stupendous turn into White Horse, as with rapidly accelerating speed they plunged into the final chaos of angry water. . . ." A few men drowned; many kept their lives but lost their boats and grubstakes.

Quickly, the ever-present Mounties instituted some regulations, allowing only expert handlers to pilot the creaky craft through the rapids—Jack London earned $3,000 that summer as a boatman. Undoubtedly, this saved countless lives and supplies from the more than 7,000 boats launched from the lakes after break-up in 1898. Soon after, an eight-km horse-drawn wooden tramway was built around the rapids from Canyon City to the present site of Whitehorse, where goods were reloaded into boats to complete the journey to Dawson City. A tent city sprang up at the tramway's lower end, and Whitehorse was born.

The town's role as a transportation hub began in 1900, when the White Pass and Yukon Railroad reached Whitehorse, finally connecting tidewater at Skagway to the Yukon by public transportation. At Whitehorse, passengers and freight transferred to riverboats for the trip down the Yukon River to Dawson City. In 1942-43 this role grew substantially, as did Whitehorse along with it, after work had begun on the Alcan Highway. In 1953, Whitehorse eclipsed declining Dawson in population and importance, and became the territorial seat of government.

SIGHTS

SS *Klondike*
Start your visit with the free 30-minute tour of this large sternwheeler, beached at the bottom of 2nd Avenue. Conducted once an hour from 9-5 by extremely knowledgeable and entertaining guides, the tour proceeds from the boiler, freight, and engine deck, up to the dining room and first-class cabins, and finally up to the bridge, one of the highest points in town. Built in 1937, the *Klondike* made 15 roundtrips a season, requiring 1½ days and 40 cords of wood for the downstream trip to Dawson, 4½ days and 120 cords back to Whitehorse. The *Klondike* is beautifully and authentically restored, right down to the 1937 *Life* magazines and the food stains on the waiters' white coats. Be sure to take this tour at least once.

Town Center
The **Visitor Centre,** 5th and Steele, open daily 8-8, has all the brochures, exhibits, and helpful personnel you've come to expect. Walk down Steele St. toward the river for the **MacBride Museum** on 1st Ave., open daily 9-9 May 15 through Sept 30, tel. 667-2709, $3. The large and varied collection includes the old government telegraph office, engine no. 51 from the WP&YR, Sam McGee's cabin, a display of stuffed Yukon wildlife, and hundreds of gold rush photographs. Notice the 1,175-kilogram copper nugget on the corner of the property.

The **Old Log Church** (1900) and rectory, at 3rd Ave. and Elliot, have been restored and opened as a religious museum ($2). Nearby, have a look (from the street) at the **log "skyscrapers."** A couple of blocks away at 2nd and Hawkins, the big modern **Territorial Administration Building** (1976) is worth exploring, open weekdays 9-5. The officials inside have built themselves the plushest office block north of Edmonton. Colorful tapestries and murals interpret the land, history, and people of the Yukon; downstairs is a good public cafeteria. The library next door has a selection of local books; open weekdays 12-9, Sat. 10-6, Sun. 1-9.

To Miles Canyon
An excellent all-day hike from Whitehorse takes you right around Schwatka Lake, with a number of historical and scenic attractions along the way. Take a lunch. Begin by crossing the bridge beside the *Klondike II.* A nature trail leads through the woods on the east bank of the Yukon River, toward the hydro dam (1959) which created Schwatka Lake and tamed the once-feared White Horse Rapids. A fish ladder allows salmon to get around the dam to their spawning grounds upriver. Above the dam is a high hill which the more energetic may want to climb for the view. Go down the other side (or around along the shore) to Chadburn Lake Road. Follow this road south till you see some paths along the lake or river; follow any one for a more enjoyable walk. Above the lake the Yukon River flows through spectacular Miles Canyon. A path along the canyon leads to Lowe Suspension (1923), first bridge across the Yukon, crossing to the west side. The views along here are superb.

In 1900, riverboats crowded Whitehorse's bustling waterfront, where goods and supplies, people, and gold were transferred to and from the new White Pass and Yukon Railroad, completing the route from tidewater at Skagway to Dawson on the Klondike.

Continue 1½ km beyond the bridge, staying on the east side, to find the site of Canyon City. The opening of the railway in 1900 put an end to river travel above Whitehorse, and Canyon City disappeared. Today, nothing remains at the site but some old tin cans and the gentle grade of the tramway, now a cross-country ski route. Return to the suspension bridge; on the west side, Miles Canyon Rd. runs five km back to Whitehorse. One km before town, follow the signs to the MV *Schwatka* excursion boat, which leaves from a dock on the lake near the dam for two-hour cruises ($13 without transportation from downtown, $20 with). Buses ($1) run along South Access Rd. into town every hour until 6:20 (except Sun.) and will stop to pick you up if you wave.

Yukon Gardens

Encompassing 22 acres, with over 1,000 species of plants, 7,000 gallons of water pumped daily, and 250,000 annuals blooming, it took seven years for construction of this, the only botanical gardens north of Vancouver. Even so, compare Vancouver's 216 frost-free days a year with Whitehorse's 72! Located at the intersection of the Alcan and South Access Rd., tel. 668-7972, open daily 9-9, $3 admission; buy some fresh vegetables while you're here.

Takhini Hot Springs

These are excellent natural mineral-water hot springs, 36° C (96° F) with no sulphur, only $3 for the whole day. Rent towels for 35 cents. Camp there for $6 and ride the horses for $8 an hour. Go 16 km from Whitehorse to the Klondike Loop Highway, turn right for five km, turn left at the sign, then go 10 km to Takhini. There's no public transportation, though you could take the Kopper King bus from the depot (see "By Bus" below) to close to the junction, then hitch the rest of the way. The 62-km RT would only add $15 to your rental car bill. A taxi is $35 OW.

PRACTICALITIES

Accommodations

Fourth Avenue Residence, 4051 4th Ave. across the street from the *Klondike,* tel. 667-4471, provides dormitory-style rooms at $30 s, $40 d, shared bath. You can also take showers here in a clean facility for $1, no time limit. **Fort Yukon Hotel,** 2nd and Black, tel. 667-2594, has spartan rooms with shared bath for $34 s and $38 d, $39 s and $50 d private bath. If you don't mind commuting, the **Kopper King Motel,** five km west on the Alaska Highway (Km 1477), tel. 668-2347, has rooms for $45 s, $50 d. **Chilkoot Trail Motel,** on 4th Ave. across from Qwanlin Mall, tel. 668-4190, has pleasant rooms with cooking facilities for $40 s, $50 d. For the same money, stay at **Whitehorse Center Motor Inn,** Jarvis and Second, tel. 668-4567.

Robert Service Campground is two km south of town by the river off South Access Rd., tel. 668-3721. For tenters only, it gets very crowded during the summer, but if you can find a site, it's not too bad for a city place, $5. Register at the office, where there's a very useful message board and a pay phone. If the Robert Service is full or you don't want to pay, continue walking south past the dam along the shoreline. Plenty of good places to pitch a tent are found in the woods just above the lake. Other unofficial places to camp are along the top of the bluff above town toward the airport (walk up Cook St. from Qwanlin Mall and along the trails to the top), and on Kishwoot Island. Head west out 2nd Ave. and look for the big parking lot across from the Chevron station. Walk by the "No Camping" sign, cross the new suspension bridge, and get lost in the undergrowth. This place is very convenient to the bus station; you can see the bridge from the depot parking lot. It's not windy, either. But stay well out of sight.

Yukon Bed and Breakfast Assn., 102-302 Steele St., Whitehorse, Yukon, Canada Y1A 2C5, tel. 633-4609, is the clearinghouse for all B&Bs in Yukon Territory (Whitehorse, Dawson, Carcross, Watson Lake, and Haines Junction). Rates start at $35 s, $45 d, and go up to $60 d for the deluxe. Gold dust is an accepted form of payment; $10 nonrefundable deposit is required. Send a SASE for more info and an application.

Food

About the cheapest place in town is the coffee shop on the second floor of **Hougen's Dept. Store** (closed Sun.). **Mr. Mike's,** 4114 4th Ave. downtown, is pretty reliable for burgers, salad bar, and such. **No Pop Sandwich Shop,** 4th and Steele, open 9 a.m.-8 p.m. Mon.-Thurs., till 9 Fri., has good wholesome sandwiches, dinners, bakery, and great atmosphere. Recommended. **Mom's Kitchen,** on 2nd by Fort Yukon Hotel, has filling breakfasts and a local-color setting, open 7 a.m.-8 p.m. Mon.-Fri., 7-3 Saturday. **McGrews,** the 24-hour coffee shop at the Yukon Inn, 4th Ave. across from the bright, bright golden arches, serves large portions at regular prices—this place comes in very handy at odd times. **Christie's Place,** 209 Main St., has great Greek pizza. **Kentucky Fried** and **Dairy Queen** are on 2nd on the *Klondike* side of Main. **The Keg,** 3rd and Jarvis, has steak, seafood, and salad bar—Gray Line drivers swear by it. Eight out of 10 readers over the past couple of years who've written in about Whitehorse have recommended the **Talisman Café** on 2nd between Main and Steele.

Foodmart at 1st and Main is a popular resupply market with the budget backpack set. **Super-Valu** in the Qwanlin Mall sells some bulk food, good produce (for Yukon), and a stunning selection of boxed juices. **Yukon Health Food Centre,** 504 Main, has nuts, dried fruits, energy bars, cereals, etc. **Food For Thought** is the other health food store, at 4th and Wood, a block beyond the No Pop.

Entertainment

Kopper King (a.k.a. the KK), five km west of town on the Alcan, hops to live country six nights a week (never on Tues.). **Trappers,** in the Westmark Klondike out 4th on the west side, usually has a Top 40 band; a DJ spins tunes the other times. **The Roadhouse,** on 2nd right between Mom's and the Fort Yukon, also gets going pretty loud with country rock bands.

Twin Cinemas is out by the mall; **Yukon Theatre** is at the corner of 3rd and Wood, around from the Visitor Centre. **Frantic Follies** is performed at the Westmark Whitehorse, 2nd and Wood, once or twice a night depending on dates, $16.

Shopping

An outstanding array of items made by the Indians and Eskimo of Canada's Northwest Territories is sold at **Northern Images,** 4th Ave. and Jarvis, tel. 668-5739. This large store is owned by a Native co-op and all of the articles are handmade. Even if you're not

TO
ALASKA HWY.

INDIAN CEMETERY

2ND AVE EXTENSION

SUSPENSION BRIDGE
TO KISHWOOT ISLAND

TO
LONG LAKE

WESTMARK

BAXTER
YUKON NATIVE
PRODUCTS

FOURTH AVE

LAUNDROMAT

KANOE
PEOPLE

THIRD AVE

**DOWNTOWN
WHITEHORSE**

RAY

BUS DEPOT

QWANLIN MALL

WP & YR RAILWAY

OGILVIE

COOK

FORT
YUKON
MOTEL

TRAIL TO AIRPORT

WHEELER

BLACK

YUKON

ALEXANDER

STRICKLAND

FIFTH AVE

NORTHERN
IMAGES

JARVIS

98 HOTEL

SEVENTH AVE

SIXTH AVE

YUKON GALLERY

MACBRIDE MUSEUM

CITY HALL

RIVER

EIGHTH AVE

WOOD AVE

NO POP
SANDWICH SHOP

STEELE

TOURIST OFFICE

RAILWAY
STATION

FIRST AVE

HOSPITAL

FEDERAL
BUILDING

CAPITAL
HOTEL

MR. MIKE'S
RESTAURANT

MAIN

POST
OFFICE

HAUGEN'S

WHITEHORSE
HEALTH
CENTER

TAKU HOTEL

ELLIOTT

T&M HOTEL

R.C.M.P.

OLD
LOG
CHURCH

LOG
SKYSCRAPER

LAMBERT

SECOND AVE

TERRITORIAL
ADMINISTRATION
BUILDING

HANSON

THIRD AVE

FOURTH AVE

HAWKINS

KENTUCKY
FRIED CHICKEN

ROGERS

FOURTH AVENUE
RESIDENCE/
SWIMMING POOL

AIRPORT

LOWE

HOGE

SS KLONDIKE II

JECKELL

LEWES BLVD

TO
MILES CANYON
& ALASKA HWY.

0   0.25 mi

0   250 m

© MOON PUBLICATIONS, INC.

buying, Northern Images is well worth a visit and is better than most museums. Get to know your endangered species! Remember that clothing or souvenirs made from animals considered endangered (including lynx, wolf, grizzly bear, and polar bear) or from marine mammals (whales, porpoises, seals, sea lions, walruses, and otters) are prohibited from entry into the United States, as is ivory. People who appreciate wildlife don't buy these articles anyway. For handicrafts made by Yukon Indians, including mukluks, parkas, and birch-bark and porcupine-quill baskets,

visit **Yukon Native Products,** 4330 4th Ave., across from McDonald's.

Mac's Fireweed, 203 Main St., has a large selection of tempting books.

Services And Information
If you haven't been immunized for diptheria, tetanus, or polio during the last 10 years, get these shots free at the Whitehorse Health Center (Mon.-Fri. 8-8:30 a.m.). This service is available to everyone. If you're camping and want a shower ($2), go to Lions Public Swimming Pool beside Fourth Avenue Resi-

dence. Take soap, shampoo, and a towel. The **Visitor Centre,** 302 Steele St., tel. 667-2915, open daily 8-8 in summer, 8-5 the rest of the year, can answer questions and has plenty of useful brochures. Ask about free guided hikes in the Whitehorse area which are often arranged by the Yukon Conservation Society; these are highly recommended. Offer to contribute something to the gas if they drive you out to a trail.

TRANSPORTATION

By Air
The airport is right above town on the bluff. Get there by going west out 4th to the Alcan and take a left, or east out 2nd and go right. On foot, follow the path along the fence around the northwest end of the runway and over to the bluff. A cab costs $8, or call Yellow Cab to arrange for the airport limo, $4 pp, which meets all flights. You can't miss the "world's largest weathervane"—the restored DC-3 mounted on a moveable pedestal which points its nose into the wind. **Canadian Airlines,** tel. 668-3535, has daily non-stop service to and from Vancouver. They also fly once a day to Edmonton. **Air North,** tel. 668-2228, flies four times a week to Fairbanks, via Dawson, which they fly to seven days a week, $650 OW. But you can get an excursion rate by booking 24 hours in advance: $170 to Dawson, another $195 to Fairbanks. **Alcan Air,** tel. 668-6616, is one of several commuter airlines with scheduled service to places like Inuvik, Old Crow, Mayo, Faro, Ross River, and Dawson City.

By Bus
The bus depot is on 1st Ave. across from the Qwanlin Mall, tel. 668-3225. Whitehorse is the northern terminus for **Greyhound;** none of their buses runs north or west of here. One bus a day departs for points east and south at noon (except Sun.).

Alaskon Express, or Gray Line of Yukon, tel. 668-3225, departs Whitehorse for Fairbanks ($135) and Anchorage ($147) on Tues., Fri., and Sat. at noon; these buses overnight in Beaver Creek (lodging not in-

cluded in price). You can get off and/or transfer in Tok. They also depart for Skagway at 4:30 p.m. Sun., Tues., Wed., and Fri., and 2:30 p.m. the other days, US$54. You can also catch the **Sourdough Shuttle** van at 2 p.m., US$50; book at the Fourth Avenue Residence.

Atlas buses also depart for Skagway (and Dawson) daily from the Sheffield. **Norline Coaches,** tel. 668-3355, goes to Dawson, at 9 a.m. from the bus depot Mon., Wed., and Fri., $72 OW. It's recommended to take this northern route through the Yukon into Alaska: more scenic, more historic, with Dawson, Top of the World Highway, Eagle, and the Taylor Highway. Note, however, that ground connections also die in Dawson. Beyond there, you can hitch or fly—your only choices.

By Train
The **White Pass and Yukon Route** trains are happily back on track (or most of it), leaving Whitehorse (by bus) at 8:30 a.m., leaving Fraser (by train) at 10:20 a.m., US$89, arriving Skagway at noon. The train depot is right downtown at the corner of 1st and Main. For reservations, call 668-RAIL.

By Boat
The most authentic way to travel from Whitehorse to Dawson is by canoe in 10-15 days, the way the stampeders did it before the advent of the sternwheelers. This is quite feasible and easily arranged; several outfits in Whitehorse supply everything required at a reasonable price. **Kanoe People** is the least expensive and most friendly, renting two-person canoes, which come with two life preservers and three paddles, $320, 16 days. Drop your boat off in Dawson with the Kanoe People agent up there. They also have shorter trips, such as to Carmacks and the Teslin River (eight days, $195), or the Big Salmon River (12 days, $250). and lead guided wilderness trips. Write Box 5152, Whitehorse, Yukon Y1A 4S3, or tel. (403) 668-4899.

Or try **Tatshenshini Expediting,** 1602 Allen, Whitehorse, Canada Y1A 3WB, tel. 632-2742, or **Yukon Tours,** tel. 667-2063. When checking around, remember to ask

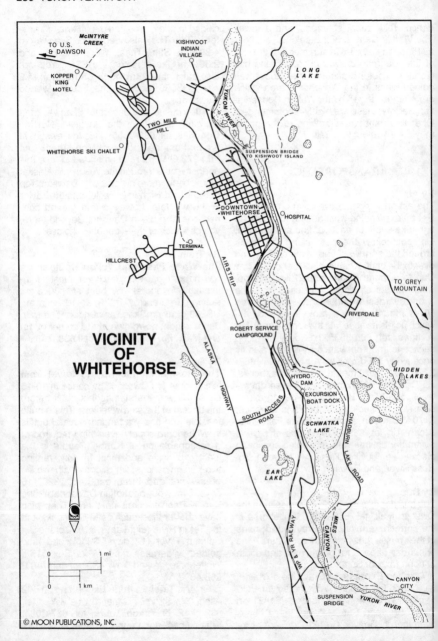

TO U.S. & DAWSON

McINTYRE CREEK

KISHWOOT INDIAN VILLAGE

LONG LAKE

KOPPER KING MOTEL

YUKON RIVER

TWO MILE HILL

WHITEHORSE SKI CHALET

SUSPENSION BRIDGE TO KISHWOOT ISLAND

DOWNTOWN WHITEHORSE

HOSPITAL

TERMINAL

HILLCREST

AIRSTRIP

TO GREY MOUNTAIN

RIVERDALE

VICINITY OF WHITEHORSE

ROBERT SERVICE CAMPGROUND

ALASKA HIGHWAY

SOUTH ACCESS ROAD

HYDRO DAM

EXCURSION BOAT DOCK

SCHWATKA LAKE

CHADBURN LAKE ROAD

HIDDEN LAKES

EAR LAKE

0   1 mi

0   1 km

WP & YR RAILWAY

MILES CANYON

CANYON CITY

SUSPENSION BRIDGE

YUKON RIVER

© MOON PUBLICATIONS, INC.

about drop-off charges, life preservers, etc. You could also buy a canoe for about $600 at the Hudson's Bay Co. and paddle yourself right into Alaska, terminating at Eagle, Circle, or the Dalton Highway.

By Thumb
To hitch west take the Porter Creek bus and ask the driver to drop you off as far out as he goes on the Alaska Highway. To hitch east take the Hillcrest bus to the corner of Alaska Highway and South Access Road.

Getting Around
Whitehorse Transit buses ($1) run Mon.-Sat. from 6:15 a.m.-7:15 p.m. (to 10:15 p.m. on Fri.). Pick up a schedule at the Visitor Centre or from the drivers. Day passes are available from drivers for $3, as are transfers. All routes begin and end beside Hudson's Bay Co. opposite Qwanlin Mall. Bus stops are clearly marked with blue-and-white signs.

Hertz, Avis, and **Norcar** rent cars at similar rates: $49-52 daily and 25-28 cents per km. All have a desk or courtesy phone at the airport.

ALASKA HIGHWAY TO BEAVER CREEK

Unless you're in a hurry to reach mainland Alaska, are heading specifically to Kluane National Park, or going to Anchorage by public transportation, it's highly recommended to take the Klondike Highway to Dawson, over the Top of the World Highway into Alaska, up to historic Eagle, and down to Tok on the Taylor Highway. This adds only 400 km (250 miles) onto the distance between Whitehorse and Fairbanks or Anchorage than the Alaska Highway (and just 192 km/120 miles if you bypass Eagle), completes the Trail of '98, and includes Dawson, a must-stop on any Northern itinerary. If you do take the "low road" to Alaska, it's 180 km (108 miles) to Haines Junction, 300 km (180 miles) from there to Beaver Creek, and 140 miles (224 km) from there to Tok.

Government campgrounds are found at Km 1543, 1602, and 1628. Thirteen km west of Whitehorse is the turnoff for Dawson (right) onto the Klondike Loop (see below). At Km 1568 is **Champagne,** which grew up in the gold rush and is now home to the Champagne Indian Band. The cemetery by the side of the highway is not for public inspection. A couple of dozen kilometers east of Haines Junction, the Kluane Icefield Ranges and the foothills of the St. Elias Mountains start to dominate the view; when it's clear, Mt. Kennedy and Mt. Hubbard loom high and white.

Haines Junction
Established in 1942 as a base camp for the U.S. Corps of Engineers connecting the Alcan with Haines, this town of 600 is the largest between Whitehorse and Tok, and growing. It has several gas stations and motels: the **Mountain View Motor Inn,** tel. 634-2646, is open year-round; also try the **Stardust,** tel. 634-2591, **Mackintosh,** tel. 634-2301, and **Kluane Park Inn,** tel. 634-2261. Restaurants include **Mother's,** which has good food; **Village Bakery,** next to the Visitor Centre, is a must. Groceries, sundries, and camping supplies are available at **Madley's General Store;** the bank and post office are also inside. A couple of the motels have pull-throughs for RVs, or head to **Kluane RV Kampground,** tel. 634-2709. Nearest public camping is at **Pine Lake,** seven km east of town on the Alaska Highway—usual excellent free Yukon facility with 33 sites, water, and firewood. Or pitch your tent unofficially behind the vehicle way station or just before the bridge on the road to Haines.

Hitching to Alaska, it's rare you'll get stuck at Haines Junction unless your ride is stopping to explore Kluane (in which case do the same!). Most hitchhikers get stuck here heading out. Either way, it's not hard to get a ride at the junction, but if your road karma is failing you temporarily, Alaskon motorcoaches pass through Haines Junction on the way to and from Alaska, stopping at the Mountain View Inn on various days of the week. Note that technically you can't buy a ticket from Haines Junction to Whitehorse since Alaskon Express is not a common carrier within the Yukon—though unofficially it's up to the driver's discretion.

KLUANE NATIONAL PARK

The lofty icecapped mountains of southwest Yukon, overflowing with glaciers and flanked by lower ranges rich in wildlife, have been set aside as Kluane National Park. Although the Alaska and Haines highways, which run along the fringe of the park, make it accessible, Kluane is a wilderness hardly touched by the hand of man; once you leave the highways you will see few other people. No roads run into the park itself, so to experience the true magnificence of this wilderness you must embark on an overnight hike. Signposts identify the trailheads, and all the trails offer splendid mountain scenery and a good chance to see wildlife. The fishing (Kluane means "Place of Many Fish") is also superb. Buy a license to fish in Kluane, as well as any national park in Canada (a territorial license is not required).

The Land

The St. Elias Range, running from Alaska through Yukon to British Columbia, is the highest mountain range in North America and the second-highest coastal range in the world (the Andes are first). Mount Logan (5,950 meters), totally inside the park, is the highest peak in Canada. The 2,500-meter-high front ranges you see from the highways are impressive enough, but only through gaps can you glimpse the fantastic Icefield Ranges lying directly behind. The many 5,000-meter-high peaks of this range are surrounded by a gigantic icefield plateau from 2,500-3,000 meters high, the largest non-polar icefield in the world, occupying a little over half the park. Radiating out from the icefield like spokes on a wheel are valley glaciers up to six km wide and 60 km long, some very active. During the late 1960s, for example, Steele Glacier advanced 11 km in only four months. Kaskawulsh Glacier is unusual in that it drains into both the Yukon River and the Pacific Ocean. Such is the importance of

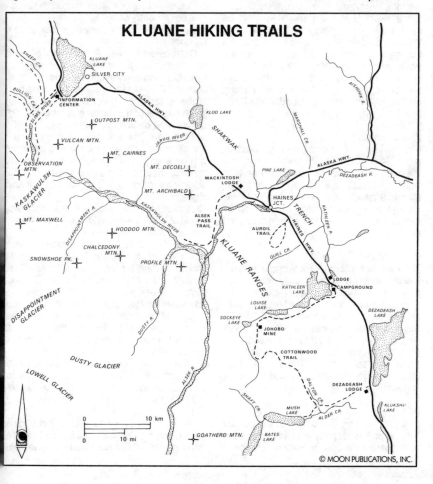

KLUANE HIKING TRAILS

© MOON PUBLICATIONS, INC.

the area that together with Wrangell-Saint Elias National Park in Alaska, Kluane has been declared a World Heritage Site by UNESCO.

Flora And Fauna

Although more than half of Kluane is ice, rock, and snow, the remainder includes a wide variety of climates and habitats, drier in the north and damper in the south; the wetter the area, the denser the vegetation. Some 4,000 Dall sheep, one of the world's largest populations, reside on the high open hillsides northwest of Kaskawulsh Glacier and elsewhere in the park. Many can be seen from the highway in the vicinity of Sheep Mountain. Kluane also has significant numbers of moose, caribou, mountain goats, and grizzly bears. Kokanee, a dwarf landlocked variety of freshwater sockeye salmon, spawn in Sockeye Lake (fishing prohibited), and also are found in the Kathleen Lakes (fishing permitted).

Flightseeing

Flightseeing over the park is available in small planes based at Burwash Lodge near the north end of Kluane Lake. The one-hour flight ($100 pp, four-passenger minimum) affords a spectacular view of Mount Logan plus several glaciers, and is highly recommended if you happen to be there on a clear day.

Practicalities

The **Kluane National Park Visitor Centre** at Haines Junction is open daily 8:30 a.m.-9 p.m. in the summer. Displays include a relief map of the park and an excellent free sight-and-sound slide show hourly from 9:30-7:30. Buy a topographical map here if you're planning to hike. The **Kathleen Lake Campground** ($3) has 41 sites with firewood, well water, and flush toilets. The waters of the lake are very clear and deep, and the fishing is good.

Hiking

Everyone setting out on an overnight hike into the park must register in advance, either at the visitor centres in Haines Junction or Sheep Mountain, or by phone (tel. 634-2251 or 634-2345). Hiking is free and no one is refused permission, but the park wardens want to know who is in the park and where. When you complete your trip, it's mandatory to call the park office again to let them know. Phones are installed at most trailheads. This system is for your own protection and, if you forget to sign out, an unnecessary and expensive search may be mounted to determine if you are in trouble. A free permit is also required for campfires. Obtain information on the trails and various attractions in the area, plus backcountry camping and campfire permits, from the Parks Canada trailer at the trailheads.

Cottonwood Trail: A minimum of four days is required to complete this 85-km loop trail from Kathleen Lake to Dezadeash (pronounced DEZ-dee-ash) Lodge on the Haines Highway (or vice versa). Some climbing is involved, several creeks must be waded across, and portions of the trail can be difficult to follow. The dividends are a great variety of plants and wildlife: many ptarmigan can be seen in the alpine areas, and watch for Dall sheep on the steep slopes. This is also prime grizzly habitat. You'll see many signs of old copper and placer gold mining sites along the way. Primitive campsites are found at Goat Creek and where Dalton Creek crosses Mush Lake Road.

From the Kathleen Lake Campground you follow an old mining road along the south shores of Kathleen and Louise lakes. Goat and Victoria creeks must be forded. Beyond Victoria Creek the road continues through the spruce forest, passing the ruins of the Johobo Mine where copper was extracted in the 1960s. From the mine continue along a trail cut through the forest, across some meadows, up a creek bed, then across a long stretch of alpine tundra to Dalton Creek and the Mush Lake Rd., which leads back out to Dezadeash Lodge. The great cheeseburgers with fries ($4) served at the lodge reward you at the end of the trail.

Auriol Trail: This 19-km loop trail begins six km south of Haines Junction and can be done in a day. There are excellent views from several points and a great variety of plant and animal life. About one km up the trail, take the fork to the right which climbs steeply to the treeline; the lefthand side is more gradual, and safer for the descent. The creek, located halfway up both forks of the trail, is narrow and easy to cross. A primitive campground is near the top on the lefthand side of the loop.

Alsek Pass Trail (Dezadeash-Alsek River Valley): This 24-km trail begins near Mackintosh Lodge, 10 km west of Haines Junction, and is relatively flat and easy to follow. The first 21 km take you on an abandoned mining road which ends at a washout; the last three km lead to Sugden Creek. Just 125 years ago this area was submerged under a lake which formed when Lowell Glacier pushed up against the west side of Goatherd Mountain, blocking the Alsek River. The lake, which once extended up the Dezadeash River well beyond Haines Junction and rose as much as 81 meters above present river levels, drained when the glacier receded. Today the old beach line is clearly visible as a sandy strip, complete with driftwood, high along the hillsides in the Dezadeash, Alsek, and Kaskawulsh river valleys. Also look for the rare plants on the sand dunes at the junction of the Dezadeash and Kaskawulsh rivers.

Slims River Trail: This is perhaps the best short (24 km OW) hike in Kluane Park because it offers old mining relics, excellent wildlife viewing, and a spectacular look at Kaskawulsh Glacier at the base of the St. Elias Mountains. The trail begins near the Sheep Mountain information trailer and leads up the west side of the Slims River. The first nine km are on an old mining road. After the road ends you have to find your way between the hillside and the riverbed. There are three major creeks to cross. The trail ends at Observation Mountain, which should be climbed for the classic view of the Kaskawulsh. Several side trails go off to the right. The first leads up to Sheep Creek Canyon (six and a half km OW) where abundant wildlife may be found. The second runs into the historic Bullion Creek placer goldmining area (9½ OW). Another route up the

east side of the Slims is often easier due to fewer creek crossings.

TO THE NEW ROAD ACROSS THE BORDER

To Beaver Creek

For 250 of the next 300 km to Beaver Creek, you're passing right next to Kluane National Park or Kluane Game Sanctuary—a comparatively well-populated, civilized, and stunningly scenic stretch of the Alaska Highway. There are three provincial campgrounds (Km 1725, 1853, and 1913), along with three little settlements, and a dozen lodges. At **Soldier's Summit,** Km 1707, a sign commemorates the official opening of the Alcan on Nov. 20, 1942, a mere eight months after construction began; a visitor info center is housed in a trailer a little east. **Destruction Bay** is the tiny town at Km 1743, with gas, motel, cafeteria, RV park, and lake tours. Only 16 km west is **Burwash Landing,** a similar settlement, but with air tours and a museum (Kluane Museum of Natural History, open 9-9, $1.50). Five lodges dot the next 120 km, then it's another 65 km into Beaver Creek.

Beaver Creek

With the last facilities before crossing the border, Beaver Creek is a tiny town with a big economy. Canadian Customs is here, and an Alaska Highway road crew. A Westmark hotel and a campground are here, where every Westours tourist between Fairbanks and Whitehorse, and every Alaskon Express passenger between Anchorage or Fairbanks and Whitehorse or Skagway, spend the night. If you're the former, your $100 room at the **Westmark Inn** is ready, and your luggage will be delivered as soon as possible.

If you're the latter, the **KOA Kampground** is $8; showers are free with a campsite. There's also free camping at Ida's (see below) if you ask permission first inside; Ida's also has motel rooms. Or mosey into the woods nearby, as always. The Westmark has a cafeteria-style restaurant and a barbecue feast and live stage show. Or get road food at **Ida's** across and down the highway. A nightly one-hour slide show, sponsored by Westmark, happens at the Civic Centre, 200 meters across from the hotel on the spur road.

Canadian Customs is three km before town if you're heading east into Canada; U.S. Customs is 22 miles beyond town. Canadian border guards are somewhat sensitive about guns; U.S. Customs officers seem to distrust young travelers, suspecting them to be transient workers or carrying drugs. Extensive searches of cars, backpacks, etc. are not uncommon, especially these days, with drug hysteria and "zero tolerance" rampant among law enforcers.

KLONDIKE LOOP

The Klondike Loop runs 521 km from its junction with the Alaska Highway (30 km northwest of Whitehorse) northwest to Dawson City, then 105 km on Top of the World Highway to the 109-mile stretch of the Taylor Highway back to the Alcan outside of Tok. Roughly following the original overland trail to Dawson, the road is almost completely paved with just a few gravel breaks. This first spell of highway was laid from Whitehorse to Stewart Crossing in 1950, then was pushed through to Dawson five years later.

Lake Laberge, 62 km from Whitehorse, is famous primarily as the site of the actual burning of the corpse in Robert Service's immortal "Cremation of Sam McGee." The excellent trout fishing here has also been well known since stampeder days, when the fish were barged to Dawson by the ton. Around 15 km north is **Fox Lake Campground** (19 sites, water). **Little Fox Lake,** 15 minutes up the road, is extremely photogenic; its tiny islands densely covered with spruce seem to smile at the camera.

Just over 190 km from Whitehorse is **Carmacks,** the first civilization since the capital. Named after George Carmack, credited with the Bonanza Creek strike that touched off the Rush of '98, the town has three gas stations, two motels, cafes and lounges, and a campground on the Yukon. Twenty-five km north of Carmacks is a pullout overlooking **Five Finger Rapids,** the halfway point on the river trip from Whitehorse to Dawson. Four rock towers here choke the river, forming five channels that the current rips through. According to the *Milepost,* only the eastern righthand channel is safe for navigation.

In another 83 km is **Pelly Crossing,** a tiny Indian town with a cafe and gas station (which might even have gas). The bridge north of town crosses the Pelly River, discovered and named by Robert Campbell, an explorer for the Hudson's Bay Co. who established Fort Selkirk in 1848 at the junction of the Pelly and Yukon rivers. Seventy km north is **Stewart Crossing,** with a bridge over the Stewart River, discovered in 1849 by James Stewart, Robert Campbell's clerk. The famous trio of Harper, Mayo, and McQuesten set up a trading post here in 1886 after placer gold was discovered. Jack London's one winter in the Yukon was spent in Stewart, snowbound on his way to the goldfields. He came down with scurvy, recovered during his short visit to Dawson, and quickly returned by way of the Yukon to California—where he turned 22. Today, Stewart Crossing has a couple of lodges, gas stations, and an information center. It's 181 km from here to Dawson; top of your tank so as not to worry.

(GORDY OHLIGER)

DAWSON CITY

Of all the destinations in the North, Dawson has the widest fame and the wildest foretime: one day after the *Portland* hit Seattle in August 1897 the entire world equated the name Dawson with a ton of gold. Within a year, 40,000 stampeders (out of an estimated 100,000 who started out) had descended on Dawson, making it the largest Canadian city west of Winnipeg—though 25,000 of its residents were American! The city's heyday, however, was as brief as its reputation was beefy, and Dawson quickly declined into another small town on the banks of the Yukon. Today, Dawson's population has grown to 1,611, doubling in population during the last decade, but still only third-largest in the territory, edged out by Watson Lake's extra 50 residents. It is, however, experiencing a second stampede, sparked by soaring gold prices. A delightful salmagundie of historic facades and abandoned buildings, tiny old cabins and huge new ones, touristy gold panning and bulldozer placer mining, Dawson's many opportunities for adventure and fortune are as authentic and valid as ever. And thousands of hopefuls are again covering the miles from all over North America, sharing on

arrival the thrill of the stampeders, and forging a living link with the past that will linger long into the future.

HISTORY

Discovery
The Klondike goldfields cover an area of 2,000 square km southeast of the city. In 1895, Robert Henderson, a prospector from Nova Scotia born with a lust for gold, was grubstaked by Joe Ladue, a trader at the tiny settlement of Ogilvie, 100 km upstream from the Thron-diuck River. Ladue pointed Henderson in the direction of what would come to be called the Klondike, and Henderson prospected for two years, finding color on the creeks, but not the fortune he was looking for. Finally, in spring 1896, he climbed what was later named King Dome and surveyed six creeks radiating out from where he stood like spokes on a wheel—six of the richest gold-bearing creeks ever known in the world. Sticking his pan into one, he found 20-30 cents' worth of gold in a single wash—four times as much as he was used to, and hurried off to tell the nearest miners about his

Dawson's original red light area was the alley between 2nd and 3rd from King to Queen. As the city became more established, the prostitutes were shifted across the Klondike to Lousetown, where they continued to do a brisk business until the respectable ladies of Dawson led a campaign to close the brothels.

prospect on his newly named "Gold-Bottom Creek." (Before the rush, the free sharing of information among miners was a code strongly subscribed to in the North, for it occasionally meant the spreading around of fortunes, and often the difference between life and death.)

Henderson and his companions worked Gold-Bottom Creek for a year. In Aug. 1896 Henderson was returning from Ogilvie with supplies when he had the fateful meeting with "Siwash" George Washington Carmack, who was fishing with his two Athabascan brothers-in-law for salmon at the mouth of the Thron-diuck ("Hammer-Water") River, named for the fish-trap stakes hammered into its bed. Invoking the miner's code, Henderson again shared his news of Gold-Bottom Creek, advising Carmack to prospect the Thron-diuck—and send word if he found anything.

On Aug. 17, 1896, Carmack struck gold where Rabbit Creek (soon to be renamed Bonanza) empties into the Klondike, in extraordinary quantities—$3-4 a pan. Barely able to contain their incredulity, he and his partners, Tagish Charlie and Skookum Jim, prospected along the creek, staked three claims, and hurried off to file in Fortymile, the largest supply settlement, a half-day's journey downstream. Carmack displayed his vial of large new nuggets to everyone he met, and Fortymile was deserted the next day.

The news then reached Ogilvie, emptying i immediately; Joe Ladue himself rushed to the Klondike and staked, but he also had the great foresight to establish a sawmill on a wedge of fetid swamp where the Klondike met the Yukon—thus founding Dawson. By fall, the news had spread to Circle City and as far as Juneau, and most of the rich groun had been claimed. Ironically, only Rober Henderson, working his Gold-Bottom Cree a few-hours' hike on the other side of the dome, didn't get word; by the time he hear it was too late to get in on the riches.

Gold Fever

The news of the strike reached the outside world a year later, when a score of prospec tors, so loaded down with gold that the couldn't handle it themselves, disembarke in San Francisco and Seattle. The spectacl created mass insanity throughout the conti nent, immediately triggering a rush the like of which the world had rarely seen before and has not seen since. Clerks, salesmen streetcar conductors, doctors, preachers generals, even the mayor of Seattle simpl dropped what they were doing and started o for the Klondike. Mining companies advertis ing in New York papers for investment capita were inundated with money. Adventurer from Europe, Australia, America, and else where set out to seek the gold. Boatloads c would-be brides sailed around Cape Horr

(top left) Jerry Deppa with a resident of Sitka's Alaska Raptor Rehabilitation Center;
(top right) Annie Turnmir preparing chum salmon in an Angoon smokehouse;
(bottom) Lino Alves and Brian Voykin man the counter at the general store in Carcross, Yukon Territory.

(top) an old skin boat and trapper's cabin along the Chitina River within Wrangell-St. Elias National Park (bottom) Floatplanes provide access to hundreds of public-use cabins in Tongass National Forest.

City dwellers, factory workers, men who had never climbed a mountain, handled a boat, or even worn a backpack, were dumped unceremoniously on the edge of an uncharted wilderness with Dawson—a thousand miles from anywhere—as the imagined grand prize.

Meanwhile, the first few hundred lucky stampeders to actually reach Dawson before the rivers froze that winter (1897) found the town in such a panic over food that people were actually fleeing for their lives. At the same time that tens of thousands of stampeders were heading toward Dawson via the Chilkoot and White passes, up the Yukon River, over the Mackenzie, Peace, and Pelly rivers from Edmonton, over the Valdez Glacier at Prince William Sound and the Malaspina Glacier at Yakutat, and up from the Skeena and Stikine rivers through interior British Columbia, others passed them on the trails heading the other way, talking of famine and starvation. Most hopefuls were caught unprepared in the bitter grip of the seven-month Arctic winter, and many froze to death, or died of scurvy, starvation, exhaustion, heartbreak, suicide, or murder. And when the break-up in 1898 finally allowed the remaining hordes to pour into Dawson the next spring, every claim worth working within 150 km had already been staked and filed.

Heyday And Paydirt

That next year, from summer 1898 to summer 1899, was a unique moment of history. As people and supplies started deluging Dawson, all the hundreds of thousands in gold, worthless previously for lack of anything to buy, was spent with a feverish abandon. The richest established the saloons, dance halls, gaming centers, trading companies, even steamship lines and banks, a much easier way to get the gold than mining it. The casinos and hotels were as opulent as any in Paris. The dancehall girls charged $5 in gold per minute for dancing (extra for slow dances), the bartenders put stickum on their fingers to poke a little dust during transactions, and the janitors who panned the sawdust on the barroom floors were known to wash out $50 nightly. Paupers became millionaires on a roll of the dice, and vice versa. Dawson burned with an intensity born of pure lust, the highlight of the entire lives of every single person who braved the trails and experienced it.

And then Dawson burned, literally, twice that year, the second time practically to the ground. Only a few die-hards had the heart to rebuild the town a third time. Also, word filtered in that gold had been discovered on the beaches of Nome, and just as the Klondike

Miners operating rockers at King Solomon's Hill up Bonanza Creek in 1898. Gravel was shoveled into the wooden boxes which were rocked back and forth manually using handles on the sides. Larger particles were screened out on top while gold, which is twice as heavy as lead, would collect in the bottom after the other material had been removed.

strike had emptied Ogilvie, Fortymile, and Circle, Nome emptied Dawson. By the summer of 1899, as the last bedraggled and tattered stampeders limped into Dawson two years after setting out (mostly overland from Edmonton) the 12-month golden age of Dawson was done.

By far the most comprehensive, colorful, and poetic history of the great gold rush is *The Klondike Fever,* by Pierre Berton (Carrol and Graf, 1958), a well-known and prolific Canadian journalist and editor who grew up in Dawson after his father crossed the Chilkoot in '98. Also, don't miss "City of Gold," a "moving slide show" written and narrated by Berton, shown at the Dawson tourist office.

SIGHTS

Dawson's plentiful free or inexpensive attractions can keep you happily busy for several days. Its expensive nightlife, however, will greedily relieve you of your daytime savings. The excellent campground is no longer free, but disappearing into the woods makes the late nights of Dawson painless, though the price of meals will quickly eat up any money left over from your lodging budget. But the vibe around this town is *party,* so save on sights and overnights, and splurge on those perennial pleasures of the flesh.

Visitor Reception Centre

As always, start your visit at the info office, right in the thick of things at Front and King streets, tel. 993-5566, open daily 9-9. This center is extremely well organized and prepared for the most common questions from the hordes of hopefuls that are, after all, Dawson's legacy. They stock books of menus, hotel rates, and gift shops, schedules of tours, hours of attractions and movies, prices of showers, and much much more. Pick up a good map of Dawson's historical buildings and one of the area, and leave your pack here for $1 a day.

Downtown

Two 45-minute walking tours leave from the Visitor Centre: the Fort Herchmer walk at 11

a.m. (so-so) and the Town Core tour at 1 and 4 (excellent). The restored riverboat SS *Keno* (1922) is beached on Front St.; tours are no longer given. You'll really appreciate the size of Whitehorse's *Klondike* by comparing it to the *Keno,* which once plied the Stewart River, bringing ore concentrates from the mining area around Mayo down to the confluence of the Yukon, where larger riverboats picked them up and transported them upriver to Whitehorse and the railhead. The exterior of the **Bank of Commerce,** near the *Keno,* hasn't changed much since Robert Service worked here in 1908. Upstairs in the old assay room is a gold display, open 10-3, free.

On King St., up a block from the Visitor Centre, is the **Palace Grand Theatre,** built in 1899 by "Arizona Charlie" Meadows, the most famous bartender/gunslinger on the Trail of '98. The original building was demolished in 1959, but an exact replica, complete with Klondike Kate's room upstairs, was erected in 1962. Catch tours of the Palace at 11, 1, 3, and 5. At 1:30 the Palace Grand shows the documentary "City of Gold," free. This was filmed by a local in the pre-tourist boom days when Dawson was withering away and Parks Canada hadn't yet come to the rescue. At 8 p.m. nightly (except Tues.), **Gaslight Follies** is performed ($12).

Parks Canada is restoring some of the historical buildings, and signboards along 2nd and 3rd avenues explain their significance; others, such as Straits Auction House at Harper and 2nd, are in authentic condition—to the continuing livelihood of Mr. Eastman and Mr. Kodak. Don't miss the excellent photographic exhibit in Harrington's Store.

Around Town

The **Dawson City Museum** in the former Territorial Administration Building (1901) on 5th Ave. and Church St. has a mind-boggling array of gold-related artifacts, historic photos, geological interpretation, even camel bones found in the area. Open daily 10-6, $3, the museum also shows silent films and slide shows. Several **locomotives** which once ran from town to the goldfields (1906-14) may be seen free in the park adjoining the museum.

The outdoor city **pool** is adjacent ($2 including shower).

Stroll three blocks uphill to 8th St. and **Robert Service's log cabin.** Irish actor-director Tom Byrne has been entertaining visitors with Robert Service's life story, famous epics, and obscure ditties for over a decade. Hear how Service, who never took shovel or pan to earth or water, wound up as a troubador-bank teller in Dawson, and made his fame and fortune unexpectedly while living here. No one has lived in this cabin since Service left Dawson a celebrity in 1912, and people have been making pilgrimages to it for 75 years. If you do one thing in Dawson, this is it—everyday at 10 and 3. Two blocks east is **Jack London's cabin,** where it was moved from Stewart; readings at 1 p.m.

Midnight Dome

If you're driving, either take Front St. out of town two km and turn left onto Dome Rd., or

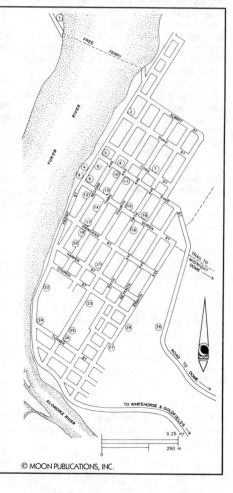

DAWSON CITY

1. Yukon River Campground
2. Yukon Sawmill
3. Information Center
4. *Keno* riverboat
5. bus station/drugstore
6. Palace Grand Theatre
7. Gold Rush Campground
8. Bank of Commerce
9. Dawson General Store
10. old post office
11. Madame Tremblay's Store
12. Farmers' Market
13. Midnight Sun
14. Westminster Hotel
15. Diamond Tooth Gertie's Gambling Hall
16. Triple J Cafeteria
17. Harrington's Store
18. main post office/mining records
19. Red Feather Saloon
20. Mary's Rooms
21. Westmark
22. Commissioner's residence
23. Dawson City Museum
24. former courthouse
25. swimming pool
26. Black residence
27. Jack London Cabin
28. Robert Service Cabin
29. pioneer cemetery

© MOON PUBLICATIONS, INC.

take the shortcut at the top of King St. (at 9th). Go one km up past the old cemeteries, then go right at the fork for another km till joining the main Dome Rd.; it's five km up to the top.

If hoofing it, a good (though steep) morning hike (so the sun's not right in your eyes, like it is later) begins by following the hydro lines at the east end of Queen St. directly up the slope to a point where it levels off, and you see two large white radio transmitters through the trees to the left. Follow a branch cable through to the transmitters and go up the dirt road to the smaller, uppermost disk. The trail to the Midnight Dome begins just behind and above this disk. Go straight up through the woods passing the abandoned Yukon Ditch, which once carried water to the dredges on the goldfields, and past an unused loop of the old road to the summit. The trail is improving and semi-marked; ask at the Visitor Centre for the latest details.

From the top of the Dome (885 meters) you get a complete 360-degree view of the area; the Yukon River stretches out in both directions and Dawson is right below you; the Ogilvie Mountains line the horizon to the northeast; to the west the Top of the World Highway winds away to Alaska; to the south you look directly up Bonanza Creek, past the wavy tailings and hillsides pitted by hydraulic monitors which still bring paydirt down for sluicing. The sign there identifies all the topographic features.

After a good look, follow the ridge down west toward the Yukon River. This trail affords an even more spectacular view of Dawson City. After passing the clear area near the end of the ridge, the path ends a couple a bushwacking hours short of the Moosehide Trail. It's easier to return to King and 8th and start fresh on this trail, which carries on to **Moosehide**, an Indian village abandoned in 1957, but now hosting again a few residents. The log cabins, cache houses, schoolhouse, St. Barnabas Anglican Church (1908), and the Indian cemetery all remain. If you decide to visit, remember that this is private property.

PRACTICALITIES

Accommodations

The only hotel in Dawson with any character left is the **Westminster Hotel,** 3rd and Queen, $45 s, $60 d. Don't let its appearance scare you; the rooms on the third floor are clean and quiet. **Mary's Rooms,** 3rd and Harper, are homey and comparably priced— $46 s and $50 d. The rest of Dawson's 276 hotel rooms (one for every six residents!) have Disneyland exteriors, Howard Johnson interiors, and charge the earth. Reports have it that a youth hostel is nearing completion near the ferry crossing; check to see if it's there when you are.

The **Yukon River Campground,** across the river from town, is large (100 sites), convenient for cars and foot traffic, and water, pit toilets, firewood ($8). Also, a free ferry, the *George Black,* with room for six to eight cars, crosses the river frequently, 24 hours a day, a fun ride even if you're not camping. It's only a half km from the crossing to the campground (turn right) or to downtown (turn left). Walk down past the campground to the sternwheeler graveyard; three big riverboats disintegrate where they were beached many years ago. (Or walk straight into the woods on the campground side to avoid paying the $8; many of Dawson's seasonal workers live hereabouts. Just don't cut down trees, leave scatalogical evidence, or abuse the campground facilities.)

Food

Dining is dear in Dawson, darling. Study the menu book at the Visitor Centre closely. If you simply must eat out here, **Nancy's** on Front St. is wholesome, with good soup, and sandwiches on homemade bread. The '98 **Drive-In,** also on Front St., is the place for road food. **Klondike Kate's** serves good, big, reasonably priced breakfasts. **Marina's** is highly touted for its pizza and Italian, as is **Claims Cafe** for baked goods and coffee. But all in all, Dawson is one of the best places in the North to buy groceries (at **Dawson General Store** next to '98 Drive-In—reportedly

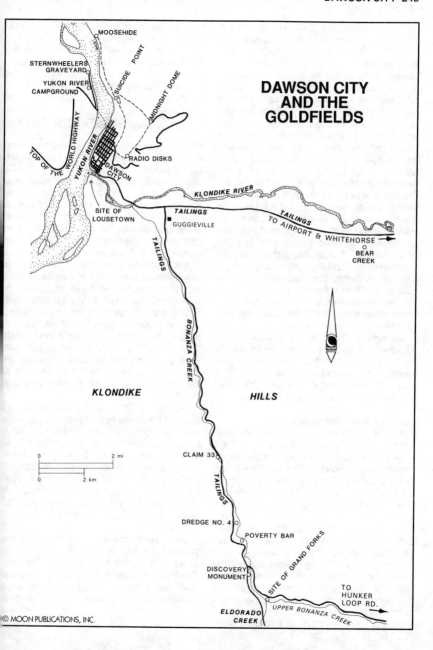

DAWSON CITY AND THE GOLDFIELDS

MOOSEHIDE

STERNWHEELERS GRAVEYARD

YUKON RIVER CAMPGROUND

SUICIDE POINT

MIDNIGHT DOME

TOP OF THE WORLD HIGHWAY

YUKON RIVER

RADIO DISKS

DAWSON CITY

SITE OF LOUSETOWN

KLONDIKE RIVER

TAILINGS

GUGGIEVILLE

TAILINGS

TO AIRPORT & WHITEHORSE

BEAR CREEK

TAILINGS

BONANZA CREEK

KLONDIKE

HILLS

0   2 mi

0   2 km

CLAIM 33

TAILINGS

DREDGE NO. 4

POVERTY BAR

SITE OF GRAND FORKS

DISCOVERY MONUMENT

TO HUNKER LOOP RD.

ELDORADO CREEK

UPPER BONANZA CREEK

© MOON PUBLICATIONS, INC.

better than **Farmer's Market**) and concoct yourself a campground culinary cudfest.

Entertainment

Diamond-Tooth Gertie's, 4th and Queen, open 8 p.m. to 2 a.m. except Sun., charges $4 *admission* into a casino that's going to take your gambling money, extract a liver and spleen for snacks and drinks, and entertain with a floor show that consists mostly of a sing-along with Gert to such geritol classics as "I've Been Working on the Railroad," "Take Me Out To The Ballgame," "She'll Be Coming Around the Mountain," and "Yankee Doodle Dandy." The can-can dancers are energetic, though, so you might justify the admission for a few leg shots. But sit in the back unless you want to take the chance of Gert pulling you on stage to high-step, or sitting on your lap while singing "Melancholy Baby." Still, it's good corny fun, and *the* thing to do at night in Dawson. Besides, the proceeds go to the Klondike Visitors Association for a good cause: the restoration of Dawson—which proceeds apace as the centennial of the gold rush looms nearer and nearer.

Gaslight Follies, in the Palace Grand Theatre on King St., is yet another vaudeville revue, 8 p.m., $12. For something a little earthier, try the two bars in the Westminster Hotel. To drink and dance with the Dawsonians, join in at the Midnight Sun.

Services And Information

The Visitor Centre is on Front St.; see "Sights" above for details. It's not too difficult to de-dust in Dawson—three establishments provide public showers. Cheapest are those at the Chief Isaac Hale building next door to the Visitor Centre: 25 cents for two minutes. Gold Rush (in town) and Guggieville (at the junction of Bonanza Creek Rd. and Klondike Hwy.) campgrounds charge 25 cents a minute. Get hours at the Visitor Centre. You can also grab a shower at the city pool.

Change your money before coming to Dawson if possible as the one bank gives a poor rate. Topographical maps are sold in the mining recorder's office adjoining the main post office, on 5th between Queen and Princess. They also sell an excellent blueprint map of the Klondike Placer Area showing all the goldfields for only $1—a bargain.

Maximillian's Gold Rush Emporium on Front St. has a great selection of paperbacks and books of northern interest, including the excellent *The Klondike Fever* by Berton.

TRANSPORTATION

Norline buses leave for Whitehorse from Arctic Drug Store on Front St. (across from the *Keno*) Mon., Wed., and Fri. at 4 p.m., $72 OW. Beyond returning to Whitehorse and catching a bus to Tok, Fairbanks, or Anchorage, Dawson is the end of the road for buses. You can hitch the 127 km across the border to the junction with the Taylor Highway, then continue the 65 miles up to Eagle or the 96 miles down to Tetlin Junction on the Alaska Highway. (**Note:** Customs at Boundary is only open from mid-May to mid-Sept., 9-9). Top of the World and Taylor highways are surprisingly well traveled during the summer; getting a ride shouldn't be too long an ordeal. The extension to Eagle is less so, and depending on karma, could be excruciatingly time-consuming. Andrew Hempstead and Nadina Purcell, hitchhikers and researchers extraordinaire, spoke to drivers lined up at the ferry crossing on the Dawson side and found a ride to Eagle.

Another option is to fly. **Air North** flies direct to Fairbanks from Dawson four times a week for US$195. Also, check with **Warbelow's Air Ventures,** which has Dawson as a flag stop on their Tues. and Thurs. mail/passenger route between Fairbanks and Eagle, $150 OW Dawson, Eagle, Fairbanks. The travel agency in the building next to the Visitor Centre can make these arrangements. Dawson's airport is 17 km east of town.

One more possibility is to catch the Westours' *Yukon Queen* to Eagle at 9 a.m. This riverboat plies the Yukon daily between Dawson and Eagle, $69 OW, and reports have been unanimous—an excellent crew, a beautiful ride, and a great ship. Buy tickets at Arctic Drug Store.

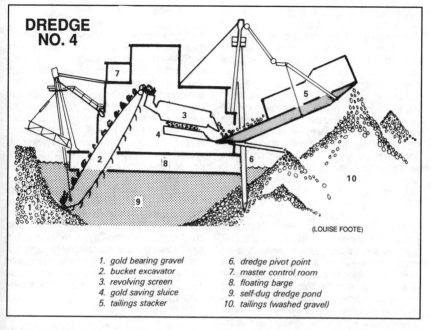

DREDGE NO. 4

1. gold bearing gravel
2. bucket excavator
3. revolving screen
4. gold saving sluice
5. tailings stacker
6. dredge pivot point
7. master control room
8. floating barge
9. self-dug dredge pond
10. tailings (washed gravel)

(LOUISE FOOTE)

Tours

Speaking of boats, the *Yukon Lou,* a miniature sternwheeler, departs the dock at the SS *Keno* for a short ride down the Yukon to Pleasure Island and a salmon bake, $24. **Atlas Tours** offers a three-hour city tour, which includes a trip out by the goldfields to Dredge No. 4, leaving at 9 a.m. and 1 p.m., $15. A couple of local tour companies also do city and goldfields tours. David Taylor (a.k.a. "Buffalo"), who operates **Gold City Tours,** 3rd and King, tel. 993-5175, is highly recommended by everybody.

VICINITY OF DAWSON

The Goldfields

For a close-up look at some of the most tore-up country in the North, and for some insight into the gold frenzy that created and continues to stimulate the area, head out Bonanza Creek Road. The mountains of tailings could cover the entire Yukon Territory with gravel, and the heavy equipment could spread it around. A monument at Discovery Claim, 16 km southeast of town, marks the spot where George Carmack pulled up $4 in his first pan in 1896. A km beyond the monument is the confluence of Bonanza and Eldorado creeks, site of the gold rush town of Grand Forks. Nothing remains at the Forks as the entire area has since been dredged. The Klondike Visitors Association owns a claim here where you may pan for gold as much as you like free of charge (bring your own pan). On the way up from Dawson you pass two commercial panning operations, **Claim 33** and **Poverty Bar,** where you pay $5 for a guaranteed (spiked) pan of gold. Still, it's good fun and practice for your technique.

The highlight of the trip, however, is **Dredge No. 4,** largest wooden-hulled gold dredge in North America. Built in 1912, this massive machine scooped paydirt from the creek beds right up until 1966. An info trailer has descriptions of the operation. You can walk right up to the control room at the top of the dredge, but that's about all; the rest of the machinery is chicken-wired shut. Wait till you get to the Jack Wade Dredge on the Taylor Highway to really climb on one of these houseboat-cranes.

Four km beyond the dredge, take a left at the fork to Upper Bonanza Creek, for miles more of mucking. You can continue along this road (which gets pretty rough in spots) all the way up to King Dome, where Robert Henderson stood, surveyed the land, and chose the wrong creek. You pass a turnoff (left) to Quartz Creek, then shortly another left to Sulphur Creek. This gravel road travels a 100-km loop into some seriously isolated country—you'll probably not see another car. It rejoins Upper Bonanza Rd. (which soon becomes Hunker Creek Rd.) only a bit beyond where it cut out. Then you start to descend along Hunker Creek Rd., for more placer operations, including another small dredge (inaccessible but photographable). Finally you come out (after a 72-km loop) at the glorious pavement of the Klondike Highway about a km on the Dawson side of the airport.

Into Alaska

Top of the World Highway from Dawson to the Taylor Highway in Alaska is the best unpaved road in the North. It's wide, smooth, and *fast*—90 km/h and fourth gear. It's a high road, cutting mainly through the upper taiga and alpine tundra of the lower White Mountains, with vast vistas in which you can see the road running along the ridgetops in the distance. It's even a basically civilized road—guard rails and well signposted. Civilization *along* the highway, however, is scanty; but for **Boundary Lodge** (cafe and gas) 111 km from Dawson, human habitation is non-existent to the junction of the Taylor and beyond. Keep a close eye on your gas gauge: the next gas after Boundary is at O'Brien Creek Lodge, 40 miles past Boundary on the Eagle Cutoff, or at Chicken, also 40 long miles on the Taylor. Note, too, that both American and Canadian Customs operate only from mid-May to mid-Sept., and only 9-9. And don't forget the time change at the border: Alaska time is an hour earlier than Yukon time.

an Inuit mask, carved from a piece of driftwood
(DIANA LASICH-HARPER)

INTERIOR

Interior Alaska is a great tilted plateau between the crests of the Alaska and Brooks ranges. The mighty Yukon and Tanana rivers are the main features of this region, but vast expanses of rolling hills are almost always in view. Interior Alaska has one medium-sized city, Fairbanks, several small towns, and a number of bush villages, the most interesting along the rivers, but also some beside the highways. Much of the region is expensive or inaccessible to visit without your own vehicle, but great adventures await on the many wild and scenic rivers, in the wildlife refuges, and in spectacular Denali National Park.

EAGLE

Eagle Cutoff

Hang a right at Jack Wade Junction; it's 65 miles to Eagle on the Eagle Cutoff. This stretch is almost more a trail than a road: very narrow and winding, with steep grades, rough surface, endless hairpin turns, and little traffic—20-30 mph max. For the same reasons, it's one of the funnest roads in the state, too. Lots of twists and turns, ups and downs, few other cars to worry about—you can really *play* on this one. The scenery is the same Interior hills and spruce trees you've been accustomed to since Whitehorse, so it's not a loss to keep your eyes glued to this road at all times; one glance away and you're driving into a ditch or off a 300-foot cliff. Until you get to Eagle, only one facility is at your service: **O'Brien's** (Mile 125, gas and booze), and one primitive BLM campground, **Liberty Creek** (Mile 131, six sites, free). Expect to spend at least two hours for these 65 miles, two hours of white-knuckle, bug-eyed, teeth-chattering thrills—hopefully without the spills.

To Go Or Not To Go

Over 160 miles from Tetlin Junction and 145 miles from Dawson, all gravel, it takes a strong desire and a serious commitment to get to Eagle. Even if you're on the way from

Dawson into Alaska, it's 130 miles, at least five hours of driving, to go to Eagle and back to the junction of Top of the World and Taylor highways. And gas when you get there is a buck-seventy a gallon. Is it worth it?

Consider this. Eagle is a total history lesson. The small photogenic town of 150 may have more square feet of museum space than anywhere else in the state. The moving-right-along walking tour can take up to *three hours*. Add to that a beautiful free campground, great shower, good food, friendly people, and Yukon River scenery, and Eagle is without hesitation worth the extra time, effort, and expense.

History

In 1881, Francis Mercier, a French-Canadian trader, established a trading post at the site of Eagle to compete with Fort Yukon and Fort Reliance, two Hudson's Bay Co. posts along this eastern stretch of the Yukon River. It was a shrewd choice of location. Just inside the

American border, stampeders fed up with Canada's heavy-handed laws and taxes in spring 1898 organized a supply town here, naming it Eagle for the profusion of these birds in the area. Also, sitting at the southern-most point on the Yukon in eastern Alaska, Eagle occupied a strategic spot for transportation, communication, and supply routes to the Interior from Valdez at tidewater. Within six months, three large trading companies developed Eagle into a major Yukon port. In 1899 the Army began building Fort Egbert next to the townsite. In 1900 Judge James Wickersham arrived to install Interior's first federal court, with jurisdiction over half the state. And by 1902, the WAMCATS telegraph line was completed between Eagle and Valdez, inaugurating the first "all-American" communication system to the Lower 48.

The biggest event in Eagle's history happened in 1905, when a Norwegian Arctic explorer appeared out of the icy fog, and somehow communicated to the townspeople

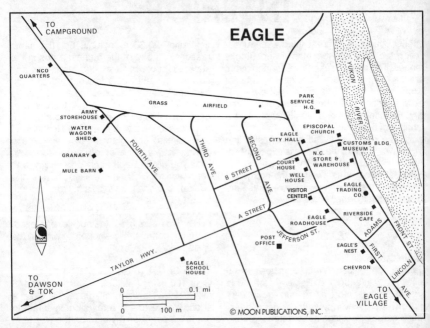

EAGLE

(he spoke no English) who he was and what he'd done. The man was Roald Amundsen, and he had just navigated the Northwest Passage (for the first time in the 350 years of attempts), and had crossed over 500 miles of uncharted country by dogsled in the deepest Arctic winter from his ice-locked ship off the coast to announce his feat to the world. The message, going out over the telegraph line, was the news story of the decade.

By then, however, Eagle's star had faded. The stampeders had moved on to Nome and Fairbanks, followed by Judge Wickersham and his court. The importance of Fort Egbert declined, till it was abandoned in 1911. WAMCATS was replaced, seven years after it was installed, by wireless transmission. Eagle's population continually dwindled, to a low of 13 in 1959. Since then, with a resurgence of gold activity near Chicken and on the Fortymile, the establishment of the Yukon-Charley Rivers National Preserve, and a general influx of independent pioneer-types, Eagle has become a revitalized community, proud of its past and present.

Sights

The Eagle Historical Society is one of, if not the, most successful and well-organized groups in the state. The care, devotion, and thoroughness with which they display Eagle's awe-inspiring array of artifacts is something to see. And their guided tour ($2), which leaves from the courthouse porch at 10 a.m. daily, is really the only way to see it. While waiting in the morning, fill up your water containers at the **wellhouse** next door to the court. The well, dug 60 feet deep by hand in 1910, still pumps the cold H_2O—delicious. Struggle through the three heavy doors and either fill your bottle at the faucet, or stretch the gas-pump-type handle to the jugs in your vehicle.

The tour begins appropriately inside the **courthouse,** built in 1901 by Wickersham for $5000. All four rooms plus the hallway on the ground floor are covered with displays of the Han Indians, geology and archaeology, early pioneers, telegraph story, etc. Be sure to check out the front page of the Dec. 7, 1905

New York Times, with Amundsen's story, plus the map of the Northwest Passage in the hall. And don't miss the amazing Nimrod's false teeth and his relief map of the vicinity (made with newspaper and moose blood). Upstairs in Wickersham's courtroom is a small gift shop run by the Historical Society—great stuff and for a good cause.

Then you mosey down to the **Customs House** on the waterfront, another two-story museum packed with history. Study the six dated shots of the freezing of the Yukon River from Oct. 13, 1899, to Jan. 12, 1900, plus the photos upstairs of "wild" animals—Fred Ferwilliger's wolf pups, and Mae Collins' pet black bear.

Next you walk up to **Fort Egbert,** where your first stop is the granary, and a photo display of the restoration of the few remaining fort buildings, sponsored by Sen. Ted Stevens and financed by the BLM from 1975 to 1979. More exhibits are on display in the waterwagon shed and mule barn—at 150 feet long and 30 feet wide, one of the largest restored buildings in Alaska. Check out the prototype Sears chain saw in the barn, as

(GORDY OHLIGER)

well as the gold mining exhibit upstairs. Don't miss this tour: it's the thing to do in Eagle.

Others

Two and a half miles out 1st Ave. (take a right coming into town) is **Eagle Village,** a picturesque Indian settlement that predates the white settlers. Fish wheels operate just offshore, and racks of salmon dry under the clouds. The residents are friendly, but please respect their privacy. Back in town read the bulletin board outside the post office to see if anything's going on.

Practicalities

Follow the signs from town left to the free campground just beyond the cemetery (a few old markers; Nimrod's buried here): big, uncrowded, nice wooded sites, free firewood, vault toilets. There's an easy nature walk between the campground and the airstrip. Or stay inside at **Eagle Trading Co.** on the riverfront, where rooms start at $50. The **Riverside Café** next door is open 6:30 a.m.-8 p.m., with burgers and fries at $5.50, and $5 specials. They also have oh-so-fine showers, $4 for 15 minutes, but nobody's counting—unless of course you try to wash any potatoes! This is also the place to inquire about any locals (or travelers) heading to Dawson, Tok, or Fairbanks if you need a ride. Eagle Trading Company sells gas from a tricky pump at $1.70 a gallon.

Transportation

No public ground transportation is available to Eagle. It's a good four hours by car from Dawson, at least another five down to Tetlin Junction, depending on how long you play in the gold country. **Warbelow's Air Ventures,** tel. 547-2213, flies daily to Fairbanks at 9:50 a.m., $88 OW, and to Dawson City on Tues. and Thurs. at 2:50 p.m., $150. Plan carefully so that you're able to fit in the walking tour in the morning. Westours' *Yukon Queen* sails to Dawson at 2 p.m., arriving around 8:30—highly recommended.

Yukon-Charley Rivers National Preserve
Eagle itself is pretty far out there, but if you really want to disappear, you can explore Yukon-Charley Rivers National Preserve. This huge, 2.5-million-acre park is primitive, with no facilities or established transportation, and a skeleton Park Service staff with headquarters on the Fort Egbert strip at Eagle. The Yukon-Charley Rivers National Preserve Visitor Center on the corner of 1st and Fort Egbert Ave. has a huge selection of video maps and advice for those contemplating a trip. For further info, write to them at Box 64, Eagle, AK 99738.

The popular raft or canoe trip is from road's end at Eagle down the Yukon to road's end at Circle; allow five to 10 days. Or you can charter a bush plane to drop you and a boat way up around the Charley headwaters and float down to the Yukon. You must be highly experienced, entirely self-sufficient, and have at least a tolerance for, if not a love of, mosquitos. Check in at HQ for advice, conditions, and to leave your intended itinerary. **Tatondak Outfitters,** Box 55, Eagle, AK 99738, tel. 547-2221, rents rafts and can fly small groups into the bush or back from Circle.

TAYLOR HIGHWAY

Coming back down from Eagle south of Jack Wade Junction, the highway remains primitive, pretty, and fun. Have "long eyes" to enjoy the distant vistas. The road itself continues to be rough, especially when it descends, about six miles past the junction, into **Fortymile** country and the old **Jack Wade** mining camp, which consists of many abandoned buildings but modern mining machinery—take care not to trespass. In another three miles you round a bend, and there, like the biggest jungle gym you've ever seen, is **Dredge No. 1.** Though half the size of Dredge No. 4 on Bonanza Creek (and Dredge No. 8 near Fairbanks), and not in use since 1942, it's still solid as a rock, and you can climb over every inch of it—monkey heaven. For the next several miles, the rough road, mountains of tailings, and mining equipment will also remind you, on a smaller scale, of Bonanza Creek Road outside of Dawson. Four miles farther, stop off at the BLM **Walker Fork Campground** to

(LOUISE FOOTE)

stretch your legs—and maybe soak your feet if it's real hot. In a beautiful site where the South and Walker forks of the Fortymile meet, a footbridge across the creek leads to a three-minute trail to the top of the limestone wall—nice view of the valley, one of innumerable similar valleys in the immense Interior.

Fortymile Canoe Route

Canoeists frequent this stretch of the road to put in to the Fortymile and its forks. Mile 49 (West Fork bridge), Mile 66 (Mosquito Fork bridge), Mile 69 (Chicken), and Mile 75 (South Fork bridge) are all good places to start, with high enough water levels. Where you take out depends on your time and prior arrangements. O'Brien Creek bridge (Mile 112) is the closest, or float to Clinton Creek in Yukon Territory, which has a 40-km unmaintained road back to the Top of the World Highway, or just keep paddling into the Yukon River and down to Eagle or Circle, or the bridge at Mile 56 on the Dalton Highway, or all the way to the Bering Sea. Like Yukon-Charley, you're entirely on your own out here (except for skeeters so thick they can blot out the sun); help can be days away. The main route (Chicken to Eagle) is rated Class I and II with some Class III rapids and one Class IV. The BLM brochure lists the 20 or so USGS topo maps for the route.

To Tok

Twelve miles south of Walker Fork Campground is **Chicken** (pop. 39), the vernacular name for ptarmigan, which the miners mucking for gold around here in 1895 were unsure how to spell. Anyone who's read *Tisha* by Ann Purdy, the story of a young teacher who overcame enormous local odds in Chicken in the '20s, might want to make a pilgrimage to her home, up the road from the post office. The **Chicken Mercantile** sells gas and the usual burgers and booze, plus famous T-shirts, *Tisha,* and local gold. A cafe and bar are attached. **Goldpanner** gift shop and grocery is next door.

From here down to Tetlin Junction, the Taylor crests some passes, descends into some valleys, and encounters almost no civ-

ilization. Make sure your gas tank and water jug levels are sufficient. The road gets progressively smoother, wider, and faster the closer you get to the Alaska Highway, till you cruise down a long hill, come around a corner, and there, like blue velvet after days of sandpaper, is pavement, glorious pavement, your first in 305 miles.

Three miles west of Tetlin Junction, evidence of the Tok River fire becomes apparent. The wildfire, which started in early July 1990, burned nearly 3.2 million acres and cost $36 million to contain, making it the most complex and costly wildfire in Alaska history. A graphic display on "How Tok Was Saved" is exhibited at the Public Lands Visitor Center in Tok.

TOK

Twelve miles west of Tetlin Junction, and 96 miles from the border, Tok (pop. 1,200; rhymes with "joke") considers itself the "gateway to Alaska," and is the service center for several Native villages in the upper Tanana Valley. Where the Tok River empties into the Tanana, the Athabascan tribes once gathered to affirm peace among them, and Tok is usually translated to mean "Peace Crossing." The town itself grew from a highway construction camp in the mid-1940s, and is still unincorporated. The turnoff to Anchorage (326 miles) is in the town center; continue straight on the Alcan 101 miles to Delta Junction.

The thing to do in Tok is to visit the Alaska Division of Tourism's **Tok Public Lands Office,** open 8-8. Similar (though smaller) to the Public Lands Information Centers in Fairbanks and Anchorage, this is the place to collect brochures and maps for the whole state, pick the personnel's brains, catch a movie or slide show, and freshen up in the large bright bathrooms. The bulletin board outside the johns might have ride info. Exhibits include stuffed animals and a good historical time line. The local information center next door in a trailer is run by the Tok Chamber of Commerce.

Practicalities

A unique **youth hostel** is eight miles west of town at Mile 1322.5—take a left at Pringle Rd. and follow the signs (avoid the six-year-olds on ATVs!) about a mile on a rough rock road to the driveway. In an army-type tent cabin with a dirt floor you'll find 10 bunk beds, a kitchen and sitting area, and outhouses. Very rustic. Pick your spot, and the houseparents, who live up the driveway, will be around to collect your $5.50 (member), $8.50 (non) fee. Otherwise, pitch your tent at the good state campground, **Tok River State Recreation Site,** which survived the fire, five miles before Tok on the Alcan, $8 pp.

The **Gateway Motel,** tel. 883-4511, across from the visitor center, has rooms with shared bath starting at $25. Several places have public showers, including the **Northway** complex and Westours **KOA** at Tundra Lodge, $2 for five minutes. A half-dozen other motels in town start at $60. And nine (count 'em) RV parks accommodate the big fat fatties.

Fast Eddy's has good pizza and subs; **Husky Lounge** next door sometimes has live music. **Young's Cafe** at the junction serves breakfast all day. You can also grab something fast at **Tastee-Freez,** or pig out at the highly visible salmon bake.

The **Burnt Paw** next door to the Westmark has an interesting sled dog and equipment display with free demos nightly at 7:30 p.m.

Transportation

For years Tok has had the notoriety of being a hitchhiker's worst nightmare. Legends abound about men growing beards and women going through menopause while standing with their thumbs out at the junction. If only 12 hitchers are in front of you, and you only spend one night on the side of the road, consider yourself lucky. Luckily, Tok is a crossroads for **Alaskon Express** buses rolling between Skagway, Whitehorse, Beaver Creek, Fairbanks, and Anchorage, and you can catch the one going in your direction at least three times a week (ask at either visitor center).

DELTA

The next junction town is another 100 miles northwest, where the Alaska Highway technically ends. Fairbanks makes a claim to being the end of the famous road, a distinction that really belongs to Delta: not only does all the historical and current travel literature list the Alcan as 1,422 miles long (as opposed to the 1,520 to Fairbanks), but the Alaska Highway mileposts end with finality at the Delta Visitor's Center. The mileposts to Fairbanks then pick up at Mile 266 (the distance from Valdez on the Richardson Highway).

The Richardson was Alaska's first road. The WW II road designers specifically aimed the Alcan to join at Delta, connecting it to both Interior Alaska and tidewater. The Richardson was originally envisioned as an "all-American route" to the goldfields along the Yukon just before the turn of the century, and a trail was constructed in conjunction with the WAMCATS telegraph cable to Eagle. But with the shift of attention to the Fairbanks area in the early 1900s, the trail was redirected there and upgraded to a wagon road in 1907 under the auspices of Wilds P. Richardson, first president of the Alaska Road Commission.

Delta began as one of the numerous roadhouses along the trail, which were spaced a day's journey apart (roughly 30 miles). Bate's Landing was opened in 1906 at the confluence of the Delta and Tanana rivers, where travelers crossed the Tanana on a government-operated ferry, which used the current for propulsion by a method the Natives had been using for at least 5,000 years.

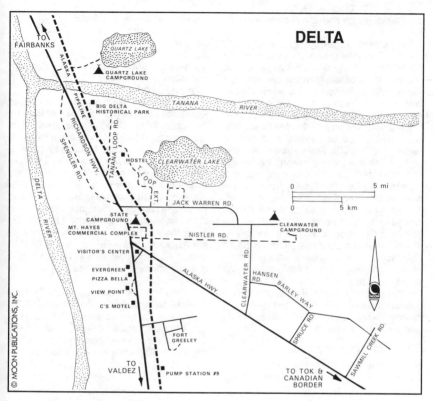

Delta hit the big time, however, with the construction of the Alcan, and when Allen Army Airbase (now Fort Greely) was established nearby as one of the many military installations along the highway. Delta received another boost when a pipeline construction camp was located here; the pipe crosses the Tanana right next to the highway—a spectacular first view of it for overland travelers. Delta services the largest agricultural area in the state, including nearly 100,000 acres (not all used) of grain farms and numerous smaller truck farms. And finally, the Delta area is also home to a herd of nearly 400 bison, which once outnumbered even caribou in Alaska, from an original 23 animals, transplanted from Montana 60-odd years ago,

Sights

As always, start at the **Visitor's Center,** in the "Triangle" at the junction. Open 8:30 a.m.-7:30 p.m., the center's exhibits include one on the Cold Regions Test Center of Fort Greely, and a Please Touch display of furs. Read the bulletin board and help yourself to coffee, peruse the books for sale, buy an "End of the Alaska Highway" certificate ($2), and eavesdrop on the innocent questions the *cheechakos* ask.

You can take a short loop through the **agricultural area** by heading back down the Alaska Highway eight miles; take a left at Sawmill Creek Rd., another left on Bailey Way, again on Hansen Rd., and one more on Clearwater, which delivers you back to the highway. Good views of the eastern peaks of the Alaska Range from the Clearwater area, if it's clear.

To get the total 360 degrees, though, head down to **Donnelly Dome,** 23 miles south on the Richardson. Go right on the gravel road at Mile 248, continue for a quarter mile past the second sharp bend; an obvious though unmarked trailhead is at the car park there. Allow half a day to the dome and back.

But if you only do one thing in Delta, take an enjoyable and educational stroll through history at **Big Delta State Historical Park,** eight miles past town toward Fairbanks, open 8 a.m.-7 p.m. Set in a scenic spot along the banks of the Tanana just below the pipeline crossing, this 20- to 30-minute self-guided walk features signs about Delta's crossroads traditions, WAMCATS, the Truckers' Rebellion, and others, as well as several restored buildings including Rika's Roadhouse, the ferryman's cabin, a barn, blacksmith shop, and ARC Garage. Ask about tours at the gift shop; have a bite at the Packhouse Pavilion. This is one of only two historical parks in the state (the other is Independence Mine near Wasilla) and is highly recommended.

Accommodations And Food

Delta has a **youth hostel,** tel. 895-4627, $5. Go seven miles toward Fairbanks and take a right on Tanana Loop Rd. (gravel). Continue one mile, go right on Tanana Loop Extension, and follow the AYH signs. The cabin has 10 beds and a kitchen.

You can pitch your tent at **Delta State Recreation Site,** a half mile west of town by the airport, $6 pp. Good view across the flats of the eastern Alaska Range. In the morning, grab a shower at the **Delta Self-Service Laundry,** another half mile west. **Fielding Lake State Recreation Site** is two miles west of the Richardson Highway at Mile 200.5 at 3,000 feet elevation. It's a rustic seven-site campground, right on the lake.

Or stay inside at the **Alaska 7 Motel,** (formerly the Alaska 6 and probably soon to be the Alaska 8), four miles up the Richardson toward Fairbanks, tel. 895-4848; $44 s, $50 d. **Kelly's Motel,** tel. 895-4667, in town has rooms for $45 s and $52 d.

Across from the Visitor Center on the Rich is **Pizza Bella;** Italian dishes start at $6.50, pizza at $9. Or pick up your own supplies at **L.P. Frontier Foods,** or **Diehl's Food Center.** And if you're nearby on July 4th, head for the Buffalo Barbecue at the junction, $8.

FAIRBANKS

Arguably no city in the North is closer to the Edge than Fairbanks. With several hundred miles of Arctic bush surrounding it on all sides, the frontier feeling is pervasive: haphazard layout, constant infrastructure improvements, heavy military presence, a hundred churches overflowing with large families on Sunday mornings, a colorful core of hard-drinking, hard-living "pioneers," and more Chevrolet Camaros and Pontiac Trans Ams per capita than anywhere else you've ever been. Second-largest town in the state, it's still no more than a quarter the size of Anchorage, with a compact, convenient, and hospitable hominess that Anchorage has long since forgotten. But it's still one of the largest population centers this far north on Earth.

The town itself isn't pretty, barely scenic, but for such an outback, plain, boxy place, Fairbanks, like the rest of Alaska, takes extrovert pride in itself; it has a lot to offer the visitors who stagger in from the bush and want to kick back or live it up for a few days. Plan on at least a couple of days here to dust off from the road and relax in comfort without abandoning the Edge—one of the best places in Alaska to combine all three.

Climate
Fairbanks has one of the widest temperature ranges of any major city in the world. The mercury can plummet to -60° F in January, and soar to 90° F in July, for a whopping 150-degree differential. In addition, one day in July could be 90 and cloudless, while the next day could be 40 and rainy. Visitors are often taken aback by Fairbanks' occasional sizzling summer days, and scramble for the few air-conditioned hotel rooms. During the mild days, the 22 hours of daylight are a novelty to travelers, but that hot sun beating relentlessly down on residents *all summer long* can make you just as crazy as 22 hours of darkness in December—and fry your pineal gland to a crisp!

The seasons here are pronounced. Spring generally occurs around Memorial Day weekend, or sometimes even over a one-day period! A 1986 Weather Service release cited May 22 as the day "the leaves finally sprouted" in Fairbanks: "The 24-hour transformation of the Fairbanks area from gray to green was quite dramatic." During the 90-day summer the foliage changes from green to yellow, orange, and red. Over Labor Day weekend, it generally goes brown. It can snow and drop into the teens anytime in September, when the first day of winter is still more than three months away. Winter solstice sees two hours of dim daylight, and then there's five more months till spring.

HISTORY

E.T. Barnette
In Aug. 1901, E.T. Barnette was traveling up the Tanana River on the *Lavelle Young* with a boatload of supplies bound for Tanacross to set up a trading center on a well-used gold rush trail. Unable to negotiate some rapids, Captain Charles Adams turned into the Chena River to try and bypass them, but got stuck on the Chena's silt-laden sandbars. Adams refused to go any farther, and Barnette refused to turn back, leaving the two men as stuck as the boat.

Peering through field glasses from a distant hill, Felice Pedrone (Felix Pedro, as he's remembered) watched the boat's progress— or lack thereof—by the smoke from its stacks. A mountain man and prospector extraordinaire, Pedro had been looking for gold in the huge wilderness north of the Tanana and Chena rivers for several years, and had found signs of color on some creeks near where he stood watching the steamer. However, running low on provisions, he was facing a several-hundred-mile roundtrip to Circle to restock, unless. . . .

Meanwhile, Capt. Adams was unceremoniously dumping Barnette, his wife, and their goods on the shore. "We cut some spruce and helped him get his freight off," Adams

The Yukon Quest is a 1,000-mile dogsled race between Whitehorse and Fairbanks.

recalled 30 years later. "We left Barnette furious. His wife was weeping on the bank. They were standing directly in front of the present site of [the heart of downtown Fairbanks]." That's when Pedro showed up, quietly informed Barnette of his prospect, and bought a winter's worth of supplies. Back at his promising creek, Pedro finally hit pay dirt.

News of the strike traveled far and fast. Miners abandoned played-out Klondike and Nome and headed for the tiny outpost on the Chena River, named after Illinois Senator Charles Fairbanks, who soon became vice president under Teddy Roosevelt. Unfortunately, Barnette wasn't content with his good fortune of owning most of the townsite of rich little Fairbanks. In 1911, he was tried for embezzling funds from his own Washington-Alaska Bank. Though he was acquitted, he left town with his family, never to return. His wife divorced him in 1920 in San Francisco; where he went from there, and when or how he died, are complete mysteries. Only one clear photograph of his face survives today: Barnette standing in a line with several other early Fairbanks bankers. But when the photo was found, old-timers were hard-pressed to identify which one was the town father. In fact, a discrepancy exists over his first name. In *E.T. Barnette,* Terrence Cole calls him Elbridge, while *The $200 Million Gold Rush Town,* by Jo Anne Wold, remembers him as Eldridge, and the city fathers commemorated him by naming an elementary school Ebenezer T. Barnette. Whatever his name, possibly no man embodies the boom-bust character of Fairbanks better than its founder, E.T. Barnette.

Gold

The Fairbanks strike differed markedly from the shiny shores of the Klondike and the golden sands of Nome—this gold was buried under frozen muck anywhere from eight to 200 feet deep. Fortune hunters quickly became discouraged and left, which rendered Fairbanks' boom much less explosive than Dawson's or Nome's. But even determined miners eventually reached the limits of both their endurance and the primitive placer-mining technology. After fires and floods, by 1913 when the road from Valdez to Fairbanks was completed, the town was in the midst of a serious bust cycle. But in 1923 the Alaska Railroad reached Fairbanks from Seward and Anchorage, which inaugurated the real Golden Age. Major mining corporations freighted up and installed the mechanical monsters required to uncover the gold, and eventually $200 million worth was dredged from the surrounding area. When the Alaska Highway was pushed through to Delta from Canada in 1942, connecting the Richardson Highway to the outside world, the city's future was assured.

Pipeline

A massive flood in the summer of 1967 nearly drowned the town, and the future looked bleak for a while, but in early '68 the Prudhoe Bay strike promised to drown the town *in oil* and Fairbanks' prospects looked bright again. Many local people invested heavily on speculation of a boom around the proposed pipeline; most went bust in the six years it took to start the project. But pipeline construction finally began in 1974, and Fairbanks boomed yet again. Of the 22,000 total pipeline workers, 16,000 were dispatched from Fairbanks' union halls. Suddenly demand far exceeded supply, making it a seller's market for everything from canned food to cocaine, from housing to hookers. In fact, there were so many hookers, and the unions grew so strong, that the hookers themselves sought union representation to get the city council and cops off their backs, so to speak.

So many people poured in with dreams of the big bucks that officials took out ads in Lower 48 newspapers telling everyone to stay away. Only half the job seekers ever got hired, and the length of the lines at the bank were only exceeded by those at the unemployment office. For three years you could barely utter or hear a sentence in Fairbanks that didn't contain the word "pipeline." The word itself eventually reached almost mystical status, with the locals blaming the exploding population, rampant crime, deteriorating social services, long separations from home and family, and every other local problem on it, while the oil companies and workers hailed it as the second coming itself. For better or for worse, Fairbanksans mined this vein for three years, and those with enough brains and self-control set themselves up for the bust that was sure to follow. And did. E.T. Barnette would've been proud. Those were the days.

Modern Times

Like the rest of the state, the town surfed the oil wave for almost a decade, and has survived the peaks and valleys ever since. "Pipeline" seems still to be the magic word, in fact. A proposed 769-mile natural gas pipeline out of Prudhoe Bay has gone the way of 16-cylinder automobiles and first novels. But Governor Hickel is currently (Sept. 1991) floating a proposal for a 3,000-mile, $150 billion *water* pipeline from Alaska to California under the Gulf and Pacific. The feasibility study has been assigned to Paul Bunyan and his faithful ox, Babe.

SIGHTS

The smoothest sight around hard-edged Fairbanks may be the rounded hills that surround the bowl at the bottom of which Fairbanks sits, flat as a mackerel. It's not a particularly colorful town, yet only the savviest tour drivers make the *Solar Borealis* (see

The Trans-Alaska Pipeline snakes above ground through the vast rolling interior.

(GORDY OHLIGER)

below), a psychedelic public art sculpture at the airport, a stop on their city tour. But the residents do their bit to beautify, and the profusion of potted, planted, and painted flowers really spruces up the place. Walk around downtown to get the frontier flavor, and be sure to wander through the nearby residential neighborhoods for the flowers, log cabins, and huge heads of cabbage. Or just loiter at the corner of 1st and Cushman, counting the Camaros.

Downtown

Start out at the **Fairbanks Visitors Bureau** (open daily 8-6:30) on 1st Ave. in a sod-roofed log cabin by the Chena River. Load yourself down with a few pounds of paper: be sure to get the excellent and venerable *Interior and Arctic Alaska Visitors Guide* tabloid put out the Fairbanks *Daily News-Miner*, and the *Fairbanks Visitor's Guide* brochure, a comprehensive listing of local practicalities, as well as the two excellent handouts, *Fairbanks Walking Tour*, describing almost 50 historical sites within a 10-square-block area downtown, and *Fairbanks Driving Tour*. Or join the informative guided walking tours which leave the office at 10 a.m. and 3 p.m. You can call the Tourist Office at 456-5774, or get their recorded "InfoLine" with the day's events at 456-INFO. A cadre of volunteers fluent in a dozen foreign languages is on call to translate for anyone who needs it.

Just outside the log cabin is the new **Golden Heart Park,** officially opened in 1987. The centerpiece is a large heroic sculpture of *The First Unknown Family,* created by Malcolm Alexander, who also did *Builders of the Pipeline* in Valdez. The statue's fountain foundation is covered with 36 bronze plaques, some of which describe the growth of the park's large corporate sponsors, while others list the names of sponsoring individuals.

Walk a block up to Cushman and 2nd Ave., to the storefront of the **Yukon Quest,** tel. 452-7954, open 10-5. The Yukon Quest race was established in 1983 as an alternative to the Iditarod dogsled race from Anchorage to Nome. The first 1,000-mile race from Fairbanks to Whitehorse by way of Circle, Eagle, and Dawson City was run in Feb. 1984 by 26 mushers. Now in its ninth year, the $50,000 purse is split by the top 15 racers, with the winner earning $15,000. The storefront displays equipment, maps, photographs, newspaper clippings, and sells yearly programs and prints of the races, along with T-shirts, sweatshirts, and calendars.

Next, walk another block up Cushman for the **Alaska Public Lands Information Center,** 3rd Ave. at Courthouse Square, tel. 451-7352, open daily 8:30 a.m.-9 p.m. in summer, 10-6 in winter. A combination museum and information bureau, this excellent facility represents eight state and federal agencies, from the Alaska Division of Tourism to the U.S. Geological Survey. You can easily spend a couple of hours here looking and playing: interesting aerial and relief maps hang on the walls, four-minute videos give thumbnail sketches on different aspects of the six geographical regions of Alaska; old-time stereoscopic viewers show three-dimensional views of historic Alaska; a touch-activated trip-planning computer is programmed with more than 200 public-land sites throughout the state; tasteful displays include photographs, taxidermy, Native artifacts, etc. You can view scheduled films in their comfortable 35-seat theater every two hours from 10-8. Starting in 1991, you can make reservations, seven to 21 days in advance, for Denali shuttle bus seats and campground sites. The office sells prints, slides, books, and tapes—take advantage of this place.

Across The River

Visit the **Immaculate Conception Church** (1904), just across the river from the Tourist Office, for its beautiful stained-glass windows. Farther north along Illinois St. are the old wooden **coal bunkers** erected in the 1930s to supply fuel to steam locomotives. They are still in use; just park your truck under a chute and pull the rope.

Keep walking north (about a mile) on Illinois and take a left at College Road. In another mile is **Creamer's Field Migratory Waterfowl Refuge,** where you might observe migratory birds and most of the common vegetation of the Interior. In early April, the

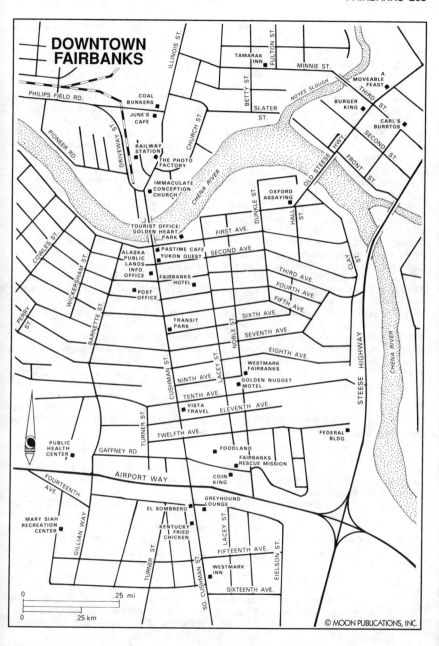

DOWNTOWN FAIRBANKS

© MOON PUBLICATIONS, INC.

field is plowed and tons of barley are spread around it. Canada geese stop off at the field in mid-April on their migratory route—a local herald for the arrival of spring. On the two-mile nature path, all eight types of trees native to the region are found, within the common local habitats: forest, shrub, muskeg, and riparian. The high point of the trail, literally, is a 20-foot-high observation platform, from which you are supposed to be able to spot wildlife—if you can see anything through the mass of skeeters buzzing around your head. The trail is mostly boardwalk over swamp, with the predictable insectoid results. Either wear lots of clothes and headgear, or just shorts and a T-shirt, and come here to jog. Pretty good jogging trail, actually, with fun ups and downs. Even though mosquitos flap their wings 1,000 times a minute, you can outrun them! The trail begins beside the Alaska Department of Fish and Game, 1300 College Rd. (Red Line). Take the long gravel driveway between Fish and Game and the Creamer's Field parking lot to the gate at the dairy; pick up a free trail guide there. The dairy is the oldest in Alaska (1904) and the northernmost in the Western Hemisphere. Charles Creamer owned it from 1928-66, when he sold it to Fish and Game for use as a migratory waterfowl refuge.

To The University

Continue on College Rd. to the **University of Alaska, Fairbanks** (UAF), main educational facility in the state. Opened in 1922 as Alaska Agricultural College, there were six students and as many faculty; today almost 4,500 students attend the 2,500-acre campus. This facility is highly regarded for its Arctic research and Alaska Native studies. The bus drops you at the Campus Commuter Terminal. Ask the driver or any student to direct you to the **Wood Campus Center** nearby, where you can pick up a free map of the grounds, check the ride board for people going in your direction, and grab a cheap breakfast or good lunch in the cafeteria or pub.

A free shuttle bus runs every 15 minutes from the Commuter Terminal around campus; grab it for a ride to the excellent **University Museum,** tel. 474-7505, open 9-7 June and July, 9-5 May and Sept., $3, $2.50 over 60 and under 12. You can also catch an express bus from the Transit Park downtown to the museum eight times a day, from 2:15 to 8:45 p.m. The museum collection is divided into the state's six geographical areas. The wildlife and gold exhibits are mind-boggling; the Russian artifacts and permafrost display are exceptional. Other highlights include a three-ton copper nugget and 425-pound quartz crystal, 1905 Sheldon car, an antler couch, a 36,000-year-old bison, polar dinosaur bones, and the aurora video from the university's research center at Poker Flats. The gift shop sells the usual books, prints, and cards, and some unusual items like fish neckties. On a clear day Mt. McKinley, across the broad Tanana Valley, can be seen in all its awesome eminence from the museum.

Monday through Fri. at 10 a.m., two-hour guided walks leave from the museum, led by a student. Other activities on campus include mining movies, daily at 2 p.m. in the Brooks Building. Tours of the Large Animal Research Station (musk ox, caribou, and reindeer) are conducted on Tues. and Sat. at 1:30 and 3 p.m., $4, on Yankovich Rd. a mile off Ballaine Rd., or go anytime and use the viewing stand. The Agricultural and Forestry Experimental Station is below the museum at the west end of campus; call 474-7653 for directions and information about the self-guided tour.

Alaskaland

This enjoyable theme park, the only one of its kind in the state, occupies the site of the 1967 state centennial celebration. Many of the buildings and exhibits are authentic, brought here from various locations around Alaska. See the gold rush town, native village, mining valley, and the genuine 1933 sternwheel riverboat, which houses the info center. There's also a 1915 carousel ride ($1), miniature golf, a train ride, Wickersham House and Harding Car, salmon bake, big playground, and Palace Saloon. Especially provocative are the Native arts and lifestyle exhibitions and performances. The parking lot is open to motor homes (no facilities, $5 a night). Alaskaland is open daily 11-9, admission free. The salmon bake is $7.95 for lunch and $16 for dinner. A free salmon bake shuttle bus runs from 4-10 p.m., and stops at the major hotels from the Polaris downtown all the way out to Sophies Plaza at University and Airport Way, plus the Norlite Campground. Good free rides. The Blue Line (Airport Way) also passes Alaskaland's gates (hourly on weekdays).

Dog Mushers' Museum

For everything you ever wanted to know about dog-sledding, check out the extensive exhibits on the history, technology, and competition of this northern sport at this fine museum. Sponsored by the Alaska Dog Mushers Association, demonstrations are given out back, around the staging area for many of the local dog-sled races. Also, videos can be turned on for you-are-there views of the big statewide competitions. A gift shop sells souvenirs of the races and the sport. At 4 Mile Farmers Loop Road, tel. 457-MUSH, open daily 9:30-4:30.

Solar Borealis

Like the *Nimbus* in Juneau, the *Solar Borealis* ("Northern Sun") was built with funds from Alaska's "Percent for Art" program, which earmarks one percent of the state's construction budget for public art. This $107,000 sculpture, selected from over 71 pieces submitted for the site, was created by San Franciscan Robert Behrens, and unveiled in June 1985. The welded-steel archway rises 50 feet above the exit from Fairbanks International Airport. Special diffraction tiles attached to the front of the sculpture reflect all shades of the spectrum, depending on what angle you view it from—so long as the sun is shining. Otherwise, the metallic trellis appears stark and silvery-white. Designed specifically for the few minutes of potential sunlight during the deepest dark of Fairbanks' long winter night, the best time to view it is on a clear bright day from 10 a.m. to 1 p.m.—guaranteed to give you acid flashbacks, even if you've never taken LSD.

ACTIVITIES

Hiking

For the local trail, see "Creamer's Field" above. Farther afield, for hiking and backpacking opportunities in the White Mountains, see p. 284; in the Pinnell Mountains, see p. 282.

Biking

Fairbanks has an excellent series of connecting bike routes: from downtown along the river to Alaskaland; from University and Airport out a ways on Chena Pump Rd.; and a great up-and-down route on Farmer's Loop Rd. from the Steese Highway to the university.

Canoeing

A quiet backwater, Noyes Slough, loops through the north side of Fairbanks from the Chena River. If you're in the mood for adventure, consider renting a Coleman canoe from **Beaver Sports**, 3480 College Rd., tel. 479-2494. They charge $25 a day for the first two days, $15 per day after that. Launch your canoe in the slough and you're off on a scenic 20-km circle trip. Take a lunch, and start by heading east for Graehl Landing to avoid having to battle the current in the Chena River later. If you run into any obstructions in the slough, just portage around them. If this sounds tame, why not paddle your canoe down the Chena River to the Tanana, then on to the town of Nenana (12 hours). Check at the Alaska Railroad station about the possibility of bringing canoe and self back to Fairbanks on the train.

Swimming

Three indoor pools are open to the public. You can swim at **Hamme Pool** at Lathrop High School, Airport and Cowles, tel. 456-2969, Tues.-Fri. 2-4 and 7-9; you can also take showers there every day from 6 a.m.-9 p.m. Call **Mary Siah Recreation Center**, 1025 14th Ave., tel. 456-6119, for their complete list of hours. **Patty Gym Pool** at UAF, tel. 474-7205, is open Mon.-Thurs. 7:30-9 p.m. for $3 per visit.

Ice Skating

No need to wait for winter freeze-up in this town. **Big Dipper Ice Arena,** 19th and Lathrop, tel. 456-6683, is open Mon.-Sat. 11:45 a.m.-1:15 p.m., plus additional odd hours. Admission with skate rental is $2.50.

Fishing

Fishing in the Chena River for grayling is fair; they must be 12 inches or longer to keep. Better grayling fishing is found at the Chatanika River, between miles 30 and 40 on the Steese Highway toward Circle. Chum, silver, and a few kings run up here from mid-July. Chena Lakes Recreation Area has good rainbow-trout fishing. Fish and Game provides a recorded hotline of fishing tips, updated once or twice a week, tel. 452-1525. For guided fishing trips to the Interior, check under "Guide Service" in the Yellow Pages.

ACCOMMODATIONS

Hostel And Camping

The summer-only **Fairbanks Youth Hostel** was shut down in 1991 when the Tanana Valley Fairgrounds refused to renew the hostel's lease. Kindly Paul Schultz, the manager, opened his house to some of the 1,000 or so overnighters, and at last report had yet to find a new location for the hostel. Ask when you arrive. The **campground** at the Fairgrounds on College Rd. at Aurora Drive charges $9 for a site (up to four people—two tents). Showers are free and campfires are allowed. This campground is in a much more natural setting than **Norlite Campground** on Peger Rd. near Alaskaland, which is like camping in a parking lot. They charge tenters $15 d, and RVs $20 for full hookup. The campground has its own laundromat, showers (25 cents for the first five minutes), store, and restaurant, but no campfires are permitted. Norlite is very convenient to Alaskaland and the salmon bake bus. Otherwise, get there on the Blue Line; the last bus out leaves at 6:45 p.m. Mon.-Friday.

A little-known campground in town is behind the university, but it's only for college-connected campers. **John Alfonsi Sr. Memorial Campground,** at the very back of UAF on S. Koyukuk Dr., has 15 walk-in and 15 drive-in sites, restrooms but no showers, and a two-week maximum stay. For showers, walk down to the Patty Gym or hockey rink. Buy the camping permit from the campground caretaker or at the ASUA offices in the Wood Center.

Chena River State Recreation Site, locally known as Chena Wayside, is a state campground on University Ave. just north of Airport Way (Red or Blue lines). It has 59 sites, running water but no showers, fireplaces, boat launch, and fishing—not bad for city camping, $12 pp. **River's Edge RV Park** is a handy new campground on Boat St. off Airport Way near University Ave, tel. 474-0286, charging $12 for tenters, with free showers.

Rooming Houses

Several houses rent rooms by the night (around $20) or week ($100) near downtown, with shared bath and kitchen. Mostly for men, they're not a bad deal if you're used to that kind of place, and not hard to get used to if you're not. Check the classifieds in the *Daily News-Miner* under "Furnished Rooms."

Moderate

A good deal for Fairbanks is the **Golden North Motel,** 4888 Airport Way, tel. 479-6201. It's a little out of town, and the nearest bus (Blue Line) passes about a quarter mile away, but their courtesy van will drop you off and pick you up if you ask nicely. The motel rooms could be larger and fresher, but have cable TV; $49.95 for one bed, $55 for two, $10 key deposit.

Downtown, the **Alaskan Motor Lodge,** 419 4th Ave., tel. 452-4800, charging $54 s, $65 d, is a little more expensive than the **Fairbanks Hotel,** 517 3rd Ave., tel. 456-6440, at $38 s or $44 d shared bath, $59 s or d private bath. But the Alaskan has nicer rooms, TV, and might be quieter. Walk around the corner and compare the two for yourself.

About a mile from downtown, within walking distance of the train depot, the **Tamarac Inn,** 252 Minnie St., tel. 456-6406, charges

$60 s, $72 d, $150 s weekly shared bath, $200 s weekly private bath, plus $25 each additional person, and is a better deal than both the above. The large shopping malls three blocks from the Tamarac make the kitchenettes in each room especially convenient and cost-cutting. The 104-room **Borealis Hotel** is out by the university, just off Geist Rd. at 700 Fairbanks St., tel. 479-3015; $40 d, showers down the hall.

Bed And Breakfasts

The B&B scene in Alaska has exploded over the last several years, with more and more private homes opening up their spare rooms and spare time to the tourist gold rush. Most charge around $40 s, $50 d, with full breakfasts and limited transportation. Get a list of roughly three dozen B&Bs in and near Fairbanks from the Visitor Center. They can come and go pretty fast, but the venerable ones (meaning they appeared in the last edition of this guide) include: **Joan's**, tel. 479-6918, **Fairbanks B&B**, tel. 452-4967, **Chena River B&B**, tel. 479-2532, and **Ravenswood**, tel. 457-6613.

Emergency Accommodations

If you're broke, **Fairbanks Rescue Mission,** tel. 452-6608, next to Foodland, offers free accommodations. Check in at 6:30 p.m. and be up by 6 a.m. for the Christian service and breakfast. The **Salvation Army Shelter,** 117 1st Ave., tel. 452-5005, has a 12-bed dormitory for men, six beds for women. Check in any time there's room, no later than 10 p.m., and be out by 8 a.m. Because these facilities are provided for locals, use them only if you have to. Freeloading might take a space that could be used by someone truly in need.

Other Emergency Accommodations

In the upper reaches, the best deal is at the **Super 8,** 1909 Airport Way, tel. 451-8888, charging $76 s, $81 d, all rooms air-conditioned. **The Great Land Hotel,** downtown at 723 1st Ave. on the river, tel. 452-6661, charges $85 s, $90 d, and their rates don't go up in summer—because they're closed in the winter! Most of the other hotels—Westmark's two, Sophie's Plaza, Captain Bartlett, etc.—

charge over $100 a night rack rates, but if you have a business card, you can try for a corporate discount.

FOOD

Breakfast

The **Bakery,** 69 College Rd. near the corner of Illinois, open Mon.-Sat. 6:30 a.m.-10 p.m., Sun. 7-4, is highly recommended for any meal, but especially for big breakfasts and fine baked goods. Look for their coupons in the *Visitors Guide* tabloid. **Maria's Place Cafe** downtown at the corner of 4th and Lacey serves breakfast all day. **Sam's Sourdough Cafe,** open 6 a.m.-10 p.m., has good coffee shop fare. Similar is **June's Cafe** on Illinois St. at the corner of Phillips Field Rd—friendly efficient service and reasonable prices. Have breakfast here before catching the train to Denali; open 6-7 Mon.-Fri., 7-5 Saturday. **Freres Jacques,** 4001 Geist Rd. in West Valley Plaza, serves authentic French cuisine and baked goods for breakfast such as crepes (and lunch and dinner); it's very popular with the locals.

Lunch

The best salad bar is in the gourmet/deli section of **Foodland Supermarket,** corner of Gaffney and Lacey, just south of downtown. Excellent selection of fruit, vegies, salads, soup, taco bar—$2.59 a pound. Pay for your salad at the cashier, then sit and eat in the deli.

Whole Earth Natural Foods sells bulk groceries Mon.-Sat. 10-7; their deli, open Mon.-Sat. 11-3, has great meatless burgers, tempeh Reubens, salads, tortilla wraps, and the like. Stroll next door to **Hot Licks,** for homemade ice cream. Or walk around the corner into the shopping center to **TCBY's,** which stands for The Country's Best Yogurt.

Souvlaki, just across the Cushman Street Bridge on Illinois near the *News-Miner,* seves good Greek gyros and salads.

Fast-food row is on Airport Way between Lathrop and Wilbur: **Wendy's, McDonald's, Denny's, Pizza Hut, Sizzler, Shakey's,** and a **7-11.** A McDonald's and Wendy's are also in the mall area near the Tamarac Inn. The two **Food Factories,** one at the Bentley Mall and the other on S. Cushman at 17th, seem to enjoy a good reputation around town, even though the prices are pretty high and the food—burgers and subs, mostly—tastes kind of like the name sounds.

Dinner

Try **Pasta Bella,** 706 2nd Ave. across from Nordstrom, for fresh pasta, homemade bread, gourmet pizza, and subs. Recommended.

Peking Gardens, best Chinese in town, moved in late 1989 to a new and large building at 1101 Noble St. at 12th.

Heading south out of town on S. Cushman you'll find two Mexican restaurants: **El Sombrero** (corner Airport Way next to the **Drop In Cafe,** which is the oldest restaurant in Fairbanks—opened in 1950) and **Los Amigos** (28th Ave.) which is the better. But for great gourmet Mexican, try **Don Diego's,** corner of College Rd. and the Old Steese in the old Arby's building—expensive but worth every penny.

For a splash, try **Clinkerdaggers,** around the corner in the Bentley Mall, College Rd.—delicious.

Also as for a splash, if you're not sick of salmon bakes by now, try the one at Alaskaland. For $15 you get the usual fish or ribs and salad bar; however, the salmon is superb, kings caught around Sitka and flown in fresh daily. The owner grew up in Juneau where his father was a commercial fisherman, so he knows his fish.

The fanciest rooms in town are the **Bear and Seal** at the Westmark Fairbanks; **Club 11,** 11 miles east on the Richardson toward North Pole; and the **Turtle Club,** 10 Mile Old Steese in Fox. For the **Pumphouse,** see "Entertainment" below.

ENTERTAINMENT

Drinkin' And Dancin'

For the best view in town, have a drink (but skip the food) at **Tiki Cove,** top of the Polaris Hotel, corner of Lacey and 1st Avenue. For a nice riverside drink and hors d'oeuvres, head out to the Pumphouse, 1.3 Mile Chena Pump Rd., tel. 479-8452. A National Historical Monument, the Pumphouse was built in 1933 to pump water up Chena Ridge to provide pressure for the hydraulic "giants" used in gold dredging. Renovated in 1978, the restaurant and bar has a fascinating interior of mining and pumping artifacts.

Don't be put off by the weird exterior of the **Greyhound Lounge,** corner of Airport and Cushman, tel. 452-7977. It's walkable from downtown, the room is large and comfortable, the dance floor is huge, and if the band is halfway decent, you've got it made. Otherwise, get your fill of droning Top 40 at **Sunset Strip,** 345 Old Richardson Highway, tel. 456-4754, the most popular night spot in town. But if you wanna *rock,* head straight for the **Howling Dog Saloon,** 11 Mile Old Steese Highway in Fox, which advertises itself (probably accurately) as the "Farthest Northern Rock 'N' Roll Bar in the World." The house band in this classic barn-type bar, The Flyers, will get you jumping up and down in a nightlong aerobic frenzy. Note the steel weld-ring hanging over the bar; when a particular local starts to get a good buzz on and hits the ring with a hammer, the sound easily overpowers the band's wall of amplifiers, and the vibrations are picked up on the university's seismograph. Also check out the flags from around the world.

Movies

The eight-screen **Goldstream Cinema** is on Airport Way at Lathrop, tel. 456-5113; a four-screen complex is at **The Center,** Airport Way and Market, tel. 479-3800. Movies might also be showing at **Alaskaland Civic Center** Mon. through Wed. at 8, $4. Finally, don't forget about the 30 free documentaries at the **Alaska Public Lands Information Center,** 3rd and Cushman.

Saloon Theaters

The **Palace Saloon** at Alaskaland, tel. 456-5960, offers a musical comedy revue nightly all summer, written and performed by Jim Bell, in his third decade at the Palace. The show (and times and prices) change every year, but are generally around 8 p.m. for $8-9. The **Malemute Saloon** in Ester, 10 miles south of Fairbanks, tel. 479-2500, has been a local institution since 1958, putting on a musical revue and Robert Service recitations nightly at 8 p.m., Fri. and Sat. at 10 p.m., $5. You sit at plywood and beer-barrel tables; the pitchers keep coming and the peanut shells mingle with the two-inch-deep sawdust. (For other entertainment in Ester, see p. 277.)

Baseball
Two local teams, the Fairbanks Goldpanners and North Pole Nicks, play in a semi-pro league (similar to Triple-A in the minors) against each other (a sizzling rivalry) and other teams throughout Alaska, Hawaii, and the West Coast. The games are played at Growden Field, 2nd and Wilbur, behind Alaskaland, starting at 7:30 p.m. The famous Midnight Sun game, played around the summer solstice, starts at 11 p.m. and goes nine innings without using the field's artificial lights.

Events
Fairbanksans have roughly 90 days a year to get their fill of outdoor extravaganzas—without having to worry about frostbite, that is—and they go at it with a vengeance. The first big event of the season is summer solstice's **Midnight Madness** (June 20-21), another excuse for department store sales. Next comes **Golden Days,** between the second and third weekends in July—a week-long party culminating in The Grand Parade. The whole town turns out, and if you happen to be there, even without your camera, you won't forget it. Next comes the **World Eskimo-Indian Olympics,** a 26-year-old event featuring Alaska Native athletic games, dance, and art. This three-day event, held at the Big Dipper Recreation Arena at 19th and Lathrop, tel. 456-6683, includes such unusual competitions as Ear Pulling, Greased Pole Walk, Kneel Jump, Knuckle Hop, Seal Skinning, Toe Kick, and Blanket Toss. It could be one of the most exotic and memorable events in Alaska. Finally, the **Tanana Valley State Fair** takes place at the Fairgrounds, College Rd., the second and third weeks of August. Dress warmly.

SHOPPING AND SERVICES

Gift shops abound downtown; **Arctic Travelers** at 201 Cushman (and Alaskaland) is the biggest. You'll find **Penney's, Nordstrom,** and **Woolworth's** nearby. If you're looking for gold nuggets at "spot" prices, go to **Oxford Assaying,** 208 Wendell. For groceries go to **Foodland,** Lacey and Gaffney; the two **Super-Value** stores, at the Gavora and Shoppers Forum malls, could have better (though more expensive) produce. But the best produce in town can be bought at **Green Gopher** fruit stand, 700 College Rd. across from the Wedgewood apartment complex. **Alaska Native Arts and Crafts Center,** 1603 College Rd., tel. 452-8164, is Native-owned and -operated, featuring handmade crafts.

Services
The **post office** is right downtown on 5th Avenue. The most convenient **laundromat** is Coin King, across from Foodland. But bring your bankroll—$3 a load to wash and dry. Next door to Coin King is a do-it-yourself **car wash;** again, bring your quarters in a wheelbarrow: 25 cents for 20 seconds of hot water. To wash your own self, **B&C Laundromats,** one at 416 3rd St. (corner of Steese Hwy.), the other at Campus Corner Mall (near University Ave.), have public showers: $2.50 for 15 minutes. Or shower then swim at **Mary Siah Recreation Center;** call 452-1451 to find out their limited hours. The bargain haircut of the North can be had at **New Concepts Beauty School,** 1019 College Rd., tel. 452-4684: $10 by students about to graduate into the real world of beauty parlors.

Vista Travel, 911 Cushman, tel. 456-7888, is the Fairbanks agent for the state ferry system, and will happily and helpfully sell you tickets for any other kind of transportation. If you'd like some film developed quickly, see Robin at the **Photo Factory,** 226 Illinois Street. If you need a doctor, the **Fairbanks Public Health Center** is at 800 Airport Way (corner of Gillam), tel. 452-1776, or look up "Health and Social Services" under State Government Offices in the blue pages of the phone book. If they can't help try the **Fairbanks Clinic,** 1867 Airport at Wilbur, tel. 452-1761—$80 to see a doctor. For emergencies, drag yourself to **Memorial Hospital** at 1650 Cowles, tel. 452-8181.

INFORMATION

For the **Fairbanks Visitors Bureau,** and the **Alaska Public Lands Information Center,** see p. 264. Topographical maps of all of Alaska are sold in Room 126 in the Federal Building, 101 12th Ave. (open Mon.-Fri. 9 a.m.-4:30 p.m.). Visit also the **Northern Alaska Environmental Center,** 218 Driveway, tel. 452-5021, north of the river near the railway station—great T-shirts.

Noel Wien Library

The Noel Wien Library, corner of Airport Way and Cowles, is a very comfortable and complete facility. One look inside tells you a lot about Fairbanks' nine months of winter. Over 60% of borough residents hold library cards, compared to an average of 15-25% nationally. Odd hours, call 452-5177 for info. Noel Wien was a pioneer bush pilot who, with his two brothers, founded Wien Airlines. The library was built in 1977 on the site of Weeks Field, the first airport in Fairbanks.

Bookstores

Ubiquitous **Book Cache** is in University Mall, corner Airport and University Ave., tel. 479-6727. **Waldenbooks** is in the Bentley Mall,

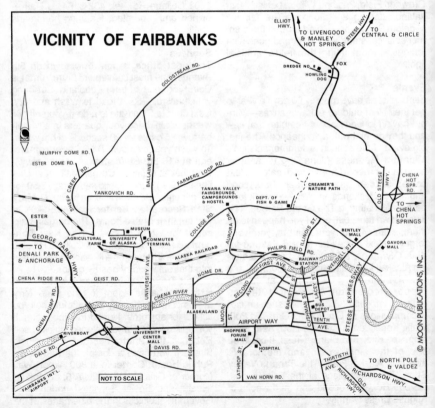

VICINITY OF FAIRBANKS

© MOON PUBLICATIONS, INC.

NOT TO SCALE

College Rd. and Steese Hwy., tel. 456-8088. **Village Bookshop,** in the Shoppers Forum (Airport Way and Cowles), has a limited selection, tel. 456-8206. **Baker and Baker,** in the North Gate Square Mall, Old Steese Highway, tel. 456-2278, has an excellent Alaskana section, including out-of-print books. **Gulliver's Books,** at Campus Corner on College Rd. and University Ave., is an Alaskan used-bookstore chain. Good bargains here.

TRANSPORTATION

By Air
Fairbanks International Airport (FAI) is six miles southwest of downtown. Greatly expanded in 1984, the second floor houses a gift shop, snack shop, and lounge. On the first floor are an unmanned info booth with a bunch of brochures, a few stuffed animals, and the Curtiss JN-4D "Jenny" biplane used by Carl Ben Eielson, one of the earliest and most famous bush pilots from the area.

Alaska Airlines, tel. 452-1661, flies five times daily between here and Anchorage; **Mark Air,** tel. 452-7577, has three flights daily. Both charge around $150 OW and $300 RT. **Air North,** tel. 474-0225, flies to Dawson ($195) and Whitehorse ($360) daily; buy your ticket at least 24 hours in advance, or else pay the price. **Warbelows,** tel. 474-0518, flies to Eagle and Dawson, as well as Central, Ft. Yukon, and a number of other bush communities in the northern Interior.

There is no city bus service out to the airport; transfers are provided by **Prestige Limo,** tel. 479-2036, $5, or **King Cab** limo service, tel. 456-5464, $5.

By Train
The **Alaska Railroad** departs Fairbanks at 8:30 a.m., arriving Denali at 12:30 p.m. ($39) and Anchorage at 8 p.m. ($108). The northbound train departs Anchorage daily at 8:30 a.m. and is scheduled to arrive at Denali Park at 3:50 p.m. ($78) and in Fairbanks at 8 p.m.; The train leaves Denali for Fairbanks at 4 p.m.; $39 OW, bicycle $2 extra. Tour-bus fares to Denali and Anchorage are comparable to the train, though minivan fares are

much cheaper. But the train is a more comfortable, enjoyable, and historical way to see this part of Alaska.

If you want to go in luxury, however, buy a ticket for the superdome vistacruisers hooked onto the end of the train, run by Tour Alaska and Westours. The train depot is at 280 N. Cushman, tel. 456-4155, only a five-minute walk to downtown, 10 minutes to the local transit terminal.

By Bus
Gray Line, Alaska Sightseeing, Royal Hiway, and **Denali Express** arrive in Fairbanks from Anchorage; Denali Express is cheapest ($75). Gray Line, Royal Hiway, and **Alaskon Express** arrive from Whitehorse and Dawson; **Alaska Sightseeing** shows up from Valdez. Keep reading for details.

From Fairbanks, bus transportation southbound is good. **Denali Express,** a newer company run by young locals, has the least expensive deal to Denali ($25) and Anchorage ($75) in a 14-seat minivan. Their van departs from the Polaris Hotel at 3 p.m., arrives Denali at 5:30, and arrives Anchorage at 11. You can call them at (800) 327-7651, or in Anchorage at 274-8539.

Alaska Sightseeing Company, 250 Cushman at Courthouse Square, tel. 452-8518, is primarily a tour operation, but they also have regularly scheduled bus service to Anchorage and Valdez. From Fairbanks, their bus leaves daily at 8:30 a.m., $42 OW to Denali and $120 OW to Anchorage. They also go to Valdez on Mon., Wed., and Fri. at 7:30 a.m. for $103.

Gray Line/Westours, tel. 452-2843, charges $100 from Fairbanks to Anchorage.

Eastbound, **Gray Line** offers a tour package from Fairbanks to Whitehorse, overnighting at their Westmark Inn in Beaver Creek, Yukon, near the border, for $299 inclusive. If you just want transportation, you can take their **Alaskon Express** bus, tel. 452-2843, from the Westmark Inn, at 9 a.m. daily, to Tok for $42, then on to Beaver Creek, where you provide your own sleeping arrangements, and to Whitehorse ($135 from Fairbanks) or Haines ($156 from Fairbanks) the next day.

Getting Around

Fairbanks' public bus system, Metropolitan Area Commuter Service (MACS) is just that: a commuter service which runs weekdays from around 6:30 a.m.-7 p.m. After that, the lines run infrequently till around 9:30 p.m.; Sat. has very limited service, and Sun. has none. The routes are color-coded, and you can pick up folded timetables of individual routes at all the info centers, travel desks, and the central Transit Park (where all routes begin and end) on Cushman and 5th Avenue. The fare is $1, unless you purchase tokens for 80 cents in advance at the Transit Park. Bus drivers are extremely helpful; don't hesitate to ask them anything. Or call MACS Transit Hotline at 452-3279.

Taxis charge $1 for the flag drop, and $1 per mile thereafter. **Prestige Limo,** tel. 479-2036, has a good service if you're traveling in a large group: $4 pp up to four people, then a maximum $15 per van load (up to 15 people) anywhere in town.

Hitchhiking

First, get as far out of town as possible on MACS, then pick a good spot on the highway. For Delta Junction and the Richardson or Alaska highways, catch the Green Line out to North Pole. For Denali and Anchorage on the George Parks Highway, take the Red Line to the corner of Geist Rd. and Fairbanks St., then walk the half mile to the highway, or take the Blue Line to the corner of Geist and Chena Pump Rd. and stand right there with the other hitchhikers.

Tours By Bus

Gray Line has travel desks in the lobbies of the Westmark Fairbanks, Noble and 8th, and Westmark Inn, Cushman and 15th. Book a city tour gold-dredge tour, or riverboat cruise at either travel desk, and catch the bus in back of either hotel. (Note, however, that the Gray Line city tour does not include the UAF Museum.) A city tour with a visit to the museum is offered by Royal Hiway Tours which leaves from the Captain Bartlett Inn, Airport Way and Lathrop.

The Binkley family, now in its third (soon to be fourth) generation of riverboat pilots, runs the **paddlewheeler cruise,** 20 miles RT on the Chena and Tanana rivers ($29.95). This is the only operating paddlewheeler in Alaska, with three riverboats in the fleet. In July 1987, *Discovery III,* designed by the Binkleys and built in Seattle, chugged into Fairbanks after a 1,000-mile voyage—the first sternwheeler to make the trip up the Yukon River in over 30 years. The cruises depart from the dock at the end of Dale Rd. out by the airport at 8:45 a.m. and 2 p.m. If you need a ride, get there with any of the tour companies.

VICINITY OF FAIRBANKS

NORTH POLE

In 1949, Con Miller was cleaning out the Fairbanks trading post he'd just bought, and found a Santa Claus suit. He liked it so much that he took to wearing it during his trips to the Interior to buy furs and sell supplies. The costume made a big impression on the Native kids. A few years later, when he moved 12 miles southeast of Fairbanks near Eielsen Air Force Base, he built a new trading post and called it Santa Claus House. Miller and his neighbors chose the name North Pole for their new town, reportedly, to attract a toy manufacturer to the area (none arrived).

Today, Santa Claus House, right on the Richardson Highway, is the largest and tackiest gift shop in the state, open daily 8-8, and North Pole is a large suburb of Fairbanks, with schools, malls, banks, bars, cops, and a mayor. Twenty-three churches are in the area, including St. Nicholas Church, and Santa Claus House has a 40-foot Santa figure out front. Street names include Kris Kingle Court and Mistletoe Lane.

The North Pole **Visitor Center** is on the Richardson Highway (corner of Mission Rd.), there's a **campground** on 5th Ave., and Chena Lakes Recreation Area (see below) is nearby. But the big thrill here is to get your letters postmarked "North Pole, Alaska." Post them from the Santa Claus House, or the post office on 5th Avenue. Throughout December, this post office is deluged with letters and cards from people wanting a North Pole postmark—the stacks can be piled 10 feet high. And that's *not* including the estimated 10,000 letters to Santa Claus himself, which are all answered by students at North Pole Middle School.

You can also buy a "holiday message from Santa," mailed in December from North Pole to any kid in the world, $2.50 ($3 international). For an extra $2.50 they'll send you a deed to one square inch of the Santa Claus Subdivision in town. Write Santa Claus House, Santa Land 5049, North Pole, AK 99705.

Chena Lakes Recreation Area

In mid-Aug. 1967, it rained seven inches in seven days, and the Chena River overflowed its banks, inundating low-lying Fairbanks under five feet of floodwaters. Half the town's residents were evacuated; damage neared $200 million. Preventing a similar disaster in the future fell to the Army Corps of Engineers, which mucked around for 15 years, building a dam at Moose Creek, a levee and spillway into the Tanana River, and this 2,000-acre park of man-made lakes and recreational facilities. Nearest beach to Fairbanks, on hot weekends the exodus is not unlike Bostonians fleeing to Cape Cod—you might be able to wedge a dishtowel onto some sand,

Santa is larger than life in North Pole.

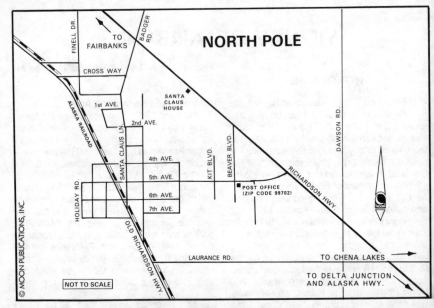

and swim in place. Most of the season, though, Chena Lakes is a delightful place to picnic, stroll, fish, and rent canoes, paddleboats, and sailboats. Camp at either the lakes campground or the river park. Fees are $3 per carload for day use, $6 for camping, $1 per bicycle rider. From Fairbanks, go five miles past North Pole, take a left on Laurance Rd., and follow the signs. Or catch the Green Line from town and have the driver drop you off on Laurance Road. Or call 452-3279, and ask if the Fairbanks transit system is running a special bus to the recreation area.

FOX

In 1901, Felice Pedroni (Felix Pedro) found color on what is now Pedro Creek and is credited with the discovery of the Cleary and Goldstream veins, which touched off the rush from the Klondike and Nome to the Fairbanks area. However, the gold here was anything but easy for the taking: this gold-laden bedrock was normally 80-100 feet under gravel, muck, and permafrost. Within 20 years of the find, the rich creeks were worked out, the shallow, low-grade ground was exhausted, and most miners couldn't afford the expense of working the deep claims. In 1923, however, the railroad was finished from Seward to Fairbanks, and brought with it the feasibility of large-scale gold production. Hydraulic giants, monster dredges, miles of tailings, and businessmen in three-piece suits replaced the lone prospector with his hammer and bucket. This second—corporate—gold rush to Fairbanks eventually produced almost $200 million worth of the precious heavy metal.

A ride 10 miles up the Steese Highway from Fairbanks to and around Fox clearly reveals the impact of this second boom (as well as the third—you pass the pipeline on the way). Huge cleared fields and stripped hillsides trace the progress of the giants and dredges, and the tailings lie in the snaking mounds they were spit into 50 years ago. Marble, gravel, and sand are for sale along the roadside. Heavy machinery dots the

(top) The Trans-Alaska Pipeline slices across the state from Prudhoe Bay to Valdez.
(bottom left) the S.S. *Klondike* in Whitehorse, Yukon Territory;
(bottom right) totem in Totem Bight State Park, Ketchikan

(top left) muskeg area near Petersburg; (top right) Mendenhall Glacier near Juneau; (bottom) verdant rainforest along McDonald Lake on Tongass National Forest

land with the bovine patience of metal and rubber. Fox boasts several roadhouse-type restaurants and a coffee shop, and the famous Howling Dog Saloon (see p. 270). Continue another 15 miles past town for the monument to Felice Pedroni, who started it all rolling only 85 years ago. Across the road is Pedro Creek; try your hand at panning for a little dust, and note the unnatural look of a creek played for gold for most of the century.

Gold Dredge No. 8

Local placer gold derives from ancient quartz veins once exposed in creek beds, now buried up to 100 feet below the surface. To get to it, first you hose off the surface layer down to two feet with hydraulic cannons or "giants," then down another few feet as the exposed frozen gravel thaws on its own. The deeper frozen muck and rock is thawed over a year or so by water pumped through pipes from the surface to bedrock, supplied by monumental aqueducts such as the Davidson Ditch. Once the earth down to bedrock is diggable, a gold dredge is brought in.

The dredge dwarfs even the most giant machine in this land of giant machines. It's a true Alaskan-size contraption that looks like a cartoon cross between a houseboat and a crane. An endless circular conveyor of up to 100 steel buckets scoops up the gravel, conveys it to the top end of a revolving screen, and dumps it. The screen separates the larger rocks, shunting them off to the tailing piles, from the golden gravel, which is sifted from the screen to riffles, where quicksilver (mercury) gleans the gold, forming an amalgam. The riffles are cleaned every couple of weeks, then further processed, assayed, and in the old days during the height of production, shipped to the mint, where it earned $35 per troy ounce ($400 today).

Gold Dredge No. 8, the only National Historic Mechanical Engineering Landmark in Alaska, is just a little larger than its official designation. One of Alaska's first steel-hulled bucketline dredges, it was installed in 1928—five stories tall, 250 feet long, weighing over 1,000 tons. The tour, $8, lasting around a half hour, starts every 45 minutes from 9 a.m.-10 p.m., then you can pan for gold—and keep what you find—for as long as you like. The grounds also contain a restaurant, bar, small hotel, and gift shop. Open daily, tel. 457-6058. To get there, drive or hitch eight miles up the Steese Highway toward Fox, take a left on Goldstream Rd. and another left on the Old Steese. No public transportation nears the place, but Gray Line leaves from the major hotels at 6:30 and 7:30 p.m.

ESTER

Like Fox, Ester had a two-boom gold rush: panning and placer mining in the early 1900s, then dredging by the Fairbanks Exploration Co. from the mid-1920s to the late '50s. Today, Ester has a few buildings that remain from the once-booming mining days, which now house a hotel, gift shop, gallery, and the famous Malemute Saloon. Since 1958 the **Hotel Cripple Creek** (now the Cripple Creek Resort), tel. 479-2500, has been in operation here, in a refurbished bunkhouse. The rooms are plain but functional and a real bargain—making Cripple Creek an attractive alternative to pricey Fairbanks if you have a car. Free continental breakfast is served in the mess hall downstairs, which also spreads out an all-you-can-eat buffet with fried chicken, reindeer stew, and halibut; the place is run by the Alaskaland salmon bake. They also have an all-you-can-eat crab buffet once a week; call for night and price.

Top off the evening with the Robert Service musical extravaganza at the Malemute Saloon (see p. 270), or take in the "Crown of Light" photosymphony ($5) at the Firehouse Theater just up the road. This 45-minute musically accompanied slide show of the northern lights on a curved 30-foot screen (affectionately known as "Aurorarama") is decidedly more high-tech than most attractions in Alaska, and wonderfully dark. The shots are individually pretty, but on the whole the show is slow-changing and ponderous. It's shown at 8 p.m.; another show, "Once Around the World," goes on at 7, and both shows together cost $9. Better is to be here in late Aug. when it gets dark, and see the real aurora.

By car, head down the George Parks Highway toward Denali 10 miles, then follow the signs for Ester and Cripple Creek Resort. All the tour companies offer packages with roundtrip transportation and the saloon show, but the resort company has its own shuttle bus, leaving around 6:15 and 7:30 p.m. from the major hotels in town. Call 479-2500 to arrange pickup.

THREE LONG RIDES TO SWIMMING POOLS

The vicinity of Fairbanks offers three outstanding opportunities to explore and experience the land and waterways, and then to luxuriate in hot springs that have soothed and refreshed travelers for a century. With the Interior's predictable good weather, the long days and low lighting, and the humbling power of this vast humanless wilderness, you'll return from any of these trips knowing a lot more about Alaska, and yourself. **Chena Hot Springs Road** boasts three exciting hiking trails, two stunning campgrounds, a choice of canoe routes and fishing spots, and a large pool resort, all within an hour's drive of town on a good paved road. The **Steese Highway** has five campgrounds, abundant canoeing and fishing, a high-country backpack that rivals much of Denali, and the fascinating evidence of gold fever—past and present. And the pool waiting at Arctic Circle Hot Springs is about as close as you'll come to hedonist heaven in central Alaska. The **Elliott Highway** is the longest, roughest, and most primitive ride of the three. Along it is one long trail close to Fairbanks, no campgrounds (to speak of), and no facilities (of any kind), all of which make the small pool and hot tubs at the road's end in friendly Manley all the more rewarding.

CHENA HOT SPRINGS ROAD

Depending on whom you believe, either Felix Pedro (1903) or the U.S. Geological Survey (1907) discovered the hot springs off the north fork of the Chena River. Shortly after, the land was homesteaded by George Wilson, who built a lodge and cabins, and enclosed the springs in a pool. The 55-mile road from Fairbanks was completed in 1967, only to be wiped out a few weeks later by the great flood. It was finally rebuilt and completely paved by 1983. From Mile 26 to 51 is Chena River Recreation Area, a well-developed and beautiful playground in Fairbanks' backyard, where numerous trails, river access, picnic areas, and two campgrounds are within an easy hour's drive from town. You could solidly fill up three or four days camping, hiking, backpacking, and canoeing (all free), and then satisfy the creature-comfort yearnings you accumulated in the backcountry with a soak in the pool and a drink at the resort at the end of the road.

By car, take the Steese Highway just north of town to the exit to Chena Hot Springs Road. It's well trafficked, so hitching shouldn't be too time-consuming. **Goldline Express**, tel. 474-0535, runs a shuttle service out to the resort for $50 RT.

Tack's General Store

The essence of one-stop shopping, Alaska style. The giant greenhouse is warm and beautiful, and will satisfy all the craving for color you've been having in this rather monochromatic environment. The cafe serves reasonably priced sandwiches on homemade bread, and your choice of at least two dozen pies—biggest slice you've ever seen for $3.25. The two-story general store houses everything from a post office to pipe fittings to the latest videos. Open daily 8-8, tel. 488-3242.

Chena River State Recreation Area

At 254,000 acres, this is Alaska's largest state recreation *area;* only Denali, Chugach, and Kachemak Bay state *parks* are larger. Chena River SRA boasts luxurious campgrounds, excellent outdoor recreational opportunities, lush greenery, towering trees (for Interior Alaska), rolling hills, the curvy Chena River, and best of all, no crowds. When town becomes oppressive, head a half hour east to some of the best that Interior has to offer.

The Granite Tors loop trail starts at Mile 39, on the righthand side just before the bridge just before the second campground. Constructed by the YCC in 1980-82, this well-maintained trail is a 15-mile, six-hour roundtrip. The first mile or so is on boardwalk over muskeg; the first tors (strange granite sculptures in the middle of the tundra) are around six miles from the trailhead on both the north or south forks of the trail. **Angel Rocks** trail begins at Mile 49 just beyond a pullout right before the fourth bridge over the Chena. It runs about a half mile along the river, then cuts in at a swampy slough (mosquitos) to the loop fork, and goes for another three miles roundtrip past spectacular rock outcroppings. Allow three to four hours. For the **Chena Dome** trail, take the northern trailhead which starts at Mile 50.5, a half mile past Angel Creek on the left side of the road; it's a three-day, 29-mile loop trail mostly along ridgetops marked by cairns—great views. A quarter mile up the trail is the sign for Chena Dome (nine miles); after a short boardwalk you start to climb and leave the mosquitos and heat behind. One mile up the trail is a good viewpoint.

The road parallels the river all the way to the hot springs, and crosses it four times, at Miles 37, 40, 44, and 49. Numerous well- marked pullouts give easy river access and your choice of the length of a canoe trip. A good place to put in is at the Mile 44 bridge—a little faster and funner than downriver. Watch for sweepers, deadheads, shallows, and especially the many impassable sloughs—stagnant, stinking, and mosquito-ridden.

Grayling fishing is great on this river, especially in July and August. You'll throw most back in, but you'll usually keep half a dozen 12-15 inchers. Four small lakes (Miles 30, 43, 46, and 48) are also well stocked with grayling and trout.

Rosehip Campground, Mile 27, right at the entrance to the recreation area, is as big and lush a campground as you could ever want, and only a half hour from town. The level gravel pullouts are big enough for 40-foot RVs, and you can almost put up a tent in one site and not see the tent in the next. The river is never more than a two-minute walk away. Twenty-five sites, pit toilets, water pumps, and numerous signboards with info about trails, wildlife, canoe routes, $6 pp. **Tors Trail Campground,** Mile 39, is a little less woodsy and inviting than the Rosehip, but it has the same excellent elbow room, facilities, river, and the Granite Tors trailhead is right across the road. Less crowded, 18 sites, $6 pp. The camping area at Chena Hot Springs is secluded and quiet, if a little mucky; $6 per site a night.

Chena Hot Springs

At Mile 57, the road ends at this sprawling resort. Along with the hot-spring-fed swimming pool and hot tub, it offers cabins and hotel rooms, and numerous activities: volleyball, croquet, badminton, billiards, cook-outs, hiking, and skiing in winter. The lodge is worth exploring for its neat little dining rooms, beautiful woodwork and furniture, and relaxing couches and library. The pool costs $6 for all day, $1 suit rental, 50-cent towels. Small cabins with no linen or running water (chemical toilets) start at $80; instead, stay in your trusty, money-saving tent at either state campground and use the resort for an afternoon and evening's entertainment. Prices at the restaurant in the lodge are reasonable. For information and reservations in Fairbanks, call 452-7867.

STEESE HIGHWAY AND ARCTIC CIRCLE HOT SPRINGS

Gold is the color of this country: the precious metal wrested with brute force from the reluctant earth, the golden-green panoramas of the alpine tundra, the golden light sparkling through the plumes of dust-fog along the

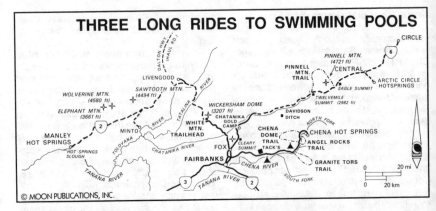

THREE LONG RIDES TO SWIMMING POOLS

© MOON PUBLICATIONS, INC.

road, and the pot of gold of the hot springs at the end of its own rainbow.

Other than the drive itself and the unlimited fishing and canoeing on the Chatanika River and Birch Creek, the excitement on the Steese can be found at the **Davidson Ditch,** on the challenging **Pinnell Mountain Trail,** and at **Arctic Circle Hot Springs** resort. The Davidson Ditch was one of the first miracle-of-engineering pipelines in this country, and unlike the oil pipeline, you can play on it! The Pinnell Trail is a three-day stroll along the windswept ridges of the White Mountains, with distant jagged horizons for the long-eyed, and stunning alpine wildflowers for the short. And after you've reached the limits of backcountry endurance, only 20 miles up the road is the biggest, deepest, hottest pool in Alaska, with not only all the conveniences and sociability you've been missing, but budget accommodations as well.

The Road
Named for Army General James G. Steese, president of the Alaska Road Commission from 1920-27 who oversaw its entire construction, the Steese Highway parallels the original Fairbanks-Circle Trail. Thousands of fortune seekers floated up and down the Yukon to Circle, then hit that trail after news of Felix Pedro's strike spread, and helped open up the Interior in the early 20th century. The road was completed in 1928 and paved for the first 44 miles in the early '50s.

Starting from Fairbanks, the highway immediately climbs into the gold-bearing hills, with a great viewpoint overlooking the Tanana Valley on the left at Hagelbarger Road. On a clear day, turn around to see if the Alaska Range is "out"—stunning panorama from Mt. McKinley to the eastern peaks of Deborah, Hess, and Hayes. Just up the road is a pullout to view the pipeline, which runs aboveground here, and an informative sign. Don't climb on this pipe. In a few miles you come to the Goldstream dredge and Fox; note the extensive tailings in the area. At the junction with the Elliot Highway (Rt. 2), take a right for the Steese (Rt. 6). At Mile 16 is a turnout with a plaque mounted on a stone monument to Felix Pedro; walk across the road to Pedro Creek, whose golden sands infected the stampeders with Fairbanks fever.

Fairbanks Exploration Company/ Poker Flats
From Pedro Creek the frost-heaved pavement climbs quickly to the Cleary Summit (elev. 2,233 feet) ski hill. The road twists and turns down to Chatanika; at Mile 28, take a hard right and climb to the site of the Fairbanks Exploration Company Gold Camp. After the completion of the Alaska Railroad in 1923, the U.S. Smelting, Refining, and Mining Co. began acquiring and consolidating many of the placer properties around Fairbanks. By 1938, the subsidiary F.E. Co. had three dredges operating between Chatanika

and Ester, had installed the Davidson Ditch (see below), and fueled the entire operation with its own power plant in Fairbanks. In its 30 years of production, F.E. Co. took out nearly $100 million in gold—and that was at no more than $35 per troy ounce, less than 10% of what it's worth today. The grounds are covered with vintage equipment and 15 restored buildings that are still maintained by machinery used during the '40s.

Bunkhouse rooms go for $27.50 d; or sleep in the 200-year-old brass bed for $58.50. Showers only are $3; the sauna is $3.75. Huge meals are cooked on a 10-foot coal-fired stove in the restaurant, which too is chock full of mining memorabilia and artifacts. Also don't miss the huge and unique Aurorium, an Alaskan-size log structure with a glass-panel roof that the owners have built on a hill behind the camp for viewing the northern lights. People from all over the world come here during winter to make use of it.

A mile up the road is the **Chatanika Lodge**, with similar room rates and restaurant prices, as well as a large bar and dance floor.

At Poker Flats, two miles farther, the **Geophysical Institute** at UAF studies the aurora and upper atmosphere with rockets launched from here, the world's only rocket-launch facility owned by a university. Tours are conducted here weekly in summer; tel. 474-7015.

Upper Chatanika River State Recreation Site—Mile 39

Another excellent state facility, this campground has 28 sites, pit toilets, water pump at the entrance, and plentiful river access for fishing (grayling) and boating, $6 pp. Head around to the back of the grounds and try for a campsite right on the river. Bring an inner tube and ride from the bridge down to your tent.

Davidson Ditch

The pavement ends at Mile 44, and the next 15 miles are rough—washboard shaky and deep gravel, slippery when dry. Take heart, though, it gets much smoother along the way. At Mile 42 is **Miner Ed's Trading Post.** Ed, the miner, quit mining 20 years ago, but is still happy to talk about the good old days and

show you his photos and mining treasures. At Mile 57 is a side road and a pullout (left). The side road leads seven miles to **Nome Creek**, a historic mining area with a designated area for recreational goldpanning. The pullout is for a long stretch of pipe, a remnant of the Davidson Ditch, the amazing engineering feat (1925) that slaked the F.E. Co. dredges' enormous thirst for water. Starting at a dam on the upper Chatanika River, the 12-foot-wide, four-foot-deep, 83-mile-long ditch, along with nearly seven miles of 48-inch pipe and a combined mile of tunnels, crossed 90 miles of hilly wilderness, directing 56,000 gallons of water per minute to the goldfields. Notice the expansion or "slip" joint in the middle of the level section of the pipe here, and the wooden saddle below it. The pipe was drained in the winter but the cold still took its toll: note the bulge in the pipe where it cuts uphill, and the repair job on the joint.

This is one of several views of the ditch in the next 10 miles, standing in mute testimony to the struggle of rugged miners against rugged terrain and harsh elements in the quest for gold. You can't help but be amazed by this project, especially when you consider that the road was barely built, the machinery was primitive, and the land unyielding. F.E. Co.'s contract did not require the removal of the pipe when gold production ceased, so here it still sits—either a blight on the landscape or evidence of the colorful history of this land, depending on your perspective. Whichever it is, watch your footing as you monkey around on the pipe.

Cripple Creek Campground And Beyond

This BLM facility at Mile 60 (there's a fee but nobody hereabouts seem to know how much) consists of an inner loop for pickups and RVs, and a walk-in section. Either take a site with the RV crowd, or park in the walk-in lot by the toilets, head to the back of the campground, and pitch your tent right by the river. The water pump is at the start of the inner loop; a signboard, nature trail, and toilets are at the other end.

The road out here gets smoother, wider, less slippery. From the back of a large pullout (right) at Mile 62 is another view of the pipe disappearing into a tunnel; it's an easy thrash through the brush to play on it. At Mile 81, natural spring water gushes cold and delicious from an open spigot, about five gallons a minute. While you've got the Davidson Ditch on your mind, multiply the pressure of the water from the spigot by 10,000 for an idea of the force with which the ditch moved its water.

Pinnell Mountain Trail And Eagle Summit

The first trailhead leaves the Steese at Mile 85 at 12-Mile Summit (elev. 2,982 feet); the second rejoins the highway near Eagle Summit (Mile 107). A short access road (right) at the first trailhead leads past a signposted section of the Fairbanks-Circle Trail to a small mountain pond—nice spot for a picnic. The trail follows a boardwalk for the first quarter mile, then climbs steadily for a long time. Most hikers prefer to start at the second trailhead, 700 feet higher, which has a great signboard full of fascinating information. This beautiful 27.3-mile, three-day trail through alpine tundra along White Mountain ridgelines is famous for its views of the Alaska and Brooks ranges and the midnight sun on solstice, plus the incomparable wildflowers (especially the state flower, forget-me-nots—striking blue dots on the tundra) which also peak in mid-June. This rolling treeless high country, with long-distance views in all directions, makes you want to stop, get out, and book all the way to the Edge. Be prepared for wind! Get info and a trail map at the Public Lands Info Center in Fairbanks.

Eagle Summit, at 3,624 feet, is the highest point on the road, a popular destination for Fairbanksans and travelers around solstice to watch the sun skirt the horizon, never setting. If the sun is *shining,* that is. It's been known to snow up here on solstice, or be socked in by clouds or fog. In fact, you might wish for a nice blizzard to hold down the skeeters, so thick and ferocious that they've been rumored to pick up men—large men—and carry them off. The mile-long access road to the summit is particularly steep and rocky; alternatively, walk up or drive a couple of miles past the turnoff just past Mile 109 and hike up the back side to save wear and

tear on your vehicle. If you drive up and down the access road, though, when you get back to the Steese it feels like pavement!

To Central

At Mile 94 a road to the right leads to undeveloped camping and the launching point for the popular **Birchcreek Canoe Trail.** Coming down from the summit, there are gorgeous views of the current gold mining activities down on the valley floor, along Mammoth and Mastodon creeks, so named for the frozen remains of large Alaskan mammals uncovered by strip mining. The tusks on display at the UAF Museum came from here. Make sure to stop at 101 Gas to check out the ancient gas pump, which recently pumped its last gas(p). Take a left at Mile 119 and go straight at the fork for **Bedrock Creek Campground** (BLM); now "closed" or unmaintained, you could certainly still camp here if you wanted.

Central

Ten miles farther is Central, whose year-round population of 100 doubles in the summer due to the influx of miners. Passions run high around here about the right of individuals to mine their claims. **Crabb's Corner** has a gas station, general store, and clean rooms ($35 d), showers ($3), and free camping. **The Circle District Museum** in the log cabin in town has mining and mushing artifacts from the early days, and a good wildflower photo display; $1, usually open noon-5. Walk around back to see the wagon-wheel camper. **Central Motor Inn and Campground** rents trailer rooms for $30 s, $37.50 d, and serves meals in a small cafe.

Arctic Circle Hot Springs

Hang a right on Hot Springs Rd. in central Central; in eight miles is the hot springs resort, tel. 520-5113. This water is hot! It bubbles out of the ground at 139° F, fills an Olympic-size swimming pool, runs through pipes to keep the lodge at a tropical 72° F when it's 72° below outside, and has been irrigating sumptuous vegetable gardens in the area since 1905. Even if you don't get out of the car between Fairbanks and here, this

(GORDY OHLIGER)

pool is worth the trip. The water is much hotter than the pool at Manley, and the sulphur is nowhere near as strong as at Chena; $6 to swim all day.

This large family resort also has a well-stocked general store and ice cream parlor, as well as a gift shop, bar, restaurant, and lodge. Rooms in the lodge, romantically furnished with brass beds and individually color-coordinated, cost $42 s, $60 d, or $90 for a deluxe suite with Jacuzzi. Furnished cabins with kitchenette, linen, and porta pottie start at $60, $15 each additional person. A better deal is the hostel rooms on the fourth floor. For $20, you crawl through the three-quarter-size door and under the attic eaves, where you sleep on your own bedding; bathroom down the hall. All rates include use of pool facilities. Or just camp for free at **Ketchum Creek Campground** (BLM) three miles before the hot springs: again, closed, unmaintained, but campable still.

Circle

Erroneously named by miners who thought the townsite was close to the Arctic Circle (which is actually 50 miles north), Circle is a long 34 miles beyond Central. The road is in good condition, just quite winding; the last 11 miles are a rally-car driver's dream. Gold was discovered on Birch Creek nearby in 1893, and Circle was a boomtown with two dozen saloons, library, hospital, even an opera house, long before anyone had heard of the Klondike. When the miners did hear of the Klondike a few weeks after the strike, Circle

immediately lost half its population. Circle gradually declined as a supply center for the Circle Mining District after the Steese Highway hooked up to Fairbanks. Today, with a population of 70, Circle is typical of end-of-the-road Alaska—couple of streets, lots of cars (mostly junked). The main attraction is the mighty Yukon. Pitch your tent at the denuded campground (free) on the banks and watch the river flow. The Yukon Trading Post has a cafe, bar, gasoline, motel rooms (from $55 d), and offers helicopter tours. Get directions here to the Pioneer Cemetery. **Warbelow's Air Ventures,** tel. 474-0518 in Fairbanks, has a flight to Central ($67 OW) and Circle ($70 OW) once daily from Fairbanks.

THE ELLIOTT HIGHWAY AND MANLEY HOT SPRINGS

The Elliott Highway, named after Major Malcolm Elliott, president of the Alaska Railroad Commission from 1927-32 (following George Steese), begins at the junction with the Steese Highway in Fox, 11 miles north of Fairbanks. The road is paved to Mile 28 (but watch for frost heaves), then turns into a very wide, occasionally smooth two-lane gravel road (actually an extension of the Dalton Highway to Prudhoe) until the junction with the Dalton, when it narrows to a one-lane rough gravel ribbon through total wilderness. Other than the BLM White Mountain Trail at Mile 28, and gorgeous views in several spots on the road (especially Miles 95-96), there's little on the way to Manley Hot Springs, a small town at the end of the highway, 152 long miles from Fox. In fact, there's only one facility (Wildwood General Store, Mile 49.5) between the Hilltop Cafe, just outside of Fox, and Manley. Most of the road is in the 40- to 50-mph range, with a few 20- to 30-mph stretches, totaling four to five hours one way from Fairbanks.

Between Fox and the Dalton junction, huge supply trucks to and from Prudhoe barrel along, raising blinding clouds of dust; by the time you get back to Fairbanks from Manley, a fine layer of dust will have settled over everything you've got, including your entire respiratory tract. It's essential to have *plenty* of water along for this ride. Also take food, as there's no Denny's at the next exit, since there aren't any exits. And don't forget your bathing suit.

To The White Mountain Trail

The road climbs quickly out of Fox, with good views of the Interior's rolling hills. One mile north of the abandoned railroad and mining town of **Olnes,** just before the Mile 11 bridge over the Chatanika River, a large gravel road on the left goes a mile in to Chatanika Pond, part of the **Chatanika River State Recreation Site:** no facilities, but fair fishing and camping. On the other side of the Mile 11 bridge is the rest of the recreation site: camping ($6), picnicking, pit toilets, fishing for grayling in the summer, whitefish (spearfishing) in the fall. At Mile 28 on the right is a parking area and the trailheads for myriad trails through the White Mountains. Read the information board carefully. Most trails are for winter use and are not maintained during the summer for hiking. The Summit Trail starts from the trailhead on the left and is designated for summer use. This 21-mile trail (OW), mostly along alpine ridgetops through the foothills of the White Mountains, ends at Beaver Creek. Across the creek is the Borealis-LeFavre Cabin, which can be reserved through the BLM, 1150 University Ave., Fairbanks, AK 99709, tel. 474-2200. As for hiking, you start out high up to begin with, and the first mile or so of the Wickersham Creek Trail takes you out of the taiga and onto a ridgetop, with a beautiful 300-degree view of the Tanana Valley, Alaska Range, and gigantic sky. Even if you're not hiking all the way, it's worth it to do this mile for the view.

Bye Bye Pavement

The pavement ends 100 yards from the trailhead. Enjoy this nice wide gravel stretch while you've got it! Nice views of the pipeline here—shining in the sunlight, twisting through the tundra, suddenly disappearing underground and surfacing again. At Mile 57 is the only official campground on the Elliot, nicknamed **Mosquito Creek Campground.** Unless you want to donate a few pints of life's precious fluid (per minute) to the local bloodsucking population, do not camp, do not get out of your car, don't even stop.

At Mile 71 is the two-mile access road to **Livengood,** a tiny mining center which flourished briefly as a pipeline construction camp. It now has a population of seven, including Grandpa Ent, who sells his handmade wooden toys, including kangaroos, from an Atco trailer. Two miles farther is Mile 0 of the Dalton Highway (see below). Take a left to stay on the Elliott.

To Manley

A bit past the junction, right after the bridge over the Tolovana River, is a little pullout (left), a nice spot for a picnic, camping, fishing, or even swimming (no facilities). Here the road narrows considerably, and you follow the two tire-packed stripes down the middle of it, hoping nobody is coming in the other direction. At Miles 95-96 is a fantastic view overlooking the Minto Flats, Tanana River, and the foothills of the Alaska Range. If you're very lucky and have charmed cloud karma, you'll get a breathtaking view of Mt. McKinley and the accompanying snowcapped peaks to its right and left, jutting straight up like a big militant fist from the lowlands. Even though the range is over 100 miles due south, the possibility of seeing it is worth the whole ride—even the dust. From here to Manley are some fun roller-coaster humps and curves; watch for porcupines, foxes, snowshoe hares, tree squirrels, and hawks.

Manley Hot Springs

This relaxing and friendly town is a couple of miles this side of the end of the Elliot at the Tanana River. Like many Interior villages, Manley Hot Springs (pop. 150) had its heyday in the early 1900s during the peak activity of nearby mines. The U.S. Army Signal Corps set up a telegraph station here in 1903, and Frank Manley built the town's first resort in 1907. Because of the geothermal activity, Manley boasts agricultural features uncommon for Interior: rich warm soil, long growing season, even earthworms, and is known for its abundant produce. Manley also has a new resort, a roadhouse, a popular landing strip, wilderness tours, and more ATVs than cars. A lot more. Best of all, the hot springs have no sulphur, so you can enjoy the soak without the stink.

Just as you come into town, take a right into **Manley Hot Springs Resort,** tel. 672-3611. For $5, you can swim all day in their pool. Rent towels and suits for a buck apiece. The lodge has a bar ($2.50 for beers), restaurant ($5.75 for burgers), a giant pool table, and a beautiful jade fireplace. The jade came from a single nugget, weighing more than a ton. Hotel rooms in a long double-wide trailer cost $55 d with toilet, $70 d with shower, $85 d with Jacuzzi, or dry cabins for $45 per night. If you're interested in a fishing trip, ask here for Frank who charges $30 an hour.

Continue toward town and take the next right to the large greenhouse, and look around for Chuck or Gladys Dart. These long-time Manley residents (the school is named after Gladys) are friendly Alaskan farmers who use the hot springs bubbling up on their property to grow tomatoes, cucumbers and other vegetables, which they sell to local residents and passersby. Inside the first greenhouse are four square concrete hot tubs with 108° spring water. After an hour's soak ($5), buy some produce, add your favorite dressing for some zing, and you'll have a true Manley experience.

Keep going toward town, and park by the bridge over Hot Springs Slough. Go right just before the bridge, and walk a half mile to the first road to the right. The first part of the trail past the cabins is private property. Then it's three miles to the tower, and two more up to Bean Ridge. Great views and camping up there. The public campground below the bridge on the other side of Hot Springs Slough in the middle of town has toilets, picnic tables, and cinder-block barbecues, $2 a night—handy to everything. The **Roadhouse,** tel. 672-3161, was built in 1906 and is a popular meeting place for local miners, trappers, and dog mushers. It has many prehistoric and historic artifacts on display, collected from around the area, along with the usual bar, restaurant, friendly atmosphere, and rooms ($40 s, $55 d, cabins $65.

The Elliott Highway continues past the landing strip and trading post two and a half miles to the end of the road at the mighty Tanana River. Here it's scenic and breezy, and you could camp here in a pinch.

Apart from driving out here in your own vehicle, the Manley Hot Springs Resort runs a van to Fairbanks once a week for groceries, and will take passengers either way ($20 OW); ring to find out what day. If there are four or more people, they'll make a special trip. **Tanana Air,** tel. 474-0301 in Fairbanks, flies Mon. through Fri. from Fairbanks at 11:45 a.m., $55 OW.

DALTON HIGHWAY

Before pipeline days, the Elliott Highway ran from just outside of Fairbanks to Livengood, where a 56-mile spur road cut north to the Yukon River. The Dalton Highway began as the "Haul Road" in 1974, constructed to run parallel to the Alaska pipeline from the Yukon River to Deadhorse, a small oil settlement on Prudhoe Bay.

The Dalton Highway, more popularly known as the Haul Road, on which materials for the North Slope oilfields were transported during the mid-'70s, was added to the Elliott, and the spur was renamed the Dalton. In 1981, the spur road and the Haul Road, a total of 414 miles, were renamed the Dalton Highway, named for James Dalton, who pioneered early oil exploration efforts on the North Slope (and not Bill Dalton, who pioneered Moon Publications). This long road traverses some of the most spectacular and remote land accessible by road in Alaska (and therefore in the country), through taiga, tundra, over the Arctic Circle, past towering snowcapped peaks, through the foothills of the Brooks Range, and within a mile of Gates of the Arctic National Park. Wildlife is abundant: caribou, Dall sheep, and wolves if you look real sharp.

The road is still primarily a truck-supply route and is fairly wide, but becomes very dusty or slippery, depending on recent weather. A permit is required to travel past Mile 211, but this is far enough to satisfy most people's curiosity and tolerance for gravel roads, especially since you then turn around and retrace the previous somewhat excruciating 7-11 hours on this tire-eating, bone-jarring, teeth-grinding, anus-clenching "highway." However, because you're looking at it from the other direction, it might appear slightly different.

A trip up the Dalton is not to be taken lightly. There are only two services along the way, which charge $35 just to hop into the tow truck, and another $35 to back it out of the garage. (And don't even *ask* the per-mile price.) Always travel with plenty of water, your headlights on, two spare tires, and *watch for trucks*. In most cases, you can see them coming from a fur piece, ahead as well as behind, from the dust trails they raise. Be prepared for all that dust to come your way.

To Coldfoot

Mile 0 of the Dalton is 73 miles north of Fairbanks along the Elliott. From here it's 56 miles to the Yukon River, with sweeping views of the undulating landscape and good glimpses of the pipeline. No developed campgrounds are maintained along the Dalton, but the first of many undeveloped areas is at **Hess Creek,** Mile 24. A 2,290-foot wooden-deck bridge crosses the might Yukon at Mile 56. On the northern side is the only service facility before Coldfoot, with gas, tire repair, restaurant, and rooms ($35 s, $70 d). An interesting pipeline interpretive display is beside the road. Cross the road and drive under the pipeine for an undeveloped camping area.

Isolated granite tors are visible to the northeast at Mile 86, and at Mile 98 are excellent views of the mountains across the tundra before the road descends again to travel along the valley floor. At Mile 115 is the Arctic Circle: latitude 66 degrees, 33 minutes. A huge sign proclaims the location. A road behind the sign leads a half mile to camping.

At Mile 132 is **Gobbler's Knob,** and the first views of the Brooks Range on the distant northern horizon. The road winds past Pump Station 5, over numerous rivers and creeks, by great fishing, and at Mile 175, rolls into Coldfoot.

Coldfoot

Gold was discovered at Tramway Bar in the upper reaches of the Koyukuk River in 1893, which attracted enough prospectors and miners to found the town of Coldfoot. Still, the town reportedly received its sobriquet when most of them got cold feet at the onset of the first winter, and left the country. Two of the original mining cabins are still in the bush at the northern end of the airstrip.

It's no wonder the old miners' feet became frosty. In Jan. 1989, Coldfoot recorded a temperature of -82° F, and for 17 days the mercury refused to rise above 62 below. Then, that summer, it got up to three degrees below 100—the 179-degree differential broke all North American records.

A visitor center puts on a daily presentation on Gates of the Arctic and the Brooks Range. Coldfoot Services calls itself the "world's northernmost truck stop," and has reasonably priced meals, gas at $1.60 a gallon, post office, and gift shop. The Arctic Acres Inn has rather costly rooms in an Atco trailer: $105 s, $110 d.

And Beyond

From Coldfoot, it's 36 miles to the turnaround point at Disaster Creek. Undeveloped camping is found at Marion Creek at Mile 180. Views across the Koyukuk River take in Wiseman, a historic mining town, and fantastic mountain scenery. Gates of the Arctic National Park boundary is high up on the slopes to the west, and at Mile 194 are the first views of Sukakpak Mountain. The road passes along the base of this rugged peak and a trail at Mile 203 leads a half mile right to the base. The strange-looking mounds between the road and the mountain are "palsas," formed by ice beneath the soil pushing upwards.

Mile 211 marks the turnaround for all vehicles without an onward-travel permit. From here the road climbs quickly up to Chandalar Shelf, a huge basin with a healthy population of grizzlies, then over Atigun Pass at Mile 244, the highest highway pass in Alaska (4,800 feet). The road winds quickly down through the Atigun Valley and onto the North Slope. At Mile 414 is Prudhoe Bay, beginning of the pipeline and home to 8,000 workers.

Hitching is conceivable in the summer, since a steady trickle of hardy travelers brave this highway. The trucks, of course, won't stop for you. Not all car rental agencies allow their vehicles on the Dalton, so ask first. **Northern Alaska Tour Company,** tel. 474-8600, offers one-day tours to the Arctic Circle, leaving Alaskaland in Fairbanks at 7:30 a.m., $85, and a bus/boat/plane trip to Mile 137 for $115. **Princess** and **Gray Line** offer package tours by bus from Fairbanks to Prudhoe Bay and by plane the other way; the three-day/two-night trip starts at $675.

TO DENALI

George Parks Highway

Completed in 1971, the George Parks Highway (Rt. 3) is named for George Parks, an early Territorial governor, not for Denali national and state parks, as is often thought. Running 359 miles from Fairbanks to Anchorage, the highway winds through the Tanana Hills south of Fairbanks (good views of the Alaska Range to the east) and passes **Skinny Dick's Halfway Inn** (it *is* halfway between Fairbanks and Nenana, which makes it an even better pun), several fireworks stands, and the **Monderosa,** just north of Nenana, whose "best burger in Alaska" is in fact a great deal—one fills up two. A large steel bridge crosses the Tanana River (pronounced TA-na-naw); notice the Nenana River (pronounced nee-NA-na) emptying into it on the right.

NENANA

Nenana (pop. 552) was an Athabascan Indian village at the confluence of the two rivers (*na* in Athabascan means "river"; Nenana means "Camping Spot at Two Rivers") until it mushroomed into a town of 5,000 in 1916 as a base for construction on the northern leg of the Alaska Railroad. At the north end of the 700-foot railroad bridge spanning the Tanana, Warren G. Harding, first president to visit Alaska, drove in the golden spike, marking the completion of the line on July 15, 1923. Harding's visit was the culmination of a long train tour across the country, during which he attempted to rally support for his flagging administration, which was dogged by suspicions of high-level corruption. Prior to his trip, Harding'd supported exploitation of Alaska's resources, but the first-hand experience changed his mind. Returning from Alaska to Seattle, he made a speech calling for more roads and agriculture, and conservation of lumber, fish, and mineral resources. "We must regard life in lovely, wonderful Alaska as an end and not a means, and reject the policy of turning Alaska over to the exploiters." Unfortunately, Harding died a week later; his new vision was buried with him.

Nenana is famous for its yearly **Ice Classic,** "Alaska's Biggest Guessing Game." It all

Ice Classic tripod on Tanana River

started in 1917, when Alaska Railroad workers started a pool for the exact time the ice on the Tanana River would break up; the pay-off was $800. Now in its 75th year, the prize is usually around $100,000, which is 50% of the gross. The rest goes to taxes, salaries, promotion, and the town till. Thousands of Alaskans place $2 bets on the day, hour, and minute of the break-up. A four-legged tripod (the town's symbol) is set up on the river ice in February, with a cable running to a clock tower on the river bank. When the ice moves, the cable stops the clock, recording the official time. Earliest break-up was April 20, in 1940; latest was May 20, in 1964. Pick up entry forms ($2) at the Visitors Center or the Tripod Gift Shop—you can mail in your guess from anywhere in the country up until April 1.

The Ice Classic and the town's active waterfront, where freight and supplies are loaded onto barges for bush towns strung along the Tanana and Yukon rivers, make Nenana a prosperous, photogenic, and friendly little place—great for a leisurely stroll to break up (sorry) the trip from Fairbanks to Denali.

Sights

Stop off at the **Visitor's Center** at the bottom of the bridge, corner of the Parks Highway and A St., open 8-6. Check out the replica of the Ice Classic cable system, and pick up the xeroxed historical map of town with descriptions of the older buildings. Behind the cabin is the *Taku Chief*, the last commercial wooden tugboat to ply the Yukon and Tanana rivers, till it was condemned in Nenana in

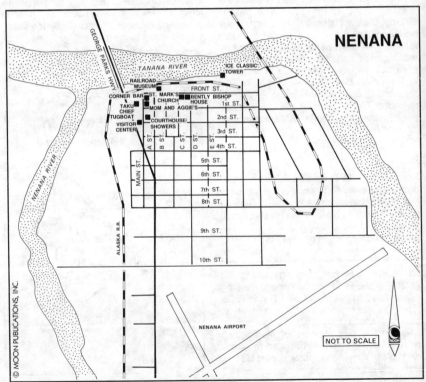

1978 where it still sits. Unfortunately you can't climb on it.

Walk down A St. toward the river. Go right on Front St. and enter the old depot. Inside is the **Alaska State Railroad Museum,** tel. 832-5500, open 9-6 daily, free, along with a small exhibit on the lifestyles of Nenana. Outside there's a monument with a memorial plaque and the once-golden spike. A block over is **St. Mark's Mission Church,** established in 1904 to educate Native children from around the Interior. On the waterfront is the Ice Classic tower; next to it is a building with the clock, and a huge book of entries, turned to the page of winners. Six information signs line the waterfront walkway. The white stones across the river on the hillside are Native graveheads. And on the way out of town, don't miss the oft-photographed log-cabin bank on the left.

Practicalities

Have a bite at **Mom and Aggie's** on A St., a classic bush cafe; have one for the road at the **Corner Bar,** on the west corner of A and Front streets. The bar across the street on the east corner is not called the Corner Bar, though it is on the corner; the Corner Bar got to the name first. Grab a shower ($3) in the clean bright laundromat behind the court-house; not a bad idea to have this facility share the courthouse building, so you can spruce up a bit before you go in front of the judge for drunk and disorderly . . . or whatever. Several gift shops line A Street. The Chevron station and mini-mart is open 24 hours a day, a handy gas stop to depend on if you're heading north and can't make it all the way to Fairbanks.

Nenana is 67 miles from the entrance to Denali National Park, and 54 miles south of Fairbanks. The Alaska Railroad passes through, but it's not a scheduled stop. You can get off there if you want to, but you can't check any baggage. Canoeing from Fairbanks to Nenana on the fat and sassy Tanana River is a wild two-day trip.

(GORDY OHLIGER)

DENALI

INTRODUCTION

Denali National Park is now Alaska's number two tourist attraction (the first is Portage Glacier). Denali attracts more visitors during its 114-day season than the entire state has residents. Most travelers come to see Mt. McKinley, highest peak in North America (20,320 feet), which towers above the surrounding lowlands and 14,000- to 17,000-foot peaks. Visible only one day in three, and often shrouded for a week or more at a time, those who get lucky and see The Mountain experience a thrill equivalent to its majesty and grandeur. Those who don't are usually consoled by lower snowcapped mountains and attending glaciers, high passes and adrenaline-pumping drops off the road, tundra vistas and "drunken forests," and the incredible abundance of wildlife, including the Big Four: caribou, moose, sheep, and bear. But even if The Mountain's socked in, the grizzlies are hiding, and the shuttle bus windows are fogged up, you're still smack in the middle of some of the most spectacular *and* accessible wilderness in the world. It was the call of the wild that brought you out here in the first place. And all you have to do is step outside and answer.

The Land And Climate

The Alaska Range is a U-shaped chain which extends roughly 600 miles from the top of the Alaska Peninsula (at the head of the Aleutians) up through the Park and down to south of Tok. It's only a small part, however, of the coastal mountains which include California's Sierra Nevada, the Northwest's Cascades, the Coast Mountains of B.C., Yukon's St. Elias and eastern Alaska's Wrangell ranges. The Park road starts out a bit north of the Alaska Range, and follows the "U" 90 miles southwest toward its heart—Mt. McKinley.

One thing that makes The Mountain so spectacular is that the surrounding lowlands are so low: the Park hotel sits at 1,700 feet, and the highest point on the road, Thoroughfare Pass, is just under 4,000. The base of Mt. McKinley is at 2,000 feet, and the north face rises at a 60-degree angle straight up to 20,000 feet—highest vertical rise in the world.

Weather patterns here differ between the south side of the range (wetter, cooler) and the north. During the summer, the prevailing winds come from the south, carrying warm moisture from the Pacific. When they run smack into the rock wall of the Alaska Range, they climb, the moisture condenses, and depending on the amount of moisture and altitude, it either rains or snows. A lot. On top of that whole system sits mighty Mt. McKinley—very high, very cold, and very alone. So alone that The Mountain has its own relationship to the weather. The combination of wind, wet, cold, and height creates weather extremely localized around McKinley, which can get violent. Storms can blow in within an hour and last weeks, dumping 10 feet of snow. Winds scream in at up to 80 mph. The mercury drops below zero in mid-July. Some of the worst weather in the world swirls around up there. But when The Mountain emerges bright white against bright blue, and you're craning your neck to see the top, it's an unforgettable sight worth waiting around for—even in the rain.

Flora And Fauna

From sea level to around 2,300 feet is the habitat for the **boreal forest,** in which the black spruce, with its somber foliage and

somber black spruce limbs
(LOUISE FOOTE)

clusters of tawny cones, is the climax tree. Younger white spruce, along with deciduous aspen, birch, and cottonwood, grow near the streams, road, and in recently burned areas. Climbing out of the forest, above 2,300 feet, you enter the **taiga,** a Russian word meaning "land of twigs." This transition zone accommodates no deciduous trees, the spruce are thinned out and runty (though they can be over 60 years old), and a green shag carpet of bush, mostly dwarf willow, layers the floor. Sitka spruce is the state tree because of its size, grandeur, and commercial value, but it's the willow that vegetates Alaska. And it has endless uses. Before synthetics like nylon, the bark was stripped, split, and braided, and made into rope, bows, wicker baskets, snowshoes, fishnets, small game and bird snares and traps. The inner bark is sweet; the sap is very sweet. Young buds and shoots are edible and nourishing, and willows are the nearly exclusive staple of the moose diet. The taiga also hosts a variety of berries: blueberries and lowbush cranberries by the ton, crowberries, bearberries, soap and salmon berries, raspberries.

Above 2,500 feet is the **tundra,** a Lapp word meaning "vast, rolling, treeless plain." There are two types of tundra: the moist, or Alaskan, tundra is characterized by the taiga's dwarf shrubbery, high grasses, berries, but no trees; and the alpine tundra, the highest zone, has grasses, moss, lichens, and small, hardy wildflowers, including the stunning forget-me-not, Alaska's state flower.

COEXISTING WITH THE BEARS

Entering Bear Country

Enter bear country with respect but not fear. Know that bears rarely attack man; you're 1,000 times more likely to be injured in a highway accident than by a bear. In fact, more people are hurt each year by moose than by bears. Bears have poor eyesight, but excellent senses of smell and hearing. Avoid unexpected encounters with bears by letting them know you're there. If you walk with a breeze hitting your back, any bears ahead of you will know you are coming. If you're unable to see everything around you for at least 50 yards, warn any hidden animals by talking, singing, clapping your hands, tapping a cup, rattling a can of pebbles, or wearing a bell. Whistling is not recommended as you might inadvertently imitate a bird. Don't get mauled because a bear mistakes you for a long-tailed jaeger! Be especially wary when traveling through thick brush or high grass, into the wind, along streams, or at twilight. Safety is also in numbers: the more of you hiking together, the more likely a bear is to sense you and stay away.

At The Campsite

When choosing a campsite, avoid places like salmon streams, ground squirrel mounds, or berry patches. Watch for fresh signs of bears (droppings, tracks, diggings). Make sure you're not on a game trail. In mid-summer bears tend to move up to the cooler alpine areas, while in fall they will be anywhere the salmon are spawning or berries are ripening. If possible, camp near a climbable tree. Keep your campsite clean! Avoid smelly foods such as fish, fresh meat, cheese, sausage, or bacon; freeze-dried food is light and relatively odorless. Keep food in airtight containers or several layers of plastic bags. Your cooking, eating, and food storage area should be at least 50 yards away from your tent. Wash up after eating. Burying garbage is useless as animals soon dig it up; burn what garbage you can, and wash and flatten tin cans. Store unburnable garbage and the clothes you were wearing while cooking in the same place. Put your food, toothpaste, and soap in a plastic bag inside a sleeping bag stuff sack and suspend it from a branch or between two trees, at least three yards off the ground. Tie two cups or pots to it so you

will hear if it's moved. In the absence of trees, store food well downwind of your tent. Many campgrounds provide handy bear-proof metal food caches. Perfumes, deodorants, and sexual smells are all thought to attract bears. Women should be especially cautious during their periods. Used tampons should be stored in air-tight containers and packed out with all other garbage.

(LOUISE FOOTE)

Other Precautions

Photographers are the main recipients of bear hugs. Never, under any circumstances, approach a bear, even if it appears to be asleep. Move off quickly if you see bear cubs, especially if one comes toward you; the mother is always close by. Dogs create dangerous situations by barking and exciting bears—leave yours at home. It is *illegal* almost everywhere to feed or harass bears, or deliberately leave food or garbage to attract them. Fed bears become garbage bears, and wildlife officials are eventually forced to destroy them. Report anyone you see feeding bears (such as from a car window) as quickly as possible, for they are not only endangering their own lives but also yours. Bear incidents of any kind should be reported to park or wildlife authorities so they can act to minimize the problem. Remember, bears are dangerous wild animals which may be encountered anywhere in the North. This is *their* country, not a zoo. By going in you accept the risk of meeting a bear.

COEXISTING WITH THE BEARS (CONT.)

Bear Encounters

If you unexpectedly come upon a bear while hiking, or if one enters your campsite, make a wide detour around it or back off and give it time to go away. A bear may feel its territory is being invaded at 200 yards, threatened at 50. If you happen to find yourself closer than this, don't panic. The worst thing you can do is run; this could trigger the chase instinct, and you *cannot* outrun a bear. Also, any sudden moves might startle the animal. Speak *quietly* and wave your hands slowly above your head to let the bear know what you are. If the bear is very close, slowly back off while continuing to face it. If the bear stands on its hind legs and waves its head from side to side it may only be trying to identify you. When it does, it will usually run away. If a bear follows as you back off, drop a hat or piece of clothing for it to smell. Move cautiously toward a climbable tree, if one is nearby. If a bear woofs and postures, don't imitate, as this is a challenge. Keep retreating! Most bear charges are also a bluff; the bear will often stop short and amble off. When it charges, however, don't move. If contact is imminent, drop down and play dead. Put your hands behind your neck, pull your legs up to your chest, and make whatever deal with the Lord your God you think will save you. Keep your pack on for protection. It takes a lot of courage to do this, but often a bear will only sniff or nip you and leave. The injury you might sustain would be far less than if you had tried to resist. If you live, keep your bargain with God.

Ursus Major

Observe all the precautions and you have little to worry about. It's a sad commentary on the human condition that many people's reaction to bears is a desire to kill them. People who **work** in bear country often carry rifles, but seldom need to use them (see accompanying story). But as an occasional hiker, or even veteran backpacker, if you feel the need to carry a rifle for protection, it's better you stay out of the wilderness. You have plenty of alternative places to go; the bears do not. Every Northerner has a bear story. Listen to them, but take them with a grain of salt. If you see a bear yourself it will probably be the most memorable event of your trip, and the one you'll talk about most to the folks back home. Let us hope the great bears always remain an intriguing part of the northern wilderness.

WALTZING AT TERROR LAKE

Kodiak has a higher population density of brown bears than anywhere else on the planet, about 3,000 of them, a bear for every five people. Arguably, one bear is as good as five people, as they've been known to stand over 10 feet tall and weigh up to 1,500 pounds. So when 500 construction workers were building a dam and power plant at Terror Lake in the Kodiak National Wildlife Refuge in 1982-85, it provided Alaska Fish and Game an excellent opportunity to ob-

Grizzly

Black Bear

Polar Bear

Alaskan Brown Bear

COEXISTING WITH THE BEARS (CONT.)

serve the man-bear choreography. Workers were trained in how to behave around bears, there were no garbage dumps nearby, and only supervisors and remote crews carried firearms. Huge bears were encountered continually, but during the course of the study, no bears or men killed or even injured each other. Only a small fraction of the local bear population was attracted to the garbage cans. A minimum of bear activity was disturbed by the blasting, building, and general bedlam. It was reported that the bears "even became somewhat accustomed to helicopters." Bears scratched their backs on power poles while crews strung wire nearby. The major impact, of course, was the shrinking of the brown bear habitat. But it's clear that brown bears and humans can learn to dance.

The animal life varies with the vegetation. In the forest, look for moose, porcupine, snowshoe hare, marten, lynx, two kinds of weasels, red or tree squirrels, and several varieties of small rodents. On the taiga—or in both the forest and tundra—you might see coyote, wolf, fox, grizzly, and ground squirrel. In the tundra, keep an eye out for caribou, wolverine, Dall sheep, marmot, vole, lemming, and shrew.

HISTORY

William Dickey

In 1896, a prospector named Bill Dickey was tramping around interior Alaska looking for gold. Like everyone who sees it, Dickey was captivated by the size and magnificence of the mountain that was then variously known as Tenada, Denali, Densmore's Mountain, Traleika, and Bulshaia. Dickey was from Ohio, William McKinley's home state, and a Princeton graduate in economics. When he came out of the bush and heard that McKinley had been nominated for president, he promptly renamed the mountain "McKinley," wrote numerous articles for stateside magazines and lobbied in Washington, D.C. in support of adoption of the name, which finally caught on after President McKinley was assassinated in 1901.

Harry P. Karstens

Karstens reached the Klondike in 1898 when he was 19, bored by Chicago and attracted by adventure and gold. Within a year he'd crossed over into American territory and wound up at Seventymile, 20 miles south of Eagle. When the local mail carrier lost everything one night in a card game and committed suicide, Karstens took his place. He became proficient in dog mushing and trail blazing, and within a few years was delivering mail between Eagle and Valdez, a 900-mile roundtrip every month (the Richardson Highway follows the same route). Later he moved on to Fairbanks, and began delivering mail to Kantishna, the mining town on what is now the west end of the Park, growing very fond of and familiar with the north side of the Alaska Range. So when a naturalist from the East Coast, Charles Sheldon, arrived in 1906 to study Dall sheep in the area, Karstens guided him around Mt. McKinley's northern foothills, delineating the habitat of the sheep. Karstens was also the co-leader of the four-man expedition which was the first party to successfully climb the true peak of Mt. McKinley, the south summit, in 1913.

OF WOLVES AND WORDS

"If societies are judged by their systems of order, justice, land rights, and family, the kingdom of the wolf is one of the most sophisticated. Few creatures, two-legged or four, honor a hierarchical system with such respect, teach and nurture their young with such diligence, defend their territories with such passion, and hunt and fight for survival with such dogged ferocity."

—ALASKA Magazine, Editors, May 1991

Meanwhile, Charles Sheldon was back in Washington, lobbying for national park status for the Dall sheep habitat, and when Mt. McKinley National Park was created in 1917, Karstens was the obvious choice to become the first Park Superintendent. He held that post from 1921-28, patrolling the Park boundaries by dogsled. He died in 1955 in Fairbanks, at age 73.

Pioneer Climbs

Many pioneers and prospectors had seen The Mountain and approached it, but Alfred Brooks, a member of the first U.S. Geological Survey expedition in Alaska (1902), first set foot on it. He approached it from the south, and reached an elevation of 7,500 feet before running out of time. He published an article in the Jan. 1903 issue of *National Geographic,* in which he recommended approaching The Mountain from the north. Following that suggestion, the next attempt was from the north, led by James Wickersham, U.S. District Judge for Alaska. Judge Wickersham was sent from Seattle to bring law and order to Eagle in 1900; he moved to Fairbanks in 1903. That summer, he had a spare couple of months, and set out to climb The Mountain, traveling more than 100 miles overland and reaching the 7,000-foot level of the north face, later named Wickersham Wall in honor of His Honor.

That same summer, Dr. Frederick Cook, who'd been with Peary's first party to attempt the North Pole (1891) and Amundsen's Antarctic expedition (1897), also attempted to climb The Mountain from the north, and reached 11,300 feet. In 1906, Cook returned to attempt McKinley from the south, but failed to get near it. His party broke up and went their separate directions, and a month later, Cook sent a telegram to New York claiming he'd reached the peak. This was immediately doubted by the members of his party, who challenged his photographic and cartographic "evidence." But through public lectures and articles, Cook's reputation as the first man to reach the peak grew. Two years later, he claimed to have reached the North Pole several months ahead of another Peary expedition, and Cook began to enjoy a cult

status in the public consciousness. Simultaneously, however, his credibility among fellow explorers rapidly declined, and Cook vanished from sight. This further fueled the controversy, and led to the Sourdough Expedition of 1910.

Four sourdoughs in Fairbanks simply decided to climb The Mountain to validate or eviscerate Cook's published description of his route. They left town in Dec., climbed to the north peak in early April, then the three members who'd actually reached the peak stayed in Kantishna to take care of business, while the fourth member, Tom Lloyd, who hadn't reached the peak, returned to Fairbanks and lied that he had. By the time the other three returned to town in June, Lloyd's story had already been published, and widely discredited. So nobody believed the other three—*especially* when they claimed they'd climbed up to the north peak and down to their base camp at 11,000 feet in 18 hours, with a thermos of hot chocolate, four doughnuts, and dragging a 14-foot spruce log that they planted up top and claimed still to be there! Finally, in 1913, the Hudson Stuck/Harry Karstens expedition reached the true summit, the south peak, and could prove it beyond a shadow of a doubt. Only then was the Sourdough Expedition vindicated: all four members of the Stuck party had seen the spruce pole still standing on the north peak!

Since then, 2,000 people have reached the south peak, from ages 16-69. For the full story on the early attempts, read the excellent *Pioneer Climbs,* by Terris Moore, and for the report on the subsequent explorations, mapping expeditions, and scientific excursions on The Mountain, read *A Tourist Guide to Mt. McKinley,* by Bradford Washburn.

Created And Expanded

Woodrow Wilson signed the bill that created Mt. McKinley National Park, Alaska's first, in 1917. The Park road was begun five years later, completed to Kantishna in 1940. In 1980, with the passage of the Alaska National Interest Lands Conservation Act (ANILCA), with its famous section d2, McKinley Park was renamed Denali National Park and

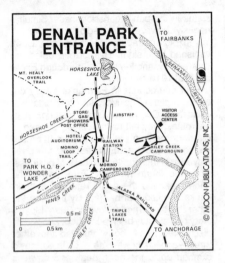

DENALI PARK ENTRANCE

TO FAIRBANKS

MT. HEALY OVERLOOK TRAIL

HORSESHOE LAKE

NENANA RIVER

HORSESHOE CREEK

STORE/ GAS/ SHOWERS POST OFFICE

AIRSTRIP

VISITOR ACCESS CENTER

© MOON PUBLICATIONS, INC.

HOTEL/ AUDITORIUM

RAILWAY STATION

RILEY CREEK CAMPGROUND

MORINO LOOP TRAIL

TO PARK H.Q. & WONDER LAKE

MORINO CAMPGROUND

HINES CREEK

ALASKA RAILROAD

RILEY CREEK

TRIPLE LAKES TRAIL

0   0.5 mi
0   0.5 km

TO ANCHORAGE

Preserve and expanded to nearly six million acres, or roughly the size of Vermont.

WHAT TO TAKE

Because of the lack of affordable indoor accommodation, the rainy and cool nature of the Park summer, the crowded conditions of the backcountry, and the small selection at both grocery stores, it's essential to be well prepared if you're planning to hang around the Park for any length of time. Experienced backpackers should have no problem making themselves at home at Denali for a week or more, but even novice campers, with the proper equipment, can be comfortable in the worst weather. If you've made it to the middle of Alaska without a tent, beg, borrow, *or buy* one. It's the only thing that stands between you and cold, wet nights (and possible hypothermia). And a good sleeping bag is worth its weight in warmth and comfort.

Bring as much food as you can carry—grocery prices around here are what you would expect, and even the most beefless burger will bludgeon your budget bloodless, bubba. Raw and dehydrated foods, along with old standby nuts, seeds, and dried fruits, will see

you through a minimalist Park experience. But with a small backpacking stove, freeze-dried and instant foods, along with grains and beans (sprouting for a few days diminishes cooking time and fuel) are convenient, filling, and sometimes even tasty. A little flour, dried milk, and cheese can be the basis for numerous sauces and stews. You might consider bringing extra fuel along for security, and don't forget matches. Layers of clothing (T-shirt or thermals, wool shirt, down vest or parka, etc.) are as useful here as everywhere else in Alaska, and hiking boots are imperative. A sponge is a handy item to have along, as are extra plastic bags (and don't forget the wire ties). For more helpful hints, see p. 52 in the Introduction.

SIGHTS

Visitor Access Center

Make sure to stop off at the Visitor Center near the beginning of the Park road. Open from 5:45 a.m.-7 p.m. daily, the $3.2 million new facility opened in May '90. In 1991, the park finally begain charging admission: $3 for visitors between 16 and 62, $5 per family. This pass is good for seven days only, or buy an annual permit for $15. At the Access Center, visit the backcountry hiking desk, the camping permit desk, and the shuttle bus token desk. It's $12 a night to camp at one of the six park campgrounds ($3 a night at the Marino walk-in campground across from the Park Hotel. Also check the bulletin board for a schedule of daily naturalist programs—guided walks, talks, slide shows, kids' programs, etc.

Shuttle buses start running at 5 a.m.; from 6 a.m. to 3 p.m., they run every 20 minutes. Reservations can be made up to two days in advance. Then get your token (free) for the next available seat on a shuttle bus. Latest reports have it that to get a seat for the same day, you need to be in line at the info center no later than 6 a.m.; otherwise, take your chances later on, or be prepared to get a token for the next day. Although the shuttle buses theoretically stop if you flag them down anywhere on the Park road, overcrowding has become such a problem that most people won't get off the bus, for fear that there won't be a seat when they want to come out of the Park, and they'll be stuck there forever. It's probably a bad idea to try to get a seat heading into the Park anywhere this side of Teklanika, or heading out of the Park any where this side of Toklat.

Denali Park Hotel

The original Lodge had 84 rooms, tennis courts, badminton room, and cigar counter; according to *McKay's Guide to Alaska,* published in 1959, a double with bath went for $17. It burned down on Labor Day, 1972, the same year that the George Parks Highway opened, the shuttle system began, and visitors doubled. In order to be ready to open the next May, construction continued all winter on a new hotel, with three wings of modular units, and a dozen Pullman sleeper and dining cars rolled in on tracks laid by the Alaska Railroad. This "emergency" accommodation still stands today, 18 years later, with the train cars in front (which never fail to confuse most tourists who pull up from the train depot!), though the Park Service has recently judged them not fit for human habitation. The lobby is dark and congenial, a good place to watch the action, meet other travelers, and succumb to your Big Mac attack (at the snack shop) or craving for a cold beer (at the Golden Spike Saloon). The gift shop has a large selection of the usual; Denali Park T-shirts and sweatshirts are the hot-selling items. You now see them all over the Lower 48.

The Park Service auditorium in back of the hotel hosts varying interpretive programs on a wide range of topics about Denali Park, at 2:30 and 7 daily. They also crank up the "Denali Wilderness" film at 11 and 1:30 daily. Sixty- to 90-minute walks leave from the hotel's front dock at 8 a.m. and 8:30 p.m. daily, led by naturalists.

Park Headquarters

One of the highlights of the Park is the Sled Dog Demonstration at the kennels behind HQ. The dogs are beautiful and accessible (the ones not behind fences are chosen for friendliness and patience with people), and the anxious collective howl they orchestrate when the lucky six dogs are selected to run is something to hear. Naturalists give a talk about the current and historical uses of dogs in the Park, their breeding and training, differ-

VICINITY OF PARK ENTRANCE

TO FAIRBANKS
HEALY ROADHOUSE
NATIONAL PARK BOUNDARY
CANYON CAMPGROUND
McKINLEY CHALET & DENALI DELI
DENALI CROWS NEST
LOG CABINS & RAFTING
McKINLEY RAFT TOURS
LYNX CREEK GAS
GROCERIES, PIZZA & PUB
McKINLEY/DENALI SALMON BAKE
HARPER LODGE
PARK HOTEL
INFORMATION
PARK H.Q.
TO WONDER LAKE
R.R. STATION
GRIZZLY BEAR CAMPER PARK
MT McKINLEY VILLAGE
DENALI RAFT ADVENTURES
DENALI CABINS
0   3 mi
0   3 km
NATIONAL PARK BOUNDARY
CARLO CREEK LODGE
TO ANCHORAGE
© MOON PUBLICATIONS, INC.

ent commands for controlling them, and sometimes the fascinating statistics of maintaining a working kennel in a national park. Then certain dogs, according to a rotating schedule, are taken from their cages or houses, hitched up to a wheel sled, and run around a gravel track. The enthusiasm of the dogs to get off the chain and into the harness is an eyebrow-raising glimpse into the consciousness of Alaskan sled dogs—they live to run.

Demonstrations are given daily at 10, 2, and 3. A free shuttle bus leaves the Park Hotel's front dock 20 minutes before the hours of the demos. Don't miss this one.

Along The Road

A few miles beyond HQ the road climbs out of the boreal forest, levels off, and travels due west through a good example of taiga. The ridgeline to the north (right) of the road is known as the **Outer Range,** foothills of the massive Alaska Range to the south (left). The Outer Range is much older than the Alaska Range, of different geological origins, much more rounded and eroded than the jagged Alaska Range. First view of The Mountain comes up at Mile 9; look southwest. The day has to be nearly perfectly clear to see McKinley from here: you're at around 2,400 feet and The Mountain is over 20,000 feet, which leaves nearly 18 grand spread over 70-odd miles of potential cloud cover. That's a lot of potential.

Next you pass Checkpoint Charlie and the **Savage River Campground,** then wind down to the river valley and cross the bridge. From the bridge, look upriver (left) and notice the broad, U-shaped, glacial valley with large gravel deposits forming braids or channels, then look right to compare the V-shaped valley obviously cut by running water. The Savage Glacier petered out right at the bridge around 15,000 years ago during the last Ice Age. Here you also kiss the pavement goodbye, then start climbing Primrose Ridge, which offers excellent hiking especially in June and early July, when the wildflowers are in full bloom. Turn around and look back at the Savage bridge; the stark rock outcrop-

ping just up from it has a distinct resemblance to an Indian's facial bone structure, which is how the Savage got its name. Just up the road is a pullout—if The Mountain's out, *make* the driver stop for the clear shot.

McKinley disappears behind jagged lower peaks as the road descends into the broad, glacial **Sanctuary River** valley. Watch for moose, caribou, fox, lynx, waterfowl, and eagles along here. Right on the other side of the Sanctuary is a good view down at a "drunken forest," one effect that permafrost has on the vegetation. Notice how many of the trees are leaning at bizarre and precarious angles, with some of them down entirely. As an adaptation to the permafrost, these spruce trees have evolved a root system that spreads horizontally across the surface soil; the tap root sinks only a foot or two. So the taller a tree grows around here, the less support it maintains, and the more susceptible it is to falling over. When the surface soil becomes saturated (due to lack of absorption over the permafrost), it sometimes shifts, either spontaneously or due to slight tremors (a major fault runs through here), taking the trees with it.

Next you descend into the broad **Teklanika River** valley, with a good view across the river at the three vegetation zones on the mountain slopes: forest, taiga, and tundra. You pass a number of small ponds in this area, known as "kettles," usually formed when a retreating glacier drops off a large block of ice, which melts, leaves a depression, and fills with rainwater. The stagnant water is very rich in nutrients, and provides excellent hatching grounds for Alaska's famous mosquitos, and as such are good feeding spots for ducks and shorebirds. Look for mergansers, goldeneyes, sandpipers, buffleheads, and phalaropes in these ponds. And in some of the higher, smaller, more private kettles, look for hikers and Park employees with no clothes on . . . maybe even join them, if you care to brave the skeeters, which have been known to show up on Park Service radar screens.

Cross the river and enter **Igloo Canyon,** where you turn almost due south. The moun-

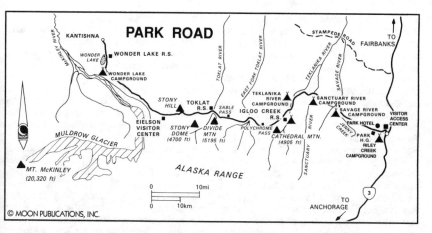

tain on the right is Igloo (4,800 feet); the one on the left is Cathedral (4,905 feet). Igloo is in the Outer Range, Cathedral in the Alaska Range. Closest distance between the two ranges, it's right on the migration route of the Dall sheep, and a great place to view the white dots on the slopes, or climb either mountain to get close. **Sable Pass** is next, at 3,900 feet the second-highest point on the road. This area is closed to hiking and photography, due to the large grizzly population. Keep your eyes peeled. Also, the next good views of The Mountain are from these highlands.

Once you cross the **East Fork River** (great hiking out onto the flats from here), you begin your ascent of Polychrome Pass, one of the most spectacular and sphincter-clamping sections of the road. If you're scared of heights or become frightened at the 1,000-foot drop-offs, just do what the driver does—close your eyes. These rocks have a high iron content; rate of oxidation and the combination of the iron with other minerals determines the different shades of rust, orange, red, and purple. The chemical toilets here are the first rest stop for the shuttle buses. Look and listen for hoary marmots in the nearby rocks, and from here almost the rest of the way to Eielson Visitor Center, watch for caribou and wolves; these are the Murie flats,

where wildlife biologist Adolph Murie studied the lifestyle of *Canis lupus*.

Descend to the **Toklat River,** the last and largest you cross before Eielson. The Toklat's source is the Sunrise Glacier, just around the bend upriver (left). You can see from the size of the river how big the glacier was 20,000 years ago. Great hiking up into the Alaska Range from here. Next you climb up **Stony Hill,** and if the weather is cooperating, when you crest the ridge, you're in for the thrill of a lifetime: Denali, The Great One, in all its immense, majestic glory. You can't believe that The Mountain is still 40 miles away! But wait, you get another five miles closer, crossing **Thorofare Pass,** highest elevation on the road (3,950 feet). Finally you arrive at Eielson Visitor Center.

Eielson Visitor Center

Open daily 9:30 a.m.-7:30 p.m., the view from here, weather cooperating, is unforgettable. Even if you can only see the bottom 12,000 or 14,000 feet, have a naturalist or your driver point to where the top of Mt. McKinley is, and visualize it in your mind's eye. Also, things change fast around here, so keep an eye out for the peak popping out of the clouds as a surprise just for you. The Visitor Center has running water and flush toilets, sells film, maps, and books, and has a nice display delineating the peaks and features in the view. Naturalists lead 30-minute "Tundra Walks" at 1 and 3 p.m. daily; leave Riley Creek by 11 a.m. to catch the second one. Rangers lead "Discovery Hikes" taking a half day or more, which are posted at the Visitor Centers. The excellent backpacking zones in this area are usually the first to fill up.

To Wonder Lake

Half the buses turn around at Eielson and travel back the same 62 miles; the other half go on another 25 miles to Wonder Lake. If The Mountain's not out, you might think twice about adding another three hours onto the bus ride. But if McKinley is visible, as soon as you get to Eielson, sign up on the waiting list for the next seat on the Wonder Lake run. The road comes within 25 miles of The Mountain, passing **Muldrow Glacier**, which is covered by a thick black layer of glacial till and vegetation. From Wonder Lake, the **Wickersham Wall** rises magnificently above the intervening plains, with the whole Alaska Range stretching out on each side. In addition, the reflection from the lake doubles your pleasure and doubles your fun, from which even the mosquitos here, some of the most savage, blood-thirsty, insatiable beasts of the realm, cannot detract.

ACTIVITIES

Hiking Around The Hotel

Horseshoe Lake Trail starts behind the McKinley Mercantile and parallels the road till the railroad crossing; then it descends to the lake, where you might see waterfowl and beaver. Pick up a self-guiding brochure at Riley Creek or at the overlook by the tracks; two and a half miles roundtrip—easy and enjoyable. **Morino Loop Trail** goes through the forest between the hotel and tenters' campground. Hiking the five-mile roundtrip **Mt. Healy Overlook Trail** is a great way to get the lay of the land, see The Mountain if it's out, quickly leave the crowds behind, and get your heart pumping. Pick up the trail near

the top of the back parking lot, or have an employee point you in the right direction. Once at the overlook, keep climbing the ridges for another several hours to get to the peak (5,200 feet).

Hiking In The Park

Grab a window seat on the left side of the shuttle bus, and ride until you get stiff, sore, or inspired. Or ask at the backcountry desk at Riley Creek, or any hotel employee you run across, where the best hiking is found. Popular areas include up the Savage River toward Fang Mountain; down the far side of Cathedral Mountain toward Calico Creek (get off the bus just before the Sable Pass closure); up Tatler Creek a little past Igloo Mountain; anywhere on the East Fork flats below Polychrome toward the Alaska Range; anywhere around Stony Hill; and the circumnavigation of Mt. Eielson (get off five to six miles past the Visitor Center, cross the hundred braids of the Thorofare River, and walk around the mountain, coming back up to the Visitor Center).

Large as it is, it's nearly impossible to get lost in the Park—you're either north or south of the road. And since the road travels mostly through open alpine tundra, there aren't any man-made trails to follow—just pick a direction and book. Usually you'll want to make for higher ground in order to: a) get out of the knee- to hip-high dwarf shrubbery of the moist tundra and onto the easy hiking of the alpine, b) get to where the breeze will keep the skeeters at bay, and c) see more. Or walk along the gravel riverbars into the mountains, though depending on the size of the gravel, it can be ankle-twisting. Hiking boots are a must, and carry water, compass, and binoculars. And keep your eyes and ears wide open for wildlife that you don't want to get close to, sneak up on, or be surprised by.

Rafting

Four raft companies run the Nenana, from two-hour canyon trips ($35-40) to four-hour long-distance floats ($50). All provide raingear, boots, and life jackets, plus transportation to and from the hotels. Pick up the different brochures, decide, and book at any of the travel desks. **Denali Raft** gets high marks from readers.

Flightseeing

If The Mountain is out and there's room on the plane, this is the time to hand over one of those precious $100 traveler's checks, or pull out the credit card. These one-hour flights ($120 pp) around McKinley will leave you flying high for days. Book at the travel desks, or at the office of Denali Wilderness Air at the train depot.

ACCOMMODATIONS

Indoors

The **Happy Wanderer Hostel** provides eight beds in a basic house with kitchen facilities; $15 for a bed for the night. There's no running water, but it's dry and clean. Look for the blue cabin on the south end (closest to the Park entrance) of the shuttle bus parking lot across from Lynx Creek. Check-in times are a bit vague—call 683-2690 for information. You can catch the Chalet shuttle buses and walk back five minutes. For a nice place with running water, hot showers, laundry, and a home-baked continental breakfast, you can stay at the **Denali Hostel** for $22. It's eight miles north, but the proprietors will pick you up (at 5 or 9 p.m.) and drop you back off in the morning at the Visitor Access Center.

The next cheapest place to stay inside is at the **Denali Salmon Bake** cabins; $55. Call 683-2733 for reservations.

A number of cabins have been built on private land around the Park entrances to the north and south. A little more rustic than the hotels, but just as comfortable, and 25-30% less expensive, are **Denali Crows Nest**, tel. 683-2723, on the hill overlooking all the activity just north of the Park on the Parks Highway, **Denali Cabins**, tel. 683-2642 or **Grizzly Cabins**, tel. 683-2696, down by McKinley Village at the south entrance.

Rick and Keri Zarcone, long-time McKinleyites and owners of the popular Lynx Creek pizza parlor, opened the **Mt. McKinley Motor Lodge** next door to Lynx Creek in

1991—the first bona fide motel in the area. With all the lodges, chalets, cabins, B&Bs, roadhouses, and campgrounds proliferating over the past decade, *why* it took a nice motel so long to arrive is curious. But *by whom* is not: Rick Zarcone has proved himself to be one of Denali's most farsighted and successful locals. The rooms, with views, color TV, and front-door parking, are $94 d, a good $20-40 more reasonable than the nearby comparable lodging. This is a true motor lodge—no shuttle transportation is provided—and an idea whose time has come to Denali. Call 683-1240 in the summer, 683-2567 the rest of the year, for reservations.

Among the hotels, the best deal is at the **McKinley Chalets,** tel. 276-7234 year-round. You've got to call and book amazingly early to get one; most are automatically blocked for the tour companies. The two-room suites go for $122, but can sleep four comfortably, five with a rollaway, and you get the use of the recreation center: pool, sauna, Jacuzzi, weight room—not a bad deal if you can get a reservation and stuff several bodies in.

If you have your own transportation and don't mind staying a little away from the action, the **Healy Roadhouse,** roughly six miles north, tel. 283-2273, has 13 motel rooms for $50 s, $55 d. The **Totem Motel,** about three miles north of there, has 36 rooms for $65.

The **Healy Historic Hotel** at Mile 248, tel. 683-2242, originally housed local Alaska Railroad workers and coal miners, and served as the community center. The Railroad sold the hotel in 1985 to Carlyle and Dee Boberg, who moved it to the intersection, and proceeded to restore it to the tune of a cool half-mil. One of 29 rooms goes for $70 d; the restaurant is open 6 a.m.-10 p.m.

Camping Inside The Park

Inside the Park seven campgrounds offer a total of 230 sites. Limited reservations are accepted at the Public Lands offices; otherwise, sign up at Visitors Access Center when you arrive. During peak season all the sites are filled by noon. It's best to get to the VAC at 7 a.m. and get in line. Sites go for $12 a night, and the maximum stay is 14 days, so plan your stay accordingly—no refunds. Just over 100 of the 230 sites are at **Riley Creek** at the Park entrance, which has flush toilets and a dump station. This campground is mostly for RVs and car campers. **Morino Campground** is for tents only next to the depot, a short walk from the hotel. It's officially listed at 10 sites, but you can usually find a patch of ground for your tent, $3. Rangers regularly comb the nearby woods looking for squatters.

You can drive to **Savage River Campground,** with 34 sites, so it fills up fast. Also, note that many of the shuttle buses are still full when they get there, so make sure to ask what time the buses that deadhead (depart empty) from the Park entrance arrive, which guarantees you a seat. The **Wonder Lake Campground** is also extremely popular for hiking and the potential to see The Mountain, especially around sunset and sunrise, when the alpenglow turns it purple and pink, and you'll expose every frame of film you have, plus make a permanent imprint on your retina.

Camping Outside The Park

The closest camping to the Park entrance is one mile north at **Lynx Creek,** tel. 683-2215, with 42 sites at $16 apiece. **KOA Kampground,** tel. 683-2379, is 10 minutes north of the Park at Healy, charging $17 d for one of 88 sites; it's a somewhat wooded area but right next to the road. **Grizzly Bear Campground,** eight miles south of the turnoff into Denali at the southern entrance, tel. 683-2696, has 59 sites which go for $15 each.

West End

The latest boom neighborhood near Denali Park, the town of Kantishna, 85 miles west of the Park entrance at the western end of the Park road, now has four roadhouses and several in the planning stages. The Kantishna area has been settled since 1905, when several thousand miners rushed to the foothills just north of Mt. McKinley to mine, as of 1978, 55,000 ounces of gold, 265,000 ounces of silver, plus millions of pounds of lead, zinc, and antimony. After 1980 and the Alaska National Interest Lands Conservation Act, which expanded Denali Park's boundaries, Kantishna found itself inside the Park, and in 1985, mining was halted by court order. Without their traditional livelihood, some of the property owners have gone into the tourism business.

Kantishna Roadhouse, Box 397, Denali, AK 99755, tel. 733-2535 or 683-2710, run by Roberta Wilson, is highly recommended for comfort, service, and friendliness, along with restaurant, bar, and gold-panning. Rates are $108 s, $140 pp with meals. At **Camp Denali** and **North Face Lodge,** Box 67, Denali, AK 99755, tel. 683-2290, rates start at $100 s and go up to $200 pp which includes meals and transportation.

OTHER PRACTICALITIES

Food

Sentimental favorite is the **Denali Dining Room** at the Park Hotel, where I worked as a waiter for a couple of years. This room also has the widest range of prices and dishes on any menu at the Park. The **Whistle Stop Snack Shop** next door has the usual $6 burgers and fish and chips; try the Polish sausage sandwich. **The Deli,** at the Chalets, is similar, but with a better sandwich selection. **Lynx Creek,** at Mile 238, a mile north of the Park entrance, serves excellent pizza, pasta, subs, and salads; it's often full of locals, seasonals, and *Alaska-Yukon Handbook* readers—recommended.

Across the street is the **Denali Salmon Bake,** serving the usual fish and ribs for $16. A better deal for salmon-bake fare is at **Alaska Cabin Night** ($18) at the lower Chalets. This is all-you-can-eat (the Salmon Bake isn't), and the dinner theater comes with the food—the waitpeople are also the entertainers. Corny but fun, you could see your shuttle or tour driver taking advantage of the large spread. **Crow's Nest** has a bar, steakhouse and a great view from the deck. The **Denali Fruit Express,** a step van outfitted like a catering truck, stops at the Park post office every Thurs. between 7:30 and 8:30 p.m., or check the bulletin boards for current schedule.

Entertainment

The Park Service puts on talks, walks, slide shows, movies, kids' programs, etc.—check the bulletin boards at Riley Creek, Eielson, and the post office. The locals hang out at the **Gold Spike Saloon** in the Park Hotel; employees hang out at Lynx Creek. Ask around for what night is dance night at Lynx these days. The lobby of the Park Hotel is a good place to catch the action. And don't forget the free *Denali Wilderness* film in the auditorium at 11 and 1:30.

Services

You can buy the necessities at either grocery store, **McKinley Mercantile** next to the Park Hotel, and **Lynx Creek** at Mile 238, but it's best to bring as much as you can carry from Fairbanks or Anchorage. Coin-operated showers ($2, no time limit) are in a small bathhouse behind McKinley Mercantile, open 7 a.m. to 10 p.m.; pay at the Mercantile. The showers and laundry rooms in the dormitory right behind the hotel and at the bottom of the road that comes up from the lower Chalets are for employees only. The closest official medical aid is a physician's assistant in Healy, 11 miles north of the Park, tel. 683-2211. The hotel company hires a nurse or even a doctor to fill one of its positions; ask around. Any emergencies should be reported immediately to the Park Service, tel. 683-2295.

Miscellaneous Information

The Park is open year-round, though the facilities are only in business from mid-May to mid-September. A skeleton winter Park Service crew patrols the Park by dogsled, and hauls out the season's garbage. After the first heavy snowfall, the Park road is only plowed to HQ, but many locals run dogs and snowshoe. The wildflowers peak around summer solstice (as do the mosquitos); the berries, rose hips, and mushrooms are best in mid-Aug. (as are the noseeums). The fall colors on the tundra are gorgeous around Labor

Day weekend, the crowds start to thin out, and the northern lights start to appear, but it can get very cold. Most questions can be answered at the Visitor Center at the Park entrance, but if you have an especially esoteric, academic, theoretic, or thermodynamic matter on your mind, try the staff or small library at Park HQ. For brochures and general info, write Denali National Park, P.O. Box 9, Denali Park, AK 99701.

TRANSPORTATION

Getting To And From

By **train**, Alaska Railroad leaves Fairbanks at 8:30 a.m. and arrives at Denali at 12:30 p.m., $39 one way, and departs Anchorage at 8:30 a.m., arriving Denali at 3:45 p.m., $78. Inside the Park depot is a railroad gift shop, storage lockers, and a big board of brochures. The train leaves the Park northbound at 3:55 p.m., southbound at 12:45 p.m.

Westours/Gray Line, Alaska Sightseeing, Royal Hiway, and **Denali Express** buses and vans head out from the Park in both directions daily, en masse. Cheapest is Denali Express, tel. 274-8539 in Anchorage, $25 to Fairbanks, $50 to Anchorage. The other tour buses are more plentiful, competitive with (though a little higher than) the railroad. Make your arrangements with the expeditors for each company at the hotels.

Getting Around

In 1971, before the George Parks Highway connected McKinley Park to Fairbanks (125 miles) and Anchorage (245 miles), you either had to take the train, or from Fairbanks you had to drive down to Delta Junction, take the Richardson Highway to Paxson, the Denali Highway to Cantwell, then the Parks Highway up to the Park entrance, for a grand total of 340 miles. From Anchorage you had to drive to Glenallen, then up the Richardson to Paxson, over to Cantwell, etc., for 440 miles. That year, nearly 45,000 visitors passed through the Park. In 1972, when the George Parks Highway radically reduced driving times from both main urban centers, almost 90,000 visitors came. In anticipation of the huge jump in tourism, the Park Service initiated the shuttle system of school buses running a regularly scheduled service along the Park road. It started out free, and 15 years later it's still technically free, though the entrance fee ostensibly covers the ride.

There's no question that the shuttle system is highly beneficial to the Park experience: the road is tricky and dangerous, crowds are much more easily controlled, there's much less impact on the wildlife (which take the buses for granted), and it's much easier to see wildlife when 40 passengers have eyeballs, binoculars, spotting scopes, and telephotos trained on the tundra.

Queues start forming at 5 a.m. for the first bus out at 6, and get longer as the day progresses. It's recommended that you catch the early-morning buses: better chance to see wildlife and The Mountain in the cool of the morning, and more time to get off the bus and fool around in the backcountry. To do so, plan on catching the bus the second (or third) day you're in the Park, and make reservations as soon as you arrive.

You can get off the bus and flag it down to get back on (if there's room) anywhere along the road. Many riders never get off the bus at all, and just stay on for the entire roundtrip. Schedules are readily available at the Visitors Centers and hotels. Take everything you need, as nothing (except books) is for sale inside the Park.

A free shuttle runs frequently between the Park Hotel and the McKinley Chalets, servicing all connections and scheduled events. This makes it easy to familiarize yourself with all the facilities in between, and barhop at night looking for what little action you might find. Another bus runs (less frequently) down to McKinley Village Hotel and Denali Cabins.

Tour

The Park tour, in Blue Bird buses that are a little more comfortable than the yellows, leaves at 6 a.m. and 3 p.m. You get a narration and box lunch, but only go as far as Toklat, 13 miles short of Eielsen Visitor Center; $44.

(GORDY OHLIGER)

(GORDY OHLIGER)

SOUTHCENTRAL

Southcentral Alaska is a land of short rivers, long mountain ranges, and wide valleys, which extends north from the Gulf of Alaska to the crest of the Alaska Range. The Kenai and Chugach mountains are a rugged strip 60 miles wide that swing northeast along the Gulf, from Cook Inlet to the Yukon border. To the north lie the Matanuska and Susitna valleys, with Mt. McKinley visible beyond. Much of the area around Prince William Sound and on the Kenai Peninsula is included in the Chugach National Forest. In many ways, Southcentral is the rich heartland of Alaska, with one big metropolis (Anchorage) and many picturesque small towns, the main agricultural region of the state, and some of the state's finest scenery and best hiking and camping opportunities. Getting around is easy by roads and a variety of public transportation, including an efficient ferry system, brings the best within reach. Southcentral Alaska offers something for everyone.

DENALI STATE PARK

Another superlative state facility, Denali State Park is actually a continuation of Denali National Park, sharing its southeast border. Its 324,240 acres, half the size of Rhode Island, provide an excellent alternative wilderness experience to the crowds and hassles of its federal neighbor. The Mountain is visible from all over the Park, bears are abundant, and you won't need to stand in line for a permit to hike or camp while you wait for McKinley's mighty south face to show itself. Several trails offer a variety of hiking experiences and spectacular views. However, the park is accessible only by car, and it's imperative to be super prepared—the nearest grocery store is 50 miles away.

Sights
If The Mountain or even "just" some of the lower peaks of the Alaska Range are out, you

won't need to read the next sentence to know what or where the sights are. The best viewpoint along the highway in the park is at the large pullout at Mile 135, a half mile north of the Mountain Haus. Set up your tripod and shoot shoot shoot. A signboard here identifies the glaciers and peaks. Other unforgettable viewpoints are at Miles 147, 158, and 162. The **Alaska Veterans Memorial,** within walking distance of Byers Lake Campground, is a shrine consisting of five monumental concrete blocks with stars carved out, commemorating the enormous contribution the armed forces have made to Alaska since its purchase by the U.S. in 1867. As usual, the state planners chose and developed this spot with care and respect. Turn your back to the monument, and if you're lucky, there's blue-white McKinley, perfectly framed by tall spruce trees.

Trails

Little Coal Creek trailhead is at mile 164, five miles south of the park's northern boundary. This is the park's gentlest climb to the alpine tundra—five miles east up the trail by Little Coal Creek, then you cut southwest along Kesugi Ridge with amazing views of the Range and glaciers; flags and cairns delineate the trail. Watch for bears! The trail goes 27.5 miles till it hooks up with Troublesome Creek Trail just up from Byers Lake Campground. About halfway there, **Ermine Lake Trail** cuts back down to the highway, an escape route in case of really foul weather. Ermine Lake Trail is not quite completed, but it is flagged well enough to follow.

Troublesome Creek Trail, so named because of frequent bear encounters, has two trailheads, one at the northeast tip of Byers Lake Mile 147), the other at Mile 138. The park brochure describes this 15-mile hike along Troublesome Creek as moderate. It connects with Kesugi Ridge Trail just up from Byers Lake, or descends to the easy five-mile **Byers Lake Loop Trail** which brings you around to both campgrounds. Just down and across the road from the Byers Lake turnoff is a family day-hike along Lower Troublesome Creek—a gentle mile.

Camping

Byers Lake Campground (61 sites, $6) offers the usual state accommodations—huge, gorgeous, uncrowded. It has abundant outhouses, water, interpretive signs, large well-maintained sites, and beautiful Byers Lake a stone's throw down the road. Just under two miles along the Loop Trail from here, or across the lake by boat, is the **Lakeshore Campground,** with six sites, outhouses, no water, but unimpeded views of The Mountain and Range from your tent flap. Across the road and a quarter mile south, **Lower Troublesome Creek Campground** has 10 sites and all the amenities of Byers Lake.

Other Practicalities

Only two commercial facilities are within park boundaries. The **Mountain Haus** at the southern entrance (mile 134) has a restaurant, lodge, and great view of The Mountain out their picture window. **Chulitna River Lodge and Café,** mile 156, is 13 miles from the north entrance, with cabins, a small menu off the grill, gas, gifts, and kids running all around. Very homey. Otherwise, the nearest civilization is 69 miles north of the northern boundary of the state park at the entrance to Denali National Park, and 48 miles south of the southern boundary at Talkeetna. Neither Denali Express nor Alaska-Denali Transit list a stop at this state park, but you could probably make arrangements with them to deliver and later collect you there for the price of a one-way through ticket.

TALKEETNA

Two closely related phenomena dominate this small bush community: The Mountain, and flying to and climbing on The Mountain. On a clear day, from the overlook a mile out on the spur road into town from the Parks Highway (mile 98), Mt. McKinley and the accompanying Alaska Range scrape the sky like a jagged white wall. Though still 60 miles northwest, you actually have to crane your neck to see the summit of the highest peak in North America. Also on a clear day, the four flightseeing and air-taxi companies take off in a continuous parade to circle McKinley, buzz up long glaciers or even land on them for a champagne lunch, then return to Talkeetna's busy airport to drop off passengers whose wide eyes, broad smiles, and shaky knees attest to the excitement of this once-in-a-lifetime thrill. In May and June, mostly, these same special "wheel-and-ski" planes might be delivering an American, European, Japa-

nese, or even African climbing expedition to the Kahiltna Glacier (elevation 7,000 feet), from where—if they're lucky—they inch their way up the popular West Buttress route 13,000 feet to the peak. On a clear day, if you're anywhere within striking distance, make a beeline for Talkeetna, and be whisked away to some of the most stunning and alien scenery you'll ever see.

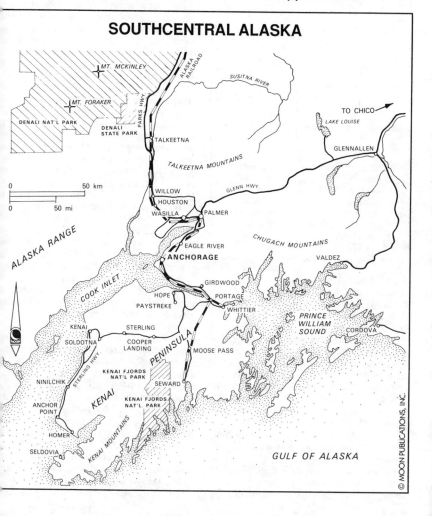

SOUTHCENTRAL ALASKA

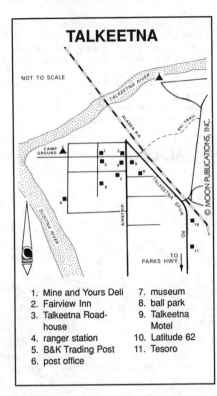

TALKEETNA

NOT TO SCALE

1. Mine and Yours Deli
2. Fairview Inn
3. Talkeetna Road-
   house
4. ranger station
5. B&K Trading Post
6. post office
7. museum
8. ball park
9. Talkeetna
   Motel
10. Latitude 62
11. Tesoro

fresh, along with a fern cookbook, and Mary's many memoirs. The gift shop also stocks rocks, crafts, burls, and souvenirs.

Turn off onto gravel roads at miles three and 12 for out-of-the-way lakes and camping spots. At Mile 13 is the big turnout with an interpretive sign on the Alaska Range and heart-stopping views—if the clouds are co operating. Then you head right into Talkeetna

For a graphic and detailed look at its his tory, check out the excellent **Talkeetna Mu seum,** open Mon.-Sat. 10-6, Sun. noon to 8 Take a left after B&K Market, which you car read all about in the museum; the museum is half a block down the side street on the righ in an old red schoolhouse. Housing hundred: of historical articles, including an eclectic li brary in the back room with eyebrow-raising old magazines and scrapbooks of newspa per clippings, the museum is dedicated t Don Sheldon and Ray Genet, hometown boys who were two of Alaska's most heroi figures. Sheldon was the honorary guiding light of Alaska's elite fraternity of bush pilot: until his untimely death from cancer in 197! at the age of 56; Genet was the all-tim record-holder of climbs on McKinley an other Alaska Range peaks until his untimel death at 27,000 feet on Mt. Everest in 197: at the age of 48. Separately and togethe they pulled off some of the most daredev rescues imaginable, and Sheldon's exploit have been immortalized in *Wager With Th Wind.* Reading the displays devoted t these giants of northern lore will give you a idea of the kind of people who gravitate t Talkeetna.

Next door to the museum is a funky littl cabin which houses the National Park Se vice ranger. Ask about wuh thappening o The Mountain, or just pull up a chair an thumb through the beat-up bookshelf copy *Wager With The Wind,* and eavesdrop on th ranger and radio! For sale are some book on mountaineering. Better yet, walk out to th airport to watch the different bush plane take off and land; strike up a conversatic with a pilot or mechanic about flying cond tions around The Weathermaker.

The ski trail signposted at the back of th small park as you enter town is hikable

Sights And Hikes

Talkeetna ("Where The Rivers Meet"), nesting at the confluence of the Talkeetna, Chulitna, and Susitna rivers, was originally settled by trappers and prospectors who paddled up the Susitna River to gain access to rich silver, coal, and fur country around the Talkeetna Mountains. The settlement got a boost when the railroad was pushed through in the early 1920s, and still remains a popular stop on the route. In 1965 the spur road from the Parks Highway to Talkeetna was completed, furthering access to the town.

A mile off the Parks Highway is **Mary Carey's** place, one of the most prolific and renowned Alaska women authors—an incredible life story. This facility, tel. 733-2428, hosts the world's only fiddlehead fern farm, selling gourmet ferns pickled, frozen, and

summer, though it'll probably be extremely muddy. To stretch your legs and keep your feet dry, saunter along the railroad tracks in either direction: graded, cleared, scenic.

Flightseeing

Best of all, *get on* one of the planes and see for yourself. Four charter companies provide service to Mt. McKinley. **Hudson's Air Service,** tel. 733-2321, offers the best deal of late: two hours flying around and landing on The Mountain, with a walk over to Base Camp, $70 pp. **Doug Geeting Aviation,** tel. 733-2366, does an 80-minute trip which includes a glacier landing, also very good value. **K2 Aviation,** tel. 733-2291, offers a variety of tours: 60-minute flightseeing, 90-minute Circle McKinley, 90-minute glacier landing, and an overnight in Kantishna, including lodging and meals ($330 pp). **Talkeetna Air Taxi,** tel. 733-2218, can give you more of the same. Inquire early in the day and you might be able to get a space or two on a partially filled flight.

Practicalities

Camp free (no amenities) at **Talkeetna River Park** at the back end of town on the banks of a slough off the river; three or four nice sites are to the left, if you can get one. Otherwise, pitch a tent anywhere along the banks here. The historic **Fairview Inn** (1923) has the best

prices of the five lodging houses—$25 s, $40 d—but their six rooms fill up fast. Take your chances and register at the bar, or write ahead to Box 379, Talkeetna, AK 99676, or call 733-2423. **Talkeetna Roadhouse,** tel. 733- 2341, has rooms for $28 s, $36 d. **Talkeetna Motel,** tel. 733-2323, charges $45 s, $55 d.

The restaurant at **Talkeetna Motel** is recommended: massive amounts of good food, reasonable prices, and relaxing surroundings. Try breakfast here, or the dinner special. **Talkeetna Roadhouse** serves family-style dinners; reserve a place before 3 p.m. **Mine and Yours Deli** has pizza, from a $5 mini cheese up to the $18.75 large kitchen sink. Sandwiches start at $6. **Sparky's** is a fast-food walk-up take-out on the left as you enter town. The **pay phone** in town is on the campground side of the Talkeetna Roadhouse.

Getting There

The turnoff to Talkeetna is 135 miles north of Anchorage and 259 miles south of Fairbanks on the George Parks Highway. The spur road is 15 miles. No buses go to Talkeetna, but hitching the spur road is easy—the locals are very friendly and they know there's only one place you can be going. They might be a little few and far between, however. Alaska Railroad's daily express "stops" at Talkeetna

You'll stay high long after you touch back down in Talkeetna from your flightseeing trip around the Great One.

(DIANA LASICH-HARPER)

every day (northbound at 11:20 a.m., southbound at 4 p.m.), and you can get on or off, but you *cannot* check any baggage, only what you can carry on. This makes it inconvenient enough to wait for the local, which leaves Anchorage Wed., Sat., and Sun. at 6:30 a.m. and arrives in Talkeetna at 9:30 a.m. **Alaska-Denali Transit** stops at Talkeetna ($25) on their way to Denali from Anchorage.

CONTINUING SOUTH

On the 45 miles from the Talkeetna cutoff to Willow, the next town, are half a dozen restaurants and gas stations, and two state campgrounds. **Montana Creek SRS,** Mile 97, is another large, attractive campground, with 89 sites, chemical toilets, water, a few short trails, and good salmon fishing in season. Two miles east of the Parks Highway on Hatcher Pass Rd. (Mile 71) is **Willow Creek SRS,** with seven sites, water, and toilets. This is a pretty and handy place to spend the night if it's getting late and you plan to travel Hatcher Pass Rd. to Independence Mine State Historical Park and Wasilla or Palmer (see below).

Willow (pop. around 200) is still a sleepy little roadside town, though 10 years ago Alaskans voted to move the state capital here; if it'd happened, Willow today would be the Brasilia (an overnight pre-fab metropolis in the middle of nowhere) of Alaska, a bureaucrat's instant wet-dream on the tundra. A multibillion-dollar city was planned, and real estate speculation went wild. However, when a second election was held in 1982 to decide whether to actually *spend* the billions, the plan was soundly defeated. For a fascinating look at this bit of Alaskan lore, read John McPhee's renowned *Coming Into The Country.* Also check out the "Capital Move Cabin" in back of the Wasilla Museum.

Nancy Lake State Recreation Area

Sixth-largest in the system, this state park has unusual topography compared with what you've become accustomed to in Interior: flat, heavily forested terrain, dotted with over 100 lakes, some interconnected by creeks.

As you might imagine, the popular activities here are fishing, boating, and canoeing, plus there's a very comfortable campground, and a couple of hiking trails. As you might also imagine, the skeeters here are thicker'n even those fabled man-eating black swarms up there in that Alaska territory.

Heading south on the Parks Highway, turn right onto a wide gravel road at Mile 67. About a quarter mile in is the Visitor Info Cabin: pick up the Nancy Lake brochure. About 1,000 feet past the cabin is a trailhead on the left to four public-use cabins (three within a few miles' hiking of the trailhead, the fourth accessible only by boat), $15 a night. For reservations, call the Parks and Recreation main office in Anchorage at 762-4565, or the Mat-Su Area Office at Finger Lakes, 745-3975. Another 1,000 feet beyond this trailhead is the **Tulik Nature Trail,** an easy walk that takes about an hour. A self-guiding brochure, wonderfully written and illustrated by creative YCC teenagers, identifies ferns, shrubs, grasses, and trees, and includes some nice legends, descriptions, and suggestions for enjoying yourself. Keep an eye out for loons, beavers, and terns, and watch for that prickly devil's club! The thorns can cause nasty infections.

The **Lynx Lake Canoe Route** begins at Milo Lakes Canoe Trailhead, mile 4.7 of the Nancy Lake Road. This 12-mile, two-leisurely-day trip hits 14 lakes, between most of which are well-marked portages, some upgraded with boardwalks over the muskeg. Hunker down for the night at any one of 10 primitive campsites (campfires in fireplaces only!). Another possibility, though requiring a long portage, is to put into the Little Susitna River at Mile 57 on the Parks Highway, and portage to Skeetna Lake, where you connect up to the southern leg of the loop trail. **Tippe Canoe Rentals** in Willow, tel. 495-6688, rents canoes for $5 an hour (up to three hours), $15 for four to eight hours, $22 up to 24 hours, up to $60 for four to seven days. They offer free pick-up and delivery to Nancy Lake, and within 15 miles of Willow.

At the end of the road is **South Rolly Lake Campground,** with 98 sites, and the usual excellent state amenities. An easy three-mile

RT trail leads to an overlook above Red Shirt Lake. Continue on this trail all the way to the lake.

HATCHER PASS ROAD

It's a boring 25 miles from Nancy Lake SRA to Wasilla on the Parks Highway. But a highly recommended side trip is the 50-mile road from Mile 71 of the Parks, two miles north of Willow, over Hatcher Pass (3,886 feet), taking in the Independence Mine State Historical Park on the way. The first 10 miles off the highway are paved, and the next 15 gravel miles are quite smooth and scenic, through beautiful forest, following Willow Creek and the route of a wagon trail built to service the gold mines along the creek. Then the road climbs four miles on rough gravel up to Summit Lake and Hatcher Pass, an area of vast vistas, high tundra, excellent hiking (and cross-country skiing), and backcountry camping. Another two miles brings you to Independence Mine.

Independence Mine State Historical Park

It's hard to imagine a park that better combines the elements of the Alaska experience: scenery, history and lore, and that noble yellow metal, gold. And it's free! This mine is very different from the panning, sluicing, deep placer, and dredging operations you've seen in Yukon and Interior. This was "hard-rock" mining, with an intricate 21-mile network of tunnels under Granite Mountain. The miners drilled into the rock, inserted explosives (which they set off at the end of shifts to give the fumes time to dissipate before the next crew went in), then "mucked" the debris out by hand, to be sorted, crushed, amalgammated, assayed, etc., a process similar to the finish operations up north.

Hard-rock or "lode" mining is often preceded by panning and placer mining. Prospectors who first took gold from Grubstake Gulch, a tributary of Willow Creek, in 1897, noticed the gold's rough, unweathered nature, which indicated a possible lode of unexposed gold nearby. In 1906, Robert Lee Hatcher staked the first lode claim, and his Alaska Free Gold Mine operated till 1924. In 1908, the Independence Mine opened on the mountain's east slope, and over the next 25 years produced several million dollars' worth. In 1937, the two mines merged into the Alaska Pacific Consolidated Mining Company, which operated Independence Mine at peak production through 1942, when WW II shut it down. A series of private sales, and public deals with the Alaska Division of Parks, culminated in 1980, leaving the state with 271 acres, including the whole mining camp, and deeding 1,000 acres to the Coronado Mining Corporation, which has active operations in the area.

A couple of dozen camp buildings are in various stages of ruin and refurbishing. Start your visit at the fascinating Visitor Center in

Independence Mine State Historical Park
(GORDY OHLIGER)

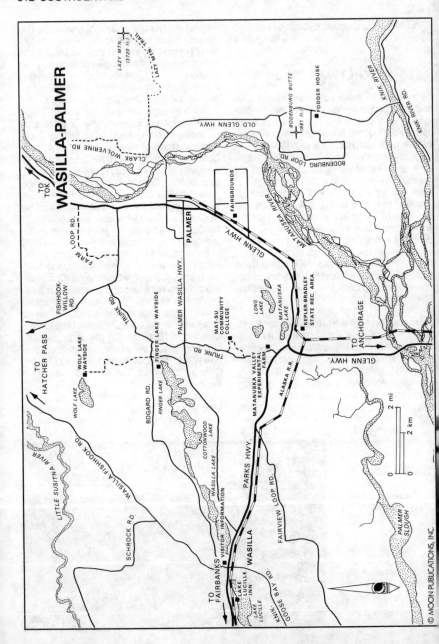

WASILLA-PALMER

© MOON PUBLICATIONS, INC.

the rehabilitated house of the camp manager, Walter Stoll. Take some time to enjoy the excellent displays: historic charts, gold-mining overview, "touch tunnel" complete with sound effects, and fascinating wage summaries of workers and management. Don't miss the spinning board which points to old black-and-white snapshots and displays vignettes about the people and scenes. Guided walks are given several times daily by park personnel ($2), but you're free to wander the whole site on your own; interpretive signs in front of most buildings describe their purpose. Independence Mine State Historical Park is a must-see on any Alaskan itinerary.

WASILLA

In 1977, Wasilla consisted of a landing strip and grocery store, which advertised the convenience of flying in from the Bush, buying Matanuska Valley produce, and flying out again—without the hassles of Anchorage. Then, when the capital looked like it might be moved to Willow, 25 miles up the highway, Anchoragites began to discover Wasilla's quiet, beauty, and affordable land, and contractors took advantage of the town's lax restrictions on development. And develop it did, with a vengeance. From 1980-82, the town's population of 1,200 doubled, then doubled again from '82-84. Stores, malls, and fast-food chains popped up faster than you could say "We do chicken right." Teeland's General Store was jacked up, moved from the corner it had sat on for over 60 years, and unceremoniously dumped in a parking lot around the block to make way for a 7-11. Even the original airstrip, which had kept Wasilla on the map for so long, is about to be moved out from the middle of all the hustle and bustle of town. Hundreds of "strip-developed" buildings along the highway are no more than three to four years old; now driving south of the Parks Highway is like passing through a space warp and reemerging in any Southern California suburb. Even the parking lots are paved!

The fact that it's such a shock, however, is instructive either way you look at it: rendering Wasilla surprisingly exotic in an Alaskan context, or enhancing one's appreciation of the rest of Alaska by comparison.

Sights
Make sure to visit **Dorothy G. Page Museum and Historical Park** on Main St. just off the Parks Highway, tel. 376-2005, open 9-6, $3. Get the eager staff-on-hand to tell the stories behind any of the museum's hundreds of artifacts, including a collection of old lenses, Mr. Herning's (a town pioneer from the '20s) original radio, and the excellent 20-year-old relief map. Downstairs through the "mining tunnel" are more displays, including an entire early dentist's office. Walk out the back door to the little settlement, with a schoolhouse, bunkhouse, smokehouse, steambath, cache, antique Ferris wheel, Teeland's General Store (built in 1914), and "Capital Move Cabin," complete with amusing bumper stickers in favor of the move. The **library** is next door; the **post office** is across the street.

Lakeshore Park at Wasilla Lake right off the highway has swimming (for the brave), picnic tables, and a great view of the craggy Chugach—great place to set up your tripod. A less crowded day-use lake area is at **Kep-**

famous Alaska-sized cabbage at the Matanuska Experimental Farm near Wasilla

ler-Bradley Lakes just beyond the junction of the Parks and Glenn highways, on the Glenn toward Palmer.

About 1,000 feet before that same intersection, take a left onto Trunk Rd. and climb the hill to the University of Alaska's **Agricultural Experimental Station.** Founded in 1917 by the U.S. Dept. of Agriculture, this 960-acre farm was deeded to the university in 1931. Agricultural information collected here was the contributing factor in colonizing this valley with Midwestern farmers in 1935. The large cabbages, giant begonias, and scores of flowers will add some vibrant color to your day. Free tours of the facility, given 8-4:30, last about an hour, and include the grounds, dairy, and lab building. Walk into the main building across from the gardens and go left on the ground floor to the tour guide office, tel. 745-3257.

Wasilla is the headquarters for the 1,049-mile **Iditarod Sled Dog Race** from Anchorage to Nome. At the company offices is a museum housing a large display of race memorabilia, Native artifacts, and pioneer and dog-mushing equipment. It's at Mile 2.2 Knik Road, open Wed. to Sun. noon to 6. Call 376-2005 for directions.

Accommodations

Several motels are strung along the highway. Heading south, the first you come to is **Kashim Inn,** tel. 376-5800, $42 d; then the **Windbreak,** tel. 376-4209, $40 d, $10 key deposit, register at the bar (the "office" upstairs is the night bartender's apartment); and the **El Toro,** tel. 376-4908, $60 d. **Mat-Su Lodge,** 1.3 Mile Bogard Rd., tel. 376-3229, charges $79 for deluxe rooms and $94 for suites. Heading south on the highway, go left on Crucey at the light, then right on Bogard for a mile.

Nearest official camping is at a state campground on **Finger Lake.** Heading south on the Parks, take a left onto Main St., then bear right at the fork onto Bogard Road. Go a few miles and turn right into Finger Lake, 42 sites, sometimes crowded. If it's full, the map on the signboard points to an overflow state campground at **Wolf Lake**—go another 1,000 feet past Finger Lake turnoff on Bogard, take a left onto Engstrom, and follow it to the left to Wolf Lake. Closest *unofficial* camping is on Lake Lucille. Go right over the railroad tracks on Snyder across from the Chevron station on the Parks. Make an immediate left and wind around to the bottom of

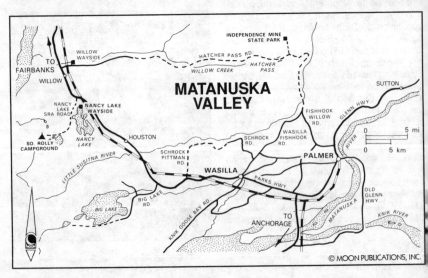

Snyder Park. Park next to the gate and stroll down to the lake, where you can set up your tent on some grassy areas right on the water out of sight of the road and houses. Good in a pinch.

Food

Wasilla has a Carrs, Safeway, Shoprite, health food stores, Roadhouse, and enough generic galloping grub to gag even a gorging glutton of a grizzly. Also keep an eye out for roadside produce stands to sample some of the valley's harvest. **Mat-Su Resort** has a good dining room with the usual prices for burgers and fried chicken. **Lake Lucille Inn,** on W. Lake Lucille Dr. at Mile 43.5 of the Parks Highway, replaced the landmark Hallea Bar. Dinner is prohibitively steep, but you can get soup and steak fries for $3 and sit by the big picture windows over the lake. The **Windbreak Café** serves good-value breakfasts and lunches.

(GORDY OHLIGER)

ANCHORAGE

It's hard to arrive in Anchorage—especially if you've been traveling around the state for a while—without some strong preconceived notions of what to expect from the place. Generally, Alaskans either love or hate Anchorage, their degree of affection or distaste usually revealed by their chosen proximity to the city. You'll certainly have heard, from well-meaning Juneau, Fairbanks, and Bush dwellers, of Anchorage's unplanned urban sprawl, its seedy downtown, traffic jams, sprouting trailer parks and condos, expensive facilities and lack of services, corporate skyscrapers, yuppie bars, airplane noise, mall mania, fast-food frenzy, crime, and pollution, that it's the antithesis of every virtue and value that God-fearing, law-abiding, and patriotic Alaskans hold sacred—in short, all the complaints about every large city in any country in the whole world. You might also have heard that Anchorage has nothing to see or do, that all the ostensible attractions are either a joke or a scam, and that if you're looking for a true

Alaskan experience, you should avoid the city altogether or try to forget that it even exists!

As a traveler you'll find yourself in Anchorage at least once on your Alaska itinerary, and all the city's drawbacks notwithstanding, you'll more than likely be pleasantly surprised by your visit. The fact is that Anchorage can be an eminently enjoyable *and* affordable place in which to hang out. You can easily fill a whole day touring downtown, another exploring its far-flung corners by bike or bus, another researching the many places to go from Anchorage and the best ways to get there, and another just lying around a downtown park for the one day in four that the sun shines. Anchorage's highlights include the Anchorage Historical and Fine Arts Museum, the 60-bed youth hostel two blocks from the Transit Center, the extensive People Mover bus system, and the 100-plus miles of biking and hiking trails. The natural beauty of the surroundings helps to lend Anchorage an

Alaskan air; if the city becomes at all oppressive, just lengthen your gaze to the Chugach Mountains, the Alaska Range, and either arm of the Cook Inlet. In addition, Anchorage is within easy striking distance of some of the most exciting and extensive hiking, climbing, fishing, kayaking, flightseeing, and wilderness areas that Alaska has to offer.

Of course, if you can't overcome the idea that "Alaska population center" is a contradiction in terms, you can simply breeze into town, make your connection, and quickly "get back to Alaska." But if you want a fully rounded experience of the 49th state, get to know Anchorage, *urban* Alaska, and come to your own conclusions.

Climate

One of the deciding factors in choosing Anchorage as a site for a main construction camp for the Alaska Railroad was its mild winters and comparatively low precipitation. The towering Alaska Range shelters Southcentral in general and the Cook Inlet Basin in particular from the frigid winter breath of the Arctic northerlies; the Kenai and Chugach mountains cast a rain shadow over the Basin, which allows only 15-20% of the annual precipitation in communities on the windward side of the ranges. Anchorage receives at most 20 inches of annual precipitation (10-12 inches of rain, 60-70 inches of snow), while Whittier, 40 miles away on the Gulf side of the Chugach, gets 175 inches. Anchorage's winter temperatures rarely drop below 10° F, with only an occasional cold streak, compared with Fairbanks' frequent 40 below; its summer temperatures rarely rise above 65° F, compared with Fairbanks' 80s and 90s.

HISTORY

Beginnings

In June 1778, Captain James Cook sailed up what's now Turnagain Arm in Cook Inlet, reaching another dead end on his amazing search for the Northwest Passage. But he did dispatch William Bligh, of HMS *Bounty* fame, to explore, and he saw some Tanaina Indians in rich otter skins. George Vancouver, who'd

also been on Cook's ship, returned in 1794 and noted Russian settlers in the area. A century later, prospectors began landing in the area and heading north to Southcentral's gold country, and in 1902 Alfred Brooks began mapping the Cook Inlet for the U.S. Geological Survey. In 1913, five settlers occupied Ship Creek, the point on the Inlet where Anchorage now stands.

A year later, Congress passed the Alaska Railroad Act and in April 1915, the route for the federally financed railroad from Seward to Fairbanks was made official: it would pass through Ship Creek, where a major staging area for workers and supplies would be located. This news traveled fast, and within a month a "ramshackle tent city" of nearly 2,000 railroad job seekers had sprung up. Things developed so quickly that in July, the U.S. Land Office auctioned off 650 parcels at the new townsite. The settlement, renamed Anchorage, grew quickly, with water, telephone and power lines, sidewalks, and schools in place within a year.

Slumps And Spurts

Railroad laborers, earning 37 cents an hour (low for Alaska), struck in 1916, after which the minimum wage was raised to 45 cents an hour. The population continued to boom, topping out at around 7,000 in 1917. With WW I and completion of the southern portion of the railroad, the number of people dropped below 2,000 in 1920, when the town incorporated, electing its first mayor and city council. Through the 1930s, Anchorage held steady at 3,000-4,000 people, but WW II changed that in a hurry. The town's strategic location led to a huge influx of military personnel, when the Army's Fort Richardson and Air Force's Elmendorf Field were constructed outside of town. By 1950, Anchorage was a prosperous "city" of over 11,000. In the following decade Anchorage also experienced the post-war boom, with the attending shortages of housing and modern conveniences, which created its own construction miniboom. In 1957, when Richfield Oil discovered black gold on the Kenai Peninsula, the oil companies started opening office buildings in the city, and the economy stabilized.

Since Statehood

Much of Anchorage collapsed in the Good Friday Earthquake, March 27, 1964, which lasted an interminable five minutes, registering 8.6 on the Richter Scale (though with today's more sensitive equipment, it's been calculated at closer to 9.2). The north side of 4th Ave. wound up eight to ten feet lower than the south side of the street. A very rich residential section on the bluff overlooking Knik Arm was destroyed. Nine people were killed and upwards of $50 million in damages were recorded. Anchorage was rebuilt, and like most of the towns around Southcentral, its appearance dates back only 25 years.

Though the pipeline doesn't come within 300 miles of Anchorage, oil money towers over town in the form of the 21-story Arco building, 20-story Hunt building, and the Chevron, Alyeska, and Teamsters office

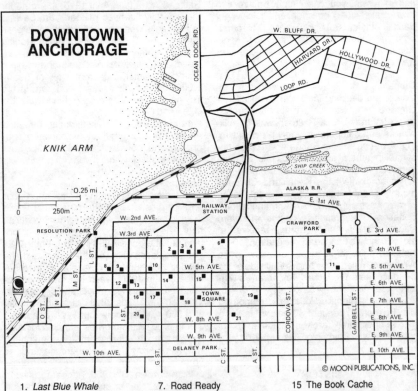

DOWNTOWN ANCHORAGE

1. *Last Blue Whale* sculpture
2. Alaska Public Lands Info. Center
3. Gray Line/Columbia Glacier Tours
4. Downtown Deli
5. McDonald's
6. downtown post office
7. Road Ready
8. Captain Cook Fountain
9. Captain Cook Hotel
10. Captain Cook Travel
11. Great Alaskan Bush Company
12. La Mex Restaurant
13. Wings 'n' Things
14. Performing Arts Center
15. The Book Cache
16. Oomingmak Producers Co-operative
17. BAC (bus accommodation center)
18. Armed Services YMCA
19. Anchorage Museum
20. youth hostel
21. Federal Building

buildings. Tourism also affects the local economy enormously, with 750,000 annual visitors spending close to $300 million. Anchorage fancies itself quite the cosmopolitan city, boasting more than 75 arts organizations, an ambitious "revitalization" program, and fancy hotels, restaurants, cafes, and bars to cater to the thousands of suits who fill the skyscrapers that gleam in the defracted light of the midnight sun. Indeed, if Juneau is bureaucratic Alaska, and Fairbanks is rank-and-file Alaska, then Anchorage is corporate Alaska.

SIGHTS

Anchorage is an easy town to get the hang of quickly. The blocks are square, with the lettered streets (A through L) going north-south and the numbered avenues (starting at 2nd Ave. just up the hill from the tracks) running east-west.

Start your tour of downtown at the **Anchorage Convention and Visitors Bureau,** corner of 4th Ave. and F St., tel. 274-3531, open 7:30-7 in summer, 8:30-6 May and Sept., 9-4 the rest of the year. Stock up on any of the brochures that interest you at the moment, to read later on your bunk bed, and be sure to take a copy of the ACVB's visitors guide magazine. Though mostly geared toward package and mainstream tourists, the walking and driving tours and two-page illustrated map of Anchorage bowl are worthwhile.

To Resolution And Elderberry Parks
Continue along the Walking Tour down the hill to the **Alaska Railroad** depot, then up the hill past the old Federal Building, which now houses the **Alaska Public Lands Information Center** (see "Information" below). Head west down 4th Ave. to the *Last Blue Whale* sculpture (between 3rd and 4th on K St.), whose happy countenance and big smile seem a bit incongruous with its name. Or maybe the felicitously figurative fiberglass fellow knows something we don't. Around the corner on L St. is **Resolution Park,** named for Captain Cook's ship, the *Resolution.* This place gets a lot of ink, and is usually crowded with visitors. But walk a block to 5th, and

down the hill to **Elderberry Park**—larger, more comfortable, and frequeted by Anchorage families. At the bottom of the park is one of the historical signposts that stand in a dozen locations around downtown; this one is all about pioneer aviation, Anchorage in 1915, and the Oscar Anderson house (next door). Also here is convenient access to the **Tony Knowles Coastal Trail,** an asphalt track that wends its way along the Knik Arm from downtown past the airport to Kincaid Park at Point Campbell, where the Knik and Turnagain arms meet. Stroll the trail a ways—at least through the tunnel, beyond which you leave downtown behind and emerge into a new world: the grand sweep of the Arm, tidal flats, rock wall up to the trail, railroad tracks, sparsely populated residential neighborhood on the hill. On nice summer weekends this trail is more like a freeway, with people on every kind of wheels imaginable: bike and unicycle riders, roller skaters and bladers, ice-skaters and cross-country skiers, skateboarders, joggers (legs pumping in a mechanical circle), babies in carriages.

Also wander around the affluent residential area beyond Elderberry Park known as The Cove; **Nulbay Park** is at the corner of 7th and O, from where you can see Mt. McKinley if it's out.

Alaska Experience
Head back up the hill and east along 6th Avenue. Across the street from the **People Mover Transit Center,** is the Alaska Experience. If you get dizzy or motionsick easily, skip this 40-minute film, shown on the hour 10-9, tel. 276-3730. The half-dome screen and special 180-degree fish-eye cinematography create a perspective so big and so melodramatic and so off, that it actually dwarfs even the vast panoramas it strives to capture, and gets quickly tiresome. One thing's for sure, though—when you walk out of the Experience, you'll know the world is round!

To Anchorage Museum Of History And Art
Continue east a block on 6th to **Town Square,** a fine flower-filled little park for falling on your face on the newly mowed lawn—custom-

The stunning Chugach Mountains backdrop Anchorage, urban Alaska

made for a daydreaming boy or girl. Scenic cityscapes here: the **Performing Arts Center** (three intimate auditoriums with wonderful acoustics; take a tour of the place Mon., Wed., Fri., and Sat. at 1 p.m., tel. 263-2901), **Egan Civic Center,** and the **Hilton** tower in the background.

A block back on G between 6th and 7th is the **Arco building,** tallest in Anchorage. Arco puts on a free multimedia show Tues. and Thurs. at 1:30, 2:30, and 3:30 p.m. in the auditorium off the lobby. Head east on 7th to the **Federal Building;** stop at the cafeteria and grab a bite at Anchorage's cheapest eatery. For more info on the Federal Building, see p. 324.

The **Museum of History and Art,** 7th between C and A streets, tel. 343-6173, is the highlight of downtown Anchorage, open daily 9-6, $3. When you walk into the Atrium, the temporary exhibits and children's gallery are to the right, the permanent collections to the left. Plan to linger a while in the permanent wing; the Cook Inlet collection is outstanding. Check out paintings of the Independence Mine, wild Fairbanks snow, even Mt. McKinley seen from the Rialto Bridge over Venice's Grand Canal. The historical art section is fascinating, especially the paintings by Sydney Laurence, one of Alaska's most famous and prolific fine artists; His six- by 10-foot oil of Mt. McKinley is the centerpiece. Upstairs is the Alaska Gallery, with Alaska-size dioramas chronicling a spectacular journey from prehistoric Alaskan archaeology all the way up to the pipeline. The library, with a collection of over 150,000 historical photographs, is open Tues.-Fri. 10 a.m.-noon. Free documentaries are shown on occasion in the comfortable auditorium. The cafe serves juices and lite fare. The museum is the perfect place to study Alaskan culture late in the afternoon while waiting for the hostel to open.

Other Museums

The **Heritage Library-Museum,** housed in the lobby of the National Bank of Alaska corporate offices on the corner of Northern Lights and C St., is open Mon. -Fri. 12-5, free; call 265-2834 for tours and special arrangements. This is one of the state's largest privately owned collections of Alaskana artifacts and books, which will keep you spellbound for hours, if you have the time. Only a handful of the highlights include: parkas made from bird skins and walrus intestines; Sydney Laurence's "Cave Woman" and other jaw-dropping paintings; Nome and Fairbanks newspapers from the early 1900s; stunning black-and-white photos made from the original glass plates of gold rush scenes; and two walls of beautiful bookcases filled with rare books and maps. Buy *The Heritage of Alaska,* a 28-page booklet full of historical vignettes and biographies, well worth the $2. This little gem is not to be missed.

Alaska Aviation Heritage Museum, 4721 Aircraft Dr. (take the Lake Hood exit off International Airport Road), tel. 248-5325, open 9-7 May through Sept., $5, displays vintage aircraft, flight uniforms and jackets, historical photos, and shows 30-minute movies on early aviation in Alaska, early Alaska Airlines footage, and recovery operations. Pick up discount coupons at the Visitor Center downtown.

Imaginarium, 5th and G streets, tel. 276-3179, open Mon.-Sat. 11-5, $4 adult, $2 kids, is a fun place if you've got young ones in tow. This is one of the "Science Discovery Centers" that is the latest trend in museums these days. "Measure up" against moose, polar bears, and king salmon, learn all about pulley and pedal power, human ears and eyes, seismics, bubbles, and much much more. Next door is the **Visual Arts Gallery,** open daily 12-6, free, where you might find just about anything.

Parks

Resolution, Elderberry, and Nulbay parks are described above, as is Town Square. A block from the youth hostel is enjoyable **Delaney Park,** running between 9th and 10th avenues from L St. to Barrow. Known as the "park strip," early in Anchorage's history it marked the boundary where the town stopped and the wilderness started, and in 1923 the strip where the park is today was cleared as a fire break. Since then it has served as a golf course, airstrip, and now hosts half a dozen softball games every night of summer, tennis and basketball courts, and large grassy sections for Frisbee, hackey sack, tai chi, sunbathing, or people-watching. Ten blocks farther south is another park strip, along **Chester Creek,** with popular bike and jogging trails.

Earthquake Park, out Northern Lights Blvd. at the city's northwest tip by the airport, has an interpretive sign about the Big One on Good Friday, 1964, an okay view of the skyline and Inlet, and a network of poorly maintained trails that all end at swamps. It's a mystery why this place gets so much press and is a main stop on the city tours. Anchorage has numerous other parks and recreational facilities. Also see "Swimming" and "Camping" below.

Alaska Zoo

Located at 4731 O'Malley Rd., two miles east of New Seward Highway, tel. 346-3242, open daily 10-6, $5 adults, $2-3 kids and seniors; also connected by a special hourly bus from the Transit Center. This zoo is not too bad from a human standpoint—nice grounds, enjoyable shady paths, bridges over creeks, plenty of restrooms and snack bars—and all the Alaskan animals, plus elephants, cougars, etc., but no monkeys. From the animals' perspective, however, this, like all zoos, is a pretty sad place. A cage is a cage is a cage. The brown bears pace the inside of their 20 by 20; the magnificent polar bear lies on a concrete shelf with its long nose sticking through the bars; six varieties of stunning owls perch on the ground, forever flightless; the foxes, wolves, lynx, and even the moose don't bother moving anymore; and the very shy wolverines, marmots, etc. don't even show themselves. If you've got kids, they'll enjoy it. And one dubious redeeming factor is that it puts taxidermy in a little better light: at least those specimens are already dead, and their souls are free. These are the living dead, never to run, hunt, fly, migrate, play, or be free again.

Military Bases

Since WW II Anchorage has thrived on military spending, as a visit to the largest of the installations, Elmendorf Air Force Base just north of downtown, will illustrate. The weekly free tour (Wednesdays, 2:30-5) of the base is highly recommended, but you must call 552-8151 a few days ahead to make a reservation. The highlight of the tour is a visit to a hangar to see an F-15 and talk to the pilot. The size and sophistication of this giant fighter-bomber base is mind-boggling; the way tourists are allowed to wander around will startle visitors from abroad. Even if you can't get on the tour, the Wildlife Museum (tel. 552-2282, open weekdays 10-5; admission free) on base is worth visiting.

ACTIVITIES

Ballooning

Anchorage is wild about ballooning. At least one hot air balloon always seems to be floating somewhere over the city, especially in the early morning or early evening. Of the several ballooning companies in Alaska, **Hot Air Affair,** 3605 Arctic Blvd., tel. 349-7333, is representative: one-hour flights with up to nine passengers, from 2,000-4,000 feet up,

VICINITY OF ANCHORAGE

ELMENDORF AIR FORCE BASE

ALASKA R.R.

GLENN HWY.

BLUFF RD.

3RD. AVE.

7 ■

PT. WORONZOF

EARTHQUAKE PARK

POSTMARK DR.

WISCONSIN ST.

15TH AVE.

MERRILL FIELD

DE BARR AVE.

6 ■

MULDOON RD.

FORT RICHARDSON MILITARY RESERVATION

FIREWEED

L ST.

SPENARD RD.

C ST.

LAKE OTIS PARKWAY

BRAGAW ST.

NORTHERN LIGHTS BLVD.

BONIFACE PARKWAY

2 ■

1 ■

3 ■

TUDOR RD.

4 ■

5 ■

AIRPORT

AIRPORT RD.

DOWLING RD.

RASPBERRY RD.

ARCTIC BLVD.

E 68th AVE.

CAMPBELL FIELD

CAMPBELL PT.

KINCAID RD.

SAND LAKE RD.

SAND LAKE

JEWEL LAKE RD.

JEWEL LAKE

MINNESOTA DRIVE

OLD SEWARD HWY.

NEW SEWARD HWY.

LAKE OTIS PARKWAY

ABBOTT LOOP RD.

ABBOTT RD.

9 ■

10 ■

11 ■

CHUGACH STATE PARK

DIMOND BLVD.

CAMPBELL LAKE

8 ■ O'MALLEY RD.

HUFFMAN RD.

HILLSIDE DR.

12 ■

DeARMOUN RD.

TURNAGAIN ARM

RABBIT CREEK RD.

0   2 mi

0   2 km

© MOON PUBLICATIONS, INC.

1. Spenard Beach Park
2. Alaska Heritage Library-Museum
3. Loussac Library
4. U. of AK, Anchorage
5. Alaska-Pacific University
6. Lions Camper Park
7. Centennial Park
8. Alaska Zoo
9. Glen Alps Trailhead
10. Prospect Heights Trailhead
11. Rabbit Creek Trailhead
12. Upper Huffman Trailhead

with a champagne toast and a framed flight certificate upon landing—all for only $150 pp. They fly an hour after sunrise and an hour before sunset, and call to inform you of the take-off site. You get there on your own, and they deliver you back to your hotel or wherever after the flight for free.

Boating And Fishing

So many charter companies, sportfishing excursions, pilot guides, fly-in lodges, cruise options, and rentals are based in Anchorage that you'll wind up with a dozen brochures even if you're an inveterate landlubber who gets seasick on a waterbed. Also consult the *Visitors Guide* for listings and advertisements, and the Yellow Pages under any of the above categories. To figure out where the fish are running and when, or what the local regulations are, call Fish and Game at 344-0541 (recorded message at tel. 349-4687) or visit the Public Lands Info Center.

Hiking And Floating

For a complete description of all the hiking trails around Anchorage and vicinity, see "Chugach State Park," p. 334. For guided trips try **Back Trails Tours,** tel. 276-5528, and **CampAlaska Tours,** 376-9438, out of Wasilla. The exciting rafting, kayaking, and canoeing trips are either down the Kenai Peninsula, or north around Nancy Lake and the Matanuska River.

Flightseeing

The best way to get a bird's-eye view of the area is to get together with three or four people who each have $75-100 handy. You can either go up with a plane that has set rates for specific routes, or charter a plane by the hour and design your own tour, which might be less expensive and more rewarding. Either way, call around and shop for the best deal; often a party of two or three people are just waiting around for one more to join them and split the cost. **Regal Air,** at Lake Hood, tel. 243-8535, charges $105 pp for a 90-minute flight over the Chugach Mountains and Knik Glacier, $180 pp for three-hour flights over Columbia Glacier or Mt. McKinley (minimum three). **Airlift Alaska,** at Merrill

Field, tel. 276-3809, charges $179 (minimum two) for McKinley and Columbia Glacier, $125 hourly for their three-seater. Rust's **Flying Service,** tel. 243-1595, charges $189 pp for Columbia Glacier, Mt. McKinley, or Harding Icefield, and $210 an hour to charter their five-seater.

Swimming

If you're lucky enough to be in Anchorage during a hot spell and want to cool off under the bright blue sky, head out to **Lake Spenard,** down Spenard Rd. toward the airport, then right on Lakeshore Dr. (routes 6 and 7). **Jewel Lake** also has swimming, on Dimond Blvd. between Jewel Lake and Sand Lake roads in the southwest corner of the city (routes 7 and 9). The most developed outdoor swimming is at **Goose Lake,** out Northern Lights between Lake Otis and Bragaw near the U. of Alaska, on the bike trail, with basketball courts, pit toilets, and a snack bar.

If you're in the mood for a swim anytime, Anchorage is a good place to experience Alaska's love affair with Olympic-size indoor pools. There are six to choose from—five at the high schools ($3.50, call 264-4474 for locations and times), and one at the university's Sports Center, tel. 786-1233.

ACCOMMODATIONS

Youth Hostels

The saving grace of accommodations for shoestring travelers, **The Anchorage Youth Hostel** moved to its present highly convenient location in 1987. At 700 H St., between 7th and 8th, two blocks south of the Transit Center, tel. 276-3635, the 60-bed facility is open for check-in from 8-10 a.m. and 5-12 p.m. At $10 for members and $13 for non, it fills up *fast* nightly; the overflow may be accommodated on the floor of the manager's apartment on the premises. You must be out by 10 a.m. after completing a 15-minute chore ($2 chore deposit); curfew is 11 p.m. The hostel has a kitchen, common rooms, washers ($1) and dryers (50 cents). Men and women are segregated by floors. Reserve your bunk by leaving your things on it. Store extra baggage for $1 per day per item. Sleeping sheets cost $1. Make reservations by sending one-night's fee deposit per person. The six-day maximum stay should be plenty for Anchorage. Best place in town to meet travelers. Also, the hostel has reasonable wintertime long-term lodging: $200-300 a month.

Budget
Budget in Anchorage translates to $50-60 for a night in a basic motel room. In this category are the **Arctic Inn Motel**, 842 W. International Airport Rd. (call for a free ride from the airport), tel. 561-1328, $52.90 cash, $56.80 credit card; **Spenard Motel**, 3960 Spenard Rd., tel. 243-6917, $55 s or d; **Kobuk Motel**, 1104 E. 5th Ave., tel 274-1650, $58 d; and the **Woods Motel**, 2005 E. 4th, tel. 274-1566, $54-59 s and d. Right downtown is the **Inlet Inn**, 539 H St., tel. 277-5541, charging $60 d.

For longer stays, check out the "For Rent, Rooms" classified sections of the *Anchorage Times* or *Daily News*, or look under "Boarding Houses" or "Rooming Houses" in the Yellow Pages. Prices for a room with shared bath and kitchen start at $150 weekly. Students visiting between mid-May and early August can stay in the dormitory at **Alaska Pacific University**, when there's space. The charge is $20 a night (ask for weekly rates) in three-bed rooms; call 561-1266 and ask for the housing director. Get there by taking routes 3, 45, or 93 to Providence Hospital, or head out Providence Dr., then up the hill to the Atwood Center.

Moderate To Expensive
Moderate means around $75 a night in a basic motel room. Try the **Puffin Inn**, 4400 Spenard, tel. 243-4044, $69 s, $74 d, highly recommended by some seasonal employees; and **Big Timber Motel**, 2037 E. 5th, tel. 272- 2541, whose $75 rooms have a four- by six-foot Jacuzzi in them ($50 deposit), $105 rooms have a six-by-six ($75 deposit). The **Anchorage Hotel**, 330 E St. right next to the Hilton, tel. 272-4553, has been recently refurbished—unique rooms starting at $100 s.

The **Westmark, Hilton, Captain Cook, Sheraton**, and **Clarion** hotels fall into the expensive zone, which is no different than any other big city in the country: $150 a night to start. The **Captain Cook**, 5th and K, tel. 276-6000, is the least expensive ($135 s, $145 d, five percent corporate discount) and the highest quality. They have very good food, interesting shops, and excellent service.

Camping
Two city parks offer pretty good camping. **Lion's Camper Park** is a small 60-site campground with showers; $12 per site, seven-day limit. Take Boniface Parkway south from the Glenn Highway and go a half mile. The campground, in Russian Jack Springs city park, is marked by two small entrance and exit signs. Or take routes 5 or 8 to E. 6th and Boniface, and walk south 1,000 feet.

Centennial Park has the same prices and facilities, and is roomier and a bit farther out the Glenn Highway from town. Take Muldoon Rd. south from the Glenn, hang your first left onto Boundary, then the next left onto the highway frontage road for a half mile to the campground. Routes 3 and 75 stop at the corner of Boundary and Muldoon.

Bed And Breakfasts
Anchorage had over 30 B&Bs at last count, and four booking agencies to handle all the details. Contact **Stay with a Friend**, 3605 Arctic Blvd., Anchorage 99503, tel. 344-4006; **Accommodations in Alaska**, Box 110624, Anchorage 99516, tel. 345-4761; **Alaska Private Lodgings**, 1236 W. 10th, Anchorage 99501, tel. 258-1717; and **Sourdough B&B Assn.**, 889 Cardigan, Anchorage 99503, tel. 563-6244.

FOOD

Good Value
One place in Anchorage has Lower 48 prices for food: the cafeteria in the **Federal Building**, 7th and C Street. Open Mon. through Fri., serving breakfast 7-10, lunch 11-1:30, and snacks 1:30-3:30, you won't believe these prices. You'll feel free to stuff yourself silly with bacon and eggs ($3!), burgers, salad and potato bars, etc. The cafeteria is in

the F wing, entrance at 8th and D. Fast food within walking distance of the hostel are: **Kentucky Fried Chicken** at the Transit Center, **McDonald's** at the corner of 4th and E, and **Wendy's** down the street from McD's.

Very close to the hostel are: **La Mex,** corner of 6th and I, where you can get a plate of nachos for $2.50 and a one-item lunch (filling) for $5; **Wings 'n' Things,** just down I St. toward 5th, open till 10 p.m., featuring 10 deep-fried chicken wings with celery and bleu cheese sauce for $4.95. A muffin shop is next door.

The **Downtown Deli**, 4th Ave. between E and F, is an Anchorage institution. Not especially budget, but with all the bagels and lox, blintzes, and pastrami sandwiches, you might think you went into a time warp and landed back on the planet near Delancey St. in Manhattan. The owner, Tony Knowles, the friendly guy serving sandwiches, is an ex-mayor of Anchorage and runner-up in the 1990 gubernatorial election.

Another Anchorage tradition (though also not necessarily cheap) is **Hogg Bros. Café,** 2421 Spenard between Fireweed and 25th Ave. (next to Chilkoots—take routes 6 or 7), which serves gigantic breakfasts ($5) and burgers ($4.50), open 7:30-5. **Legal Pizza** is now at 4th and L, open 11-11, with good pizza, salad bar, and live music on weekends. Other good pizza can be scarfed at **Fletcher's,** where Anchorage waitpeople and cooks go after work.

Midtown

The Anytown, USA, commercial strip in Anchorage is known as Midtown, encompassed by Northern Lights and Benson boulevards between Minnesota Dr. and Old Seward Highway. Here you'll find all the malls, shopping centers, supermarkets, fast food, and other stores you could possibly need. Starting from Northern Lights and Old Seward and heading west, you pass Tastee-Freez, Dunkin' Donuts, Denny's, Chuck E. Cheese, McDonald's, Taco Bell, Sizzler, Burger King, Shakey's, and Dairy Queen. Heading back east on Benson are One Guy From Italy, Peking Palace, California Roll, Skipper's, and Baskin-Robbins. It's only a 20-minute walk from the hostel to Midtown, and almost any southbound bus gets you there in 10.

For A Splash

On L St. overlooking the Inlet are three classy establishments. **Simon and Seaforts** is the flagship of Restaurants Unlimited's excellent chain (Stanley and Seaforts in Tacoma, Ryan's in Honolulu, Skate's by the Bay in Berkeley, etc.). This company has come up with a highly successful combination—the eclectic menu, excellent food and service, and splendid view are worth the splurge; open for lunch daily, dinner at 5 Mon.-Saturday. **Elevation 92** and the **Kayak Club** have similar prices and views, but serve mainly meat and fish. Considered right up there in quality with Simon and Seaforts is the **Marx Bros. Cafe,** 3rd and I streets, open 6-9:30 Mon.-Sat., with hors d'oeuvres starting at $6 and dinners at $16.

Ethnic

Dynasty Chinese, 420 G St. between 4th and 5th, is a small, well-established restaurant with unusually high standards for Oriental food in the frozen north. The **Thai Restaurant** on H St. near 5th is recommended by Anchoragites. **Maharaja's,** 4th and K, serves an Indian buffet for lunch, which at $7.50-8.50 is not too expensive; dinners 5:30-10 Mon.-Sat. are a little less of a bargain. And for the most exotic room in Anchorage, head out to the **Olde Vic Tea Shop** in the Country Village Mall, Seward Highway and E. Benson, serving high tea between 2 and 4:30—real scones, English cookies, and crumpets.

For the second-most exotic, try the **Warsaw Restaurant,** 7550 Old Seward Highway., tel. 344-8193, open 11-11, Sun. 4-11. This is Eastern European with a surprisingly light touch.

To shop for yourself, stop off at **Sagaya,** 3309 Spenard, open 10-7 Mon.-Sat., 12-6 Sunday. This major Oriental market sells almost everything—25- and 50-pound sacks of rice, saki, sushi, and tea sets, spices, noodles, and beans, sushi and pot stickers to go, excellent and exotic produce, plus live crabs, clams, and mussels. Stop off here just for a visit.

Salmon Bakes

The **Old Anchorage Salmon Bake,** 251 K St. between 2nd and 3rd, is nestled in a tent city at Anchorage's original townsite. For $15.95, you get two pieces of salmon, halibut, reindeer sausage, or crab legs, plus the usual salad bar, baked beans, sourdough rolls, etc., served 4-10. For the price of the meal, you can also take in a saloon show; and while you're there, pan for gold, stock up on packaged fish, and eavesdrop on the conversations comparing this salmon bake to the ones in Denali, Fairbanks, Tok, Valdez, Homer, Dawson, Skagway, Juneau, Ketchikan. . . . The Clarion Hotel's **Lakeside Cook-Out** adds corn on the cob, corn bread, and fruit salad to the usual fare, 5-9 p.m., $15.

ENTERTAINMENT

Drinking And Dancing

Anchorage is a "Cheers"-type town, with lots of corner bars and local pubs tucked away. Downtown, a popular place is **F Street Station** between 3rd and 4th next to the Hilton, which also serves good-value lunches (soup and half sandwich for $2.50). Also, **Darwin's Theory** on G between 4th and 5th attracts a good after-work crowd. If you luck into a clear evening, are lugging something a little dressy, and don't mind blowing two-days' budget on a beer, head up to the **Crow's Nest** atop the Captain Cook Hotel or the **Penthouse Lounge** in the Westmark—the view from both is worth the effort. For a different kind of view, take in the famous **Great Alaskan Bush Company** on 4th across from the Sheraton, where strippers strut their stuff at eye level for the price of a beer. The new **Bush Company II,** on International Airport Rd. and Old Seward Highway, is, amazingly enough, tastefully designed, with high-powered ventilation, beautiful bodies, and a heavy military audience—about as unsleazy as a strip joint could be.

The only non-yuppie dance bar left in Anchorage is **Chilkoot Charlies,** 2435 Spenard Rd., just south of Fireweed. It's sort of a Howling Dog south, a ramshackle building where you can do some serious jumping up

and down to real rock 'n' roll, play horseshoes out back, generally have a night of good raunchy fun—so long as you don't ask the wrong guy's girl (or the wrong girl's guy) to dance. More "live" music (Top 40 tends to get deadening) can be found at **Yesterdays,** at Dimond and New Seward Highway; big dance floor and great sound system (but skip the food).

Spenard

Joe Spenard, one of Anchorage's more colorful pioneers, owned one of the first automobiles in the new town, which he put to work as City Express, a taxi, delivery, and emergency service. He also opened a roadhouse and beach resort on Jeter Lake, which he renamed Lake Spenard, at that time several miles south of town. Today, Spenard Road is the undisputed vice district of Anchorage, where most of society's fringe element decamped to, after revitalization desleazed downtown. In the Mischief Mile between Northern Lights Blvd. and International Airport Rd., you'll find it all: junk shops, pawn shops, lots of liquor stores, rough-and-tumble bars, adult bookstores, massage parlors, escort services, strip joints, motel rooms by the hour, bikers, hookers on the corner, and one prominent Baptist church. This strip also boasts Anchorage's official greeter, Floyd, who stands and waves from the corner of Spenard and 36th all day, every day. The **Fly-By-Night Club,** 4811 Spenard, has a highly recommended saloon-type show till 10:30 p.m. ($10), and dancing afterward. The **Clarion Hotel,** 4800 Spenard, has a yuppie bar overlooking Lake Hood, within a lodge-type atmosphere complete with taxidermy and a huge cozy fireplace.

Mr. Whitekey's Fly By Night Club is now at 3300 Spenard, tel. 279-SPAM. The "Gormay Kweezeen" menu explains the phone number: with delicacies such as Spam with Nachos and Cajun Spam ("Paul Prudhomme's own spices"). Anything with Spam is half price when ordered with champagne, and free with Dom Perignon. There's also a 50-cent Budweiser "tax"—for all the nitwits who *still* want Bud in spite of the huge selection of imported and obscure beers. The "Whale Fat Follies" is a multi-media revue that the Department of Tourism definitely does not want you to see. This hilarious send-up ends with a woman doing a reverse strip-tease with her husband's clothes. If you never though that putting clothes *on* could be sexy, check it out.

Movies

Free documentary flicks are shown several times a day at the **Public Lands Information Center** (see below) and the **Museum of History and Art** (see above). **Denali Theater,** 1230 W. 27th at Spenard Rd., tel. 279-2332, shows double features for $1—one of the best deals in town. The movies are mostly second-run, but at two for a buck, you could stand seeing them again. Take routes 7 or 9. The other half dozen cinemas are all multi-theater and United Artists-owned, showing first-run single features that, at $6, you can either do without or wait for the video. But if you're craving a big-screen experience, there should be something playing at **Totem Theater's** 10 cinemas (3101 Muldoon, tel. 333-8222, routes 5, 75, and 79), **Fireweed Theater's** eight cinemas (Fireweed and New Seward, tel. 277-3825, Routes 60, 92, and 97), and eight each at **University** and **Polar** theaters.

SHOPPING

Gift Shops

Downtown, 3rd and 4th streets are lined with gift shops selling an enormous selection of Alaskan arts and crafts—everything from $2 tourist trinkets to $20,000 jade sculpture. In an hour or two of strolling up 3rd and back down 4th, you can shop for ceramics, clocks, belt buckles, dishes and cups, pendants, placemats, posters, slides, T-shirts, stuffed animals, candles, notecards, *Alaska Krosswords,* postcards, videotapes, wall hangings, and a score of other souvenirs—all with Alaska shapes, scenes, graphics, typography, and none more than $20. From there, you can work your way up through Native commercial and fine art: ivory, jade, and soapstone carvings, scrimshaw, totems, *ulu,*

masks, dolls, weaving, and jewelry, which can max out your credit line in a single bound. If you've been traveling around the state for a while, you might have an idea of what you'd like to buy, and here in the big city you'll probably come close to what you're looking for, though the prices are inflated to help the storekeepers meet the high overhead. If you're a *cheechako,* look, shop, compare, and wait. Either you'll find what you like cheaper elsewhere, or you'll pass through Anchortown again for a second look.

An unusual and expensive purchase to consider is *qiviut:* caps, scarves, shawls, sweaters, baby booties, hand-knitted by Natives from the wool of domestic musk-oxen. Supposedly many times warmer and lighter than down, these fine knits can be seen and salivated over at **Oomingmak Co-op,** 609 H St., tel. 272-9225. Another shop not to miss is **Alaska Native Arts and Crafts,** on 4th Ave. in the Post Office Mall.

Another place not to miss is **Myron Rosenberg's Gallery,** at 4th and D streets. This guy is not only an amazing photographer, but he has his marketing trip down pat. You can buy his images on any price medium, from $1.25 greeting cards to $4 mini-posters up to $350 giant framed prints. Bring money; you'll definitely buy something.

In fact, the entire corner at 4th and D is an attraction of its own: Rosenberg's Gallery, the **Wendel Building** next door (oldest building in Anchorage, from 1915) with Alaska Heritage Art inside, including Native carvers working in the windows, plus a fantastic new mural of the Alaska coastline across the street.

Also, whenever you're down there, stop in at **Classic Toys,** in the lobby of the Captain Cook, which might be frequently if you're hip: the Cook, a Hickel hotel, is the best one downtown by far.

Secondhand Stores

Anchorage is a great place to buy used clothes and gear of all sorts. The largest secondhand stores are **Bishop's Attic,** 11th and Gambel, tel. 279-6328, and **Value Village,** 5437 E. Northern Lights Blvd., tel. 337-2184. The latter has an enormous selection of surprisingly excellent clothing. On the unique side is **The Second Chance,** 3106 Spenard, tel. 277-2748. It's a pigsty with junk all over the yard, basement, roof, and a great place to buy used bunny boots. The owner is a character who seems to price things according to how feisty you are in return!

INFORMATION

One of the best things about Anchorage is the ease with which it's possible to collect all the information you could possibly need. Before the opening of the Public Lands Information Center, you had to get to five different offices all over town to find out about national parks and forests, state parks and recreation areas, federal lands, and fish and wildlife. But now, three stops within five blocks of each other right downtown can supply you with a ton of fliers, brochures, booklets, guides, schedules, maps, and charts, plus the synthesizing expertise of the extremely solicitous and knowledgeable staffs to help you make sense of it all. For info about the Municipality of Anchorage, stop in at the **Anchorage Convention and Visitors Bureau;** for all state and national parks, preserves, and other public lands, hit the **Alaska Public Lands Information Center,** 4th and E; and for topo maps and oceanographic charts, go to the **Federal Building,** 7th and C.

Anchorage Convention And Visitors Bureau

The ACVB, at 4th and F in a small log cabin with a sod roof, tel. 274-3531, is open 7:30-7 June through Aug., 8:30-6 May and Sept., 9-4 the rest of the year. Pick up a copy of *Visitors Guide* magazine, which includes the downtown Walking Tour and Around Anchorage driving tour, plus numerous listings of practicalities. You can also call their Info line at 276-3200 for a recorded message on special events, call 274-3531 to book any local activities, and call 276-4118 to receive assistance in any one of 20 foreign tongues. The ACVB also maintains the visitor centers at the airport, one in the domestic terminal and the other in the international. Ask at the desk for the bike trail map of Anchorage.

Alaska Public Lands Information Center

Opened on Aug. 1, 1987, this excellent facility, corner of 4th and E, tel. 271-2737, open daily 9-7, combines the resources of eight federal and state land and water management agencies. This center is much roomier and brighter than the one in Fairbanks, with similar videotapes but quite different exhibits, including taxidermy, relief maps, and an excellent "talking map" of the local fishing scene. The Alaska Natural History Assn. has a bookstore here, and the large auditorium shows great free documentaries on the Great Land.

Federal Building

While partaking of a snack or meal at Lower 48 prices in the cafeteria, be sure to stop in at the **United States Geological Survey** office next door—just to dig the amazing maps on the walls, or pick up interesting free reading material such as the 28-page booklet on topo maps, or "How To Obtain Aerial Photographs" from the National Mapping Program. Topographical maps are available for every nook and cranny of the state; ask the helpful office staff for assistance in locating your particular nook or cranny. Right next door is the **National Oceanographic and Atmospheric Administration,** which can supply you with nautical charts for Alaska's immense coastline.

Library

The **Z.J. Loussac Library** is a gorgeous facility which opened in Sept. 1986. At 36th and Denali (routes 2, 60, 79, and 93), tel. 261-2975, open Mon.-Thurs. 12-9, Fri. and Sat. 10-6, and Sun. noon to 6 p.m. Named after a pioneer pharmacist, politician, and philanthropist who made his fortune selling drugs to early Alaskans, you can easily lose an afternoon just wandering among the stacks, enjoying the cozy sitting rooms on Level 3, studying the huge relief map of the state, browsing among the excellent artwork hanging on the walls, or picking a book at random from the large Alaskana collection and filling yourself up with arcane information that will no doubt color the rest of your trip. Highly recommended.

(GORDY OHLIGER)

Be sure to pick up your bike trail map and discount coupons at the ACVB.

Bookstores

The **Book Cache** has this town all sewed up. At last count a dozen branches were scattered around the Basin. The downtown store, at 5th and G, has a mind-boggling selection of books and magazines, including the best collection of current Alaskana—from $50 picture books to $1.95 self-published excursions into Alaskan trivia, humor, recipes, anecdotes, autobiographies, and the like. Another convenient and eclectic bookstore is **Cyrano's,** 413 D at 4th; have a cappuccino while you're browsing. **Walden's** is in the Fifth Avenue Mall; **Dalton's** is in the Penney's Mall.

GETTING THERE

By Air

Anchorage styles itself as the "air crossroads of the world." Every day 140 flights of 13 major airlines arrive at the airport, which handles almost six million passengers a year. Almost everybody who flies into the state from the Lower 48 lands at Anchorage, even if just to connect to other carriers around Alaska. While waiting for your luggage, take a look at the collection of stuffed Alaskan animals and fish on the upper level. The city skyline and Chugach Mountains are visible from up here; go out, breathe the air, dig the view, and indulge in a private smile—you finally made it to Alaska.

Anchorage International Airport (ANC) is six miles southwest of downtown. Manned information booths are found in both the domestic and international terminals. Neither has lockers; baggage storage is at the far end of the lower level of the domestic terminal. Open 5:30-1:30 a.m., prices vary, but it's mostly $2 per day per piece. People Mover route 6 (75 cents) runs from the lower level into downtown Anchorage every hour Mon.-Fri. from 7 a.m.-9 p.m., every two hours from 9 a.m.-6 p.m. on Sat., no service on Sunday or holidays.

By Car And Bus

If you're driving into the city, all roads from the Interior feed into the Glenn Highway (Route 1), which turns into 5th Ave. and delivers you right into the heart of downtown Anchorage. The Parks Highway (Route 3) from Fairbanks and Denali joins the Glenn at Wasilla, 35 miles north; the Richardson Highway (Route 4) from Delta Junction and Valdez (along with the Tok Cutoff extension of the Glenn) merges at Glennallen, 187 miles northeast.

Several bus companies serve Anchorage daily. **Alaskon Express** (Gray Line's public transportation) departs Haines on Fri., Sat., and Tues. at 8:15 a.m. with an overnight at Beaver Creek, arriving Anchorage at 7:15 p.m. $182 OW. They depart Skagway at 7:30 a.m. on the same days ($194) and White-horse at 12 noon ($147), also overnighting at Beaver Creek (not included in price) and arriving Anchorage 7:15 p.m.

Denali Express does a daily run from Fairbanks, $100. **Alaska Sightseeing** has a daily bus from Fairbanks, $120. **Valdez Anchorage Bus Lines** departs Valdez at 9:30 a.m. ($55), stopping at Glennallen at 1:30 p.m. and Palmer at 4:15 p.m., arriving Anchorage at 5:15 p.m., daily except Monday.

By Train
Alaska Railroad has a daily express from Fairbanks, stopping in Denali, Talkeetna, and Wasilla, and arriving in Anchorage at 8 p.m. They also run a local train from Honolulu (Alaska) on Wed., arriving Anchorage at 3:55 p.m., and one from Denali on Sat. and Sun., leaving at 3:30 p.m., stopping at around 30 milk-run points along the way, arriving in Anchorage at 10 p.m. From Seward, catch a train at 6 p.m. Thurs. through Mon., arriving Anchorage at 10 p.m., $35 OW.

GETTING AROUND

By Bus
People Mover, Anchorage's public bus system, does a remarkable job, considering that it began operating less than 15 years ago,

carries 14,000 passengers a day, and covers the entire sprawling Anchorage Basin and beyond. Because it is mostly a commuter line, weekday service is extensive, with all 26 routes operating from 6 a.m. to 11 p.m. On Sat., most lines run from 8 a.m. to 10 p.m., but 90% of the company rests on Sunday. The Transit Center is at 6th and G, where you can pick up a timetable of all routes for 50 cents (the Book Cache there also sells them if the ticket counter is closed). The Transit Center is open 7-6 Mon.-Fri., or call 343-6543 for specific instructions on where and when to catch the People Mover to your destination.

Signs above the windshield display the route number and destination. Exact fare (75 cents) is required. Transfers are valid only on a different bus traveling in the same direction within two hours of the time of receipt.

By Bicycle
Anchorage is wild about bicycles. Parks and Recreation has provided nearly 120 (and growing) miles of urban bike and jogging and cross-country skiing trails. Bike trail maps are available at the ACVB. A great ride goes from Point Woronzof way out on the western tip of the city, past Earthquake Park and West-chester Lagoon, along Chester Creek and around to Goose Lake, where you can take a dip if you're hot. Another popular ride is to get on C St. heading south to Dimond Blvd., head west (right) along Campell Creek to Campbell Lake. Or just bomb around to wherever the wind blows you.

A couple of companies rent cycles, if your budget permits the luxury of a 10-speed or mountain bike. **America Rents,** 3600 Arctic Blvd. and 36th (pretty far out there; take route 9), tel. 563-3600, charges $13 a day for either (7:30 a.m.-7:30 p.m.) with a $50 deposit or credit card. **Big Boy Toys,** 6511 Brayton Dr. *(really* far out there on the frontage road of Seward Highway between Dimond and Dowling; take route 60), tel. 349-1425, charges $12.50 a day (9-6) and a $50 deposit. Also try **Borealis Backcountry Cycling,** tel. 562-4493.

By Taxi

Taxis, of course, are expensive. Most charge about $1 flag drop and $1 per mile thereafter. But they're not regulated and some competition does exist among them; call around to find out the cheapest rates: **Alaska Cab**, tel. 258-3434; **Yellow Cab**, tel. 272-2422; and **Checker Cab**, tel. 274-3333. Common fares include: downtown anywhere, $3; downtown to Midtown, $5-7; downtown to the airport, $10-12.

By Rental Car

Rental cars are very hard to come by in Anchorage during the summer. A little planning even just a few days in advance comes in handy. But as much as a week or two can be needed to get a car. Both Rent-A-Wreck and Rent-A-Dent have gone out of business since the last edition of this book. Now, the best deal in town can be had from **Road Ready,** 4th and Eagle (in a service station), tel. 279-7287. They charge $27 per day ($165 weekly) for Chevettes and Colts with 50 free miles and 18 cents per mile thereafter. Their mid-size cars (Fairmonts, Phoenixes) are only $29 a day ($176 weekly), with the same mileage charges.

Practical, tel. 276-1230, gets $30 a day with 50 free plus 18 cents. Almost as good as Road Ready. Starting at $49 daily and 30 cents a mile, you might think twice about Hertz, Avis, National, Budget, etc. Of the bunch, Payless, 243-3616, has the lowest rates, at $49 with 100 free and then 30 cents.

By Rental Motorhome

Let **Number One Motorhomes'**, tel. 277-7575, prices speak for themselves: their smallest camper-van units (one-ton chassis, queen-size bed, stove and fridge but no shower) have a three-day minimum at $140 a day and 20 cents a mile. Their medium-size (26-foot) units are $155 daily plus 20 cents per mile, and their honkin' Alaska-size nuthahs—the ones you sit behind for miles as they waddle down the road at 30 mph and get four miles to the gallon—cost $190 daily and 20 cents per mile.

FROM ANCHORAGE

By Air

If you're planning to fly out from Anchorage, but don't already have a ticket, it'll be very worth your while to exhaust all possibilities before you shell out almost $400 for a one-way ticket to Seattle. First, consider taking the Alaskon Express bus to Whitehorse ($140), then Greyhound to anywhere else you're going. If you're not up for a five-day sentence on The Dog, but aren't in a hurry, read the "Travel-Transportation" section of the classifieds in the daily newspapers. People are always selling the unused portion of their roundtrip tickets at a substantially reduced price—usually half the total fare. The departure date can't be changed, so you might consider fooling around on the Kenai Peninsula or Prince William Sound to kill time while you wait to fly. Just make sure the name on the ticket matches your gender. If you're really in a hurry, though, buy a roundtrip ticket to Seattle or your final destination; you'll usually be able to sell the return trip.

By Bus

Over-the-road bus companies in Alaska turn over faster than Mary Lou Retton doing somersaults down the North Face of Mt. McKinley. There is no central bus station in Anchorage (or anywhere else in Alaska, for that matter), and schedules and prices change frequently. The information below is intended only as a guide, and should be rechecked carefully before setting out.

Alaskon Express buses depart for Haines ($182), Whitehorse ($147), and Skagway ($194) every Sun. Wed., and Fri. at 7 a.m. All these runs overnight at Beaver Creek. They arrive Haines and Skagway at 6:30 p.m., Whitehorse at 4:30 p.m. **Denali Express,** tel. 273-3234, runs 14-seat vans to Haines on Sat. at 8 a.m. from the Sheraton Anchorage, overnighting in Tok, arriving in Haines in time to meet the Sun. evening ferry out, $115. They also go daily to Fairbanks ($75) by way of Denali ($50), leaving also at 8 a.m. **Alaska Sightseeing** goes to Fairbanks daily, leaving the major downtown hotels at 7 a.m., arriving Fairbanks at 6:30, $120.

Anchorage-Valdez buses leave the Sheraton Anchorage at 9 a.m. for Palmer ($7), Glennallen ($34), and Valdez ($55, arriving at 5 p.m.). **Seward Bus Lines,** tel. 278-0800, runs a 10-seat van from the Samovar Inn, 7th and Gambell, to Seward, leaving 2:30 p.m., arriving 5:30 p.m., $25.

By Train

The daily express to Fairbanks on **Alaska Railroad,** 1st Ave., tel. 265-2494, has prices comparable to the tour buses, but is a much more comfortable, historical, enjoyable, and leisurely ride. The express departs Anchorage May 10 through Sept. 19 at 8:30 a.m. for Denali (arriving around 3:45 p.m., $78) and Fairbanks (arriving 8 p.m., $108). The express also stops in Wasilla, Talkeetna, and Nenana, and you can hop off there, but you're not allowed to check any luggage—only what you can carry on. The local service departs Anchorage at 6:30 a.m. on Wed. for Honolulu (south side of Broad Pass *before* Denali). The local runs all the way to Denali on Sat. and Sun., also leaving at 6:30 a.m., $13 to Wasilla (arriving 7:50 a.m.), $30 to Talkeetna (9:30 a.m.), and $60 to Denali (12:25 p.m.). Sometimes they run a Saturday special at half price; be sure to inquire.

Westours and **Tour Alaska** hook their superdome vistacruisers up to the back of the express for an old-fashioned luxury rail experience. These are mostly for package tourists, but they also sell seats to independents.

There's also service from Anchorage to Whittier on Prince William Sound (for ferry and glacier cruise connections). A motorcoach departs the train depot at 11:45 a.m., transferring in Portage to the shuttle, arriving Whittier 2 p.m., $18 OW. You can drive to Portage, but not Whittier; the train runs under the Chugach Mountains through two three-mile tunnels Thurs. through Mon. six times a day from 8 a.m.-9:30 p.m., Tues. and Wed. four times daily from 1:30-9:30 p.m. ($8 OW, $32 for car and driver). You line up in Portage and drive onto flatbeds, and sit in your vehicles, rocking and rolling through the tunnels.

By Thumb

To hitch south down the Kenai, routes 92 and 101 take you all the way out to DeArmoun Rd. at the intersection with New Seward Highway. But since these are park-and-ride commuter buses, the first one doesn't get down there till 3 p.m., which could be a little late to start thumbing. Route 60 messes around down there all day, dropping you off at Dare and Old Seward Highway, north of DeArmoun, starting at 6:45 a.m. Walk a half mile to New Seward, and if you've paid adequate homage to Mercury, god of hitchhikers, you should be in Portage within the hour.

To hitch north, route 102 is the park-and-ride commuter, first reaching the north end of Eagle River at 5:30 p.m. Routes 76 and 78 are the milk runs, starting out at 7:55 a.m. from the Transit Center.

TOURS

By Pedicab

They're not exactly Balinese *becak* or Chinese trishaws, but if you enjoy being pedaled around town in the open air by a knowledgeable guide with thunder thighs, call **Alaska Pedicab** at 272-2030. They offer a variety of tours, from a 30-minute romp downtown ($35 d) to a two-hour Point Woronzof marathon ($80 d). All tours include a snack or picnic of the usual Alaskan fare.

By Bus

At least half a dozen tour companies are happy to sell you tours of Anchorage and the surrounding area. Unless you're very short on time and long on tender, skip the city tour which rates number one in complaints from the package tourists. Besides, half the fun of cities is finding your own way around. They also all do Matanuska Valley and Portage Glacier/Alyeska Ski Resort loops; the smaller companies often specialize—one focusing on Hatcher Pass and Independence Mine, another doing the zoo and Potter Game Refuge and Historic Park.

Gray Line, 457 4th Ave. across from the ACVB, tel. 277-5581, charges $20 for their two-and-a-half-hour city tour, $30 for a six-hour Matanuska Valley circuit (includes

Eklutna, Experimental and musk ox farms, and Palmer), and $30 for the six-hour Portage Glacier day trip. **Royal Hiway,** in the Tour Alaska office next to Woolworth's, tel. 276-7711, is a xerox of Gray Line. **Alaska Sightseeing,** 543 4th Ave., tel. 276-1305, is the city tour to take if you must—their $20 trip goes out to Elmendorf. **Eagle Custom Tours,** 614 4th Ave., tel. 258-2901, and **Personalized Tours,** tel. 344-1458, offer smaller, more custom-tailored trips. Eagle also has a six-hour tour to the must-see Independence Mine and Hatcher Pass, $40.

By Boat

In late Aug. 1987, the **MV *Miki Miki*** started operating a cruise of the upper Cook Inlet out of Anchorage—the only one. These four three-hour cruises correspond to mealtimes: continental breakfast cruise (9 a.m. to noon, $45), salmon buffet cruise (1-4 p.m., $49), seafood dinner cruise (6-9 p.m., $75), and sunset cruise (10 p.m. to 1 a.m., $49). For tickets, go to **Alaska Cook Inlet Adventures,** 527 W. 3rd Ave., tel. 272-TOUR.

Anchorage is a good place to check out the different boat trips across Prince William Sound. **Alaska Marine Highway's** southwest ferry routes do not reach Anchorage, but you can connect up with the system in Whittier via the Alaska Railroad. The ferry to Valdez passes within sight of massive Columbia Glacier, the budget way to see the Sound; continue on to Cordova, Seward, Homer, Kodiak, etc., or take the bus back to Anchorage via the magnificent Richardson Highway. **Gray Line** runs the *Glacier Queen* right up to Columbia Glacier on its boat-hotel-bus tour ($249), or a fly/cruise ($198), as does **Alaska Sightseeing.** Or get to Whittier on your own and hop on one of the three tour boats that also make the run by the glacier to Valdez (see p. 342). Also in Whittier is a new cruise, initiated by Phillips Tours, 509 4th Ave., tel. 276-8023, passing by 26 glaciers in College and Harriman fjords ($99); for $129 you can include the roundtrip train ride from Anchorage to Whittier.

(GORDY OHLIGER)

CHUGACH STATE PARK TO WHITTIER

Alaska's second-largest state facility, Chugach State Park encompasses nearly half a million acres, half the size of Delaware. Designating as parkland the entire Chugach Range from Eagle River, 25 miles north of Anchorage to Girdwood, 35 miles south, it could take a committed hiker years to cover all its trails, ridges, peaks, and passes. From the easy three-and-a-half-mile RT hike to Flattop Mountain in Anchorage to the 25-mile OW trek from the Eagle River Visitor Center along the historic Iditarod Trail over Crow Pass down to Girdwood, you have a wide range of choices of trail length, elevation, difficulty, access, and crowds.

Pick up the brochure at the Public Lands Info Center in Anchorage, decide on a trail, then dress for rain! The clouds often sit down on these city-surrounding mountaintops and when it's sunny and hot in Anchorage, it could be hailing only a few minutes away on the trails. But don't let that stop you. This whole park is within a few miles of the largest city north of Vancouver and west of Edmonton, where over 60% of Alaska's entire population huddles, but up in these mountains it's easy to pretend you're a hundred years ahead of the crowds, and all the hustle and bustle on the Inlet flats is far in the future.

Activities

Hiking is the main one, with about a dozen well-maintained, well-used, moderate-to-difficult trails. You share this wilderness with the usual land and air creatures; photography and wildlife-watching go hand in hand with hiking. Rock climbing is poor due to the sedimentary and metamorphic composition of the mountains, but snow and ice climbing are possible year-round, with permanent freezing conditions above the 6,000-foot level. Small boating is popular at Eklutna Lake, and rafters and kayakers on Class II Eagle River can put in at two access points (miles 7.5 and 9) on Eagle River Road.

Practicalities

Developed campgrounds are found at Eklutna Lake and Eagle River north of Anchorage and Bird Creek south. The latter two are almost always filled to capacity; all three have four-day limits, outhouses, water, and starting in '88 "Iron Rangers" began collecting $5 at Eklutna and Bird, and $10 at Eagle River. Please comply. The Visitor Center is in Eagle River, at the end of 12-mile Eagle River Rd., which leaves the Glenn Hwy. at mile 13. It's open Fri. through Mon. 11 a.m.-7 p.m. staffed by state park rangers, tel. 694-2108. For a 24- hour recorded message about naturalist programs, guided hikes, and trail conditions, call 694-6391. To file a trip plan with the main office of Chugach rangers, call 345-5014. And to talk to the State Park administrative personnel for some reason call 762-2616.

NORTH OF ANCHORAGE

Eklutna Lake Area

Heading south down the Glenn Hwy., get off at the exit for Eklutna Rd., which follows Eklutna River 10 miles to Eklutna Lake. A small campground is at the end of the auto road at the lake, with outhouses and a large picnic area. A 13-mile trail follows the west side of the lake, with a trail to **East Twin Peak** near the start of it, and two trails at the end take the right-hand trail along the **East Fork Eklutna River,** or the left-hand trail up to **Eklutna Glacier.**

Just off the exit ramp on the other (west) side of Eklutna Rd. are the **St. Nicholas Russian Orthodox Church** and the **Tanaina Spirit Houses.** From this point, at the site of the first Tanaina (a branch of Athabascan) settlement on the Inlet, down through the western Kenai Peninsula, Kodiak, and the Aleutians, Russian Orthodoxy is strongly over-laid on the Native culture. The ancestors of most of these Indians were converted by Russian missionaries, and the church dating from the 1830s, is the oldest building in the Anchorage area. The miniature log chapel, against a backdrop of colorful "spirit-house" graveheads, is one of the most photographed.

A mile south of Eklutna Rd. is the exit for **Thunderbird Falls.** Drive a quarter mile to the big gravel parking lot, then hike an easy mile down to Thunderbird Creek. From there follow your ears to the falls.

Eagle River Area

Take the Eagle River exit at Mile 13 of the Glenn, then take your first right onto Eagle River Rd., a dazzling, paved, 12-mile ride right into the heart of the Chugach. The road ends at the parking lot to the **Visitor Center** (see above for hours), which features a "close-up corner" with furs and a track book, as well as an aurora display, and T-shirts and postcards for sale. The **Rodak Nature Trail** is a wide gravel route, half mile RT, with six artistic and informative signs on snow, glaciers, forest, the sun, etc. It's 15 minutes well spent. For a longer walk, take the three-and-a-half-mile RT **River Trail** down to Eagle River.

For one of the longest hikes in the park, get on the 25-mile **Iditarod Trail.** This stretch combined with Resurrection Pass Trail to provide an overland route from the port at Seward through the Chugach to the Interior. It was used until 1919, when the Alaska Railroad replaced it. The gradual climb to Crow Pass fords several streams, including Eagle River midway along the trail. It might be wise to camp overnight, and cross the river in the morning, when the glacial runoff is lower. Raven Glacier and Crystal Lake are scenic highlights near Crow Pass, where you leave Chugach State Park and continue on **Crow Pass Trail** in immense Chugach National Forest. From here it's four miles via Crow Pass down to the trailhead on rough Crow Creek Rd., then another five miles to the Alyeska Ski Resort access road.

From the Eagle River exit on the Glenn, it's another two miles to the Hiland Rd. exit, and one and a half miles to the **Eagle River Campground,** on the south side of Eagle River, 36 sites, $10. At Mile 6 on the Glenn is the exit to Ski Bowl Rd., which runs seven miles to the parking lot at the Arctic Valley ski area. A trailhead about a mile before road's end leads to long **Ship Creek Trail,** which (with a little cross-country hiking) hooks up with Bird Creek and Indian Creek trails (see p. 337) via the passes of the same names. From the parking lot a two-mile trail goes up to **Rendezvous Peak,** an easy hike with great views of the city, Inlet, and even Mt. McKinley if you're lucky.

Getting There

Bus route 75 stops at Arctic Valley Rd. and Glenn Hwy.; you either have to walk or hitch the six miles to Ship Creek trailhead and another mile to Rendezvous Peak trailhead. Route 74 reaches about a mile down Eagle River Rd. (corner of Eagle River Loop Rd.); the remaining 11 miles to the Visitor Center is an easy hitch on this well-traveled road. Closest you can get to Eklutna is Peters Creek at Mile 21 on routes 76 and 78, the farthest north People Mover goes. This is still five miles short of the Eklutna exit off the Glenn.

HIKING AROUND ANCHORAGE

Four trailheads on the city's southeastern outskirts give access to a network of crisscrossing and connecting trails in the section of the range that hems in Anchorage Bowl. They're all off of Hillside Dr., which skirts a suburb of sparkling glass houses and gorgeous views of the skyline, Inlet, and Mt. Susitna to the west. Route 92 buses stop at the corner of DeArmoun Rd. and Hillside Drive. From there, continue on Hillside Dr. uphill till you come to Upper Huffman Rd., and go right. In a half mile go right again onto aptly named Toilsome Hill Drive. Toil uphill for 2½ miles to get to the trailhead for aptly named **Flattop Mountain,** a popular 3½-mile RT hike with an elevation gain of 1,500 feet, steep near the top. Also from the Glen Alps trailhead are several moderate hikes: **Little O'Malley Peak,** 7½ miles; **the Ramp** and **Wedge,** 11 miles each; and **Williwaw Lakes,** 13 miles.

Continue on Hillside past Upper Huffman Rd. and take a left on O'Malley Road. The second left leads you to Prospect Heights trailhead to Wolverine Peak, 10.5 miles. The 13-mile trip from Prospect Heights to Knoya Peak and the 15-mile route to Tikishla Peak are undeveloped and require lots of experience.

SOUTH OF ANCHORAGE

Potter Area

At Mile 116 of the Seward Hwy. is **Potter Marsh Nesting Area,** with a boardwalk over the edge of the marsh. This is a good spot to look for over 80 kinds of waterfowl, including Canada geese, trumpeter swans, and even the flyin'-fool arctic terns. Bring binoculars. This marsh was created when the railroad builders installed an embankment to protect the track from Turnagain Arm's giant tides, which dammed the freshwater drainage from the mountains. A mile south on the other side of the highway is the **Potter Section House,** a small railroad museum of interpretive displays and signs outside, and inside the restored original "section" house. Check out the nine-foot rotary snowplow (to clear avalanches), the track display, and an excellent signboard on today's Alaska Railroad's use of high-tech: microwave repeaters, solar crossing guards, electromagnetic tampers, articulated flatcars, etc. A small gift shop sells railroad memorabilia and books. Open 8-8 June through Aug., 10-8 in May and September.

Old Johnson Trail

Across the highway is the parking lot for **Potter Creek trailhead,** the first access to the Old Johnson Trail, built to transport railroad workers and supplies, which parallels the highway for a ways. In three miles is **McHugh Creek Wayside,** a day-use picnic area (open 9-9; gate locked) and trailhead for hikes up to McHugh Peak and a four-mile trail to Rainbow Valley Rd., which connects back up to the Seward Hwy. at Mile 108. The O.J. Trail runs another two miles to Windy Corner at Mile 106; the entire 10-mile trail takes roughly six hours.

On the highway at mile 110 is **Beluga Point,** a good place to see these white whales cavorting in Turnagain Arm in late May and late August. Or just have a picnic and wait for the Cook Inlet's famous **bore tides.** The tides here, at 30 feet, are among the world's highest, and the lead breaker can be up to eight feet high, a half mile across and move at over 10 miles per hour. This is the only bore tide in the U.S., created when a large body of water (Cook Inlet) is forced by strong tidal action into a narrow shallow one (Turnagain Arm). Look for a series of small swells (two to three feet high, larger depend

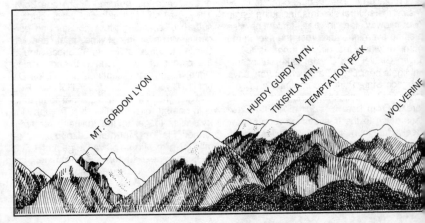

ing on the wind) which crash against the rocks and send up a mighty spray. You won't soon forget the roar of the bore, which goes by Beluga Point roughly two hours after low tide in Anchorage—check the tide tables in the daily newspapers.

Indian And Bird Creeks

At Mile 102, right before Turnagain Restaurant in Indian (an old gold "town"), take a right on the gravel road and head 1½ miles through Indian Valley to the **Indian Creek Trailhead.** This trail, which follows Indian Creek over Indian Pass (especially rewarding during Indian summer), is six miles of easy walking on a well-maintained trail. You can then continue for several miles of undeveloped hiking till you hook up with the Ship Creek Trail, which runs 21 miles to Arctic Valley north of Anchorage. The **Powerline Pass Trail,** 11 miles from the Glenn Alps trailhead, also nearly reaches this trail; you cross-country hike about a quarter mile on the ridge to hook up.

Two miles down the highway from the turnoff to Indian Creek is the **Bird Creek** area. It features two trails, the first up the ridge and the second along Bird Creek to Bird Pass (especially enjoyable if you're hiking with Larry Bird), and the **Bird Creek Campground,** at Mile 100. This thickly forested 19-site campground is almost always full of anglers working Bird Creek. The bike trail between Anchorage and Girdwood runs right through the middle of it. **Bird House** bar is on the left side heading south; keep an eye out for it. I'm not going to describe it. You simply have to see it for yourself.

GIRDWOOD

At Mile 90 you leave Chugach State Park and cross into immense Chugach National Forest, which encompasses the entire Prince William Sound area, and includes a chunk of the Kenai Peninsula and a chunk of Kodiak Island. From here to Seward, the land and all its facilities are managed by the U.S. Forest Service.

Go left at Girdwood Station (Mile 90), site of the town before it was leveled by the earthquake. The access road runs three miles to new Girdwood and Alyeska Ski Resort. Only 40 scenic miles from 250,000 people, this winter resort even in summer is a favorite destination for Anchoragites, package tourists, unsuspecting travelers, and the occasional backpacker who likes a quick ride to the alpine tundra. Don't mistake the end of the road for a tour bus convention—it's okay to park your car here, too.

First check out the resort itself, a classic Alaskan tourist trap. If you're still solvent after

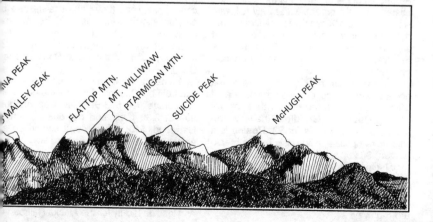

the food, dessert, T-shirts, souvenirs, etc., fork over $10 for the 15-minute chairlift ride up to the Skyline Restaurant and follow the well-marked trail to the alpine overlook onto cute Alyeska Glacier. Ten-dollar views up here.

Other Activities

A mile before the resort is another gravel access road (six miles) to **Crow Pass Trailhead.** It's 3½ miles to the pass, with a 2,000-foot elevation gain. You pass old mining ruins and a Forest Service cabin; a half mile beyond the pass is Raven Glacier, where you re-enter Chugach State Park and join the Iditarod Trail (see above). **Glacier Aviation,** tel. 783-2144, does flightseeing trips from Girdwood airport. You can also jump out of planes around here, by signing up with **Northland Skydiving,** tel. 783-2690. These guys use special dual harnesses for tandem jumps with your instructor. The first costs $150; second, third, and fourth jumps cost $100 each. It's $60 for each of four "transition jumps," or $625 for the whole package. After all this instruction, practice, and expense, you're such a hot skydiver that you're able to jump without a parachute.

Practicalities

Heading toward the resort on the access road, go right on Timberline, pass gorgeous ski chalets, then right again on Alpina. Around a couple of curves is the new youth hostel. This is a great place, rarely full, with six beds in the sleeping loft, kitchen, and bathroom downstairs, and wood-burning sauna out back; $8 members, $10 non. Make reservations or confirm them at the Anchorage YH.

Girdwood itself, on the other side of the access road, has several restaurants, a post office, and a laundromat with showers ($1.50). **Girdwood Griddle** is the local coffee shop, serving BLTs for $3. **Rosies** is a little more upscale, with basic boring breakfasts at $6.25, and interesting specials like their lemon-pepper chicken burger for $6.

You'll also find some of the best bakery and deli food at the **Alpine Café** at the intersection of the Girdwood spur road and the Seward Highway.

But the place to go for the best meal around Anchorage, if not Alaska, is the famous **Double Musky Inn,** a quarter mile up Crow Creek Rd. on the left, open 5-10 Tues.-Thurs. and 4-10 Fri.-Sun., no reservations taken. Owned by Bob and Deanna Persons, this 100-seat restaurant serves 300 dinners on a typical night—in other words, crowded, loud, long wait, and brief visits from the waitpeople. But as soon as the food comes, none of that makes any difference. No need to sample the appetizers, unusual though they may be; save *all* your room for dinner. Mountain Cajun shrimp, prawns, scallops, halibut, and salmon dishes go for $16-20, chicken is $16, and steaks from $18-30 comes with vegetables, potatoes, and trendy rolls. The house specialty is French Pepper Steak, $18, which is the biggest, juiciest, and tastiest slab you've ever been served. I'd managed to polish off a good third of it, when my tipsy Scottish companion looked over and exclaimed, "Have you not *started* your steak yet?" If you're like me, you can get dinner and five sandwiches out of it.

Finally, stop off at the **Candle Factory,** on the access road a half mile from Seward Hwy., tel. 346-1920. The candles they sell are not only a unique and inexpensive souvenir or gift item, they also burn till the cows come home without smoke or odor. The candlemakers start with a soapstone sculpture of a wildlife image from which they form a silicone mold. Then they pour in a mixture of paraffin, stearic acid, Alaska crude, and sea oil byproduct, heat at 200 degrees for seven hours, *et voilà!* Small candles start at $3, large guys go for around $12. Don't miss the Candle Factory.

You can take the **Seward Bus Lines** mini van from the Samovar Inn, 7th and Gambell, Anchorage, tel. 562-0712, leaving Anchorage at 2:30 p.m., and get dropped off in Girdwood, $18. Otherwise, it should be an easy hitchhike down the Seward Hwy.

PORTAGE VALLEY

At Mile 80 of the Seward Hwy. is the staging and loading facility for the Alaska Railroad

Whittier. If you're driving, get toward the rear of the line (cuts the diesel fumes in the tunnel), and pay the ticket sellers who step off the train $32 for car and driver, $8 without the car. One mile farther is the 5½-mile access road (left) through Portage Valley to Portage Glacier. This is the number-one tourist attraction in Alaska, with roughly 650,000 visitors counted in 1989. If you're here on a clear weekend day, you might think that all 650,000 of them are here with you, too.

In 1986 the Forest Service opened the $8 million **Begich, Boggs Visitor Center,** a beautiful facility named after Nicholas Begich (U.S. representative from Alaska) and Hale Boggs (majority leader of the U.S. Senate) whose plane disappeared in the area in 1972; they were never found. The large picture-window tunnel overlooks the narrow outlet of Portage Lake, where icebergs jam up after floating down from Portage Glacier. The Visitor Center boasts an amazing array of displays, including an ice cave, a "live" iceberg hauled in from the lake, an engrossing relief map of the local icefields, and everything you ever wanted to know about glaciers, including moving displays on glacial motion and crevasses. Don't miss the vial of tiny iceworms (related to earthworms and snow worms), which inhabit the surface of glaciers, feeding on pollen grains and red algae, and surviving within a very delicate near-freezing temperature range. Life! There's also good footage on iceworms in the 20-minute movie, *Voices From The Ice* shown every 45 minutes from 9:30 a.m.-5:30 p.m., $1 suggested donation.

Hiking

Two hikes are within walking distance of the Visitor Center. The **Moraine Loop Trail,** accessible from the path to the lodge, is a five-minute stroll through some typical moraine vegetation; Portage Glacier occupied this ground only 100 years ago. Interpretive signs explain some of the vegetation, and here's an awesome overlook of the parking lot. Follow the access road past the Visitor Center (south) just under a mile. At the back of the parking lot starts the **Byron Glacier Trail,** an easy three- quarter mile walk along

the runoff stream to below the hanging glacier.

Practicalities

Three Forest Service campgrounds along the access road contain 58 sites: large, woodsy, water, toilets, $5. **Portage Glacier Lodge** has a cafeteria with surprisingly reasonable prices; try the cross-cut fries for your crunch craving. To get to Portage Glacier, take the **Seward Bus Lines** minivan (see above), or take the day trip offered by all the package tour companies from Anchorage, $30. The shuttle train betweeen Portage and Whittier is $7.50; it's a mile to the access road, and 5½ miles to the Visitor Center.

In 1989, Westours began operating a small tour boat on Portage Lake; catch the *Ptarmigan* from its dock near the end of the Byron Glacier road, $18.

WHITTIER

Several thousand tourists pass through this tiny town (pop. 330) every week, transferring from the cruise ships, ferries, and tour boats to the Alaska Railroad between Anchorage and Prince William Sound. But possibly only two dozen ever *see* Whittier. The vast majority steps off the boat right onto the train, and misses one of the most unusual, friendly, and appealing places in Alaska. Since at least five train trips daily hook up to Portage or Anchorage, it's a simple matter to catch the early or late train and avail yourself of Whittier's unique charm—there's nowhere else quite like it in Alaska, if not the world.

History

While less well known than the Alaska Hwy., the construction of the railway to Whittier was one of the great engineering feats of WW II. Two tunnels, 1,497 and 3,990 yards long, were carved through the Chugach Mountains to link the military bases in Anchorage and Fairbanks to a secret saltwater port. Seward, the main ice-free port in Southcentral Alaska at that time, was considered too vulnerable to Japanese attack, so from 1941 to 1943 the Army blasted through the mountains and laid the tracks which would ensure the flow of

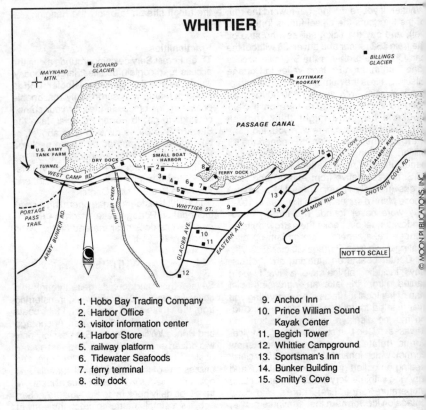

WHITTIER

MAYNARD MTN.

LEONARD GLACIER

BILLINGS GLACIER

KITTINAKE ROOKERY

PASSAGE CANAL

U.S. ARMY TANK FARM

TUNNEL

WEST CAMP RD.

DRY DOCK

SMALL BOAT HARBOR

FERRY DOCK

SMITTY'S COVE

SALMON RUN

PORTAGE PASS TRAIL

ARMY BUNKER RD.

WHITTIER CREEK

WHITTIER ST.

GLACIER AVE.

EASTERN AVE.

SALMON RUN RD.

SHOTGUN COVE RD.

NOT TO SCALE

© MOON PUBLICATIONS, INC.

1. Hobo Bay Trading Company
2. Harbor Office
3. visitor information center
4. Harbor Store
5. railway platform
6. Tidewater Seafoods
7. ferry terminal
8. city dock
9. Anchor Inn
10. Prince William Sound Kayak Center
11. Begich Tower
12. Whittier Campground
13. Sportsman's Inn
14. Bunker Building
15. Smitty's Cove

supplies for the defense of Alaska. After the defeat of Japan, the military pulled out of Whittier, but a year later they were back as the Cold War began with the Soviet Union. Whittier became a permanent base and large concrete buildings were built at that time. The 14-story Begich Tower (1948-54), an unlikely skyscraper in this small village, is near another anomaly, the "City Under One Roof," which once housed 1,000 men and was the largest building in Alaska. The base was deactivated in 1960 and the buildings were damaged in the 1964 earthquake. The Begich Tower has been restored and converted into apartments. The military presence today is limited to an oil pipeline which supplies the military installations at Anchorage.

Sights

Most travelers never get farther than the tou ist action on the waterfront but the town well worth exploring. Stop off first at the rai road car donated by the Alaska Railroad i 1982, which houses the **Visitor Center,** ope daily 11-8. Pick up train and charter boat inf and ask the "pioneer volunteers" anything o your mind. The **Small Boat Harbor** acros the road is a misnomer—this large facility h a some very big boats.

Follow the signs for Whittier down past th dry dock, then go left across the tracks on Whittier Street. Take a right on Glacier Av to the **Begich Tower.** In its 198 condos li most of the town's population; the rest resi in the 70 condos at Whittier Manor (a.k.

Sportsman's Inn). Your typical three-bedroom sells for $35,000-40,000, or rents for $350 a month. Many are owned by Anchoragites who use them as weekend and summer getaways, which boosts Whittier's summer population to nearly 1,000.

In room 107 of Begich Tower is the town **museum,** which houses one of the state's wildest and most eclectic collections of artifacts. Open daily 11-5 (free), you'll almost always have the volunteer staff member entirely to yourself. Check out the Alaskan white, brown, and black coral, the shellfish display preserved by Babs Reynolds (owner of Hobo Bay; see below), the teeth of the wolf fish, 1951 photo of Whittier, Russian coins, and sealskin etchings. Marvel over the walrus-jaw boot-jack, the two-by-eight board punched clean through a 22-inch truck tire by the 1964 tidal wave, and Lori Simonds' collection of Alaska matchbooks. The **post office** is also on the first floor; the **library** is upstairs.

But a very interesting place to stop by is the new **Seamen's Center** on the first floor of Begich. This is a low-pressure Christian respite for the weary cruise-ship crews (Indonesian, Filipino, Pole, etc.) who work seven days a week, 12-15 hours a day, belowdecks, who are forbidden to go above for fresh air or communicate with the passengers. They get no days off, except for the eight-hour layover in Whittier! So they go to the Seamen's Center to sing, pray, call home, and have lemonade and chocolate chip cookies fixed by the local church ladies. A real eye opener.

Follow Eastern Ave. to the Sportsman's Inn; climb the stairs to the **Seaquarium,** open 9-7 daily. Peek inside to decide if you want to shell out, as it were, the $3 admission. Continue another quarter mile to quiet, scenic Smitty's Cove, where one of Whittier's very few private residences sits. Here there's a great view across Passage Canal waterfalls, a kittiwake rookery, and giant Billing's Glacier.

Hikes

In back of Begich Tower is a road up a ways along Whittier Creek; from the end of the road at the creek you could bushwack up to the waterfall and close to Whittier Glacier. But the popular trail is up to **Portage Pass.** In the early days when gold was discovered around Hope on the Kenai Peninsula, Hope-bound hopefuls would boat to this harbor, portage their supplies over the glacier pass, and float down up the Turnagain Arm to their destination. This highly recommended day-hike from Whittier affords splendid views of Passage Canal, Portage Glacier, and the Chugach Mountains. On a clear day the views of the glacier from the Portage Pass area are far superior to those from the Portage Visitor Center, which is accessible by road from Anchorage. From Whittier station, walk back a mile along the road beside the railway line to the oil tanks and tunnel at the foot of Maynard Mountain. Cross the tracks on the dirt road to the left, but do not cross the river. Take the road to the right and climb southwest along the flank of the mountain up a wide, easy track. If you walk briskly, you can be at Portage Pass (elev. 700 feet) in less than an hour. There are places to camp beside Divide Lake, but beware of strong winds at the pass. From the lake follow the stream down toward the glacier, then find a way via a tributary on the right up onto one of the bluffs for a view of Portage Lake. Deep crevasses in the blue glacial ice are clearly visible from here. Portage Glacier has receded far enough that the gold rush route is now impossible, due to the lake, unless you're packing an inflatable raft. You must go back the way you came. This hike is highly recommended; allow a minimum of three hours RT. Note that there is no clear trail beyond Divide Lake; you must find your own way. Do not attempt to walk on the glacier itself, as the crevasses can be deadly.

Other Activities

Prince William Sound Kayak Center, a block in front of Begich Tower, tel. 472-2452, mainly rents kayaks, but also offers instruction and guided tours, $30 pp and up. For charters and tour boat rides, see "Tours" below.

Practicalities

Sportsman's Inn out on Eastern Ave. has large hotel rooms for $45 s and $50 d; **Anchor Inn** is similar. The Sportsman's Inn's shuttle bus to the dock is big and brown; the Anchor Inn's is small and yellow. Both have restaurants and bars, though at Anchor Inn the two are combined and you eat among drinkers and pool shooters, with the TV or jukebox on. Designated camping behind Begich Tower is good and plenty, with secluded spots, clearings for tents, and a shelter for cooking and socializing in the rain. You can use the bathrooms on the first floor of Begich Tower if the outdoor pit toilet is uncouth.

The **Hobo Bay Trading Company** on the waterfront is open for lunch and dinner: fresh fish, burgers, burritos, good pies. Something busily local is usually happening here; for a long story, ask Babs how she preserved the shellfish at the museum. Also on the wharf, the **Dog House** has hot dogs, milkshakes, and ice cream, and behind the ferry terminal is a barbecue joint and **Tidewater Seafood,** for chowder, smoked fish, and catch of the day. Both the hotels have small grocery stores, but don't miss the classic **Harbor Store,** a combination grocery/dry goods/ sporting goods/clothing/hardware/bait and tackle supermarket-department store—in an ATCO trailer. The post office is in the Tower; get showered at the Harbor Office, next to Hobo Bay.

Transportation

Almost everybody comes in by boat and leaves by train, or vice versa. The **MV Bart-lett** arrives in Whittier daily, except Thurs., at 2:15 p.m., and departs for Valdez at 3. The Mon. sailing to Cordova is the only trip th doesn't pass Columbia Glacier. The **Glaci Seas** is the Alaska Sightseeing tour boa Westours' is the **Glacier Queen.**

The **Alaska Railroad** spur makes at lea four roundtrips a day to Portage, 12 miles, 3 minutes, $8 pp, add $24 OW for a car. Yo line up by the tracks, drive up the ramp on flatcars, and ride the train behind your stee ing wheel. Try to get toward the back: les diesel fumes in the long eerie tunnel. Hitc the 45 miles to Anchorage, or head down th Kenai, from Portage. Note that Portage nothing more than a parking lot; there's n even a depot. From Whittier, the bus to A chorage connects with the 3:30 shuttle tra to Portage, arriving Anchorage at 5:30, $1 OW. This makes an excellent day-trip fro the city.

Tours

Wiso Charters, tel. 472-2304, does sigh seeing, fishing, and kayak drop-off, $250 f four hours (max. six people). Anchorage A semblyman Don Smith's **Blackstone Gl cier** cruise does a five-hour lunch trip ($99 leaving at 9 a.m., and a four-hour dinn cruise ($89), leaving Whittier 3 p.m. (fro Anchorage add $30), tel. 279-8790. But th popular new kid on the Sound, the **Klondik** does a 26-glacier cruise around College a Harriman fjords, 11:30 a.m. to 5:30 p.m., $ ($99 from Anchorage), tel. (800) 544-052 Inquire around the dock or at the Visitor Ce ter for these tickets.

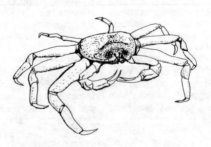

PALMER TO VALDEZ

Glenn Highway

Named for Captain Edwin Glenn, an early army explorer of the area, this road (Route 1) stretches 328 miles from downtown Anchorage to Tok, where it joins the Alaska Highway. Most of the Glenn was built during the corridor construction craze of 1942, first from Tok to Gulkana, where it joins the Richardson Highway, then from Glennallen, where it leaves the Richardson, to Palmer. Palmer was already connected to Anchorage by rail; the final 42 miles of road were completed a few years later. Head out 6th Ave. from downtown Anchortown, past Merrill Field, the Northway Mall, Fort Richardson, and onto the highway. In 10 miles you pass the exit for Eagle River and the northern section of Chugach State Park. At Mile 29, take a right onto the Old Glenn Highway, the scenic alternate route to Palmer.

PALMER

For its first 20 years, Palmer (pop. 3,000) was little more than a railway depot for Alaska Railroad's Matanuska branch. Then, in May 1935, during the height of both the Depression and a severe drought in the Midwest, Roosevelt's New Deal Federal Emergency Relief Administration selected 200 farming families from the relief rolls of northern Michigan, Minnesota, and Wisconsin, and shipped them here to colonize the Matanuska Valley. Starting out in tent cabins, the colonists cleared the dense virgin forest, built houses and barns, and planted crops pioneered at the U. of Alaska's Agricultural Experimental Station in Wasilla. These hardy transplanted farmers endured the inevitable first-year hardships, including disease, homesickness, mismanagement, floods, and just plain bad luck. But by the fall of 1936, the misfits had been weeded out, a record-setting 120 babies had been born in the colony, fertile fields and long summer days were filling barns with crops, and the colonists celebrated with a three-day harvest festival, the forerunner of the big state fair. Palmer had already become not only a flourishing town, but also the center of a bucolic and beautiful agricultural valley unique in Alaska—which it remains today. The 125-pound pumpkins, 75-pound cabbages, 10-pound onions, and two-pound radishes you might have heard about come from here.

Sights

Driving into Palmer from Wasilla along the Palmer-Wasilla Highway is a lot like driving into Wasilla from the bush on the Parks Highway—time warp. The contrast between Palmer, a 50-year-old farming community, and Wasilla, with its patented spontaneous combustion of helter-skelter development over the past five years, is startling. Start your visit at the **Palmer Information Center,** corner of S. Valley Way and E. Fireweed, open daily 9-6 in summer. Load up with brochures, especially "Alaska Fresh," a listing of where to visit farms and buy produce, and visit the small display downstairs of a colonial workshop and kitchen.

Walk two blocks east on E. Elmwood to visit the **Church of a Thousand Logs,** built by the colonists in 1936-37.

Another block east brings you to the **Agricultural Experiment Station** headquarters, where you can check out the greenhouses and arboretum across the street. About a mile south of town, down the Glenn Hwy. is the **Alaska State Fairgrounds;** the fair is held from the last week in Aug. through Labor Day. At the fairgrounds is the **Museum of Alaska Transportation and Industry,** open Tues.-Sat. 8-4. This indoor/outdoor attraction is crammed full of every imaginable kind of vehicle on wheels: don't miss the "Auto Railer," a small school bus for railroad tracks, or the "Oil Pull" from the '20s in Fairbanks. Also at the fairgrounds is **Colony Village,** which preserves some of Palmer's early buildings, including houses, a barn, and church. The Village is free, open Mon.-Sat. 10-4.

Farms

While in Palmer, take the opportunity to visit the world's only domestic **Musk Ox Farm** to see these prehistoric Arctic creatures. The 100 or so musk-ox are clearly visible through fenced walkways, while the guide explains how the fleece is woven in Eskimo cottage industries into qiviut products, which are also for sale in the gift shop. Open 10-6 daily, $2-3. Take the Glenn Highway north of town to mile 50, turn left on Archie Rd. (first left past Fishhook Rd.). Then, continue another

mile to **Wolf Country USA,** Mile 51.8, tel 745-0144, open 9-8 daily, $3. See the hybrid wolves and maybe even buy a hybrid wolf cub.

Heading north through downtown, take a right on Arctic Ave., which turns into the Old Glenn Highway. Go about four miles to Bodenberg Loop Rd., a five-mile Sunday drive through some of the most gorgeous farmland in the valley, with the Chugach's Pioneer Peak towering over it. You hardly know you're in Alaska. To see some of the

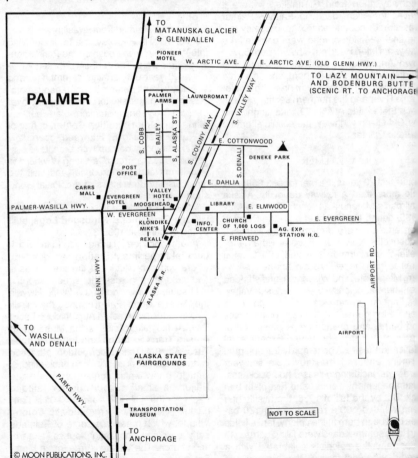

original colonial farms, head out the Glenn Highway nine miles to Farm Loop Road.

Hiking And Activities

Two excellent hikes are accessible off the Old Glenn Highway east of Palmer. Heading north from downtown, go right on Arctic Ave., which becomes the Old Glenn. Just beyond the bridge across the Matanuska River, go left onto Clark-Wolverine Rd., then continue about a mile till the next junction. Take a right on Huntley Rd., go about a mile and bear right at the fork, then drive past the caretaker's cabin to the large gravel parking lot. The trailhead is not marked, but it's obvious at the upper end of the lot. It's two hours to the top of **Lazy Mountain** (3,270 feet). A better view and shorter hike is from the top of **Bodenberg Butte** (881 feet). Keep going south on the Old Glenn, pass the first right onto the Loop Rd., and take the second (just before Fodder House Restaurant). In a quarter mile, just beyond a gravel pit, is a steep unmarked trail (you'll see it), eroded from the traffic of horses. A 40-minute huff rewards you with a 360 of the valley, Chugach, Talkeetnas, Knik Glacier, and some of the uncleared forest which graphically illustrates what the colonists confronted in "clearing the land."

The joyride in the area is taking an "air boat" from the Old Glenn Highway up the Knik River to the Knik Glacier. Twin companies run three three-hour tours a day, which include a snack. **Knik Glacier River Tours,** tel. 745-0675, charges $95. **Knik Glacier Scenic Tours,** tel. 373-2628, charges $90. They both offer free roundtrip transportation from hotels in Palmer.

Accommodations

Palmer has an unbeatably convenient city campground, **Deneke Park,** only three blocks from the information center on S. Dahlia. The sites are wooded and semi-private, $5, 10-day limit, with showers in the johns, 50 cents for eight minutes. The only time this place gets crowded is during the state fair—then forget it. To stay inside, try the **Everglen,** 326 W. Evergreen Ave. near City Hall, $25 s, $35 d. **Palmer Arms Apartments,** 1½ S. Alaska at the corner of Arctic, tel. 745-3787, has

rooms with kitchenettes for $40 s, $45 d; you can take showers here from 9-9, $3. **Old Towne Laundromat and Showers** is across the street. Around the corner on Arctic is **Pioneer Motel,** tel. 745-3425, at $40 s, $45 d.

Food And Entertainment

Possibly one of the cheapest places to eat in Alaska is the lunch counter in back of the old-fashioned **Rexall** dry-goods and drug store right downtown on Colony Way across from the Information Center. Hamburgers start at $2, sandwiches at $2.25—order two. Two doors down is **Klondike Mike's Saloon,** which has live rock 'n' roll Wed. through Sat. starting at 9:30 p.m. Around the corner on W. Evergreen is the **Frontier Coffee Shop,** open 6 a.m.-10 p.m., with usual prices and a salad bar. But if you get hungry or thirsty or sleepy at witching hours, rest assured that all your needs can be met at the **Golden Eagle** 24-hour restaurant, motel, and lounge downtown on Colony Way.

Transportation

Valdez-Anchorage buses depart daily (except Mon.) from the Sheraton Anchorage at 9 a.m., arriving Palmer at 10:15 a.m., $7. **Alaska Railroad** only runs to Palmer during the state fair. For tours of the Matanuska Valley out of Anchorage, see p. 332.

TO GLENNALLEN

Just outside of Palmer, the Glenn enters some hilly forested wilderness. Only 12 miles from town, at Mile 54, is **Moose Creek Campground,** a small but useful overnight alternative if Palmer is too crowded or expensive for your taste. But at Mile 76 is **King Mountain Wayside,** a large beautiful campground with water, outhouses, and choice spots right on the Matanuska River (though the interior loop might be less windy). The site faces King Mountain across the river—a perfect triangular peak. **King Mountain Lodge** is only 100 yards up the road. You could easily spend an idyllic day and night simply enjoying this spot. Or stop off at **Long**

Lake State Recreation Site, Mile 85, another beautiful location for camping along the Glenn. But if you're looking for easy access to the Matanuska Glacier, the highlight of this highway, pitch your tent at the **Matanuska Glacier State Recreation Site,** at Mile 101 on a hillside overlooking the ice giant, with the usual excellent state facilities.

Matanuska Glacier

This glacier is so close, safe, and spectacular that it's worth the price of admission. Admission? To a glacier? That's right, folks. For a low, low $5—cheaper than a movie or even a paperback these days—you can be the first on your block to get muddy on the Matanuska Glacier. This unique concept combines homesteading, sightseeing, and conservation, all in the same neat package. John Kimball, the friendly visionary toll-booth attendant, homesteaded 400 acres from near the highway up to the face of the glacier in 1966, then spent two years and a considerable bankroll building a road and bridges to a bluff overlooking the ice. Since 1968, Kimball has "managed" the glacier with foresight and care.

Take a right at the sign ("Glacier Park Resort—Bad Food, Warm Beer") at Mile 102, then go a mile to the lodge. Stop in and have a drink, burger, or just pay the toll. You can camp anywhere on the property; for an amusing exercise in new math, ask John about two-night charges for, say, seven people. The gate raises and you drive another two miles on an okay gravel road (rough at the end) to the parking lot. Today, this glacier is 27 miles long and four miles wide; 8,000 years ago it reached to where the lodge is, and 18,000 years ago it occupied Palmer, but it hasn't done much in the last 400 years. The terminal moraine is mostly solid, though some spots are quicksandy—wear hiking boots and expect to get a bit muddy. You can muck around right to the face, though the closer you get, the slicker it gets. Bring black-and-white film and a polarizing lens.

Glennallen

At Mile 187 of the Glenn, just before the junction with the Richardson, is this small

(GORDY OHLIGER)
Matanuska Valley and Pioneer Peak

service town, named for both Edwin Glenn (see above) and Henry Allen, leader of the first expedition up the Copper River. Strung along both sides of the road, Glennallen (pop. 449) is all practicalities. The state campground, **Dry Creek,** is five miles north of the junction. Or go half a mile west of Caribou Cafe, turn north at the library, and go an eighth mile to around the baseball fields. The tables, pit toilets, and woods would make an adequate unofficial campsite in a pinch.

Otherwise, stay at the **Caribou Motel,** which has rooms in an ATCO trailer annex for $35, and in the new motel for $60. **Caribou Cafe** serves three meals—a bit expensive. Get road food at the **Tastee-Freez,** pizza and salad bar at **Last Frontier Pizza,** open 11-11 on Post Office Rd., or wander the aisles of the grocery store. Fill your tank at Chevron, Tesoro, or Union 76.

Hitchhiking to Valdez usually isn't a problem; 115 miles on one road. But northbound thumbists: try using a destination sign for the first day or two, then bite the bullet on one of the many buses that pass through here. The **Alaskon Express bus stop** these days (since the Ahtna Lodge closed down in 1987) is at the Caribou Cafe. Call or stop in for the latest schedules and prices; public bus systems around here change faster than Dolly Parton's costumes. Good luck.

RICHARDSON HIGHWAY SOUTH

These 115 miles, running between the rugged Chugach and the massive Wrangell mountains, are so chock full of history, scenery, wilderness, and fish that you could easily spend your entire Alaskan experience between Glennallen and Valdez. This route—the oldest road in Alaska—was blazed during the stampede of 1898, and has since been used as a footpath, telegraph right-of-way, wagon trail, and auto thoroughfare. It provides access to Wrangell-St. Elias, largest national park in the country; the Edgerton Highway (Route 10) goes 96 miles from the Richardson through Chitina, which boasts superb river salmon fishing, to McCarthy and the Kennecott copper mine, deep in the heart of the national park. Finally, the last 25-mile stretch to Valdez ranks in the top three of the most scenically varied and spectacular roads in the North—right up there with the Denali Park road around Eielson and the Icefields Parkway between Lake Louise and Jasper. And that's not all. Read on.

Copper Center

Copper Center (pop. 150) is 15 miles south of Glennallen, at Mile 100 on the Richardson. Settled in 1896, this was the first non-Native town in the interior of Southcentral, opened up by all the explorations on the mighty Copper River. This was also the point where the perilous trail over Valdez Glacier came down from the mountains. When the stampeders arrived, they found a score of tents, several log cabins, a post office, and Blix Roadhouse, built in 1898 for $15,000, with spring beds and modern bath. **Copper Center Lodge,** which replaced the roadhouse in 1932, charges $45 s, $50 d, has a restaurant open 7 a.m.-9 p.m., and a bar. The **Ashby Museum** next door is open Wed. and Thurs. 1-4 p.m., Fri. 1-4 and 6-8 p.m., free. Across the highway, **The Chapel on the Hill,** built by Army volunteers in 1942, has a free slide show on Copper River country.

Edgerton Highway
To Chitina—And Beyond?

At Mile 82, 18 miles south of Copper Center, is the turnoff of Route 10 to Chitina and on to McCarthy. The Edgerton, named after yet another Alaska road commissioner, is a 33-mile highway, the first 20 of them paved. It ends in Chitina (pronounced CHIT-nuh, from the Athabascan *chiti* meaning "copper," and *na,* meaning "river"). The Chitina Indians used copper tools to hammer copper nuggets into plates, which they traded with the Tlingits; the owner of five or six plates was a millionaire. Chitina became an important junction in 1909, when the Copper River and Northwest Railroad arrived; a spur road connected the track to the original Richardson wagon trail to Fairbanks. The town began its decline in 1938 when the railroad shut down, and its future was further eroded by the Good Friday Earthquake of 1964, which knocked out several bridges linking Cordova and Chitina by the Copper River Highway. The highway project was abandoned at that time.

However! The summer of 1991 saw big doings on 80 miles of the 120-mile "Copper River Highway," 40 miles of which is south of Chitina, 40 north of Cordova, along the west bank of the mighty Copper River. Governor Hickel appears to have perpetrated an "end-run" around numerous federal, state, and Native requirements by secretly authorizing $250,000 in scarce road-maintenance funds to get out there and gouge a one-lane wilderness track to connect Cordova to the rest of the world by land. Ahtna Corp., the Native landowner, claims the state is trespassing and destroying historic and cultural sites. The Army Corps of Engineers ordered the state to cease and desist the practice of bulldozing fill into waterways. A local fishermen's lobby has decried the loss of spawning habitat. And a number of environmental groups are very pissed off in general. For now, though, it's Wally's World.

Chitina (pop. 42) is famous for its dipnetting season in June, when Alaskan residents converge on the confluence of the Copper and Chitina rivers, "dip" 35-gallon nets on 10-foot-long aluminum poles into the water, and lift out eight-pound reds and 25-pound kings by the score. The gutting and cleaning along the shore invariably engenders the nickname "Blood Beach," immortalized in 1987 by a sign which still hangs at the Howling Dog Saloon in Fox. Chitina has one motel, gas station, pay phone, Park Service station, and a couple of restaurants. The nearest official camping is at BLM's **Liberty Falls** campground 10 miles before town, but tents spring up around Town Lake, and along the three-mile appendage road south of town.

McCarthy Road

This could be the longest 60-mile road in the North—plan on at least four hours, several more if it's clear and you stop for the views of the Wrangells. At Mile 17 get ready for an adrenaline-pumping drive across the Kuskulana River on a narrow railroad bridge 300 feet above the water. Just before the end of the road is a spectacular overlook of McCarthy, the surrounding mountains, and the Kennicott and Root glaciers. The road ends at the Kennicott River, where you climb up on an open platform, and pull yourself the length of a football field, hand over hand on two trams, to get to the other side. Walk up the hill into McCarthy.

McCarthy

This beautiful little settlement (pop. 17) was another boomtown from the early 1900s till 1939, serving the copper workers at Kennecott Mine and the railroad workers on the Copper River and Northwestern. The mines, in their nearly 30 years of operation, eventually extracted $220 million in ore: nearly pure chalcocite up to 70% copper, and a little silver and gold on the side. The Alaska Syndicate (owned by J.P. Morgan and Daniel Guggenheim) held the controlling interest; it also owned the CR&NW railroad which freighted the ore to tidewater, plus the Alaska Steamship Co. which shipped the ore to various smelters. The mines shut down in 1938, when world copper prices dropped, and the cost of production became prohibitive. The abandoned town of Kennicott and mines of Kennecott (the original misspelling of the mines was never corrected) are a long day

hike or easy overnight trip from McCarthy (or pay $15 for a ride).

In McCarthy, stay at **McCarthy Lodge,** where a bed in the bunkhouse (sleeps 12) runs $15 including a continental breakfast; private rooms are $70 s, $80 d, which includes three meals. At the restaurant, bacon and eggs are $6, a bowl of chili or stew $3, and family-style dinners during the week are $8.95 (higher on Fri. and Sat.).

Wrangell-St. Elias National Park

Though somewhat less accessible than Denali, this park is an excellent alternative to the crowds, clouds, wows, and crying-out-louds. The mountains (Chugach, Wrangells, and St. Elias) are incredible, and Mt. Wrangell (14,163 feet), highest volcano in Alaska, usually puffs away on Earth's crustal cigarette. The icefields are world class, and their glacial tentacles rival any in the state. The Copper River can provide weeks-long raft or canoe rides, with all the fish you can stand. The wildlife is as abundant and visible as Denali's, and this park even has beaches on the Gulf of Alaska. Two roads plunge deep into the park's wildlands, and bus service is available. This is the largest national park in the country (larger than southern New England), with 13.2 million acres (8.4 million park, 4.8 million preserve); along with Kluane National Park across the Canadian border, the whole area was the first designated U.N. World Heritage Site. Finally, you don't need backcountry permits to traipse around or camp on this federal land—just pick a direction, and backpack till you crack.

Ground access is via the Edgerton Highway-McCarthy Rd. which cuts off from the Richardson at Mile 82, and runs almost 100 miles into the heart of the park, and the 43-mile road from Slana at Mile 65 of the Tok Cutoff (Glenn Highway) to the abandoned mining town of Nabesna. Air taxis and charter services can drop you off anywhere in the park; check around Glennallen or Cordova.

Park HQ is in Glennallen: write Superintendent, Box 29, Glennallen, AK 99588, tel. 822-5234. The visitor center is at Mile 105 on the Richardson, 23 miles south of the Edgerton Cutoff. It's open 8 a.m.-6 p.m. during the season; the rangers can help you with trip planning, sell you USGS topo maps, and record your proposed itinerary in case of emergency. Small ranger stations are also located at Slana, Chitina, and Yakutat.

To Valdez

The next 75 miles are a wonderful drive through green forested hillsides along surging creeks with countless waterfalls emanating from ice patches and small glaciers atop the jagged Chugach. If you're terminally enchanted by this stretch of road and want to linger, two state recreation sites offer camping: **Squirrel Creek** at Mile 79 and **Little Tonsina** at Mile 65. But it keeps getting more spellbinding. Near Mile 33, you come around a bend, unsuspecting, and the **Worthington Glacier** looms into view, its three fingers creeping out of Girls Mountain like a grotesque hand in a horror movie. In another few miles is the turnoff to the state site, on a very rough road about a quarter mile to the overlook parking lot. There's no established campground here, only an open cinder-block shelter with interpretive signs and a view down on the longest glacial finger. Trails cover the short distance to the glacier. Contrary to popular misconception, this glacier is not named after Cal Worthington, largest automobile franchiser on the West Coast.

It gets better. A mere three miles down (or more accurately, *up)* the road is **Thompson Pass,** elevation 2,771 feet. A long row of serrated peaks, like a cosmic cross-cut saw with only a few dull or missing teeth, lines the high horizon. Blueberry and Summit lakes are accessible by a loop road about a mile on the Valdez side of the pass; the small campground at Blueberry is beautiful—though exposed, especially if Thompson Pass is in the process of maintaining its record-setting precipitation levels. But there's more to come.

In about seven miles, you drop from the pass to **Keystone Canyon,** one of the most gorgeous sights in Alaska, even in the rain. This four-mile section is steeped in gold rush and copper frenzy history. At the height of

Klondicitis, accounts of the heavy tax and strict regulations that Canadian authorities imposed on the stampeders (which saved countless lives) were passed down the coast, and rumors of an old Indian-Russian trail from Valdez to the Yukon circulated simultaneously. The vague story of an "all-American route" to the gold sent 4,000 would-be prospectors headlong to Valdez—a measure of the madness that gripped the land. Suicidally unprepared, like lemmings they attempted to cross the brutal Valdez Glacier. Also responding to the rumors, the U.S. Army dispatched Capt. William Abercrombie in 1898 to find or blaze a route from Valdez to the Interior. Abercrombie had been on the original American expedition to Copper River country in 1884. He *knew* the land and the conditions; when he crossed Valdez Glacier in 1898, he postponed his trail-blazing assignment in order to deal with the horror that he found (see p. 350 for the rest of this tragedy). Abercrombie returned in 1899 and thoroughly explored and mapped the whole area, locating and naming the Lowe River, Keystone Canyon, and the Thompson Pass route to the Interior.

Then in 1906, during the often violent race to build a railroad from tidewater to the Kennecott copper mines, two of the competing construction companies clashed over the right-of-way through this Keystone Canyon; one man was killed. The ensuing trial further fanned the flames, and the "Shoot-out at Keystone Canyon" became a great issue between the opposing sides. All this is highly dramatized in Rex Beach's popular novel, *The Iron Trail.*

Today, you drive along the raging Lowe River, at the bottom of nearly perpendicular 300-foot cliffs; the entire canyon is a psychedelic green; every crack and crevice in the sheer walls is overgrown with bright lime moss. Waterfalls tumble over the walls to the river below, spraying the road with a fine mist. Bridal Veil and Horsetail falls live up to their names. And now you're ready to enter Valdez.

VALDEZ

At the end of Valdez Arm and completely surrounded by snowcapped peaks, Valdez (pronounced val-DEEZ) is not only one of the most picturesque towns in Alaska, but with the pipeline terminal, it's one of the most prosperous. It's also one of the most progressive, the city leaders planning ahead for when the oil money inevitably stops flowing and Valdez reverts to Anytown, Alaska. The new $50 million floating container dock is the largest of its kind in the world. The Copper Valley hydroelectric plant supplies power for distant towns (the power lines along the Richardson all the way to Glennallen emanate from here). Its tailing waters are used by Solomon Gulch Hatchery, working to ensure large runs of salmon for the future. Valdez is proud of its $3 million Civic Center, $1.3 million teen center, $1.5 million softball and recreation complex, new library, hospital, pioneer home, mushrooming community college, etc.; even the slick 30-minute video singing Valdez's praises looks like a million-dollar production. Finally, with year-round access by road, ferry, and air, and well-developed tourist facilities, charter fishing opportunities, tour boat cruises to popular Columbia Glacier, and seemingly endless wilderness around it, Valdez's pivotal place in Alaska's future is well assured. . . .

. . . As long as the dust settles from the Exxon Valdez oil spill. In the mad summer of 1989, Valdez was turned on its head by the "Exxon Economy," and Valdez residents' lives and livelihoods were changed, possibly irreparably, possibly forever. Only time will tell.

History
Cook sailed into and named Prince William Sound in 1778; Spanish explorer Don Salvador Fidalgo entered "Puerto de Valdez" in 1790, naming it after Spain's Marine Minister. In 1898, Valdez was a tent city of stampeders similar to Skagway—except for one critical detail: no trail to the Interior. Still, between

4,000 and 6,000 cheechakos crossed the death-defying Valdez Glacier that year. Army Capt. William Abercrombie described the foolhardy newcomers as "terrifyingly incompetent . . . wholly unprepared physically and morally for what they would face." They barely knew how to strap packs on their backs, and few thought to carry the two basic necessities: water and wood. Many were blinded by the sun's reflection off the ice. Many got lost in howling storms, where it was impossible to see or hear the man ahead. Of those who managed to reach the summit, many lost their loads and lives on slick downhill slides into oblivion. And those who actually got off the glacier intact had to contend with the fast cold waters of the runoff. Many men with heavy packs on lost their footing and drowned in knee-deep water. Some attempted to build boats and float down the Klutina River to Copper Center; few made it. And those stuck between the glacier and river had nothing.

In the final count, all but 300 (and the countless dead) of those who'd set out from Valdez during the spring and summer of '98 had returned to Valdez the way they came by fall. Abercrombie found them destitute and broken. Many had gone mad, some had scurvy, most had frost-bitten hands, feet, faces. Facilities were squalid. And there was no food. Abercrombie postponed his orders to blaze a trail into the Interior for six months to feed, clothe, house, and arrange transportation home for those men.

But the town of Valdez was growing up around them. Only four or five years later, a corporate copper rush kicked off a fierce competition between Valdez, Cordova, and a town called Katalla to be selected as the tidewater terminus of the proposed railway to the copper mines. A dozen projects were conceived, and one was even begun out of Valdez (see "To Valdez" above), but Cordova won out in the end. For the next 60 years, Valdez was a sleepy fishing and shipping

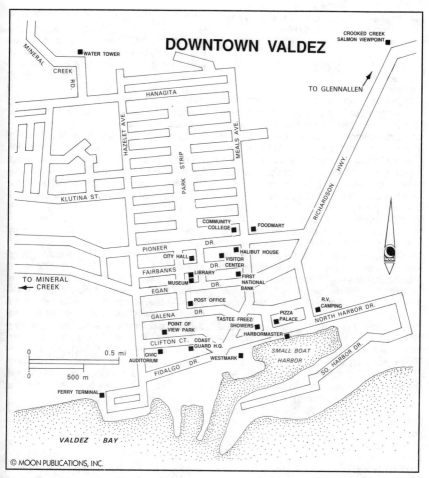

DOWNTOWN VALDEZ

CROOKED CREEK SALMON VIEWPOINT

TO GLENNALLEN

MINERAL CREEK RD.

WATER TOWER

HANAGITA

HAZELET AVE.

MEALS AVE.

PARK STRIP

RICHARDSON HWY.

KLUTINA ST.

COMMUNITY COLLEGE

FOODMART

PIONEER DR.

CITY HALL

HALIBUT HOUSE

VISITOR CENTER

FAIRBANKS DR.

TO MINERAL CREEK

LIBRARY

MUSEUM

FIRST NATIONAL BANK

EGAN DR.

POST OFFICE

GALENA DR.

R.V. CAMPING

NORTH HARBOR DR.

POINT OF VIEW PARK

TASTEE FREEZ/ SHOWERS

PIZZA PALACE

CLIFTON CT.

COAST GUARD H.Q.

HARBORMASTER

SMALL BOAT HARBOR

0   0.5 mi

CIVIC AUDITORIUM

WESTMARK

FIDALGO DR.

SO. HARBOR DR.

0   500 m

FERRY TERMINAL

VALDEZ   BAY

© MOON PUBLICATIONS, INC.

port, competing with Seward, then Whittier, for access to the Interior. Then in 1964 the Good Friday Earthquake struck, wiping out the entire old town, which was rebuilt four miles inland on property donated by a local. Finally, in 1974, the town leaders sold the virtues of Valdez—its ice-free port, 800-foot-deep harbor, and proximity to the Interior—to the pipeline planners, who chose the town as their terminus.

Everything went along miraculously smoothly and without serious incident until March 29, 1989, almost 25 years to the day after the Good Friday Earthquake, when the *Exxon Valdez* ran aground on Bligh Reef a few hours after leaving the pipeline terminal in Valdez, dumping 11 million gallons of North Slope crude into Prince William Sound. The unthinkable had happened. And it remains to be seen when and if the 1,100 miles of coastline fouled by the hardened sludge will recover from this devastating blow.

SIGHTS

Downtown

For its size, **Heritage Center Museum,** right in the middle of town on Egan, open 9-8, tel. 835-2764, $2, has an extraordinary amount of comprehensive displays. Check out the fascinating photo display on the pipeline's "impact," and the early black-and-whites, especially one of a steamship at the Columbia Glacier in 1928. Some rare early maps and charts include a Russian one from 1737; look for the beautiful engraving by Webber, Cook's prolific ship's artist. Informative displays illustrate Indian, mining, and telegraph history; the 1840 lighthouse lens and the 1907 Ahrens steam engine are the highlights. Spend some time reading the descriptions of the earthquake—unbelievable. And if you have any grief and amazement to spare after that, read about Valdez's namesake supertanker.

Up Meals Ave. toward the mountains is **Prince William Sound Community College;** a number of wooden sculptures by Peter Toth dot the grounds, including one magnificent Indian head. Down Meals Ave. by the harbor, bear left onto Clifton, and go up past Coast Guard HQ to the **Civic Center.** An interpretive signboard describes the pipeline terminal across the bay. Climb the steep stairs up to **Point of View Park,** for the good view of town.

Out Of Town

Crooked Creek spawning area is out the Richardson about a half mile from town. In late summer, walk out on the boardwalk and watch the salmon go through the final act of their incredible life cycle; cross the road to see what happens to them after they spawn. Continue out the Rich about 3½ miles to where a historical sign points to Old Valdez. The only thing left of the old townsite besides the post office foundation and memorial plaque are the mileposts on the Rich: zero

still starts here. In another three miles, turn right onto Dayville Rd.; in several miles you come to the hydroelectric plant and salmon hatchery. Pause here to see the powerful falls at Solomon Gulch, take the brief self-guided tour around the hatchery (staff will usually answer your questions), and hike the steep 2½-mile RT Alaska Power Authority trail up to the dam and lake, just to the left as you face the plant.

Continue two miles to the front gate of the pipeline terminal. The sculpture is by Malcolm Alexander, who did the similar one at Fairbanks' Golden Heart Park. The information center moved out to the airport during the unfortunate episode of Iraqi genocide in the winter of 1991 for security reasons; it might be back at the gate when you get there. Wherever it is, the center has a row of signboards explaining everything from the history of Valdez to pipeline "pigs"—capsule-type rotors sent through the pipe periodically to scrape the waxy yellow buildup on the inner walls. Check out the graphic comparison between a *Bartlett*-size ferry and a two-million-barrel oil tanker, one of four that the terminal docks can accommodate. For a point of reference, the *Valdez* was Exxon's largest supertanker. The center itself basically only sells T-shirts and souvenir jimjacks; the proceeds help the Alyeska consortium meet the payroll. Alyeska sponsors a free bus tour through the pipeline terminal three times a day.

ACTIVITIES

Hiking

A good walk is out beautiful **Mineral Creek Rd.**—a stunning canyon leading to a turn-of-the-century stamp mill. The 5½-mile road is very narrow and bumpy, better used as a trail; a mile beyond the end is Smith Stamp Mill, which crushed ore from mines up the mountain to process through sluice boxes. Go up Hazelet to Hanagita, turn left, then right on Mineral Creek Rd.; allow five to six hours for this 13-mile RT.

Another pretty walk is out Egan west of town beyond the bridge over Mineral Creek;

Take a tour boat cruise for a seal's eye view of glaciers and icebergs.
(GORDY OHLIGER)

or take a left just before the bridge and walk up the hill past Blueberry Hill B&B. Very scenic.

A couple of miles past the campground out the airport road is a huge gravel-pit dead-end at a stream in front of the deadly **Valdez Glacier.** Sharp echo off the sheer rock wall along the road. Scramble straight up the ridge for the view. This is a good walk after a big breakfast at the campground.

Rafting And Cruising
Keystone Raft and Kayak Adventures, at Mile 17 of the Richardson, tel. 835-2606, offers an exciting two-hour raft trip down the Class III Lowe River through Keystone Canyon. With five trips daily, you can almost always fit one into your schedule, $30 pp, $35 with transportation from town. Rainsuits, life jackets, and rubber boots are provided. A similar trip goes down Mineral Creek Canyon, so you can hike up and ride back, if you plan carefully. Also ask about their charter trips around the Interior and Copper River country. **Alaska Waterways,** tel. 835-5151, does a day-long trip to the Shoup Glacier on the *Peggy J,* a motorized pontoon boat, including hiking, wildlife watching, and a hot lunch, $70 pp.

Valdez has two dozen charter fishing and cruising boats for hire by sportsmen and tour-

ists. The central booking agency is **Hook, Line, and Sinker Charter Boat Booking Service,** Box 1345, Valdez, AK 99686, tel. 835-4410.

To Columbia Glacier
Columbia Glacier is the most visited tidewater glacier in the state. Glacier Bay's popularity is as long-standing, and a few new challengers (Kenai and College fjords) siphon off some tourists, but they're all private, fairly expensive cruises. Columbia is the only one passed by the state ferry, from which most people view this stunning grandfather of glaciers in Prince William Sound. Covering about 440 square miles, Columbia Glacier is 42 miles long and more than three miles wide at its face, which rises up to 300 feet above the water and plunges an incredible 2,000 feet below. Although it's the second-largest of its kind in Alaska, and still extends 32 miles out into its ancestral fjord, Columbia Glacier is but a minor remnant of the vast glacier that only a few thousand years ago filled Prince William Sound, and whose face reached a height of 4,000 feet. Yet only in the past five years or so has this glacier begun to recede, after having held relatively steady since measurements on it first began in the early 1900s.

Only 25 air miles from Valdez, the state ferry *Bartlett* pauses a couple of miles out on its trip between Valdez and Whittier. At least four tour boats cruise right up to the face, threading their way among icebergs with seals sunning themselves. Trips come in many combinations, including plane-boat, bus-boat, train-boat, or just the roundtrip cruise from Valdez. **Stan Stephens Charters,** tel. 835-4731, runs the *Glacier Spirit;* **Glacier Charter Service,** tel. 835-5141, runs the *Lu-Lu Belle; Glacier Queen* is the original **Westours** vessel, tel. 835-2357; and *Glacier Seas* is run by **Alaska Sightseeing,** tel. 835-4558. Shop by phone or around the Small Boat Harbor for the price ($79-99) and time that suits you best.

Flightseeing

Get a bird's-eye view of the Sound and see how big Columbia Glacier and its icefield really are, by air. **Valdez Aero Services,** tel. 835-4304, has regular 45-minute Columbia Glacier trips for $50 pp in their three-seater, and you can arrange other charter flights at $175 an hour. Or knock around on the ubiquitous **ERA** helicopters, tel. 835-2636.

PRACTICALITIES

Accommodations

Creative camping is the name of this game. RV parks abound right in town, mostly along the waterfront, but the closest official campground is five miles away. Go back out the Richardson, turn left toward the airport, and continue another mile past it—look closely for the small signboards at the A-frame on the left, poorly marked. This huge campground has outhouses, water, and is quite scenic and free, though obviously barely accessible to people on foot. Otherwise, to camp free walk around the corner from the ferry terminal and take a left on Egan Dr.; a quarter mile out will hide you in the trees. You can also pitch your tent on the grassy area across from the parking lot around the bend from the ferry, though it's exposed and close to the canneries. Or disappear on the hill behind the waterfront. The **Bear Paw RV Park** on the waterfront accepts tenters for $10 (includes showers). Or head halfway

around Harbor Drive; on the left is a large city park with good views and lots of seasonals. You can camp here for $5.

All hotel rooms in Valdez cost upwards of $100. The best deal here is to rent one of the 16 cottages out back of the Village Inn, tel. 835-4445. For $99 a night, you get private bath, kitchenette, and beds for six (two doubles, four bunk beds). This is the way to go if you get together a few people, shop and cook, *and have a reservation.*

True to new Alaskan form, the Valdez "Facilities and Services" brochure lists 51 bed and breakfasts. Ring up **One Call Does It All,** tel. 835-4988, for B&B reservations, as well as tours, sight and flightseeing, rafting and fishing charters.

Food

Lots of choices here. The **Totem Inn** is busiest with locals for breakfast—a big dark dining room, with aquariums, wildlife displays, and big-screen video. **Alaska Halibut House,** on Meals Ave. across from the college, has good local fast-food fish, or get the salmon bake lunch for $7, dinner for $15. To get there, go out N. Harbor Dr. past Bear Paw and around the bends.

Wait in line for an hour for pizza and Italian food at **Pizza Palace,** also on N. Harbor next to **Tastee-Freez,** which has plastic breakfasts but very cheap burgers and fried chicken (and the showers). **Fu Kung** Chinese is in a Quonset hut on Kobuk behind the Totem Inn. The buffet at the **Village Inn** is almost worth the $11.25—eat with the Alaska Sightseeing package tourists.

Services And Information

The public showers are at the rear of Tastee-Freez, open 6 a.m.-10 p.m., $3, no time limit and not too funky, but sinks and toilets are up front in the restaurant. The car wash on the outside back wall of the Tastee-Freez is $1.75 for five minutes. Or try the swimming pool at the high school out on Hanagita usually closed most of August. The helpful friendly **Visitor Center** is across from City Hall at 200 Chenega St., tel. 835-2984, open daily 8-8. Check out the free flicks on the earthquake and pipeline.

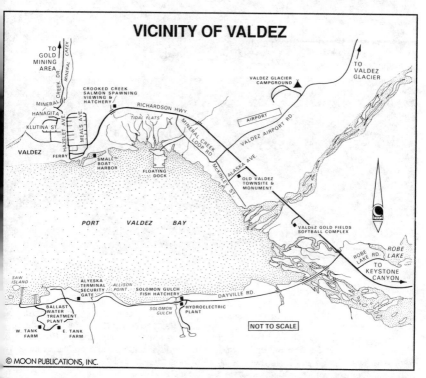

VICINITY OF VALDEZ

NOT TO SCALE

© MOON PUBLICATIONS, INC.

Transportation

Valdez is 366 miles from Fairbanks on the Richardson; from Anchorage it's 189 miles on the Glenn Highway to Glennallen, then another 115 on the Richardson. **Valdez-Anchorage Bus Lines** leaves the Totem Inn at 9:30 a.m., $55 to Anchorage, arriving at 5:15 p.m. **Alaska Sightseeing** has a bus from the Village Inn to Fairbanks, leaving at 7:30 a.m. on Tues., Thurs., and Sat., $103 and to Valdez from Fairbanks on Mon., Wed., and Fri., leaving from the Golden Nugget Motel. **ERA** and **Wilburs** have scheduled flights to and from Anchorage and Cordova several times a day. The airport is four miles outside of town; a Yellow cab, tel. 835-2500, runs around $3. Note all the abandoned ATCO trailers and brothel/bars out by it—a reminder of Valdez's population boom (up to around 10,000) during pipeline days.

Alaska Marine Highway's **E.L. Bartlett** leaves Valdez every day except Thurs. for Whittier ($56); it also runs between Whittier and Cordova on Mon. ($56), and Valdez and Cordova on Wed. ($28). Note that the *Bartlett* is the only state ferry *without* showers—painful. The *Tustemena* leaves Valdez on Sat. and Sun. on its way around Prince William Sound and over to Seward, Homer, and Kodiak, but different weeks have different times; check the schedule and prices carefully.

Avis, tel. 835-4774, rents cars for $49 daily and 37 cents a mile after 150 miles. **Hertz,** tel. 835-4402, is similar. **Beaver Sports** on Galena down from the post office rents two one-speed clunkers, $4.50 per hour, $24 for all day. They're open Mon.-Fri. 9 a.m.-7 p.m., Sat. 9 a.m.-6 p.m.

(GORDY OHLIGER)

CORDOVA

Cordova (pop. 2,585) is noticeably less populated, less prosperous, and less accessible than its big-sister city Valdez—and most people like it that way. Though only a six-hour ferry ride away, its setting is its own, its climate is milder and wetter, and its vibration is nothing like Valdez's. Cordova might feel more at home somewhere between Petersburg and Juneau: connected only by boat and plane, with a large commercial fishing fleet, mild and very wet climate, lush forests and small islands and snowcapped peaks. Many travelers, especially those who gravitate to the coast, use Cordova as the stepping stone from Southeast to Southcentral and the mainland, bypassing the hundreds of miles of overland travel through Yukon and Interior. But Cordova is more than just the coast; it's also Chugach National Forest, Prince William Sound, and their abundant outdoor recreation; the Copper River and its wild rides and massive delta; railroad history and the Million Dollar Bridge. Amidst all of this is a bustling little community bursting at its seams during the summer fishing season, but also glued together by that magical fishing lifestyle. Cordova was much harder hit than Valdez by the actual oil from the spill and the future remains unsure. But drift over to Cordova and spend a couple of days exploring this special corner of Alaska—you'll be glad you did.

History

In 1884, Abercrombie surveyed the Copper River delta, which made the area known to a few hardy prospectors. Then the crazed stampede of 1897-98 opened up the area to settlement. Still, in 1905, Cordova was little more than a couple of canneries processing the pinks and silvers from the Sound. Then Michael J. Heney showed up. After years of surveying rights-of-way, watching railroad ventures to the rich coal and copper mines nearby start and fold, and failing to convince the Morgan-Guggenheim Alaska Syndicate not to start their road from Katalla, Heney invested his entire savings and in 1907 began laying track from Cordova toward Kennecott Mine. After the Katalla facilities were destroyed by a storm, the Syndicate purchased the Copper River and Northwest line from Heney, and completed it in 1911 at a total cost of $23 million; by 1917 it had hauled over $100 million in ore to Cordova for transshipment to smelters. Cordova was a boomtown till the Kennecott Mine closed in 1938. Since then the town's economy has reverted to fishing and canning. The year-round population doubles in the summer, and in good years there's plenty of work.

SIGHTS

The **Cordova Museum** is in the Centennial Building at First and Adams, adjoining the library. Open 1-5 p.m. Tues.-Sun., plus 5-7 p.m. on Sat., this museum (free) is small but packed with artifacts, including an old Linotype, an ancient slot machine, a three-seat bidarka, and an amusing exhibit on Cordova's world-famous Iceworm Festival (held each Feb.). Look for the aerial views of earthquake damage to the Million Dollar Bridge. The 30-minute *Story of Cordova* is shown on Sat. evening at 7:30. The **library** is open 1-9 p.m. except Wed., Sat. 9-5 p.m., and Sun. 1-5 p.m. This is a good place to read, rest, even sleep, and meet fellow travelers while waiting for the ferry.

Many buildings around town were built during its original construction in 1908, including (all on First St.) the Alaskan and Cordova hotels, the Ambrosia Pizza building, and the Red Dragon, oldest building in town, which served weekdays as a rowdy clubhouse, but on Sundays turned into a church when the altar was let down by ropes from the beams. Pick up the historic walking-tour map of the museum for a complete list of the old buildings.

Million Dollar Bridge

There aren't enough superlatives in the English language to describe adequately the 50-mile ride out the Copper River Highway from Cordova to this amazing bridge. The scenery—mountains, glaciers, river, delta—rivals any 50 miles on the continent, let alone the state. The wildlife—thousands of shorebirds and ducks, Canada geese, huge trumpeter swans, bald eagles, moose, bears, and spawning salmon—gives Denali a run for its money. The history encompasses punching an early 20th-century railroad 200 miles into the Interior to starting a road in the '60s on its right-of-way, only to be destroyed by the largest earthquake ever recorded in North America. The crowning glory of the trip, as visible in rain or fog as in bright sunshine, built at great expense and great danger in 1910 between the faces of two moving glaciers and left mostly standing by the earthquake, is the Million Dollar Bridge, the vista from which is unsurpassed in a land of unsurpassed vistas.

Just outside of town, the Copper River Highway passes beautiful Eyak Lake at the base of Eyak Mountain. Notice how the lake is two colors, deep blue and light green, which don't merge. From around Mile 6 at the bridge over Eyak River to Mile 12 where the pavement ends, keep a sharp eye out for waterfowl and wildlife in the runoff sloughs from nearby Scott Glacier. Take a left at Mile 12 for the airport, and a two-mile gravel road up to Cabin Lake where there're trout fishing, picnic tables, and trails to three other lakes. At Mile 14, another left and another two miles of gravel bring you to the Mt. Sheridan trailhead; hike a mile on the 4WD extension spur and scramble up on the ridge to look out over the two-finger glacier flowing down either side of the mountain, and the iceberg-clogged lake at its face. A side road to the right at Mile 17 goes off to **Alaganik Slough;** the three rough miles are excellent for viewing shorebirds.

At Mile 27, you cross the first of nearly a dozen bridges and causeways to the other "side" of the Copper River, more than 10 miles distant, which might remind you of the south Florida Keys. Long Island, from Mile 28 to Mile 33.5, sits smack in the middle of the mighty river delta. Good canoeing in the ponds along here, which connect up with a minimum of portage. Out here you can understand why, out of 196 miles of track from Cordova to Kennicott, 96 miles were built over bridges or trestles.

Finally, at Mile 48, you arrive at Million Dollar Bridge. This bridge, which cost a little

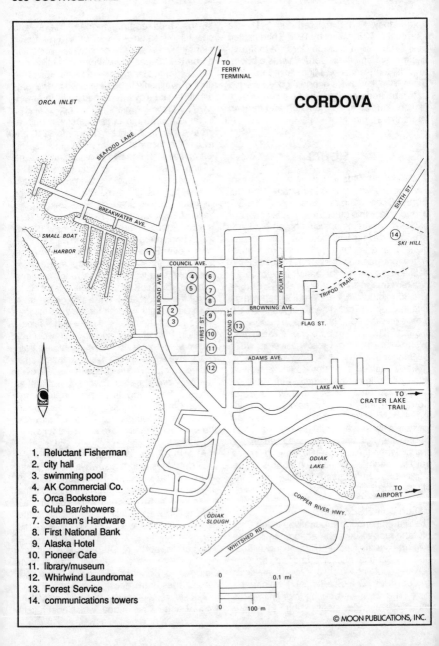

ORCA INLET

CORDOVA

TO
FERRY
TERMINAL

SEAFOOD LANE

BREAKWATER AVE.

SMALL BOAT
HARBOR

SIXTH ST.

SKI HILL

14

COUNCIL AVE.

RAILROAD AVE.

TRIPOD TRAIL

FOURTH AVE.

4   6
5   7
     8
2   9
3   10
     11
12

FIRST ST.

SECOND ST.

BROWNING AVE.

FLAG ST.

13

ADAMS AVE.

LAKE AVE.

TO
CRATER LAKE
TRAIL

ODIAK
LAKE

TO
AIRPORT

COPPER RIVER HWY.

ODIAK
SLOUGH

WHITSHED RD.

1. Reluctant Fisherman
2. city hall
3. swimming pool
4. AK Commercial Co.
5. Orca Bookstore
6. Club Bar/showers
7. Seaman's Hardware
8. First National Bank
9. Alaska Hotel
10. Pioneer Cafe
11. library/museum
12. Whirlwind Laundromat
13. Forest Service
14. communications towers

0   0.1 mi

0   100 m

© MOON PUBLICATIONS, INC.

over a million dollars to build in 1910, was the culmination of Michael Heney's vision, faith, and employee loyalty—not to mention the uncanny abilities of his civil engineers. It had to be built entirely in winter, when the two glaciers that sandwiched it were dormant. The working conditions were unbearable at best and the danger was extreme, especially as the builders raced to finish the final span even as its supports were being washed away by break-up. But it *was* completed, Heney sold the whole show to the Syndicate, and according to Rex Beach in *The Iron Trail*, married the girl of his dreams and lived happily ever after.

The north span collapsed in the earthquake, but the state jury-rigged a ramp down to the abutment, and it's a fun little joyride to the other side. (Governor Wally's road "maintenance" crews have been busy working on the Copper River Highway on the other side of the bridge. No telling what it might look like when you get there.) On the bridge, look to your left at the massive face of the **Childs Glacier**; look right about three miles across Miles Lake to the **Miles Glacier**, which has receded two miles since 1910. A short side road on the left just before the bridge leads past a small concrete shack used by Fish and Game while counting the salmon escapement, down to the rocky beach across the river from the unbelievable Childs. Plan to spend all afternoon here as the glacier creaks, groans, and cracks, dropping calves into the narrow river channel. *Be careful* of particularly big calves, whose waves can splash all the way up the embankment. To get out here, see "Getting Around" below.

Hiking

Two trails climb **Mt. Eyak**—one through the forest, the other up the ski slope. The unmarked **Tripod Trail** is a little hard to find, but if you cut to the right between a cabin and a driveway near the end of 5th St., you'll see the trailhead. This is a pretty hike through forest primeval, with salmonberries (a little bitter but juicy) ripe for the picking in August. Otherwise, head straight up Council Ave., bear left onto 6th, and follow it around the Alascom communications apparatus. You

can start right up the mountain from there, and you don't have to go far to get a great view of the town and harbor. You could camp around here in a pinch.

The excellent **Crater Lake Trail** begins opposite Skaters Cabin on Eyak Lake, two miles from town beyond the old cemetery, seaplane base, and municipal airstrip. The trail climbs 1,500 feet in two miles through a beautiful forest, with panoramic views near the top of Eyak Lake and the Heney Range. The terrain around Crater Lake is fairly open and it would be easy to scale the surrounding summits, if you have the time and energy. Allow a minimum of two hours RT from the road to the lake. The trail is solid and very easy to follow; even if a wet wind is blowing, it will be relatively still in the forest, but be careful not to slip. Don't miss this one.

At the end of Power Creek Rd., six miles from town, a trail leads about a mile up to Ohman Falls—and when you see it you'll definitely say, "Oh man!"

The Forest Service maintains the **Lydick Slough Trail** (3.2 miles), starting at Mile 7 of the Copper River Highway, the **Lake Elsner Trail** (four miles), from the end of Cabin Lake Rd., the **Pipeline** (two miles) and **McKinley Lake** (two miles) trails, both from Mile 19.8 of the highway, and the **Mt. Sheridan Trail** (two miles), from the end of Glacier Road. Pick up a Xeroxed handout on these hikes at the Forest Service office (see "Services and Information" below).

Recreation Cabins

Over a dozen Forest Service cabins are available for rent ($15) in the Cordova area; all but three are accessible only by plane or boat. There are cabins at both ends of the McKinley Lake Trail. If you've never seen one, hike for two minutes up the McKinley Lake Trail (Mile 19.8) and peer in the windows. To reserve, go to the Forest Service office on 2nd Ave. (see below).

PRACTICALITIES

Accommodations

One motel and two hotels are on 1st St., the main drag, all above or connected to bars.

Least expensive is the **Alaska Hotel,** above the Alaska Bar, $35 s without bath, $40 with; add $5 for each additional person. Next door, the **Cordova Hotel,** above the Cordova Bar, charges $36.50 s (or double—if a couple), $41.50 for doubles of the same sex. Check into both at the bars downstairs. The **Prince William Sound Motel,** behind the Club Bar and Cafe, charges $65 s or d. You can also take showers next door at the laundromat. The manager, Penny, is a very kind and accommodating Cordovan, who'll store your backpack from 8-8 while you wander around town, and doesn't mind seeing you during the day. The **Reluctant Fisherman** down on Railroad Ave. is the classy place—rooms start at $100, if you can get one. The **Oystercatcher B&B,** run by John and Mary Davis, rents rooms for $50, including bacon and eggs, tel. 424-5154.

A municipal parking area for RVs is a half mile out Whitshed Rd. beside what was once the city dump. Camping on this gravel-surfaced area overlooking Orca Inlet is $5; showers are available to non-campers. Many people pitch their tents on top of the bluff opposite the ferry terminal, by the green water tower. Or get lost on the ski hill, or head out of town in any direction for a half mile.

Food

Two coffee shops open at 6 a.m., which'll give you some place to go when you arrive on the early ferry. The **Windsinger,** behind the Club Bar on 1st Ave., serves the usual bacon and eggs for $6; the **Reluctant Fisherman** coffee shop is similar. Both stay open till 9 p.m. If you can hold out for an hour in the morning, a great place to eat is the **Killer Whale Cafe** in the Orca Bookstore on 1st Avenue. Wholesome West Coast-type breakfast fare starts at $4; sit upstairs for the view of the harbor (or the store). They also serve unusual combination sandwiches, such as teriyaki chicken, ham, and pineapple for lunch ($5.50), and excellent bakery goods till 4 p.m. The **Munchie Hut** is a fast-food wagon down Breakwater Ave. next to the Anchor Bar. **Ambrosia Pizza** and **OK Chinese Restaurant** are also on 1st Avenue.

Frenchy's serves Baskin-Robbins ice cream; **Town Bakery** does donuts and coffee. **Powder House,** out a mile on the highway, does a thriving business in soup and sandwiches; sit on the deck overlooking the lake.

Alaska Commercial Co. is the larger supermarket in town, just up Council Ave. from the Reluctant Fisherman. **Davis Foods** is the smaller one, right on 1st Avenue.

Entertainment

Don't come to Cordova for the nightlife; other than drinking with the seafood folks, it's strictly make your own. The **Club Bar** has live music most nights, dancing some nights when someone wild instigates it. The **Alaska** and **Cordova** bars next to each other on 1st Ave., and the **Anchor Bar** on Breakwater Ave., are hard core. The best view is from the bar at the **Reluctant Fisherman,** with prices to match. At the **Powder House** a mile out the Copper River Highway, you can have a drink on the deck on Eyak Lake; a bluegrass band jams most weekends—if they're not burned out from fishing.

Services And Information

Showers are available across the alley from the Prince William Sound Motel. Pick up the key ($2.50) from the motel office, and get quarters for the hot-water meter, 25 cents for three minutes. They have a sink and mirror—much roomier and nicer than the Valdez Tastee-Freez. Or plan to get to the pool on Railroad Ave. at the appropriate hours: Mon.-Sat. for open swim and adult laps 5:45-8:30 p.m., $4 first half hour, $1 each additional hour. You can also shower at the RV area on Whitsled Road. Anything you want to know about the business side of Cordova you can find out at the **Chamber of Commerce,** in a narrow office on 1st Ave., especially if Kathy Sherman is working. Supposedly open 9-noon Mon.-Thurs.; keep checking. Stop at the **USFS** office, on the third floor of the old post office building on 2nd Avenue. Big maps on the wall, plus local maps, handouts, info on cabins; ask for the 21-page handout on the many trails in the area. Open 8-5 Mon.-Friday.

TRANSPORTATION

By Ferry

The **MV** *Bartlett* services Cordova three times a week in the summer, leaving Valdez at 11:45 p.m. on Tues. and Wed., arriving at 5:30 a.m. Wed. and Thurs. ($26), and leaving Whittier (not via Columbia Glacier) at 3 p.m. Mon. and arriving Cordova at 10 p.m. ($56). The **MV** *Tustemena* leaves Valdez at 1:30 p.m. Sat. and arrives at 7 p.m. The *Tustemena* has showers; the *Bartlett* doesn't. It's a 20-minute walk from the Cordova ferry terminal to town; take a right at the fork onto Railroad Ave. to avoid the 1st Ave. hill, then walk up Council Ave. from the Reluctant Fisherman.

By Air

Alaska Airlines flies into Cordova once daily (twice on Fri. and Sun.) on its way to and from Juneau, $170 OW. Although expensive, this is how you can hop over from Southeast to Southcentral, connecting up from the one ferry to the other, while skipping the long distances overland. **Wilbur's Flight Operations** flies from Anchorage three times daily (once on Sun.). They also fly regularly from Valdez. The airport is 12 miles from town out the Copper River Highway. Reluctant Fishermen has an airport van for $5; Wilbur's and J.V. Transportation might also be running one.

Getting Around

If you just want to hang around town, everywhere is walkable in 10 minutes. If you want to go back and forth from the campground or out to the lake or to some of the trailheads, **Whiskey Ridge Cycle Shop,** tel. 424-3354, down Breakwater next to the Fathom Gallery, rents mountain bikes for $10 a day.

But if you want to get out to the glaciers or Million Dollar Bridge, you'll have an interesting challenge on your hands. You can ferry your own car across from Valdez for $128 RT (make reservations far in advance). If that sounds steep, compare it to renting a car from the Reluctant Fisherman: $75 a day, 50 cents a mile, plus insurance, plus gas, plus city tax (four percent). With no trouble you can rack up $200 for the day. Also check with Imperial Car Rental, tel. 424-5695; their rates are somewhat more reasonable.

Hitchhiking is possible, especially on a fair day when an occasional local might pick you up on his or her joyride; visitors' vehicles tend to be crowded with travelers sharing expenses. Or you could grab an airporter van out to the end of the pavement and try hitching from there; if you don't get picked up, you don't have that far to come back. **Copper River Express,** tel. 424-5463, will run out to the bridge for a minimum of three people. Or you could call around to the charter companies and ask if their drivers or vehicles happen to be heading out there for one reason or another.

What your intrepid author finally did was find someone who knew someone who had a teenage son with a 4WD pickup who wasn't doing anything that day. What a ride!

KENAI PENINSULA

The Kenai Peninsula is like a mini-Alaska, compressing all of the country's features—mountains, icefields and glaciers, fjords and offshore islands, large fish-filled rivers and lakes, swampy plain, varied climate and precipitation, a few scattered port towns and a sprawling population center—into an area roughly 1/35th the size of the state. The outdoor recreational opportunities are practically inexhaustible, with innumerable choices of every pedestrian, pedaled, paddled, piloted, port-holed, piscatory, predatory, and picaresque particular you could ever ponder. You, and 300,000 other folks from the neighborhood, that is. The Kenai is the major playground for Anchoragites and travelers, and possibly the most popular all-around destination for all Alaskans. But don't let that deter you. The resources are abundant, well-developed, and often isolated. And besides, what's wrong with a little company along the trail or under sail?

The Land

At 16,056 square miles, Kenai Peninsula is a little smaller than Vermont and New Hampshire combined. The Kenai Mountains form the Peninsula's backbone, with the massive Harding Icefield dominating the lower lumbar. The east side, facing Prince William Sound, hosts a spur of the Chugach Mountains, with the glimmering Sargent Icefields; the west side, facing Cook Inlet, is outwash plain, sparkling with low-lying swamp, lakes, and rivers. The icefields, glaciers, and plains are all a result of ice sculpting over the million-year course of the Pleistocene, with its five major glacial periods. During the last, the Wisconsin Period, Portage Glacier filled the entire Turnagain Arm, 50 miles long and a half mile high. Portage stopped just short, 10,000 years ago, of carving a fjord between Prince William Sound and Turnagain Arm; otherwise, Kenai Peninsula would've been Kenai Island. Still, this peninsula is so digitated with peninsulettes that it has over 1,000 miles of coastline. The land is almost completely controlled by the feds; Chugach National Forest, Kenai National Wildlife Refuge, and Kenai Fjords National Park account for nearly 85% of it.

History

You begin to feel strongly the Russian influence in this neck of the woods. Baranov's first shipyard was located somewhere along Resurrection Bay down from Seward. Russians built a stockade near Kasilof in 1786, and a fort at Kenai in 1791. Other than these brief incursions, the land belonged to the Kenai Indians, part of the great Athabascan tribe, till the gold rush, when color was uncovered around Hope and Sunrise on Turnagain Arm, and at Moose Creek halfway to Seward. First trails ran between the mining communities, then wagon roads, and finally the railroad pushed from Seward through Anchorage to Fairbanks by the early 1920s. The Seward and Sterling highways were completed in 1952, opening the Kenai's western frontier. When Atlantic Richfield tapped into oil (1957) and gas (1962) off the west coast the Peninsula's economic star began to twinkle. And today, the Kenai Peninsula Borough's 40,000 people are occupied with fishing, outfitting, tourism, and services.

TO HOPE

Five miles past Portage, the Seward Highway starts climbing into the Chugach Mountains. Don't despair or do anything rash if you get stuck behind a rental RV fishtailing along at 30 mph; a passing lane arrives just in time. You enter Kenai Peninsula Borough at Turnagain Pass (Mile 68.5, elev. 988 feet), where rest areas rest on both sides of the road. Stop and stretch in this pretty alpine area. In 2½ miles at Mile 65 is **Bertha Creek Camp**

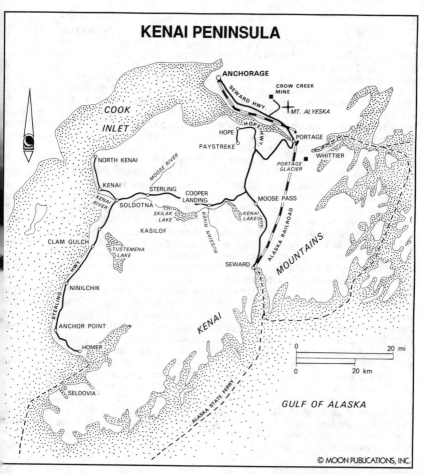

KENAI PENINSULA

round, 12 sites, $5. At Mile 64 is the north-ern trailhead to **Johnson Pass Trail,** which oes 23 miles over relatively level terrain and merges at Mile 33 of the Seward. The For-st Service facilities are very poorly marked. ou get no warning about upcoming turnoffs rom the highway to the facility, and only a mall sign indicates the junction with the ighway. (The difference between the care nd cash that the state invests in its re-ources, and the federal trickle that gets out

this far, is clear.) Forget about the irate guy in the pickup who's breathing down your neck and go slowly, being ready to pull off as soon as the small sign appears.

To Hope, bear right just beyond Mile 57 onto the Hope Highway. This road is sparsely trafficked, especially compared to the Sew-ard. It follows Sixmile Creek north back up to Turnagain Arm; pan for gold along the first five miles of the crick. The entire 16½ miles to Hope is pavement, divine pavement.

Hope

Gold was discovered on Resurrection Creek in 1888, and by 1896, 3,000 people inhabited this boom neighborhood, between Hope and Sunrise on Sixmile Creek. Many came by way of the Passage Canal where Whittier now squats, portaging their watercraft over the Chugach glacial pass to Turnagain Arm, which is how Portage Glacier got its name. Large-scale mining prospered into the '40s, but then Sunrise was abandoned and left to the ghosts, and Hope hangs on today with minor mining and logging supporting the town's 225 people. Turn right off the highway into downtown Hope. Take a quick left for old Hope to see the photogenic **Social Hall,** the original Alaska Commercial Co. store, and the tidal flats (caused by the earth sinking seven feet in the '64 quake; and dangerous—don't walk on them!). Go back and turn left for new Hope, with its post office, red schoolhouse, and beautiful new and old log cabins.

At the end of Hope Highway is **Porcupine Campground,** featuring an uncommon paved loop road, 24 sites, and red raspberry hors d'oeuvres; $5. Across the road is unique **Davidson Grocery Store,** with its all-glass front. The unmarked **Mt. Baldy Trail** is a cat track just beyond the end of the guard rail at the head of the campground. Walk along Porcupine Creek for a quarter mile, then head up to a knob that overlooks the Arm. From here you can hike forever on the ridgeline. The **Seaview** in old Hope charges $28 s, and sells firewood for $5. Fill up on breakfast and good dinner specials ($5.95) at **Discovery Café,** a little out Hope Highway.

Resurrection Creek And Trail

Head out the highway and go right on Palmer Creek Road. In three-quarters of a mile is a fork: go straight for seven long miles to **Coeur D'Alene Campground,** or go right on Resurrection Creek Road. In just under four rough miles is the trailhead, with parking, information signboard, and a fun bridge across the crick. This popular backpack trip leads 38 miles down to Cooper Landing on the Sterling Highway, or you can cut across on **Devil's Pass Trail** to Mile 39 on the Seward. Eight USFS cabins ($20 a night—just as

easy to camp) are spaced along the route, but most people divide the trip into four or five segments. You could also walk right onto Russian Lakes Trail on the other side of the Sterling at Cooper Landing, which goes 16 miles to the Resurrection River Trail, and hike another 16 miles to Exit Glacier Road outside of Seward. This 12-day hike covers the Peninsula from head to toe. Recreational miners pan for gold between the bridge at this trailhead and Paystreke, a half mile upstream.

Paystreke

In the early 1980s, Tom Williams, a congenial, handsome bear of a modern-day prospector was looking for gold around Hope, when he heard about a parcel of privately owned land on Resurrection Creek, surrounded by Forest Service wilderness. He cut a deal with the owner, who stipulated that if Williams installed a $100,000 placer operation on the creek, he'd deed over the title at the end of two years. Williams mined the parcel for two years, and lost his shirt in the process, but wound up with the land. In 1985, sitting around one night with the other miners and bemoaning the lack of any women around Paystreke, he got the idea to run an ad in an Anchorage daily for traditional mail-order brides. The ad ran for only a week, but got picked up by the wire services, and the story went out all over the world. Williams was deluged with 8,000 letters from prospective brides, from Georgia to Germany, from South Dakota to South Korea. He finally picked a 20-year-old woman from Tumwater, Washington, got married in Japan, appeared on "Donahue" in San Francisco, sold their story to Hollywood . . . then went back to Paystreke, Alaska, population 11 (all guys), in December, to live happily ever after. The happy bride lasted three months.

Stop by Paystreke to see what shenanigans might be in progress at the moment.

TO SEWARD

A wide road with passing lanes heads up to scenic **Summit Lake.** At Mile 46 is **Tenderfoot Creek Campground,** in a beautiful area on the shores of this alpine water. Next to it is the incomparable **Summit Lake Lodge,** open 7 a.m.-11 p.m. year-round. Cozy and well placed, the food here is consistently rec-

HIKING TRAILS: ANCHORAGE TO SEWARD

© MOON PUBLICATIONS, INC.

ommendable. Breakfast ($6) is served till 2 p.m., after which you have your choice of burgers, salads, entrees, or a Garbage Grinder or Miss Piggy. The original lodge was built in 1953; the big fireplace and chimney are the only part of the building that survived the '64 quake. The new building is constructed of local logs.

Just after Mile 40 and a mile before the Seward-Sterling junction is **Devil's Pass** trailhead; this trail leads nine miles to the pass, then another mile to where it joins the Resurrection Pass Trail. The Devil's Pass trailhead is very poorly marked—be prepared. The **Carter Lake Trail** leaves the highway at Mile 33, climbs 1,000 feet in just over two miles to Carter Lake, and continues another mile around Carter Lake to Crescent Lake. A half mile beyond the trailhead is the southern trailhead to **Johnson Pass Trail** (whose northern trailhead is at Mile 64). And just beyond that is **Trail Lakes Fish Hatchery,** open 8-4:30, which has a fascinating annotated color-photo display about spawning and stocking salmon. Definitely stop and see why Alaska Fish and Game estimates an output of four million kings, six million silvers, and 30 million reds by 1992.

At Mile 30 you slow down for Moose Pass, a town slightly larger than Hope, famous for Ed Estes' waterwheel, and for its wild solstice celebrations. Continue six miles to the turnoff for **Trail River Campground,** just over a mile off the highway: large, empty, $5, with some choice sites on the lakeshore loop. Next up on the left at Mile 23 is **Ptarmigan Creek Campground,** 25 sites, $5. A trail climbs three and a half miles along the creek to Ptarmigan Lake. **Kenai Lake** comes into view just south of here: huge, beautiful, blue-green, with snowcapped peaks all around. Breathe deeply. Three-mile **Victor Creek Trail** starts at Mile 20; in three miles is the turnoff to **Primrose Campground,** a mile from the Seward on Kenai Lake, 10 sites, $5. Primrose Trail climbs 1,500 feet in five miles to Lost Lake, where you can hook up to **Lost Lake Trail** and come out at Mile 5 near Seward. **Grayling Lake, Golden Fin,** and Lost Lake trails complete your journey from Portage—if you've hiked all the trails, overnighted at all the campgrounds, talked to all the townspeople, and kept Kodak and Fuji in business—to Seward, two months later.

SEWARD

Seward (pop. 2,400) is another pocket-size port town on a sparkling bay surrounded by snowcapped peaks, the only large town on the east side of the Kenai Peninsula. It's hooked up by bus, ferry, and plane, has a maritime climate, and a large seafood industry, just like a half dozen other places you've visited so far—but with a difference: Seward is right on the doorstep of Kenai Fjords National Park. This pup of a park, still in its formative years, contains some of the most inhospitable visitable country in the state. Its Harding Icefield, a prehistoric frozen giant with three dozen frigid digits, rivals Glacier Bay for scenery and wildlife, but is decidedly less expensive to visit. Combine this with Seward's convenient camping, good food, excellent access via public transportation, and more bars on Main Street than in any other town in Alaska, and you've got all the elements for a wild time in this old town.

William H. Seward

History

In 1791, Baranov, on a return voyage to Kodiak from around his Alaskan domain, waited out a storm in this bay on Sunday of Resurrection, a Russian holiday. Its sheltered waters prompted Baranov to install a shipyard, and 110 years later, surveyors for the Alaska Central Railroad laid out the townsite for their port. This private enterprise, financed by Seattle businessmen, established Seward, laid 50 miles of track, and went broke. In 1911, Alaska Northern Railroad extended the track almost to present-day Girdwood. In 1912, the U.S. government began financing the completion of this line, which reached Fairbanks 470 miles north, in 1923. From then, Seward's history parallels Valdez's as the two ice-free year-round ports with shipping access to Interior, Seward's by rail, Valdez's by road. Like Valdez, Seward was nearly completely destroyed by the Good Friday Earthquake. Today, fishing and processing (especially halibut) keep Seward in business, with help from cruise ships touching the Peninsula here, and tour boats cruising the national park.

Sights

Start out at the **Visitor Info Center** in the Seward Rail Car on 3rd St. at Jefferson, tel. 224-3094, open 9-5 daily. Pick up the "Visitors Guide," which has a walking tour and some interesting history. The rail car served Seward from 1936 to 1960, and was President Warren Gamaliel Harding's dining car on his way to Nenana in 1923—even as his wife was plotting to insure Harding's place in history by poisoning him. Next, head a few steps south to **Seward Museum**, at Jefferson and 3rd, open 11-4 daily, 50 cents. Buy statehood and Alaska Purchase stamps here, check out the office equipment from the original Brown and Hawkins store, the cross section of a 350-year-old Sitka spruce, the Seward slide show (ask the volunteer to turn it on), and more. The **library,** at 6th and Adams, open Mon.-Fri. 1-8 p.m., till 6 p.m. on Sat., shows movies every summer at different times; inquire.

Seward Marine Center operates University of Alaska's marine research facility at the

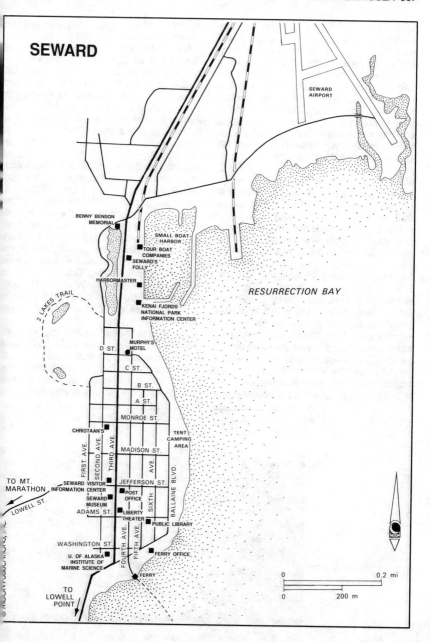

SEWARD

SEWARD AIRPORT

BENNY BENSON MEMORIAL

2 LAKES TRAIL

SMALL BOAT HARBOR

TOUR BOAT COMPANIES

SEWARD'S FOLLY

HARBORMASTER

RESURRECTION BAY

KENAI FJORDS NATIONAL PARK INFORMATION CENTER

D ST.

MURPHY'S MOTEL

C ST.

B ST.

A ST.

MONROE ST.

TENT CAMPING AREA

CHRISTAAN'S

MADISON ST.

FIRST AVE.

SECOND AVE.

THIRD AVE.

FOURTH AVE.

FIFTH AVE.

SIXTH AVE.

BALLAINE BLVD.

JEFFERSON ST.

TO MT. MARATHON

LOWELL ST.

SEWARD VISITOR INFORMATION CENTER

POST OFFICE

SEWARD MUSEUM

LIBERTY THEATER

ADAMS ST.

PUBLIC LIBRARY

WASHINGTON ST.

U. OF ALASKA INSTITUTE OF MARINE SCIENCE

FERRY OFFICE

TO LOWELL POINT

FERRY

0   0.2 mi

0   200 m

base of 3rd, open Mon.-Sat. for tours, movies, slide shows. etc. Finally, head out 4th toward the highway for the buzzing Small Boat Harbor. **Kenai Fjords Visitor Center** is next to the Harbormaster, open daily 8-7 from Memorial Day to Labor Day, 8-5 the rest of the year, tel. 224-3175, and has an excellent exhibit on the Harding Icefield and little-known sights of the Park, and sells books of local interest, including *Guide to Alaska's Kenai Fjords,* by David Miller (Wilderness Images, 1984).

Activities

For an enjoyable short walk on a winding trail through the forest, look for the **Two Lakes Trail** behind AVTEC First Lake Facility, 2nd and C. There's a picnic area at the trailhead. The high, bare slope which hangs over Seward is **Mt. Marathon.** Every 4th of July there's a foot race up and down the mountain and many do it in under an hour, but if you've come to enjoy yourself, allow four at least. Follow Jefferson St. due west up Lowell Canyon and look for the trailhead to the right just beyond a pair of large water tanks. You can run all the way back down the mountain on a steep gravel incline if your legs and nerves are good, but beware of slipping on the solid rock face near the bottom. The trail does not actually reach the summit of Mt. Marathon (4,560 feet), but rather the broad east shoulder, which offers a spectacular view of Seward and the entire surrounding area.

Alaska Treks 'n' Voyages, at the Small Boat Harbor, tel. 224-3960, is a highly recommended outfitter and guide company for all sorts of expeditions all over the place. From Seward, they lead sea kayak voyages (up to a week) and one- to three-day treks into the Park, offer instruction in sea kayaking, and rent kayaks ($45 s daily, $75 d).

Exit Glacier

Head out the Seward Highway for four miles, and take a left at the sign, then your first right (where there may or may not be a sign pointing to the glacier). Go seven miles out this rough gravel road to the trailhead of the 16-mile **Resurrection River Trail,** which completes the 70-mile, three-trail system from Kenai's top to bottom. Resurrection River Trail leads to the 16-mile Russian Lakes Trail, which hooks up near Cooper Landing to the 38-mile Resurrection Pass Trail to Hope. A Forest Service cabin is six miles from the trailhead; check with the USFS office in Seward (see below) for availability.

On the other side of the new bridge across Resurrection River is the national park. A mile beyond, past the small walk-in campground, is the end of the road, at the Ranger Station/Visitor Center. Inside, a spectacular satellite photo shows what a tiny fraction of the

all-encompassing view from the shoulder of Mt. Marathon

The Kenai Fjords cruise from Seward on Resurrection Bay is one of Alaska's best trips for seeing marine wildlife.
(DIANA LASICH-HARPER)

Harding Icefield Exit Glacier is. A dozen taped-together topo maps create a giant image of the Peninsula. A one-mile RT nature trail offers an easy, quiet, forest walk. The main trail to the glacier goes a half mile, crosses a creek, then climbs a steep quarter mile up to the 150-foot face. A third trail, 6½ miles OW, forks off just after the bridge over the creek, and climbs to 3,500 feet and the Icefield. Plan on at least four hours. Maybe carry cross-country skis and slide around on the crevasse-free Icefield.

Accommodations
The fashionable, reasonable, and venerable **Van Gilder Hotel** is a great place to stay. Take my word for it. Rates start at $50 and go up to $95. Contact Deane Nelson at Box 2, Seward, AK 99664, tel. 224-3525, for reservations and rates. At **New Seward Hotel** on 5th Ave. downtown, tel. 224-8001, you can get a "bargain basement" room for $48, or spend up to $91 for a double. Murphy's Motel, 911 4th Ave., tel. 224-8090, looks inexpensive, but charges $59 s, $70 d.

A dozen and a half B&Bs are listed on the C of C's info sheet. Rates range from $30 for a "sleeping room" at **Le Barn,** tel. 224-8706, and $25 per adult at **Mom Clock's,** tel. 224-3195, up to $95 for a king at **The Farm,** tel. 224-5691. Most hover between $50-60.

City officials have seen fit to provide a fine stretch of "campground" along the shore across from Ballaine Blvd., with outhouse, picnic shelter, beautiful view, lots of company, and $5 fee if anyone shows up to collect. You can also camp at the other city grounds at Mile 2 out the Seward—large trees, some highway noise, $4.25. Or pitch your tent in the small **national park campground** at Exit Glacier. It has only 10 sites, with a small parking lot. There's water at the entrance; otherwise, this is minimalist camping, on strange moraine terrain.

A **youth hostel** is near Mile 16 of the Seward, one mile south of Primrose Campground, convenient to hikers coming off the Lost Lake Trail. In 1986-87, the hostel was in the home of Dennis and Robin Helminski, but they've built a spanking-new hostel building next door, with 12 beds, two baths, kitchen and common room downstairs, $10 members, $13 non. Open 5 p.m.-8 a.m. Write HCR 64, Box 425, Seward, AK 99664 for reservations.

Food And Entertainment
Walk up and down 4th Ave. and read the menus. **Apollo Pizza** charges $10 for a spaghetti lunch, while **Niko's** down the block charges $6. Niko's pizza is also reasonable, though the Mexican food is high, but you

won't need to eat again for at least a couple of hours. **Christaan's Restaurant,** 3rd and Monroe, serves the cheapest burger in Alaska (97 cents) and proves the rule that you get what you pay for. But 97 cents *is* 97 cents. Order three. Very popular with the business lunch crowd, with slow service to match. **Ray's** at the Small Boat Harbor is especially convenient for grabbing a bite while you wait for your tour boat (or for a hot drink when you get back), and a great place to have dinner. **Peking,** on 4th Ave. downtown, is open till 10 p.m.; try their kung pao halibut.

Every other storefront on 4th is a bar. There's the **Yukon, Tony's, Pioneer, Showcase,** and **DJ's**—take your pick. DJ's has rock 'n' roll nightly; the Pioneer has music on weekends. **Liberty Theater** on Adams shows movies twice nightly, $5.

Services And Information
For Seward maps and brochures, go to the train car on 3rd and Jefferson; for Kenai Fjords info, go to their center at the Small Boat Harbor (see "Sights" above for both). The **Forest Service** office is on 4th near Jefferson, open 8-5, tel. 224-3374. They can tell you about all the hikes and cabins, but they can't make up your mind which of the dozen to choose. Soap and rinse your entire naked body in the large locker room-type facility at the Harbormaster, open 8 a.m.-10

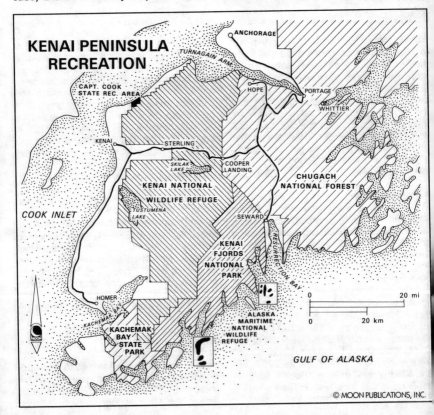

p.m., for a very reasonable 75 cents (coin-op) per five minutes.

Transportation
An Alaska Railroad train leaves Anchorage daily from May 25 through Sept. 8 at 7 a.m. and arrives Seward at 11 a.m., then returns to Anchorage at 6 p.m., $35 OW, $60 RT. Note that the train does not stop at Portage to pick up or drop off foot passengers. You have to take a bus between Portage and Anchorage and catch the Seward train in Anchorage.

Seward Bus Lines, tel. 278-0800 in Anchorage, leaves Anchorage (7th and Gambell) at 2:30 p.m., arriving at 5:30, then leaves Seward from 4th and Washington at 9 a.m., arriving Anchorage at noon, $25 OW, tel. 224-3608 in Seward. **Alaska Marine Highway's** trusty *Tustemena* calls in at its home port four times a week at all different hours of the day and night, on its way to and from Kodiak ($44), Homer ($80), and Dutch Harbor ($210).

Renting a car in Seward is no fun: from **National Car Rental** at the New Seward Hotel, you'll pay $50 daily and 30 cents a mile (first 100 miles free). Also check Avis' rates at Murphy's Motel.

A trolley runs around town frequently; 75 cents.

Tours
Trails North, tel. 224-3587, does a scheduled three-hour tour of town and Exit Glacier Fri. to Sun., $15. Call and make a deal during the week; they leave from the Small Boat Harbor. The most exciting thing to do in Seward, however, is to get on a tour boat out into Resurrection Bay or into some nearby fjords. This is *the* cruise for seeing marine wildlife. On a good day, you could see three kinds of whales, including humpbacks and orcas, plus porpoises, seals, sea otters, sea lions, hundreds of puffins, kittiwakes, auklets, and the occasional bald eagle and oystercatcher. Several tour companies offer half-day and full-day cruises. **Kenai Fjord Tours,** tel. 224-3068, is representative: $50 half day (9-1 and 1:30-5), $75 full day (8-5). **Kenai Coastal**

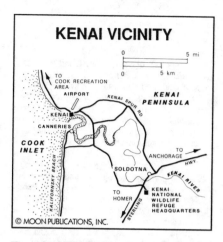

KENAI VICINITY

Tours, tel. (800) 937-9119, does a five-hour tour from 11:30 to 6:30 for $95. **Major Marine Tours,** tel. 224-8030, offers a wildlife dinner cruise with all-you-can-eat crab and shrimp. Locate all the tour boats in the Small Boat Harbor. Binoculars and telephotos are handy, seven layers of overclothes are imperative. This trip is guaranteed to be one of the highlights of your Alaskan visit.

TO SOLDOTNA/KENAI

The junction of the **Sterling Highway** is at Mile 37 of the Seward Highway; the mileposts along Sterling also start counting at 37 from this point. Between the junction and Cooper Landing (Mile 49) are three USFS campgrounds: **Tern Lake** (25 sites, water, $5), **Quartz Creek** (paved loop road, 32 sites, flush toilets, beautiful site, $6), and **Crescent Creek** (three miles down Crescent Creek Rd., nine sites, $5). A 6½-mile trail climbs 1,000 feet from the Crescent Creek parking lot to Crescent Lake.

Cooper Landing
This is the first of many service centers which sprawl along both sides of the Sterling all the way to Kenai on the west side of the Peninsula. The main attraction here is the raft trip

SALMON

Five species of salmon are found in Alaskan waters. All are anadromous, spending time in both fresh and salt water. All five species also have at least two common names, making them confusing to newcomers. Most female salmon spawn in creeks and rivers during late summer throughout Alaska, digging holes in the gravel with their tails before laying hundreds of small red eggs. The males fight for position to fertilize the eggs as soon as they're laid. Shortly after spawning the salmon die, creating a stench that permeates late summer evenings in the woods. The yearly return of salmon is a major event for all animals in Alaska. Fishermen search out the migrating schools in the ocean as they prepare to head up creeks to spawn. Bears pace the creek banks ready to pounce on salmon in the shallow water. Eagles, ravens, gulls, and other birds wait for the salmon to weaken or die before feeding on them. Crab and halibut move into the areas near creek mouths, eating salmon carcasses that wash downstream.

If you want to try your luck at fishing, purchase a 14-day nonresident fishing license for $20, or a three-day license for $10. Licenses are available in sporting goods stores throughout Alaska or by writing to the Dept. of Revenue, Fish and Game Licensing, 1111 W. 8th St., Juneau, AK 99801. Before you head out, pick up a copy of the fishing regulations. Forest Service interpreters onboard the ferries can help you find good places to fish. Many backpackers carry a small collapsible fishing pole for their trips out of town. These work well with trout and smaller salmon, but may not survive an encounter with a 10-pound coho.

TYPES OF SALMON

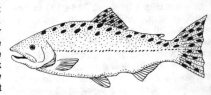

Pink (Humpback)

The smallest (3-4 pounds) and most abundant salmon in Southeast Alaska are the pinks. "Humpie" runs sometimes turn creeks into a seething mass of fish. They are considered a "trash fish" by many Alaskans, but are fine when caught in salt water. Once they reach fresh water they develop a very prominent humpback and large teeth. Pinks are the major commercial fish in Southeast and are the mainstay of many canneries.

down the Kenai River. Half a dozen raft companies offer this 14-mile ride to Jim's Landing, which includes some Class II rapids at Schooner Bend. **Osprey Outfitters,** just over the Kenai bridge on the left, tel. 595-1265, is representative: two four-hour trips leave at 11 a.m. and 4 p.m. and include a hot lunch, $40 pp. They also do an overnight 30-mile float from Kenai Lake, which passes through Class III Kenai River Canyon and ends up at Skilak Lake. **Alaska River Co.,** at Mile 50, tel. 595-1226, has similar itineraries, but also does custom wilderness trips, kayak and canoe instruction, and guided fishing expeditions.

Just beyond Cooper Landing is **Cooper Creek Campground,** with sites ($6) on both sides of the road. A mile and a half past that is the large **Russian River Campground,** one of the best places in the state to catch sockeye salmon, and one of the worst places to have a peaceful night when the reds are running (mid-June and mid-July). A ranger at the USFS entrance station at the end of the two-mile access road takes your $6 fee and assigns you a site. Park in the lot ($2) if you just want to hike on the 21-mile **Russian Lakes Trail** or take the "fisherman's path" along the river to Russian River Falls, where salmon leap. The **Resurrection Pass Trail** crosses the Sterling Highway at Mile 53.

Kenai National Wildlife Refuge

This large habitat supports so many moose, Dall sheep, bear, salmon, and other wildlife

SALMON (CONT.)

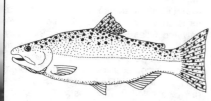

King (Chinook)
The largest of all Pacific salmon, the king commonly exceeds 30 pounds (the record is 126 pounds) and is considered by many the most highly prized and best-tasting sport fish in Alaska.

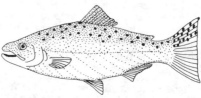

Coho (Silver)
The silvery-colored cohos generally weigh 5-15 pounds and are a beautiful fish that can be caught in both fresh and salt water.

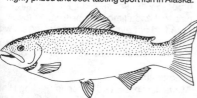

Sockeye (Red)
Much smaller (4-8 pounds) and difficult to catch, sockeyes are considered almost equal in flavor to kings. They turn bright red with an olive-green head when ready to spawn.

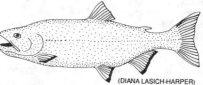

(DIANA LASICH-HARPER)

Chum (Dog)
Chum are also quite large (5-15 pounds) but are not considered as tasty as kings, sockeye, and coho. Spawning time turns them into grotesque monsters with huge dog-like teeth. The name dog salmon may also refer to their use as food for sled dog teams in central Alaska.

that it was designated a refuge by President Roosevelt in 1941. The National Interest Lands Act (1980) changed the name from Kenai National Moose Range, and expanded the refuge to its present two-million-plus acres, managed by the federal Fish and Wildlife Service. An information cabin is at Mile 58, right at the junction of the Sterling and rough and dusty 20-mile **Skilak Lake Loop Road.**

From here to Sterling (Mile 81) on both roads are so many campgrounds, trailheads, lakes, creeks, and accompanying recreational opportunities that even listing them is beyond the scope of this edition. For more information about the seven free campgrounds, more than a dozen trails, and hundreds of miles of boating and fishing lanes, inquire at the USFWS greeting cabin or the HQ in Soldotna (see below), or use the excellent *Guide to the Kenai Peninsula* booklet, and the useful book, *55 Ways to the Wilderness in Southcentral Alaska.*

By far the most popular salmon fishing along this stretch is at the **Kenai-Russian Rivers Campground,** Mile 55, where a privately operated, cable-guided, current-powered ferry shuttles anglers between the campground and the sockeye-rich opposite bank.

Sterling
You'll know you're in salmon country in Sterling (pop. 2,800), Mile 83, where the widening Kenai River merges with the Moose

River, and the fish-hook frenzy pervades all your senses (especially the olfactory). The height of the activity is on either side of the bridge, with a private fish camp on the west side, and **Izaak Walton State Recreation Site** on the east. This pretty campground has 17 sites, paved loop roads, toilets, and water, $6. Archaeological excavations conducted here suggest that Eskimos occupied this fish-rich confluence up to 2,000 years ago.

Oil was discovered in 1957 in the northern wilderness near the Swanson River; the 18-mile gravel road built to the oilfields also opened up this lake-studded lowlands. Two canoe routes, **Swanson River Route** (80 miles, 40 lakes) and **Swan Lake Route** (60 miles, 30 lakes) are accessible by Swanson River Rd., a right turn off the Sterling at Mile 84 by the old log school. Also, 13 miles in on Swanson River Rd. is **Dolly Varden Lake Campground**: free, uncrowded, nice views, right on the lake, frequent moose visits. Pick up the USFWS brochure *Canoeing in the Kenai National Wildlife Refuge* for detailed info.

From Sterling to Soldotna is a highly civilized 13-mile stretch bristling with guides and outfitters, fish camps, fish exchanges and markets, bait and tackle shops, charters, marine stores, boat rentals, boat engine sales and repairs, propellor sharpening shops, etc.—essential infrastructure in the eternal struggle between sportsmen and salmon. You'll either be in angler ecstasy or claustrophobia central.

SOLDOTNA

If Kenai is a mini-Alaska, Soldotna (pop. 3,818) is a mini-Anchorage. Just as Anchorage was established as a supply center for the railroad, Soldotna grew up in the 1940s around the junction of the Sterling Highway and Kenai Spur Road. It's still supported by the same Cook Inlet oil money that stabilized Anchorage's economic base. And the sprawling suburban burgh is the seat of the borough government, has a branch of the U. of AK, and has been mauled by malls, festooned by fast food, and fashioned by fish—it's got everything but the skyscrapers.

Sights
Kenai Peninsula Visitor Information Center is on Sterling Highway south of the river between Miles 95 and 96, open 9-5 daily. Stop by to see the great wildlife photography and the 94-pound king salmon, one of the largest salmon ever caught by a sport fisherman. For the **Wildlife Refuge Visitor Center**, take a left at Kalifornsky, then an immediate right, and go a mile up Ski Hill Rd., tel. 262-7021, open 8-4:30 Mon.-Fri., 10-6 weekends. Buy books and posters, and see their 15-minute video hourly noon-4 p.m. weekdays, or free wildlife documentaries (noon-5 weekends). Stroll the mile-long nature trail and climb the observation tower.

To find out everything that's going on with everybody who's anybody in town, read the community bulletin board at **Pay 'n' Save**.

Practicalities
All the action is found either on Sterling Highway in town or on Kalifornsky Beach Rd (named for an early settler from California) which crosses the Kenai River one more time right at its mouth just before Kenai town. **Centennial Park City Campground** charges $6 a night to camp, $2 a day to park and fish on the river; cross the bridge on the Sterling take a right at the light onto Kalifornsky, then another immediate right into the campground. Another two miles out Kalifornsky **Duck Inn,** tel. 262-5041, which has reasonable rooms, $60. The Duck also has a comfortable bar and dining room, and the **Orca** cinema is next door.

Take your pick of rapid rations in Soldotna. **Grand Burrito,** open 11 a.m.-1 p.m., will fill you up for under $4—if you can ever choose among four kinds of meat three kinds of cheese, two kinds of tortilla and your main dish. Or try the old stand-by **Sizzler,** with its good burgers and salad bar on the corner of Kalifornsky and Sterling Hwy. across from the Centennial Campground.

KENAI

he town of Kenai (pop. 6,000-plus) sits on a
luff above the mouth of the Kenai River
verlooking Cook Inlet. Across the inlet to the
outhwest rise mounts Redoubt and Iliamna,
ctive volcanos at the head of the Aleutian
Range. The Alaska Range is visible to the
orthwest. Great white beluga whales enter
he mouth of the river on the incoming tides to
ook for fish. Kenai is the second-oldest permanent settlement in Alaska, founded by Rus-
ian fur traders who built St. Nicholas Re-
oubt in 1791. The U.S. Army built their own
fort, Kenay, in 1869, two years after the Great
Land changed hands. Oil was discovered in
1957 offshore, and now Kenai is the largest
and most industrial city on the Peninsula.

Sights
All the sights of Kenai are in one small area,
which you can tour on foot in 1½ hours. Start
at the **Visitor Center,** at Main St. and Kenai
Spur Rd., tel. 283-7989, open 9-5 weekdays.
Walk down toward the bluff on Overland Ave.
to the replica of **Fort Kenay,** built in 1967 for
the Alaska Centennial. The small museum
upstairs is open 10-5, Mon. through Saturday. Next door is **Holy Assumption Rus-**

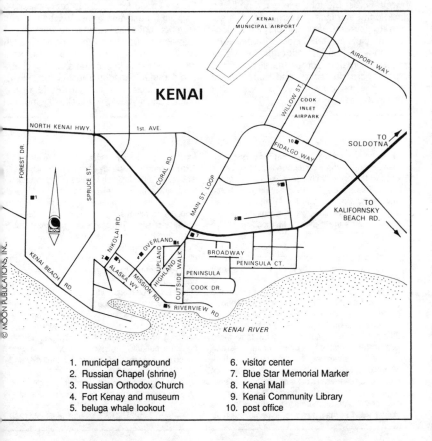

1. municipal campground
2. Russian Chapel (shrine)
3. Russian Orthodox Church
4. Fort Kenay and museum
5. beluga whale lookout
6. visitor center
7. Blue Star Memorial Marker
8. Kenai Mall
9. Kenai Community Library
10. post office

sian Orthodox Church, built in 1896. Peek through the windows at the painted altar and brass chandelier. **Saint Nicholas Memorial Chapel** (1906) nearby, built over the grave of Kenai's first priest, also reflects the traditional Russian Orthodox architectural style. Walk east on Mission Rd. for two viewpoints over the bluff; from the first, look out over the riverside canneries, with the Kenai Mountains behind and the Aleutian and Alaska ranges strung out across the Inlet. The second has an interpretive sign about beluga whales.

Practicalities

Camp at **Kenai Municipal Park**—go past town to Forest Dr., take a left, and go half a block to the entrance. It's large, comfy, free, with pit toilets and water, and only a half block from the bluff. Several places to eat, including Bookey's Burgers, surround the visitor center; the mall is across the street. Don't forget about the salad and soup bar at Carrs—just the thing when you're passing through Kenai.

TO HOMER

From Kenai, backtrack on Kalifornsky over the Kenai River, go right at the fork to the coast; this spur road joins the Sterling at Mile 109 at **Kasilof** (ka-SEE-loff), gateway to huge Tustemena Lake, whose turnoff is at Mile 110. At Mile 117 is the turnoff for **Clam Gulch State Recreation Area,** a two-mile gravel road down to the campground and clamgrounds. Make sure you have a sport fishing license ($5 for one day, $15 for 10), a shovel, bucket, and gloves before you dig in the cold sand for the sharp razor clams, 60 bag limit, best during low low tide in early summer, but possible anytime from April to September. Watch how the pros first spot the small hole in the sand, then dig a few shovelsful and reach fast for the escaping clam. If you'd rather get formal instruction, stop at **Ipswich Plaza,** Mile 118, tel. 262-5545, for a guided dig; if you don't feel like digging at all

CLAMMING

Opinions vary as to the best method to go after a clam. Some clammers say one should place his back to the ocean with his shovel in front of the clam's depression. Others maintain you should start on the side, and still others center the shovel so the first scoop lifts away the dimple. My wife Lacey prefers the "Safeway Method," and buys her clams for 98 cents a can.

The best digging is in muddy sand. Once the vibrations start from above, the razor clam takes the fast elevator down. I have my most consistent success by taking three fast scoops directly over the dimple, then throwing my shovel aside and plunging into the hole with both arms. Though some feel throwing the shovel is optional, it is not. The distance of the toss is barometer of enthusiasm and a signal to the body than more adrenaline is needed. A good shovel toss can accelerate the capture of a clam by as much as 30 seconds. Sometimes, also, if one does not maintain an awareness of his proximity to the sea, it serves as an offering to the god, Neptune.

Once the arms are buried to the elbows in a wet clam hole, the main thing to remember is you

must get as dirty as possible. This is the fun part. A razor clam is evidently awed by an individual who is not afraid to lie on his side in the sand and muck, and extend his arm past the clavicle, fingers groping for its shell. Sometimes, the mollusk will stop its own excavating just to get a good look at its gutsy pursuer. If this should occur and something hard is touched, one must refrain from prematurely making the triumphant an nouncement that "I've got one!" It may be a clam, but it may also be a rock or the distributor cap to a '49 Ford. It is unnnecessary to provide veteran diggers with the stimulus for additional mirth.

Razor clams should be cleaned as soon after the capture as possible, preferably by someone else. The process requires a surgeon's understanding of anatomy, and it often takes longer than the pursuit. The neck is tough, and best saved for chowder and erasers, but the body and "foot" are tender and delicious.

When I figure gas, towing, and dry cleaning, my razor clams cost more than 50 bucks a pound.

—Alan Liere, *ALASKA* Magazine, Sept. 1988

(GORDY OHLIGER)

eat at **Clam Shell Lodge** nearby and pay the price. Clamming is excellent from here all the way down to Anchor Point.

This next 40-mile stretch of the Sterling gives you yet another impression of Alaska's incredible diversity: except for a few back lanes in Southeast, this is the state's only extended coastal road. The view across the Cook Inlet is of the Aleutian crown, Mt. Redoubt (10,197 feet) to the north and Mt. Iliamna (10,016 feet) to the south—both within rhyming Lake Clark National Park. On a very clear day you can also see active Mt. Augustine, a solitary volcanic island with a well-defined cone at the bottom of the Inlet.

Ninilchik

This small town, located where the Ninilchik River empties into the Inlet, has a long history. Settled at the turn of the 19th century by retired Russian-America Co. workers who took Native wives, the old village is down a short side road off the Sterling. The modern town (pop. 750) is strung along the highway. Stop at the **library** (sign outside says "Tourist Information"), open 11-4 weekdays, tel. 567-3333, and pick up the excellent *Tour of Ninilchik Village*. A dozen historical buildings and signs are along the way; a short footpath leads up to the **Russian Orthodox Church,** built on an overlook in 1900. Bear left on this side road just before you cross the river for camping and the Small Boat Harbor. **Kenai State Fairgrounds** hosts a large fair on the third weekend in August. Just before town (Mile 134) is **Ninilchik State Recreation Site,** with 35 sites, water, and toilets. On a bluff a few hundred feet above the beach, this facility, like **Stariski SRS** at Mile 152 (20 sites), has one of the best views of any state campground.

HOMER

Homer has a dazzling reputation for possessing some of the finest scenery, the mildest climate, heaviest halibut, biggest bays, longest spits, coolest people, and best quality of life in the state and beyond, and in fact, it is one of Alaska's peerless dead-end towns. Homer does have an undeniably beautiful setting, with the unruly coastline, lingulate fjords, and cavalcading Kenai Mountains across magnificent Kachemak Bay. The temperatures are generally mild year-round, though winter's freezing rain tends to dampen the enthusiasm of many townspeople. The halibut often tip the scales at over 200 pounds, and for $100-plus you can try your luck with a line. And an abundance of fine artists and craftspeople call Homer home, selling their wares at small galleries full of rare and tempting stuff. But its real virtue for the traveler lies less in what's in Homer than what's nearby: most of the hiking, kayaking, photography, natural history, and artist colonies are around the bay. So if you arrive in town with realistic expectations, along with an agenda flexible enough to allow for out-of-town exploration, you're sure to come away with an approbatory, if not acclamatory, impression of Homer.

History

The Russians knew of the limitless coal in this area in the early 1800s, and Americans were mining the seams only a decade after the Alaska Purchase. The gold rush began

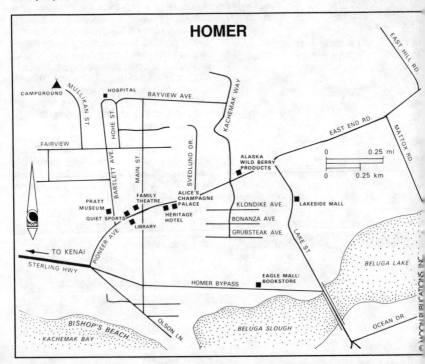

HOMER

*Homer Spit juts into
Kachemak Bay.*
(GORDY OHLIGER)

delivering men and supplies to the small port at the end of the Spit on their way to the goldfields at Hope and Sunrise up the Inlet in the mid-1890s. One of the most flamboyant prospectors to pass through, Homer Pennock, left his name on the settlement. Mining the hundreds of millions of tons of accessible bituminous fuel continued until 1907, when a combination of fire in Homer, federal policy, and falling prices burned out the market. Slowly, the inevitable fishermen and homesteaders began settling in during the 1920s, and they found a lifetime supply of home-heating fuel free for the taking right on the beach. Homer remained a small fishing and canning port till the early '50s, when the Sterling Highway finally connected the town with the rest of the continent. Since then, the population has steadily grown to just over 4,000 today, with seafood processing, shipping, and tourism supporting the economy, the Bradley Lake hydroelectric project across the bay making slow progress, and the possibility of oil drilling in the future around the lower Cook Inlet.

Around Town

Start out at the **Chamber of Commerce,** at 3776 Lake St., open business hours, tel. 235-7740. Be sure to pick up the "Walking Tour" brochure, and the *Visitors Guide,* among the 10 pounds of flyers for lodging, meals, charters, tours, etc. **Pratt Museum,** on Bartlett just up from the corner of Pioneer, tel. 235-8635, open daily 10-5, $3, was an excellent local museum until it was completely reorganized in 1989, and is now even better. The historical, lifestyle, industry, and artifact displays will engross you for hours, the Russian exhibit is fascinating, but the best is the case full of early Homer objects, with captions handwritten by the fourth-grade class of Homerite, hostess-with-the-mostest, mile-a-minute-Janet Fink. The collection of flora and fauna is one of the state's most outstanding: the beaked whale skeleton extends nearly the length of one room; follow the story of how it was shot and washed up onto a Homer beach, then was taken apart and put back together piece by piece. Some fantastic ivory model boats sport baleen sails. The rest of the fish, shellfish, otter, shorebirds, and aquarium displays fill the Marine Gallery.

The Spit

This tenuous four-mile finger of real estate jutting boldly into the bounteous and tolerant bay has seen several docks come and go, a railroad and roundhouse, shipwreck, fire, drought, and an earthquake that lowered the land six feet. Today, the Spit hosts the Small Boat Harbor, canneries, two touristy boardwalks, the renowned Salty Dawg Saloon, beautiful Land's End Hotel, public camping, and lazy beachcombing with an incomparable view. If you haven't been to town or the

Chamber of Commerce is closed, be sure to stop in at the **Info Center** here across from Thompson's Fishing Village, open daily.

For details on all the practicalities and activities, see the specific sections below.

Scenic Drives

Head back out the Sterling and take a right on West Hill Rd.; just after the pavement ends, go right at the fork (a left puts you on Diamond Ridge Rd. which drops you back down to the Sterling) onto **Skyline Drive.** You climb pretty high, among expensive homes, till you see the famous view of the Spit, bay, and march of mountains on the southern coast, all framed by fireweed. Continue on Skyline Dr. and go left on Ohlson Mtn. Rd., till it ends at Ohlson Peak (1,513 feet).

Pioneer Ave. through town turns into **East End Road,** which also has beautiful homes and great views of the Spit and bay, and it's paved for 12 miles. Out here is a suburb of Homer, with Fritz Creek General Store, the Homestead (entertainment weekends), and increasingly jaw-dropping views of the bay, glaciers, and Bradley Lake project. The road ends at the school bus turnaround, 20 miles from town. If you don't want to drive all that way, take a hard right onto Kachemak Dr. only a few miles out of town, and head back down to the Spit.

But the best views from up on the hill here are from **East Hill Rd.,** which is a left turn one mile out East End Road. The pavement ends, and then it turns into Skyline, which continues up to an unsigned intersection. Get to Ohlson Mountain by the road on the left. It's another three miles from there to the end of Skyline Drive. Unsurpassed views all the way.

Halibut Cove

Even if you only have two days in Homer, spend half of one visiting this enchanted village (pop. 50 year-round). In an unbelievably beautiful and lush setting, you can stroll the boardwalks, visit two galleries, dine on the deck of the famous **Saltry,** or hike into the surrounding jungle. The fishing-boat ferry, *Danny J,* departs from behind the Salty Dawg

at noon and 5, $40 RT. The noon trip cruises up to Gull Island bird sanctuary, which Alfred Hitchcock should've known about; wear a hat and breath through your nose. The 5 p.m. cruise is only for Cove residents, or visitors with dinner or lodging reservations. The return trips are at 4 and 9 p.m. Call 235-7847 for information and reservations.

Seldovia

Another sleepy fishing village, (pop. 560), Seldovia (from the Russian for "herring") was once the bustling metropolis that Homer is now. The road, the earthquake, and fate exchanged their roles. On the same latitude as Oslo, Norway, Seldovia was first settled by Russians in the early 1800s, and became an active fur-trading post. Through the years, Seldovia has had many ocean-oriented industries, from the short-lived herring boom to salmon, king crab, and tanner.

Catch a ride over from Homer on the state ferry once a week, or on the tour boats, and stroll along Main Street. Stop off at **Synergy Art Shop** to see the local crafts and get visitor information; make sure you grab a map of Seldovia and the Otterbahn Hiking Trail. The Russian Orthodox Church is open 1-2 p.m. Walk along the last remaining section of original boardwalk (wiped out in the earthquake) just up from the small boat harbor. Rent a bike and pedal out Seldovia St. to Outside Beach or Jakalof Bay. The **Rocky River Road Trail** at the end of Jakalof Bay Rd. is a local favorite. The well-marked **Otterbahn Trail** leads a mile and a half from the schoolgrounds, around the headland, to Outside Beach. Dan Delmissier at Quiet Sports in Homer has full details on hiking, biking, and kayaking around Seldovia.

Several hotels offer rooms starting at $65, but **Annie McKenzie's Boardwalk Hotel,** tel. 234-7816, right on the harbor is worth the extra money ($84 d). Camp for free at Outside Beach a short hike out Jakalof Bay Road; no running water.

Grab a meal at **Kachemak Kafé,** or for a treat head just under three miles up Rocky St. to the **Harmony Point Wilderness Lodge,** tel. 234-7858, which serves great seafood dinners for $20 pp. You can also buy groceries (pricey) at **Stampers Family Market.**

Dancing Eagles, tel. 234-7627, rents kayaks for $5 an hour or $20 for all day, and mountain bikes at $10 a day.

The *Tustemena* sails over on Tues. and Wed., taking 90 minutes and laying over for an hour or two, then returning to Homer, $32 RT, reservations required, tel. 235-8449. At least three companies offer natural history and sightseeing cruises across Kachemak Bay, with two-hour layovers in Seldovia. Cheapest is the *Endeavor,* which departs daily from the Spit at midday, $35 RT. Purchase tickets at the Homer Spit Campground, tel. 235-8206, by 11 a.m. **Rainbow Tours** offers the same basic cruise for a couple more bucks. Make arrangements at their office on Cannery Row on the Spit, or call 235-7272. A few local bush-plane companies also do the roundtrip. **Southcentral**

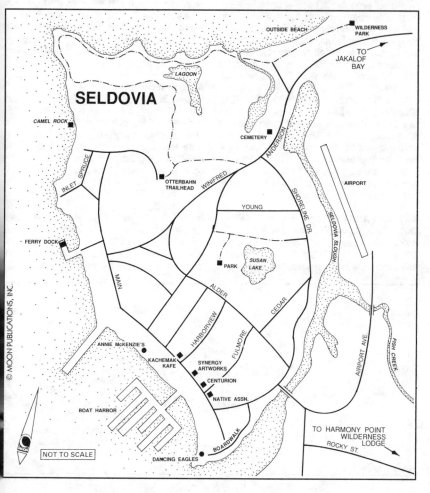

Air, tel. 235-6172, charges $46.50 RT, and **Homer Air,** tel. 235-8591, charges $47 RT.

Others Across The Bay

If you have three days in Homer, spend one of them on the Kachemak Bay **Natural History Tour,** with the Center for Alaskan Coastal Studies at China Poot Bay. Local naturalists guide you around tidepools and rainforest, and give you an appreciation for the marine world that you'll carry for life. The nine-hour experience costs a bargain-basement $35, which includes the ride across on Rainbow Tours' *Sizzler.* Bring your own lunch, raingear, rubber boots (some are available at the Center), binoculars, camera, etc. For reservations, call Rainbow Tours, 235-7272; for more info, call China Poot Bay Society, tel. 235-6667.

Saint Augustine Charters, tel. 235-7847 (Central Booking Agency), does tours of the bay on their 38-foot wooden cutter sailboat *St. Augustine's Fire.* Their day sail, 9 a.m.-4:30 p.m., costs $90 and includes lunch; a two-hour trip around Gull Island is $35; go halibut fishing, take sailing lessons, or arrange a trip over to Sadie Cove to tour Jim Landis' custom sailboat shop.

Kayaking And Fishing

Quiet Sports, 144 W. Pioneer Ave., tel. 235-8620, open 10 a.m.-5:30 p.m., rents kayaks at $60 s for two days, $85 d. It's an hour and a half across the bay—an excellent way to see all the sights if you know how to kayak. If you don't, contact **Ageya** in Anchorage, tel. 248-7140; they give kayaking courses in Kachemak Bay. Homer has at least a dozen fishing charter outfits to help you go out and bag yourself a big halibut. Easiest is to contact **Central Charter Booking Agency,** tel. 235-7847, to make your special arrangements.

But if you just want to drive into town and cast a line in the water, head out to the Spit, across from Glacier Drive-In and Kachemak Gear Shed to the "fishing hole." Fish and Game stocks this little pond with salmon, which return in such big numbers that the place is occasionally opened up to snagging. Classic roadside fishing stop for RVers, kids, lazy locals, and the like

.

Accommodations

Ocean Shores Motel, 3500 Crittendon just below Homer Junior High, tel. 235-7775, charges $45 for rooms with kitchenettes. The two next cheapest hotels in town are the **Heritage Hotel,** on Pioneer next to Alice's, tel. 235-7787, and **Driftwood Inn,** down on Bishop's Beach, tel. 235-8019. Both charge around $50 without bath, and each has its own charm. The Heritage, rooming lodgers since 1948, has cozy rooms and comfortable baths. The Driftwood is right on the water (coming into town on the Sterling, pass Pioneer Ave. on the left and take the next right onto the dirt road), and you can stuff four bodies into all their rooms for the same $45.

KACHEMAK BAY

© MOON PUBLICATIONS, INC.

Seekins Bed and Breakfast, two miles up East Hill Rd., tel. 235-8996, offers two guest cottages with gorgeous views, plus sauna, $45 s, $50 d.

Many other bed and breakfasts in town offer rooms starting at $45: try **Pioneer,** tel. 235-5670; **JP,** tel. 235-7362; and **Beach House,** tel. 235-5945. Or contact **Central Charters Booking Agency,** tel. 235-7897.

Camping on the Spit, however, is what most people do. The ocean-side beach has a 14-day limit; at other designated areas you can camp all summer with the cannery workers. Pay $5 a night to the fee collectors that circulate, or at the Harbormaster's office. Another city campground is near downtown on Mulligan; heading up from the Sterling on Pioneer, go left on Bartlett, left on Fairview, then right on Mulligan, $5.

Food

Consider breakfast at **Land's End,** the hotel at the tip of the Spit. The prices are competitive, the portions are large, the food is delicious, and the view is, well, words fail. Otherwise, get your dose of unreconstructed hippiedom at **Fresh Sourdough Express Bakery,** a little ways up Ocean Dr. from the Spit. Try their reindeer scramble for $6.25. They also serve sandwiches for lunch and full dinners. Or just stuff yourself on the coffee and baked goods.

Back on the Spit, **Addie's Big Paddies** has good prices on great burgers and is open 24 hours; the same people run the **Porpoise Room,** which spreads out an amazing seafood buffet nightly 5:30-10:30, $18.95. **Casa di Pizza** gets the raves from locals; on the boardwalk next to Central Charters, owner Barbara Ault uses recipes pioneered by her father; open 11:30 a.m.-midnight, tel. 235-6153. **Boardwalk Fish and Chips,** across from the Harbormaster and Salty Dawg, is open 11-9; their scallop basket ($7.50) and halibut fish and chips ($5.25) will have you smackin' your chops.

In town, the locals go to **Chow's** for Chinese, open 11-8:30 Mon.-Saturday. **Don Jose's** has the good Mexican food. **McDonald's** opened in 1986.

Homer Natural Foods is now called **Smoky Bay Cooperative,** at the corner of Pioneer and Bartlett across from the museum. It's open 8- 8 Mon.-Sat., 10-6 Sunday. The deli has been expanded, now serves a variety of specials and sandwiches, and is one of the main coffee centers in Homer.

Entertainment

Alice's Champagne Palace next to Heritage Hotel downtown is along the lines of the Howling Dog and Chilkoot Charlie's; this place rocks all night, even on Mondays. If you just want to drink, cross the street to **Hobo Jim's Alaska Bar.** Two miles east of town on East End Rd. is **Down East Saloon,** which also has dancing nightly. **Family Theatre,**

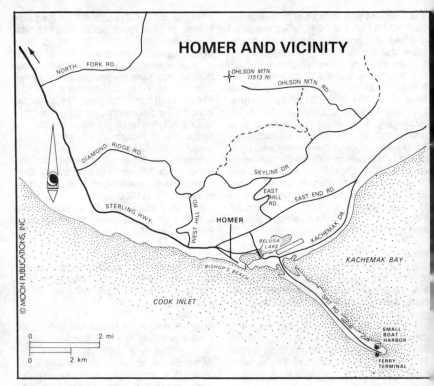

HOMER AND VICINITY

OHLSON MTN. (1513 ft)

NORTH FORK RD.

OHLSON MTN. RD.

DIAMOND RIDGE RD.

SKYLINE DR.

EAST HILL RD.

EAST END RD.

STERLING HWY.

WEST HILL RD.

KACHEMAK DR.

HOMER

BELUGA LAKE

KACHEMAK BAY

BISHOP'S BEACH

COOK INLET

SPIT RD.

SMALL BOAT HARBOR

FERRY TERMINAL

© MOON PUBLICATIONS, INC.

0   2 mi

0   2 km

Pioneer and Main, shows movies; $5, tel. 235-6728.

The **Salty Dawg Saloon** out near the end of the Spit could be Homer's most famous landmark. The original building dates from 1897, the second building from 1909, and the tower from the mid-'60s. Each building housed 12 different companies in eight different locations before settling down here on the Spit. Open from 11 a.m. till the last patron staggers out the door, have a beer for the experience.

Homer has a high proportion of talent, and some of the performers who've been shining for years in the spotlights of Christmas variety shows and springtime cabin-fever talent shows have gotten together to do **Pier One Theater,** across from Glacier Drive-In on the Spit. Whatever plays they're doing it's guaranteed to be one of the finest theater experiences in the state. Also, keep your ears open for **Fresh Produce,** a local improvisational group that performs occasionally.

Galleries And Shopping

Speaking of artists, a few local showcases are must-sees on any Homer itinerary. The most eclectic and endlessly inspiring collection is exhibited at **Ptarmigan Arts** on Pioneer across from Wild Berry Products. Here you might see anything from crystal and alabaster sculpture to shoji screens, windsock banners to wooden toys, notecards to handknit sweaters. In the back are a few artisans' workshops. Nearby is **8X10 Studio,** for berry fine art. Also check out **Homer Artists,** in the

Mariner Mini-Mall next to Alaska Wild Berry, open 10-6 Tues.-Sat., for watercolors, prints, cards, woodwork, and art supplies.

Halibut Cove Artists is on the boardwalk at Halibut Cove. Diana Tillion's octopus ink paintings are something to see. **Pratt Museum** also has rotating exhibits of local artwork.

Wild Berry Products, 523 East Pioneer Ave. (you can't miss it) is Homer's classic Alaskan tourist trap. Any trinkets you meant to buy at Woolworth's but didn't, you'll have a second shot at here. The jellies and jams do make nice gifts.

The **Eagle Mall,** on Homer Bypass heading toward the Spit, opened in April 1989. Step into the **Carr's** and it's like you never left Anchorage. **The Bookstore** has moved into the mall, open 10-7 Mon.-Sat., 12-5 Sunday. Pick up copies of local author Tom Bodett's books and read the vignettes inspired by the place you're visiting. **Homer Travel** is here too.

Stop at Lakeside Mall on Lake St. for **Bagdad Cafe,** open 10:30-5, selling used books, plus soup and sandwiches. Nice place.

Services And Information

For clean clothes and underarms, go to **Washboard Laundromat,** up from Sourdough Bakery on Ocean Drive. This sparkling facility is enormously appreciated by travelers and locals alike; $2.50 to shower in bright rooms, no time limit. For the same price you can also stand under the blessed hot water at Homer Spit Campground. For the Chamber of Commerce downtown, and their Info Center on the Spit, see "Sights" above. **Central Charter Booking Agency** can book almost anything there is to do in Homer—a good place to call first, tel. 235-7847.

The **post office** is now on Ocean Dr. at Waddell—notice the eagle done by a stained-glass class at the community college. In fact, the college, the Kachemak Bay Campus of Kenai Peninsula College of the University of Alaska, occupies the old post office building on Pioneer. It's up to 600 students these days and is growing fast.

Getting There

Alaska-Denali Transit has service between Homer and Anchorage for $39, stopping everywhere along the way; call 733-2601 (in Talkeetna).

Another way to get to Homer by surface transportation is to take the minivan or train to Seward, and connect to Homer (via Kodiak) on the trusty *Tustemena,* $94. Study the schedule very carefully; misreading it could cost you a week, maybe two. The Homer ferry dock is near the end of the Spit, which is convenient for camping.

ERA, tel. 243-3300, flies to Homer from Anchorage twice a day. The fare is not unreasonable, and you get an incredible view of the Peninsula. See if they're offering any standby deals, which usually saves you 20%. ERA hooks into Alaska Air in Anchorage. **Southcentral** is the other carrier to Homer, which hooks into Delta, tel. 235-6172. The **airport** is out E. Kachemak Rd., which forks off from the Spit road at Beluga Lake.

Getting Around

There's no local public transportation around Homer. The **Seekins,** who run a great B&B, also do tours of the area, tel. 235-8996. **Quiet Sports,** 144 W. Pioneer Ave., tel. 235-8620, open 10-5:30, rents mountain bikes for $4 hourly, $15 daily.

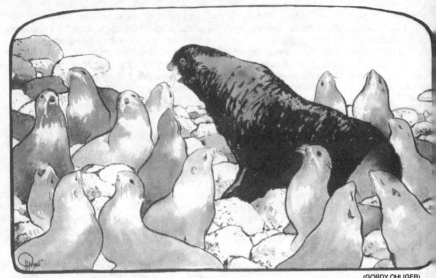

(GORDY OHLIGER)

SOUTHWEST ALASKA AND THE ARCTIC COAST

Southwest Alaska and the Arctic coast include the Kodiak Island group, the Alaska Peninsula, the barren, windswept Aleutian Islands, and the mainland's vast west and north coasts, spotted with such small far-flung settlements as Kodiak, Dutch Harbor, Dillingham, Bethel, Nome, Kotzebue, and Barrow. Kodiak is accessible and reasonable, but the other western and northern sections of the state are extremely remote, making them difficult and expensive to reach, but also exotic and fascinating to visit. Fur seals, sea otters, walrus, and other marine animals abound around the Aleutians and more northern Pribilofs; the islands are also a bird-watcher's paradise. Due to climatic conditions there are no forests west of northern Kodiak Island and the adjacent mainland; most of the Alaska Peninsula and all the Aleutians are open tundra. Several national

parks, monuments, and preserves on the Alaska Peninsula, in the Brooks Range, and around Kotzebue offer exciting possibilities for hikers and river runners in search of adventure. Any trip into these areas means passing out hundred-dollar traveler's checks like candy, but you'll be rewarded with a unique and unforgettable experience.

Southwest Alaska

From Denali National Park the Alaska Range swings southwest to become the Aleutian Range, and marches right into the North Pacific as the Alaska Peninsula and Aleutian Islands. This 1,500-mile arc from the northern end of the Alaska Peninsula to the western tip of the Aleutians is an area of extraordinary volcanic and seismic activity, accounting for an amazing 10% of the world's earthquakes. Kodiak Island sits uneasily on

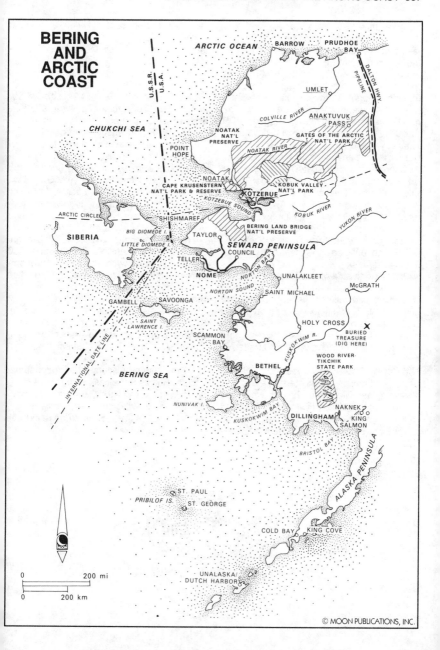

BERING
AND
ARCTIC
COAST

© MOON PUBLICATIONS, INC.

the edge of the Aleutian Trench; Kodiak is non-volcanic, yet bears the brunt of its fiery neighbors. Great collapsed craters at Katmai and Aniakchak are now administered by the National Park Service, and the 50-60 volcanos along the archipelago comprise the longest and straightest line of smoke-belchers and ash-spewers anywhere on Earth. The vegetation is a thick, luxurious shag carpet of grass and brush; you can travel for hundreds of miles here without seeing a single tree. The climate is particularly disagreeable—fog, rain, snow, wind. The trusty *Tustemena* sails out as far as Dutch Harbor once a month, but only in summer; Reeve Aleutian Airlines and Peninsula Airways connect Anchorage to many of the small towns, mostly occupied by Aleuts and Eskimos. With ferry service from Homer and Seward three times a week, Kodiak is the only easily accessible place in Southwest Alaska.

On the north side of the Alaska Peninsula is Bristol Bay, considered the world's most productive red salmon fishery. Dillingham (pop. 2,000) is home to 500 salmon fishing boats, dozens of sportfishing companies, and is the gateway to remote Wood-Tikchik State Park, at 1.4 million acres Alaska's largest.

The Bering And Arctic Coasts

Bethel and vicinity, in western Alaska, is a low-lying, lake-filled delta through which the Kuskokwim and Yukon rivers spread out and finally empty into the Bering Sea. Eskimo villages are scattered across the stark, tree-less plain. Farther north is Nome, a gold rush town where dredging continues today. Farther northward, across the rounded mountains of the Seward Peninsula, is the large Eskimo town of Kotzebue and, at the top of the continent on the Arctic Ocean, Barrow. Package tour companies have expensive day and overnight excursions to Nome and Kotzebue out of Anchorage, and to Barrow out of Fairbanks. From these Arctic coast settlements you can catch bush planes to Gates of the Arctic, Kobuk Valley, and Cape Krusenstern national parks, or Bering Land Bridge and Noatak national preserves. Gray Line and Princess Tours also offer a three-day bus-plane trip up the Dalton Highway to Prudhoe Bay/Deadhorse, which includes a hop over to Barrow, and the return to Fairbanks.

Traveling among the Eskimo, you might sense a certain tension. For the past 200 years, they have watched the marine mammals and caribou herds, once the foundation of their society, ruthlessly depleted by white men using advanced technology. Whenever a valuable resource has been discovered in their homeland—be it fur, gold, or oil—strangers have arrived to grab it for themselves. Also, the Eskimos' subsistence lifestyle has been seriously undermined by alcohol, American education, and the consumer society. But, as is the case everywhere in the world, if you travel lightly, approach the people with sensitivity, and carry yourself with dignity, you'll learn a lot about traveling, the people, and yourself.

KODIAK ISLAND

Kodiak Island is an unlikely land of superlatives. At 60 by 100 miles, it is the largest island in Alaska, and second-largest in the U.S. (after Hawaii's Big Island). Kodiak has Alaska's longest history and largest fishing fleet, plus the country's biggest brown bears and Coast Guard station, third-highest grossing port, most expensive bridge to nowhere, and weirdest golf tournament. The island is home to nearly 15,000 people, of whom 12,000 live in and around the town of Kodiak, which sits on the island's northeast side in St. Paul Harbor, protected from the wild Gulf by the photogenic wooded islands in Chiniak Bay. Kodiak town is an exciting place to visit even when it's totally fogged in and the fishing fleet is out. Even then it's clear that the honest, dangerous, and romantic lifestyle of commercial fishing in one of the world's richest and roughest fisheries is the only common denominator a community could ever need. It's also clear, even if you don't like fish, that Kodiak's livelihood is one of the most appropriate manifestations of the mystique of the Alaskan experience. Only 250 air miles (one hour, $138) from Anchorage, or 84 nautical miles (12 hours, $46) from Homer, Kodiak is a highly accessible and pleasurable place to visit.

The Land And Climate
The Kodiak Island group, an extension of the Chugach-Kenai ranges, was possibly once connected to the mainland, but is now separated by the "entrances" to Cook Inlet and Shelikof Strait. The group perches on the continental shelf, right on the edge of the Aleutian Trench. This makes it highly susceptible to the after-effects of volcanic and seismic activity, such as the ash of Novarupta and the tsunamis of the Great Earthquake. However, glaciation, not volcanism, has been the primary agent in the shaping of Kodiak's geologic features. Snow and ice almost completely covered the group during the last ice age, and the alpine is chiseled roughly—steep slopes, short fast runoff streams, rounded kettles. Kodiak's coastline, in addition, is so lingulated by long fjords that even with a maximum width of 60 miles, no point on the island is over 20 miles from tidewater. Kodiak is also the western front of the spruce forest, and you can see from the intense green of the understory why Kodiak is nicknamed "The Emerald Isle."

Expect cool, wet, and windy weather. The average temperature in Aug., the "hottest" month, is 54° F. Kodiak's record high is 86, but only half a dozen summer days even exceed 70. Kodiak receives 75 inches of rain a year, of which 12½ fall from June to September. Locals claim that some sun shines one out of every three days, and that figure averages out pretty reliably—but it can be clear or partly clear for three glorious days, then soupy for the other nine in a row! Dress warm, and if you intend to explore the back-country, bring rain gear and rubber boots.

History And Economy

Russian fur trader Glotoff "discovered" Kodiak in 1763, and told Grigori Shelikof about the abundant sea otters there. The island's second-highest peak (4,450 feet) was named for Glotoff, but Shelikof is remembered as the founder of the Russian America Company and the first European settlement in Alaska, at Three Saints Bay, Kodiak, in 1784. Alexander Baranof arrived in 1791 to manage the company and colony; he promptly relocated the whole settlement to St. Paul's Harbor (present-day Kodiak town), after a tsunami nearly wiped out the existing town. The Eskimo-related Koniag population wasn't sorry to see the Russians and their Aleut slaves move again, in 1800, to New Archangel (Sitka)—except that the sea otters in their vicinity had been almost completely eradicated and, as happened in the Queen Charlottes off the north coast of British Columbia, the 8,000 Native inhabitants were reduced by more than half in just a couple of decades due to introduced disease and conflict.

Kodiak survived the 19th century on fur, whaling, fishing, even ice-making (Russian die-hards began producing ice in the 1850s to supply California gold rush boom towns; they introduced the first horses and built the first roads in Alaska). Salmon fishing really caught on in the early 1900s, and the living was easy until the awesome explosion of Novarupta on Katmai across the strait in 1912. It showered ash down on the town, "which blanketed fields and villages, crushed roofs, and changed the green island into a gray-brown desert overnight." After 48 hours of total blackness and ash-choked gasping for air, a U.S. revenue cutter evacuated 450 residents in a daring rescue. It took over two years for life to return to normal.

Kodiak, like the rest of Alaska, was mobilized during WW II, but the fortifications here had a more urgent quality: forts, gun emplacements, submarine bases, and command centers were installed to protect the island from Japanese invasion and to manage the Aleutian campaign. Thousands of servicemen left a large economic legacy as well, but the major economic boom for the island came later, in the form of the famous Kodiak king crab, harvested by the hundreds of millions of pounds in the early '60s. Then the Good Friday Earthquake struck in 1964, quaking the earth for over five minutes, then flooding the town for the next 12 hours with several "waves," which first sucked the tidewater out, exposing the harbor bottom, then swept half the town from its moorings with swells up to 35 feet high. For a gripping description of that terrible night (and a fascinating first-hand look at the Kodiak fishing life) read *Highliners*, by William B. McKloskey.

Since then, Kodiak has rebuilt and retooled for the harvesting of salmon, halibut, shrimp, herring, and bottom fish (king crab has long been nearly fished out). The bottom-fishing industry—pollock, rock fish, cod, among others—is one of the fastest growing in Alaska; these "junk fish" are processed into surimi, imitation crab and shrimp meat that tastes like salted cardboard. Today, Kodiak has regained first place among the ranks of U.S. ports in value of fish landed.

Finally, in the summmer of '89, everything changed, when Kodiak was overrun with oil, the Exxon economy, and uncertainty about the future.

SIGHTS

Downtown

The **Visitor Information Center** shares the same building with the ferry office on Marine Way and Center St., right at the terminal, tel. 486-4070, open 8-5:30 daily. Pick up the excellent "Kodiak Island Map" and their "Visitors Guide," and recheck the ferry departure schedule while you're there. They'll also hold your backpack if you want to scout around a little. Right across the street is **Baranof Museum,** housed in the oldest Russian building in North America, built in 1793 as a storehouse for sea otter pelts. Open 10-3 weekdays, noon-4 weekends, tel. 486-5920, admission $1. Displays include Koniag, Aleut, and Russian artifacts.

Just across the green on Mission Rd. and Kashevaroff St. is **Holy Resurrection Ortho-**

dox Church, under the distinctive blue onion domes. This is the third church in which Kodiak's Orthodox faithful have worshipped since the parish was founded in 1794, and it shelters the earthly remains of St. Herman of Spruce Island, the only Russian Orthodox saint in the Western Hemisphere (canonized in 1970). The interior contains many colorful icons and religious paraphernalia, with a good view of the room from the balcony. To get inside, either put on clean clothes and attend a service (Thurs. at 7:30 p.m., Sat. at

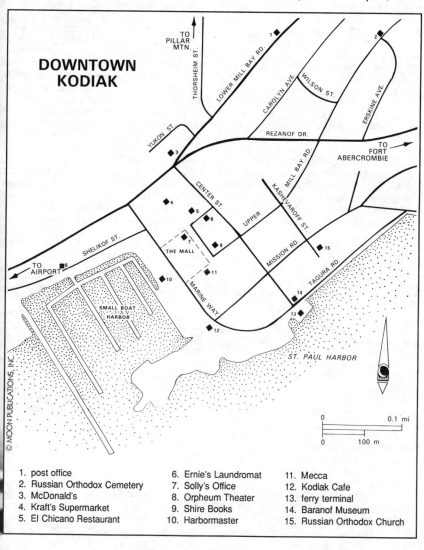

DOWNTOWN KODIAK

TO PILLAR MTN.

THORSHEIM ST.

LOWER MILL BAY RD.

CAROLYN AVE.

WILSON ST.

ERSKINE AVE.

YUKON ST.

REZANOF DR.

TO FORT ABERCROMBIE

CENTER ST.

MILL BAY RD.

KASHEVAROFF ST.

UPPER

MISSION RD.

SHELIKOF ST.

THE MALL

TO AIRPORT

MARINE WAY

TAGURA RD.

SMALL BOAT HARBOR

ST. PAUL HARBOR

MOON

0   0.1 mi

0   100 m

© MOON PUBLICATIONS, INC.

1. post office
2. Russian Orthodox Cemetery
3. McDonald's
4. Kraft's Supermarket
5. El Chicano Restaurant
6. Ernie's Laundromat
7. Solly's Office
8. Orpheum Theater
9. Shire Books
10. Harbormaster
11. Mecca
12. Kodiak Cafe
13. ferry terminal
14. Baranof Museum
15. Russian Orthodox Church

6:30 p.m., or Sun. at 9:30 a.m.), or hang around at 1 p.m. daily when the doors are unlocked for the organized tour.

To get the full history as well as the modern flavor of the Russian Orthodox religion, walk up toward the bridge overpass to the **Veniaminov Museum** at St. Herman's Theological Seminary, one of three such seminaries in the U.S. Look for Oleg, the museum curator and librarian and a teacher at the seminary, who'll show you around this fascinating room. Ask him about the eight original missionaries working around Kodiak in the late 1700s, and you'll hear how only Herman, through total faith, devotion, and holiness, managed to build up a following of thousands of Koniags and Aleuts, performing miracles and accurately prophesying along the way. Even more amazing, though, is the story of Ivan Veniaminov, physical scientist, anthropologist, ethnographer, linguist, inveterate traveler, and modern administrator, the guiding light behind the crusade in Russian America to incorporate the Native societies into Orthodoxy. Notice the antique Bibles—the right-hand pages in Russian, the left-hand pages in Aleut. Veniaminov went on to become first bishop of Alaska, then of Siberia, then one of the most important religious figures in all of Russia. Possibly the most moving image in the room is the photograph of the seminary membership—Natives, Russians, children, all dressed up in religious garb. Russian Orthodoxy is not just history, but a living, breathing, dynamic religious organization, with 85 churches and roughly 20,000 members in Alaska. Don't miss St. Herman's, open daily 1-4:30 p.m. It's a real education.

Head left out of the ferry terminal and around the corner on Marine Way to Kodiak's **Small Boat Harbor,** without a doubt the state's most crowded. When the fleet is in, all the masts, rigging, and fishing equipment make the harbor an almost impenetrable thicket. On Marine Way, stop at **National Bank of Alaska,** known as the "Crab Bank," for the display of the king crab life cycle in the outer vestibule. **First National Bank of Anchorage,** around the corner on Center St., is known as the "Bear Bank" for the huge stuffed brown bear in the lobby. Continue left down Shelikof St. to cannery row.

Toward The Airport

Heading out Rezanof Dr. West, in about a mile you pass the *Kalakala,* one of the world's first streamlined modernistic ferries, built by Boeing and used from the mid-'30s to mid-'60s, then converted into a cannery. Veteran commuters from Bremerton will grow misty-eyed here from more than the weather. Continue another three miles to the U.S. Fish and Wildlife Service **Visitor Center** and headquarters for Kodiak National Wildlife Refuge, established along with the Kenai NWR in 1941 to preserve the brown bear habitat. The refuge encompasses 1.8 million acres in the southwestern two-thirds of the island (and a small portion of Afognak Island). The Visitor Center, tel. 487-2600, open weekdays 8-4:30, weekends noon-4:30, has a beautiful annotated relief map of the island, a "please touch" exhibit of furs, and a 15-minute Time-Life video called "Kodiak Island," about bears and the incredible life cycle of salmon—stunning footage, don't miss it. Scan the list of 23 other screen presentations and take your pick. They also sell books, and have handouts on animals, birds, and cabins in the wildlife refuge. **Buskin State Recreation Site** is just down the access road on the Buskin River.

Cruise by the airport to the overlook of the **Coast Guard Station.** Largest in the U.S., this support center is home to four large cutters and almost 2,500 personnel. Main activities include patrolling the 200-mile fishing zone for illegal fishing (offenders are mostly Japanese and Russian trawlers) and illegal drug trafficking, as well as search and rescue for disabled, distressed, or disappeared local fishing boats.

Right between the Visitor Center and airport is the turnoff to beautiful **Anton Larsen Bay,** on the island's northwest tip. This 12-mile gravel road goes by a huge crab-pot storage area, overgrown WW II bunkers, communications apparatus, golf course, trailheads to pointy Pyramid Peak, and finally to the boat launching area on this scenic protected fjord. The drive is worth the time, even if it's foggy or raining, to see this part of the Emerald Isle.

Fort Abercrombie State Park

Five miles east of town out Mill Bay Rd. or Rezanof Dr. East is this state historical and recreational site. The peninsula it's set on, in Monashka Bay, supports an incredible rainforest of huge Sitka spruce, with thick chartreuse moss thriving on the volcanic ash from Novarupta, clinging to these stately trees. Check out the gun emplacements on the cliff above the bay, ancient cannons that could never have hit the broad side of any Japanese (floating) barn. From this overlook, watch for puffins, sea otters, sea lions, and cormorants. On the other side of the ranger/ visitor center is the outdoor theater where "Cry of the Wild Ram," an enactment of the tragic life of Baranof, is performed rain or shine by local people each night in early August. On a clear night, with a wooded hill for a backdrop and the bay beyond, the play takes on a dramatic value unequaled indoors. In July, catch rehearsals in the evening. This park is a beautiful, evocative place.

Pillar Mountain And Scenic Drives

A good road climbs right up to the top of Pillar Mountain, from which all the overviews of Kodiak town are photographed. Start out at Thorsheim St. and go as far as Maple, where you turn left and go up Pillar Mountain Road. The route can be confusing as it passes through a subdivision, so ask someone along the way. Or you can scramble up the front of the mountain from Rezanof Drive West of town—steep, but much faster than walking up the road. The Pillar Mountain Golf Tournament is held on the side of this mountain on the spring equinox. This deranged, one-hole, par-70 course, cleared by spotters with machetes, runs 1,400 feet to the peak, where a bucket in the snow serves as the hole, and lime jello is the green. Wild.

All told, Kodiak Island has nearly 100 miles of road (14 paved, one traffic light): up to Anton Larsen Bay (see above), around Monashka Bay from Abercrombie State Park, over to Cape Chiniak on the island's eastern tip, and all the way down to the Pasagshak Bay and State Park in the southeast. A detailed mileage guide for all the roads is found in the "Kodiak Island Visitors Guide."

Hiking

Twenty-four hikes are listed in the Visitor Association's "Kodiak Island Map," almost all of them moderate to difficult. Trailheads are so poorly marked and trails so poorly maintained that you might think Alaska Parks is worried you'll run into a bear or something. Still, a few popular trails are accessible and hikable. Pillar Mountain is described above. **Barometer Mountain Trail** is a steep five-mile hike to the 2,500-foot peak. It starts at an unmarked (but recognizable) trailhead on the first road to the right past the airport runway out Rezanof Dr. West. **Fort Abercrombie** has a network of trails around the edge of the peninsula. **Pyramid Peak** has two trailheads off Anton Larsen Bay Road. And **Termination Point Trail** begins at the end of Monashka Bay Rd., as does **Monashka Creek Trail.** Before you set out, be sure to talk over any

---

PETROGLYPHS

Petroglyphs (ancient rock carvings) are found along the coast from Kodiak to the Columbia River, although the greatest concentration is between Sitka and Puget Sound. The coastal type is very different from the petroglyphs of the interior plateau and central Oregon, but there are similarities with carvings in the Amur River region of Siberia. Although a single style can be followed down the coast, no one knows who carved the petroglyphs, when they were carved, or why. Contemporary Indians have no knowledge of them. Many, such as designs found near Wrangell, face west and were carved on rocks below the high-tide mark. Were they territorial boundary signs? Greetings to returning salmon? Sacred places? As with Stonehenge, we can only speculate. Some have supposed the petroglyphs were just the idle doodles of some ancient graffiti artist. This is unlikely not only from a cultural sense, but also due to the difficulty of pecking out a design in these hard, fine-grained rocks using only stone tools.

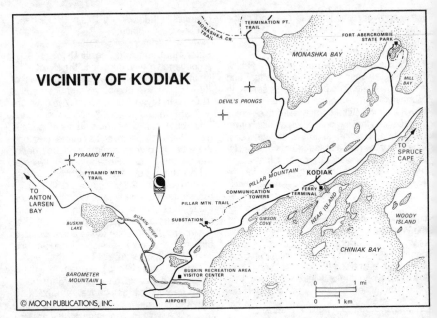

VICINITY OF KODIAK

© MOON PUBLICATIONS, INC.

of these hikes with personnel at either visitor center, or with the park rangers at Fort Abercrombie.

PRACTICALITIES

Accommodations
Hotels are expensive. **Kodiak Star Motel,** 119 Yukon St. (just before McDonald's, go left off Mill Bay), tel. 486-5657, has rooms starting at $60 d, cheapest in town. **Shelikof Lodge,** 211 Thorsheim Ave. behind McDonald's, tel. 486-4141, charges $67 s or d. The **Buskin River Inn,** tel. 487-2700, right at the airport, has rooms for $84 d. Add 10% hotel tax. Make your reservations well in advance.

Closest official campground is at **Buskin River State Recreation Site,** four miles south of town on Buskin Beach Rd. next to the airport. Hitching shouldn't be a problem, or check to see if there's any transportation these days to and from the airport. This is an okay site on the water, with shelters, pit toilets, trails, and the runways right in your ear, $6, seven-day limit. Better is to camp at **Fort Abercrombie State Park,** on the eastern tip of town, five miles away. Even if all 14 sites are occupied, you can pitch your tent somewhere close. It's worth the hitch, bike ride, or extra miles on the rental car—this is a magical place to pass your nights on Kodiak, $6.

Pasagshak River SRS, 45 miles from town at the very end of the road, also has good camping. It's illegal to camp in town, but in a pinch you could walk across "the bridge to nowhere" (completed in 1986 to the tune of $14.5 million to provide access to Near Island, to which the Small Boat Harbor is expanding) and lose yourself in the woods of this city-owned land.

Food
The place to go for breakfast or lunch is **Kodiak Cafe,** open 24 hours, right across from the public launch ramp at the Small Boat Harbor. This place hums inside just like the harbor hums outside. Breakfasts are huge, and the $5 grilled halibut (thick, juicy, one-pound slab) and fries for lunch will keep you satisfied all afternoon. **El Chicano,** on the

second floor of Center St. Plaza next to Krafts, has unexpectedly authentic Mexican food, with chiles rellenos, tasty homemade tamales, chorizo con huevos, and even a little menudo for your hangover. Good prices, too. **Solly's Office** has good lunch specials. **The Fox Inn** at Shelikof Lodge has good dinner specials. Up at the main intersection of Rezanof Dr. and Center St. are **McDonald's, Kodiak Burger, Peking Chinese,** and **Captain's Keg.**

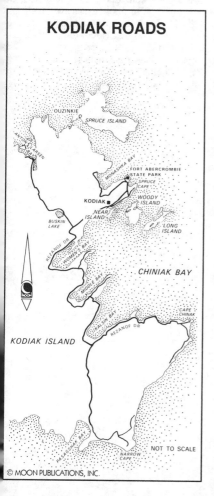

KODIAK ROADS

OUZINKIE
SPRUCE ISLAND
ANTON LARSEN
MONASHKA BAY
FORT ABERCROMBIE
STATE PARK
SPRUCE
CAPE
KODIAK
WOODY
ISLAND
NEAR
ISLAND
BUSKIN
LAKE
LONG
ISLAND
REZANOF DR.
WOMENS BAY
CHINIAK BAY
MIDDLE BAY
CAPE
CHINIAK
KALSIN BAY
REZANOF DR.
KODIAK ISLAND
NOT TO SCALE
PASAGSHAK BAY
NARROW
CAPE

© MOON PUBLICATIONS, INC.

Entertainment
You'd expect a town whose inhabitants live close to the Edge to party hearty, and Kodiak definitely won't disappoint you. You don't even have to venture any farther than the Mall downtown, whose dozen or so storefronts are *half* occupied by bars, *big* bars. The **Mecca** has what might be the largest dance floor in Alaska; this place competes with the *ocean* for rockin' and rollin'! **Solly's Office** is only slightly more sedate, with a Top 40 band and a less rowdy clientele. For hard drinking with the highliners, sit down at **Tony's** or **Ship's Tavern. Tropic Lounge** is a huge bar where some people go bowling. Otherwise, take in a flicker at **Orpheum Theater** on Center St., $3.75, or in Aug., attend the outdoor theater (see "Fort Abercrombie State Park" above).

Services And Information
For an *indoor* shower, head straight to **Ernie's Laundromat,** across the street from the main ramp down to the Small Boat Harbor on Shelikof. A $3.25 token gets you 20 minutes of blessed steaming, thundering hot water; a mere 50 cents avails you of a dry towel, open 7-10 Mon.-Sat., 8-8 Sunday. The **Visitor Information Center** (and Chamber of Commerce) is in the ferry terminal on Marine Way around the corner from the harbor, and the **Kodiak National Wildlife Refuge Visitor Center** is out by the airport (see "Sights" above for both). The **library** on Mill Bay Rd. downtown has an enormous collection of books on Alaskan history, open 10-9 weekdays, 10-5 weekends. **Shire Books** at 422 Marine Way is a good place to pick up *Highliners* and immerse yourself in local lore. Down the hall is **Local Color,** an interesting gift shop which sells gorgeous salmon leather wallets (almost affordable).

Transportation
Mark Air and ERA Aviation have a 14-day APEX fare from Anchorage for $170 RT, but you have to stay over a Sat. night. Their regular coach fare is $138 OW. ERA's 14-day APEX is $138 *roundtrip* from Homer, though you change planes in Anchorage. ERA's regular coach from Homer is $83 OW. Mark Air also has a two-day tour package, $306,

which includes a night at the Westmark Kodiak. You can also arrange to join their Marine Tour, cruising by the nearby islands. If you're a little short on time and don't want to ride the ferry, this is the way to get to and experience Kodiak.

On the way down, if you're very lucky and it's clear, sit on the right side of the plane for a view of mounts McKinley and Foraker down to mounts Spurr, Redoubt, Illiamna, and even Augustine—nearly 500 miles of spectacular peaks with just a slight twist of your head. On the way back, also sit on the right to see the vast Harding Icefield and Kenai Mountains. The airport is two miles from Kodiak town. It's walkable, or catch a cab. The Airporter wasn't running in 1991.

If you're long on time and want to save up to 75% on transportation, catch the trusty *Tustemena* in Homer at varying times depending on the week of the summer, arriving Kodiak 10 hours later, $46. Or get on at Seward, $52.

Several car rental companies have desks at the airport. Best deal is **Rent-A-Heap,** tel. 486-5200, at $25 daily plus 25 cents a mile, or $38 with unlimited mileage. **National Car Rental, Avis,** and **Budget** charge roughly $45 per day with unlimited miles. Or rent a two-wheeler from **Elkay Bicycle Shop,** at 1620 Mill Bay Rd. about a mile from town, tel. 486-4219, for $10-a-day used bikes, $15-a-day mountain bikes. Hours are noon-6, but call ahead to arrange pick-up at 8 a.m. But don't even think about getting a cab—$3 flag drop and $2.50 per mile, or a whopping $13 out to Fort Abercrombie.

ALASKA PENINSULA

Katmai

Katmai National Park occupies a large chunk of the Alaska Peninsula, over four million acres (roughly the size of Connecticut and Rhode Island), just northwest of Kodiak Island across Shelikof Strait. In June 1912, one of the great cataclysms of modern history took place here as Mt. Novarupta blew its top, violently spewing volcanic glass, ash, and sulfurous fumes for three days. One of the explosions was heard in Ketchikan, 860 miles away. The fallout choked Kodiak, whose 450 inhabitants were evacuated in a daring marine rescue. Hot ash and pumice piled up 600 feet deep over a 50-square-mile area. Massive amounts of dust cloaked the vicinity in pitch blackness for 60 hours and circulated in the upper atmosphere for two years, changing weather patterns worldwide.

Robert Griggs, a botanist sent in by the National Geographic Society, discovered in 1916 the nearby Valley of Ten Thousand Smokes, where hot gases released when the hot ash contacted buried rivers and springs, surfaced via tens of thousands of holes and cracks. Only a few fumaroles remain today. A national monument was created here in 1918; it has since been expanded five times to encompass the large brown bear habitat. In 1980, under the Alaska National Interest Lands Conservation Act, it was declared a national park.

Today, as Katmai approaches the 80th anniversary of the Noveruption, volcanologists are studying this unique phenomenon—a young, intact volcano created by a single event—to determine the hazards from such future eruptions. Novarupta, however, is only one of 15 active volcanoes monitored within Katmai National Park. The last to spew was Trident Volcano, in 1968.

If you're especially scared of bears, cross Katmai off the list. They're big, they're bad, and they're ubiquitous, thanks to the million-plus salmon that run up the Naknek River drainage system from Bristol Bay each year. Dozens of other mammal, bird, and fish species thrive in the park. Katmai experiences weather similar to the rest of the Aleutian arc—cool, wet, and wildly windy.

Katmai is extremely remote, and so expensive to reach that it should stay that way for a while. To get there, first you fly Mark Air from Anchorage to King Salmon, then you transfer to a Katmai Air Service six-seater floatplane, which puts you down at Brooks Camp, right at the Park Service Visitor Center. That's for openers. A 44-mile, eight-hour (RT) bus tour runs from the Visitor Center to a viewpoint over the Valley of Ten Thousand Smokes. And if you want to stay the night at Brooks Lodge, be prepared to shell out a couple hundred dollars nightly, plus $10 for breakfast, $12 for lunch, and $18 for dinner. The lodge sells a few groceries. Mark Air also has an overnight package, $432 for all air transportation and one night's lodging at Brooks Lodge—not a bad deal. There's a campground at Brooks Camp. For info, write Superintendent, Katmai, Box 7, King Salmon, AK 99613, tel. 246-3305.

McNeil River State Game Sanctuary

Wedged above the northeast corner of Katmai, this state sanctuary is where most of the famous photographs of brown bears, salmon, and gulls (in the same frame) are taken. In fact, during the salmon runs, more brown bears congregate here than in any other single site on Earth— recently, 130 were counted in one day. And when you place 10 or so people observing the action up close, you have an apt symbol for wild Alaska.

National Geographic photographer Cecil Rhode first published frames of McNeil River—without identifying it—in 1954, right after which the federal government closed the area to hunters. It became a state game sanctuary in 1967, and the limited permit system was installed in '73. And in 1979, the river was completely closed to sport fishing. Even with the number of visitors increasing (from 110 in 1980 to 310 in 1988), the number of bears has also grown (from 60 in 1980 to 125 in 1989), yet there have been no casualties among the people or the bears.

However, one of the state's major controversies has been brewing for several years now, over a nearly completed project to build a fish ladder at Paint River, three miles north of McNeil River outside the existing sanctuary, to allow salmon to spawn above a prohibitive 35-foot falls. Proponents argue that even more bears will arrive to take advantage of the new food source, that the sanctuary will be extended to include the Paint, and that a potentially huge new spawning ground will replenish the lower Cook Inlet's diminished supply of wild salmon. Opponents, on the other hand, hold that the fish ladder will have a seriously negative impact on the McNeil River bear habitat. Construction on the fish ladder was begun in spring 1991, but halted in late summer when the Army Corps of Engineers decided to prepare a new environmental impact statement.

In 1991, nearly 2,000 applications to visit McNeil River were received by Alaska Fish and Game; only 200 were granted. To get into the in-group of those allowed to visit, write to Alaska Fish and Game, 333 Raspberry St., Anchorage, AK 99502, by early April, requesting an application. Fill it out, enclose $5, and get it back by May 1; a lottery is held on May 15 to select the lucky 10 visitors a day who are taken up to "the falls" (prime habitat) by biologist/ranger Larry Aumiller. The best time to go for bear watching is mid-July to early Aug., but it's also the time that most people apply to visit. Second choice is as close to peak as possible on the earlier side; later the excitement tapers off. You're given four days at the Sanctuary—take them all. But even if you don't get a permit, there's a very good chance you can go standby, if you hang out long enough in Homer: waiting either for somebody not to show up, or for somebody at base camp to leave early, or for somebody not to hike the two hours up to the falls that day. **Kachemak Air Service** in Homer, tel. 235-8924, is a super-friendly mom-and-pop flying service that has been doing the trip daily across the Inlet for 20 years, like a bus. According to owner Bill de Creeft, almost everybody who wants to go over eventually does. They fly Beavers and Otters; times are determined by the morning and evening tides, $300 RT.

Beluga Lake Float Plane Service handles the stand-by passengers in conjunction with Fish and Game in Homer.

Wood-Tikchik State Park

This 1.6-million-acre state facility, largest state park in the country, is 300 miles southwest of Anchorage. The park preserves a vast system of rivers and lakes, primarily the upper Tikchik and Wood River lakes. Here is some of the finest sport fishing in the world: trophy salmon, trout, arctic char, northern pike. Dillingham, gateway to the area, is serviced by Alaska Airlines and Peninsula Air; bush planes drop you at your designated site, usually one of five fishing lodges in the park. Wood River Lodge, for example, charges $3900 pp per week. For more information write the park at Box 3022, Dillingham, AK 99576.

THE ALEUTIAN ISLANDS

From the tip of the Alaska Peninsula, an arc of 200 islands curves 1,050 miles southwest to Attu Island, separating the North Pacific Ocean from the Bering Sea. The Aleutian Islands are part of the circum-Pacific "ring of fire," one of the most geologically unsettled regions on Earth, where titanic tectonic forces clash as the Pacific plate pushes under the North American plate right at the deep Aleutian Trench, making the earth rumble, quake, and spew. The 14 large and 65 smaller islands (plus tiny islets) are all dismal, windswept outposts in the northern Pacific, where the meeting of the mild Japanese Current with the icy Bering Sea causes a climate of much fog, rain, and wind, and little sun. Compounding this is a meteorological phenomenon known as the "Aleutian low," a low-pressure atmospheric valley which funnels a number of intense storms east into North America. In short—it's not the greatest place to get a tan.

High peaks drop abruptly to the sea. There is no permafrost, but the constant strong winds inhibit tree growth; only tundra and muskeg vegetation survive. Frequent storms blow through (Unalaska experiences almost 250 rainy days a year), but due to the warm currents the sea never freezes. Given these extreme climatic cnditions, it's perhaps surprising that, prior to the arrival of the Rus-

sians, every island was inhabited by Aleut people, close relatives to the Inuit. On the other hand, it's not surprising, given the abundance of the ocean, that the Aleut were skillful hunters who lived in balance with the fish, marine mammals, and birds of their islands. The Russians enslaved and slaughtered them, and their numbers plummeted from approximately 25,000 in 1741 to perhaps 2,000 a century later. The Russians also hunted the sea otters and fur seals of the islands to near extinction, and the single-minded exploitation of the islands' resources continues even today. The U.S. Coast Guard must keep a careful watch for plunderers, as Asian and Russian fishing boats steal in to the now uninhabited islands under the most extreme weather conditions (when they know the patrol planes will be grounded), and sweep the sea clean of fish. Nothing is returned.

THE WAR IN THE ALEUTIANS

The Japanese Challenge

During the spring of 1942, Japan was sweeping triumphantly across the Pacific to the gates of Australia and Hawaii. However, the strength of the U.S. aircraft carriers, none of which had been lost at Pearl Harbor, worried Fleet Admiral Isoroku Yamamoto, comman-

A string of volcanoes from the Alaska Peninsula to the edge of the Aleutians is an active part of the Pacific "Ring of Fire."

der-in-chief of the Japanese navy. He knew that time was on the side of the United States. To win, he would have to draw the American carriers into a great naval battle where his superior forces could crush them and end the war. His target was Midway, a tiny island at the end of the Hawaiian chain, where the U.S. had recently built a base. But to first split the American forces, Yamamoto ordered a diversionary thrust at the Aleutians. In June 1942, Japanese carrier-based planes struck twice at Dutch Harbor, a large new U.S. naval base in Unalaska Bay, but inflicted only slight damage, and the base continued to function. Meanwhile, at Midway, the U.S. had broken the Japanese naval code, and Yamamoto's plans were falling apart. Their own strength divided, one Japanese carrier after another sank before American momentum. As a face-saving move, the retiring Japanese occupied undefended Attu and Kiska at the west end of the Aleutians in the hope that bases on these islands would shield northern Japan and drive a wedge between the U.S. and Russia.

The Struggle For The Islands

In Aug. 1942, the U.S. Navy occupied Adak Island and built an airfield from which to attack nearby Attu and Kiska. In Jan. 1943, the Navy leapfrogged to Amchitka Island, right next door to Kiska, to provide an advance base. Continuous bombing and a naval blockade weakened Japanese resistance and, on May 11, 1943, 16,000 U.S. troops landed on Attu. Of these, 549 Americans were killed before the 2,650 Japanese troops entrenched in the mountains were overcome. On May 29 about 800 remaining Japanese staged a *banzai* charge. At first they overran the American lines but their thrust was finally quelled by reserve forces. Only 28 Japanese prisoners were taken, and the 6,000 Japanese on Kiska seemed about to face a similar fate.

Late in July, however, Japanese destroyers slipped through the U.S. blockade in dense fog and evacuated their soldiers. On Aug. 15 some 34,000 U.S. and Canadian troops landed, unopposed, on Kiska. Though there was no one to attack and rout, incredibly, they suffered a shocking 99 dead and 74 wounded through landing mishaps and other

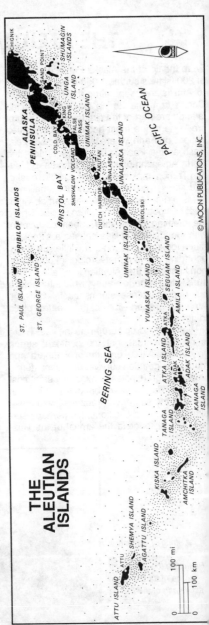

THE ALEUTIAN ISLANDS

© MOON PUBLICATIONS, INC.

accidents. Writing in the Jan. 1988 issue of *ALASKA* Magazine, Irving Payne described the scene: "The American and Canadian troops [coming in from 2 directions] mistook each other for the enemy and opened fire. Everything left by the Japanese was booby-trapped." With their masterful evacuation, the Japanese had ended the Aleutian campaign.

THE ISLANDS TODAY

Of the 80 named Aleutian Islands, only eight are occupied by humans. Sea otters are making a strong comeback from the edge of extinction, and the rich variety of other marine mammals and seabirds is protected within the Aleutian Islands National Wildlife Refuge, particularly the black brant in Izembek Refuge near Cold Bay at the tip of the Alaska Peninsula.

Unalaska/Dutch Harbor

Unalaska Bay cuts into the north side of mountainous Unalaska Island, creating a great sheltered harbor. Dutch Harbor is on Amaknak, a small island in the bay opposite the village of Unalaska (combined population 2,000). The two towns are linked by a 500-foot bridge. During Russian times, Unalaska was the main trading center in the Aleutians and a Russian Orthodox church remains. Captain Cook spent three weeks at Unalaska in 1778, sharing experiences with Russian explorers. Today the many canneries at Dutch Harbor service the rich fisheries of nearby Bristol Bay. Crab canning is a specialty. Akutan (pop. 189), on a small island just northeast of Dutch Harbor, is also an important fishing center.

Others

The Air Force maintains a low-level radar base on **Shemya** and the Navy has an anti-submarine warfare base on **Adak,** but security clearance is required to visit either. The town of Adak is a modern settlement with some 2,000 residents, and everything from bowling alleys to gymnasiums, an indoor swimming pool, theater, library, bank, stores, and a television station.

UNALASKA

© MOON PUBLICATIONS, INC.

The Aleut villagers of **Attu** were deported to Japan in 1942 by the Japanese. On their return to Alaska after the war, the U.S. government refused to allow them to resettle on their island. Today the only inhabitants of Attu are the staff of the Coast Guard Loran station. Tiny Aleut villages exist at Atka and Nikolski. Despite its fragile geological situation, the U.S. used this remote volcanic island for underground nuclear testing until as late as 1971. In its first public action, the Vancouver-based environmental organization, Greenpeace, sent a protest vessel into the area and the resulting controversy led to the cancellation of the tests.

Getting There

One of Alaska's affordable adventures to the remote bush is on the state ferry *Tustemena,* which departs Homer once a month from May through Sept. for a one-week RT cruise out to Dutch Harbor, by way of Kodiak, Chignik, Sand Point, King Cove, and Cold Bay. The trip takes three and a half days OW, and can be somewhat rough, especially in Sept., $245 OW. The *Tustemena* has showers, cafeteria, bar, and gift shop. It's advisable to bring some food and drink, plus plenty of books, tapes, and other recreational items. Sleep in the solarium with the Therma-Rest and Fiberfill crowd. If, for some reason, you want to stick around one of the villages, or you don't want to take the ferry back the way you came, you can catch a **Reeve Aleutian** plane, tel. 243-4700 in Anchorage, back from Cold Bay or from King Cove. **Peninsula Airways,** tel. 243-2485 in Anchorage, flies back from Dutch Harbor twice a day, as does Mark Air, though the weather stops Mark Air's jets more frequently, while Pen Air's smaller planes rarely cancel.

PRIBILOF ISLANDS

The remote, teeming Pribilofs "sit like matzo balls amid the richest plankton soup north of the Galapagos." Lying in the middle of the Bering Sea 250 miles north of the Aleutians, 300 miles west of the mainland, and 1,000 miles from Anchorage, the two main islands—St. Paul (pop. 592—world's largest Aleut community) and St. George (pop. 176)—and two minor ones host the largest concentration of mammals and seabirds anywhere on Earth. Each summer over one and a half million northern fur seals, 75% of the world's population, return to the Pribilofs (1.3 million to St. Paul, 250,000 to St. George) to breed and give birth. In addition, over 190 species of birds have been identified, including millions of murres, and thousands of puffins, cormorants, kittiwakes, and fulmars. Harbor seals, sea otters, Steller's sea lions, and long-tusked walruses round out this brawling, bawling, and caterwauling marine mammalian gumbo. Nowhere else in North America, and arguably the world, is wildlife so easily seen in such numbers. If you're set on doing something really wild during your trip north (west), this would be it.

Volcanic in origin, two of the four islands in the group are now inhabited. Tiny Walrus and Otter islands also support thousands of seals and birds. Saint Paul's highest elevation is 500 feet; St. George has a sheer wall rising from the sea to almost 1,000 feet, with millions of waterfowl breeding in its nooks and crannies. The weather is similar to the Aleutians—cool, damp, foggy, and windy; summer temperatures average 50° F, with an occasional 60° day in July.

Soon after Russian fur finder Gerassim Pribilof discovered the uninhabited islands in June 1786, his fur company brought Aleut slaves to harvest the seals. Accounts vary, one claiming that the Russians slaughtered the seals here nearly to extinction, the other that in 1867 the population had regenerated to record numbers and it was the Americans who trimmed their skins by the millions. In either case, by 1911 the seal population had dwindled to under 150,000 animals, less than 10% of what it had been. That same year, the U.S., Russia, England, and Japan signed a treaty banning ocean hunting and limiting the number allowed to be taken on land. Today, a U.S. government-sponsored "harvest" takes up to 30,000 three- to four-year-old bachelors, which fortuitously also have the most marketable fur. The Aleut hunters have been perfecting their technique for nearly 200 years, and can stun (with a blow to the head), kill (with a knife to the heart), and skin a fur seal in less than 90 seconds. The carcasses are processed into "sealburger" and oil.

For years, Greenpeace has interfered with the carnage. They claim that the seal population is declining at a rate of five percent a year, that the market for this kind of fur is super-saturated, and that worldwide patience for the hunt has run out. In addition, the U.S. subsidy for the the hunt amounts to $5 million for every $1 million earned. Fortunately, with new harbors built on the islands, conversion to a fishing economy offers an attractive alternative. Let's hope that the Aleut, Greenpeace, and the fur seals can work out a compromise that balances tradition, progress, and survival.

Seeing It All

Two tour companies offer package trips to the Pribilofs, one company for each island. **Marktours,** tel. (800) 426-6784 (in Anchorage tel. 243-6285), takes large groups to St

(LOUISE FOOTE)   *puffin*

photo opportunities right from the village; this tour is also more personalized, and the smaller groups allow participants more direct input. It's also a bit more expensive, but meals are included, which comes close to making up the difference.

It's possible to save a fair amount of money and have a more complete experience of the Pribilofs if you take the independent route. **Reeve Aleutian Airways,** tel. 243-4700, has a seven-day APEX fare from Anchorage; **Peninsula Airways,** tel. 243-2485, also flies to St. George. They also have a scheduled flight between the islands one day a week, depending on Reeve's schedule, but often fly between the two when they're out there. There's no camping on either island; you must stay in the one hotel on each. Saint George Hotel charges $80 pp, and officially you can't get in on the tour package meals, but you can cook in the kitchen. King Eider Hotel on St. Paul charges $56 pp, $30 pp for the meal plan, and $25 for the tour. If Tanaq's 18-passenger van on St. George isn't maxed out, you can get on it; there's almost always room for another paying body on the Marktour of St. Paul. In sum, for a little over $1100, you can fly roundtrip Anchorage to St. Paul, stay two nights at the King Eider, take the tour and get the meal plan, fly roundtrip St. Paul to St. George, stay two nights at the hotel and take the tour. Also, you can get off at Cold Bay on the way back and lay over for 24 hours at no extra charge. If you want to combine the package with your own arrangements, go for Marktour's two-night deal, then extend your return reservations. When you're arranging all this, make sure there's room at both hotels, that Pen Air is flying back and forth, and that the tour numbers are small enough for you to insinuate yourself onto them. Good luck!

Paul; they charge $736 for two nights. The price includes accommodation at King Eider Hotel (bath down the hall), sightseeing, and local transportation, but meals are extra and there's no children's discount.

St. George Tanaq Tours, tel. 562-3100 in Anchorage, is the locally owned company with tours to St. George (more birds, fewer seals). When you call their number in Anchorage, you talk to either residents of the islands or highly knowledgeable staff. Tanaq Tours uses Peninsula Airways' Conquest nine-passenger prop-jets and flies direct to St. George. This is the more scenic island, with

THE ARCTIC COAST

NOME

The town of Nome (pop. 4,500, of whom nearly 2,500 are Native) sits on the south side of the Seward Peninsula on the edge of Norton Sound facing the Bering Sea, only 190 miles east of Siberia, and 2,300 nautical miles north of Seattle. (Flying time is 80 minutes from Anchorage.) Nome was named when a cartographer marked its unnamed location on a map as "? Name," and a second mapmaker misread it as "C. [for Cape] Nome." One hundred fifty miles south of the Arctic Circle, Nome is on roughly the same latitude as Fairbanks, and shares similar hours of daylight, as well as warmer temperatures than its Arctic coast cousins, Kotzebue and Barrow—though the mercury rests around zero F in January, and soars to a sizzling 50° in July!

History
Word reached Dawson in late spring 1899 of fabulous deposits of gold at Anvil Creek near Nome. By fall, 10,000 stampeders had arrived, and set up tents on the beach, only to have them blown away by a fierce September storm which prompted a migration inland. There, more gold was found; in fact, placer deposits were carried by most streams which emptied into the Bering Sea. By 1900, 20,000 prospectors crowded the coast, a full third of the white population of Alaska at the time. A railroad had been built to Anvil Creek, which produced several dozen million-dollar claims. Judge James Wickersham brought law and order to Nome in 1902, after the first judge was convicted of corruption. In 1925, a diphtheria epidemic required emergency delivery of serum from Nenana 650 miles overland by dogsled, the forerunner of today's famous Iditarod Sled Dog Race from Anchorage to Nome, which takes place every March, and turns Nome into a late winter carnival. During WW II Nome was a major transfer point for lend-lease aircraft being sent to Russia. Almost 8,000 planes were turned over to Soviet airmen at Nome airfield. Nome is still gold-dredge central—with over two dozen of the mechanical monsters nearby. Some have been reactivated as rising gold prices have sparked a resurgence of activity.

Nome Today
Oil and gas leases to Norton Sound (Nome is on the edge of the sound along the Bering Sea) were sold in 1983. Reindeer herding occupies a significant portion of the Nome economy, as does ivory carving, and the arrival of 12,000 tourists every season. Of course, the Iditarod Race focuses international attention on Nome every March. But the big Nome news these days is the Russian connection. Bering Air has been flying between Nome and Providenya in Siberia since July 1989, thus far transporting over 3,000 Natives, tourists, schoolchildren, researchers, and officials between the "divided twins." In fact, so many Soviets are seen in Nome that the Chamber of Commerce has launched a unique campaign to get local merchants to accept rubles for payment—even though doing so might land the Russian citizens in jail for exporting rubles, and the Alaska merchants could not reconvert rubles into dollars.

Sights
Start out at the **Visitor Center** on Front St. across from City Hall. Pick up the walking tour brochure of Nome, mostly focusing on historical attractions, such as the nearby dredges. The center also dispenses several dozen interesting, well-organized, and highly informative local brochures and booklets. Spend some time with the scrapbooks and photo albums. Open business hours Mon.-Saturday. The **Carrie McLean Museum** is in the basement of the library a few doors east on Front St., tel. 443-2566. They have a fascinating Soviet exhibit. Over 200 miles of roads fan out from Nome, allowing you to explore the Arctic countryside around Seward Peninsula (see below for rental car information).

Practicalities

Cheapest accommodation is at the **Polaris Hotel** downtown, tel. 443-2000, $40 pp in the old section, shared bath. It's $80 d with private bath. **Oceanview Manor,** tel. 443-2133, is a B&B with singles for $45, doubles for $50. **Betty's Igloo,** tel. 443-2419, rents rooms for $50 s, $60 d. Also try **Ponderosa,** tel. 443-5737, $65-85, and **Nugget Inn,** tel. 443-2323, $85-95. You might be able to camp on the beach.

Eat at the popular **Polar Cub Cafe.** Nome also has a couple of pizzerias, a Chinese restaurant, and a handful of diners.

Alaska Airlines flies into Nome Airport, a mile west of town. Cheapest by far is to book the two-day Nome-Kotzebue package tour through Gray Line (see below).

Rent 2WD pickups from **Alaska Cab Garage,** tel. 443-2939, $75 daily with unlimited mileage; 4WDs go for $85. **Bonanza,** tel. 443-2221, also rents 2WDs for $65, 4WDs and sports utilities for $80. **Stampede Rent-a-Car,** tel. 443-5252, has similar prices, and rents vehicles by the hour.

KOTZEBUE

Kotzebue (pop. 3,594), on Kotzebue Sound near the mouths of the Noatak, Kobuk, and Selawik rivers, is 26 miles north of the Arctic Circle. The sun rises on June 3 and doesn't set for 36 days. Otto von Kotzebue, a Russian sailor, happened upon this Inupiat village in 1816, then called Kikiktagruk ("Almost An Island") at the edge of Baldwin Peninsula. The Natives today lead a traditional lifestyle (with snowmobiles and VCRs thrown in), which includes herding reindeer. They make use of the entire animal: for meat; mukluks, parkas, mittens, and socks from the hide; and aphrodisiac powders from the ground-up antlers sold to Asians.

The big news around Kotzebue these days, though, is the Red Dog Mine, largest zinc mine in the world, 100 miles north of town. Half a billion dollars have been invested in the giant operation, $175 million by the state, the rest by a consortium of international bankers. Red Dog is jointly owned by Cominco Canada and Northwest Alaska Native Association (NANA), which owns the land near the Noatak Preserve. The storage warehouse that will hold an estimated eight million tons ($5 billion worth) of lead and zinc is the largest building north of the Arctic Circle. A new borough was created to oversee and profit from this massive project.

Kotzebue boasts two museums. **NANA Museum of the Arctic,** on Second Ave., has a multimedia show, crafts demonstrations,

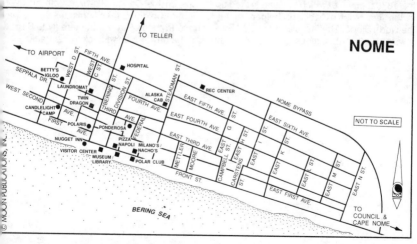

and the famous blanket toss. **Ootukahkuk-tuvik,** which means "museum" in Inupiat, is on First Ave., and you have to be able to pronounce the name to get in. Stroll around town to absorb the Native flavor. The only hotel is the **Nul-luk-vik,** tel. 442-3331; rooms start at $100. If those prices don't agree with you, you can pitch your tent out past the airport on the beach. Eat at the **Dairy Queen, Hamburger Hut, Pizza House,** or **Arctic Dragon.** Drink and dance at the **Ponderosa.** The **Gray Line** tour flies Anchorage-Kotzebue, where you overnight, then goes on to Nome and back to Anchorage the next day.

BARROW

Barrow (pop. 3,185) is 350 miles north of the Arctic Circle, at 71° latitude, 800 miles northeast of Nome. It receives over 80 days of uninterrupted sunlight in summer, almost 70 days of darkness in winter. It sits on the edge of the Arctic Ocean, which remains virtually frozen 10 months of the year—an amazing sight in itself. This stretch of coast was first mapped in 1826 by Capt. Beech of the British navy, who named it after Sir John Barrow, an English nobleman who encouraged and outfitted numerous Northwest Passage and polar expeditions. Whalers began arriving in the 1870s, many of which became locked up in the ice; relief expeditions helped survey the North Slope. The first plane reached Barrow in 1926, and famous bush pilot Wiley Post and humorist Will Rogers crashed and died there in 1935. Today, Barrow is the seat of the vast 88,000-square-mile North Slope Borough, and has profited greatly (a $100 million annual budget) from the oil pipeline—as can be seen in the modern buildings and services.

The thing to do in Barrow is just look around—at the people, the prices, the icepack, the pallor, the paradoxes. Visitor information is available at the Chamber of Commerce across from the Mark Air terminal. The cheapest hotel room is in the **Arctic Hotel,** $90 s. For the most expensive Mexican food you could ever imagine, eat at **Pepe's North of the Border**—a taco-enchilada combination plate is $14, and worth it! The owner, Fran Tate, is a sort of one-woman Barrow publicity machine, having appeared on "The Tonight Show" and been written up in *Time.* Also try **Mattie's Eskimo Cafe** for the burgers and whaling artifacts, **Arctic Pizza** (small cheese $13), and **Burger Barn** to hang out with the teen scene. **Mark Air** has the monopoly on flights to Barrow. A one-day Mark tour from Fairbanks costs $344 RT; the overnighter (with a stay at Top of the World Hotel) from Fairbanks is $388. You can also hop over to Prudhoe Bay on the overnighter for another $100. **Gray Line** and **Princess Tours** offer a three-day tour overland which runs up the Dalton Highway, with an overnight at Coldfoot, then continues all the way up to Prudhoe Bay. From there fly to Barrow for the day tour, then back to Fairbanks.

BOOKLIST

DESCRIPTION AND TRAVEL

Alaska Geographic. Alaska Geographic Society, Box 4-EEE, Anchorage, AK 99509, USA. A quarterly magazine with the emphasis on color photography.

A Moneywise Guide to North America. Presidio Press, 31 Pamaron Way, Novato, CA 94947, USA. Although short on maps and necessarily selective in what it covers, this book is an indispensible companion on any trip across or around the United States or Canada. It contains a wealth of the most interesting and unusual information, as well as specific instructions on how to survive on a tight budget. Concise and delightful.

Buryn, Ed. *Vagabonding in the U.S.A.* A cornucopia of bizarre travel ideas, guaranteed to turn your wanderlust into a lifelong trip; a kaleidoscope of Americana.

Colby, Merle. *A Guide to Alaska.* New York, MacMillan, 1939. This Federal Writers' Project guide to Alaska half a century ago has never been surpassed. Look for it in a good library.

Exploring Alaska's Mount McKinley National Park. Anchorage, Alaska Travel Publications, 1976. This outstanding guidebook makes up for the lack of trails in the park by mapping and describing 25 recommended hikes off the road. Unfortunately, it is presently out of print.

Heller, Herbert L. *Sourdough Sagas.* Cleveland, World Publishing Co., 1967. Colorful tales of mishap and adventure about Alaska's prospecting pioneers.

Higgins, John. *The North Pacific Deckhand's and Alaska Cannery Worker's Handbook.* Albacore Press, Box 355, Eastsound WA 98245 USA. Get this book for the evocative photographs, description of the fishing industry, and practical instructions on how to become part of it all.

Marshall, Robert. *Alaska Wilderness.* Berkeley, University of California Press, 1970. A thrilling account of the author's exploration of the Central Brooks Range.

McGinniss, Joe. *Going to Extremes.* New York, New American Library, 1980. One man's journey to Alaska leads him to a series of characters as diverse as the state itself.

McPhee, John. *Coming into the Country.* New York, Bantam Books, 1979. Perhaps the best portrayal of Alaskan lifestyles ever written. Read it before your trip.

Moore, Terris. *Mt. McKinley, The Pioneer Climbs.* Seattle, The Mountaineers, 1981. An exciting history of man's challenge to North America's highest mountain.

Muir, John. *Travels in Alaska.* New York, Houghton Mifflin Co., 1915. Muir's classic narration of his experiences on the Stikine River and at Glacier Bay during 1879, 1880, and 1890.

Murie, Adolph. *A Naturalist in Alaska.* New York, Devin-Adair, 1961. Excellent insight into the fauna of Alaska.

Nienhueser, Helen, and Nancy Simmerman. *55 Ways to the Wilderness in Southcentral Alaska.* The Mountaineers, 300 Third Ave. W, Seattle, WA 98119, USA. A compact trail guide, complete with maps, photos, and descriptions of the best the region has to offer.

Piggot, Margaret. *Discover Southeast Alaska with Pack and Paddle.* The Mountaineers, 300 Third Ave. W, Seattle, WA 98119, USA. A superb guide to the trails and canoe routes of Southeast—full of photos, hiking maps, and useful tips. Highly recommended.

The Milepost. Alaska Northwest Publishing Co., Box 4-EEE, Anchorage, AK 99509, USA. For motorists, the best guidebook to Alaska and Western Canada. The highway maps and description make *The Milepost* a must if your're driving north. Although the information is accurate and comprehensive, specific listings of hotels, bars, and restaurants are limited to advertisers.

Wayburn, Peggy. *Adventuring in Alaska.* Sierra Club Books, 530 Bush St., San Francisco, CA 94108, USA. A guide to the remote wilderness regions of Alaska and how to get there. This book is recommended for anyone planning a major canoe, kayak, or rubber raft expedition of the state.

Williams, Howel, ed. *Landscapes of Alaska.* Berkeley, University of California Press, 1958. A superb geography text.

HISTORY

Burton, Pierre. *Klondike.* Toronto, McClelland and Stewart, 1972. Brings alive the unforgettable characters who came out of the last great gold rush.

Chevigny, Hector. *Lord of Alaska.* Portland, Binfords & Mort, 1971. The biography of Alexander Baranof, manager of the Russian-American Company from 1791 to 1817.

Cohen, Stan. *The Forgotten War.* Pictorial Histories Publishing Co., 713 South 3rd W, Missoula, Montana 59801, USA. A pictorial history of WW II in Alaska and northwestern Canada.

Morgan, Murray. *One Man's Gold Rush, A Klondike Album.* Seattle, University of Washington Press, 1967. A feast of gold rush photography.

Okun, S.B. *The Russian-American Company.* Cambridge, Harvard University Press, 1951. This translation from the Russian gives a different view of the period up to 1867.

Sherwood, Morgan B. *Exploration of Alaska, 1865-1900.* New Haven, Yale University Press, 1965. The story of the opening of the interior.

Speck, Gordon. *Northwest Explorations.* Portland, Binford & Mort, 1954. Fascinating tales of the early explorers.

POLITICS AND GOVERNMENT

Alaska magazine. Alaska Northwest Publishing Co., Box 4-EEE, Anchorage, AK 99509 USA. A monthly magazine of life in the las frontier.

Mixon, Mim. *What Happened to Fairbanks?* Boulder, Colorado, Westview Press, 1978 The social impact of the Trans-Alaska Oi Pipeline on Fairbanks, Alaska.

Hanrahan, John, and Peter Gruenstein. *Los Frontier, The Marketing of Alaska.* New York Norton & Co., 1977. A piercing analysis o what the transnationals have in store fo Alaska.

Kresge, David T. *Issues in Alaska Develop ment.* Seattle, University of Washingto Press, 1977. A scholarly examination of th issues facing the state today.

Watkins, Mel, ed. *Dene Nation, The Colon Within.* Toronto, University of Toronto Press 1977. The struggle of the Athapaskan Indi ans of Canada for a settlement similar to th one granted their brothers in Alaska.

ANTHROPOLOGY

Boas, Franz. *Race, Language, and Culture* New York, MacMillan, 1940. Boas' anthro lopological work on the Northwest Coast In dians was definitive.

Bruemmer, Fred. *Seasons of the Eskimo, Vanishing Way of Life.* Greenwich, New Yor Geographic Society, 1971. A photo essay o the Eskimos of Canada today.

Dekin, Jr., Albert A. *Arctic Archeology, A Bibliography and History.* New York, Garland Publishing, 1978.

Fejes, Claire. *Villagers.* New York, Random House, 1981. An account of contemporary Athapaskan Indian life along the Yukon River.

Swanton, John R. *The Indian Tribes of North America.* Washington, Smithsonian Institution, 1952. Specifically identifies all native groups.

ART AND LITERATURE

Bancroft-Hunt, Norman. *People of the Totem, The Indians of the Pacific Northwest.* New York, Putnam's Sons, 1979. A beautifully illustrated history of the art of these people.

London, Jack. *The Call of the Wild.* This gripping tale of a sled-dog's experience along the gold rush trail was Jack London's most successful rendering of the spirit of the North. *Masterpieces of Indian and Eskimo Art from Canada.* Paris, Musee de l'Homme, 1969.

Service, Robert. *Collected Poems.* New York, Dodd, Mead & Co., 1959. No one has ever better captured the flavor of northern life than the poet, Robert Service.

Stewart, Hilary. *Looking at Indian Art of the Northwest Coast.* Vancouver, Douglas & McIntyre, 1979. A concise analysis of the art forms of this powerful culture.

The Far North, 2000 Years of American Eskimo and Indian Art. Washington, National Gallery of Art, 1977. A catalog of an exhibition of native art.

REFERENCE

Hulten, Eric. *Flora of Alaska and Neighboring Territories.* Stanford, Stanford University Press, 1968. A huge manual of the vascular plants—highly technical, but easy to consult.

Lada-Mocarski, Valerian. *Bibliography of Books on Alaska Published Before 1868.* New York, Yale University Press, 1969.

Murie, Olaus. *A Field Guide to Animal Tracks.* Boston, Houghton Mifflin, 1954. All North American mammals are included in this valuable publication.

Orth, Donald J. *Dictionary of Alaska Place Names.* Washington, U.S. Government Printing Office, 1967.

Robbins, Chandler S., et al. *Birds of North America.* New York, Golden Press, 1966. A guide to field identification.

The Alaska Almanac. Alaska Northwest Publishing Co., Box 4-EEE, Anchorage, AK 99509, USA. A rich source of useful information about the state, all in one compact volume.

Tourville, Elsie A. *Alaska, A Bibliography, 1570-1970.* Boston, G.K. Hall & Co., 1974. Includes a simplified subject index.

Wickersham, James. *A Bibliography of Alaskan Literature, 1724-1924.* Fairbanks, Alaska Agricultural College, 1927.

INDEX

Page numbers in **boldface** indicate the primary reference. Page numbers in *italics* indicate information in captions, call-outs, charts, illustrations, or maps.

ABOUT THE AUTHORS

Deke Castleman

Massachusetts, New York, Florida, and Nebraska before finally reaching the West Coast. He received his M.S. in Wildland Resource Science (fire ecology) from UC Berkeley in 1981. Since graduating he has spent his summers in Alaska, working first on a fire research project in Wrangell-St. Elias National Park and then in Tongass National Forest for five years as a trail crew foreman and wilderness ranger. He has also written *Berkeley Inside/Out* (Heyday Books, 1989) and *Wyoming Handbook* (Moon Publications), while taking photographs for two other books about Wyoming. He took all the photos for the color pages of this book, and his photos have appeared in numerous other Alaskan books and calendars.

When Deke Castleman first visited Alaska in 1977, he became enchanted with McKinley (now Denali) National Park. For the next six summers, he was employed there as a shuttle and tour bus driver, waiter, luggage handler, and hotel locksmith. Thereafter, he worked as bellcaptain for four years at the Travelers Inn (now Westmark Fairbanks). These days he doesn't work in Alaska anymore—just travels to update this guidebook.

Don Pitcher stumbled into travel writing almost by accident. Trained as an ecologist, he picked up a copy of the first edition of *Alaska-Yukon Handbook* while working in Alaska, and his long letter of feedback to Moon Publications eventually resulted in his researching and writing the Southeast chapter of the second, third, and fourth editions. Born in Georgia, Pitcher also lived in Maine,

Don Pitcher

Moon Handbooks—The Ideal Traveling Companions

Open a Moon Handbook and you're opening your eyes and heart to the world. Thoughtful, sensitive, and provocative, Moon Handbooks encourage an intimate understanding of a region, from its culture and history to essential practicalities. Fun to read and packed with valuable information on accommodations, dining, recreation, plus indispensable travel tips, detailed maps, charts, illustrations, photos, glossaries, and indexes, Moon Handbooks are ideal traveling companions: informative, entertaining, and highly practical.

To locate the bookstore nearest you that carries Moon Travel Handbooks or to order directly from Moon Publications, call: (800) 345-5473, Monday-Friday, 9 a.m.-5 p.m. PST

The Pacific/Asia Series

BALI HANDBOOK by Bill Dalton
Detailed travel information on the most famous island in the world. 12 color pages, 29 b/w photos, 68 illustrations, 42 maps, 7 charts, glossary, booklist, index. 428 pages. **$12.95**

INDONESIA HANDBOOK by Bill Dalton
This one-volume encyclopedia explores island by island the many facets of this sprawling, kaleidoscopic island nation. 30 b/w photos, 143 illustrations, 250 maps, 17 charts, booklist, extensive Indonesian vocabulary, index. 1,000 pages. **$19.95**

SOUTH KOREA HANDBOOK by Robert Nilsen
Whether you're visiting on business or searching for adventure, *South Korea Handbook* is an invaluable companion. 8 color pages, 78 b/w photos, 93 illustrations, 109 maps, 10 charts, Korean glossary with useful notes on speaking and reading the language, booklist, index. 548 pages. **$14.95**

SOUTHEAST ASIA HANDBOOK by Carl Parkes
Helps the enlightened traveler discover the real Southeast Asia. 16 color pages, 75 b/w photos, 11 illustrations, 169 maps, 140 charts, vocabulary and suggested reading, index. 873 pages. **$16.95**

BANGKOK HANDBOOK by Michael Buckley
Your tour guide through this exotic and dynamic city reveals the affordable and accessible possibilities. Thai phrasebook, color and b/w photos, maps, illustrations, charts, booklist, index. 214 pages. **$10.95**

PHILIPPINES HANDBOOK by Peter Harper and Evelyn Peplow
Crammed with detailed information, *Philippines Handbook* equips the escapist, hedonist, or business traveler with thorough coverage of the Philippines's colorful history, landscapes, and culture. Color and b/w photos, illustrations, maps, charts, index. 587 pages. **$12.95**

HAWAII HANDBOOK by J.D. Bisignani
Winner of the 1989 Hawaii Visitors Bureau's Best Guide Book Award and the Grand Award for Excellence in Travel Journalism, this guide takes you beyond the glitz and high-priced hype and leads you to a genuine Hawaiian experience. 12 color pages, 86 b/w photos, 132 illustrations, 86 maps, 44 graphs and charts, Hawaiian and pidgin glossaries, appendix, booklist, index. 879 pages. **$15.95**

KAUAI HANDBOOK by J.D. Bisignani
Kauai Handbook is the perfect antidote to the workaday world. 8 color pages, 36 b/w photos, 48 illustrations, 19 maps, 10 tables and charts, Hawaiian and pidgin glossaries, booklist, index. 236 pages. **$9.95**

MAUI HANDBOOK: Including Molokai and Lanai by J.D. Bisignani
"No fool-'round" advice on accommodations, eateries, and recreation, plus a comprehensive introduction to island ways, geography, and history. 8 color pages, 60 b/w photos, 72 illustrations, 34 maps, 19 charts, booklist, glossary, index. 350 pages. **$11.95**

OAHU HANDBOOK by J.D. Bisignani
A handy guide to Honolulu, renowned surfing beaches, and Oahu's countless other diversions. Color and b/w photos, illustrations, 18 maps, charts, booklist, glossary, index. 354 pages. **$11.95**

BIG ISLAND OF HAWAII HANDBOOK by J.D. Bisignani
An entertaining yet informative text packed with insider tips on accommodations, dining, sports and outdoor activities, natural attractions, and must-see sights. Color and b/w photos, illustrations, 20 maps, charts, booklist, glossary, index. 347 pages. **$11.95**

SOUTH PACIFIC HANDBOOK by David Stanley
The original comprehensive guide to the 16 territories in the South Pacific. 20 color pages, 195 b/w photos, 121 illustrations, 35 charts, 138 maps, booklist, glossary, index. 740 pages. **$15.95**

MICRONESIA HANDBOOK:
Guide to the Caroline, Gilbert, Mariana, and Marshall Islands by David Stanley
Micronesia Handbook guides you on a real Pacific adventure all your own. 8 color pages, 77 b/w photos, 68 illustrations, 69 maps, 18 tables and charts, index. 287 pages. **$9.95**

FIJI ISLANDS HANDBOOK by David Stanley
The first and still the best source of information on travel around this 322-island archipelago. 8 color pages, 35 b/w photos, 78 illustrations, 26 maps, 3 charts, Fijian glossary, booklist, index. 198 pages. **$8.95**

TAHITI-POLYNESIA HANDBOOK by David Stanley
All five French-Polynesian archipelagoes are covered in this comprehensive guide by Oceania's best-known travel writer. 12 color pages, 45 b/w photos, 64 illustrations, 33 maps, 7 charts, booklist, glossary, index. 225 pages. **$9.95**

NEW ZEALAND HANDBOOK by Jane King
Introduces you to the people, places, history, and culture of this extraordinary land. 8 color pages, 99 b/w photos, 146 illustrations, 82 maps, booklist, index. 546 pages. **$14.95**

OUTBACK HANDBOOK by Marael Johnson
Australia is an endlessly fascinating, vast land, and *Outback Handbook* explores the cities and towns, sheep stations and wilderness areas of the Northern Territory, Western, and South Australia. Full of travel tips and cultural information for adventuring, relaxing, or just getting away from it all. Color and b/w photos, illustrations, maps, charts, booklist, index. 450 pages. **$14.95**

BLUEPRINT FOR PARADISE: How to Live on a Tropic Island by Ross Norgrove
This one-of-a-kind guide has everything you need to know about moving to and living comfortably on a tropical island. 8 color pages, 40 b/w photos, 3 maps, 14 charts, appendices, index. 212 pages. **$14.95**

The Americas Series

NORTHERN CALIFORNIA HANDBOOK by Kim Weir
An outstanding companion for imaginative travel in the territory north of the Tehachapis. 12 color pages, b/w photos, 69 maps, illustrations, booklist, index. 759 pages. **$16.95**

NEVADA HANDBOOK by Deke Castleman
Nevada Handbook puts the Silver State into perspective and makes it manageable and affordable. 34 b/w photos, 43 illustrations, 37 maps, 17 charts, booklist, index. 400 pages. **$12.95**

NEW MEXICO HANDBOOK by Stephen Metzger
A close-up and complete look at every aspect of this wondrous state. 8 color pages, 85 b/w photos, 63 illustrations, 50 maps, 10 charts, booklist, index. 375 pages. **$13.95**

TEXAS HANDBOOK by Joe Cummings
Seasoned travel writer Joe Cummings brings an insider's perspective to his home state. 12 color pages, b/w photos, maps, illustrations, charts, booklist, index. 483 pages. **$11.95**

ARIZONA TRAVELER'S HANDBOOK by Bill Weir
This meticulously researched guide contains everything necessary to make Arizona accessible and enjoyable. 8 color pages, 194 b/w photos, 74 illustrations, 53 maps, 6 charts, booklist, index. 505 pages. **$13.95**

UTAH HANDBOOK by Bill Weir
Weir gives you all the carefully researched facts and background to make your visit a success. 8 color pages, 102 b/w photos, 61 illustrations, 30 maps, 9 charts, booklist, index. 452 pages. **$12.95**

ALASKA-YUKON HANDBOOK by Deke Castleman and Don Pitcher
Get the inside story, with plenty of well-seasoned advice to help you cover more miles on less money. 8 color pages, 26 b/w photos, 95 illustrations, 92 maps, 10 charts, booklist, glossary, index. 400 pages. **$13.95**

WASHINGTON HANDBOOK by Dianne J. Boulerice Lyons and Archie Satterfield
Covers sights, shopping, services, transportation, and outdoor recreation, with complete listings for restaurants and accommodations. 8 color pages, 92 b/w photos, 24 illustrations, 81 maps, 8 charts, booklist, index. 400 pages. **$13.95**

OREGON HANDBOOK by Stuart Warren and Ted Long Ishikawa
Brimming with travel practicalities and insider views on Oregon's history, culture, arts, and activities. Color and b/w photos, illustrations, 28 maps, charts, booklist, index. 422 pages. **$12.95**

IDAHO HANDBOOK by Bill Loftus
A year-round guide to everything in this outdoor wonderland, from whitewater adventures to rural hideaways. Color and b/w photos, illustrations, maps, charts, booklist, index. 275 pages. **$12.95**

WYOMING HANDBOOK by Don Pitcher
All you need to know to open the doors to this wide and wild state. Color and b/w photos, illustrations, over 60 maps, charts, booklist, index. 427 pages. **$12.95**

MONTANA HANDBOOK by W.C. McRae and Judy Jewell
The wild West is yours with this extensive guide to the Treasure State, complete with travel practicalities, history, and lively essays on Montana life. Color and b/w photos, illustrations, maps, charts, booklist, index. 393 pages. **$13.95**

COLORADO HANDBOOK by Stephen Metzger
Essential details to the all-season possibilities in Colorado fill this guide. Practical travel tips combine with recreation—skiing, nightlife, and wilderness exploration—plus entertaining essays. Color and b/w photos, illustrations, maps, charts, booklist, index. 550 pages. **$15.95**

BRITISH COLUMBIA HANDBOOK by Jane King
With an emphasis on outdoor adventures, this guide covers mainland British Columbia, Vancouver Island, the Queen Charlotte Islands, and the Canadian Rockies. 8 color pages, 56 b/w photos, 45 illustrations, 66 maps, 4 charts, booklist, index. 381 pages. **$11.95**

CATALINA HANDBOOK: A Guide to California's Channel Islands by Chicki Mallan
A complete guide to these remarkable islands, from the windy solitude of the Channel Islands National Marine Sanctuary to bustling Avalon. 8 color pages, 105 b/w photos, 65 illustrations, 40 maps, 32 charts, booklist, index. 262 pages. **$10.95**

BAJA HANDBOOK by Joe Cummings
A comprehensive guide with all the travel information and background on the land, history, and culture of this untamed thousand-mile-long peninsula. Color and b/w photos, illustrations, maps, charts, booklist, index. 400 pages. **$13.95**

YUCATAN HANDBOOK by Chicki Mallan
All the information you'll need to guide you into every corner of this exotic land. 8 color pages, 154 b/w photos, 55 illustrations, 57 maps, 70 charts, appendix, booklist, Mayan and Spanish glossaries, index. 391 pages. **$12.95**

CANCUN HANDBOOK and Mexico's Caribbean Coast by Chicki Mallan
Covers the city's luxury scene as well as more modest attractions, plus many side trips to unspoiled beaches and Mayan ruins. Color and b/w photos, illustrations, over 30 maps, Spanish glossary, booklist, index. 257 pages. **$10.95**

BELIZE HANDBOOK by Chicki Mallan
Complete with detailed maps, practical information, and an overview of the area's flamboyant history, culture, and geographical features, *Belize Handbook* is the only comprehensive guide of its kind to this spectacular region. Color and b/w photos, illustrations, maps, booklist, index. 212 pages. **$11.95**

JAMAICA HANDBOOK by Karl Luntta
From the sun and surf of Montego Bay and Ocho Rios to the cool slopes of the Blue Mountains, author Karl Luntta offers island-seekers a perceptive, personal view of Jamaica. Color and b/w photos, illustrations, maps, charts, index. 350 pages. **$12.95**

The International Series

EGYPT HANDBOOK by Kathy Hansen
An invaluable resource for intelligent travel in Egypt. 8 color pages, 20 b/w photos, 150 illustrations, 80 detailed maps and plans to museums and archaeological sites, Arabic glossary, booklist, index. 510 pages. **$14.95**

PAKISTAN HANDBOOK by Isobel Shaw
For armchair travelers and trekkers alike, the most detailed and authoritative guide to Pakistan ever published. 28 color pages, 86 maps, appendices, Urdu glossary, booklist, index. 478 pages. **$15.95**

MOSCOW-LENINGRAD HANDBOOK by Masha Nordbye
Provides the visitor with an extensive introduction to the history, culture, and people of these two great cities, as well as practical information on where to stay, eat, and shop. 8 color pages, 36 b/w photos, 20 illustrations, 16 maps, 9 charts, booklist, index. 205 pages. **$12.95**

NEPAL HANDBOOK   by Kerry Moran
Whether you're planning a week in Kathmandu or months out on the trail, *Nepal Handbook* will take you into the heart of this Himalayan jewel. Color and b/w pages, illustrations, 50 maps, 6 charts, glossary, index. 450 pages.   **$12.95**

NEPALI AAMA   by Broughton Coburn
A delightful photo-journey into the life of a Gurung tribeswoman of Central Nepal. Having lived with Aama (translated, "mother") for two years, first as an outsider and later as an adopted member of the family, Coburn presents an intimate glimpse into a culture alive with humor, folklore, religion, and ancient rituals. B/w photos. 165 pages.   **$13.95**

Moonbelts

Made of heavy-duty Cordura nylon, the Moonbelt offers maximum protection for your money and important papers. This all-weather pouch slips under your shirt or waistband, rendering it virtually undetectable and inaccessible to pickpockets. One-inch-wide nylon webbing, heavy-duty zipper, one-inch quick release buckle. Accommodates traveler's checks, passport, cash, photos. Size 5 x 9 inches. Black.   **$8.95**

IMPORTANT ORDERING INFORMATION

FOR FASTER SERVICE: Call to locate the bookstore nearest you that carries Moon Travel Handbooks or order directly from Moon Publications:

(800) 345-5473 · Monday-Friday · 9 a.m.-5 p.m. PST · fax (916) 345-6751

PRICES: All prices are subject to change. We always ship the most current edition. We will let you know if there is a price increase on the book you ordered.

SHIPPING & HANDLING OPTIONS:
 1) Domestic UPS or USPS first class (allow 10 working days for delivery):
  $3.50 for the first item, 50 cents for each additional item.

Exceptions:
 · **Moonbelt** shipping is $1.50 for one, 50 cents for each additional belt.
 · Add $2.00 for same-day handling.
 2) UPS 2nd Day Air or Printed Airmail requires a special quote.
 3) International Surface Bookrate (8-12 weeks delivery):
  $3.00 for the first item, $1.00 for each additional item. Note: Moon Publications cannot guarantee international surface bookrate shipping.

FOREIGN ORDERS: All orders which originate outside the U.S.A. must be paid for with either an International Money Order or a check in U.S. currency drawn on a major U.S. bank based in the U.S.A.

TELEPHONE ORDERS: We accept Visa or MasterCard payments. Minimum order is US $15.00. Call in your order: 1 (800) 345-5473. 9 a.m.-5 p.m. Pacific Standard Time.

ORDER FORM

Be sure to call (800) 345-5473 for current prices and editions or for the name of the bookstore nearest you that carries Moon Travel Handbooks · 9 a.m.-5 p.m. PST (See important ordering information on preceding page)

Name:_____Date:_____

Street:_____

City:_____Daytime Phone:_____

State or Country:_____Zip Code:_____

Quantity	Title	Price

Taxable Total	
Sales Tax (7.25%) for California Residents	
Shipping & Handling	
TOTAL	

Ship: ☐ 1st class   ☐ UPS (no P.O. Boxes)   ☐ International Surface

Ship to: ☐ address above   ☐ other_____

_____

_____

Make checks payable to:
Moon Publications Inc., 722 Wall Street, Chico, California 95928 U.S.A.
We Accept Visa and MasterCard
To Order: Call in your Visa or MasterCard number, or send a written order with your Visa or MasterCard number and expiration date clearly written.

Card Number: ☐ **Visa**   ☐ **MasterCard**

☐☐☐☐ ☐☐☐☐ ☐☐☐☐ ☐☐☐☐

Exact Name on Card: ☐ same as above   expiration date:_____

☐ other_____

signature_____